T0305661

International Macroeconomics

International Macroeconomics

A Modern Approach

STEPHANIE SCHMITT-GROHÉ
MARTÍN URIBE
MICHAEL WOODFORD

PRINCETON UNIVERSITY PRESS
Princeton and Oxford

Published by Princeton University Press
41 William Street, Princeton, New Jersey 08540
99 Banbury Road, Oxford OX2 6JX

press.princeton.edu

Library of Congress Control Number: 2022932465

ISBN 9780691170640
ISBN (e-book) 9780691189543

British Library Cataloging-in-Publication Data is available

Editorial: Joe Jackson, Josh Drake
Jacket Design: Wanda España
Production: Erin Suydam
Publicity: Kate Hensley, Charlotte Coyne

Jacket art : Dmytro Razinkov / Alamy Stock Vector

This book has been composed in MinionPro and Univers

Printed on acid-free paper ∞

Printed in the United States of America

10 9 8 7 6 5 4 3 2 1

Contents

Preface

Ever since the microfoundations revolution of the 1970s, research in macroeconomics—both at universities and in policy institutions—has been based on an approach that derives the relationships between macroeconomic variables from the intertemporal decision problems of individual households and firms. Yet undergraduate textbooks in macroeconomics have often continued to follow a reduced-form ad hoc approach, creating an ever-widening gap between current research and what is taught in the classroom. And this has nowhere been more true than in the case of textbook treatments of international macroeconomics topics.

Of course, international macroeconomics is complex; one must deal with all of the issues that arise in the macroeconomics of a closed economy (and that are treated in general macroeconomics texts), but many additional complications as well. This leads many instructors to assume that an explicitly microfounded framework simply cannot be afforded if one wishes to treat international issues. Moreover, courses in international macroeconomics are generally expected to focus even more on economic challenges faced in particular parts of the world than is true in general macroeconomics courses; and some instructors likely fear that insistence upon a rigorous and theoretically elegant approach would mean talking insufficiently about real macroeconomic problems. This book aims to show that these challenges can be met, bringing undergraduate instruction in international macroeconomics in line with current economic research.

A defining characteristic of this text is that it consistently maintains a microfounded, optimizing, dynamic general equilibrium approach throughout its presentation of the material. The same theoretical framework is used in all chapters. A basic framework is introduced, with appropriate variations then brought in to address all of the central topics in the field, including the determinants of the current account in small and large economies; processes of adjustment to temporary, permanent, and anticipated shocks; the determinants of the real exchange rate; the role of fixed and flexible exchange rates in models with nominal rigidities; interactions between monetary and fiscal policy; the role of capital controls in the presence of financial frictions; and balance of payments crises.

The goal of the book is to present undergraduate and master's students an analysis of questions relevant for economic policy using the same basic analytical approach as is employed in the research literature. This is made possible by introducing two simplifications for pedagogical purposes: first, in most of the book the assumption of an infinite horizon economy is replaced by a two-period framework.

And second, stochastic economies are replaced in many cases by perfect foresight economies. Sometimes only one of these two simplifications is needed to make the material intuitive and accessible to students. For example, a two-period model is a suitable environment for understanding the role of uncertainty shocks in the determination of a country's current account, though in this case it is important to depart from perfect foresight. This simple environment proves useful to shed light on the role of the Great Moderation in global imbalances. Similarly, only the assumption of perfect foresight is needed to explain why a balance of payments crisis should result from a fiscally inconsistent fixed exchange rate regime, though for this problem it is important to consider an economy as lasting for more than two periods.

Throughout the book, the predictions of the theoretical models are confronted with data. These tests are used to highlight the power of a particular theory in providing insight into a real-world problem, but also to mark its limits and to motivate critical thinking. An essential component of the book are the exercises at the end of each chapter. These range from relatively simple questions intended to help students master the materials covered in the chapter, to more advanced questions, that should help students to think about how the tools they have learned can be used for understanding economic problems beyond those explicitly treated. The exercises not only train the students' theoretical skills, but also challenge them to scrutinize the empirical relevance of the models by confronting them with actual data.

Over the years, preliminary drafts of this book have been used as a main text in courses in International Macroeconomics and International Finance, taught at both the undergraduate and MA levels in countries in many parts of the world. At Columbia, in undergraduate courses in International Macroeconomics or International Finance, we typically first cover Chapters 1–10, which expose students to the determinants of the current account and the real exchange rate in small and large economies. We then select topics from the more advanced chapters presented in Parts III and IV of the book, such as exchange rate policy and unemployment in models with nominal rigidities (Chapter 13) or financial frictions (Chapter 12). At the MA level, we place more emphasis on the advanced materials by beginning with Chapters 3 and 5, and then skipping ahead to Chapters 10–15. In the Intermediate Macroeconomics course, we have taught Chapters 3 and 5, which present the macroeconomic adjustment to aggregate shocks in endowment and production economies and derive the saving and investment schedules from microfoundations. We then use this apparatus to study the determination of the equilibrium interest rate in closed and open economies (Chapter 7) and to introduce students to fiscal policy analysis, emphasizing the conditions for Ricardian equivalence and its failure (Chapter 8).

We would like to thank the many students, especially our teaching and research assistants, who over the years have helped us develop and test in the classroom various incarnations of this book. Special thanks go to Alberto Ramos, Sanjay Chugh, Marco Airaudo, Debajyoti Chakrabarty, Xuan Arthur Liu, Kyoobok Lee, Javier García-Cicco, Sarah Zubairy, Wendy Werstuik (né Wang), Sebastian Rondeau, Ozge Akinci, Matthieu Bellon, Pablo Ottonello, Samer Shousha, Tuo Chen, Mengxue Wang, Yoon J. Jo, Hyoseok Kim, Ken Teoh, Emilio Zaratiegui, Seungki

Hong, Yang Jiao, Ryan Chahrour, Wataru Miyamoto, Carlos Montes-Galdón, Mariana García-Schmidt, and Seunghoon Na.

Among the instructors at other institutions who have used the book while it was under development, we are particularly grateful for detailed comments from Roberto Perotti, Linda Tesar, Geert Van Moer, Marc Alexandre Sénégas, and Bill Yang. We also would like to thank our first editor at Princeton University Press, Seth Ditchik, for believing that this was a project worth pursuing, and Joe Jackson, who took over as editor after Seth left the Press, for smoothly and patiently overseeing the project to completion. Finally, we would like to thank Alison Britton for excellent copyediting.

CHAPTER 1

Global Imbalances

Over the past decades, the world has witnessed the emergence of large external debt positions in some countries and large external asset positions in others. The United States became the largest external debtor in the world in the late 1980s and has maintained this position ever since. At the same time, China, Japan, and Germany hold large asset positions against the rest of the world. This phenomenon has come to be known as *global imbalances*.

The *heat map* in Figure 1.1 presents the accumulated current account balances from 1980 to 2017 for 182 countries. As we will explain in more detail later in this chapter, to a first approximation the current account equals the change in a country's net foreign asset position. Current account surpluses increase a country's net foreign asset position and current account deficits decrease it. By accumulating the current account balances of each country over time, we can obtain an idea of which countries have been playing the role of lenders and which the role of borrowers. Cumulative current account surpluses appear in green and cumulative current account deficits in red. Darker tones correspond to larger cumulative surpluses or deficits. If the cumulative current accounts of all countries were more or less balanced, then the heat map would be filled in with only light colors. The fact that the map has several dark green and dark red patches is therefore an indication that some countries have been consistently borrowing from the rest of the world and others consistently lending over the past 38 years.

The United States appears in dark red and China in dark green, reflecting the fact that the former is the world's largest external debtor and the latter one of the world's largest creditors. More generally, the pattern that emerges is that over the past four decades, the lenders of the world have been Japan, China, Germany, and oil- and gas-exporting countries (Russia, Norway, Saudi Arabia, Kuwait, United Arab Emirates, and Qatar). The rest of the world, especially the United States, has been borrowing from these countries.

This chapter presents an anatomy of external debt and its components in the United States and other countries and traces them across time. It will answer questions such as what international transactions contributed the most to making the United States the largest external debtor in the world? How much of the U.S. external debt stems from imbalances with China? And how do changes in asset prices,

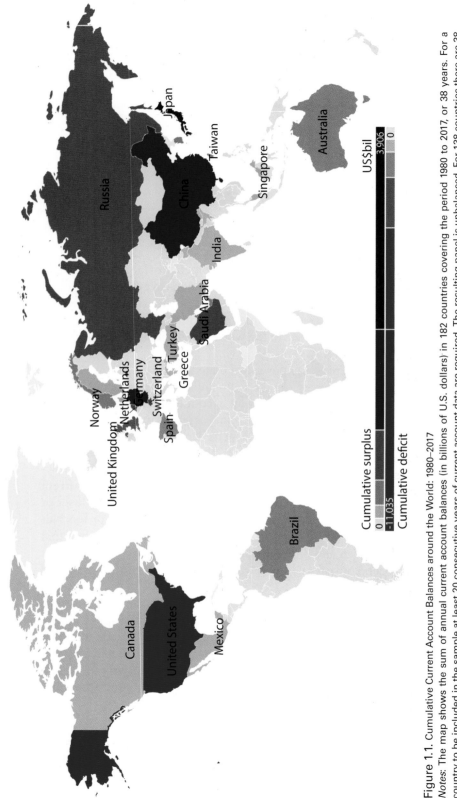

Figure 1.1. Cumulative Current Account Balances around the World: 1980–2017

Notes: The map shows the sum of annual current account balances (in billions of U.S. dollars) in 182 countries covering the period 1980 to 2017, or 38 years. For a country to be included in the sample at least 20 consecutive years of current account data are required. The resulting panel is unbalanced. For 138 countries there are 38 observations, and for the average country there are 35 observations. Cumulative current account surpluses appear in green and cumulative current account deficits in red. There are six shades of red and green corresponding to, respectively, at least one half, one fourth, one eighth, one sixteenth, and one thirty-second of the maximum cumulative current account surplus (Japan: $3,906bn) and the maximum cumulative current account deficit (U.S.: −$11,035bn). Countries with less than 20 years of data appear in gray. Country names are displayed for the countries with the top 10 largest cumulated current account surpluses and deficits. The data source is Philip R. Lane and Gian Maria Milesi-Ferretti (2017), "International Financial Integration in the Aftermath of the Global Financial Crisis," IMF Working Paper 17/115.

such as stock prices and exchange rates, affect the net foreign asset position of a country? Before addressing these and other related questions, the chapter begins by introducing some basic concepts related to a country's external accounts.

1.1 The Balance of Payments

A country's international transactions are recorded in the *balance of payments accounts* (also called *international transactions accounts*, ITA). In the United States this data is produced by the Bureau of Economic Analysis (BEA). The balance of payments has two main components: the *current account* and the *financial account*. The current account records exports and imports of goods and services and international receipts or payments of income. Exports of goods and services and income receipts enter with a plus and imports of goods and services and income payments enter with a minus. For example, if a U.S. resident buys a smartphone from South Korea for $500, then the U.S. current account goes down by $500. This is because this transaction represents an import of goods worth $500. If the French car maker Peugeot pays €100 in dividends to an American shareholder and the exchange rate is $1.1 per euro, then the U.S. current account increases by $110, because this transaction represents an international income receipt of a U.S. resident in this amount.

The financial account keeps record of transactions in financial assets between residents and nonresidents. Sales of assets to nonresidents represent an export of an asset and are given a positive sign in the financial account. Purchases of assets from nonresidents represent an import of a financial asset and enter the financial account with a negative sign. For example, in the case of the import of the smartphone, suppose the U.S. resident pays for the phone with U.S. currency, then this represents a sale (export) of U.S. financial assets (currency) to a South Korean resident (Samsung Electronics, say) in the amount of $500. Accordingly, the U.S. financial account records a positive entry of $500. In the example of the dividend receipt, the American resident "imports" €100 from the French company Peugeot, so the U.S. financial account goes down by $110 (or €100).

The smartphone and dividend receipt examples illustrate a fundamental principle of balance of payments accounting known as *double-entry bookkeeping*. Each transaction enters the balance of payments twice, once with a positive sign and once with a negative sign. To illustrate this principle with another example, suppose that an Italian friend of yours comes to visit you in New York and stays at the Lucerne Hotel. He pays $400 for his lodging with his Italian VISA card. In this case, the United States is exporting a service (hotel accommodation), so the U.S. current account increases by $400. At the same time, the Lucerne Hotel (a U.S. resident) purchases (imports) a financial asset worth $400 (the promise of VISA-Italy, a nonresident, to pay $400), which decreases the U.S. financial account by $400. (Can you figure out how this transaction would be recorded in the Italian balance of payments accounts?)

An implication of the double-entry bookkeeping methodology is that any change in the current account must be reflected in an equivalent change in the country's financial account; that is, the current account equals the difference between a country's purchases of assets from foreigners and its sales of assets to them, which is the financial account preceded by a minus sign. This relationship is known as the *fundamental balance of payments identity*. Formally,

$$\text{Current Account Balance} = -\text{Financial Account Balance} \qquad (1.1)$$

There is a third component of the balance of payments (and thus a third term in the balance of payments identity), called the capital account. It keeps record of international transfers of financial capital. The major types of entries in the capital account are debt forgiveness and migrants' transfers (goods and financial assets accompanying migrants as they leave or enter the country). The capital account is insignificant in the United States, but it can be important in other countries. For instance, in July 2007 the U.S. Treasury Department announced that the United States, Germany, and Russia were providing debt relief to Afghanistan of more than $11 billion. This is a significant amount for the balance of payments accounts of Afghanistan, representing about 99 percent of its foreign debt obligations. But the amount involved in this debt relief operation is a small figure for the balance of payments of the three donor countries. Because the capital account is quantitatively irrelevant for the balance of payments of most countries, we will ignore it in the remainder of the book and will focus on the current account and the financial account.

Let's now take a closer look at each side of the fundamental balance of payments identity (1.1). A more detailed breakdown of the current account is given by

$$\text{Current Account Balance} = \text{Trade Balance}$$
$$+ \text{Income Balance}$$
$$+ \text{Net Unilateral Transfers.}$$

In turn, the trade and income balances each include two components, as follows

$$\text{Trade Balance} = \text{Merchandise Trade Balance}$$
$$+ \text{Services Balance}$$

and

$$\text{Income Balance} = \text{Net Investment Income}$$
$$+ \text{Net International Compensation to Employees.}$$

The *trade balance*, or *balance on goods and services*, keeps record of *net exports* (i.e., the difference between exports and imports) of goods and services. The *merchandise trade balance*, or *balance on goods*, is given by net exports of goods, and the *services balance* is given by net exports of services, such as transportation, travel expenditures, and legal assistance.

In the *income balance*, *net investment income* is given by the difference between income receipts on U.S.-owned foreign assets and income payments on foreign-owned U.S. assets. Income receipts on U.S.-owned foreign assets enter the income balance with a positive sign. It includes items such as international interest and dividend receipts and earnings (distributed or reinvested) of U.S.-owned firms operating abroad. Income payments on foreign-owned U.S. assets enter the income balance with a negative sign. Examples of such income payments are interest paid on U.S. government bonds, interest paid on U.S. corporate bonds, and dividends paid on U.S. stocks. In the United States, net investment income is by far the most important component of the income balance.

The second component of the income balance, *net international compensation to employees*, includes, as positive entries, compensation receipts from earnings of U.S. residents employed temporarily abroad, earnings of U.S. residents employed by foreign governments in the United States, and earnings of U.S. residents employed by international organizations located in the United States, such as the United Nations, the International Monetary Fund, and the International Bank for Reconstruction and Development. Negative entries to net international compensation to employees include payments by U.S. residents or institutions to foreign workers (mostly from Canada and Mexico) who commute to work in the United States, foreign students studying in the United States, foreign professionals temporarily residing in the United States, and foreign temporary workers in the United States. In the United States, net international compensation to employees is so small that the income balance is basically equal to net investment income.

The third component of the current account, *net unilateral transfers* (also called secondary income in the ITA accounts), keeps record of the difference between gifts—that is, payments that do not correspond to purchases of any good, service, or asset, received from the rest of the world and gifts made by the United States to foreign countries. One big item in this category is private remittances. For example, payments by a U.S. resident to relatives residing in Mexico would enter with a minus in net unilateral transfers. Another prominent type of unilateral transfer is U.S. government grants, which represent transfers of real resources or financial assets to foreigners for which no repayment is expected.

The financial account has two main components:

Financial Account = Increase in foreign-owned assets in the United States

− Increase in U.S.-owned assets abroad.

Foreign-owned assets in the United States include U.S. securities held by foreign residents, U.S. currency held by foreign residents, U.S. borrowing from foreign banks, and foreign direct investment in the United States. U.S.-owned assets abroad include foreign securities, U.S. bank lending to foreigners, and U.S. direct investment abroad.

As mentioned earlier, the double-entry bookkeeping method requires that every international transaction result in two entries in the balance of payments accounts. The two examples at the beginning of this chapter—namely, importing a smartphone and paying for it with cash, and the Italian tourist paying the New York hotel with a credit card—each gives rise to one entry in the current account and one entry in the financial account. However, an international transaction does not necessarily have to give rise to one entry in the current account and one entry in the financial account. It can be the case that it gives rise to two offsetting entries in the financial account or two offsetting entries in the current account. International transactions that involve the exchange of financial assets generate two entries in the financial account and no entry in the current account. For example, if a U.S. resident purchases shares from Fiat Italy paying with dollars, then the financial account receives both a positive entry (the sale, or export, of dollars to Italy) and a negative entry (the purchase, or import, of equity shares from Italy). As an example of an international transaction that generates two offsetting entries in the current account, suppose the United States donates medications worth $10 million to an African country afflicted by malaria. This gift gives rise to a positive entry of $10 million in the merchandise trade balance (the export of the malaria medication), and a negative entry in the same amount in net unilateral transfers.

1.2 The Trade Balance and the Current Account

What does the U.S. current account look like? Take a look at Table 1.1, which displays the U.S. international transactions recorded in the current account for 2020. In that year, the United States experienced a large current account deficit of $647.2 billion or 3.1 percent of gross domestic product (GDP) and also a large trade deficit of $681.7 billion, or 3.3 percent of GDP.

Looking inside the trade balance, Table 1.1 shows that in 2020 the United States was a net importer of goods, with a deficit in the trade of goods of 4.4% of GDP, and, at the same time, a net exporter of services, with a service balance surplus of 1.1% of GDP. The United States has a comparative advantage in the production of human-capital-intensive services, such as professional consulting, higher education, research and development, and health care. At the same time, the United States imports basic and manufactured goods, such as primary commodities (e.g., minerals, fuels, and oils), consumer electronics (e.g., cellphones and computers), and transportation equipment (e.g., motor vehicles and motor vehicle parts).

Table 1.1. The Current Account of the United States in 2020

Item	Billions of dollars	Percentage of GDP
Current Account	−647.2	−3.1
Trade Balance	−681.7	−3.3
Balance on Goods	−915.6	−4.4
Balance on Services	233.9	1.1
Income Balance	181.6	0.9
Net Investment Income	190.9	0.9
Compensation of Employees	−9.3	−0.0
Net Unilateral Transfers	−147.1	−0.7
Private Transfers	−127.1	−0.6
U.S. Government Transfers	−20.0	−0.1

Data Source: Authors' calculations based on data from ITA Tables 1.1 and 5.1 and NIPA Table 1.1.5. of the BEA, available at www.bea.gov.

In 2020 the trade balance and the current account were roughly equal to each other in magnitude, -3.3 versus -3.1 percent of GDP. This means that the sum of the other two components of the current account, the income balance and net unilateral transfers, was small. Individually, however, these two components of the current account were sizable, close to 1 percent of GDP, but of opposite sign.

The income balance in 2020 was positive and equal to $181.6 billion, or 0.9 percent of GDP. Almost all of this amount was accounted for by net investment income (net international receipts of interest, dividends, profits, etc.), with compensation of employees representing a negligible figure. The sizable positive value of net investment income is puzzling because, as the heat map in Figure 1.1 suggests, the United States is a large net external debtor, so one would expect that on net it makes payments to rather than receives payments from the rest of the world. In Section 1.7, we discuss what could be behind this paradoxical fact.

Table 1.1 displays a negative balance for net unilateral transfers in 2020 equal to $-$$147.1 billion, or -0.7 percent of GDP. This means that in 2020 the United States made more gifts to other nations than it received. This is typically the case. A large fraction of these international gifts are remittances of foreign workers residing in the United States to relatives in their countries of origin. Typically, U.S. residents send much larger remittances abroad than foreign residents send to the United States. In fact, income from international remittances is so small that it is often not reported separately in the ITA.

Overall, net remittances are a small fraction of the U.S. current account. But for some countries, they can represent a substantial source of income. For example, in 2016 Honduras received remittances for $3.9 billion, almost exclusively coming from the United States. This figure represents 18.4 percent of Honduras' GDP, but only 0.02 percent of the United States'. The same is true for other small countries in Central America. For El Salvador, for example, the flow of dollars coming from the United States has been so large that in 2001 its government decided to adopt the U.S. dollar as legal tender. Even for much larger economies, remittances can represent a nonnegligible source of income. For example, in 2016 Mexico received $28.7 billion in remittances amounting to 2.7 percent of its GDP. As in the cases of Honduras and El Salvador, virtually all of the remittances received by Mexico originated in the United States, for which they represented only 0.15 percent of GDP.

U.S. net unilateral transfers have been negative ever since the end of World War II, with one exception. In 1991, net unilateral transfers were positive because of the payments the United States received from its military allies in compensation for the expenses incurred during the Gulf War.

Deficits in the trade balance and the current account have been consistently observed in the United States since the early 1980s. Figure 1.2 displays this pattern. It graphs the current account and the trade balance as percentages of GDP over the period 1960 to 2020. Until the mid-1970s, the trade balance and the current account were positive albeit small, less than 1 percent of GDP. In the early 1980s, both accounts turned into deficits which grew over time, reaching a peak of about 5.5 percent of GDP in 2008, just before the beginning of the global financial crisis. After 2008, the current account and the trade balance deficits shrunk to about 3 percent of

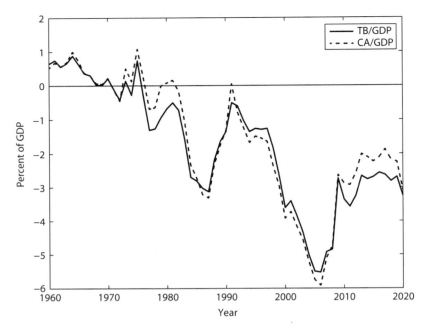

Figure 1.2. The U.S. Trade Balance and Current Account as Percentages of GDP, 1960–2020

Notes: *TB* and *CA* stand for trade balance and current account, respectively. Authors' calculations based on data from ITA Table 1.1 and NIPA Table 1.1.5 of the BEA.

GDP. In sum, for the past 40 years, the United States has displayed current account and trade balance deficits of about equal magnitude.

1.3   The Trade Balance and the Current Account across Countries

We just saw that in the United States the current account and the trade balance typically have the same sign and size. However, this need not be the case for every country. In principle, the current account can be larger or smaller than the trade balance. Furthermore, the trade balance and the current account can be both positive, both negative, or of opposite signs.

Figure 1.3 illustrates this point. It displays the trade balance and the current account as percentage of GDP, denoted TB/GDP and CA/GDP, respectively, in 2019 for 82 countries. Most countries lie either in the first quadrant or the third quadrant. This means that for most countries the trade balance and the current account have the same sign. Furthermore, many (TB/GDP, CA/GDP) pairs fall around the 45-degree line. This means that for many countries the trade balance and the current account have not only the same sign but also roughly the same magnitude. Put differently, the clustering around the 45-degree line suggests that, as in the United States, in many countries, the trade balance is the dominant component of the current account.

In Figure 1.3 the space (TB/GDP, CA/GDP) is divided into six regions, depending on the signs of the trade balance and the current account and on their relative

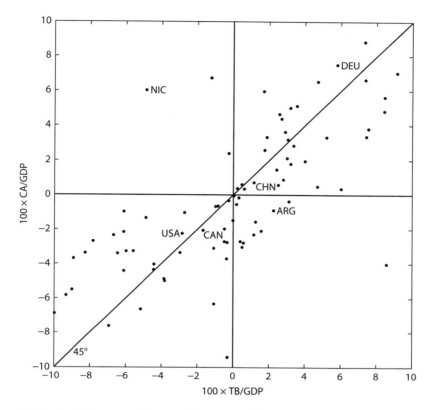

Figure 1.3. Trade Balance and Current Account as Percentage of GDP across Countries in 2019
Notes: TB denotes the trade balance and CA denotes the current account balance. The data source is World Development Indicators (WDI), available at databank.worldbank .org. There are 82 countries included in the figure. Country names are shown using ISO abbreviations. Countries in the WDI database with trade balances or current account balances in excess of ±10 percent of GDP were excluded.

magnitudes. Table 1.2 extracts six countries from the 82 countries shown in Figure 1.3, one from each of the six regions into which the figure is divided.

China is an example of a country that in 2019 ran surpluses in both the trade balance and the current account, with the trade balance exceeding the current account (a dot in the first quadrant and below the 45-degree line). The trade balance surplus (0.9 percent of GDP) was larger than the current account surplus (0.7 percent of GDP) because China ran a deficit in the income balance (−0.3 percent of GDP); in particular, in net investment income. This is surprising because, as the heat map in Figure 1.1 suggests, China is a large net creditor to the rest of the world, so one would expect that its net investment income (such as net interest, dividend, and earnings income) be positive. In Section 1.7.3, we document that this phenomenon has occurred not only in 2019 but persistently over the past quarter century and explain why it might be taking place.

Table 1.2. The Current Account of Selected Countries as Percentage of GDP in 2019

Item	ARG	CAN	CHN	DEU	NIC	USA
Current Account	−0.9	−2.1	0.7	7.5	6.0	−2.2
Trade Balance	2.9	−1.6	0.9	5.7	−4.3	−2.7
Income Balance	−4.0	−0.3	−0.3	3.2	−3.7	1.1
Net Investment Income	−4.0	−0.1	−0.3	3.2	−3.7	1.2
Compensation of Employees	−0.0	−0.3	0.0	0.0	0.0	−0.1
Net Unilateral Transfers	0.2	−0.1	0.1	−1.4	14.0	−0.7
Private Transfers	0.0	−0.3	0.1	−0.6	14.0	−0.6
Government Transfers	0.2	0.2	−0.0	−0.8	0.0	−0.1

Notes: The table presents the current account of Argentina, Canada, China, Germany, Nicaragua, and the United States in 2019 expressed as a percentage of GDP.

Data Sources: Authors' calculations based on data from World Development Indicators, available online at databank.worldbank.org, and the IMF's Balance of Payments and International Investment Position Dataset, available online at data.imf.org.

Like China, Germany displays both a current account and a trade balance surplus. However, unlike China, the German current account surplus is larger than its trade balance surplus (a dot in the first quadrant and above the 45-degree line). This difference can be explained by the fact that Germany, unlike China, receives positive net investment income (3.2 percent of GDP) on its positive net foreign asset position. Nicaragua provides an example of a country with a current account surplus (6.0 percent of GDP), in spite of a sizable trade balance deficit of −4.3 percent of GDP (a dot in the second quadrant). The positive current account balance is the consequence of large personal remittances received (14 percent of GDP), which come mostly from the United States. Canada, the United States, and Argentina all experienced current account deficits in 2019. In the case of Canada and the United States, the current account deficits were associated with trade deficits of about equal sizes. In Canada the current account deficit was larger than the trade deficit (a dot on the third quadrant and below the 45-degree line). This is because Canada had a deficit on the income balance. In particular, the balance on net international compensation to employees was −0.3 percent of GDP, stemming mainly from wages paid by Canadian residents to U.S. residents who commute to work in Canada. Finally, Argentina displays a negative current account balance in spite of running a trade balance surplus (a dot in the fourth quadrant). In this case, the difference between the trade balance and the current account balance is accounted for by a 4.0 percent of GDP deficit in net investment income.

1.4 Imbalances in U.S. Trade with China

Figure 1.4 displays the U.S. merchandise trade balance since 1960 and its bilateral merchandise trade balance with China since 1990. The starting date for China

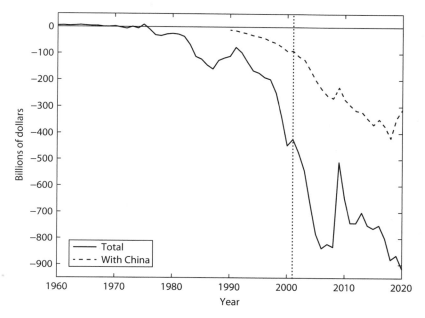

Figure 1.4. The U.S. Merchandise Trade Balance with China, 1990–2020
Notes: The data source for the U.S. merchandise trade balance is ITA Table 1.1. The data source for the bilateral merchandise trade balance between the United States and China is the OECD, http://stats.oecd.org, for the period 1990 to 2002 and ITA Table 1.3 for the period 2003 to 2020. The vertical line marks the year 2001, when China became a member of the World Trade Organization.

is dictated by data availability. Most likely, however, the bilateral trade balance prior to 1990 was as small as or even smaller than in 1990 because of legal and political impediments to Sino-American trade. During the 1960s, trade was limited by an existing embargo. Despite the fact that, following his famous trip to China, President Nixon lifted the U.S. trade embargo on China in 1971, and despite the fact that the U.S. Congress passed a trade agreement conferring contingent Most Favored Nation status on China in 1980, trade impediments persisted because of existing laws linking trade benefits with human rights policies of communist countries.

Figure 1.4 shows that the U.S. merchandise trade deficit with China has widened since China became a member of the World Trade Organization (WTO) in December 2001. When a country joins the WTO, it gains improved access to global markets and, in return, must grant other countries better access to its domestic market. In the case of China, the WTO agreement obliged this country to cut import tariffs and give foreign businesses greater access to domestic insurance, banking, and telecommunications markets. In 2001 the deficit on the U.S. bilateral merchandise trade balance with China was $90 billion, or 21 percent of the overall U.S. merchandise trade deficit. By 2015, the deficit with China had risen to $368 billion, or 48 percent of the overall U.S. merchandise trade deficit. By the end of the sample, the bilateral trade deficit fell significantly. In 2020 it stood at $310 billion, or 34 percent of the overall U.S. merchandise trade deficit. Two candidate explanations for this narrowing of the bilateral trade imbalances are an increase in trade triangulation after the imposition of import tariffs by the Trump administration starting in 2018 and the COVID-19 pandemic.

1.5 The Current Account and the Net International Investment Position

One reason why the concept of current account balance is economically important is that it reflects a country's net borrowing needs. For example, in 2020 the United States ran a current account deficit of $647.2 billion (Table 1.1). To pay for this deficit, the country must either reduce its international asset position or increase its international liability position, or both. In this way, the current account is related to changes in a country's *net international investment position* (NIIP). This term is used to refer to a country's net foreign wealth; that is, the difference between the value of foreign assets owned by the country's residents and the value of the country's assets owned by foreign residents. When the NIIP is negative, it is referred to as the country's net external debt.

The NIIP is a stock, while the current account is a flow. To understand the difference between a flow and a stock variable in this context, think of a water tank. The level of water in the tank (a stock) is the NIIP of the country. The current account is the flow of water that might enter or leave the tank through pipes. When the flow of water that enters the tank through pipes (exports, interest and dividends received from investments in foreign countries) is larger than the flow of water that leaves the tank (imports, interest and dividends paid on foreign-owned investments in the country), the current account is positive, and the stock of water in the tank, the NIIP, rises over time. By contrast, when the flow of water that leaves the tank is larger than the flow of water that enters the tank, the current account is negative, and the level of water in the tank, the NIIP, falls over time.

Figure 1.5 shows the U.S. current account and NIIP expressed in percent of GDP over the periods 1960 to 2020 and 1976 to 2020, respectively. (The later starting date of the NIIP series is determined by data availability.) The U.S. net international investment position was positive at the beginning of the sample. However, in the early 1980s, the United States began running large current account deficits. By 1989 these deficits had eroded the net foreign wealth of the United States and the country became a net debtor to the rest of the world for the first time since World War I.

The U.S. current account deficits of the 1980s did not turn out to be temporary. As a consequence, by the end of the 1990s, the United States had become the world's largest external debtor. The current account deficit continued to rise for 25 more years. Only shortly before the onset of the global financial crisis of 2008 did the downward trend stop and current account deficits became smaller.

By the end of 2020, the net international investment position of the United States stood at −$14.1 trillion or −67 percent of GDP. This is a big number, and many economists wonder whether the observed downward trend in the NIIP is sustainable over time.[1] The concern stems from the fact that countries that accumulated

---

[1] Chapter 2 analyzes this concern in detail.

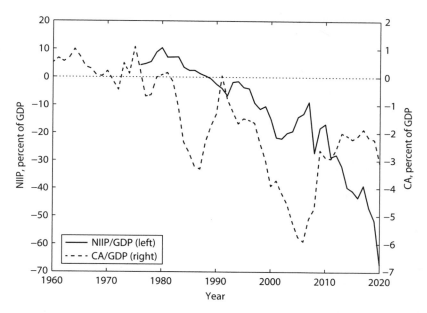

Figure 1.5. The U.S. Current Account and Net International Investment Position
Notes: CA, NIIP, and *GDP* stand for current account, net international investment position, and gross domestic product, respectively. The sample period for CA is 1960 to 2020 and for NIIP 1976 to 2020. Authors' calculations based on data from ITA Table 1.1, IIP Table 1.1, and NIPA Table 1.1.5 of the BEA.

large external-debt-to-GDP ratios in the past, such as many Latin American countries in the 1980s, Southeast Asian countries in the 1990s, and more recently peripheral European countries, have experienced sudden reversals in international capital flows that were followed by costly financial and economic crises. These episodes are known as *sudden stops*.[2] The 2008 financial meltdown in the United States brought this issue to the fore.

1.6 Valuation Changes and the Net International Investment Position

The current account is not the only source of changes in a country's NIIP. It can also change due to variations in the prices of the financial instruments that comprise a country's international asset and liability positions. So we have that

$$\Delta NIIP = CA + \text{valuation changes}, \tag{1.2}$$

where $\Delta NIIP$ denotes the change in the net international investment position and CA denotes the current account balance.

---

[2] Chapters 10 and 13 present historical examples of sudden stops and develop tools to analyze them.

1.6.1 EXAMPLES OF VALUATION CHANGES

To understand how valuation changes can alter a country's NIIP, consider the following hypothetical example. Suppose a country's international asset position, denoted A, consists of 25 shares in the Italian company Fiat. Suppose the price of each Fiat share is €2. Assume that the exchange rate is $2 per euro. Then, the country's foreign asset position is $A = 25 \times 2 \times 2 = \$100$. Suppose that the country's international liabilities, denoted L, consist of 80 units of bonds issued by the local government and held by foreigners. Suppose further that the price of local bonds is $1 per unit, where the dollar is the local currency. Then we have that total foreign liabilities are $L = 80 \times 1 = \$80$. The country's NIIP is given by the difference between its international asset position, A, and its international liability position, L, or $NIIP = A - L = 100 - 80 = \$20$.

Suppose now that the euro suffers a significant depreciation, losing half of its value relative to the dollar. The new exchange rate is therefore $1 per euro. Since the country's international asset position is denominated in euros, its value in dollars automatically falls. Specifically, its new value is $A' = 25 \times 2 \times 1 = \$50$. The country's international liability position measured in dollars does not change, because it is composed of instruments denominated in dollars. As a result, the country's new net international investment position is $NIIP' = A' - L = 50 - 80 = -\$30$. It follows that just because of a movement in the exchange rate, the country went from being a net creditor of the rest of the world to being a net debtor. This example illustrates that, all else equal, a depreciation of the foreign currency can reduce a country's net foreign asset position.

Consider now the effect of an increase in foreign stock prices on the NIIP of the domestic country. Specifically, suppose that the price of the Fiat stock jumps up from €2 to €7. This price change increases the value of the country's foreign asset position to $25 \times 7 = €175$ or, at an exchange rate of $1 per euro, to $175. The country's international liabilities do not change in value. The net international investment position then turns positive again and equals $175 - 80 = \$95$. This example shows that, all else equal, an increase in foreign stock prices can improve a country's NIIP.

Finally, suppose that because of a successful fiscal reform in the domestic country, the price of local government bonds increases from $1 to $1.5. In this case, the country's international asset position remains unchanged at $175, but its international liability position jumps up to $80 \times 1.5 = \$120$. As a consequence, the NIIP falls from 95 to $175 - 120 = \$55$.

1.6.2 VALUATION CHANGES IN THE UNITED STATES

The above hypothetical examples illustrate how a country's NIIP can display large swings because of movements in asset prices or exchange rates. This is indeed the case in actual data as well. Valuation changes have been an important source of movements in the NIIP of the United States, especially since 2000.

Figure 1.6 displays valuation changes between 1977 and 2020. The figure reveals a number of noticeable characteristics of valuation changes. First, valuation changes can be large, exceeding ± 10 percent of GDP in some years. Second, large valuation

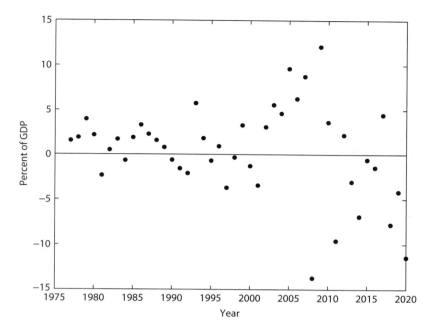

Figure 1.6. Valuation Changes in the U.S. Net International Investment Position, 1977–2020

Notes: The figure shows year-over-year changes in the U.S. net international investment position arising from valuation changes expressed in percent of GDP. Authors' calculations based on data from ITA Table 1.1, IIP Table 1.1, and NIPA Table 1.1.5 of the BEA.

changes are a recent phenomenon. Until 2000, the typical valuation change was between −1 and 2 percent of GDP. Third, the period 2000 to 2020 has also been characterized by higher volatility in valuation changes, as both increases and decreases in valuation became larger. Fourth, over the period 2000 to 2010 the United States experienced mainly valuation gains, whereas over the period 2011 to 2020 it experienced mainly valuation losses.

Why have valuation changes become so large lately? One reason is that gross international asset and liability positions have exploded since the 2000s, as shown in Figure 1.7. Gross positions grew from about 80 percent of GDP in 2000 to over 160 percent by 2020. When gross positions are large relative to net positions, just a small change in the price of an asset that is asymmetrically represented in assets and liabilities can result in large changes in the value of the net position. For example, most of the United States' international liabilities are denominated in dollars, whereas most of its international asset position is denominated in foreign currency. As a result, a small appreciation of the dollar vis-à-vis other currencies can cause a significant deterioration of the NIIP, if the gross positions are large.

Valuation changes played a dominant role in the evolution of the U.S. net international investment position in the run-up to the global financial crisis of 2008. The period 2002–2007 exhibited the largest current account deficits since 1976, which is the beginning of our sample. In each of these years, the current account deficit

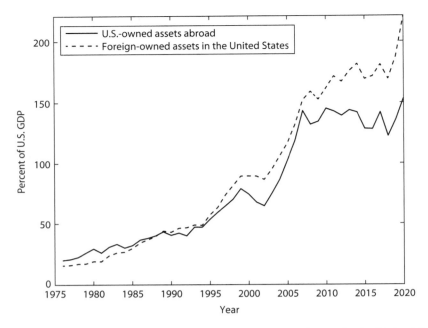

Figure 1.7. U.S.-Owned Assets Abroad and Foreign-Owned Assets in the United States, 1976–2020
Notes: The figure shows that the gross U.S. foreign asset position and the gross U.S. foreign liability position have risen sharply since the mid 1990s. Authors' calculations based on data from IIP Table 1.1 and NIPA Table 1.1.5 of the BEA.

exceeded 4 percent of GDP, with a cumulative deficit of $3.9 trillion, or 32 percent of GDP. Nevertheless, the NIIP actually improved by $80 billion. The discrepancy of almost $4 trillion between the accumulated current account balances and the change in the NIIP was the result of increases in the market value of U.S.-owned foreign assets relative to foreign-owned U.S. assets.

What caused these large changes in the value of assets in favor of the United States? Milesi-Ferretti, of the International Monetary Fund, identifies two main factors.[3] First, the U.S. dollar depreciated relative to other currencies by about 20 percent. This is a relevant factor because, as we mentioned earlier, the currency denomination of the U.S. foreign asset and liability positions is asymmetric. The asset side is composed mostly of foreign-currency-denominated financial instruments, while the liability side is mostly composed of dollar-denominated instruments. As a result, a depreciation of the U.S. dollar increases the dollar value of U.S.-owned assets, while leaving more or less unchanged the dollar value of foreign-owned assets, thereby strengthening the U.S. net international investment position. Second, the stock markets in foreign countries significantly outperformed the U.S. stock market. Specifically, a dollar invested in foreign stock markets in 2002 returned $2.90 by the end of 2007. By contrast, a dollar invested in the U.S. market in

[3] Gian Maria Milesi-Ferretti, "A $2 Trillion Question," VOX, January 28, 2009, available online at http://www.voxeu.org.

2002 yielded only $1.90 at the end of 2007. These gains in foreign equity contributed to an increase in the net equity position of the United States from an insignificant level of $40 billion in 2002 to $3 trillion in 2007.

The large positive valuation changes observed in the period 2002–2007, which allowed the United States to run unprecedented current account deficits without a concomitant deterioration of its net international investment position, came to an abrupt end in 2008. Look at the dot corresponding to 2008 in Figure 1.6, which shows that valuation losses in that year were almost 15 percent of GDP. The source of this drop in value was primarily the stock market. In 2008, stock markets around the world plummeted. Because the net equity position of the United States had grown so large by the beginning of 2008, the decline in stock prices outside of the United States inflicted large losses on the value of the U.S. equity portfolio.

Since 2010, and especially during the COVID-19 pandemic, the U.S. NIIP has suffered mostly valuation losses (see Figure 1.6). This has been the consequence of three developments. First, both the U.S. foreign portfolio equity asset and liability positions more than doubled during this period. This means that the U.S. NIIP became more sensitive to changes in stock prices. Second, the U.S. net foreign portfolio equity position has narrowed, as equity liabilities grew faster than equity assets. And third, for most years since 2010 U.S. stock prices have outperformed foreign stock prices. Every time the U.S. stock market goes up, the value of U.S. portfolio equity liabilities (U.S. stocks held by foreign investors) goes up. And when the foreign stock market goes up, the dollar value of the U.S. portfolio equity asset position (foreign stocks held by U.S. investors) goes up. Thus, if U.S. stocks outperform foreign stocks, as they did in most years since 2010, the value of the U.S. net foreign portfolio equity position, and, all else equal, the value of its NIIP go down.

1.6.3   A HYPOTHETICAL NIIP THAT EXCLUDES VALUATION CHANGES

Another way to visualize the importance of valuation changes is to compare the actual NIIP with a hypothetical one that results from removing valuation changes. To compute a time series for this hypothetical NIIP, start by setting its initial value equal to the actual value. Our sample starts in 1976, so we set

$$\text{Hypothetical } NIIP_{1976} = NIIP_{1976}.$$

Now, according to identity (1.2), after removing valuation changes in 1977, the change in the hypothetical NIIP between 1976 and 1977 equals the current account in 1977; that is,

$$\text{Hypothetical } NIIP_{1977} = NIIP_{1976} + CA_{1977},$$

where CA_{1977} is the actual current account in 1977. The hypothetical NIIP in 1978 is given by the NIIP in 1976 plus the accumulated current accounts from 1977 to 1978, that is,

$$\text{Hypothetical } NIIP_{1978} = NIIP_{1976} + CA_{1977} + CA_{1978}.$$

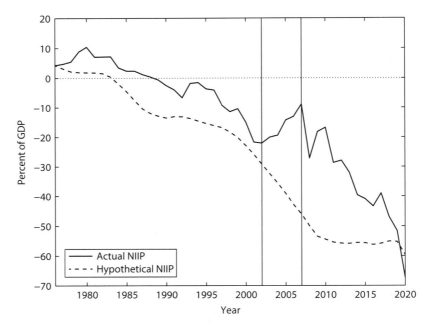

Figure 1.8. Actual and Hypothetical U.S. *NIIP* in Percent of GDP, 1976–2020
Notes: The hypothetical *NIIP* for a given year is computed as the sum of the *NIIP* in 1976 and the cumulative sum of current account balances from 1977 to the year in question. The vertical lines indicate the years 2002 and 2007, respectively. Authors' calculations based on data from IIP Table 1.1, ITA Table 1.1, and NIPA Table 1.1.5 of the BEA.

In general, for any year $t > 1978$, the hypothetical NIIP is given by the actual NIIP in 1976 plus the accumulated current accounts between 1977 and t. Formally,

$$\text{Hypothetical } NIIP_t = NIIP_{1976} + CA_{1977} + CA_{1978} + \cdots + CA_t.$$

Figure 1.8 plots the actual and hypothetical NIIPs over the period 1976 to 2020 in percent of GDP. Until 2002, the actual and hypothetical NIIPs were not that different from each other, implying that valuation changes were not sizable. In 2002, however, the hypothetical NIIP started to fall at a much faster pace than its actual counterpart. This means that after 2002 the United States started to benefit from large valuation gains. Between 2001 and 2007, the gap between the actual and hypothetical NIIPs widened from 4 percent to 37 percent of GDP. Without this lucky strike, all other things equal, the U.S. net foreign asset position in 2007 would have been an external debt of 46 percent of GDP instead of the actual 9 percent. The reversal of fortune that came with the global financial crisis of 2008 is evident from the narrowing of the gap between the two NIIPs. By 2019 this gap had shrunk to only 4 percent of GDP, a figure not significantly different from the ones observed prior to the exuberant quinquennial 2002–2007. In 2020, in spite of the economic crisis brought about by the COVID-19 pandemic, the U.S. stock market boomed and outperformed international equity markets. As a result, the United States suffered large valuation losses

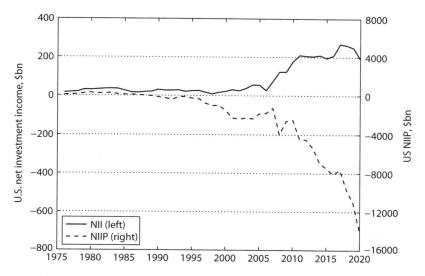

Figure 1.9. Net Investment Income and the Net International Investment Position, United States 1976–2020

Notes: Authors' calculations based on data from IIP Table 1.1 and ITA Table 1.1 of the BEA.

of 11.4 percent of GDP, which closed the gap between the hypothetical and actual NIIPs for the first time since 1976. In fact, by the end of 2020, the actual NIIP was 8 percentage points of GDP below the hypothetical one, indicating that over the period 1976 to 2020 the United States experienced a cumulative valuation loss.

1.7 The *NIIP—NII* Paradox

We have documented that since 1989, the U.S. net international investment position (*NIIP*) has been negative (Figure 1.5). This means that since 1989 the United States has been a net debtor to the rest of the world. One would therefore expect that during this period the United States paid more interest and dividends to the rest of the world than it received. In other words, one would expect that the net investment income (*NII*) component of the current account be negative. This is, however, not observed in the data. Take a look at Figure 1.9. It shows net investment income and the NIIP of the United States since 1976. Net investment income is positive throughout the sample, whereas the NIIP has been negative since 1989. How could it be that a debtor country, instead of having to make payments on its debt, receives income on it? We call this puzzling pattern the *NIIP—NII paradox*. We next discuss two possible explanations.

1.7.1 DARK MATTER

One explanation of the *NIIP—NII* paradox, proposed by Ricardo Hausmann and Federico Sturzenegger, is that the BEA may underestimate the net foreign asset holdings of the United States.[4] The source of the underestimation according to this explanation is that U.S. foreign direct investment contains intangible capital, such as entrepreneurial capital and brand capital, whose value is not correctly reflected in the official balance of payments. At the same time, the argument goes, this intangible capital invested abroad may generate income for the United States, which is appropriately recorded. It thus becomes possible that the United States could display a negative net foreign asset position and at the same time positive net investment income. Hausmann and Sturzenegger refer to the unrecorded U.S.-owned foreign assets as *dark matter*.

To illustrate the dark matter argument, consider a McDonald's restaurant operating in Moscow. This foreign direct investment will show in the U.S. foreign asset position with a dollar amount equivalent to the amount McDonald's invested in items such as land, the building, cooking equipment, and restaurant furniture. However, the market value of this investment may exceed the actual amount of dollars invested. The reason is that the brand McDonald's provides extra value to the goods (the burgers) the restaurant produces. It follows that in this case the balance of payments, by not taking into account the intangible brand component of McDonald's foreign direct investment, would underestimate the U.S. international asset position. On the other hand, the profits generated by the Moscow branch of McDonald's are observable and recorded, so they make their way into the income account of the balance of payments.

How much dark matter was there in 2020? Let *TNIIP* denote the "true" net international investment position and *NIIP* the recorded one. Then we have that

$$TNIIP = NIIP + \text{Dark Matter}.$$

Let r denote the interest rate on net foreign assets. Then, net investment income equals the return on the country's true net international investment position,

$$NII = r \times TNIIP.$$

In this expression, we use *TNIIP* and not *NIIP* to calculate *NII* because, according to the dark matter hypothesis, the recorded level of *NII* appropriately reflects the return on the true level of net international investment. In 2020, *NII* was $0.1909 trillion (see Table 1.1). Suppose that r is equal to 5 percent per year, which is about the historical average real rate of return on equities. Then, we have that $TNIIP = 0.1909/0.05 = \$3.8$ trillion. The recorded *NIIP* at the beginning of 2020 was $-\$11.1$ trillion. So, according to the dark matter hypothesis, the United States doesn't owe $11.1 trillion to the rest of the world. On the contrary, the rest of the world owes $3.8 trillion to the United States. This means that dark matter, the difference between the true NIIP and the observed NIIP, was $3.8 - (-11.1) = \$14.9$ trillion. This seems like a big number to go under the radar of the BEA. It thus seems in order to consider a competing explanation of the *NIIP—NII* paradox.

---

[4]Ricardo Hausmann and Federico Sturzenegger, "U.S. and Global Imbalances: Can Dark Matter Prevent a Big Bang?," working paper CID (Center For International Development), Harvard University, 2005.

1.7.2 RETURN DIFFERENTIALS

An alternative explanation for the paradoxical combination of a negative net international investment position and positive net investment income is that the United States earns a higher interest rate on its foreign asset holdings than foreigners earn on their U.S. asset holdings. The rationale behind this explanation is the observation that the U.S. international assets and liabilities are composed of different types of financial instruments. Foreign investors typically hold low-risk U.S. assets, such as Treasury bills. These assets carry a low interest rate. At the same time, American investors tend to purchase more risky foreign assets, such as foreign stocks and foreign direct investment, which earn relatively high returns.

How big does the spread between the interest rate on U.S.-owned foreign assets and the interest rate on foreign-owned U.S. assets have to be to explain the paradox? Let A denote the U.S. gross foreign asset position and L the U.S. gross foreign liability position. Further, let r^A denote the interest rate on A and r^L the interest rate on L. Then, we have that

$$NII = r^A A - r^L L. \tag{1.3}$$

Let's put some numbers in this expression. According to the BEA, in 2020 A was $32.2 trillion and L was $46.3 trillion. From Table 1.1, we have that in 2020 NII was $0.1909 trillion. Suppose we set r^L equal to the return on U.S. Treasury securities. In 2020, the rate of return on one-year U.S. Treasuries was 0.37 percent per year, so we set $r^L = 0.0037$. Now let's plug these numbers into expression (1.3) to get

$$0.1909 = r^A \times 32.2 - 0.0037 \times 46.3,$$

which yields $r^A = 0.0112$ or 1.12 percent. That is, we need an interest rate spread of 75 basis points ($r^A - r^L = 1.12\% - 0.37\% = 0.75\%$) to explain the paradox. This figure seems more empirically plausible than $14.9 trillion of dark matter.

The analysis thus far assumes that foreign investors hold only U.S. bonds in their international asset portfolio. This is a good simplification of reality until 2010. But since then, as mentioned in Section 1.6, we have observed a significant increase in the relative participation of U.S. equity in the U.S. international liability position. The ratio of equity to bonds in the U.S. international liability position is closer to 1; that is, roughly half is in equity and half in bonds. Suppose that the return on equity is the same domestically and abroad. Accordingly, the rate of return on U.S. foreign liabilities, r^L, is $r^L = \frac{1}{2}(r^A + r^B)$, where $r^B = 0.0037$ is the rate of return on U.S. Treasury securities we used in the baseline exercise. Then we have that equation (1.3) becomes

$$NII = r^A A - \frac{1}{2}(r^A + r^B)L.$$

Evaluating this expression using actual numbers gives

$$0.1909 = r^A \times 32.2 - \frac{1}{2} \times (r^A + 0.0037) \times 46.3,$$

which gives $r^A = 3.06$ percent. The corresponding premium of equity over government bonds is 2.69 percent ($r^A - r^B = 3.06\% - 0.37\%$), which is a more realistic number than the 0.75 percent premium obtained when all of L was assumed to be in U.S. bonds.

1.7.3 THE FLIP SIDE OF THE *NIIP — NII* PARADOX

If we divide the world into two groups, the United States and the rest of the world, then the rest of the world should display the flipped paradox—that is, a positive net foreign asset position and negative net investment income. The reason is that what is an asset of the United States is a liability for the rest of the world and vice versa. The same is true for net investment income. International income receipts by the United States are international income payments by the rest of the world. So we have that

$$NIIP^{US} = A^{US} - L^{US} = L^{RW} - A^{RW} = -NIIP^{RW}$$

and

$$NII^{US} = r^A A^{US} - r^L L^{US} = r^A L^{RW} - r^L A^{RW} = -NII^{RW},$$

where the superscripts *US* and *RW* refer to the United States and the rest of the world.

This means that at least one set of countries in the rest of the world must display the flipped paradox. A possible candidate is China, for two reasons: first, as we observed when discussing global imbalances (see the heat map in Figure 1.1), China has been accumulating large current account surpluses for the past quarter century, so it is a likely candidate to have a positive *NIIP*. Second, Figure 1.3 and Table 1.2 show that in 2016 the Chinese trade balance surplus was larger than the current account surplus. There, we pointed out that this was due to a negative *NII*.

Figure 1.10 plots the *NIIP* and *NII* of China for the period 1982 to 2020. It shows that until the country's accession to the WTO in 2001, the NIIP was near zero. Since 2001, China's net foreign asset position grew rapidly, reaching $2.2 trillion by 2020. At the same time, China's net investment income, *NII*, was close to zero until 2001 and then became mostly negative, fluctuating around −$50 billion. Thus, China displays the flipped *NIIP—NII* paradox, a positive NIIP and a negative NII.

A possible explanation of the Chinese flipped paradox is that China saves largely in safe, low-return assets, such as U.S. government bonds, while foreign investment in China is predominantly in the form of high-return assets, such as foreign direct investment.

What about countries other than China and the United States? Because the sizes of *NIIP* and *NII* are smaller in absolute value in China than in the United States, it must be the case that the flipped *NIIP—NII* paradox is observed in the rest of the world taken together.

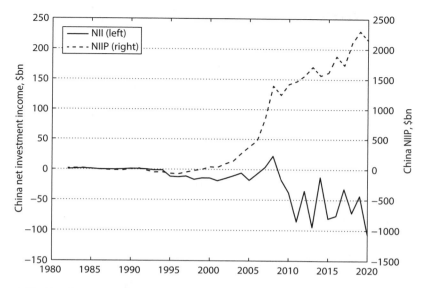

Figure 1.10. Net Investment Income and the Net International Investment Position, China 1982–2020

Notes: The figure shows that China displays the flipped *NIIP–NII* paradox. Since accession to the WTO in 2001, with the exception of the global financial crisis years (2007 and 2008), China recorded a positive *NIIP* and a negative *NII*.

Data Sources: *NIIP* for 1982 to 2017 is from Lane and Milesi-Ferretti, op. cit., and for 2018 to 2020 from International Financial Statistics (IFS). *NII* is from IFS. Reprinted by permission of the authors.

1.8 Summing Up

This chapter introduces the concepts of global imbalances, the current account, the trade balance, and the NIIP, and documents how these variables have evolved over time in the United States and other countries.

- Worldwide, the distribution of external debts and credits is not even. Some countries, like the United States, are large net external debtors and some, like China, are large net external creditors. This pattern is known as global imbalances.
- The balance of payments keeps record of a country's international transactions.
- The balance of payments has two accounts, the current account and the financial account.
- The current account records transactions in goods, services, income, and unilateral transfers between residents and nonresidents.
- The financial account records transactions involving financial assets between residents and nonresidents.
- The current account has three components: the trade balance, the income balance, and net unilateral transfers.

- For most countries, including the United States, the trade balance is the largest component of the current account.
- In the United States, the trade balance and the current account move closely together over time.
- The United States has been running large current account deficits since the early 1980s.
- Current account deficits deteriorate a country's NIIP, which is the difference between a country's international asset position and its international liability position.
- Due to its large current account deficits, the United States turned from being a net external creditor in the early 1980s to being the world's largest net external debtor since the late 1990s.
- A second source of changes in a country's NIIP is valuation changes, originating from changes in exchange rates and in the price of the financial instruments that comprise a country's international asset and liability positions.
- In the United States, valuation changes became large in the early 2000s, reaching values as high as ±15 percent of GDP in a single year. Valuation changes were mostly positive between 2001 and 2010 and mostly negative between 2011 and 2020. On net, between 1976 and 2020, positive and negative valuation changes have roughly offset each other.
- The *NIIP—NII paradox* refers to the phenomenon that the United States has a negative net international investment position, $NIIP < 0$, and positive net investment income, $NII > 0$.
- Two stories that aim to explain the *NIIP—NII* paradox are the dark matter hypothesis and the rate-of-return differential hypothesis.
- The *NIIP—NII* paradox in the United States must have a flipped paradox in the rest of the world. China has had a positive *NIIP* and negative *NII* since the 2000s, so it displays the flipped *NIIP—NII* paradox.

1.9 Exercises

Exercise 1.1 (TFU) Indicate whether the following statements are true, false, or uncertain and explain why.

1. The trade balance, exports, and imports are all flow variables.
2. Net investment income (NII) is a stock variable.
3. The net international investment position of South Africa was $-70.5 billion in 2010 and $-19.7 billion $ in 2011. The current account in 2011 was -10.1 billion USD. There must be an error in the official numbers. The correct figure should be a net international investment position of -80.6 billion USD in 2011.
4. The fact that the United States made large valuation gains between 2002 and 2007 means that the rest of the world as a whole made equally large valuation losses. After all, this is a zero-sum game.
5. The United States has large unrecorded foreign asset holdings.

6. According to the return differential hypothesis, China pays a higher rate of return on its international liabilities than on its international assets.

7. According to the dark matter hypothesis, the Chinese statistical agency overestimates the level of China's net international investment position (NIIP).

Exercise 1.2 (Balance of Payments Accounting) Describe how each of the following transactions affects the U.S. balance of payments. (Recall that each transaction gives rise to two entries in the balance of payments accounts.)

1. Jorge Ramírez, a landscape architect residing in Monterrey, Mexico, works for three months in Durham, North Carolina, creating an indoor garden for a newly built museum and receives wages of $35,000.

2. Jinill Park's mother, a resident of South Korea, pays her son's tuition to Columbia University via a direct deposit.

3. Columbia University buys several park benches from Spain and pays with a $120,000 check.

4. Floyd Townsend, of Tampa, Florida, buys $5,000 worth of British Airlines stock from Citibank New York, paying with U.S. dollars.

5. A French resident imports American blue jeans and pays with a check drawn on her account with J.P. Morgan Chase Bank in New York City.

6. An American company sells a subsidiary in the United States and with the proceeds buys a French company.

7. A group of American friends travels to Costa Rica and rents a vacation home for $2,500. They pay with a U.S. credit card.

8. The U.S. dollar depreciates by 10 percent vis-à-vis the euro.

9. The United States sends medicine, blankets, tents, and nonperishable food worth $400 million to victims of an earthquake in a foreign country.

10. Olga Rublev, a billionaire from Russia, enters the United States on an immigrant visa (that is, upon entering the United States she becomes a permanent resident of the United States). Her wealth in Russia is estimated to be about $2 billion.

11. The United States forgives debt of $500,000 to Nicaragua.

Exercise 1.3 Find the most recent data on the U.S. current account and its components. Present your answer in a form similar to Table 1.1; that is, show figures in both current dollars and as a percentage of GDP. For current account and GDP data visit the BEA's website. Compare your table with Table 1.1.

Exercise 1.4 Suppose Columbia University, a U.S. resident, acquires $100,000 worth of shares of Deutsche Telekom from a German resident. How does this transaction affect the U.S. balance of payments accounts and the U.S. NIIP in each of the following three scenarios. Be sure to list the entries in the U.S. current account and the U.S. financial account separately.

1. Columbia pays for the shares with U.S. dollar bills.

2. Columbia pays for the shares with an apartment it owns in midtown New York.

3. The German resident attends Columbia College and settles the tuition bill with the Deutsche Telekom shares.

4. Do all three scenarios have the same effects on the U.S. current account and on the U.S. NIIP?

Exercise 1.5 (Bigger Debtor Nation) On July 4, 1989, the New York Times reported, under the headline "U.S. is Bigger Debtor Nation," that *"The United States, already the world's largest debtor, sank an additional $154.2 billion into the red last year as foreign money poured in to plug the nation's balance-of-payments gap. .... The increasing debt is likely to mean that American living standards will rise a bit more slowly than they otherwise would, as interest and dividend payments to foreigners siphon off an increasing share of the United States' output of goods and services."* With the benefit of hindsight, critically evaluate the last statement.

Exercise 1.6 This question is about the balance of payments of a country named Outland. The currency of Outland is the dollar.

1. Outland starts a given year with holdings of 100 shares of the German car company Volkswagen. These securities are denominated in euros. The rest of the world holds 200 units of dollar-denominated bonds issued by the Outlandian government. At the beginning of the year, the price of each Volkswagen share is €1 and the price of each unit of an Outlandian bond is $2. The exchange rate is $1.5 per euro. Compute the net international investment position (NIIP) of Outland at the beginning of the year.

2. During the year, Outland exports toys for $7 and imports shirts for €9. The dividend payments on the Volkswagen shares were €0.05 per share and the coupon payment on Outlandian bonds was $0.02 per bond. Residents of Outland received money from relatives living abroad for a total of €3 and the government of Outland gave $4 to a hospital in Guyana. Calculate the Outlandian trade balance, net investment income, and net unilateral transfers in that year. What was the current account in that year? What is the Outlandian NIIP at the end of the year?

3. Suppose that at the end of the year, Outland holds 110 Volkswagen shares. How many units of Outlandian government bonds are held in the rest of the world? Assume that during the year, all financial transactions were performed at beginning-of-year prices and exchange rates.

4. To answer this question, start with the international asset and liability positions calculated in item 3. Suppose that at the end of the year, the price of a Volkswagen share falls by 20 percent and the dollar appreciates by 10 percent. Calculate the end-of-year NIIP of Outland.

Exercise 1.7 (Balance of Payments in a Two-Country World) Suppose the world consists of two countries, country A and country C.

1. Let $NIIP^A$ denote the net foreign asset position of country A. Find the net foreign asset position of country C.

2. Let CA^A denote the current account balance of country A. Find the current account balance of country C.

3. Let A^A denote foreign assets owned by residents of country A and L^A denote country A's assets owned by residents of country C. Find the foreign asset and liability positions of country C denoted A^C and L^C, respectively.
4. Assume that the value of country A's foreign liabilities increases by 20 percent. Find the change in the net foreign asset position of country A and country C.

Exercise 1.8 (*NIIP—NII* Paradox) A country exhibits the paradoxical situation of having negative net investment income (*NII*) of -100 and a positive net international investment position (*NIIP*) of 1000. Economists' opinions about this are divided. Group A thinks that the explanation lies in the fact that, because of the bad reputation of the country in world financial markets, foreign investors charge a higher interest rate when they lend to this country, relative to the interest rate the country receives on its investments abroad. Group B believes that domestic investors inflate their gross international asset positions to look like big players in the world market.

1. Calculate the interest rate premium that would explain the paradox under group A's hypothesis, assuming that the interest rate on assets invested abroad is 5 percent and that the country's gross international asset position is 4000.
2. Calculate the amount by which domestic investors inflate their gross foreign asset positions under group B's hypothesis, assuming that the interest rate on assets and liabilities is 5 percent.

Exercise 1.9 (NIIP and NII in a Two-Country World) The international asset position of country 1, denoted A, consists of $10 in bonds issued by the government of country 2, and $20 in shares of firms residing in country 2. The international liabilities of country 1, denoted L, consist of $35 in bonds issued by the government of country 1 and held by foreign residents, and $5 in shares of firms residing in country 1 held by foreigners. Suppose that the rate of return on government bonds is 2 percent and that the rate of return on shares is 6 percent.

1. Calculate the net international investment position (NIIP) and net investment income (NII) in country 1.
2. Suppose you observe the NIIP and NII of country 1 (refer to the numbers you obtained in question 1), but not the rate of return on bonds and shares. Suppose further that your explanation for the observed values of NIIP and NII is dark matter. Assuming a rate of return of 3 percent on all assets, how big is dark matter and what is the "true" net international investment position, TNIIP, in country 1?

Exercise 1.10 (NIIP and NII in a Three-Country World) The international asset and liability positions of countries 1, 2, and 3 are as follows:

Country 1:
- International Asset Position (A^1)
  $50 in shares of firms residing in country 2, and $50 in shares of firms residing in country 3.

- International Liability Position (L^1)
  $200 in bonds issued by country 1 and held by foreign residents.

Country 2:
- International Asset Position (A^2)
  $100 in bonds issued by the government of country 1.
- International Liability Position (L^2)
  $75 in shares of firms residing in country 2 and held by foreign residents.

Country 3:
- International Asset Position (A^3)
  $100 in bonds issued by the government of country 1, and $25 in shares of firms residing in country 2.
- International Liability Position (L^3)
  $50 in shares of firms residing in country 3 and held by foreign residents.

Suppose that the rate of return of bonds issued by the government of country 1 is $r^1 = 1$ percent, that the rate of return on shares of firms residing in country 2 is $r^2 = 2$ percent, and that the rate of return on shares of firms residing in country 3 is $r^3 = 3$ percent.

1. Calculate the net international investment positions of countries 1, 2, and 3, denoted $NIIP^1$, $NIIP^2$, and $NIIP^3$, respectively.
2. Calculate the net investment income of countries 1, 2, and 3, denoted NII^1, NII^2, and NII^3, respectively.
3. Suppose an analyst only observes the pairs ($NIIP^i$, NII^i), for $i = 1, 2, 3$. What would she most likely find paradoxical about them? Knowing all of the data, how would you explain those apparent paradoxes?
4. Take the country with a negative NIIP and positive NII. What would a believer in dark matter say is the true NIIP, denoted TNIIP? What would she say is dark matter? Suppose that in her calculations, this analyst uses the average rate of return across all securities; that is, $(r^1 + r^2 + r^3)/3$.

Exercise 1.11 (Valuation Changes) Suppose that over the period 2020 to 2022, the net international investment position of a country was $NIIP_{2020} = 100$, $NIIP_{2021} = 125$, and $NIIP_{2022} = 130$. Suppose that over the same period, the current account was $CA_{2020} = 30$, $CA_{2021} = 20$, and $CA_{2022} = 10$. Calculate valuation changes in 2021 and 2022.

Exercise 1.12 (Dark Matter versus Return Differentials I) Suppose net investment income is $NII = 200$, the international asset position is $A = 3000$, the international liability position is $L = 4000$, and the rate of return is 5 percent, $r = 0.05$.

1. Economist John Green, a strong advocate of the dark matter hypothesis, believes that A is not accurately recorded. Calculate the amount of dark matter and the "true" international asset position, which we will denote TA, consistent with Green's view.
2. Financial analyst Nadia Gonzalez does not believe in the dark matter hypothesis. Instead, she believes that A is accurately measured. In her view

5 percent is actually the rate of return on assets $r^A = 0.05$, and the rate of return on the country's international liabilities, r^L, is different. Find the value of r^L consistent with Gonzalez's view.

Exercise 1.13 (Dark Matter versus Return Differentials II) Suppose net investment income is $NII = 300$, the net international investment position is $NIIP = -2000$, the international liability position is $L = 5000$, and the rate of return on assets is 4 percent ($r^A = 0.04$).

1. Economic consultant Jim Taylor, a strong advocate of the return differential hypothesis, maintains that the rate of return on the country's international liabilities, denoted r^L, is different from the return on its net international assets. Find the value of r^L consistent with Taylor's view.
2. Economist Teresa Jones does not support the idea of return differentials. Instead, she defends the dark matter hypothesis. Specifically, she believes that A is not accurately recorded and that the rate of return is 4 percent on both, A and L. Calculate the amount of dark matter and the "true" international asset position, which we will denote TA, consistent with Jones's view.

Exercise 1.14 (Net Foreign Asset Positions around the World) Download data on current accounts and net foreign asset positions from the External Wealth of Nations Database put together by Philip Lane and Gian Maria Milesi-Ferretti. For each country that has current account and net foreign asset position data starting in 1980, sum the current account balances from 1980 to the latest date available and find the change in the NIIP over the corresponding period. Then plot the change in the net foreign asset position against the cumulated current account balances. Discuss your results. In particular, comment on whether cumulative current account balances represent a good measure of global imbalances (refer to Figure 1.1). What does your graph suggest, if anything, about the quantitative importance of valuation changes for the majority of countries in your sample?

Exercise 1.15 Section 1.6 analyzes how valuation changes affected the *NIIP* of the United States over the past decades. In this question, you are asked to analyze how valuation changes affected the *NIIP* of China.

1. Download data on China's current account, net foreign asset position, and gross domestic product from the External Wealth of Nations Database put together by Philip Lane and Gian Maria Milesi-Ferretti. Use these time series to construct the hypothetical *NIIP* of China and then, using a software like Matlab or Excel, plot the actual *NIIP* and the hypothetical *NIIP* for China, both expressed in terms of GDP. Your plot should be a version of Figure 1.8 but using Chinese instead of U.S. data. Compare and contrast your findings to those obtained for the United States.
2. Then construct a time series for valuation changes in China's net foreign asset position. Plot valuation changes as a share of GDP. Use the same scale for the vertical axis as that of Figure 1.6. Then compare and contrast the

valuation changes experienced by China with those experienced by the United States. What may account for the observed differences?

Exercise 1.16 (Dark Matter over Time) Use data from the BEA to construct a time series of dark matter using the methodology explained in subsection 1.7.1. Construct a time series as long as the available data permits. Discuss the plausibility of the dark matter hypothesis based not on its size, but on its volatility over time.

Exercise 1.17 (The Effects of the 2017 Tax Cuts and Jobs Act (TCJA) on Components of the International Transactions Accounts)

1. Read "Apple, Capitalizing on New Tax Law, Plans to Bring Billions in Cash Back to U.S.," which appeared online in the New York Times on January 17, 2018. We will use this article to learn what the TCJA is about and to see if we can follow the algebra given in the article.
    (a) Based on the information given in the article, how much corporate cash held abroad is Apple repatriating?
    (b) What is the tax saving from the repatriation under the new one-time lower tax relative to the pre-reform tax rate?
    (c) What is the potential maximum tax saving for Apple from the repatriation under the new one-time lower tax rate relative to the post-reform tax rate of foreign corporate cash holdings? That is, how high is the incentive to repatriate the cash, taking as given that the tax law changed?
    (d) The article states that "By shifting the money under the new terms, Apple has saved $43 billion in taxes." Given the information provided in the article, do you agree or disagree with this figure?
2. Assume that Apple Ireland is owned by Apple USA and that 2018 earnings of Apple Ireland are 0. Assume that nevertheless Apple Ireland paid Apple USA cash dividends in the amount of $100 billion. Read the short BEA FAQ article "How are the International Transactions affected by an increase in direct investment dividend receipts," June 20, 2018, available at https://www.bea.gov/help/faq/166 and then answer the following questions.
    (a) How will this cash repatriation enter the U.S. current account?
    (b) How will this cash repatriation enter the U.S. financial account?
    (c) Finally, discuss whether the repatriation of earnings of foreign subsidiaries of U.S. companies will or will not improve the U.S. current account deficit.

PART I

Determinants of the Current Account

CHAPTER 2

Current Account Sustainability

A natural question that arises from our description of the recent history of the U.S. external accounts is whether the observed trade and current account deficits are sustainable in the long run. In this chapter, we develop a framework to address this question.

2.1 Can a Country Run a Perpetual Trade Balance Deficit?

The answer to this question depends on the sign of a country's initial net international investment position. A negative net international investment position means that the country is a debtor to the rest of the world. Thus, the country must generate trade balance surpluses either now or at some point in the future in order to service its foreign debt. Similarly, a positive net international investment position means that the country is a net creditor of the rest of the world. The country can therefore afford to run trade balance deficits forever and finance them with the interest revenue generated by its credit position with the rest of the world.

Let's analyze this idea more formally. Consider an economy that lasts for two periods, period 1 and period 2. Let TB_1 denote the trade balance in period 1, CA_1 the current account balance in period 1, and B_1 the country's net international investment position (or net foreign asset position) at the end of period 1. If $B_1 > 0$, then the country is a creditor to the rest of the world in period 1 and if $B_1 < 0$, then the country is a debtor. For example, if the country in question was the United States and period 1 was meant to be the year 2020, then $CA_1 = -\$647.2$ billion, $TB_1 = -\$681.7$ billion, and $B_1 = -\$14.1$ trillion (see Table 1.1 and Section 1.5 in Chapter 1).

Let r denote the interest rate paid on assets held for one period and B_0 denote the net foreign asset position at the end of period 0. Then, the country's net investment income in period 1 is given by

$$\text{Net investment income in period } 1 = rB_0.$$

This expression says that net investment income in period 1 is equal to the return on net foreign assets held by the country's residents between periods 0 and 1.

In what follows, we ignore net international payments to employees, net unilateral transfers, and valuation changes, by assuming that they are always equal to zero. Given these assumptions, the current account equals the sum of net investment income and the trade balance; that is,

$$CA_1 = rB_0 + TB_1 \tag{2.1}$$

and the change in the net international investment position, $B_1 - B_0$, equals the current account,

$$B_1 - B_0 = CA_1. \tag{2.2}$$

Combining equations (2.1) and (2.2) to eliminate CA_1 yields:

$$B_1 = (1 + r)B_0 + TB_1.$$

A relation similar to this one must also hold in period 2. So we have that

$$B_2 = (1 + r)B_1 + TB_2.$$

Combining the last two equations to eliminate B_1 we obtain

$$(1 + r)B_0 = \frac{B_2}{(1 + r)} - TB_1 - \frac{TB_2}{(1 + r)}. \tag{2.3}$$

Now consider the possible values that the net foreign asset position at the end of period 2, B_2, can take. If B_2 is negative ($B_2 < 0$), it means that in period 2 the country is holding debt maturing in period 3. However, in period 3 nobody will be around to collect the debt because the world ends in period 2. Thus, no one in the rest of the world will be willing to lend to residents in our country in period 2. This means that B_2 cannot be negative, or that B_2 must satisfy

$$B_2 \geq 0.$$

If this terminal restriction on asset holdings is not satisfied, then the country is leaving unpaid debts at the end of the world. It is known as the *no-Ponzi-game constraint*, after Charles K. Ponzi, who introduced pyramid schemes in the 1920s in Massachusetts.[1] Can B_2 be strictly positive? The answer is no. A positive value of B_2 means that the country is lending to the rest of the world in period 2. But the country will be unable to collect this debt in period 3 because, again, the world ends in period 2. Thus, the country will never choose to hold a positive net foreign asset position at the end of period 2; that is, it would always choose $B_2 \leq 0$. If B_2 can be

---

[1] To learn more about the remarkable criminal career of Ponzi, visit http://www.mark-knutson.com. A more recent notable example of a Ponzi scheme is given by financier Bernard L. Madoff's fraudulent squandering of investments valued around $64 billion in 2008. For more than 20 years, Madoff's scheme consisted in paying steady returns slightly above market to a large variety of clients ranging from hedge funds to university endowments to low-income retirees. When Madoff's own investments failed to produce such returns, the scheme required the acquisition of new clients to survive. In the financial crisis of 2008 the flow of new clients dried up and his scheme imploded overnight. In June 2009, Bernard Madoff, then 71 years old, was sentenced to 150 years in prison. Madoff died in prison at the age of 82 on April 14, 2021.

neither positive nor negative, then it must be equal to zero,

$$B_2 = 0.$$

This condition is known as the *transversality condition*. Using the transversality condition in (2.3), we obtain

$$(1+r)B_0 = -TB_1 - \frac{TB_2}{(1+r)}. \qquad (2.4)$$

This equation states that a country's initial net foreign asset position (including interest) must equal the present discounted value of its future trade deficits. Our earlier claim that a negative initial net foreign asset position implies that the country must generate trade balance surpluses, either currently or at some point in the future, can now be easily verified using equation (2.4). Suppose that the country is a net debtor to the rest of the world ($B_0 < 0$). Clearly, if it never runs a trade balance surplus ($TB_1 \leq 0$ and $TB_2 \leq 0$), then the left-hand side of (2.4) is negative while the right-hand side is nonnegative, so (2.4) would be violated. In this case, the country would be running a Ponzi scheme against the rest of the world.

Now suppose that the country's initial asset position is positive ($B_0 > 0$). This means that initially the rest of the world owes a debt to our country. Then, the left-hand side of equation (2.4) is positive. If the country runs trade deficits in periods 1 and 2, then the right-hand side of (2.4) is also positive, which implies no inconsistency. Thus, the answer to the question of whether a country can run a perpetual trade balance deficit is yes, provided the country's initial net foreign asset position is positive. Of course, the country cannot run arbitrarily large trade deficits. Equation (2.4) states that their present discounted sum is bounded above by the country's initial net foreign asset position gross of interest.

Because the United States is currently a net foreign debtor to the rest of the world, it follows from our analysis that it will have to run trade balance surpluses at some point in the future. This result extends to economies that last for any number of periods, not just two. Indeed, the appendix to this chapter shows that the result holds for economies that last forever (infinite horizon economies).

2.2   Can a Country Run a Perpetual Current Account Deficit?

In a finite horizon economy like the two-period world we are studying here, the answer to this question is, again, yes, provided the country's initial net foreign asset position is positive. To see why, note that an expression similar to (2.2) must also hold in period 2, that is,

$$B_2 - B_1 = CA_2.$$

Combining this expression with equation (2.2) to eliminate B_1, we obtain

$$B_0 = -CA_1 - CA_2 + B_2.$$

Imposing the transversality condition, $B_2 = 0$, it follows that

$$B_0 = -CA_1 - CA_2. \qquad (2.5)$$

This equation says that a country's initial net foreign asset position must be equal to the sum of its present and future current account deficits. Suppose the country's initial net foreign asset position is negative; that is, $B_0 < 0$. Then for this country to satisfy equation (2.5), the sum of its current account surpluses must be positive ($CA_1 + CA_2 > 0$); that is, the country must run a current account surplus in at least one period. However, if the country's initial net foreign asset position is positive; that is, if $B_0 > 0$, then the country can run a current account deficit in both periods, which in the present two-period economy is tantamount to a perpetual current account deficit.

The result that a debtor country cannot run a perpetual current account deficit but a net creditor can is valid for any finite horizon. This means that the result applies not only to economies that last for only two periods, as in the present example, but also to economies that last for any finite number of periods, even if this number is very large, say 1 million years.

However, the appendix shows that in an infinite horizon economy, a negative initial net foreign asset position does not preclude an economy from running perpetual current account deficits. The requirement for an infinite horizon economy not to engage in a Ponzi scheme is that it pay periodically part of the interest accrued on its net foreign debt to ensure that the foreign debt grows at a rate less than the interest rate. In this way, the present discounted value of the country's debt would be zero, which is to say that in present discounted value terms the country would pay its debt. Because in this situation the country's net foreign debt is growing over time, the economy must devote an ever larger amount of resources (i.e., it must generate larger and larger trade surpluses) to servicing part of its interest obligations with the rest of the world. The need to run increasing trade surpluses over time requires domestic output to also grow over time. For if output did not grow, the required trade balance surpluses would eventually exceed GDP, which is impossible.

2.3 Saving, Investment, and the Current Account

In this section, we show how to link, using accounting identities, the current account to a number of familiar macroeconomic aggregates, such as national saving, investment, gross domestic product, and domestic absorption. These accounting identities allow us to view current account deficits from a number of perspectives and will be of use when studying the determination of the current account in a general equilibrium model.

2.3.1 THE CURRENT ACCOUNT AS THE GAP BETWEEN SAVING AND INVESTMENT

The current account is in deficit when investment exceeds saving. To see this, begin by recalling, from Chapter 1, that the trade balance equals the difference between exports and imports of goods and services. Letting X_t denote exports in period t and IM_t denote imports in period t, we have that

$$TB_t = X_t - IM_t.$$

Let Q_t denote the amount of final goods and services produced domestically in period t. This measure of output is known as *gross domestic product*, or GDP. Let C_t denote the amount of goods and services consumed domestically by the private sector in period t, G_t government consumption in period t, and I_t the amount of goods and services used for domestic investment (in plants, infrastructure, etc.) in period t. We will refer to C_t, G_t, and I_t simply as consumption, government spending, and investment in period t, respectively. Then we have that

$$Q_t + IM_t = C_t + I_t + G_t + X_t.$$

This familiar national accounting identity states that the aggregate supply of goods, given by the sum of GDP and imports, can be used in four ways—private consumption, investment, public consumption, or exports. Combining the above two equations and rearranging, we obtain

$$TB_t = Q_t - C_t - I_t - G_t. \tag{2.6}$$

Equation (2.1) must hold not only in period 1, but in any period t, so we have that

$$CA_t = rB_{t-1} + TB_t.$$

Using this expression to eliminate TB_t from equation (2.6) yields

$$CA_t = rB_{t-1} + Q_t - C_t - I_t - G_t.$$

The sum of GDP and net investment income, $Q_t + rB_{t-1}$, is called national income, or *gross national product* (GNP). We denote national income in period t by Y_t; that is,

$$Y_t = Q_t + rB_{t-1}.$$

Combining the last two expressions results in the following representation of the current account:

$$CA_t = Y_t - C_t - I_t - G_t. \tag{2.7}$$

National saving in period t, which we denote by S_t, is defined as the difference between national income and the sum of private and government consumption; that is,

$$S_t = Y_t - C_t - G_t. \tag{2.8}$$

It then follows from this expression and equation (2.7) that the current account is equal to saving minus investment,

$$CA_t = S_t - I_t. \tag{2.9}$$

According to this relation, a deficit in the current account occurs when investment exceeds saving. Conversely, a current account surplus obtains when investment falls short of saving.

2.3.2 THE CURRENT ACCOUNT AS THE GAP BETWEEN NATIONAL INCOME AND DOMESTIC ABSORPTION

A country's absorption, which we denote by A_t, is defined as the sum of private consumption, government consumption, and investment,

$$A_t = C_t + I_t + G_t.$$

Combining this definition with equation (2.7), the current account can be expressed as the difference between income and absorption:

$$CA_t = Y_t - A_t. \tag{2.10}$$

Thus, the current account is in deficit when domestic absorption of goods and services exceeds national income.

You should keep in mind expressions (2.9) and (2.10) represent accounting identities that must be satisfied at all times in any economy. They do not provide any explanation, or theory, of the determinants of the current account. For example, the identity $CA_t = S_t - I_t$, by itself, does not provide support to the pessimistic view that the U.S. current account is in deficit because Americans save too little. Nor does it lend support to the optimistic view that the U.S. current account is in deficit because American firms invest vigorously in physical capital.

To understand what determines the current account we need a model—that is, a story of the economic behavior of households, firms, governments, and foreign residents. This is the focus of the following chapters.

2.4 Appendix: Perpetual Trade Balance and Current Account Deficits in Infinite Horizon Economies

In a world that lasts for only two periods, forever means for periods 1 and 2. Therefore, in such a world a country runs a perpetual trade deficit if the trade balance is negative in periods 1 and 2. Similarly, in a two-period world a country runs a perpetual current account deficit if it experiences a negative current account balance in periods 1 and 2. In the body of this chapter, we showed that a two-period economy can run a perpetual trade balance deficit only if it starts with a positive net international investment position. A similar condition holds for the current account: a two-period country can run a perpetual current account deficit only if its initial net international asset position is positive. In this appendix we study how these results change in a setting in which the economy lasts for an infinite number of periods.

Suppose that the economy starts in period 1 and lasts forever. Suppose, for simplicity, that the interest rate is constant over time and equal to r. Then, the net foreign asset position at the end of period 1 is given by

$$B_1 = (1+r)B_0 + TB_1.$$

Solve for B_0 to obtain

$$B_0 = \frac{B_1}{1+r} - \frac{TB_1}{1+r}. \tag{2.11}$$

Now shift this expression one period forward to obtain

$$B_1 = \frac{B_2}{1+r} - \frac{TB_2}{1+r}.$$

Use this formula to eliminate B_1 from equation (2.11), which yields

$$B_0 = \frac{B_2}{(1+r)^2} - \frac{TB_1}{1+r} - \frac{TB_2}{(1+r)^2}.$$

Shifting (2.11) two periods forward yields

$$B_2 = \frac{B_3}{1+r} - \frac{TB_3}{1+r}.$$

Combining this expression with the one right above it, we obtain

$$B_0 = \frac{B_3}{(1+r)^3} - \frac{TB_1}{1+r} - \frac{TB_2}{(1+r)^2} - \frac{TB_3}{(1+r)^3}.$$

Repeating this iterative procedure T times results in the relationship

$$B_0 = \frac{B_T}{(1+r)^T} - \frac{TB_1}{1+r} - \frac{TB_2}{(1+r)^2} - \cdots - \frac{TB_T}{(1+r)^T}. \tag{2.12}$$

In an infinite horizon economy, the no-Ponzi-game constraint becomes

$$\lim_{T \to \infty} \frac{B_T}{(1+r)^T} \geq 0. \tag{2.13}$$

This expression says that the net foreign debt of a country must grow at a rate lower than the interest rate. A debt trajectory that grows at the rate r or higher is indeed a scheme in which the principal and the interest accrued on the debt are perpetually rolled over. That is, it is a scheme whereby the debt is never paid off. The no-Ponzi-game constraint precludes this type of situation.

At the same time, the country will not want to have a net credit with the rest of the world growing at a rate r or higher, because that would mean that the rest of the world forever rolls over its debt and interest with the country in question, never paying either one. Thus the path of net international investment position must satisfy

$$\lim_{T \to \infty} \frac{B_T}{(1+r)^T} \leq 0.$$

This restriction and the no-Ponzi-game constraint (2.13) can be simultaneously satisfied only if the following transversality condition holds:

$$\lim_{T \to \infty} \frac{B_T}{(1+r)^T} = 0. \tag{2.14}$$

According to this expression, a country's net foreign asset position must converge to zero in present discounted value. Letting T go to infinity in equation (2.12) and using the transversality condition (2.14), we have

$$B_0 = -\frac{TB_1}{1+r} - \frac{TB_2}{(1+r)^2} - \cdots = -\sum_{t=1}^{\infty} \frac{TB_t}{(1+r)^t}.$$

This expression is the infinite horizon counterpart of equation (2.4) in the two-period economy. It states that the initial net foreign asset position of a country must equal the present discounted value of the stream of current and expected future trade deficits. If the initial net foreign asset position of the country is negative ($B_0 < 0$), then the country must run trade balance surpluses at some point. We conclude that regardless of whether we consider a finite horizon economy or an infinite horizon economy, a country that starts with a negative net foreign asset position cannot perpetually run trade balance deficits.

We next revisit the question of whether a country can run perpetual current account deficits. Suppose that the initial net foreign asset position of the country is negative ($B_0 < 0$). That is, the country starts out as a net debtor to the rest of the world.

Consider an example in which each period the country generates a trade balance surplus sufficient to pay a fraction α of its interest obligations. That is, assume that

$$TB_t = -\alpha r B_{t-1}, \tag{2.15}$$

where the factor α is between 0 and 1. According to this expression, whenever the country is a net debtor to the rest of the world; that is, whenever $B_{t-1} < 0$, it generates a trade balance surplus. (We are assuming that the interest rate is positive, or $r > 0$.)

Note that the evolution of the country's net foreign asset position in a generic period $t = 1, 2, 3, \ldots$ can be written as

$$B_t = (1+r)B_{t-1} + TB_t.$$

Using the debt-servicing policy (2.15) to eliminate TB_t from this expression, we obtain

$$B_t = (1+r-\alpha r)B_{t-1}. \tag{2.16}$$

Because we are supposing that B_0 is negative and that $1+r-\alpha r$ is positive, we have that the net foreign asset position of the country will be forever negative; that is, $B_t < 0$ for all $t \geq 0$. Furthermore, under the assumed debt-servicing policy the country will run a perpetual current account deficit. To see this, recall that the current account in period t is given by $CA_t = rB_{t-1} + TB_t$. Now use the debt-servicing policy, equation (2.15), to eliminate TB_t to obtain

$$CA_t = r(1-\alpha)B_{t-1},$$

which is negative because $r(1-\alpha)$ is positive and, as just shown, $B_{t-1} < 0$ for all $t \geq 1$.

To determine whether these perpetual current account deficits are sustainable, the key question is whether the country satisfies the transversality condition (2.14).

If the transversality condition is not satisfied, then the trajectory of current account deficits is unsustainable, because in that case either the country would be playing a Ponzi game on the rest of the world or vice versa.

The law of motion of B_t given in equation (2.16) implies that

$$B_t = (1 + r - \alpha r)^t B_0.$$

Divide both sides of this expression by $(1 + r)^t$ to obtain

$$\frac{B_t}{(1+r)^t} = \left[\frac{1 + r(1 - \alpha)}{1 + r} \right]^t B_0.$$

Because $1 + r(1 - \alpha) < 1 + r$, $\frac{B_t}{(1+r)^t}$ converges to zero as t converges to infinity. This implies that even though under the proposed debt-servicing policy the country is running perpetual current account deficits, the transversality condition (2.14) is satisfied.

But this is not the end of the story. Notice that under the assumed policy the trade balance evolves according to

$$TB_t = -\alpha r [1 + r(1 - \alpha)]^{t-1} B_0.$$

That is, the trade balance is positive and grows unboundedly over time at the rate $r(1 - \alpha) > 0$. Recall that the trade balance equals GDP minus domestic absorption

$$TB_t = GDP_t - A_t,$$

where $A_t = C_t + I_t + G_t > 0$ denotes domestic absorption. It follows from this expression that in order for a country to be able to generate unboundedly large trade balance surpluses, its GDP must grow over time at a rate equal to or greater than $r(1 - \alpha) > 0$. If this condition is satisfied, then the repayment policy described in this example, equation (2.15), would allow the country to run perpetual current account deficits even if its initial net foreign asset position is negative.

2.5 Summing Up

This chapter studies conditions under which given paths of the trade balance and the current account are sustainable. It derives the following results:

- A country that is a net external debtor cannot run a perpetual trade balance deficit.
- A country that is a net external debtor cannot run a perpetual deficit in the current account. This result applies to economies that last for any finite number of periods. For infinite horizon economies, perpetual current account deficits are possible even if the country is an external debtor, if the economy is growing and dedicates a growing amount of resources to pay interest on its external debt.
- The current account can be expressed as the gap between saving and investment, $CA_t = S_t - I_t$, as the gap between national income and domestic absorption, $CA_t = Y_t - A_t$, as the change in the country's net foreign asset

position, $CA_t = B_t - B_{t-1}$, or as the sum of net investment income and the trade balance, $CA_t = rB_{t-1} + TB_t$. All four expressions are identities that must hold at any time in any country.

2.6 Exercises

Exercise 2.1 (TFU) Indicate whether the following statements are true, false, or uncertain and explain why.

1. An economy that starts with a positive net international investment position will run a trade balance deficit at some point.
2. A country has been having trade balance deficits for 40 years. Four decades ago, the country was a net creditor, but after so many trade deficits it became a debtor. Clearly, this economy will have to run trade surpluses at some point.
3. A two-period economy runs trade surpluses in both periods. It follows that the current account in period 1 can have either sign (depending on the magnitude of TB_1), but the current account in period 2 must be positive.
4. When the interest rate is negative, a two-period economy can run perpetual trade deficits even if its initial net foreign asset position is negative.
5. When the interest rate is negative, a two-period economy cannot run perpetual current account deficits if its initial net foreign asset position is negative.
6. A country starts 2022 as a net creditor. The interest rate on its net asset position is 10 percent. That year, it runs a current account deficit. It follows that the trade balance in 2022 was also negative.
7. The fact that since the 1980s the United States has run larger and larger current account deficits is proof that American household saving has been shrinking.
8. A policy of balanced trade (i.e., the requirement that the trade balance must be zero at all times) is only feasible if there is free capital mobility.

Exercise 2.2 (Current Account Sustainability in a Three-Period Economy) Can a three-period economy run a perpetual trade balance deficit? Can it run a perpetual current account deficit? To address these questions, derive step-by-step adaptations of equations (2.4) and (2.5) to a three-period horizon.

Exercise 2.3 (Saving, Investment, and the Net International Investment Position) In a two-period economy, saving in periods 1 and 2 is 5 ($S_1 = S_2 = 5$) and investment in both periods is 10 ($I_1 = I_2 = 10$).

1. What is the current account in periods 1 and 2 (CA_1 and CA_2)?
2. What is the initial net international investment position (B_0)?
3. Assuming that the interest rate is 4 percent ($r = 0.04$), what is the trade balance in periods 1 and 2 (TB_1 and TB_2)?

Exercise 2.4 (Living Beyond One's Means) Consider a two-period economy that has at the beginning of period 1 a net foreign asset position of -100. In period 1, the country runs a current account deficit of 5 percent of GDP, and GDP in both periods is 120. Assume the interest rate in periods 1 and 2 is 10 percent.

1. Find the trade balance in period 1 (TB_1), the current account balance in period 1 (CA_1), and the country's net foreign asset position at the beginning of period 2 (B_1).

2. Is the country living beyond its means? To answer this question find the country's current account balance in period 2 and the associated trade balance in period 2. Is this value for the trade balance feasible? [Hint: Keep in mind that the trade balance cannot exceed GDP.]

3. Now assume that in period 1, the country runs instead a much larger current account deficit of 10 percent of GDP. Find the country's net foreign asset position at the end of period 1, B_1. Is the country living beyond its means? If so, explain why.

CHAPTER 3

An Intertemporal Theory of the Current Account

Why do some countries borrow and others lend? Why do some countries run trade balance deficits and others trade balance surpluses? This chapter addresses these and other related questions by building a model of an open economy to study the determinants of the trade balance and the current account. At the heart of this theory is the optimal intertemporal allocation of expenditure. Countries will borrow or lend to smooth consumption over time in the face of uneven output streams.

This chapter analyzes the determination of the current account in a small open economy. Chapter 7 extends the theory to a large open economy. We say that an economy is open when it trades in goods and financial assets with the rest of the world. We say that an economy is small when prices of internationally traded goods and services, as well as prices and rates of return on internationally traded financial assets, are independent of domestic economic conditions. For example, if consumption of beef doubles in a small open economy, then the world price of beef does not increase because the local beef market is too small relative to the world market. In turn, the local market could be small because the country's population is small or because consumption of beef per capita is small (e.g., people do not have a taste for beef or are too poor to afford it). Similarly, if in a small economy saving doubles, the interest rate in world financial markets does not fall, as the local capital market is too small relative to its world counterpart.

Most countries in the world are small open economies. Examples of developed small open economies are the Netherlands, Switzerland, Austria, New Zealand, Australia, Canada, and Norway. Examples of emerging small open economies are Argentina, Chile, Peru, Bolivia, Greece, Portugal, Estonia, Latvia, and Thailand. Examples of large developed open economies are the United States, Japan, and Germany. China and India are examples of large emerging open economies. There are not many examples of completely closed economies. Perhaps the closest examples are North Korea, Cuba, Iran, and in the past few years, Venezuela.

The economic size of a country may not be related to its geographic size. For example, Australia and Canada are geographically large, but economically small. On the other hand, Japan and Germany are geographically small but economically large. Also, demographic and economic size may not be correlated. For example, Indonesia is demographically large, but remains economically small.

3.1 The Intertemporal Budget Constraint

Consider an economy in which people live for two periods, 1 and 2, and are endowed with Q_1 units of goods in period 1 and Q_2 units in period 2. Suppose that goods are perishable in the sense that they cannot be stored from one period to the next. Think of fresh food in a tropical island without refrigeration. Although in the present economy households are unable to store goods, they can reallocate resources between periods 1 and 2 via the international financial market. Specifically, assume that in period 1 each household is endowed with B_0 units of a bond. These bond holdings generate interest income in the amount $r_0 B_0$ in period 1, where r_0 denotes the interest rate. In period 1, the household's income is therefore given by the sum of interest income, $r_0 B_0$, and the endowment of goods, Q_1; that is, period 1 income is equal to $r_0 B_0 + Q_1$.

The household can allocate its income to two alternative uses: purchases of consumption goods, which we denote by C_1, and purchases (or sales) of bonds, $B_1 - B_0$, where B_1 denotes bond holdings at the end of period 1. Thus, in period 1 the household faces the following budget constraint:

$$C_1 + B_1 - B_0 = r_0 B_0 + Q_1. \tag{3.1}$$

Similarly, in period 2 the household faces a budget constraint stating that consumption expenditure plus bond purchases must equal income,

$$C_2 + B_2 - B_1 = r_1 B_1 + Q_2, \tag{3.2}$$

where C_2 denotes consumption in period 2, r_1 denotes the interest rate on bonds held between periods 1 and 2, and B_2 denotes bond holdings at the end of period 2.

As explained in Chapter 2, by the no-Ponzi-game constraint households are not allowed to leave any debt at the end of period 2; that is, B_2 must be greater than or equal to zero. Intuitively, the no-Ponzi-game constraint says that it is forbidden to leave an unpaid debt in period 2, knowing that one is not going to be around when it comes due in period 3. Also, households will choose not to hold any positive amount of assets at the end of period 2, as they will not be around in period 3 to spend those savings on consumption goods. Thus, since it can be neither positive nor negative, B_2 must be zero,

$$B_2 = 0. \tag{3.3}$$

As discussed in Chapter 2, this terminal condition is known as the *transversality condition*.

Combining the period budget constraints (3.1) and (3.2) with the transversality condition (3.3) to eliminate B_1 and B_2 yields the *intertemporal budget constraint* of the household,

$$C_1 + \frac{C_2}{1 + r_1} = (1 + r_0) B_0 + Q_1 + \frac{Q_2}{1 + r_1}. \tag{3.4}$$

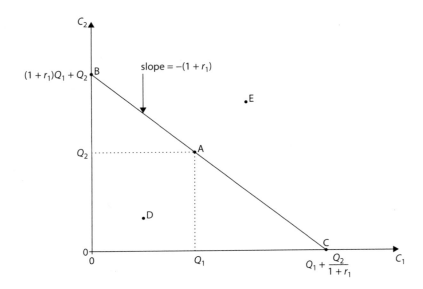

Figure 3.1. The Intertemporal Budget Constraint
Notes: The downward-sloping line represents the consumption paths (C_1, C_2) that satisfy the intertemporal budget constraint (3.4). The figure is drawn under the assumption that the household's initial asset position is zero, $B_0 = 0$.

The intertemporal budget constraint states that the present discounted value of consumption (the left-hand side) must be equal to the initial stock of wealth plus the present discounted value of the endowment stream (the right-hand side). The household chooses consumption in periods 1 and 2, C_1 and C_2, taking as given all other variables appearing in the intertemporal budget constraint (3.4), namely, r_0, r_1, B_0, Q_1, and Q_2.

Figure 3.1 displays the pairs (C_1, C_2) that satisfy the household's intertemporal budget constraint (3.4). For simplicity, we assume for the remainder of this section that the household's initial asset position is zero; that is, we assume that $B_0 = 0$. Then, the consumption path $C_1 = Q_1$ and $C_2 = Q_2$ (point A in the figure) satisfies the intertemporal budget constraint (3.4). In words, it is feasible for the household to consume its endowment in each period.

But the household's choices are not limited to this particular consumption path. In period 1 the household can consume more or less than its endowment by borrowing or saving. For example, if the household chooses to allocate all of its lifetime wealth to consumption in period 2, it can do so by saving all of its period 1 endowment. In period 2, its wealth is the period 1 savings including interest, $(1 + r_1)Q_1$, plus its period 2 endowment, Q_2. Then, C_2 equals $(1 + r_1)Q_1 + Q_2$ and C_1 is, of course, nil. This consumption path is located at the intersection of the intertemporal budget constraint with the vertical axis (point B in the figure). At the opposite extreme, if the household chooses to allocate its entire lifetime wealth to consumption in period 1, it would borrow $Q_2/(1 + r_1)$ units of goods in period 1. Then, C_1 equals the period 1 endowment plus the loan, $Q_1 + Q_2/(1 + r_1)$. In period 2, the household must pay the principal of the loan, $Q_2/(1 + r_1)$, plus interest,

$r_1 Q_2/(1+r_1)$, or a total of Q_2, to cancel its debt. As a result, period 2 consumption is zero, $C_2 = 0$, since all of the period 2 endowment must be used to retire the debt. This consumption path corresponds to the intersection of the intertemporal budget constraint with the horizontal axis (point C in the figure). All points on the straight line that connects points B and C belong to the intertemporal budget constraint and represent feasible consumption choices.

The intertemporal budget constraint dictates that if the household wants to increase consumption in one period, it must reduce consumption in the other period. Specifically, for each additional unit of consumption in period 1, the household has to give up $1 + r_1$ units of consumption in period 2. This is because the alternative to consuming an extra unit in period 1 is to save that unit in an interest-bearing asset, which yields $1 + r_1$ units in the next period. Graphically, this tradeoff between consumption in period 1 and consumption in period 2 is reflected in the intertemporal budget constraint being downward sloping, with a slope equal to $-(1 + r_1)$.

The intertemporal budget constraint depicted in Figure 3.1 allows us to see which consumption paths entail saving or borrowing in period 1. Saving is defined as the difference between income and consumption. Thus, letting S_1 denote saving in period 1, we have $S_1 = r_0 B_0 + Q_1 - C_1$. Consumption paths on the budget constraint located southeast of point A (all points between A and C), are associated with negative saving ($S_1 < 0$); that is, with borrowing. Because in the figure we are assuming that the household starts with zero assets ($B_0 = 0$), we have that all points on the budget constraint located southeast of point A are associated with $B_1 < 0$; that is, with the household starting period 2 as a debtor. Similarly, points on the budget constraint located northwest of point A (all points between A and B) are associated with positive saving in period 1 ($S_1 > 0$), or a positive asset position at the beginning of period 2 ($B_1 > 0$).

Consumption paths (C_1, C_2) located below and to the left of the intertemporal budget constraint (such as point D in Figure 3.1) are feasible, but do not exhaust the household's lifetime wealth. The household could consume more in one period without sacrificing consumption in the other period or could consume more in both periods. Such consumption paths violate the transversality condition (3.3), as the household leaves resources on the table at the end of period 2 ($B_2 > 0$).

Consumption paths located above and to the right of the intertemporal budget constraint (such as point E in the figure) are not feasible, as they have a present discounted value larger than the household's lifetime wealth. These consumption paths violate the transversality condition, equation (3.3), because they imply that the household ends period 2 with unpaid debts ($B_2 < 0$).

3.2 The Lifetime Utility Function

Which consumption path (C_1, C_2) on the intertemporal budget constraint the household will choose depends on its preferences for current and future consumption. We assume that these preferences can be described by the function

$$U(C_1) + \beta U(C_2). \tag{3.5}$$

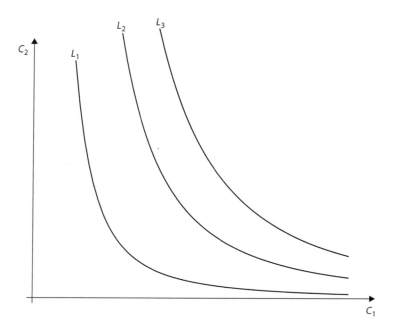

Figure 3.2. Indifference Curves
Notes: The level of the lifetime utility associated with each of the three indifference curves is L_1, L_2, and L_3, respectively. All consumption paths (C_1, C_2) on a given indifference curve provide the same level of lifetime utility. Across indifference curves, the lifetime utility increases as one moves northeast in the figure; that is, $L_1 < L_2 < L_3$.

This function is known as the *lifetime utility function*. It indicates the level of satisfaction (or felicity) derived by the household from different consumption paths (C_1, C_2). The function $U(\cdot)$ is known as the *period utility function* and the parameter β is known as the *subjective discount factor*. We assume that consumption in periods 1 and 2, C_1 and C_2, are both goods; that is, items for which more is preferred to less. In other words, we assume that households enjoy consuming goods in periods 1 and 2. This means that the period utility function is increasing and that the subjective discount factor is positive, $\beta > 0$. The subjective discount factor is a measure of impatience. The smaller is β, the more impatient the consumer will be. In the extreme case in which $\beta = 0$, consumers care only about period 1 consumption. Typically, β is set to a value greater than 0 and less than or equal to 1, which implies that households do not care more about future than present consumption.

A useful graphical representation of preferences is the *indifference map*, displaying the household's *indifference curves*. An indifference curve is the collection of consumption paths (C_1, C_2) that provide a given level of utility. Figure 3.2 displays the indifference curves for three levels of lifetime utility, L_1, L_2, and L_3. All consumption paths (C_1, C_2) on a given indifference curve provide the same level of utility. Because consumption in both periods are goods, the indifference curves are downward sloping. An increase in period 1 consumption requires a decrease in period 2 consumption if the household is to remain indifferent. As one moves northeast in the space (C_1, C_2), utility increases. Thus, in Figure 3.2 we have that

$L_1 < L_2 < L_3$. Figure 3.2 displays only three indifference curves, but the positive quadrant is densely populated with indifference curves. In fact, every point in the positive quadrant—that is, every consumption path (C_1, C_2)—belongs to one (and only one) indifference curve.

An important property of the indifference curves drawn in Figure 3.2 is that they are convex toward the origin, so that at low levels of C_1 relative to C_2, the indifference curves are steeper than at relatively high levels of C_1. Intuitively, at low levels of consumption in period 1 relative to consumption in period 2, the household is willing to give up relatively many units of period 2 consumption for an additional unit of period 1 consumption. Similarly, if period 1 consumption is high relative to period 2 consumption, then the household will not be willing to sacrifice much period 2 consumption for an additional unit of period 1 consumption. Put differently, as consumption in period 1 decreases, the household will demand larger increments of consumption in period 2 to keep its level of utility unchanged.

To obtain the slope of an indifference curve, proceed as follows. Fix the level of lifetime utility at some constant, say L. Then the indifference curve associated with a level of lifetime utility L is given by all the paths (C_1, C_2) satisfying

$$U(C_1) + \beta U(C_2) = L.$$

Now differentiate this expression with respect to C_1 and C_2 to obtain

$$U'(C_1)dC_1 + \beta U'(C_2)dC_2 = 0,$$

where $U'(\cdot)$ denotes the derivative of $U(\cdot)$. The objects $U'(C_1)$ and $U'(C_2)$ are known as the *marginal utility of consumption* in periods 1 and 2, respectively. The marginal utility of consumption in period 1 indicates the increase in lifetime utility derived from consuming one more unit in period 1, and $\beta U'(C_2)$ indicates the increase in lifetime utility derived from consuming one more unit in period 2. Rearranging the above expression, we obtain that the slope of the indifference curve, dC_2/dC_1, is given by

$$\text{slope of the indifference curve} = -\frac{U'(C_1)}{\beta U'(C_2)}.$$

The assumed convexity of the indifference curves requires that this slope become smaller in absolute value as C_1 increases. Now, when C_1 increases, C_2 decreases, because we are moving along a given indifference curve. The only way the indifference curve can become flatter as C_1 increases and C_2 decreases is if $U'(C_1)$ is decreasing in C_1; that is, if the derivative of the marginal utility is negative, $U''(C_1) < 0$. We have therefore arrived at the result that the convexity of the indifference curve requires that the period utility function $U(\cdot)$ be concave.

An example of a lifetime utility function that delivers downward sloping and convex indifference curves is the *logarithmic lifetime utility function* without time discounting, which is given by

$$\ln C_1 + \ln C_2, \tag{3.6}$$

where ln denotes the natural logarithm. In this example, $U(C_i) = \ln C_i$, for $i = 1, 2$, and $\beta = 1$. Because the natural logarithm is an increasing and concave function, this lifetime utility function is increasing in consumption in both periods, and its associated indifference curves are convex toward the origin. To see that the indifference curves implied by these preferences are downward sloping and convex, fix the level of lifetime utility at some arbitrary level, say 3. Then, the indifference curve corresponding to this utility level is given by all the consumption paths (C_1, C_2) satisfying $\ln C_1 + \ln C_2 = 3$. Solving for C_2, we obtain $C_2 = \frac{20.1}{C_1}$. This expression says that along the indifference curve associated with a level of lifetime utility of 3, C_2 is a decreasing and convex function of C_1.

The negative of the slope of the indifference curve is known as the *intertemporal marginal rate of substitution* of C_2 for C_1. The intertemporal marginal rate of substitution indicates how many units of period 2 consumption the household is willing to give up for one additional unit of period 1 consumption if its lifetime utility is to remain unchanged. The assumption of convexity of the indifference curves can then be stated as saying that along a given indifference curve, the intertemporal marginal rate of substitution decreases with C_1. For example, in the logarithmic lifetime utility function given above, the intertemporal marginal rate of substitution associated with a level of lifetime utility of 3 is equal to $\frac{20.1}{C_1^2}$, which is decreasing in C_1.

Before moving on, it is important to point out that what matters for all of the analysis that follows is that the indifference curves be decreasing and convex. For this property to obtain, it is not necessary that the lifetime utility function be concave in (C_1, C_2). Any increasing monotonic transformation of the lifetime utility function (3.5) will deliver the same map of indifference curves. For example, the lifetime utility function $C_1 C_2$ is not concave, but delivers the same indifference curves as the logarithmic lifetime utility function given in equation (3.6). This is because $C_1 C_2 = \exp(\ln C_1 + \ln C_2)$ and because the exponential function is strictly increasing. Can you show, for example, that the indifference curve that crosses the consumption path $C_1 = 3$ and $C_2 = 2$, is the same under both lifetime utility functions?

3.3 The Optimal Intertemporal Allocation of Consumption

The household chooses C_1 and C_2 to maximize the lifetime utility function (3.5) subject to the intertemporal budget constraint (3.4), taking as given the initial wealth, $(1 + r_0)B_0$, the endowments, Q_1 and Q_2, and the interest rate, r_1.

Figure 3.3 illustrates the determination of the optimal consumption path. To maximize utility, the household chooses a consumption path (C_1, C_2) that is on the intertemporal budget constraint and on an indifference curve that provides the highest level of lifetime utility; that is, an indifference curve that is as far northeast as possible. At the feasible consumption path that maximizes the household's lifetime utility, the indifference curve is tangent to the budget constraint (point B in Figure 3.3).

To obtain the optimal levels of consumption in periods 1 and 2, begin by solving the intertemporal budget constraint (3.4) for C_2 to obtain

$$C_2 = (1 + r_1)\left[(1 + r_0)B_0 + Q_1 + \frac{Q_2}{1 + r_1} - C_1\right].$$

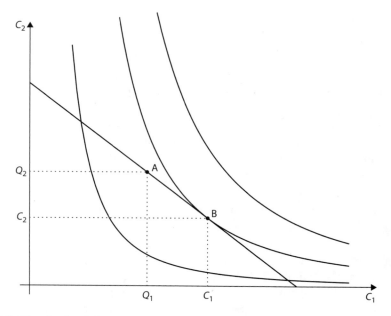

Figure 3.3. The Optimal Consumption Path
Notes: The optimal consumption path (C_1, C_2) is at point B, where an indifference curve is tangent to the intertemporal budget constraint. As the figure is drawn, the household borrows in period 1 $(C_1 > Q_1)$ and pays back its debt in period 2 $(C_2 < Q_2)$. The figure is drawn under the assumption of a zero initial net foreign asset position, $B_0 = 0$.

Define

$$\bar{Y} = (1 + r_0)B_0 + Q_1 + \frac{Q_2}{1 + r_1}.$$

Here, $\bar{Y}$ represents the household's lifetime wealth, which is composed of its initial asset holdings and the present discounted value of the stream of income (Q_1, Q_2). This short notation is handy because the household takes $\bar{Y}$ as given. We can then rewrite the intertemporal budget constraint as

$$C_2 = (1 + r_1)(\bar{Y} - C_1). \tag{3.7}$$

Use this expression to eliminate C_2 from the lifetime utility function (3.5) to obtain

$$U(C_1) + \beta U((1 + r_1)(\bar{Y} - C_1)). \tag{3.8}$$

The optimization problem of the household then reduces to choosing C_1 to maximize (3.8), taking as given $\bar{Y}$ and r_1. The first-order optimality condition associated with this maximization problem results from taking the derivative of this expression with respect to C_1 and setting it equal to zero. This yields

$$U'(C_1) - \beta U'((1 + r_1)(\bar{Y} - C_1))(1 + r_1) = 0.$$

Rearranging and using the fact that $C_2 = (1 + r_1)(\bar{Y} - C_1)$ yields

$$U'(C_1) = (1 + r_1)\beta U'(C_2). \tag{3.9}$$

The optimality condition (3.9) is known as the consumption *Euler equation* and is quite intuitive. Suppose that the household sacrifices one unit of consumption in period 1. This reduces its utility by $U'(C_1)$. Thus, the left-hand side of the Euler equation represents the utility cost of reducing period 1 consumption by one unit. Suppose further that the household saves this unit of consumption in a bond paying the interest rate r_1. Then, in period 2, the household receives $1 + r_1$ units of consumption, each of which increases its lifetime utility by $\beta U'(C_2)$. Thus the right-hand side of the Euler equation represents the utility gain of sacrificing one unit of period 1 consumption. If the left-hand side of the Euler equation is greater than the right-hand side, then the household can increase its lifetime utility by saving less (and hence consuming more) in period 1. Conversely, if the left-hand side of the Euler equation is less than the right-hand side, then the household will be better off saving more (and consuming less) in period 1. At the optimal allocation, the left- and right-hand sides of the Euler equation must be equal to each other, so that at the margin the household is indifferent between consuming an extra unit in period 1 and consuming $1 + r_1$ extra units in period 2.

To see that the Euler equation (3.9) is equivalent to the requirement that at the optimum (point B in Figure 3.3) the indifference curve be tangent to the budget constraint, divide the left- and right hand sides of the Euler equation by $-\beta U'(C_2)$ to obtain

$$-\frac{U'(C_1)}{\beta U'(C_2)} = -(1 + r_1).$$

The left-hand side of this expression, $-\frac{U'(C_1)}{\beta U'(C_2)}$, is the negative of the marginal rate of intertemporal substitution of C_2 for C_1 at the consumption path (C_1, C_2), which, as we saw earlier, is the slope of the indifference curve. The right-hand side, $-(1 + r_1)$, is the slope of the budget constraint.

3.4 The Interest Rate Parity Condition

We assume that households have unrestricted access to international financial markets. This assumption is known as *free capital mobility*. It means that the country can borrow from or lend to the rest of the world without any impediments. Free capital mobility tends to eliminate differences between the domestic interest rate, r_1, and the interest rate prevailing in the rest of the world, which we denote by r^*. This is because if the domestic interest rate were higher than the world interest rate ($r_1 > r^*$), then a pure *arbitrage opportunity* would arise whereby financial investors could make infinite profits by borrowing from abroad at the rate r^* and lending domestically at the rate r_1. This would drive down the domestic interest rate, as the country would be flooded with credit. Conversely, if the domestic interest rate were lower than the world interest rate ($r_1 < r^*$), then an arbitrage opportunity would allow financial investors to make infinite profits by borrowing domestically at the rate r_1 and lending internationally at the rate $r^* > r_1$. This would drive up the domestic interest rate, as all funds would move abroad. Arbitrage opportunities disappear when the domestic interest rate equals the world interest rate; that is, when

$$r_1 = r^*.$$

This expression is known as the *interest rate parity condition*. Chapter 11 studies empirically the extent to which financial capital can move across countries. For many countries, especially in the developed world, free capital mobility is not an unrealistic description of the functioning of their financial markets. For other countries, especially in the emerging world, large deviations from free capital mobility are often observed. In later chapters, we will study how the present economy works when financial capital is not free to move across borders, so that the interest rate parity condition does not hold. For the time being, however, we assume that the interest rate parity condition does hold.

3.5 Equilibrium in the Small Open Economy

We assume that all households are identical. Thus, by studying the behavior of an individual household, we are also learning about the behavior of the country as a whole. For this reason, we will not distinguish between the behavior of an individual household and that of the country as a whole.

The country is assumed to be sufficiently small so that its saving decisions do not affect the world interest rate. Because all households are identical, at any point in time all domestic residents will make identical saving decisions. This implies that domestic households will never borrow or lend from one another and that all borrowing or lending takes the form of purchases or sales of foreign assets. Thus, we can interpret B_t $(t = 0, 1, 2)$ as the country's net foreign asset position, or net international investment position (*NIIP*), at the end of period t.

Furthermore, the assumption that all households are identical implies that the intertemporal budget constraint of an individual household, given by equation (3.4), can be interpreted as the country's *intertemporal resource constraint*.

An equilibrium then is a consumption path (C_1, C_2) and an interest rate r_1 that satisfy the country's intertemporal resource constraint, the consumption Euler equation, and the interest rate parity condition; that is,

$$C_1 + \frac{C_2}{1 + r_1} = (1 + r_0)B_0 + Q_1 + \frac{Q_2}{1 + r_1}, \tag{3.10}$$

$$U'(C_1) = (1 + r_1)\beta U'(C_2), \tag{3.11}$$

and

$$r_1 = r^*, \tag{3.12}$$

given the exogenous variables r_0, B_0, Q_1, Q_2, and r^*. In general, the term *exogenous variable* refers to variables whose values are determined outside of the model. In the

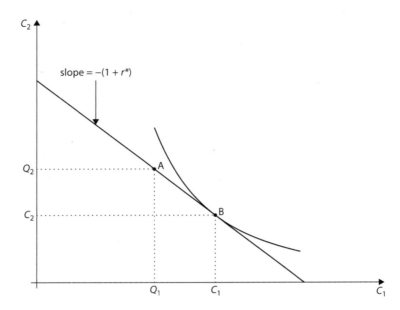

Figure 3.4. Equilibrium in the Endowment Economy
Notes: The figure displays the equilibrium in a small open economy with free capital mobility and a zero initial net foreign asset position, $B_0 = 0$. The equilibrium is at point B, where an indifference curve is tangent to the intertemporal budget constraint. Because of free capital mobility, the domestic interest rate is equal to the world interest rate, r^*, so that the slope of the intertemporal resource constraint is $-(1 + r^*)$. As the figure is drawn, the country runs trade and current account deficits in period 1, $C_1 > Q_1$.

present model economy, the initial net foreign asset position B_0 is determined in period 0, before the beginning of the economy. The world interest rate, r^*, is determined in world financial markets, which our economy cannot affect because it is too small. And the endowments, Q_1 and Q_2, represent manna-type receipts of goods whose quantity and timing are independent of the individual or collective behavior of households. By contrast, *endogenous variables* are variables that are determined within the model. Clearly, households choose consumption in both periods, so C_1 and C_2 are endogenous variables. The domestic interest rate, r_1, although taken as given by individual households, is nonetheless an endogenous variable because it is determined collectively by domestic and foreign market participants as they exploit arbitrage opportunities.

The equilibrium conditions (3.10) to (3.12) are represented graphically in Figure 3.4. The equilibrium path of consumption is at point B. Point B is on the economy's intertemporal resource constraint, as required by equilibrium condition (3.10). Also, at point A an indifference curve is tangent to the intertemporal resource constraint, which means that equilibrium condition (3.11) is satisfied. And the slope of the intertemporal resource constraint is $-(1 + r^*)$, which says that the domestic interest rate equals the world interest rate; that is, equilibrium condition (3.12) holds.

3.6 The Trade Balance and the Current Account

In the present economy the trade balance in period 1 equals the difference between the endowment of goods in period 1, Q_1, and consumption of goods in period 1, C_1, that is,

$$TB_1 = Q_1 - C_1. \qquad (3.13)$$

Similarly, the trade balance in period 2 is given by

$$TB_2 = Q_2 - C_2.$$

The current account is equal to the sum of net investment income and the trade balance. Thus in period 1 the current account is given by

$$CA_1 = r_0 B_0 + TB_1, \qquad (3.14)$$

and the current account in period 2 is given by

$$CA_2 = r^* B_1 + TB_2.$$

Combining the period 1 budget constraint (3.1) with the above expressions for the trade balance and the current account, equations (3.13) and (3.14), we can alternatively express the current account in period 1 as the change in the country's net foreign asset position,

$$CA_1 = B_1 - B_0.$$

A similar expression holds in period 2, except that because period 2 is the last period of the economy, B_2 is nil. So we have that

$$CA_2 = -B_1,$$

which says that in the last period the country retires any outstanding debt if $B_1 < 0$ or spends any asset holdings if $B_1 > 0$.

Look again at Figure 3.4. As we saw earlier, the equilibrium is at point B. Because B is located southeast of the endowment point A, consumption in period 1 exceeds the endowment, $C_1 > Q_1$. Equation (3.13) then implies that the country runs a trade deficit in period 1; that is, $TB_1 < 0$. Also, recalling that the figure is drawn under the assumption that foreign asset holdings in period 0 are nil ($B_0 = 0$), by equation (3.14) the current account in period 1 equals the trade balance in that period, $CA_1 = TB_1 < 0$. Thus, in equilibrium, the current account is in deficit in period 1. In turn, the current account deficit in period 1 implies that the country starts period 2 as a net debtor to the rest of the world ($B_1 < 0$). As a result, in period 2 the country must generate a trade surplus to repay the debt plus interest; that is, $TB_2 = -(1 + r^*)B_1 > 0$.

In general, the equilibrium need not feature trade and current account deficits in period 1. In Figure 3.4, the endowments, preferences, and the world interest rate are such that point B lies southeast of point A. But under different preferences, endowments, or world interest rates, the equilibrium may lie northwest of the endowment point A. In that case, the country would run trade balance and current account surpluses in period 1.

3.7 Adjustment to Temporary and Permanent Output Shocks

What is the effect of an increase in output on the current account? It turns out that this question, as formulated, is incomplete and, as a result, does not have a clear answer. The reason is that in a world in which agents make decisions based on current and future expected changes in the economic environment, one needs to specify not only what the current change in the environment is, but also what the future expected changes will be. The information that current output increases does not tell us in what direction, if any, future output is expected to move. Consider the following example. A self-employed income earner of a family falls ill and is unable to work full time. How should the members of the household adjust their consumption expenditures in response to this exogenous shock? It really depends on the severity of the illness affecting the head of the household. If the illness is transitory (a cold, say), then the income earner will be expected to be back on a full-time schedule in a short period of time (within a week, say). In this case, although the family is making less income for one week, there is no reason to implement drastic adjustments in spending patterns. Consumption can go on more or less as usual. The gap between spending and income during the week in which the breadwinner of the family is out of commission can be covered with savings accumulated in the past or, if no savings are available, by borrowing a little against future earnings. Future consumption should not be much affected either. For due to the fact that the period during which income was reduced was short, the interest cost of the borrowing that took place during that time is small relative to the level of regular income. However, if the affliction is of a more permanent nature (a chronic back injury, say), then one should expect that the reduction in the work week will be of a more permanent nature. In this case, the members of the household should expect not only current but also future income to go down. As a result, consumption must be permanently adjusted downward by cutting, for instance, items that are not fully necessary, such as extra school activities or restaurant meals.

The general principle that the above example illustrates is that forward-looking, optimizing individuals will behave differently in response to an income shock, depending on whether it is temporary or permanent. They will tend to finance temporary income shocks by increasing savings if the temporary shock is positive or by dissaving if the temporary shock is negative. On the other hand, they will adjust in response to permanent income shocks by cutting consumption if the permanent shock is negative or by increasing consumption if the permanent shock is positive. This same principle can be applied to countries as a whole. In this section, we develop this idea more formally in the context of the model of current account determination laid out above.

3.7.1 ADJUSTMENT TO TEMPORARY OUTPUT SHOCKS

Consider the adjustment of a small open economy to a temporary variation in output. For example, suppose that Ecuador loses 20 percent of its banana crop due to

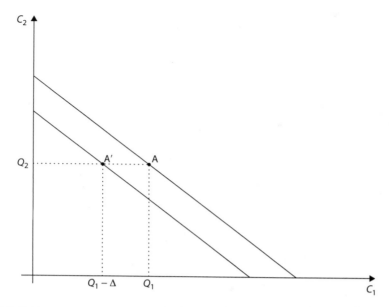

Figure 3.5. A Temporary Decline in Output and the Intertemporal Budget Constraint
Notes: In response to a decline in Q_1 equal to Δ, the intertemporal budget constraint shifts to the left by Δ. Point A indicates the endowment point prior to the output decline and point A' indicates the endowment point after the decline.

a drought. Suppose further that this decline in output is temporary, in the sense that it is expected that next year the banana crop will be back to its normal level. How would such a shock affect consumption, the trade balance, and the current account? Intuitively, Ecuadorian households will cope with the negative income shock by running down their savings or borrowing against their future income levels, which are unaffected by the drought. In this way, they can smooth consumption over time by not having to cut current spending by as much as the decline in current output. It follows that the temporary drought will induce a deterioration of the trade balance and the current account.

Formally, assume that the negative shock produces a decline in output in period 1 from Q_1 to $Q_1 - \Delta < Q_1$, but leaves output in period 2 unchanged. The situation is illustrated in Figure 3.5, where A indicates the endowment point before the shock (Q_1, Q_2) and A' the endowment point after the shock $(Q_1 - \Delta, Q_2)$. Because Q_2 is unchanged, points A and A' have the same height. As a consequence of the decline in Q_1, the budget constraint shifts toward the origin. The new budget constraint is parallel to the old one because the world interest rate is unchanged. The household could adjust to the output shock by reducing consumption in period 1 by exactly the amount of the output decline, Δ, thus leaving consumption in period 2 unchanged. However, if both C_1 and C_2 are *normal goods* (i.e., goods whose consumption increases with income), the household will choose to smooth consumption by reducing both C_1 and C_2. Figure 3.6 depicts the economy's response to the temporary output shock. As a result of the shock, the new optimal consumption path, B', is located southwest of the pre-shock consumption allocation, B. In

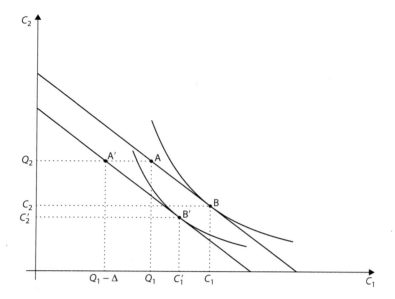

Figure 3.6. Adjustment to a Temporary Decline in Output
Notes: The figure depicts the adjustment of the economy to a decline in the period 1 endowment equal to Δ. The endowment point shifts left from point A to point A' and the optimal consumption path shifts from point B to point B'. Period 1 consumption declines by less than Δ. The period 1 trade balance becomes more negative, $Q_1 - \Delta - C_1' < Q_1 - C_1$.

smoothing consumption over time, the country runs a larger trade deficit in period 1 (recall that it was running a trade deficit even in the absence of the shock) and finances it by acquiring additional foreign debt. Thus, the current account deteriorates. In period 2, the country must generate a larger trade surplus than the one it would have produced in the absence of the shock in order to pay back the additional debt acquired in period 1.

The important principle to take away from this example is that temporary negative income shocks are smoothed out by borrowing from the rest of the world rather than by fully adjusting current consumption by the size of the shock. A similar principle applies for positive temporary income shocks. In this case, the trade balance and the current account improve, as households save part of the increase in income for future consumption.

3.7.2 ADJUSTMENT TO PERMANENT OUTPUT SHOCKS

The pattern of adjustment to changes in income is quite different when the income shock is of a more permanent nature. To continue with the example of the drought in Ecuador, suppose that the drought is not just a one-year event, but is expected to last for many years due to global climate change. In this case, it would not be optimal for households to borrow against future income, because future income is expected to be as low as current income. Instead, Ecuadorian consumers will have to adjust to the new climatic conditions by cutting consumption in all periods by roughly the size of the decline in the value of the banana harvest.

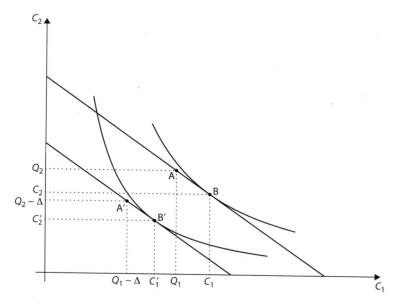

Figure 3.7. Adjustment to a Permanent Decline in Output
Notes: The figure depicts the adjustment to a decline in Q_1 and Q_2 equal to Δ. The endowment point A shifts down and to the left to point A'. The intertemporal budget constraint shifts down in a parallel fashion. The optimal consumption path (C_1, C_2) shifts from point B to point B'. The figure is drawn for the case $B_0 = 0$. The period 1 trade balance is little changed.

Formally, consider a permanent negative output shock that reduces both Q_1 and Q_2 by Δ. Figure 3.7 illustrates the situation. As a result of the decline in endowments, the budget constraint shifts to the left in a parallel fashion. The new budget constraint crosses the point $(Q_1 - \Delta, Q_2 - \Delta)$. As in the case of a temporary output decline, consumption-smoothing agents will adjust by reducing consumption in both periods. If consumption in each period fell by exactly Δ, then the trade balance would be unaffected in both periods. In general, the decline in consumption should be expected to be close to Δ, implying that a permanent output shock has few consequences for the trade balance and the current account.

Comparing the effects of temporary and permanent output shocks on the current account, the following general principle emerges: *Economies will tend to finance temporary shocks (by borrowing or lending on international capital markets) and adjust to permanent ones (by varying consumption in both periods up or down)*. Thus, temporary shocks tend to produce large movements in the current account whereas permanent shocks tend to leave the current account largely unchanged.

3.8 Anticipated Income Shocks

Suppose households learn that the endowment will be higher next period. For example, suppose that in an island with banana trees, the weather forecast anticipates an increase in rainfall next year, and that more rain will make the banana crop more abundant. Suppose further that current climatic conditions did not change, so that the present banana harvest is unchanged.

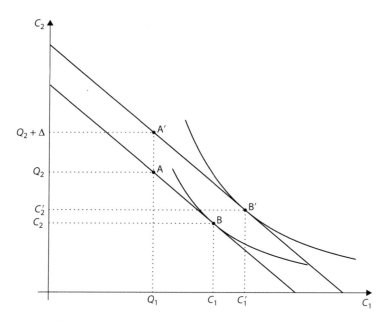

Figure 3.8. Adjustment to an Anticipated Increase in Output
Notes: The figure depicts the adjustment to an anticipated increase in Q_2 equal to
$\Delta > 0$. The initial net foreign asset position is assumed to be zero, $B_0 = 0$. The anticipated increase in Q_2 shifts the intertemporal budget constraint up by Δ. The increase
in the period 2 endowment causes an increase in period 1 consumption from C_1 to
C_1'. Because the endowment in period 1 is unchanged, the period 1 trade balance
deteriorates.

How does the economy adjust to an anticipated output shock of this type? Intuitively, households feel richer, as the present discounted value of their endowment
stream went up. As a result, they will wish to consume more in both periods. But
because the endowment in period 1 is unchanged, the increase in consumption
causes the trade balance to deteriorate. The effect of an anticipated increase in
income is illustrated in Figure 3.8. The initial endowment path is (Q_1, Q_2) and
corresponds to point A. The initial consumption path, (C_1, C_2), is point B. The
indifference curve that crosses point B is tangent to the intertemporal budget constraint. At point B, the economy runs a trade balance deficit in period 1, as C_1 is
larger than Q_1. The figure is drawn under the assumption that the initial net international investment position, B_0, is nil. Consequently, the current account equals
the trade balance, and is therefore also negative.

Suppose now that in period 1 everybody learns that the endowment in period
2 will increase from Q_2 to $Q_2 + \Delta$, with $\Delta > 0$, and that the endowment in period
1 remains constant at Q_1. The new endowment path is given by point A', located
exactly above point A. The expanded endowment in period 2 produces a shift up in
the intertemporal budget constraint. The vertical distance between the new and the
old intertemporal budget constraints equals the anticipated output change Δ. The
two intertemporal budget constraints are parallel because the interest rate did not
change. Since households are richer, they want to consume more in both periods.

In the figure, the new consumption path is marked by point B′, located northeast of point B. To expand consumption in period 1, the country must run a larger trade balance deficit (recall that Q_1 is unchanged). The current account deficit increases one for one with the trade balance.

In sum, the model predicts that an anticipated increase in output causes an expansion in consumption and a deterioration of the trade balance and the current account.

3.9 An Economy with Logarithmic Preferences

We now illustrate, by means of an algebraic example, the results obtained thus far. Let the utility function be of the log-linear type without discounting given in equation (3.6); that is,

$$U(C_1) + \beta U(C_2) = \ln C_1 + \ln C_2.$$

Households choose the consumption path (C_1, C_2) to maximize this lifetime utility function subject to the intertemporal budget constraint

$$C_1 + \frac{C_2}{1+r_1} = \bar{Y},$$

where, as before, $\bar{Y} = (1+r_0)B_0 + Q_1 + \frac{Q_2}{1+r_1}$ is the household's lifetime wealth. Solving the intertemporal budget constraint for C_2 and using the result to eliminate C_2 from the lifetime utility function, we have that the household's optimization problem reduces to choosing C_1 to maximize

$$\ln(C_1) + \ln((1+r_1)(\bar{Y} - C_1)).$$

The first-order condition associated with this problem is

$$\frac{1}{C_1} - \frac{1}{\bar{Y} - C_1} = 0.$$

Solving for C_1 yields

$$C_1 = \frac{1}{2}\bar{Y}.$$

This result says that households find it optimal to consume half of their lifetime wealth in the first half of their lives.

Using the definition of $\bar{Y}$ and the fact that under free capital mobility the domestic interest rate must equal the world interest rate, or $r_1 = r^*$, we have that C_1, C_2, TB_1, and CA_1 are given by

$$C_1 = \frac{1}{2}\left[(1+r_0)B_0 + Q_1 + \frac{Q_2}{1+r^*}\right] \tag{3.15}$$

$$C_2 = \frac{1}{2}(1+r^*)\left[(1+r_0)B_0 + Q_1 + \frac{Q_2}{1+r^*}\right] \tag{3.16}$$

$$TB_1 = \frac{1}{2}\left[Q_1 - (1+r_0)B_0 - \frac{Q_2}{1+r^*}\right] \tag{3.17}$$

$$CA_1 = r_0 B_0 + \frac{1}{2}\left[Q_1 - (1 + r_0)B_0 - \frac{Q_2}{1 + r^*} \right] \qquad (3.18)$$

Consider now the effects of temporary and permanent output shocks on consumption, the trade balance, and the current account. Assume first that income falls temporarily by one unit; that is, Q_1 decreases by one and Q_2 is unchanged. From equation (3.15), we see that consumption falls by 1/2 in period 1 and by $(1 + r^*)/2$ in period 2. Intuitively, households smooth the effect of the negative endowment shock by reducing consumption in both periods by roughly the same amount. Because consumption in period 1 falls by less than the fall in the endowment, the trade balance must deteriorate. In turn, the deterioration of the trade balance requires an increase in international borrowing, or a current account deterioration. These effects can be confirmed by inspecting equations (3.17) and (3.18), which indicate that a unit fall in the period 1 endowment causes a fall in TB_1 and CA_1 of 1/2.

Suppose next that income falls permanently by one unit; that is, Q_1 and Q_2 both fall by one. Then the trade balance and the current account decline by $\frac{1}{2}\frac{r^*}{1+r^*}$. Consumption in period 1 falls by $\frac{1}{2}\frac{2+r^*}{1+r^*}$. For realistic values of r^*, the predicted deterioration in the trade balance and current account in response to the assumed permanent negative income shock is close to zero and in particular much smaller than the deterioration associated with the temporary negative income shock. For example, assume that the world interest rate is 10 percent, $r^* = 0.1$. Then, both the trade balance and the current account in period 1 fall by 0.046 in response to the permanent output shock and by 0.5 in response to the temporary shock. That is, the current account deterioration is 10 times larger under a temporary shock than under a permanent one. Intuitively, if income falls by one unit in both periods, cutting consumption by roughly one unit in both periods leaves the consumption path as smooth as before the shock. So households do not need to use the financial market (the current account) to smooth consumption.

Finally, consider an anticipated unit increase in the period 2 endowment, with the period 1 endowment unchanged. By equations (3.15)–(3.18) we have that consumption in period 1 increases by $\frac{1}{2(1+r^*)}$ and the trade balance and the current account both deteriorate by the same amount. The intuition is clear. The increase in the future endowment makes households richer, inducing them to increase consumption in both periods. With Q_1 unchanged, the increase in current consumption causes an increase in the trade deficit, which must be financed by external borrowing; that is, by a current account deterioration. Thus, good news about the future causes a deterioration of the current account. This shows that current account deficits are not necessarily an indication of a weak economy.

3.10 Summing Up

This chapter presents an intertemporal model of the current account. The main building blocks of the intertemporal model are:

- Households face an intertemporal budget constraint that allows them to consume more than their current income by borrowing against future income or to consume less than their current income by lending to the rest of the world.

- Households have preferences over present and future consumption. Their preferences are described by indifference curves that are downward sloping and convex toward the origin.
- Households choose a consumption path that maximizes lifetime utility subject to the intertemporal budget constraint. At the optimal consumption path, the intertemporal budget constraint is tangent to an indifference curve.
- Free capital mobility implies that the domestic interest rate must equal the world interest rate.

The intertemporal model of the current account delivers the following key insight:

- In response to temporary income shocks, countries use the current account to smooth consumption over time. Positive temporary shocks cause an improvement in the current account and negative temporary shocks cause a deterioration. In response to permanent income shocks, countries adjust consumption without much movement in the current account.
- Finally, a second important prediction of the intertemporal model is that in response to an anticipated increase in future income, the trade balance and the current account deteriorate, as forward-looking, consumption-smoothing households borrow against their higher future expected income to expand current spending.

3.11 Exercises

Exercise 3.1 (The Initial Net International Investment Position and Consumption) Countries A and B are identical in all respects, except that the initial net international asset position (B_0) of country A is lower than that of country B. Indicate whether the following statements are true, false, or uncertain and explain why.

1. It must be the case that consumption in country A is lower than consumption in country B.
2. It must be the case that the trade balance in country A in period 1 is higher than in country B.
3. It must be the case that the current account in country A in period 2 is higher than in country B.
4. All of the above statements are true.

Exercise 3.2 (Endowment Shocks) Consider a two-period lived household, whose preferences for consumption are described by the lifetime utility function

$$-C_1^{-1} - C_2^{-1},$$

where C_1 and C_2 denote consumption in periods 1 and 2, respectively.

1. Do these preferences give rise to indifference curves that are downward sloping and convex? Show your work.

2. Suppose that the household starts period 1 with financial wealth equal to $(1 + r_0)B_0$, where B_0 is an inherited stock of bonds and r_0 is the interest rate on assets held between periods 0 and 1. In addition, the household receives endowments of goods in the amounts Q_1 and Q_2 in periods 1 and 2, respectively. In period 1, the household can borrow or lend at the interest rate $r_1 > 0$ via a bond denoted B_1. Find the optimal levels of consumption in periods 1 and 2 as functions of the household's lifetime wealth, $\bar{Y} \equiv (1 + r_0)B_0 + Q_1 + Q_2/(1 + r_1)$ and the interest rate r_1.

3. Find the responses of consumption in period 1, ΔC_1, the trade balance in period 1, ΔTB_1, and the current account in period 1, ΔCA_1, to a temporary increase in the endowment, $\Delta Q_1 > 0$ and $\Delta Q_2 = 0$.

4. Find the responses of consumption in period 1, ΔC_1, the trade balance in period 1, ΔTB_1, and the current account in period 1, ΔCA_1, to a permanent increase in the endowment, $\Delta Q_1 = \Delta Q_2 > 0$.

5. Compare your findings to those obtained under log preferences as presented in section 3.9.

Exercise 3.3 (A Zero Interest Rate Economy) Consider a two-period economy populated by households with preferences described by the utility function $\sqrt{C_1} + \sqrt{C_2}$. The household starts period 1 with zero assets ($B_0 = 0$) and receives endowments $Q_1 = 2$ and $Q_2 = 4$ in periods 1 and 2, respectively. The economy has free capital mobility, and the world interest rate is zero, $r^* = 0$. Calculate the equilibrium levels of consumption and the trade balance in period 1 (C_1 and TB_1).

Exercise 3.4 (An Anticipated Output Shock I) Consider a two-period, small open endowment economy populated by a large number of households with preferences described by the lifetime utility function

$$C_1^{\frac{1}{10}} C_2^{\frac{1}{11}},$$

where C_1 and C_2 denote, respectively, consumption in periods 1 and 2. Suppose that households receive exogenous endowments of goods given by $Q_1 = Q_2 = 10$ in periods 1 and 2, respectively. Every household enters period 1 with some debt, denoted B_0, inherited from the past. Let B_0 be equal to -5. The interest rate on these liabilities, denoted r_0, is 20 percent. Finally, suppose that the country enjoys free capital mobility and that the world interest rate on assets held between periods 1 and 2, denoted r^*, is 10 percent.

1. Compute the equilibrium levels of consumption, the trade balance, and the current account in periods 1 and 2.

2. Assume now that the endowment in period 2 is expected to increase from 10 to 15. Calculate the effect of this anticipated output increase on consumption, the trade balance, and the current account in both periods. Provide intuition.

Exercise 3.5 (An Anticipated Output Shock II) Consider a two-period, small open endowment economy. The lifetime utility functions of households takes the form, $C_1^{1/5} C_2^{2/5}$. Households receive endowments Q_1 and Q_2 in periods 1 and 2, respectively. Assume that the world interest rate is 33.3 percent ($r^* = 1/3$) and that the initial net foreign asset position is zero ($B_0 = 0$). Find the change in the current account in periods 1 and 2 in response to news in period 1 that the period 2 endowment will increase by ΔQ_2. Provide an intuitive explanation for your findings.

Exercise 3.6 (Debt Forgiveness) Consider a small open economy where households live for two periods and have logarithmic preferences,

$$\ln C_1 + \beta \ln C_2,$$

where the subjective discount factor β equals $\frac{10}{11}$. Suppose that households receive a constant endowment over time equal to 10, $Q_1 = Q_2 = 10$. Suppose that households start period 1 with debt including interest equal to 5, $(1 + r_0)B_0 = -5$ and that $r_0 = 0.1$. Finally, assume that the country enjoys free capital mobility and that the world interest rate is 10 percent, $r^* = 0.1$.

1. Calculate the equilibrium values of consumption, the trade balance, and the current account in period 1.
2. Suppose now that foreign lenders decide to forgive all of the country's initial external debt including interest. Calculate the effect of this external gift on consumption, the trade balance, and the current account in period 1. Provide an intuitive explanation of your findings.

Exercise 3.7 (A Three-Period Open Economy) Consider a three-period, small open endowment economy populated by a large number of households with preferences given by the lifetime utility function

$$\ln C_1 + \ln C_2 + \ln C_3,$$

where C_1, C_2, and C_3 denote, respectively, consumption in periods 1, 2, and 3. Suppose that households receive exogenous endowments of goods given by Q_1, Q_2, and Q_3 in periods 1, 2, and 3, respectively. Every household enters period 1 with an asset position, including interest, equal to $(1 + r_0)B_0$, where r_0 denotes the interest rate prevailing in period 0. Finally, suppose that the country enjoys free capital mobility and that the world interest rate is constant over time and equal to r^*.

1. Write the household's budget constraint in periods 1, 2, and 3.
2. Write the no-Ponzi-game constraint.
3. Derive the intertemporal budget constraint.
4. Compute the equilibrium levels of consumption, the trade balance, and the current account in periods 1, 2, and 3.
5. Assume that in period 1 the economy receives a temporary increase in the endowment equal to $\Delta Q > 0$, that is, assume that Q_1 increases by ΔQ and that Q_2 and Q_3 remain unchanged. Calculate the changes in consumption,

the trade balance, and the current account in period 1, denoted ΔC_1, ΔTB_1, and ΔCA_1, respectively.

6. Now assume that the endowment shock is permanent; that is, the endowments in periods 1, 2, and 3 all increase by $\Delta Q > 0$. Calculate the changes in consumption, the trade balance, and the current account in period 1.

7. Compare your answers to the ones obtained in the two-period economy.

8. Answer questions 5 and 6 in the general case of a T-period economy, where T is any integer larger than 2.

Exercise 3.8 (Durability and the Countercyclicality of the Trade Balance) Consider a two-period, small open endowment economy with durable consumption goods. Purchases of durable consumption goods in period 1, denoted C_1, continue to provide utility in period 2. The service flow households receive from the stock of durables in period 2 depends on new purchases of durables in period 2, C_2, and on the undepreciated stock of durables purchased in period 1. Durable consumption goods are assumed to depreciate at the rate $\delta \in [0, 1]$. Preferences are described by the following utility function

$$\ln(C_1) + \ln(C_2 + (1 - \delta)C_1).$$

Assume that the world interest rate, r^*, is 10 percent per year, that the endowment in period 1, denoted Q_1 is 1, and that the endowment in period 2, denoted Q_2, is equal to 1.1. Finally assume that the initial asset position, B_0, is zero.

1. State the household's budget constraints in periods 1 and 2.

2. Characterize the equilibrium allocation under free capital mobility. At this point do not use numerical values. Express the equilibrium levels of consumption in terms of the exogenous variables, Q_1, Q_2, r^* and the parameter δ.

3. Assume now that $\delta = 1$. Find the equilibrium values of consumption and the trade balance in periods 1 and 2.

4. Suppose that in period 1 the country experiences a persistent increase in output. Specifically, assume that output increases by 1 in period 1 and by $\rho \in (0, 1)$ in period 2. Continue to assume that $\delta = 1$; that is, that consumption is nondurable. Is the trade balance in period 1 countercyclical—that is, does the change in the trade balance have the opposite sign to the change in Q_1? Why or why not? Find the change in the trade balance in period 1 and provide intuition for your answer.

5. Continue to assume that the economy experiences a positive and persistent output shock; that is, Q_1 increases by 1 and Q_2 increases by $\rho \in (0, 1)$. But now do not impose that $\delta = 1$. Find the pairs (δ, ρ) such that the response of the trade balance in period 1 is countercyclical (i.e., negative) and consumption purchases, C_1 and C_2, are positive. Provide intuition for your answer.

Exercise 3.9 (Habit Formation and the Trade Balance) Consider a two-period, small open economy populated by a large number of identical households with preferences described by the utility function

$$\ln C_1 + \ln(C_2 - \alpha C_1),$$

where C_1 and C_2 denote consumption in periods 1 and 2, respectively, and $\alpha \in (0, 1)$ is a parameter measuring the degree of habit formation. This preference specification nests the standard case of no habits when α is zero. The reason why these preferences capture consumption habits is that current consumption influences the marginal utility of future consumption. Specifically, the marginal utility of period 2 consumption is given by $1/(C_2 - \alpha C_1)$, which is higher for $\alpha > 0$ than for $\alpha = 0$. Intuitively, the more the household eats in period 1, the hungrier it will wake up in period 2.

Households are endowed with $Q > 0$ units of consumption goods each period and can borrow or lend at the world interest rate, r^*, which, for simplicity, we assume is equal to zero. Households start period 1 with no assets or debts from the past ($B_0 = 0$).

1. Derive the household's intertemporal budget constraint.
2. Calculate the equilibrium levels of consumption and the trade balance in period 1 as functions of the structural parameters of the model, α and Q. Compare the answer to the one that would have obtained in the absence of habits and provide intuition.

Exercise 3.10 (External Habit Formation) The specification of habits considered in exercise 3.9 is known as internal habit formation, because the individual consumer internalizes the fact that his choice for current consumption, C_1, affects his marginal utility of consumption in the next period. Now assume instead that the utility function is of the form

$$\ln C_1 + \ln(C_2 - \alpha \tilde{C}_1),$$

where $\tilde{C}_1$ denotes the cross-sectional average level of consumption in period 1. This preference specification is known as external habits or catching up with the Joneses, because the individual consumer's happiness is affected by the consumption of others.

1. Calculate the equilibrium values of consumption and the trade balance in period 1 as functions of the structural parameters of the model, α and Q. Hint: in taking first-order conditions, consider $\tilde{C}_1$ as a parameter. This is right because the individual consumer regards the average level of consumption in the economy as out of his control. However, after you have derived the first-order conditions, you have to take into account that, because all households are identical, in equilibrium $\tilde{C}_1$ is equal to C_1.
2. Compare the answers you obtained in question 1 with the ones obtained in the case of internal habits studied in exercise 3.9 and provide intuition.
3. Discuss to what extent the economy with external habits under- or oversaves relative to the economy with internal habits. To this end, compute and compare the current account in period 1 under internal and external habits. Provide meaning to the terms oversaving or undersaving, by computing the level of lifetime welfare under internal and external habits. Provide intuition for your findings.

CHAPTER 4

Terms of Trade, the World Interest Rate, Tariffs, and the Current Account

In Chapter 3, we studied an economy with a single good, a constant world interest rate, and free trade. In this chapter we show how the current account is determined when we relax these assumptions.

We had in mind, for example, an island with banana trees. Sometimes households choose to consume fewer bananas than the trees produce. In these periods, the country exports bananas. Sometimes households wish to consume more bananas than the trees produce, and therefore the country imports bananas. Thus, the country imports or exports the same good, bananas. In the real world, however, the type of goods a country exports may be different from the type of goods a country imports. For instance, some countries in the Middle East are highly specialized in the production of oil. These countries export most of their oil production and import most of the goods they consume (food, electronics, clothing, etc.). To capture this aspect of the real world, in this chapter we study a model of current account determination that allows for differences in the type of goods imported and exported. The relative price of exports in terms of imports is known as *the terms of trade*. We will pay special attention to how movements in the terms of trade affect the trade balance and the current account.

A second simplification of the model of Chapter 3 is that the world interest rate is constant over time. In reality, however, the interest rate prevailing in world financial markets moves over time and is a critical determinant of the current account and aggregate demand in open economies around the world. When the world interest rate falls, households have fewer incentives to save and more incentives to consume. Similarly, a fall in the world interest rate induces firms to increase investment spending on items such as machines, equipment, and plants. The resulting fall in saving and increase in investment implies a deterioration in the current account. With this motivation in mind, in this chapter we study the adjustment of the current account in response to world interest rate shocks.

A third simplification of the model of Chapter 3 is that there is free trade. This assumption is not a bad approximation for some countries in the world—in particular, those belonging to a free trade agreement like the North American Free Trade

Agreement (NAFTA) or the World Trade Organization (WTO). But even for WTO members there are some tariffs and those tariffs can change over time. For example, in 2019 the United States (a WTO member) increased tariffs on imports from China (another WTO member). This change in trade policy was supposed to reduce the U.S. trade deficit with China. In this chapter, we analyze the effects of changes in import tariffs on the trade balance and the current account.

4.1 Terms of Trade Shocks

As we just mentioned, the model of Chapter 3 assumes that the good households are endowed with, Q_1 in period 1 and Q_2 in period 2, is the same as the good they like to consume, C_1 in period 1 and C_2 in period 2. For example, households are endowed with wheat and also like to consume wheat. Let us now make the model more realistic by assuming that the good households like to consume, say wheat, is different from the good they are endowed with, say oil. In such an economy, both C_1 and C_2 must be imported, while Q_1 and Q_2 must be exported. Let P_1^M and P_1^X denote the prices of imports and exports in period 1, respectively. A country's terms of trade in period 1, denoted TT_1, is the ratio of the price of its exports to the price of its imports; that is,

$$TT_1 \equiv \frac{P_1^X}{P_1^M}.$$

Continuing with the example, if the price of oil is \$90 per barrel and the price of wheat is \$10 per bushel, then $P_1^X = 90$, $P_1^M = 10$, and the terms of trade is 9, or $TT_1 = 9$. Here, TT_1 represents the price of oil in terms of wheat and indicates the amount of wheat that the country can afford to import if it exports one barrel of oil. Put differently, $TT_1 = 9$ means that with one barrel of oil the country can buy 9 bushels of wheat. In general, we have that Q_1 units of endowment are worth $TT_1 Q_1$ units of consumption goods.

The household's budget constraint in period 1 is then given by

$$C_1 + B_1 - B_0 = TT_1 Q_1 + r_0 B_0.$$

The left-hand side displays the uses of income; namely, consumption spending C_1, and saving in the form of new purchases of bonds, $B_1 - B_0$. The right-hand side displays the sources of income, given by the value of the endowment expressed in units of consumption goods, $TT_1 Q_1$, and interest income from bond holdings, $r_0 B_0$.

The budget constraint in period 2 is

$$C_2 + B_2 - B_1 = TT_2 Q_2 + r_1 B_1.$$

The above two budget constraints are identical to the budget constraints of the one-good economy of Chapter 3, given in (3.1) and (3.2), except that here the terms of trade are multiplying the endowments.

Using the transversality condition $B_2 = 0$, and combining the budget constraints in periods 1 and 2 to eliminate B_1, one obtains the following intertemporal budget constraint:

$$C_1 + \frac{C_2}{1+r_1} = (1+r_0)B_0 + TT_1 Q_1 + \frac{TT_2 Q_2}{1+r_1}.$$

Comparing this intertemporal budget constraint with the one pertaining to the one-good model presented in Chapter 3, equation (3.4), it is clear that terms of trade shocks are just like output shocks. For the household, it makes no difference whether its income in period 1, $TT_1 Q_1$, changes because of a change in the terms of trade, TT_1, or because of a change in the endowment, Q_1. The same is true for period 2. What matters is the level of income in terms of the consumption good, $TT_1 Q_1$ and $TT_2 Q_2$, but not the breakdown into price and quantity.

Consequently, the adjustment to terms of trade shocks is identical to the adjustment to endowment shocks, which we analyzed in Chapter 3. Thus, in response to a transitory deterioration of the terms of trade—that is, a fall in TT_1 with TT_2, Q_1, and Q_2 unchanged—in period 1 the economy will not lower consumption by as much as the fall in income. Instead, it will borrow on the international capital market, which will result in deteriorations in the trade balance, $TB_1 = TT_1 Q_1 - C_1$, and the current account, $CA_1 = TB_1 + r_0 B_0$. Similarly, in response to a permanent terms of trade decline, a fall in both TT_1 and TT_2 with Q_1 and Q_2 unchanged, the country will adjust consumption in both periods down by a proportion similar to the deterioration of the terms of trade, with little change in the trade balance or the current account.

We conclude that the key prediction of the one-good economy also applies in the two-good economy: The country finances temporary changes in the terms of trade by increasing the current account in response to positive shocks and decreasing the current account in response to negative shocks. This allows for consumption smoothing over time. On the other hand, the country adjusts to permanent terms of trade shocks by mostly changing consumption (downwardly if the terms of trade deteriorate and upwardly if they improve), with little movement in the current account.

4.2 Terms of Trade Shocks and Imperfect Information

The central prediction of the intertemporal theory of the current account is that consumption, the trade balance, and the current account react differently to temporary and permanent shocks. In reality, however, agents have imperfect information. When a shock hits the economy, it is not always easy to tell whether the shock is permanent or temporary. Agents must form expectations about the duration of the shock, which may or may not be validated by future developments. When expectations are not fulfilled, the behavior of the economy may ex-post look at odds with the predictions of the intertemporal theory of current account determination. The following example illustrates this point.

Consider an economy in which initially $TT_1 = TT_2 = TT$ and $Q_1 = Q_2 = Q$. Suppose now that in period 1 the terms of trade appreciate by Δ, where $\Delta > 0$, and that in period 2 they increase by 2Δ; that is, the terms of trade increase in period 1 and increase by even more in period 2. How does the current account adjust to this development? The answer depends on what people in period 1 expect TT_2 will be. If the expectation is that the terms of trade improvement in period 1 is temporary—that is, if they wrongly think that $TT_2 = TT$—then the current account in period 1 will improve, as agents will save some of the period 1 windfall for future consumption. However, if households correctly anticipate that the terms of trade will rise further in period 2 to $TT + 2\Delta$, then the current account in period 1 will deteriorate, as they will borrow against their higher expected future income.

The takeaway from this hypothetical example is that what matters for the determination of the current account is not only the actual path of income, but also the expected path of income. This point is important for analyzing actual historical episodes, as the example in the next section illustrates.

4.3 Imperfect Information, the Price of Copper, and the Chilean Current Account

In this section, we take a look at the Chilean current account dynamics in response to the copper price boom in the early 2000s.[1] We will show that one can understand the observed current account behavior if one takes into account that Chile underestimated how long the copper price boom would last and to what heights the copper prices would rise.

Copper is the main export product of Chile, representing more than 50 percent of that country's exports. Consequently, the Chilean terms of trade are driven to a large extent by movements in the world copper price. After two decades of stability, the price of copper began to grow vigorously in the early 2000s. As shown in Figure 4.1, between 2003 and 2007 the real price of copper (the crossed broken line) increased from 120 to 350. This development turned out to be long lasting; although during the global financial crisis of 2007–2009 the price temporarily fell to 250, it quickly recovered and stabilized at around 300 by 2013.

If in 2003 Chilean households had had perfect foresight about the future path of the copper price—that is, if they had correctly anticipated that the price would stay high for many years to come—then according to the intertemporal model, the current account should have deteriorated. Households would have felt richer and increased their demand for consumption goods, causing the current account to deteriorate as a way to finance the expansion in aggregate demand. In turn, the current account deficit would have been paid for by the expected future increases in the price of copper. But this prediction of the model did not materialize. Instead of deteriorating, the current account actually improved. As can be seen from Figure 4.2, the Chilean current account experienced a significant improvement between 2003 and 2007, from deficits of around 1 percent of GDP to surpluses of about 3 percent of GDP.

Concluding that the intertemporal theory of current account determination fails to explain this evidence, however, requires us to assume that when the price of

[1]This example is taken from Jorge Fornero and Markus Kirchner, "Learning About Commodity Cycles and Saving-Investment Dynamics in a Commodity-Exporting Economy," *International Journal of Central Banking* 14 (March 2018): 205–262. We thank Markus Kirchner for sharing the data shown in Figures 4.1 and 4.2.

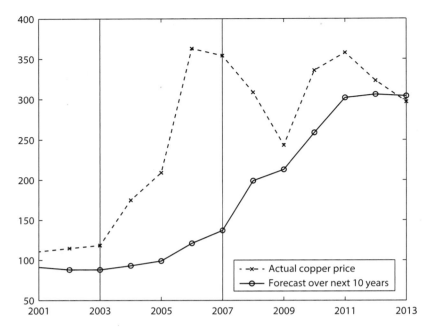

Figure 4.1. Forecast versus Actual Real Price of Copper, Chile, 2001–2013
Notes: The crossed broken line shows the actual real price of copper. The circled solid line shows the forecast of the average real price of copper over the next 10 years. The boom in the price of copper between 2003 and 2007 was expected to be temporary. The forecast of the average copper price over the next 10 years rose but by only a small fraction of the rise in the actual price.
Data Source: Central Bank of Chile.

copper started to increase agents correctly anticipated that the improvement would last for a long period of time (as it actually did). Figure 4.1 shows that this assumption is misplaced. The figure displays the actual real price of copper (the crossed broken line) and the forecast of the average real price of copper over the next 10 years produced by Chilean experts (the circled-solid line). Despite the fact that the actual price of copper grew rapidly between 2003 and 2007, the experts did not expect the price to be much higher for the next 10 years. Indeed, until 2007 they expected that over the coming 10 years it would be only slightly higher than at the beginning of the decade. That is, experts expected the improvement in the price of copper to be temporary. Only in the second half of the 2000s did forecasters begin to raise their predictions for the average price of copper over the next 10 years.

In light of these expectations, the behavior of the current account is no longer in conflict with the predictions of the intertemporal model. For it predicts that in response to an improvement in the terms of trade that is expected to be short-lived, the current account should improve, which is what indeed happened.

4.4 World Interest Rate Shocks

What happens in an open economy when the world interest rate changes? This question is important because sizable changes in the world interest rate occur

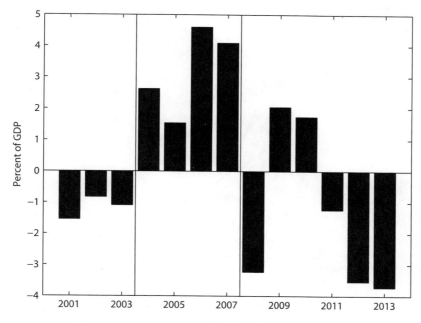

Figure 4.2. The Current Account, Chile, 2001–2013
Notes: The graph shows that between 2003 and 2007, the Chilean current account improved from a deficit of around 1 percent of GDP to a surplus of about 3 percent of GDP. This behavior of the current account is in line with the view that the boom in the copper price that took place during this period was expected to be temporary.
Data Source: Central Bank of Chile.

frequently and are considered to be an important factor driving business cycles and the external accounts in economies that are open to trade in goods and financial assets.

An increase in the world interest rate, r^*, has two potentially opposing effects on consumption in period 1. On the one hand, an increase in the interest rate makes saving more attractive because the rate of return on foreign assets is higher. This effect is referred to as the *substitution effect*, because it induces people to substitute future for present consumption through saving. By the substitution effect, a rise in the interest rate causes consumption in period 1 to decline and therefore the current account to improve. On the other hand, an increase in the interest rate makes debtors poorer and creditors richer. This effect is called the *income effect*. By the income effect, an increase in the interest rate leads to a decrease in consumption in period 1 if prior to the change in the interest rate the country was a debtor at the end of period 1 ($B_1 < 0$), reinforcing the substitution effect, and to an increase in consumption in period 1 if prior to the increase in the interest rate the country was a creditor ($B_1 > 0$), offsetting (at least in part) the substitution effect. In the case that the income and the substitution effects have opposing effects on saving, we will assume that the substitution effect dominates the income effect, so that saving increases unambiguously in response to an increase in the interest rate. Under this assumption, an increase in the world interest rate, r^*, induces a decline

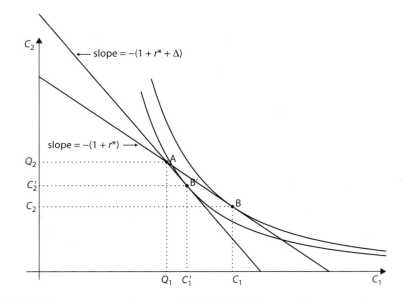

Figure 4.3. Adjustment to an Increase in the World Interest Rate
Notes: Prior to the interest rate increase, the optimal consumption path is point B. Then the world interest rate increases from r^* to $r^* + \Delta$. This causes the intertemporal budget constraint to rotate clockwise around the endowment point A. The new optimal consumption path is point B'. The increase in the interest rate causes period 1 consumption to fall from C_1 to C_1' and period 2 consumption to increase from C_2 to C_2'. The figure is drawn under the assumption that $B_0 = 0$.

in consumption and an improvement in the trade balance and the current account in period 1.

Figure 4.3 describes the adjustment to an increase in the world interest rate from r^* to $r^* + \Delta$. Initially, the slope of the intertemporal budget constraint is given by $-(1 + r^*)$. (If you don't remember why, read again Section 3.1 of Chapter 3.) The increase in the world interest rate makes the budget constraint steeper. The new slope is $-(1 + r^* + \Delta)$. The figure is drawn under the assumption that the household starts period zero with no debts or assets, $B_0 = 0$. Thus, the endowment point, point A in the figure, lies on both the old and the new budget constraints. This means that as the world interest rate increases from r^* to $r^* + \Delta$ the budget constraint rotates clockwise around point A. The initial optimal consumption point is given by point B, where in period 1 consumption is larger than the endowment and therefore the household is borrowing ($B_1 < 0$). The new optimal consumption path is point B', which is located west of point B. The increase in the world interest rate is associated with a decline in C_1 and thus an improvement in the trade balance and the current account in period 1. Because prior to the increase in the interest rate the household was a debtor ($B_1 < 0$), the income and substitution effects triggered by the rise in the interest rate reinforce each other: households consume less and save more in period 1 because bonds become more attractive and because the increase in the interest rate makes them poorer. So, saving increases unambiguously.

Let us now consider the adjustment to an increase in the world interest rate in the economy with log preferences studied in Section 3.9 of Chapter 3. There, we deduced that in equilibrium the economy consumes half of its lifetime wealth,

$$C_1 = \frac{1}{2}\left[(1+r_0)B_0 + Q_1 + \frac{Q_2}{1+r^*}\right]$$

and therefore the trade balance, $TB_1 = Q_1 - C_1$, and the current account, $CA_1 = r_0 B_0 + TB_1$, are given by

$$TB_1 = \frac{1}{2}\left[-(1+r_0)B_0 + Q_1 - \frac{Q_2}{1+r^*}\right]$$

and

$$CA_1 = \frac{1}{2}\left[(-1+r_0)B_0 + Q_1 - \frac{Q_2}{1+r^*}\right].$$

In response to an increase in r^*, in period 1 consumption falls and both the trade balance and the current account improve. Note that the decline in consumption in period 1 is independent of whether prior to the increase in r^* the country is a net foreign borrower or a net foreign lender in period 1. This is because for the particular preference specification considered in this example (log-linear preferences), the substitution effect always dominates the income effect.

4.5 Import Tariffs

In this section, we analyze how import tariffs affect the trade balance. In particular, we study whether an increase in import tariffs will reduce imports and thereby improve the trade balance as it is sometimes claimed in policy debates. The main result of this section is that an increase in import tariffs can have either a positive, a negative, or no effect on a country's trade balance, depending on whether the present import tariff is expected to be larger than, smaller than, or equal to future import tariffs.

To embed import tariffs into our model, it is most natural to think of an environment with at least two goods, one imported and one exported. Thus, we will develop the argument in the two-good economy that we studied in Section 4.1 earlier in this chapter when we analyzed the effects of terms of trade shocks.

Import tariffs affect households in two ways. One is that they change the effective price that consumers must pay for imported goods. The higher the tariff, the higher the effective price of imports. For example, suppose that the imported good is wheat and that its international price is 100. If the government imposes an import tariff of 10 percent, then the effective price of wheat that the consumer has to pay is 110. The second way in which tariffs affect the household is fiscal in nature. The imposition of an import tariff generates revenues for the government. We must make an assumption of how the government uses these revenues. We will assume that the government uses these funds to make lump-sum transfers to households.

The above discussion implies that we must introduce two modifications to the household's budget constraint, one to reflect the effect of import tariffs on the price of goods and one to reflect government transfers. Let $\tau_1 \geq 0$ denote the import tariff in period 1 and $\tau_2 \geq 0$ the import tariff in period 2. Then a household that wishes to consume imported goods in period 1 must pay $1 + \tau_1$ per unit of imported good. We also assume that households receive a lump-sum transfer from the government in the amount L_1 in period 1 and L_2 in period 2. The household's budget constraints can then be written as

$$(1 + \tau_1)C_1 + B_1 = TT_1 Q_1 + L_1 + (1 + r_0)B_0 \qquad (4.1)$$

and

$$(1 + \tau_2)C_2 = TT_2 Q_2 + L_2 + (1 + r_1)B_1. \qquad (4.2)$$

The household takes the tariff rates, τ_1 and τ_2, and the lump-sum transfers, L_1 and L_2, as exogenously given. To characterize the household's optimal consumption choice, we proceed in the usual fashion. We first combine the period 1 and period 2 budget constraints, equations (4.1) and (4.2), into a single present value budget constraint, by solving the period 2 budget constraint for B_1 and using the resulting expression to eliminate B_1 from the period 1 budget constraint. This yields

$$(1 + \tau_1)C_1 + \frac{(1 + \tau_2)C_2}{1 + r_1} = \bar{Y}, \qquad (4.3)$$

where $\bar{Y} = TT_1 Q_1 + L_1 + (1 + r_0)B_0 + (TT_2 Q_2 + L_2)/(1 + r_1)$ is lifetime wealth, which the household takes as given. The household's optimization problem consists in choosing C_1 and C_2 to maximize its utility function

$$U(C_1) + \beta U(C_2)$$

subject to the intertemporal budget constraint (4.3). Solving the intertemporal budget constraint, (4.3), for C_2 and using the resulting expression to eliminate C_2 from the utility function, the household's optimization problem can be expressed as

$$\max_{\{C_1\}} \quad U(C_1) + \beta U\left(\frac{1 + r_1}{1 + \tau_2}(\bar{Y} - (1 + \tau_1)C_1)\right).$$

The first-order condition associated with this problem is the Euler equation

$$U'(C_1) = \frac{1 + \tau_1}{1 + \tau_2}\beta(1 + r_1)U'(C_2). \qquad (4.4)$$

If the period 1 import tariff is the same as the period 2 import tariff, $\tau_1 = \tau_2$, then the Euler equation is the same as in the economy without import tariffs. In this case, the import tariffs do not distort the intertemporal allocation of consumption. Because consumption is taxed at the same rate in both periods, shifting consumption from one period to another does not result in any gain for the household. On the other hand, suppose the tariff in period 1 is higher than the tariff in period 2. Then it is relatively more expensive to consume in period 1 than in period 2 and the household will shift consumption away from period 1 and into period 2. To see this, note that in the above Euler equation the right-hand side goes up with τ_1. For the Euler equation to continue to hold, we need either C_1 to go down or C_2 to go up or both. Recall that the marginal utility of consumption, $U'(C)$, is decreasing in consumption.

Let's now turn to the government. We assume that the government returns all of the tariff revenue to households in the form of lump-sum transfers. The budget constraints of the government in periods 1 and 2 then are

$$\tau_1 C_1 = L_1 \tag{4.5}$$

and

$$\tau_2 C_2 = L_2. \tag{4.6}$$

Finally, we assume free international capital mobility so that the domestic interest rate is equal to the world interest rate,

$$r_1 = r^*. \tag{4.7}$$

Combining the household's present value budget constraint, (4.3), with the budget constraints of the government, (4.5) and (4.6), and the interest rate parity condition, (4.7), we obtain that in equilibrium the economy-wide resource constraint is given by

$$C_1 + \frac{C_2}{1+r^*} = TT_1 Q_1 + (1+r_0)B_0 + \frac{TT_2 Q_2}{1+r^*}. \tag{4.8}$$

Notice that the import tariff does not appear in this resource constraint; that is, the economy's lifetime wealth, $TT_1 Q_1 + (1+r_0)B_0 + \frac{TT_2 Q_2}{1+r^*}$, is the same as in an economy without the import tariff. The reason is that the value of the country's endowment of the export good is not affected by the import tariff, and while the household must pay import tariffs on consumption, this tariff is paid to the domestic government, which returns it in a lump-sum fashion to the households, so the economy as a whole does not lose any resources because of the import tariff.

The equilibrium consumption path, (C_1, C_2), and the equilibrium interest rate, r_1, must satisfy the Euler equation (4.4), the interest rate parity condition (4.7), and the resource constraint of the economy (4.8), for given values of tariffs, τ_1 and τ_2. This represents a system of three equations in three unknowns. Once the equilibrium values of C_1, C_2, and r_1 have been found, it is straightforward to obtain the equilibrium values of other variables of interest such as the trade balance, $TB_1 = TT_1 Q_1 - C_1$, and the current account, $CA_1 = TB_1 + r_0 B_0$. In what follows, we present a graphical analysis of the effects of transitory, permanent, and anticipated changes in import tariffs. Exercise 4.7 asks you to perform the same analysis algebraically.

4.5.1   A TEMPORARY INCREASE IN IMPORT TARIFFS

Suppose that initially import tariffs are zero, $\tau_1 = \tau_2 = 0$. Figure 4.4 displays this situation. The downward-sloping line is the resource constraint, (4.8). The slope of this line is equal to $-(1+r^*)$. The equilibrium is at point B, where an indifference curve is tangent to the intertemporal resource constraint. Assume now that

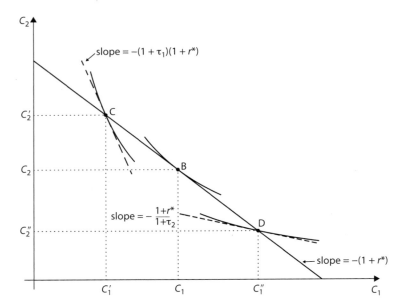

Figure 4.4. Adjustment to Changes in Import Tariffs
Notes: Prior to the imposition of import tariffs ($\tau_1 = \tau_2 = 0$), the optimal consumption path is at point B. Changes in import tariffs leave the intertemporal resource constraint (the downward-sloping solid line) unchanged. A temporary increase in import tariffs ($\tau_1 > 0$ and $\tau_2 = 0$) pushes the optimal consumption path to point C, where the slope of the indifference curve (the broken line) is steeper than at point B, $(1 + \tau_1)(1 + r^*) > (1 + r^*)$. The increase in import tariffs causes period 1 consumption to decline ($C_1' < C_1$), and the trade balance to improve. An anticipated future increase in import tariffs ($\tau_2 > 0$ and $\tau_1 = 0$) pushes the optimal consumption path to point D, where the slope of the indifference curve is flatter, $(1 + r^*)/(1 + \tau_2) < (1 + r^*)$. The expected future increase in import tariffs causes period 1 consumption to increase from C_1 to C_1'' and the trade balance to deteriorate.

the government imposes an import tariff in period 1, $\tau_1 > 0$, but imposes no tariff in period 2, $\tau_2 = 0$. The new equilibrium is at point C. The economy-wide resource constraint, (4.8), is unaffected by the change in import tariffs. This implies that the new equilibrium has to be on the same resource constraint. By the Euler equation, the slope of the indifference curve at the optimal consumption path satisfies

$$\text{slope of indifference curve} = -\frac{U'(C_1)}{\beta U'(C_2)} = -(1 + \tau_1)(1 + r^*) < -(1 + r^*),$$

which implies that the slope of the indifference curve at the new optimal consumption path must be steeper than that of the budget constraint. This in turn requires that consumption in period 1 falls. The new equilibrium levels of consumption are labeled C_1' and C_2'. With consumption lower and output unchanged in period 1, the trade balance, $TT_1 Q_1 - C_1$, improves in period 1. We conclude that a temporary increase in import tariffs improves the trade balance.

The improvement in the trade balance, however, comes at a cost. Notice that the indifference curve associated with the after-tariff consumption path, point C, lies southwest of the indifference curve associated with the original consumption path, point B, and that therefore the level of utility is lower at point C than at point B. This implies that temporary increases in tariffs are welfare reducing. Why is this so? The reason is that the import tariff distorts the intertemporal price of consumption. The economy as a whole exchanges one bushel of wheat today for $1 + r^*$ bushels of wheat tomorrow in world markets (the slope of the intertemporal resource constraint). However, households perceive that the price of one bushel of wheat today is $(1 + \tau_1)(1 + r^*)$ bushels tomorrow (the slope of the indifference curve at point C). Thus, at the equilibrium allocation, households are indifferent between sacrificing a bushel of wheat today and consuming an extra $(1 + \tau_1)(1 + r^*)$ bushels of wheat tomorrow. As a result, if households were to consume one additional bushel today, they would be better off, because world markets would ask them for only $1 + r^*$ units tomorrow, which is less than the $(1 + \tau_1)(1 + r^*)$ units that would leave them indifferent.

4.5.2 A PERMANENT INCREASE IN IMPORT TARIFFS

Consider now the case that import tariffs in both periods increase by the same amount so that $\tau_1 = \tau_2 > 0$. This implies that $(1 + \tau_1)/(1 + \tau_2) = 1$. In this case, neither the intertemporal resource constraint (4.8) nor the equilibrium Euler equation (4.4) are affected by the increase in import tariffs, and therefore the new consumption path is the same as the one without tariffs (point B in Figure 4.4). The reason the consumption path does not change is that the permanent import tariff raises the price of consumption by the same proportion in both periods. As a result the tariff does not change the intertemporal relative price of consumption, which continues to be equal to the world intertemporal price, $1 + r^*$. Because consumption is unaffected by the permanent import tariff, the trade balance is unchanged. Thus, if the government's intention was to improve the trade balance through an import tariff, making it permanent defeats its purpose.

Since the tariff leaves the path of consumption unchanged, welfare is also unchanged. Thus, a permanent tariff is innocuous. This result relies on the assumption that households do not consume the export good. To see this, consider again the example of an economy that imports food and is endowed with oil. Suppose that households like to consume not only food but also oil (for heating or transportation, say). This economy imports all of the food it consumes and exports its endowment of oil net of domestic oil consumption. A permanent import tariff does not change the intertemporal price of food but alters the intratemporal price of food in terms of oil in both periods. In particular, the tariff makes food relatively more expensive than oil in periods 1 and 2. This policy-induced change in domestic relative prices leads households to shift consumption away from food and toward oil. This substitution is inefficient because it does not reflect the true relative price of food in terms of oil, which is given by the terms of trade prevailing in world markets. As a result, a permanent import tariff reduces welfare. The trade balance is unaffected because the tariff does not alter the intertemporal relative price of either good. The reduction in the food trade deficit is offset by a reduction in the oil trade surplus of equal size. Exercise 4.8 formalizes this intuition in the context of a numerical example.

4.5.3 AN ANTICIPATED FUTURE INCREASE IN IMPORT TARIFFS

Finally, suppose that import tariffs in period 1 are zero ($\tau_1 = 0$) but that households learn that an import tariff will be imposed in period 2, $\tau_2 > 0$. The adjustment is also shown in Figure 4.4. As before, prior to the announcement the equilibrium is at point B. Because the economy-wide resource constraint is unaffected by the imposition of the import tariff, the adjustment is given by a move along the resource constraint. By the Euler equation the new optimal consumption path, denoted (C_1'', C_2''), must satisfy

$$\frac{U'(C_1'')}{\beta U'(C_2'')} = \frac{(1+r^*)}{(1+\tau_2)} < (1+r^*).$$

The increase in τ_2 lowers the right-hand side of this expression. Since $U'(C)$ is a decreasing function, we have that for the left-hand side to fall, either C_1 must increase, or C_2 must fall, or both. Since the equilibrium must occur on the original resource constraint, we have that the fall in the left-hand side must materialize via an increase in C_1 and a fall in C_2. The new consumption path is given by point D in Figure 4.4. Intuitively, with future import tariffs higher, households choose to consume more in period 1 and less in period 2. With income in period 1 unchanged (and equal to $TT_1 Q_1$), the increase in period 1 consumption is financed with external borrowing and a worsening of the trade balance. Like the increase in tariffs in period 1, the increase in tariffs in period 2 is welfare decreasing. To see this, note that the indifference curve that cuts the intertemporal budget constraint at point D lies southwest of the indifference curve associated with the no-tariff equilibrium, point B.

In sum, we have shown that import tariffs, in general, do not improve the trade balance. They only do so if current import tariffs increase relative to future import tariffs. Furthermore, we have shown that import tariffs whenever they distort the intertemporal relative price of consumption are welfare reducing.

4.6 Summing Up

This chapter analyzes the effects of terms of trade shocks and interest rate shocks in the context of the intertemporal model of the current account developed in Chapter 3.

- The terms of trade is the relative price of export goods in terms of import goods.
- Terms of trade shocks have the same effects as endowment shocks: the economy uses the current account to smooth consumption over time in response to temporary terms of trade shocks, and adjusts consumption with little movement in the current account in response to permanent terms of trade shocks.

- Interest rate shocks have a substitution and an income effect.
- By the substitution effect, an increase in the interest rate discourages current consumption and incentivizes saving, causing the current account and the trade balance to improve.
- The income effect associated with an increase in the interest rate depends on whether the household is a debtor or a creditor prior to the increase in the interest rate.
- If the household is a debtor prior to the increase in the interest rate, the increase has a negative income effect, as it makes it poorer. As a result, consumption falls and the trade balance and the current account improve. In this case, the income and substitution effects go in the same direction.
- If the household is a creditor prior to the increase in the interest rate, the income effect associated with the increase in the interest rate is positive and leads to higher consumption and a deterioration in the trade balance and the current account. In this case, the income and substitution effects go in the opposite direction, partially offsetting each other. Under log preferences the substitution effect dominates.
- An increase in import tariffs need not improve the trade balance or the current account. Only if import tariffs are temporary will they lead to an improvement in the trade balance and the current account. Future expected increases in import tariffs deteriorate the trade balance. Permanent changes in tariffs leave the trade balance unchanged.
- In the present economy, import tariffs are welfare decreasing.

4.7 Exercises

Exercise 4.1 (The Terms of Trade and the Current Account) Consider the following chart showing commodity prices in world markets:

	Price	
Commodity	Period 1	Period 2
Wheat	1	1
Oil	1	2

In the table, prices of oil are expressed in dollars per barrel and prices of wheat in dollars per bushel. Kuwait is a two-period economy that produces oil and consumes wheat. Consumers have preferences described by the lifetime utility function

$$C_1 C_2,$$

where C_1 and C_2 denote, respectively, consumption of wheat in periods 1 and 2, measured in bushels. Kuwait's per capita endowments of oil are 5 barrels in each period. The country starts period 1 with net financial assets carried over from period 0 worth 1.1 bushels of wheat (i.e., $(1 + r_0)B_0 = 1.1$, with $r_0 = 0.1$). There is free capital mobility and the world interest rate is 10 percent ($r^* = 0.1$). Financial assets are denominated in units of wheat.

1. What are the terms of trade faced by Kuwait in periods 1 and 2?
2. Calculate consumption, the trade balance, the current account, and saving in periods 1 and 2 (expressed in bushels of wheat).
3. Answer the previous question assuming that the price of oil in the second period is not $2 but $1 per barrel. Provide intuition.

Hint: Recall that the optimal allocation of consumption by households is invariant to increasing monotonic transformations of the lifetime utility function. So, for example, the utility function $C_1 C_2$ implies the same optimal consumption path as the log-linear function $\ln C_1 + \ln C_2$.

Exercise 4.2 (Anticipated Terms of Trade Shock) Consider a two-period small open endowment economy populated by a large number of households with preferences given by the lifetime utility function

$$\sqrt{C_1 C_2},$$

where C_1 and C_2 denote consumption of food in periods 1 and 2. Suppose that households receive exogenous endowments of copper given by $Q_1 = Q_2 = 10$ in periods 1 and 2. The terms of trade in periods 1 and 2 are $TT_1 = TT_2 = 1$. Every household enters period 1 with no assets or liabilities inherited from the past, $B_0 = 0$. Finally, suppose that there is free capital mobility and that the world interest rate on assets held between periods 1 and 2, denoted r^*, is 5 percent.

1. Compute the equilibrium levels of consumption, the trade balance, and the current account in periods 1 and 2.
2. Assume now that the terms of trade in period 2 are expected to increase by 50 percent. Calculate the effect of this anticipated terms of trade improvement on consumption, the trade balance, and the current account in periods 1 and 2. Provide intuition.
3. Relate your findings to those discussed in the case study of the copper price appreciation experienced by Chile in the early 2000s presented in Section 4.3. In particular, explain why the results obtained in items 1 and 3 make the behavior of the Chilean current account in the period 2003–2007 inconsistent with the intertemporal theory of current account determination under the (counterfactual) view that in the early 2000s Chileans had perfect foresight about the future path of the price of copper.

Hint: See the hint for Exercise 4.1.

Exercise 4.3 (A World Interest Rate Shock I) Consider an individual who lives for two periods, $t = 1, 2$. Her preferences for consumption in each period are described by the lifetime utility function

$$-C_1^{-1} - C_2^{-1},$$

where C_1 and C_2 denote consumption in periods 1 and 2. Suppose that the consumer starts period 1 with financial wealth equal to $(1 + r_0)B_0$, where B_0 is an inherited stock of bonds and r_0 is the interest rate on bonds held between periods 0 and 1. Suppose further that the individual receives endowments of goods in the amounts Q_1 and Q_2 in periods 1 and 2. In period 1, the individual can borrow or lend at the interest rate r_1 via a bond denoted B_1.

1. Find the optimal levels of consumption in periods 1 and 2 as functions of the individual's lifetime wealth, $\bar{Y}$, and the interest rate r_1.
2. Assume for the remainder of the problem that $r_1 = 0$. Find the optimal level of B_1 in terms of Q_1, Q_2, and $(1 + r_0)B_0$.
3. Find the response of consumption in period 1, ΔC_1, to an increase in the interest rate, $\Delta r_1 > 0$.
4. Show that if prior to the interest rate increase $B_1 = 0$, then $\Delta C_1 < 0$. Provide intuition.
5. Find conditions on Q_1, Q_2, and $(1 + r_0)B_0$ such that $\Delta C_1 > 0$ in response to the interest rate increase; that is, such that the income effect dominates the substitution effect. Find the associated condition for B_1. Provide intuition.

Exercise 4.4 (A World Interest Rate Shock II) Consider an individual who lives for two periods, $t = 1, 2$. Her preferences for consumption in each period are described by the lifetime utility function $U(C_1) + U(C_2)$, where C_1 and C_2 denote consumption in periods 1 and 2 and

$$U(C) = \frac{C^{1-\sigma} - 1}{1 - \sigma}.$$

The parameter $\sigma > 0$ denotes the inverse of the intertemporal elasticity of substitution. Suppose that the individual starts period 1 with no financial wealth, $B_0 = 0$. Suppose further that the individual receives endowments of goods in the amounts Q_1 and Q_2 in periods 1 and 2. In period 1, the individual can borrow or lend at the interest rate r_1 via a bond denoted B_1.

1. Find the optimal levels of consumption in periods 1 and 2 as functions of the individual's endowments, Q_1 and Q_2, the intertemporal elasticity of substitution $1/\sigma$, and the interest rate r_1.
2. Find the optimal level of saving in period 1 as a function of the individual's endowments, Q_1 and Q_2, the intertemporal elasticity of substitution $1/\sigma$, and the interest rate r_1. Characterize conditions under which the individual will save in period 1; that is, conditions such that $S_1 > 0$. Provide intuition.
3. Find the partial derivative of the optimal level of consumption in period 1 with respect to the interest rate r_1. Show that if $S_1 < 0$, then this derivative is negative; that is, an increase in the interest rate unambiguously lowers the optimal level of consumption in period 1. If $S_1 > 0$, characterize conditions on $1/\sigma$, r_1, Q_1, and Q_2 such that the substitution effect dominates the income effect; that is, conditions such that an increase in the interest rate r_1 reduces desired consumption in period 1. Provide an intuitive explanation of your answers.
4. Show that when $\sigma = 1$, then the substitution effect always dominates regardless of the sign of S_1; that is, the optimal level of period 1 consumption always falls when the interest rate increases.

5. Show that when $\sigma = 2$ and $r_1 = 0$, then the response of consumption in period 1 to an increase in the interest rate is the same as the one obtained in subquestion 3 of Exercise 4.3 in the case that $B_0 = 0$.

Exercise 4.5 (Oil Discovery and Extraction Costs) Consider an island populated by households with preferences given by

$$-C_1^{-1} - C_2^{-1},$$

where C_1 denotes consumption of food when young and C_2 denotes consumption of food when old. Households are endowed with 8 units of food when young and 5 units when old. Households are born with assets worth 2 units of food $((1 + r_0)B_0 = 2)$, where $r_0 = 5$ percent denotes the interest rate in period 0 and B_0 denotes the inherited stock of bonds. Suppose that households have access to the international financial market, where the interest rate, denoted r^*, is 10 percent.

1. Calculate the equilibrium levels of consumption, the trade balance, and the current account when young and when old.
2. Now assume that when young, each household discovers 20 barrels of oil reserves in its backyard. Households will be able to sell their oil in the international market only when they are old. The price of a barrel of oil in terms of units of food is expected to be 0.2 in period 2. Calculate the equilibrium levels of consumption, the trade balance, and the current account when young and old.
3. Now assume that extracting the oil requires investment in period 1 equal in value to 3.5 units of food. The investment must be made when young in order for the oil to be available for sale when old. Does it pay to make the investment? Calculate consumption and the trade balance when young.
4. Assume that households revise their expectations and now believe that the price of oil will be only 0.1 when old. Is it still profitable to extract the oil? Show your work.
5. More generally, what does the intertemporal approach to the current account predict should be the effects of oil discoveries on a country's balance of payments both at the time of the discovery and at the time of actual oil production?

Exercise 4.6 (Unfulfilled Expectations) Consider a two-period, small open economy populated by households whose preferences are given by

$$\ln C_1 + \ln C_2,$$

where C_1 and C_2 denote consumption of food in periods 1 and 2, respectively. Households are endowed with 1 ton of copper in each period and start period 1 with a zero net asset position. The relative price of copper in terms of food is 1 in both periods, and the world interest rate is zero.

1. What is consumption and the trade balance in periods 1 and 2?
2. Suppose now that in period 1 the relative price of copper continues to be 1, but that the expected relative price of copper in period 2 increases to 1.5. Calculate consumption and the trade balance in both periods.

3. Finally, continue to assume that in period 1 the relative price of copper is 1 and households are 100 percent sure that the relative price of copper in period 2 is going to be 1.5. However, assume that when period 2 arrives, expectations are not fulfilled, and the price remains at 1. What is consumption and the trade balance in periods 1 and 2? Provide intuition.

Exercise 4.7 (Import Tariffs) Consider a two-period open economy in which households have preferences given by

$$\ln C_1 + \ln C_2,$$

where C_1 and C_2 denote consumption of food in periods 1 and 2, measured in tons. The country does not produce food. Households are endowed with Q_1 and Q_2 barrels of oil in periods 1 and 2. In both periods, a barrel of oil sells for one ton of food in international markets. The economy starts period 1 with no assets, $B_0 = 0$. The world interest rate is r^* and there is free capital mobility. The government imposes tariffs on food imports in periods 1 and 2, denoted τ_1 and τ_2, and rebates the revenue generated by the tariffs to the public using lump-sum transfers, denoted L_1 and L_2.

1. What are the terms of trade in periods 1 and 2?
2. Derive the household's intertemporal budget constraint.
3. Write down the optimization problem of the household.
4. Derive the first-order conditions of the household's optimization problem.
5. Write down the budget constraints of the government in periods 1 and 2.
6. Combine the household's intertemporal budget constraint with the government budget constraints to find the economy's intertemporal resource constraint in equilibrium. Do the policy variables τ_1, τ_2, L_1, or L_2 appear in this constraint? Why?
7. Let $Y \equiv Q_1 + Q_2/(1 + r^*)$ denote the present discounted value of the endowment path. Express the equilibrium values of consumption in periods 1 and 2 in terms of Y, r^*, τ_1, and τ_2.
8. Write the equilibrium trade balance in period 1 in terms of Y, r^*, Q_1, τ_1, and τ_2. Compare the trade balance under free trade, i.e., $\tau_1 = \tau_2 = 0$, to the following cases: (a) $\tau_1 = \tau_2 > 0$; (b) $\tau_1 > 0$ and $\tau_2 = 0$; and (c) $\tau_1 = 0$ and $\tau_2 > 0$.
9. Define $x = \frac{1 + \tau_1}{1 + \tau_2}$. Use the equilibrium values of C_1 and C_2 derived in question 7 to eliminate these two variables from the household's utility function. Find the value of x that maximizes the household's welfare. Interpret your result.

Exercise 4.8 (Intratemporal Distortions of Tariffs) Consider a two-period open economy in which households consume food and oil and have preferences given by

$$\ln C_1^f + \ln C_1^o + \ln C_2^f + \ln C_2^o,$$

where C_t^f and C_t^o denote the consumption of food and oil in period $t = 1, 2$. In each of the two periods, households are endowed with one unit of oil and the terms of trade equal one. There is free capital mobility and the world interest rate equals zero.

1. Find the equilibrium levels of consumption of food and oil in periods 1 and 2. Find imports and exports of each type of good in periods 1 and 2. Find the trade balance in periods 1 and 2. Find the household's level of utility. The answer to this question is a set of numbers.

2. Answer question 1 under the assumption that the government imposes a tariff of 50 percent on imports of food in both periods. What changes qualitatively with respect to the case in which households consume only food (Exercise 4.7)? Place particular emphasis on consumption of food, the trade balance, and welfare.

CHAPTER 5

Current Account Determination in a Production Economy

In Chapters 3 and 4, we studied endowment economies. In those environments, there are no firms, physical capital, or investment in new capital goods. As a result, the current account, which, as we saw in Chapter 2, is given by the difference between saving and investment, is simply determined by the saving decision of households. The assumption that investment is zero is useful, because it allows us to understand the determination of the trade balance and the current account in the simplest possible model economy. But it is also unrealistic. Investment, which consists of spending on goods such as machines, new structures, equipment, and inventories, is an important component of aggregate demand amounting to around 20 percent of GDP in most countries. Further, investment is the most volatile component of aggregate demand and, as such, it is important for understanding movements in the current account over the business cycle.

In this chapter, we extend our theory by studying the determination of the current account in a production economy with investment in physical capital. In this new environment, factors affecting the firm's investment decision will have a direct effect on the current account even if saving were unchanged. In equilibrium, factors that affect investment will in general also affect households' saving decisions through, for example, income effects, and thus will indirectly also affect the current account.

5.1 The Investment Decision of Firms

Consider an economy populated by a large number of firms and households. As before, the economy lasts for two periods, denoted period 1 and period 2. In this economy, however, output is no longer an endowment but is produced by firms.

Suppose that in period 1 firms invest in physical capital, which they use in period 2 to produce goods. Specifically, output in period 2, denoted Q_2, is produced according to the *production function*

$$Q_2 = A_2 F(I_1),$$

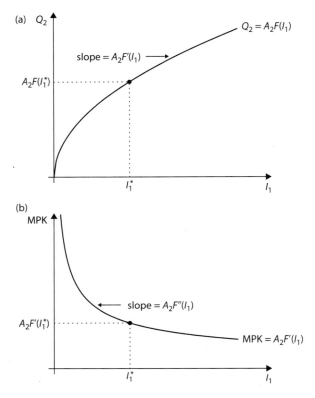

Figure 5.1. The Production Function and the Marginal Product of Capital

Notes: Panel (a) displays the production function. It depicts output in period 2, Q_2, as an increasing and concave function of capital invested in period 1, I_1, with a zero intercept. Panel (b) displays the marginal product of capital, *MPK*, as a positive and decreasing function of I_1. Panels (a) and (b) are related by the fact that at any given level of capital, say I_1^*, the slope of the production function equals the level of the marginal product of capital.

where $A_2 > 0$ is an efficiency parameter capturing factors such as the state of *technology*, $F(I_1)$ is a function, and I_1 denotes *investment* in *physical capital* in period 1, which becomes productive in period 2. The production function $A_2F(I_1)$ describes a technological relation specifying the amount of output obtained for each level of capital input. Panel (a) of Figure 5.1 plots the production function. We impose a number of properties on the production technology. First, we assume that output is zero when investment is zero, $A_2F(0) = 0$. Second, we assume that output is increasing in the amount of physical capital, $A_2F'(I_1) > 0$, where $F'(I_1)$ denotes the derivative of $F(I_1)$. Another way of stating this assumption is to say that the *marginal product of capital* (or MPK) is positive. The marginal product of capital is the amount by which output increases when the capital stock is increased by one unit,

$$\text{MPK} = A_2F'(I_1).$$

Finally, we assume that the production function is concave in capital, $A_2 F''(I_1) < 0$, where $F''(I_1)$ denotes the second derivative of $F(I_1)$. When the production function is concave, output increases with capital at a decreasing rate. It means, for example, that increasing the number of tractors from 1 to 2 in a 100-acre farm yields more additional output than increasing the number of tractors from 20 to 21. This property of the production function is known as *diminishing marginal product of capital*.

Panel (b) of Figure 5.1 displays the marginal product of capital as a function of the level of capital. Panels (a) and (b) are related by the fact that the slope of the production function at a given level of investment equals the level of the marginal product of capital at the same level of investment. For example, in the figure, the slope of the production function when the capital stock equals I_1^* equals the level of the marginal product of capital when the capital stock also equals I_1^*. The marginal product of capital schedule is downward sloping, reflecting the assumption of diminishing marginal product.

As an example, consider the production function

$$Q_2 = \sqrt{I_1}.$$

In this case, $A_2 = 1$ and $F(I_1)$ is the square root function. According to this technology, output is nil when the capital stock, I_1, is zero, and is increasing in the stock of capital. The marginal product of capital is given by

$$\text{MPK} = \frac{1}{2\sqrt{I_1}},$$

which is decreasing in the level of capital.

Consider now the effect of a productivity improvement on the production function and the MPK schedule. Suppose specifically that the efficiency parameter increases from A_2 to $A_2' > A_2$. After the productivity improvement, the firm can produce more output at every level of capital. Figure 5.2 displays the effect of this productivity shock on the production function and the marginal product of capital. Panel (a) shows that the production function shifts upward, rotating counterclockwise around the origin. This means that the production function becomes steeper for a given level of investment. In other words, the technological improvement causes the marginal product of capital to be higher for a given level of investment. This effect is shown in panel (b) as a shift up and to the right of the marginal product of capital schedule.

Changes in productivity can be permanent or temporary. Permanent productivity changes typically stem from technological improvements. For example, the introduction of the assembly line by Henry Ford in 1913 reduced the time to build a car from 12 hours to two and a half hours. In the U.S. farming sector, over the past 50 years, the average cow increased its milk production from 5,000 pounds to 18,000 pounds, due to improvements in breeding, health care, and feeding techniques. Examples of temporary productivity changes are weather conditions in the farming sector, which can alter yields from one year to the next, and new technologies that turn out to be less productive than previously existing ones, like the

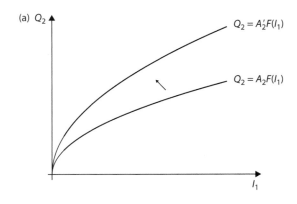

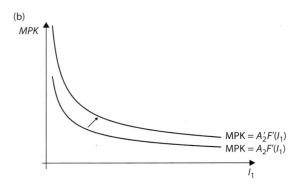

Figure 5.2. Effect of an Increase in Productivity on the Production Function and the Marginal Product of Capital Schedule
Note: A positive productivity shock that increases the level of technology from A_2 to $A_2' > A_2$ rotates the production function counterclockwise around the origin and shifts the marginal product of capital schedule up and to the right.

Boeing 737 MAX jet airliner, introduced in 2017, whose maneuvering characteristics augmentation system (MCAS) automatically and repeatedly forced the aircraft to nosedive, causing aviation authorities around the world to ground it and Boeing to suspend its production and sales in 2019.

Thus far we have discussed purely technological relationships involving no economic choices on the part of the firm. We now turn to the optimal investment and production decisions of firms. We assume that firms borrow in period 1 to finance purchases of investment goods, such as new machines and structures. Let D_1^f denote the amount of debt assumed by the firm in period 1. We then have that

$$D_1^f = I_1. \tag{5.1}$$

Firms repay the loan in period 2. Let the interest rate on debt held from period 1 to period 2 be r_1. The total repayment in period 2, including interest, is then given by $(1 + r_1)D_1^f$. The firm's profits in period 2, denoted Π_2, are given by the difference

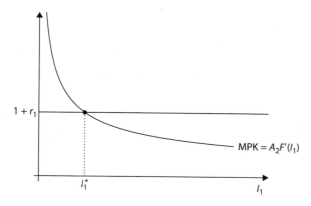

Figure 5.3. The Optimal Level of Investment
Notes: The downward-sloping line is the marginal product of capital schedule. The horizontal line depicts the marginal cost of capital schedule, which is equal to the gross interest rate, $1 + r_1$, for any level of investment. Firms invest up to the point where the marginal product of capital equals the marginal cost of capital, I_1^*. Profits are given by the triangle below the marginal product of capital schedule and above the marginal cost of capital.

between revenues from the sale of output and repayment of the investment loan; that is,

$$\Pi_2 = A_2 F(I_1) - (1 + r_1) D_1^f. \tag{5.2}$$

Using equation (5.1) to eliminate debt from this expression, we can express period 2 profits simply in terms of investment and the interest rate

$$\Pi_2 = A_2 F(I_1) - (1 + r_1) I_1. \tag{5.3}$$

Firms choose I_1 to maximize profits, taking as given the interest rate r_1 and the productivity factor A_2. The first-order condition associated with this profit maximization problem is the derivative of the right-hand side of (5.3) with respect to I_1 equated to zero. Performing this operation yields, after a slight rearrangement,

$$A_2 F'(I_1) = 1 + r_1. \tag{5.4}$$

This optimality condition is quite intuitive. Figure 5.3 displays the left- and right-hand sides of (5.3) as functions of I_1. The left-hand side is the marginal product of capital, $A_2 F'(I_1)$, which, as discussed before, is a decreasing function of the level of capital, I_1. The right-hand side is the marginal cost of capital, $1 + r_1$, and is a horizontal line because it is independent of the level of investment. Each additional unit of capital costs the firm $1 + r_1$ in period 2. This is because for each unit of capital used in period 2, the firm must take a loan in the amount of one unit in period 1 and must pay back this loan plus interest, $1 + r_1$, in period 2. For low values of capital, investment is highly productive so that the marginal product of capital, $A_2 F'(I_1)$, exceeds the marginal cost of capital, $1 + r_1$. In this case, the firm can increase profits by buying an additional unit of capital in period 1. The firm will continue to buy

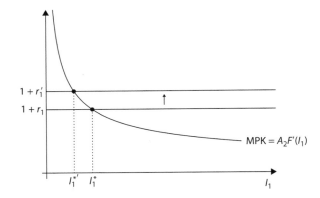

Figure 5.4. Effect of an Increase in the Interest Rate on Investment

Notes: An increase in the interest rate from r_1 to $r_1' > r_1$ shifts the marginal cost schedule up. As a result, the optimal level of investment falls from I_1^* to $I_1^{*'}$. An increase in the interest rate lowers profits, which are given by the area below the marginal product of capital schedule and above the marginal cost schedule.

additional units of capital as long as the marginal product exceeds the marginal cost. As investment increases, however, the marginal productivity of capital diminishes. For sufficiently large levels of investment, the marginal product of capital falls below the marginal cost of capital. In this range—that is, for $I_1 > I_1^*$ in the figure—an additional unit of capital reduces profits, as the amount of additional output it generates, $A_2 F'(I_1)$, is less than its cost, $(1 + r_1)$. Consequently, the firm can increase profits by reducing I_1. The optimal level of investment is reached when the marginal product of investment equals its marginal cost; that is, when equation (5.4) holds. At the optimal level of investment, I_1^* in the figure, profits of the firm are given by the area below the marginal product of capital curve and above the marginal cost of capital curve.

Figure 5.4 illustrates the effect on investment of an increase in the interest rate from r_1 to $r_1' > r_1$. When the interest rate is r_1, the optimal level of investment is I_1^*. As the interest rate increases, the horizontal marginal cost function shifts upward. At I_1^*, the marginal product of capital is now below the marginal cost of capital, $1 + r_1'$, so it pays for the firm to reduce investment. The firm will cut investment up to the point at which the marginal product of capital meets the higher cost of capital, $1 + r_1'$, which occurs at $I_1^{*'}$. It follows that investment is a decreasing function of the interest rate.

Consider next the effect of a productivity shock. Assume that the efficiency factor of the production function increases from A_2 to $A_2' > A_2$. A positive productivity shock causes the marginal product of capital schedule to shift up and to the right, as shown in Figure 5.5. Because capital is now more productive, all of the investment projects that were profitable before become even more profitable. In addition, investment opportunities that were not profitable before the increase in productivity now became profitable. As a result, it is optimal for firms to increase investment. In the figure, investment increases from I_1^* to $I_1^{*'}$ as the level of technology increases

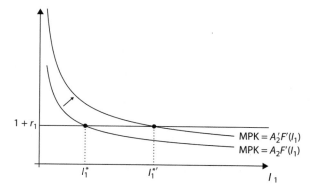

Figure 5.5. Effect of an Increase in Productivity on Investment

Notes: A positive productivity shock shifts the MPK schedule up and to the right. The firm expands investment until the new MPK schedule meets the marginal cost of capital schedule. Investment increases from I_1^* to $I_1^{*'}$. Profits increase, because the area below the MPK schedule and above the marginal cost schedule gets larger.

from A_2 to A_2'. It follows that, all other things equal, investment is an increasing function of the technology factor A_2.

5.2 The Investment Schedule

Aggregate investment is the sum of the investment decisions of individual firms. If we assume that all firms have the same technology and face the same interest rate, we have that all firms will make the same investment decisions. As a result, total investment in the economy will behave just like investment at the firm level. We then have that aggregate investment is a function of the interest rate and the productivity factor and write

$$I_1 = I(\underset{-}{r_1}; \underset{+}{A_2}), \tag{5.5}$$

where now I_1 denotes aggregate investment in period 1. We will refer to this function as the *investment schedule*. It is decreasing in the interest rate and increasing in the level of productivity. Figure 5.6 depicts the investment schedule in the space (I_1, r_1) for a given level of A_2. As the interest rate in period 1 increases, all other things equal, aggregate investment falls.

Suppose now that a technological improvement causes the efficiency parameter of the production function to increase from A_2 to A_2'. As we discussed earlier, firms now have an incentive to increase investment for every level of the interest rate. This means that the investment schedule shifts up and to the right in response to the positive productivity shock, as shown in Figure 5.7.

5.2.1 THE PROFIT FUNCTION

As discussed in Section 5.1, the firm's profit is given by the area below the marginal product of capital schedule and above the marginal cost of capital

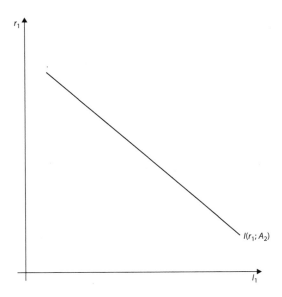

Figure 5.6. The Investment Schedule
Notes: The investment schedule relates the aggregate level of investment and the interest rate, given the productivity factor A_2. The investment schedule slopes downward because the profit-maximizing level of investment is decreasing in the marginal cost of capital.

schedule. Figure 5.4 shows that an increase in the interest rate from r_1 to $r_1' > r_1$ causes this area, and therefore profits, to shrink. This makes sense, because an increase in the interest rate raises the financing cost of investment. Thus, all else constant, profits are a decreasing function of the interest rate.

Consider now the effect on profits of an increase in the productivity of capital. Take another look at Figure 5.5, which shows that an increase in the productivity factor from A_2 to $A_2' > A_2$ shifts the marginal product of capital schedule up and to the right. As a result, period 2 profits increase by an amount equal to the expansion of the triangular area below the new marginal product of capital schedule and above the marginal cost of capital schedule. Thus profits, like investment, are an increasing function of the technology factor A_2.

We can then write the optimal level of profits as

$$\Pi_2 = \Pi_2(\underset{-}{r_1}, \underset{+}{A_2}),$$

where the function $\Pi_2(\cdot, \cdot)$ is decreasing in its first argument, the interest rate, and increasing in its second argument, the productivity factor.

You might have noticed that we have concentrated on the profit maximization problem of the firm in period 2, and have said nothing about profits in period 1. The reason for this omission is that profits in period 1 are determined by investment decisions made before period 1. As a result, there is nothing the firm can do in

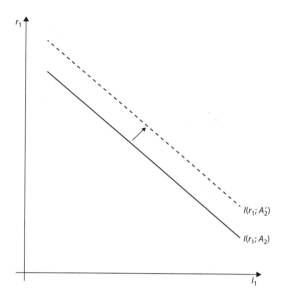

Figure 5.7. Effect of an Increase in Productivity on the Investment Schedule
Notes: The figure depicts the effect of an increase in the productivity parameter from A_2 to A_2'. The positive productivity shock shifts the investment schedule up and to the right because for every level of the interest rate, the profit-maximizing level of investment is now higher.

period 1 to alter its profitability. Specifically, profits in period 1, denoted Π_1, are given by

$$\Pi_1 = A_1 F(I_0) - (1 + r_0) D_0^f, \tag{5.6}$$

with

$$D_0^f = I_0. \tag{5.7}$$

The variables I_0, D_0^f, and r_0 are all predetermined in period 1 and are therefore taken as exogenous by the firm in period 1. The level of productivity, A_1, is indeed determined in period 1, but is out of the control of the firm. As a result, period 1 profits are determined in period 1, but are not affected by any decision made by the firm in that period. Higher interest rates (r_0) lower profits as the firm has to make higher interest payments to its creditors, and a higher productivity factor in period 1 (A_1) raises profits as it increases the amount of output that the firm can produce with the predetermined level of investment, I_0. Thus, as we did with profits in period 2, we can express profits in period 1 as:

$$\Pi_1 = \Pi_1(\underset{-}{r_0}, \underset{+}{A_1}),$$

where the function $\Pi(\cdot, \cdot)$ is decreasing in its first argument (the interest rate, r_0) and increasing in its second argument (the period 1 productivity factor, A_1).

5.3 The Consumption-Saving Decision of Households

Households in the present economy are quite similar to those in the endowment economy studied in Chapter 3. One difference is that now households are the owners of firms. Consequently, instead of receiving an endowment each period, households receive profit payments from firms, $\Pi_1(r_0, A_1)$ in period 1 and $\Pi_2(r_1, A_2)$ in period 2.

At the beginning of period 1, the household is endowed with B_0^h units of bonds, which yield the interest income $r_0 B_0^h$. We use the notation B_0^h to refer to bonds held by households, and will continue to reserve the notation B_t to refer to the country's net foreign asset position in period t. The distinction is now relevant. In previous chapters, the only agent in the economy holding liability or asset positions was the household. Now firms also participate in the financial market. As a result, the net asset position of households may be different from that of the country as a whole.

Total household income in period 1 equals $\Pi_1(r_0, A_1) + r_0 B_0^h$. The household uses its income for consumption, C_1, and additions to its stock of bonds, $B_1^h - B_0^h$. Its budget constraint in period 1 is then given by

$$C_1 + B_1^h - B_0^h = \Pi_1(r_0, A_1) + r_0 B_0^h. \tag{5.8}$$

Similarly, the household's budget constraint in period 2 takes the form

$$C_2 + B_2^h - B_1^h = \Pi_2(r_1, A_2) + r_1 B_1^h, \tag{5.9}$$

where B_2^h denotes the stock of bonds the household holds at the end of period 2.

As discussed in Chapter 3, in the last period of life, the household will not want to hold any positive amount of assets maturing after that period. Consequently, the household will always find it optimal to choose $B_2^h \leq 0$. At the same time, the household is not allowed to end period 2 with unpaid debts (the no-Ponzi-game constraint), so that $B_2^h \geq 0$. Therefore, the household's financial wealth at the end of period 2 must be equal to zero (the transversality condition),

$$B_2^h = 0.$$

Using this expression to eliminate B_2^h from the period 2 budget constraint (5.9) yields

$$C_2 = (1 + r_1) B_1^h + \Pi_2(r_1, A_2). \tag{5.10}$$

In turn, combining (5.8) and (5.10) to eliminate B_1^h gives the household's intertemporal budget constraint,

$$C_1 + \frac{C_2}{1 + r_1} = (1 + r_0) B_0^h + \Pi_1(r_0, A_1) + \frac{\Pi_2(r_1, A_2)}{1 + r_1}. \tag{5.11}$$

This expression is similar to the intertemporal budget constraint corresponding to the endowment economy of Chapter 3, equation (3.4), with the only difference that the present discounted value of endowments, $Q_1 + Q_2/(1+r_1)$, is replaced by the present discounted value of profits $\Pi_1(r_0, A_1) + \Pi_2(r_1, A_2)/(1+r_1)$. Note that the household takes the entire right-hand side of the intertemporal budget constraint (5.11) as given, since it has no control over the path of profits, $(\Pi_1(r_0, A_1), \Pi_2(r_1, A_2))$, its initial wealth, $((1+r_0)B_0^h)$, or the interest rate (r_1). Thus, we can define

$$\bar{Y} \equiv (1+r_0)B_0^h + \Pi_1(r_0, A_1) + \frac{\Pi_2(r_1, A_2)}{1+r_1}$$

to be the household's lifetime wealth, just as we did in the endowment economy of Chapter 3. The intertemporal budget constraint of the household, equation (5.11), can then be written as

$$C_2 = (1+r_1)(\bar{Y} - C_1). \tag{5.12}$$

Figure 5.8 depicts the household's intertemporal budget constraint in the space (C_1, C_2). It is a downward-sloping straight line with slope $-(1+r_1)$. The figure is drawn under the assumption that the household starts period 1 with no assets or liabilities ($B_0^h = 0$). As a result, the path of profits $(\Pi_1(r_0, A_1), \Pi_2(r_1, A_2))$ is on the intertemporal budget constraint (point A in the figure).

Households are assumed to derive utility from consumption in periods 1 and 2. Their preferences are described by the utility function

$$U(C_1) + \beta U(C_2), \tag{5.13}$$

which is the same as the lifetime utility function of households in the endowment economy of Chapter 3, given in equation (3.5). The household chooses C_1 and C_2 to maximize its utility function subject to the intertemporal budget constraint (5.12), taking as given $\bar{Y}$ and r_1. The household optimization problem is then identical to that of the endowment economy.

Figure 5.8 depicts the household's optimal intertemporal consumption choice. The optimal consumption path is at point B on the intertemporal budget constraint. At point B the intertemporal budget constraint is tangent to an indifference curve. This means that, as before, at the optimal consumption path the slope of the indifference curve is equal to $-(1+r_1)$. Recalling that the slope of the indifference curve is equal to the marginal rate of substitution, we have that the optimal consumption path must satisfy the Euler equation

$$\frac{U'(C_1)}{\beta U'(C_2)} = 1 + r_1. \tag{5.14}$$

Again, this optimality condition is identical to the one pertaining to the endowment economy (see equation (3.9)).

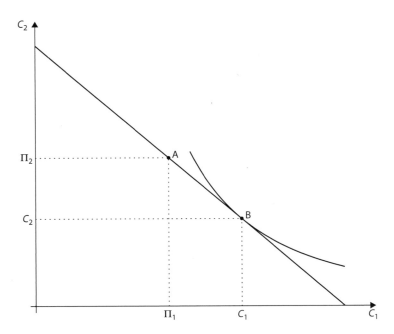

Figure 5.8. The Optimal Intertemporal Consumption Choice in the Production Economy

Notes: The figure depicts the optimal choice of consumption in periods 1 and 2. The intertemporal budget constraint is the straight downward-sloping line. It crosses the profit path $(\Pi_1(r_0, A_1), \Pi_2(r_1, A_2))$ at point A and has a slope equal to $-(1 + r_1)$. The optimal consumption path (C_1, C_2) is at point B, where an indifference curve is tangent to the intertemporal budget constraint. The figure is drawn under the assumption that the household starts period 1 with a zero net asset position, $B_0^h = 0$.

5.3.1 EFFECT OF A TEMPORARY INCREASE IN PRODUCTIVITY ON CONSUMPTION

Suppose now that unexpectedly the economy experiences an increase in the productivity of capital in period 1. Specifically, suppose that the efficiency parameter of the production function increases from A_1 to $A_1' > A_1$. Assume further that the productivity shock is transitory, so that A_2 remains unchanged. Assume also that the interest rate, r_1, is unchanged. The increase in A_1 could reflect, for example, an improvement in weather conditions in the farming sector that is not expected to last beyond the present harvest. The increase in A_1 raises firms' profits from $\Pi_1(r_0, A_1)$ to $\Pi_1(r_0, A_1')$. The capital stock in period 1, I_0, does not change because it is predetermined. Profits in period 2 are unchanged, because the temporary weather improvement does not affect A_2.

The effect on the optimal consumption path is shown in Figure 5.9. Before the shock, the profit path is at point A. The new profit path is point A' located at the same height and to the right of the original profit path. The increase in period 1 profits shifts the intertemporal budget constraint in a parallel fashion out and to the right. The slope of the intertemporal budget constraint is unchanged because

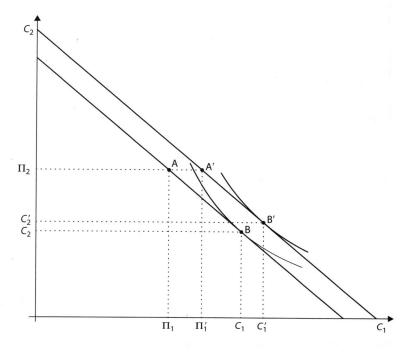

Figure 5.9. Effect of a Temporary Increase in Productivity on Consumption
Notes: The figure depicts the adjustment of consumption to an increase in the productivity of capital in period 1 from A_1 to A_1' holding constant the productivity of capital in period 2, A_2, and the interest rate, r_1. To save notation, Π_1, Π_1', and Π_2 are used in lieu of $\Pi_1(r_0, A_1)$, $\Pi_1(r_0, A_1')$, and $\Pi_2(r_1, A_2)$, respectively. Prior to the productivity shock, the profit path is at point A and the optimal consumption path is at point B. When productivity increases, period 1 profits increase from Π_1 to Π_1', and period 2 profits remain unchanged. The new profit path is at point A'. The intertemporal budget constraint shifts in a parallel fashion out and to the right. The new consumption path is at point B' and features higher consumption in both periods. Period 1 consumption increases by less than period 1 profits, so household saving increases. The figure is drawn under the assumption that the household starts period 1 with a zero net asset position, $B_0^h = 0$.

the interest rate, r_1, is unchanged. The increase in profit income induces households to consume more in both periods. The new consumption path, (C_1', C_2'), is at point B', located northeast of the initial consumption path, point B. The increase in consumption in period 1 is smaller than the increase in profit income, because households save part of the increase in period 1 income for future consumption. As a result, the temporary productivity shock causes an increase in household saving.

5.3.2 EFFECT OF AN ANTICIPATED FUTURE PRODUCTIVITY INCREASE ON CONSUMPTION

Next, let us analyze the effect of an anticipated increase in the productivity of capital. Specifically, suppose that in period 1 households learn that because of a

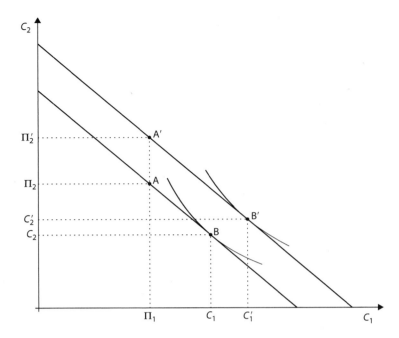

Figure 5.10. Effect of an Anticipated Future Productivity Increase on Consumption
Notes: The figure depicts the effect of an increase in the productivity of capital in period 2 from A_2 to A'_2, holding constant the productivity of capital in period 1, A_1, and the interest rate, r_1. To save notation, Π_1, Π_2, and Π'_2 are used in lieu of $\Pi_1(r_0, A_1)$, $\Pi_2(r_1, A_2)$, and $\Pi_2(r_1, A'_2)$, respectively. The initial path of profits is at point A, and the initial optimal consumption path is at point B. The anticipated positive productivity shock increases period 2 profits from Π_2 to Π'_2. The new path of profits is at point A'. The intertemporal budget constraint shifts out and to the right in a parallel fashion. The new consumption path is at point B' and features higher consumption in both periods. The increase in period 1 consumption is financed by an increase in borrowing. The figure is drawn under the assumption that the household starts period 1 with a zero net asset position, $B_0^h = 0$.

technological improvement being developed, the efficiency parameter of the production function will increase in period 2 from A_2 to A'_2. Assume further that the productivity of capital in period 1, A_1, and the interest rate, r_1, are unchanged. The expected increase in productivity raises period 2 profits from $\Pi_2(r_1, A_2)$ to $\Pi_2(r_1, A'_2)$. Period 1 profits are unchanged as A_1 is assumed to stay the same.

Figure 5.10 displays the adjustment of consumption to the anticipated productivity increase. The initial profit path is at point A and the one after the news about future technological advances is at point A', located straight north of point A. As a result, the intertemporal budget constraint shifts out and to the right in a parallel fashion. As in the case of an increase in period 1 profits, the increase in period 2 profits makes households richer and because consumption in both periods are normal goods, consumption rises in both periods. The new consumption path is at point B' located northeast of the original consumption path, point B.

Because period 1 profits are unchanged, the household must finance the expansion in period 1 consumption by borrowing. Thus, the anticipated positive productivity shock causes a fall in household saving.

5.3.3 EFFECT OF AN INCREASE IN THE INTEREST RATE ON CONSUMPTION

Consider now the effect of an increase in the interest rate from r_1 to $r_1' > r_1$. The situation is depicted in Figure 5.11. The initial profit path is at point A and the associated optimal consumption path is at point B. As before, the figure is drawn under the assumption of zero initial assets ($B_0^h = 0$), so the intertemporal budget constraint passes through point A. The household is initially borrowing the amount $C_1 - \Pi_1 > 0$. As in the endowment economy, the increase in the interest rate makes the intertemporal budget constraint steeper, because now consuming an extra unit in period 1 requires sacrificing $r_1' - r_1 > 0$ extra units of consumption in period 2. But in the production economy, the increase in the interest rate has an additional effect on the intertemporal budget constraint that was absent in the endowment economy. Specifically, at the higher interest rate firms make less profits

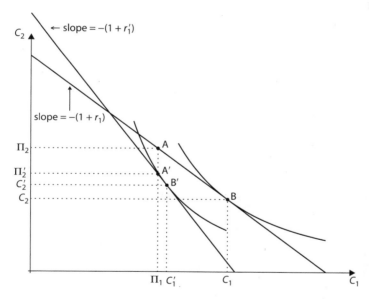

Figure 5.11. Effect of an Increase in the Interest Rate on Consumption
Notes: To save notation, Π_1, Π_2, and Π_2' are used in lieu of $\Pi_1(r_0, A_1)$, $\Pi_2(r_1, A_2)$, and $\Pi_2(r_1, A_2')$, respectively. The initial path of profits is at point A on the intertemporal budget constraint, and the initial optimal consumption path is at point B where the intertemporal budget constraint is tangent to an indifference curve. The figure is drawn under the assumption of zero initial assets ($B_0^h = 0$). The increase in the interest rate causes a reduction in profits in period 2, from Π_2 to $\Pi_2' < \Pi_2$, so the new path of profits, point A', is directly below the original one, point A. In addition, the increase in the interest rate makes the intertemporal budget constraint steeper. The new optimal consumption path, (C_1', C_2'), is point B' and features lower consumption in period 1.

in period 2, which reduces the household's income in that period from $\Pi_2(r_1, A_2)$ to $\Pi_2(r_1', A_2) < \Pi_2(r_1, A_2)$. Profits in period 1 are unaffected by the increase in r_1. As shown in the figure, the new profit path, given by point A′, is located directly below the original profit path (point A). Thus, the increase in the interest rate causes two changes in the position of the intertemporal budget constraint: it rotates it clockwise and at the same time it shifts it downward.

The new consumption path is point B′ and features lower consumption in period 1 ($C_1' < C_1$). The reduction in period 1 consumption is due to three effects. Two of them are the familiar substitution and income effects studied in the endowment economy of Chapter 3. As we discussed there, when the interest rate increases, the substitution effect always induces households to consume less in the current period, as interest-bearing assets become a more attractive option. The income effect is also negative in this example because the household was a debtor prior to the increase in the interest rate ($B_1^h < 0$), so that the increase in the interest rate makes it poorer. The third and novel effect is a negative income effect stemming from the reduction in profit income in period 2. The three effects discourage consumption in period 1. Consequently, we have that the increase in the interest rate causes a fall in borrowing (from $C_1 - \Pi_1(r_0, A_1)$ to $C_1' - \Pi_1(r_0, A_1)$), or equivalently an increase in household saving (from a negative figure to a less negative one).

Collecting the results from the analysis of the three previous subsections, we have that private consumption in period 1 is a decreasing function of the interest rate and an increasing function of current and expected future productivity. Thus we can write

$$C_1 = C(\underset{-}{r_1}, \underset{+}{A_1}, \underset{+}{A_2}). \tag{5.15}$$

5.4 The Saving Schedule

In Chapter 2 we saw that national saving, S_1, is the difference between national income, Y_1, and private and government consumption, $C_1 + G_1$; see equation (2.8). In the present economy there is no government, so that $G_1 = 0$ and national saving is simply the difference between national income and private consumption,

$$S_1 = Y_1 - C_1. \tag{5.16}$$

Recall that national income is the sum of net investment income and output,

$$Y_1 = r_0 B_0 + Q_1,$$

where B_0 is the country's net foreign asset position at the beginning of period 1, and Q_1 is output in period 1. The country's net foreign asset position at the beginning of period 1 is the sum of the household's net asset position, B_0^h, and the firm's net asset position, $-D_0^f$; that is,

$$B_0 = B_0^h - D_0^f. \tag{5.17}$$

Since B_0^h, D_0^f, and r_0 are all determined prior to period 1, we can regard net investment income as exogenously given. Output in period 1 is given by

$$Q_1 = A_1 F(I_0).$$

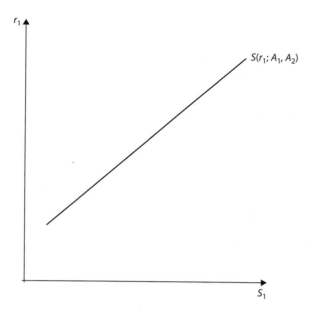

Figure 5.12. The Saving Schedule
Notes: The saving schedule relates national saving to the interest rate. It slopes upward because an increase in the interest rate induces households to postpone current consumption and increase their holdings of interest-bearing assets.

The stock of capital in period 1, I_0, is determined prior to period 1 and the productivity parameter, A_1, is determined in period 1, but is exogenous. Thus, we can regard period 1 output also as exogenously given. It follows that period 1 national income is an increasing function of productivity, A_1, and is independent of both the interest rate, r_1, and future expected productivity, A_2. We can then write national income as

$$Y_1 = Y(\underset{+}{A_1}).$$
(5.18)

Combining expressions (5.15), (5.16), and (5.18), yields

$$S_1 = Y(\underset{+}{A_1}) - C(\underset{-}{r_1}, \underset{+}{A_1}, \underset{+}{A_2}).$$

It is clear from this expression that national saving is increasing in the interest rate, r_1, and decreasing in the future expected level of productivity, A_2. But what about current productivity, A_1? On the surface, an increase in A_1 has an ambiguous effect on saving, as it causes an increase in both national income and consumption. However, we saw in the previous section that a positive temporary productivity shock (an increase in A_1) induces an increase in consumption that is smaller than the increase in income, as consumption-smoothing households prefer to save part of the increase in profit income for future consumption. Thus, national saving increases unambiguously with an increase in A_1. We can summarize these results by writing national saving as

$$S_1 = S(\underset{+}{r_1}; \underset{+}{A_1}, \underset{-}{A_2}).$$
(5.19)

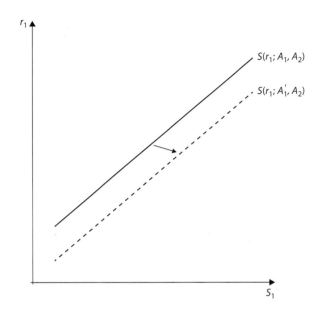

Figure 5.13. Effect of a Temporary Productivity Increase on the Saving Schedule
Notes: The figure depicts the effect of an increase in the productivity parameter in period 1 from A_1 to $A_1' > A_1$, holding A_2 constant. A positive temporary productivity shock shifts the saving schedule down and to the right, because at every level of the interest rate households save part of the additional profit income generated by the increase in productivity for future consumption.

This expression is the *saving schedule* and is depicted in Figure 5.12. The saving schedule is upward sloping in the space (S_1, r_1), because an increase in the interest rate, holding constant A_1 and A_2, encourages saving.

Consider the effect of a temporary productivity shock that increases A_1, with A_2 unchanged. Graphically, a temporary productivity shock shifts the saving schedule down and to the right, as shown in Figure 5.13. The shift in the saving schedule reflects the fact that the temporary increase in productivity induces households to save more at every level of the interest rate.

What about an anticipated increase in productivity in period 2; that is, an increase in A_2 holding A_1 constant? This type of shock causes the saving schedule to shift up and to the left, as shown in Figure 5.14. The reason is that at every given level of the interest rate, the increase in future productivity discourages saving.

5.5 The Current Account Schedule

In Section 2.3 of Chapter 2, we deduced that the current account is the difference between saving and investment (see equation (2.9)),

$$CA_1 = S_1 - I_1.$$

Using the saving and investment schedules given in equations (5.19) and (5.5), we can write

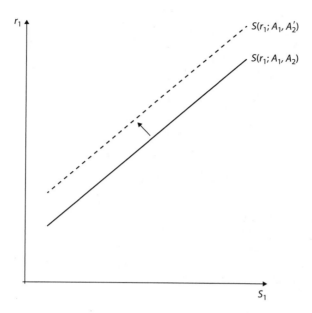

Figure 5.14. Effect of an Anticipated Future Productivity Increase on the Saving Schedule

Notes: The figure depicts the effect of an increase in the productivity parameter from A_2 to $A_2' > A_2$ on the saving schedule. The anticipated productivity shock shifts the saving schedule up and to the left. The increase in future productivity leaves current income unchanged but increases future income. In period 1, households consume more in anticipation of the future increase in profit income. Consequently, at every given level of the interest rate saving declines.

$$CA_1 = S(r_1; A_1, A_2) - I(r_1; A_2).$$
$$+ \quad + \quad - \qquad - \quad +$$

This expression implies that the current account is an increasing function of the interest rate. It also implies that the current account is increasing in the level of productivity in period 1 and decreasing in the expected level of productivity in period 2. We can therefore write

$$CA_1 = CA(r_1; A_1, A_2). \tag{5.20}$$
$$+ \quad + \quad -$$

This expression is the *current account schedule*. Figure 5.15 presents a graphical derivation of the current account schedule.[1] Panel (a) plots the investment and saving schedules. The plot of the investment schedule reproduces Figure 5.6 and the plot of the saving schedule reproduces Figure 5.12. Panel (b) plots the horizontal difference between the saving and investment schedules, which is the current account schedule. Suppose that the interest rate is r^a. From panel (a) we see that

---

[1] The graph in Figure 5.15 is known as the Metzler diagram after Lloyd A. Metzler (1913–1980). It was presented at a lecture in 1960 and published in 1968 as Lloyd A. Metzler, "The Process of International Adjustment under Conditions of Full Employment: A Keynesian View," in *Readings in International Economics*, Volume XI, edited by Richard E. Caves and Harry G. Johnson (Homewood, IL: Richard D. Irwin, 1968), 465–486.

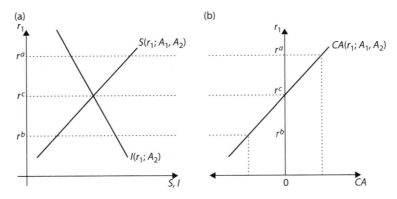

Figure 5.15. Saving, Investment, and the Current Account
Notes: This figure presents a graphical derivation of the current account schedule. Panel (a) depicts the saving and investment schedule. Panel (b) depicts the current account schedule, which is the horizontal difference between the saving and investment schedule.

at this level of the interest rate, saving exceeds investment. Accordingly, panel (b) shows that when $r_1 = r^a$ the current account is in surplus. If the interest rate is equal to r^c, then investment equals saving and the current account is zero. The interest rate r^c is the one that would prevail in a financially closed economy; that is, in an economy that does not have access to international capital markets. Financially closed economies are said to be in *financial autarky*. For interest rates below r^c, such as r^b, investment is larger than saving so that the country runs a current account deficit. In general, as the interest rate decreases, the current account deteriorates; therefore, as shown in panel (b), the current account is an increasing function of the interest rate. With the help of this graphical apparatus, it is now straightforward to analyze the equilibrium determination of saving, investment, and the current account in the production economy, as well as the effect of various aggregate shocks of interest.

5.6 Equilibrium in the Production Economy

As we discussed in Chapter 3, in an open economy with free capital mobility, the domestic interest rate, r_1, must equal the world interest rate, r^*; that is,

$$r_1 = r^*. \tag{5.21}$$

The world interest rate r^* is exogenous not only to households and firms but also to the country as a whole, because we are assuming that the domestic economy is too small to affect international asset prices.[2] Thus, we can find the equilibrium level of the current account by simply evaluating the current account schedule at $r_1 = r^*$ as shown in Figure 5.16. In the case depicted in the figure the current account

---

[2]In Chapter 7, we relax this assumption and analyze the determination of the current account in a large open economy.

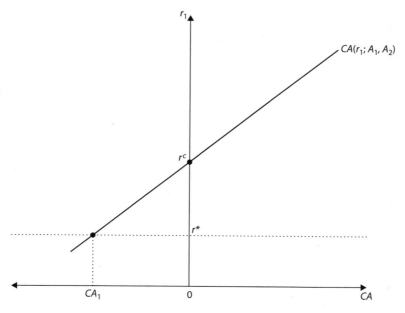

Figure 5.16. Current Account Determination in the Production Economy
Notes: This figure displays the current account schedule and the world interest rate in the space (CA, r_1). Under free capital mobility the current account is determined by the intersection of the current account schedule and the world interest rate, r^*. In a closed economy the current account is nil, and the domestic interest rate is r^c and is determined by the intersection of the current account schedule with the vertical axis.

balance is negative in equilibrium. If the economy were closed to trade in goods and financial assets, then the current account would always be nil, and the equilibrium value of the domestic interest rate would be determined by the intersection of the current account schedule with the vertical axis, r^c, in the figure.

5.6.1   ADJUSTMENT OF THE CURRENT ACCOUNT TO CHANGES IN THE WORLD INTEREST RATE

Suppose the world interest rate increases from r^* to $r^{*\prime} > r^*$. Figure 5.17 depicts the adjustment of the current account to this external shock. At the initial interest rate r^*, the country runs a current account deficit equal to CA_1. The increase in the world interest rate does not change the position of the current account schedule, but represents a movement along it. The new equilibrium value of the current account is given by CA_1', where the current account schedule intersects the new higher world interest rate, $r^{*\prime}$. The economy thus experiences an improvement in the current account. The higher interest rate encourages domestic saving, as bonds become more attractive, and discourages firms' investment in physical capital, because the interest cost of financing spending in capital goods goes up. If the economy were closed, it would be isolated from world financial markets and, as a result, no domestic variable would be affected by the change in the world interest rate. The first two columns of Table 5.1 summarize these results.

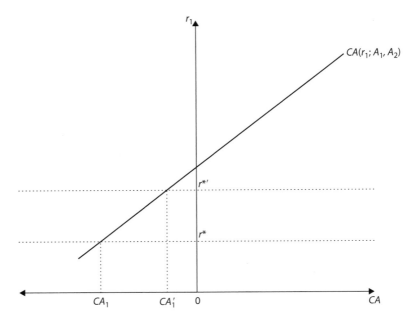

Figure 5.17. Current Account Adjustment to an Increase in the World Interest Rate
Notes: The initial world interest rate is r^* and the equilibrium current account is CA_1.
The world increases from r^* to $r^{*\prime}$. The higher interest rate leads to an improvement
in the current account from CA_1 to $CA_1^{\prime}$.

5.6.2   ADJUSTMENT OF THE CURRENT ACCOUNT TO A TEMPORARY INCREASE IN PRODUCTIVITY

Consider next the effect of a temporary increase in productivity—that is, an increase in A_1 holding A_2 constant. Specifically, suppose that the productivity parameter of the production function increases from A_1 to $A_1^{\prime} > A_1$. Figure 5.18 depicts the adjustment of saving, investment, and the current account. Prior to the productivity change, saving equals S_1, investment equals I_1, and the current account equals CA_1. In the figure, at the world interest rate r^*, saving is lower than investment and therefore the economy runs a current account deficit, $CA_1 < 0$. The temporary increase in productivity shifts the saving schedule down and to the right because for any given level of the interest rate, households save part of the increase in profit income for future consumption. The investment schedule does not shift because investment is not affected by temporary changes in productivity. The rightward shift in the saving schedule implies that at any given interest rate the difference between saving and investment is larger than before the increase in A_1. As a result, the current account schedule shifts down and to the right. At the world interest rate r^*, which is unchanged, saving equals $S_1^{\prime} > S_1$, investment continues to be I_1, and the current account equals $CA_1^{\prime} > CA_1$. Thus, we have that a temporary increase in productivity produces an increase in saving, no change in investment, and an improvement in the current account.

The adjustment in a closed economy is quite different. The equilibrium is always at the intersection of the saving and investment schedules and the current account is

Table 5.1. Adjustment of the Production Economy to Changes in the World Interest Rate and Productivity in Open and Closed Economies

	$r^* \uparrow$		$A_1 \uparrow$		$A_2 \uparrow$	
	Open	Closed	Open	Closed	Open	Closed
S_1	$\uparrow$	—	$\uparrow$	$\uparrow$	$\downarrow$	$\uparrow$
I_1	$\downarrow$	—	—	$\uparrow$	$\uparrow$	$\uparrow$
CA_1	$\uparrow$	—	$\uparrow$	—	$\downarrow$	—
r_1	$\uparrow$	—	—	$\downarrow$	—	$\uparrow$

Notes: This table summarizes the effect of three different shocks on saving (S_1), investment (I_1), the current account (CA_1), and the domestic interest rate (r_1). The shocks considered are an increase in the world interest rate ($r^* \uparrow$), a temporary increase in productivity ($A_1 \uparrow$), and a future expected increase in productivity ($A_2 \uparrow$). Two different economic environments are considered: free capital mobility (Open) and a closed economy (Closed).

always nil. The rightward shift in the saving schedule causes the equilibrium interest rate to fall from r^c to $r^{c\prime}$. The intuition behind the decline in the equilibrium interest rate in the closed economy is as follows: households wish to save part of the expansion in profit income caused by the increase in A_1. However, at the original interest rate r^c, firms do not demand more funds, because an increase in A_1 does not change their incentives to invest in physical capital. Thus, at the interest rate r^c there is an excess supply of funds in the loan market. For the market to clear, the interest rate must fall. In the new equilibrium both saving and investment increase. The increase in saving is smaller than in the open economy because the fall in the interest rate partially offsets the positive effect of the increase in A_1. The middle two columns of Table 5.1 summarize the adjustment of the open and closed economies to a temporary increase in productivity.

5.6.3 ADJUSTMENT OF THE CURRENT ACCOUNT TO AN ANTICIPATED FUTURE PRODUCTIVITY INCREASE

Suppose that in period 1 agents learn that in period 2 the productivity of capital will increase. Specifically, suppose that the efficiency parameter of the period 2 production function is expected to increase from A_2 to $A_2^\prime > A_2$. This type of news triggers an investment surge, as firms choose to increase investment in period 1 for any given level of the interest rate. Consequently, the investment schedule shifts up and to the right, as depicted in panel (a) of Figure 5.19. The world interest rate is constant at r^*. Thus, the new equilibrium level of investment is $I_1^\prime > I_1$. The increase in A_2 also affects the position of the saving schedule, $S(r_1; A_1, A_2)$. At any given level of the interest rate, the expectation of higher future profit income fosters consumption in period 1 and discourages saving. Thus, the saving schedule shifts up and to the left. The equilibrium level of saving falls from S_1 to $S_1^\prime$. These shifts in the investment and saving schedules imply that the current account schedule shifts up and to the left as shown in panel (b). Consequently, the current account deteriorates from CA_1 to $CA_1^\prime$.

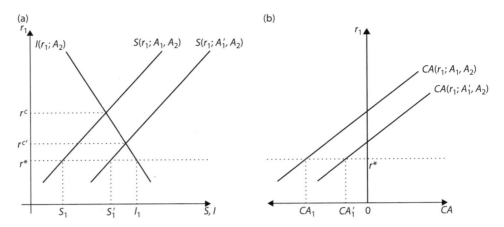

Figure 5.18. Current Account Adjustment to a Temporary Increase in Productivity
Notes: Productivity in period 1 increases from A_1 to $A'_1 > A_1$. The increase in A_1 shifts the saving schedule down and to the right. The investment schedule is unchanged. The current account schedule shifts down and to the right. In the new equilibrium the current account improves to CA'_1, saving increases to S'_1, and investment remains unchanged. In the closed economy, the increase in A_1 causes a fall in the domestic interest rate from r^c to $r^{c'}$ and higher saving and investment.

If the economy were closed, the investment surge would trigger a rise in the domestic interest rate from r^c to $r^{c'}$ and thus investment would increase by less than in the open economy. The last two columns of Table 5.1 collect these results. Note that the result that investment and saving increase in the closed economy need not necessarily hold, for it depends on the assumption that the horizontal shift in the saving schedule is smaller than that of the investment schedule. But this does not always have to be the case. Depending on preferences and technology, the shift in the saving schedule may be larger or smaller than the shift in the investment schedule. For the particular functional forms assumed for the utility function and the production function in the algebraic example presented later in this chapter (see in particular, Section 5.7.3), it will indeed be the case that in a closed economy an increase in future productivity increases saving and investment, as indicated in the last column of Table 5.1. However, for the functional forms assumed in Exercise 5.6, the shifts in the saving and investment schedules exactly offset each other so that in equilibrium saving and investment remain unchanged in response to an increase in A_2.

5.7 Equilibrium in the Production Economy: An Algebraic Approach

In Section 5.6 we used a graphical approach to characterizing the equilibrium determination of the current account and other macroeconomic indicators in a small open economy with production. Here, we perform the characterization of equilibrium using an algebraic approach. We begin by deriving the economy's intertemporal resource constraint.

In Section 5.3, we saw that the household's intertemporal budget constraint is given by

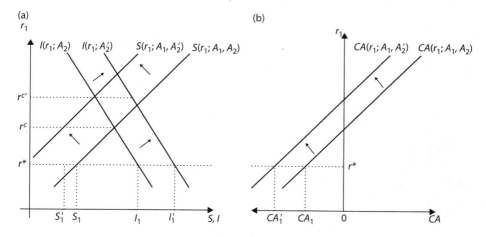

Figure 5.19. Current Account Adjustment to an Expected Future Increase in Productivity

Notes: The productivity parameter is expected to increase from A_2 to A_2'. The investment schedule shifts to the right and the saving schedule shifts to the left, although by less than the shift in the investment schedule. The current account schedule shifts to the left. In the open economy, investment increases from I_1 to I_1', saving falls from S_1 to S_1', and the current account deteriorates from CA_1 to CA_1'. In the closed economy, the interest rate increases from r^c to $r^{c'}$.

$$C_1 + \frac{C_2}{1+r_1} = (1+r_0)B_0^h + \Pi_1 + \frac{\Pi_2}{1+r_1}.$$

Using the definitions of profits in periods 1 and 2 given by equations (5.3) and (5.6) to eliminate Π_1 and Π_2 and equation (5.17) to eliminate B_0^h and D_0^f, we can rewrite this expression as

$$C_1 + \frac{C_2}{1+r_1} + I_1 = (1+r_0)B_0 + A_1F(I_0) + \frac{A_2F(I_1)}{1+r_1}. \qquad (5.22)$$

This equation is the economy's intertemporal resource constraint. The left-hand side is the present discounted value of domestic absorption (consumption plus investment). The right-hand side is the sum of initial wealth and the present discounted value of output.

An equilibrium in the production economy with free capital mobility is an allocation $\{C_1, C_2, I_1, r_1\}$ satisfying the firm's optimality condition (5.4), the household's Euler equation (5.14), the interest parity condition (5.21), and the economy's intertemporal resource constraint (5.22). The complete set of equilibrium conditions is therefore given by

$$A_2F'(I_1) = 1 + r_1, \qquad (R5.4)$$

$$\frac{U'(C_1)}{\beta U'(C_2)} = 1 + r_1, \qquad (R5.14)$$

$$r_1 = r^*, \qquad\qquad\qquad\qquad\text{(R5.21)}$$

and

$$C_1 + \frac{C_2}{1+r_1} + I_1 = (1+r_0)B_0 + A_1 F(I_0) + \frac{A_2 F(I_1)}{1+r_1}, \qquad\text{(R5.22)}$$

given the initial capital stock, I_0, the initial net foreign asset position including interest, $(1+r_0)B_0$, the world interest rate r^*, and the levels of productivity in periods 1 and 2, A_1 and A_2.

Equilibrium conditions (5.4), (5.14), (5.21), and (5.22) represent a system of four equations that can be solved for the four unknowns C_1, C_2, I_1, and r_1. Consider the following example. Suppose that the period utility function is the square root function,

$$U(C) = \sqrt{C},$$

and that technology is a power function of capital,

$$F(I) = I^\alpha,$$

where $\alpha \in (0, 1)$ is a parameter governing the rate at which the marginal product of capital diminishes with the stock of capital itself. With this production function, equilibrium condition (5.4) becomes

$$\alpha A_2 I_1^{\alpha-1} = 1 + r_1.$$

The left-hand side is the marginal product of capital, given by the derivative of the production function with respect to I_1. Solving for I_1 yields the following investment schedule

$$I_1 = \left(\frac{\alpha A_2}{1+r_1} \right)^{\frac{1}{1-\alpha}}. \qquad\qquad\text{(5.23)}$$

This is the investment schedule, a special case of equation (5.5). As expected, investment is a decreasing function of the interest rate, r_1, and an increasing function of the expected level of productivity, A_2.

Under the assumed functional form for the period utility function, the Euler equation (5.14) becomes

$$\frac{\sqrt{C_2}}{\beta\sqrt{C_1}} = 1 + r_1. \qquad\qquad\text{(5.24)}$$

Using the interest rate parity condition (5.21) to eliminate r_1, the investment schedule (5.23) to eliminate I_1, and the Euler equation (5.24) to eliminate C_2 from the economy's intertemporal resource constraint (5.22) yields the following expression for the equilibrium level of consumption in period 1:

$$C_1 = \frac{1}{1+\beta^2(1+r^*)} \left[(1+r_0)B_0 + A_1 I_0^\alpha + \left(\frac{1-\alpha}{\alpha} \right) \left(\frac{\alpha A_2}{1+r^*} \right)^{\frac{1}{1-\alpha}} \right]. \qquad\text{(5.25)}$$

Intuitively, this expression says that in equilibrium current consumption is a decreasing function of the world interest rate, r^*, an increasing function of productivity in periods 1 and 2, A_1 and A_2, and an increasing function of the country's initial net international investment position, $(1 + r_0)B_0$. Also, current consumption is decreasing in the subjective discount factor β. Recall that this parameter measures the degree of impatience (the smaller β is, the more impatient households will be). So it makes sense that as households become more impatient, they devote more resources to consumption early in their lives, leading to larger capital inflows (or smaller capital outflows).

Saving in period 1, S_1, is given by the difference between national income and consumption in period 1. National income is given by $r_0 B_0 + A_1 I_0^\alpha$, which is the sum of net investment income, $r_0 B_0$, and output (or GDP), $Q_1 = A_1 I_0^\alpha$. So we have that

$$S_1 = r_0 B_0 + Q_1 - C_1.$$

Then, using equation (5.25) to eliminate C_1 we can write saving in period 1 as

$$S_1 = r_0 B_0 + A_1 I_0^\alpha$$

$$- \frac{1}{1 + \beta^2(1 + r^*)} \left[(1 + r_0)B_0 + A_1 I_0^\alpha + \left(\frac{1-\alpha}{\alpha} \right) \left(\frac{\alpha A_2}{1 + r^*} \right)^{\frac{1}{1-\alpha}} \right]. \quad (5.26)$$

This is the saving schedule, a special case of equation (5.19). Saving is decreasing in the world interest rate, r^*, for two reasons. First, an increase in the interest rate makes saving in bonds more attractive. So households substitute future for present consumption. This effect is captured by the factor $1/[1 + \beta^2(1 + r^*)]$. Second, an increase in the interest rate reduces the profitability of firms in period 2, which in turn reduces the household's profit income in that period. Feeling poorer, households cut consumption in period 1. Since the increase in r^* does not affect income in period 1, the cut in consumption increases saving one for one.

The current account in period 1, CA_1, is given by the difference between saving and investment,

$$CA_1 = S_1 - I_1.$$

Using the investment and saving schedules given in equations (5.23) and (5.26), we can write

$$CA_1 = \underbrace{r_0 B_0 + A_1 I_0^\alpha}_{\text{national income}}$$

$$\underbrace{- \frac{1}{1 + \beta^2(1 + r^*)} \left[(1 + r_0)B_0 + A_1 I_0^\alpha + \left(\frac{1-\alpha}{\alpha} \right) \left(\frac{\alpha A_2}{1 + r^*} \right)^{\frac{1}{1-\alpha}} \right]}_{\text{consumption}}$$

$$\underbrace{- \left(\frac{\alpha A_2}{1 + r^*} \right)^{\frac{1}{1-\alpha}}}_{\text{investment}}. \quad (5.27)$$

This is the current account schedule, a special case of equation (5.20). The expression looks complicated. But as will become clear in our discussion of how various disturbances affect the current account schedule, it is indeed quite intuitive.

5.7.1 ADJUSTMENT TO AN INCREASE IN THE WORLD INTEREST RATE

Suppose that the world interest rate, r^*, increases. As is clear from (5.27), national income in period 1 is unchanged, and consumption and investment both fall. As a result, the increase in r^* causes an improvement in the current account. The increase in the world interest rate depresses domestic spending in consumption and capital goods, freeing up resources that are allocated to purchases of foreign assets. This result is in line with the result we obtained graphically in subsection 5.6.1.

5.7.2 ADJUSTMENT TO A TEMPORARY INCREASE IN PRODUCTIVITY

Suppose now that the economy experiences a positive temporary productivity improvement whereby A_1 increases by $\Delta A_1 > 0$. From equation (5.27) we have that the change in the current account in period 1 is given by

$$\Delta CA_1 = \Delta A_1 I_0^\alpha - \frac{1}{1+\beta^2(1+r^*)}\Delta A_1 I_0^\alpha > 0,$$

which, in accordance with the results obtained graphically in subsection 5.6.2, says that the current account improves in response to a temporary increase in productivity. The intuition is straightforward. The first term on the right-hand side of the above expression is the increase in period 1 income caused by the improvement in productivity. The second term is the increase in period 1 consumption, which is a fraction $1/[1+\beta^2(1+r^*)] < 1$ of the increase in output. Households consume only a fraction of the increase in period 1 output because they prefer to leave part of the windfall for future consumption.

How would the closed economy adjust to the increase in A_1? Take another look at equation (5.27). Set the left-hand side to zero, since in the closed economy the current account must always be nil. Also, replace r^* with r_1, since in the closed economy the domestic interest rate has to adjust to make the current account zero. This yields

$$0 = \underbrace{\underbrace{r_0 B_0 + A_1 I_0^\alpha}_{\text{national income}} - \underbrace{\frac{1}{1+\beta^2(1+r_1)}\left[(1+r_0)B_0 + A_1 I_0^\alpha + \left(\frac{1-\alpha}{\alpha}\right)\left(\frac{\alpha A_2}{1+r_1}\right)^{\frac{1}{1-\alpha}}\right]}_{\text{consumption}}}_{\text{saving}}$$

$$- \underbrace{\left(\frac{\alpha A_2}{1+r_1}\right)^{\frac{1}{1-\alpha}}}_{\text{investment}}. \tag{5.28}$$

This expression says that in the closed economy saving must equal investment. All other things equal, as we just discussed, the increase in A_1 produces an increase in the right-hand side of (5.28), as national income increases by more than consumption and investment is unaffected. This would violate equation (5.28), as saving would exceed investment. This means that the interest rate cannot remain unchanged. Clearly, the right-hand side of (5.28) is decreasing in r_1. So restoring equilibrium requires a fall in r_1. Intuitively, the excess supply of funds resulting from the increase in A_1 puts downward pressure on the domestic interest rate r_1, which stimulates consumption and investment, restoring the equality of saving and investment. Thus, in the closed economy a temporary increase in productivity causes an expansion in consumption, investment, and saving, and a decline in the interest rate.

5.7.3   ADJUSTMENT TO AN ANTICIPATED FUTURE INCREASE IN PRODUCTIVITY

Finally, consider the effect of an anticipated increase in productivity. Specifically, suppose that in period 1 agents learn that the productivity of capital will increase in period 2. It is clear from equation (5.27) that an increase in A_2 causes a deterioration in the current account. The reason is that consumption and investment are both stimulated by the expected increase in productivity, while national income is unchanged. This result is consistent with the graphical analysis of subsection 5.6.3.

What happens in the closed economy? We need to look again at equation (5.28). Since its right-hand side is decreasing in A_2 and increasing in r_1, we have that an increase in A_2 causes an increase in r_1. Intuitively, the increase in future productivity makes investment more profitable and fosters consumption as households feel richer. So investment expands and saving shrinks, creating an excess demand for funds in the loan market. The interest rate must therefore increase to restore equilibrium.

Note that $1 + r_1$ increases but proportionally less than A_2. To see this, note that if $1 + r_1$ were to increase by the same proportion as A_2, investment would remain unchanged but consumption would fall, which would imply an excess of saving over investment, or a violation of equation (5.28). We therefore have that in the closed economy, in response to an anticipated increase in productivity (A_2), saving, investment, and the interest rate all increase while national income remains unchanged. Since period 1 consumption, C_1, equals national income minus saving, we have that C_1 falls in spite of the fact that the economy expects good news in period 2 (an increase in A_2). This prediction is quite different from what happens in the open economy, where consumption expenditure increases unambiguously in response to an increase in A_2.

5.8   The Terms of Trade in the Production Economy

In Chapter 4, we arrived at the conclusion that terms of trade shocks are just like endowment shocks. This section shows that this result extends to the production economy. Specifically, it shows that terms of trade shocks have the same effects as productivity shocks.

Suppose, as we did in Chapter 4, that the good households like to consume is different from the good the economy produces. For example, suppose that households have preferences over the consumption of food and that the economy produces oil. Profits in periods 1 and 2 are now given by

$$\Pi_1 = TT_1 A_1 F(I_0) - (1 + r_0)I_0$$

and

$$\Pi_2 = TT_2 A_2 F(I_1) - (1 + r_1)I_1,$$

where TT_1 is the terms of trade in period 1, defined as the relative price of the export good (oil) in terms of the import good (food). A similar definition applies to TT_2. Here, we are assuming that capital is imported and that the relative price of capital in terms of food is unity.[3] Notice that the terms of trade appear always multiplying the productivity parameter; that is, where we used to have A_1 we now have $TT_1 A_1$ and where we used to have A_2 we now have $TT_2 A_2$.

In period 1, the firm chooses I_1 to maximize Π_2 taking A_2, TT_2, and r_1 as given. The profit maximization condition of the firm is

$$TT_2 A_2 F'(I_1) = 1 + r_1.$$

This optimality condition is exactly like the one obtained in the one-good economy, equation (5.4), except that instead of A_2 it features $TT_2 A_2$. It follows that a change in the terms of trade in period 2 has exactly the same effect on investment as a change in productivity in period 2. Thus, we can write the investment schedule as

$$I_1 = I(\underset{-}{r_1}; \underset{+}{TT_2 A_2}).$$

The household's intertemporal budget constraint continues to be (5.11), with the only difference that now profits in periods 1 and 2 depend, respectively, on $TT_1 A_1$ and $TT_2 A_2$ instead of A_1 and A_2. We can therefore write

$$C_1 = C(\underset{-}{r_1}, \underset{+}{TT_1 A_1}, \underset{+}{TT_2 A_2}).$$

National income equals $r_0 B_0 + Q_1 = r_0 B_0 + TT_1 A_1 F(I_0)$, which also depends on the product of TT_1 and A_1. We therefore have that saving, the difference between national income and consumption, behaves exactly as in the one-good economy except that, again, $TT_1 A_1$ and $TT_2 A_2$ take the place of A_1 and A_2, respectively. Thus, we write

$$S_1 = S(\underset{+}{r_1}; \underset{+}{TT_1 A_1}, \underset{-}{TT_2 A_2}).$$

Finally, the same principle applies to the current account schedule, since it is the difference between saving and investment,

$$CA_1 = CA(\underset{+}{r_1}; \underset{+}{TT_1 A_1}, \underset{-}{TT_2 A_2}).$$

---

[3]In Exercise 5.3 , we consider the case that the relative price of capital in terms of food is not equal to unity, and ask you to characterize the adjustment of the current account in response to a change in this relative price.

It follows that the current account adjustment to terms of trade shocks can be read off Table 5.1 by replacing A_1 by TT_1 and A_2 by TT_2. In particular, a temporary terms of trade improvement (an increase in TT_1 with TT_2 unchanged) produces an increase in saving, an improvement in the current account, and no change in investment. And an anticipated future improvement in the terms of trade (an increase in TT_2 with TT_1 unchanged) causes a fall in saving, an expansion in investment, and a deterioration of the current account.

5.9 An Application: Giant Oil Discoveries

Are the predictions of the open economy model with production studied in this chapter empirically compelling? To answer this question, we examine a number of natural experiments that took place in different countries and at different points in time. The natural experiments are giant oil discoveries. In the context of the model, the news of a giant oil discovery can be interpreted as an anticipated increase in the productivity of capital; that is, as an anticipated increase in A_2. The reason why a discovery is an anticipated productivity shock is that it takes time and extensive investment in oil production facilities to extract the oil and bring it to market. The average delay from discovery to production is estimated to be between 4 and 6 years.

The macroeconomic effects of a giant oil discovery can be analyzed with the help of Figure 5.19. Upon the news of the discovery, the investment schedule shifts up and to the right and the saving schedule shifts up and to the left. The current account schedule shifts up and to the left. The world interest rate does not change. Thus, the model predicts that when an oil discovery occurs, the country experiences an investment boom, a decline in saving, and a deterioration in the current account. Once the oil is brought to market (period 2 in the model, and 4 to 6 years post-discovery in reality), output (oil production) increases, investment falls, saving increases (to pay back the debt accumulated in period 1 for the construction of oil facilities and for consumption), and the current account improves. Are these predictions of the model borne out in the data?

Rabah Arezki, Valerie Ramey, and Liugang Sheng of the International Monetary Fund, the University of California at San Diego, and the Chinese University of Hong Kong, respectively, analyze the effect of giant oil discoveries in 180 countries from 1970 to 2012.[4] A giant oil discovery is defined as a discovery of an oil and/or gas field that contains at least 500 million barrels of ultimately recoverable oil equivalent. In turn, ultimately recoverable oil equivalent is the amount that is technically recoverable given existing technology. The sample contains in total 371 giant oil discoveries, which took place in 64 different countries (so 116 of the 180 countries experienced no giant oil discoveries over the sample period). The peak period of giant oil discoveries was the 1970s and, not surprisingly, the region with the largest number of oil discoveries is the Middle East and North Africa. Giant oil discoveries are really big, with a median value of 9 percent of a year's GDP.

---

[4]Rabah Arezki, Valerie A. Ramey, and Liugang Sheng, "News Shocks in Open Economies: Evidence from Giant Oil Discoveries," *Quarterly Journal of Economics* 132 (February 2017): 103–155.

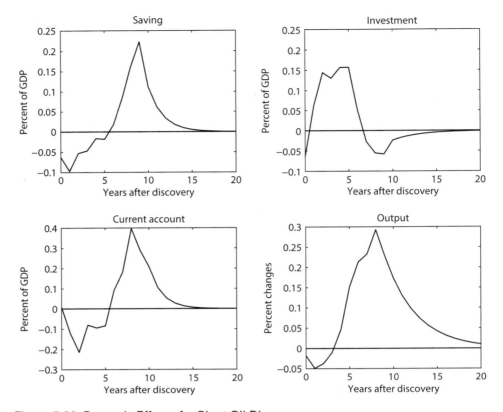

Figure 5.20. Dynamic Effect of a Giant Oil Discovery
Notes: The figure displays the dynamic effect of an oil discovery on saving, invest-
ment, the current account, and output. The size of the oil discovery is 9 percent of
GDP. Saving, investment, and the current account are expressed in percent of GDP.
Output is expressed in percent deviation from trend.
Data source: Rabah Arezki, Valerie A. Ramey, and Liugang Sheng, "News Shocks
in Open Economies: Evidence from Giant Oil Discoveries," *Quarterly Journal of
Economics* 132 (February 2017): 103–155, online appendix, Table D.I.

Figure 5.20 displays the dynamic response to a giant oil discovery of saving, investment, the current account, and output. The size of the oil discovery is
9 percent of GDP, the typical size in the data.[5] Upon news of the giant oil discovery, investment experiences a boom that lasts for about 5 years. Saving declines and
stays below normal for about 5 years, before rising sharply for several years. The
current account deteriorates for 5 years and then experiences a reversal with a peak
in year 8. Finally, output is relatively stable until the fifth year, and then experiences
a boom. Remarkably, the investment boom and the fall in saving and the current
account last for the entire delay between discovery to production that is typical in

[5]The dynamic responses are estimated using an econometric technique called dynamic panel model estimation with distributed lags. Essentially, one runs a regression of the variable of interest, say the current account,
onto its own lags, and current and lagged values of the giant oil discovery, and other control variables, such as
a constant and time and country fixed effects.

the oil industry, which is about 5 years. This result is noteworthy because it is not built into the econometric estimation of the dynamic responses.

All of the empirical responses are consistent with the predictions of the theoretical model: The giant oil discovery induces oil companies to invest in the construction of drilling platforms. In addition, households anticipate higher profit income from the future exports of oil and as a result increase consumption and cut saving. Both the expansion in investment and the contraction in saving contribute to current account deficits in the initial years following the discovery.

We conclude that the observed macroeconomic dynamics triggered by giant oil discoveries give credence to the intertemporal model of the current account studied in this chapter. This result is important because the model developed in this chapter is the backbone of many models in international macroeconomics.

5.10 Summing Up

In this chapter, we studied the workings of an open economy with production and investment.

- Firms borrow in period 1 to purchase capital goods. In period 2, firms use capital to produce final goods, pay back the loan including interest, and distribute profits to households.
- Firms invest up to a point at which the marginal product of capital equals the gross interest rate.
- The optimal level of investment is a decreasing function of the interest rate and an increasing function of the expected level of productivity in period 2.
- The negative relationship between investment and the interest rate is the investment schedule. In the space (I_1, r_1) the investment schedule is downward sloping. An expected increase in the productivity of capital shifts the investment schedule up and to the right.
- Households maximize their lifetime utility subject to an intertemporal budget constraint. On the income side, this constraint includes the present discounted value of profits received from firms.
- The optimal level of saving is an increasing function of the interest rate and the current productivity of capital and a decreasing function of the future expected level of productivity.
- The positive relationship between the interest rate and saving is the saving schedule. In the space (S_1, r_1), the saving schedule is upward sloping. An increase in the current productivity of capital shifts the saving schedule down and to the right. An expected increase in future productivity shifts the saving schedule up and to the left.
- The current account schedule is the horizontal difference between the saving and the investment schedules. In the space (CA_1, r_1) the current account schedule is upward sloping. An increase in the current productivity of capital shifts the current account schedule down and to the right. An expected increase in future productivity shifts the current account schedule up and to the left.

- An increase in the world interest rate causes an improvement in the current account, an increase in saving, and a decrease in investment.
- A temporary increase in the productivity of capital produces an improvement in the current account, an increase in saving, and no change in investment.
- An expected future increase in the productivity of capital causes a deterioration in the current account, a fall in saving, and an expansion in investment.
- Terms of trade shocks are just like productivity shocks. So their effects can be read off the last two bullets.
- The observed dynamics of saving, investment, and the current account triggered by giant oil discoveries around the world over the period 1970 to 2012 are consistent with the predictions of the intertemporal model of current account determination developed in this chapter.

5.11 Exercises

Exercise 5.1 (TFU) Indicate whether the following statements are true, false, or uncertain and explain why.

1. Good news about future productivity leads to a trade deficit today.
2. A deterioration in the terms of trade causes a fall in consumption and a deterioration in the current account.
3. Countries A and B are identical in all respects, except that the initial net international asset position (B_0) of country A is larger than that of country B. It must be the case that:
   (a) Consumption in country A is higher than consumption in country B in all periods.
   (b) Investment in country A is higher than investment in country B.
   (c) The trade balance in country A is higher than in country B.
   (d) None of the above.
4. A country populated by more impatient households (i.e., a country with a lower β) will consume more and invest less in period 1.
5. An improvement in productivity in period 1 (higher A_1) causes an increase in net investment income in period 2.
6. An increase in the world interest rate (higher r^*) causes an increase in the current account in period 1 and a decrease in the current account in period 2.
7. Good news about future productivity increases consumption already now regardless of whether the economy is open or closed.
8. All else constant, investment is more stable in open economies than in closed economies because funding is not limited to the domestic capital market.
9. Anticipated declines in future productivity raise net investment income in the future.

Exercise 5.2 (A Change in the Initial Interest Rate) Suppose in period 1, unexpectedly the initial interest rate increases from r_0 to $r_0' > r_0 > 0$. This could happen, for example, if in period 0 households took debt at a floating (as opposed to a fixed) interest rate. Present a graphical analysis of the effects of this shock on consumption, saving, investment, and the current account in period 1. Distinguish the case in which the country is initially a net creditor of the rest of the world ($B_0 > 0$) from the case in which the country is initially a net debtor ($B_0 < 0$). Provide intuition. *Hint:* In the chapter, we wrote the saving schedule as $S_1 = S(r_1; A_1, A_2)$ because we did not consider changes in r_0. But r_0 also affects saving, so one could write $S_1 = S(r_1; A_1, A_2, r_0)$.

Exercise 5.3 (The Relative Price of Investment and the Current Account) In Section 5.8, we studied an economy in which households consume a good different from the good produced by firms (the example we gave was food and oil). There, we analyzed the effects of changes in the terms of trade. An assumption of that economy was that consumption and investment were both imported and that the relative price of the investment good in terms of the consumption good was constant and equal to one. In this exercise, you are asked to modify that economy as follows. Assume that the domestic economy produces only consumption goods. Domestic output can either be domestically consumed or exported. Investment goods are not domestically produced and must be imported. The price of investment goods in terms of consumption goods is equal to PK_1. The economy is small in the sense that it cannot affect the price PK_1. The production function of domestic firms is equal to $A_t I_{t-1}^\alpha$, for $t = 1, 2$ and $\alpha \in (0, 1)$, where I_t denotes investment measured in units of investment goods.

1. Characterize the schedule for expenditures on investment in period 1 expressed in units of consumption goods. That is, derive an expression like (5.5), where now on the left-hand side are expenditures on investment goods (as opposed to the quantity of investment goods) and the arguments on the right-hand side are not only r_1 and A_2 but also PK_1. How would an increase in PK_1 shift this investment schedule?
2. Characterize the saving schedule in period 1. That is, derive an expression like (5.19) for the present economy. Does an increase in PK_1 shift the saving schedule left or right or does it leave it unchanged?
3. Characterize the current account schedule in period 1. That is, derive an expression similar to (5.20) for the present economy. Does an increase in PK_1 shift the current account schedule left or right or does it leave it unchanged?
4. Suppose that the economy is small and open to international trade in goods and assets and that free capital mobility prevails. What is the effect of an increase in PK_1 on the equilibrium levels of saving, investment, and the current account?
5. How does the answer to the previous question change if the economy is assumed to be closed to trade in financial assets but open to trade in goods?

Exercise 5.4 (Investment Decision of a Gas Producer) In period 2, a firm produces gas using the technology $I_1^{1/3}$, where I_1 denotes investment in equipment in period 1. Suppose that the price of gas is $2, the price of equipment is $1, and the interest rate is 20 percent (i.e., if you borrow $1 in period 1, you owe $1.2 in period 2). What is the optimal level of investment in period 1? How much gas will be produced in period 2?

Exercise 5.5 (An Open Economy With Investment I) Consider a two-period model of a small open economy with a single good each period. Let preferences of the representative household be described by the utility function

$$\ln C_1 + \ln C_2,$$

where C_1 and C_2 denote consumption in periods 1 and 2. Each period the household receives profits from the firms it owns, denoted Π_1 and Π_2. Households and firms have access to financial markets where they can borrow or lend at the interest rate r_1. The production technologies in periods 1 and 2 are given by

$$Q_1 = A_1 I_0^\alpha$$

and

$$Q_2 = A_2 I_1^\alpha,$$

where Q_1 and Q_2 denote output in periods 1 and 2, I_0 and I_1 denote the capital stock in periods 1 and 2, A_1 and A_2 denote the productivity factors in periods 1 and 2, and α is a parameter. Assume that $I_0 = 16$, $A_1 = 3\frac{1}{3}$, $A_2 = 3.2$, and $\alpha = \frac{3}{4}$. At the beginning of period 1, households have $B_0^h = 8$ bonds. The interest rate on bonds held from period 0 to period 1 is $r_0 = 0.25$. In period 1, firms borrow the amount D_1^f to purchase investment goods that become productive capital in period 2, I_1. Assume that there exists free international capital mobility and that the world interest rate, denoted r^*, is 20 percent.

1. Compute output and profits in period 1.
2. Compute the optimal levels of investment in period 1 and output and profits in period 2.
3. Solve for the optimal levels of consumption in periods 1 and 2.
4. Find the country's net foreign asset position at the end of period 1, denoted B_1, saving, S_1, the trade balance, TB_1, and the current account, CA_1.
5. Now consider an interest rate hike in period 1. Specifically, assume that as a result of turmoil in international financial markets, the world interest rate increases from 20 percent to 50 percent in period 1. Find the equilibrium levels of saving, investment, the trade balance, the current account, and the country's net foreign asset position in period 1. Provide intuition.
6. Suppose that the interest rate is 20 percent, and that A_1 increases to 4. Calculate the equilibrium values of output, consumption, saving, investment, and the current account in period 1. Provide an intuitive interpretation of the adjustment to the transitory productivity shock.
7. Suppose that the interest rate is 20 percent, that $A_1 = 3\frac{1}{3}$, and that A_2 increases from 3.2 to 4. Calculate the equilibrium values of consumption, saving, investment, and the current account in period 1. Explain your findings.

Exercise 5.6 (An Open Economy With Investment II) Answer questions 2–4 and 6–7 of Exercise 5.5 assuming that $B_0 = 0$ and $I_0 = 16$. Do this twice, once under the assumption that the economy is open and once under the assumption that the economy is closed. Discuss the extent to which your numerical solution conforms (or does not conform) with the qualitative solution given in Table 5.1.

Exercise 5.7 (Terms of Trade Shocks in a Production Economy) Oil represents a large share of exports in Russia. Suppose that the price of oil is expected to fall significantly next year. Use a graphical approach to analyze the effect in the present year of this expected future change in the price of oil on saving, investment, and the current account. Consider two cases: (a) Russia is a small open economy; (b) Russia is a closed economy.

CHAPTER 6

Uncertainty and the Current Account

Thus far, we have studied the response of the current account to changes in fundamentals that are known with certainty. The real world, however, is an uncertain place. Some periods display higher macroeconomic volatility than others. A natural question, therefore, is how the overall level of *uncertainty* affects the macroeconomy and, in particular, the external accounts. This chapter is devoted to addressing this question. It begins by documenting that between the mid-1980s and the mid-2000s the United States experienced a period of remarkable aggregate stability, known as *the Great Moderation*, which coincided with the emergence of large current account deficits. The chapter then expands the open economy model of Chapter 3 to introduce uncertainty. This modification allows us to understand the effect of changes in the aggregate level of uncertainty on consumption, saving, the trade balance, and the current account.

6.1 The Great Moderation

A number of researchers have documented that the volatility of U.S. output declined significantly starting in the early 1980s. This phenomenon has become known as *the Great Moderation*.[1] Figure 6.1 depicts the quarterly growth rate of real per capita gross domestic product in the United States over the period 1947Q2 to 2017Q4. It also shows, with a vertical line, the beginning of the Great Moderation in 1984. It is evident from the figure that output growth is much smoother in the post-1984 subsample than it is in the pre-1984 subsample.

The most commonly used measure of *volatility* in macroeconomic data is the standard deviation. According to this statistic, postwar U.S. output growth became half as volatile after 1983. Specifically, the standard deviation of quarter-to-quarter

---

[1] Early studies documenting the Great Moderation are Chang-Jin Kim and Charles R. Nelson, "Has the U.S. Economy Become More Stable? A Bayesian Approach Based on a Markov-Switching Model of the Business Cycle," *Review of Economics and Statistics* 81 (1999): 608–616; and Margaret M. McConnell and Gabriel Perez-Quiros, "Output Fluctuations in the United States: What Has Changed since the Early 1980's?," *American Economic Review* 90 (December 2000): 1464–1476. James H. Stock and Mark W. Watson, in "Has the Business Cycle Changed and Why?," in *NBER Macroeconomics Annual 2002*, vol. 17, ed. Mark Gertler and Kenneth Rogoff (Chicago: University of Chicago Press, 2003), 159–218, present a survey of this literature.

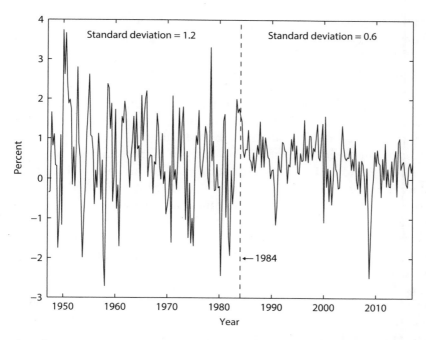

Figure 6.1. Quarterly Real per Capita GDP Growth in the United States, 1947Q2–2017Q4

Notes: The figure shows that the growth rate of real GDP per capita in the United States has been less volatile since the beginning of the Great Moderation in 1984.

Data Source: http://www.bea.gov.

real per capita output growth was 1.2 percent over the period 1947 to 1983, but only 0.6 percent over the period 1984 to 2017. Some economists believe that the Great Moderation ended in 2007, just before the onset of the global financial crisis, while others argue that the Great Moderation is still ongoing, as the volatility of output has returned to pre-crisis levels. The standard deviation of output growth is less than 0.1 percentage points lower over the period 1984 to 2006 than it is over the period 1984 to 2017. The discussion that follows includes the entire post-1984 period in the definition of the Great Moderation.

6.2 Causes of the Great Moderation

Researchers have put forward three alternative explanations of the Great Moderation: good luck, good policy, and structural change. The *good luck hypothesis* states that by chance, starting in the early 1980s the U.S. economy has been blessed with smaller shocks. The *good policy hypothesis* maintains that starting with former Fed chairman Paul Volcker's aggressive monetary policy that brought to an end the high inflation of the 1970s and continuing with the low inflation policy of Volcker's successor Alan Greenspan, the United States experienced a period of extraordinary macroeconomic stability. Good regulatory policy has also been cited as a cause of the Great Moderation. Specifically, the early 1980s witnessed the demise of Regulation Q (or Reg Q), which imposed a ceiling on the interest rate that banks could pay on deposits. It became law in 1933, and its objective was to make banks more stable. Competition for deposits was thought to increase costs for banks and to force them into making riskier loans with higher expected returns. Thus, allowing banks to pay interest on deposits was believed to contribute to bank failures.[2] However, Regulation Q introduced a financial distortion. Because of the ceiling on the interest rate on deposits, when expected inflation goes up (as it did in the 1970s) the real interest rate on deposits, given by the difference between the interest rate on deposits and expected inflation, falls and can even become negative, inducing depositors to withdraw their funds from banks. As a consequence, banks are forced to reduce the volume of loans, generating a credit-crunch-induced recession.

Lastly, the *structural change hypothesis* maintains that the Great Moderation was in part caused by structural change, particularly in inventory management and in the financial sector. These technological developments, the argument goes, allowed firms to display smoother flows of sales, production, and employment, thereby reducing the amplitude of the business cycle.

We will not dwell on which of the proposed explanations of the Great Moderation has more merit. Instead, our interest is in possible connections between the Great Moderation and the significant current account deterioration observed in the United States over the post-1984 period.

6.3 The Great Moderation and the Emergence of Current Account Imbalances

The beginning of the Great Moderation coincided with a significant change in the sign and absolute size of the U.S. current account. Figure 6.2 displays the ratio of the current account to GDP in the United States over the period 1947Q1–2017Q4. The behavior of the current account is familiar from Chapter 1. During the period 1947–1983, the United States experienced on average positive current account balances of 0.34 percent of GDP. Starting in the early 1980s, large current account deficits averaging 2.8 percent of GDP opened up.

Is the timing of the Great Moderation and the emergence of protracted current account deficits pure coincidence, or is there a causal connection between the two? To address this issue, we will explore the effects of changes in output uncertainty on the trade balance and the current account in the context of our theoretical framework of current account determination.

6.4 An Open Economy with Uncertainty

In the economy studied in Chapter 3, the endowments Q_1 and Q_2 are known with certainty. What would be the effect of making the future endowment, Q_2, uncertain? How would households adjust their consumption and saving decisions in period 1 if they knew that the endowment in period 2 could be either high or low with some

---

[2] For more information on Reg Q, see R. Alton Gilbert, "Requiem for Regulation Q: What It Did and Why It Passed Away," *Federal Reserve Bank of St. Louis Review* 68, no. 2 (February 1986): 22–37.

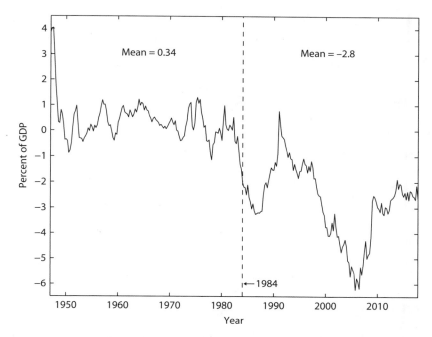

Figure 6.2. The Current Account to GDP Ratio in the United States, 1947Q1–2017Q4
Notes: The figure shows that the emergence of persistent current account deficits in
the United States coincided with the beginning of the Great Moderation in 1984.
Data Source: http://www.bea.gov.

probability? Intuitively, we should expect the emergence of *precautionary saving* in
period 1. That is, an increase in saving in period 1 to hedge against a bad income
realization in period 2. The desired increase in saving in period 1 must be brought
about by a reduction in consumption in that period. With the period 1 endowment unchanged and consumption lower, the trade balance must improve. By the
same token, a decline in income uncertainty, like the one observed in the United
States since the early 1980s, should be associated with a deterioration in the trade
balance.

To formalize these ideas, consider initially an economy in which the stream of
output is known with certainty and is constant over time. Specifically, suppose that
$Q_1 = Q_2 = Q$. Assume further that the lifetime utility function is given by

$$\ln C_1 + \ln C_2.$$

To simplify the analysis, assume that initial asset holdings are nil, $B_0 = 0$, and that
the world interest rate is zero, or $r^* = 0$. In this case, the intertemporal budget
constraint of the representative household is given by $C_2 = 2Q - C_1$. Using this
expression to eliminate C_2 from the utility function, we have that the household's
utility maximization problem consists in choosing C_1 to maximize $\ln C_1 + \ln(2Q -
C_1)$. The first-order condition associated with this maximization problem is the
derivative of this expression with respect to C_1 equated to zero, or $\frac{1}{C_1} - \frac{1}{2Q - C_1} = 0$.
Solving for C_1, we obtain $C_1 = Q$. It follows that the trade balance in period 1,

$TB_1 = Q - C_1$, is zero. The current account, given by $CA_1 = rB_0 + TB_1$ is also nil. Intuitively, in this economy, households do not need to save or borrow in order to smooth consumption over time because the endowment stream is already perfectly smooth.

Suppose now that the endowment in period 1 continues to be equal to Q, but that Q_2 is not known with certainty in period 1. Specifically, assume that with probability $1/2$ the household receives a positive endowment shock in period 2 equal to $\sigma > 0$, and that with equal probability the household receives a negative endowment shock in the amount of $-\sigma$. That is,

$$Q_2 = \begin{cases} Q + \sigma & \text{with probability } 1/2 \\ Q - \sigma & \text{with probability } 1/2 \end{cases}.$$

Relative to the economy without uncertainty, this is a *mean preserving increase in uncertainty* in the sense that the expected value of the endowment in period 2, given by $\frac{1}{2}(Q + \sigma) + \frac{1}{2}(Q - \sigma)$ equals Q, the endowment that the household receives in period 2 in the economy without uncertainty.

The standard deviation of the endowment in period 2 is given by σ. To see this, recall that the standard deviation is the square root of the variance and that, in turn, the variance is the expected value of squared deviations of output from its mean. The deviation of output from its mean is $Q + \sigma - Q = \sigma$ in the high-output state and $Q - \sigma - Q = -\sigma$ in the low-output state. Therefore, the variance of output in period 2 is given by $\frac{1}{2} \times \sigma^2 + \frac{1}{2} \times (-\sigma)^2 = \sigma^2$. The standard deviation of period 2 output is then given by $\sqrt{\sigma^2} = \sigma$. It follows that the larger σ is, the more volatile the period 2 endowment will be.

We must specify how households value uncertain consumption paths. We will assume that households care about the expected value of utility. Specifically, the lifetime utility function is now given by

$$\ln C_1 + E \ln C_2, \tag{6.1}$$

where E denotes expected value. Note that this preference formulation encompasses the preference specification we used in the absence of uncertainty. This is because when C_2 is known with certainty, then $E \ln C_2 = \ln C_2$.

The budget constraint of the household in period 2 is given by $C_2 = 2Q + \sigma - C_1$ in the good state of the world and by $C_2 = 2Q - \sigma - C_1$ in the bad state of the world. Therefore, expected lifetime utility is given by

$$\ln C_1 + \frac{1}{2} \ln(2Q + \sigma - C_1) + \frac{1}{2} \ln(2Q - \sigma - C_1).$$

The household chooses C_1 to maximize this expression. The first-order optimality condition associated with this problem is

$$\frac{1}{C_1} = \frac{1}{2} \left[\frac{1}{2Q + \sigma - C_1} + \frac{1}{2Q - \sigma - C_1} \right]. \tag{6.2}$$

The left-hand side of this expression is the marginal utility of consumption in period 1. The right-hand side is the expected marginal utility of consumption in period

2. This means that the optimal consumption choice equates the marginal utility of consumption in period 1 to the expected marginal utility of consumption in period 2.

Consider first whether the optimal consumption choice associated with the problem without uncertainty, given by $C_1 = Q$, represents a solution in the case with uncertainty. If this were the case, then it would have to be true that

$$\frac{1}{Q} = \frac{1}{2}\left[\frac{1}{2Q+\sigma - Q} + \frac{1}{2Q-\sigma - Q}\right].$$

This expression can be simplified to

$$\frac{1}{Q} = \frac{1}{2}\left[\frac{1}{Q+\sigma} + \frac{1}{Q-\sigma}\right].$$

Further simplifying, we obtain

$$1 = \frac{Q^2}{Q^2 - \sigma^2},$$

which is impossible, given that $\sigma > 0$. We have thus shown that $C_1 \neq Q$. That is, a mean preserving increase in uncertainty induces households to choose a different level of period 1 consumption than the one they would choose under certainty.

Figure 6.3 provides a graphical representation of this result. It plots with a solid line the marginal utility of period 1 consumption as a function of C_1 (the left-hand

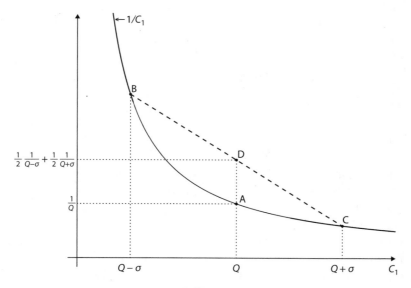

Figure 6.3. Uncertainty and Precautionary Saving
Notes: The solid line plots the marginal utility of consumption in period 1, $1/C_1$, as a function of C_1. In the case that $C_1 = Q$, the marginal utility of consumption in period 1, point A, lies below the expected marginal utility of consumption in period 2, given by point D.

side of equation 6.2). Suppose $C_1 = Q$. Then the marginal utility of period 1 consumption is equal to $1/Q$ (point A in the figure). In this case consumption in period 2 is either $(Q - \sigma)$ or $(Q + \sigma)$ and the marginal utility in period 2 is either $1/(Q - \sigma)$ or $1/(Q + \sigma)$ (point B or C, respectively). The expected marginal utility in period 2 is then given by $\frac{1}{2}\frac{1}{Q-\sigma} + \frac{1}{2}\frac{1}{Q+\sigma}$ (point D in the figure). Point D is above point A (because the marginal utility is convex), therefore when $C_1 = Q$ the marginal utility of period 1 consumption is below the expected marginal utility of period 2 consumption. Therefore, we have shown that if we set $C_1 = Q$, then the left-hand side of optimality condition (6.2) is less than the right-hand side. In other words, if the consumer chose $C_1 = Q$, then the marginal utility of consumption in period 1 would be smaller than the expected marginal utility of consumption in period 2. Intuitively, the household would be better off consuming less in period 1 and more in period 2.

To see this more formally, notice that the left-hand side of optimality condition (6.2) is decreasing in C_1, whereas the right-hand side is increasing in C_1. It follows that the value of C_1 that satisfies optimality condition (6.2) must be less than Q,

$$C_1 < Q.$$

This means that an increase in uncertainty induces households to consume less and save more. By saving more in period 1, households avoid having to cut consumption by too much in the bad state of period 2. This type of saving is known as precautionary saving.

The trade balance in period 1, TB_1, equals $Q - C_1$. It follows immediately that an increase in uncertainty causes an improvement in the trade balance. The current account in period 1, CA_1, equals $TB_1 + r_0 B_0$. Since we assume that the economy starts with zero debt ($B_0 = 0$), we have that the current account equals the trade balance. Thus, we have that an increase in uncertainty leads to an improvement in the current account. Intuitively, in response to an increase in uncertainty, households use the current account as a vehicle to save in period 1.

Viewed through the lens of this model, the reduction in output volatility that came with the Great Moderation should have contributed to the observed concurrent deterioration of the U.S. current account.

It is evident from Figure 6.3 that the positive relationship between uncertainty and precautionary saving depends on the convexity of the marginal utility of consumption. In other words, it is important that the third derivative of the period utility function $U(C)$ be positive. This requirement is satisfied in the economy analyzed here, where households have logarithmic period utility functions. Exercise 6.2 considers the case of a linear period 2 utility function. In this case, households are said to display *risk neutrality*. Exercise 6.3 considers the case of quadratic utility, which delivers *certainty equivalence*. In both cases the marginal utility of consumption ceases to be convex and therefore the connection between uncertainty and precautionary saving breaks down.

In the next section, we will analyze an environment in which precautionary saving disappears regardless of whether the marginal utility of consumption is convex or not.

6.5 Complete Asset Markets and the Current Account

In the model economy analyzed thus far, households face *uninsurable income risk*. This is because the only financial instrument available to them is one whose period 2 payoff is the same in the good and bad states. If possible, households would like to buy a portfolio of assets that pays more in the state in which the endowment is low than in the state in which the endowment is high. Here, we introduce such possibility by assuming the existence of *state contingent claims*. In this environment, households do not need to rely on precautionary saving to cover themselves against the occurrence of the low-endowment state.

6.5.1 STATE CONTINGENT CLAIMS

Suppose that in period 1 the household can buy an asset that pays one unit of good in period 2 if the state of nature is good and zero units if the state is bad. Assume also that the household can buy an asset that pays one unit of good if the state of nature is bad and zero otherwise. Assets of this type are called *state contingent claims*. Let P^g and P^b denote the prices of the assets that pay in the good and bad states, respectively, and B^g and B^b the quantity of each asset purchased by the household in period 1. This economy is said to feature *complete asset markets*, because households can buy asset portfolios with any payoff pattern across states in period 2. For example, if the household wishes to have a portfolio that pays x units of goods in the good state and y units in the bad state, then it must simply purchase x units of the asset that pays in the good state ($B^g = x$) and y units of the asset that pays in the bad state ($B^b = y$). This portfolio costs $P^g x + P^b y$ in period 1. By contrast, the single-bond economy studied in Section 6.4 has *incomplete asset markets*, because households are restricted to buying asset portfolios with the same payoff in all states of nature in period 2.

The quantities B^g and B^b could be positive or negative. This means that households are allowed to maintain *long asset positions* or *short asset positions* in the different state contingent claims. For example, the household could sell contingent claims that pay in the good state ($B^g < 0$) and buy contingent claims that pay in the bad state ($B^b > 0$).

The existence in period 1 of one state contingent claim for each possible state of nature in period 2 makes any other asset redundant, in the sense that its payoff can be replicated by an appropriate portfolio of state contingent claims. Consider, for example, a risk-free bond, like the one available to households in the incomplete asset market economy of Section 6.4. A risk-free bond is an asset that costs one unit of good in period 1 and pays $1 + r_1$ units of good in every state of period 2, where r_1 is the risk-free interest rate. Consider now constructing a portfolio of contingent claims that has the same payoff as the risk-free bond; that is, a portfolio that pays $1 + r_1$ in every state of period 2. This portfolio must contain $1 + r_1$ units of each of the two contingent claims. The price of this portfolio in period 1 is $(P^g + P^b)(1 + r_1)$. This price must equal the price of the risk-free bond, namely 1; otherwise a pure arbitrage opportunity would allow agents to become infinitely rich. So we have that

$$1 + r_1 = \frac{1}{P^g + P^b}. \tag{6.3}$$

Thus, the gross risk-free interest rate is the inverse of the price of a portfolio that pays one unit of good in every state of period 2.

6.5.2 THE HOUSEHOLD'S PROBLEM

The budget constraint of the household in period 1 is

$$C_1 + P^g B^g + P^b B^b = Q. \tag{6.4}$$

In period 2, there are two budget constraints, one for the good state and one for the bad state:

$$\text{period 2 budget constraint} \begin{cases} C_2^g = Q + \sigma + B^g & \text{with probability } 1/2 \\ C_2^b = Q - \sigma + B^b & \text{with probability } 1/2 \end{cases} \tag{6.5}$$

where C_2^g and C_2^b denote consumption in period 2 in the good and bad states, respectively. Using the period 1 budget constraint and the period 2 budget constraint (equations (6.4) and (6.5), respectively) to eliminate C_1, C_2^g, and C_2^b from the lifetime utility function (equation (6.1)), we can state the household's utility maximization problem as choosing an asset portfolio $\{B^g, B^b\}$ to maximize

$$\ln(Q - P^g B^g - P^b B^b) + \frac{1}{2}\ln(Q + \sigma + B^g) + \frac{1}{2}\ln(Q - \sigma + B^b).$$

The first-order optimality conditions associated with this utility maximization problem are

$$\frac{P^g}{C_1} = \frac{1}{2}\frac{1}{C_2^g} \tag{6.6}$$

and

$$\frac{P^b}{C_1} = \frac{1}{2}\frac{1}{C_2^b}. \tag{6.7}$$

The intuition behind these expressions is as follows: Consider the first optimality condition. The left-hand side is the welfare cost of purchasing in period 1 a state contingent claim that pays one unit of consumption in the good state in period 2. To see this, note that the price of such asset is P^g units of period 1 consumption. In turn, each unit of period 1 consumption yields $1/C_1$ units of utility because, with log preferences, $1/C_1$ is the marginal utility of consumption. So the total utility cost in period 1 of a state contingent claim that pays one unit of consumption in the good state in period 2 is P^g/C_1. The household equates this cost to the expected utility of an additional unit of consumption in the good state in period 2, given by $\frac{1}{2C_2^g}$.

An equivalent interpretation of the first optimality condition is that it equates the marginal rate of substitution between consumption in period 1 and consumption in the good state in period 2, $\frac{1}{2}\frac{1/C_2^g}{1/C_1}$, to the relative price of goods in the good state in period 2 in terms of goods in period 1, P^g. The second optimality condition has a similar interpretation.

Comparing the optimality conditions of the household's problem in this economy with the ones in the incomplete asset market model, given by equation (6.2), we see that now we have one first-order condition per state of nature in period 2, whereas in the incomplete asset market economy we had just one. The reason is that under complete markets the household can buy as many independent assets as there are states, whereas in the incomplete market economy the household has access to fewer assets than states (one asset in an environment with two states).

6.5.3 FREE CAPITAL MOBILITY

As in the incomplete asset economy studied in Section 6.4, we assume that there is free international capital mobility. This means that the domestic prices of the state contingent claims must be equal to the corresponding world prices. Letting P^{g*} and P^{b*} denote the world prices of the state contingent claims that pay in the good and bad states, respectively, we have that under free capital mobility

$$P^g = P^{g*}$$

and

$$P^b = P^{b*}.$$

By the same logic as the one used to derive the pricing equation (6.3), we have that the world interest rate, denoted r^*, must satisfy

$$1 + r^* = \frac{1}{P^{g*} + P^{b*}}.$$

We assume that foreign investors make zero profits on average.[3] The revenue of a foreign investor who sells in period 1 B^g and B^b units of state contingent claims is $P^{g*}B^g + P^{b*}B^b$. Suppose that the foreign investor uses these funds to buy risk-free bonds. In period 2, the foreign investor receives from this investment $(1+r^*)(P^{g*}B^g + P^{b*}B^b)$. In period 2 the foreign investor must pay to the agents who bought the contingent claims B^g if the state is good and B^b if the state is bad. It follows that the profits of the foreign investor are state contingent and given by

$$\text{profit of foreign investor} = \begin{cases} (1+r^*)(P^{g*}B^g + P^{b*}B^b) - B^g & \text{with probability } 1/2 \\ (1+r^*)(P^{*g}B^g + P^{b*}B^b) - B^b & \text{with probability } 1/2 \end{cases}$$

Expected profits are then given by

$$\text{expected profit of foreign investor} = \left[(1+r^*)P^{g*} - \frac{1}{2}\right]B^g + \left[(1+r^*)P^{b*} - \frac{1}{2}\right]B^b.$$

[3]Zero expected profits can arise if the international capital market is competitive and foreign lenders are risk neutral. They can also be the result of a competitive environment in which foreign investors are risk averse but hold a highly diversified portfolio. Think, for example, of a world populated by a continuum of small open economies identical to the one we are analyzing in which the endowment process is independent across countries. If foreign investors can invest in all countries, their profits become deterministic and equal to the expected value of profits in each individual country.

The assumption that the foreign investor makes zero expected profits on any portfolio $\{B^g, B^b\}$ implies that

$$(1+r^*)P^{g*} = \frac{1}{2}$$

and

$$(1+r^*)P^{b*} = \frac{1}{2}.$$

Finally, we assume, as we did in the economy with incomplete asset markets studied in Section 6.4, that the world interest rate is zero, $r^* = 0$, so that

$$P^{g*} = P^{b*} = \frac{1}{2}.$$

6.5.4 EQUILIBRIUM IN THE COMPLETE ASSET MARKET ECONOMY

Using the result that $P^g = P^b = 1/2$ to replace P^g and P^b in the first-order conditions of the household, given in equations (6.6) and (6.7), we obtain

$$C_1 = C_2^g = C_2^b.$$

This means that the presence of complete asset markets allows households to completely smooth consumption across time and states.

Combining the result that $C_1 = C_2^g = C_2^b$ with the budget constraints in periods 1 and 2, given in equations (6.4) and (6.5), respectively, yields

$$B^g = -\sigma,$$
$$B^b = \sigma,$$

and

$$C_1 = C_2^g = C_2^b = Q.$$

The first two expressions say that the household takes a short position in contingent claims that pay in the good state and a long position in claims that pay in the bad state. In this way, households can transfer resources from the good state to the bad state in period 2, which allows them to smooth consumption across states. Notice the difference with the single-bond economy of Section 6.4. There, households cannot transfer resources across states, because the financial instruments to do so are unavailable. Instead, to self-insure, households in period 1 must engage in precautionary saving to transfer resources to both states in period 2 through the single bond traded in the market. This is an inferior option because it forces them to transfer resources from period 1 to the good state in period 2, where they are not needed.

The trade balance in period 1 is given by

$$TB_1 = Q - C_1 = 0.$$

Because households are assumed to start period 1 with zero net assets, the current account equals the trade balance and is therefore also equal to zero,

$$CA_1 = 0.$$

This result obtains regardless of the amount of uncertainty in the economy; that is, independently of the value of σ. We have therefore established that under complete financial markets precautionary saving is zero and the link between the level of uncertainty and the current account disappears. Thus, the main result of Section 6.4—namely, that a decrease in uncertainty leads to a deterioration in the current account—relies on the assumption that financial markets are incomplete. It is therefore natural to ask whether reality is better approximated by the assumption of complete markets or by the assumption of incomplete markets. Domestic financial markets could be incomplete for various reasons. For example, it could be the case that world financial markets themselves are incomplete. This is not an unreasonable scenario. In the real world there are many more states of nature than just good and bad, as assumed here. Disturbances of many natures, including those stemming from policymaking, weather, natural catastrophes, epidemics, and technological innovations, create a large, possibly infinite number of states of nature. In this context, it is not inconceivable that the number of available assets is insufficient to span all possible states of nature. Furthermore, even if international financial markets were complete, domestic financial markets may be incomplete if policymakers restrict access to a subset of international financial markets. For example, the government may prohibit trade in derivatives or in short-term assets. To the extent that asset markets are not complete, uncertainty will continue to induce precautionary saving and hence variations in uncertainty will lead to variations in the current account.

Although with complete asset markets the current account is zero independently of the degree of uncertainty, σ, there can be significant amounts of international borrowing and lending in this economy. Specifically, even though the country's net international asset position is nil, $B^g + B^b = 0$, the gross positions, B^g and B^b, are not. We saw that in equilibrium the country holds a long position (saves) in bonds that pay in the bad state, $B^b = \sigma$, and a short position (borrows) in bonds that pay in the good state, $B^g = -\sigma$. Moreover, the gross asset and liability positions, B^b and B^g, are increasing in the amount of uncertainty in the economy, σ. The intuition is simple: the more uncertain the economy is, the larger the need to hedge against bad outcomes will be, and hedging involves saving in assets that pay in bad future states and borrowing in assets that pay in good states.

6.6 Summing Up

In this chapter we studied the effect of uncertainty on the current account. A summary of the main results is:

- In the postwar United States, GDP growth was about half as volatile after 1984 than before. This phenomenon is known as the Great Moderation.

- Three main explanations of the Great Moderation have been proposed: good luck, good policy, and structural change.
- The Great Moderation coincided with the beginning of sizable and persistent current account deficits in the United States.
- A model of an open economy with uncertainty about future realizations of income predicts that an increase in income volatility causes an increase in precautionary saving. In turn, the increase in precautionary saving leads to an improvement in the current account. Thus, the model predicts that the Great Moderation should have been associated with a worsening of the external accounts.
- The prediction that an increase in uncertainty results in elevated precautionary saving depends on the assumption that financial markets are incomplete. Under complete markets, households are able to insure against output volatility without resorting to precautionary saving. Consequently, under complete markets the positive relationship between the level of uncertainty and the current account disappears.
- When markets are complete, the country's net international asset position is independent of the amount of uncertainty in the economy. But the gross international asset positions are increasing in the level of uncertainty.

6.7 Exercises

Exercise 6.1 (TFU) Indicate whether the following statements are true, false, or uncertain and explain why.

1. The risk-free interest rate goes up with uncertainty in an open economy but not in a closed one.
2. All else constant, the more complete international financial markets are, the bigger the gap between output and consumption volatility will be.

Exercise 6.2 (Risk Neutrality) Redo the analysis in Section 6.4, assuming that households are risk neutral in period 2. Specifically, assume that their preferences are logarithmic in period 1 but linear in period 2 consumption, $\ln C_1 + EC_2$. Assume that $Q = 1$.

1. Assume that $\sigma = 0$. Find the equilibrium values of C_1 and B_1.
2. Now assume that $\sigma > 0$. Find the equilibrium value of B_1. What is the predicted effect of the Great Moderation on the current account? Explain.

Exercise 6.3 (Certainty Equivalence) Consider a two-period, small open endowment economy populated by households with preferences described by the lifetime utility function

$$-\frac{1}{2}(C_1 - \bar{C})^2 - \frac{1}{2}E(C_2 - \bar{C})^2,$$

where $\bar{C}$ represents a satiation level of consumption, and E denotes the mathematical expectations operator. In period 1, households receive an endowment $Q_1 = 1$ and have no assets or liabilities carried over from the past ($B_0 = 0$). Households can borrow or lend in the international financial market at the world interest rate $r^* = 0$. Compute consumption and the current account in periods 1 and 2 under the following two assumptions regarding the endowment in period 2, denoted Q_2:

1. Q_2 is known with certainty and is equal to 1.
2. Q_2 is random and takes the values 0.5 with probability 1/2 or 1.5 with probability 1/2.

Provide intuition for your findings.

Exercise 6.4 (The Current Account as Insurance against Catastrophic Events)
Consider a two-period endowment economy populated by identical households with preferences defined over consumption in period 1, C_1, and consumption in period 2, C_2, and described by the utility function

$$\ln C_1 + E \ln C_2,$$

where C_1 denotes consumption in period 1, C_2 denotes consumption in period 2, and E denotes the expected value operator. Each period, households receive an endowment of 10 units of food. Households start period 1 carrying no assets or debts from the past ($B_0 = 0$). Financial markets are incomplete. There is a single internationally traded bond that pays the interest rate $r^* = 0$.

1. Compute consumption, the trade balance, the current account, and national saving in period 1.
2. Assume now that the endowment in period 1 continues to be 10, but that the economy is prone to severe natural disasters in period 2. Suppose that these negative events are very rare, but have catastrophic effects on the country's output. Specifically, assume that with probability 0.01 the economy suffers an earthquake in period 2 that causes the endowment to drop by 90 percent with respect to period 1. With probability 0.99, the endowment in period 2 is 111/11. What is the expected endowment in period 2? How does it compare to that of period 1?
3. What percent of period 1 endowment will the country export? Compare this answer to what happens under certainty and provide intuition.
4. Suppose that the probability of the catastrophic event increases to 0.02, all other things equal. Compute the mean and standard deviation of the endowment in period 2. Is the change in probability mean preserving?
5. Calculate the equilibrium levels of consumption and the trade balance in period 1.
6. Compare your results with those pertaining to the case of 0.01 probability for the catastrophic event. Provide interpretation.

Exercise 6.5 (Interest Rate Uncertainty I) Consider a two-period economy inhabited by a large number of identical households with preferences described by the utility function

$$\ln C_1 + \ln C_2,$$

where C_1 and C_2 denote consumption in periods 1 and 2, respectively. Households are endowed with $Q > 0$ units of consumption goods each period, and start period 1 with no assets or debt carried over from the past ($B_0 = 0$). In period 1, households can borrow or lend by means of a bond, denoted B, which pays the world interest rate, denoted r^*. Assume that $r^* = 0$.

1. Derive the optimal levels of consumption in periods 1 and 2, as functions of Q. Derive the equilibrium levels of the trade balance, the current account, and net foreign assets at the end of period 1.

Now assume that the world interest rate is not known with certainty in period 1; that is, the one-period bond carries a floating rate. Specifically, assume that r^* is given by

$$r^* = \begin{cases} \sigma & \text{with probability } 1/2 \\ -\sigma & \text{with probability } 1/2 \end{cases},$$

where $\sigma \in (0, 1)$ is a parameter. In this economy, financial markets are incomplete because agents have access to a single bond in period 1. Preferences are described by the expected utility function

$$\ln C_1 + E \ln C_2,$$

where E denotes the expectations operator. The present economy nests the no-uncertainty economy described above as a special case in which $\sigma = 0$.

2. State the household's budget constraints in periods 1 and 2. To this end, let C_2^H and C_2^L denote consumption in period 2 when the world interest rate is σ and $-\sigma$, respectively.
3. Derive the optimality conditions associated with the household's problem.
4. Show whether the equilibrium level of consumption in period 1 is greater than, less than, or equal to the one that arises when $\sigma = 0$.
5. Find the trade balance in equilibrium. Compare your answer to the one for the case $\sigma = 0$ and provide intuition. In particular, discuss why a mean-preserving increase in interest rate uncertainty affects the trade balance in period 1 the way it does.
6. Are the results obtained above due to the particular (logarithmic) preference specification considered? To address this question, show that all of the results obtained above continue to obtain under a more general class of preferences—namely, the class of *CRRA preferences*

$$\frac{C_1^{1-\gamma} - 1}{1 - \gamma} + E\frac{C_2^{1-\gamma} - 1}{1 - \gamma},$$

for $\gamma > 0$, which encompasses the log specification as a special case when $\gamma \to 1$.
7. Finally, show that interest rate uncertainty does have real effects when the equilibrium net foreign asset position at the end of period 1 in the absence of uncertainty is nonzero. To this end, return to the log preference

specification and assume that the endowment in period 1 is zero and that the endowment in period 2 is $Q > 0$. How does the trade balance in period 1 compare under no uncertainty ($\sigma = 0$) and under uncertainty ($\sigma > 0$)?

Exercise 6.6 (Interest Rate Uncertainty II) Consider a two-period, small open economy inhabited by a large number of identical households with preferences described by the utility function

$$\ln C_1 + \ln C_2,$$

where C_1 and C_2 denote consumption in periods 1 and 2, respectively. Households are endowed with Q_1 and Q_2 units of consumption goods each period, and start period 1 with no assets or debt carried over from the past ($B_0 = 0$). In period 1, households can borrow or lend by means of an international bond, denoted B_1, which pays the world interest rate, denoted r^*. Assume that $r^* = 0$.

1. Find the equilibrium values of C_1, C_2, the trade balance, the current account, and net foreign assets in period 1. Express your answers as functions of Q_1 and Q_2.

Now assume that the world interest rate is not known with certainty in period 1. Specifically, assume that r^* is given by

$$r^* = \begin{cases} \sigma & \text{with probability } 1/2 \\ -\sigma & \text{with probability } 1/2 \end{cases},$$

where $\sigma \in (0, 1)$ is a parameter. Preferences are described by the expected utility function

$$\ln C_1 + E \ln C_2,$$

where E denotes the expectations operator.

2. State the household's budget constraints in periods 1 and 2. To this end, let C_2^H and C_2^L denote consumption in period 2 when the world interest rate is σ and $-\sigma$, respectively.
3. Now assume that $Q_1 > 0$ and $Q_2 = 0$. Find the equilibrium level of consumption in period 1 for the case that (i) $\sigma = 0$ and (ii) $\sigma \in (0, 1)$. Does this increase in uncertainty lead to precautionary saving in period 1? Interpret your findings.
4. Does the increase in uncertainty increase the mean and the variance of period 2 consumption? Provide intuition.

Exercise 6.7 (Complete Asset Markets and the Risk-Free Interest Rate) The model with complete financial markets studied in Section 6.5 assumes that the risk-free world interest rate is nil, $r^* = 0$. Derive the results of that section under the assumption that r^* is positive and then answer the following questions:

1. Do households continue to perfectly smooth consumption across states? Explain.

2. Do households continue to perfectly smooth consumption across time? Explain.
3. Find the sign of the current account in period 1 and provide intuition.
4. Does the model continue to predict that the level of uncertainty has no effect on the current account? Why or why not?
5. How does the current account in period 1 compare with the one that would obtain in the absence of uncertainty ($\sigma = 0$)?

CHAPTER 7

Large Open Economies

Thus far, we have analyzed the determination of the current account in a small open economy. A defining feature of a small open economy is that even if the country borrows or lends a large sum relative to its output in international financial markets, it will not affect the world interest rate. The reason is that the economy is too small to make a dent in the world supply of or demand for funds. The story is different when the country is large. Suppose, for example, that due to an expected increase in future output, the United States at current world interest rates wishes to increase its current account deficit by 5 percent of GDP. In this case, the world financial market will face an additional demand for funds of about $1 trillion. This development is likely to move world interest rates up, which would have repercussions both in the United States and in the rest of the world.

In this chapter, we present a framework suitable for analyzing the determination of the current account, the world interest rate, and other macroeconomic indicators in large open economies. The model will build on the microfoundations derived in previous chapters. This makes sense, because the problem of a household or a firm should not be different whether the household or the firm is located in a large or small economy. The main takeaway of the chapter is a theory of the joint determination of international lending and the world interest rate.

7.1 A Two-Country Economy

Let's divide the world into two regions, the United States (US) and the rest of the world (RW). Because a U.S. current account deficit represents the current account surplus of the rest of the world and conversely, a U.S. current account surplus is a current account deficit of the rest of the world, it follows that the world current account must always be equal to zero; that is,

$$CA^{US} + CA^{RW} = 0,$$

where CA^{US} and CA^{RW} denote the current account balances of the United States and the rest of the world.

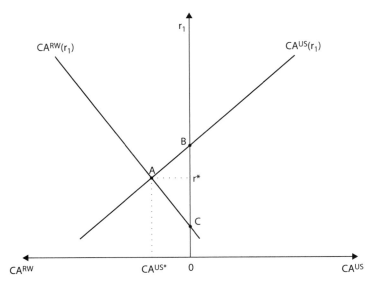

Figure 7.1. Current Account Determination in a Large Open Economy

Notes: The figure depicts the current account schedules of the United States, $CA^{US}(r_1)$, and the rest of the world, $CA^{RW}(r_1)$. The horizontal axis measures from left to right the current account balance of the United States and from right to left the current account balance of the rest of the world. Equilibrium occurs at the intersection of the current account schedules of the United States and the rest of the world and is marked by point A. In equilibrium, the current account is $CA^{US*} < 0$ in the United States and $-CA^{US*} > 0$ in the rest of the world. The equilibrium interest rate is r^*. If the two economies were closed, the equilibrium would be at point B in the United States and at point C in the rest of the world.

As we saw in Section 5.5 of Chapter 5, the current account schedule is an increasing function of the interest rate and other variables. So, we can write

$$CA_1^{US} = CA^{US}(r_1),$$
$$\phantom{CA_1^{US} = CA^{US}(}+$$

where CA_1^{US} denotes the current account balance in the United States in period 1, r_1 is the interest rate in period 1, and $CA^{US}(\cdot)$ is an increasing function. Intuitively, an increase in the interest rate induces U.S. households to increase saving in period 1 and U.S. firms to cut investment in the same period. As a result, the current account of the United States improves as the interest rate increases.

Similarly, the current account of the rest of the world is an increasing function of the interest rate,

$$CA_1^{RW} = CA^{RW}(r_1),$$
$$\phantom{CA_1^{RW} = CA^{RW}(}+$$

where CA_1^{RW} denotes the current account balance of the rest of the world in period 1, and $CA^{RW}(\cdot)$ is an increasing function.

Figure 7.1 shows the current account schedules of the United States and the rest of the world. The current account of the United States is measured from left to right, so the current account schedule of the United States is upward sloping in the graph. The current account of the rest of the world is measured from right to left, so it is downward sloping. To the left of 0 the rest of the world runs a current account surplus and the United States a current account deficit; whereas to the right of 0, the United States runs a current account surplus and the rest of the world a current account deficit.

Equilibrium in the world capital markets is given by the intersection of the current account schedules of the United States and the rest of the world. In the figure, the equilibrium is marked by point A. At that point the current account of the United States is $CA^{US*} < 0$ (a deficit), the current account of the rest of the world is $-CA^{US*} > 0$ (a surplus), and the world interest rate is r^*.

If the United States were a closed economy, its equilibrium would be at point B, where its current account is nil. The U.S. interest rate would be larger than r^*. This makes sense, because at r^* the desired current account balance in the United States is negative, so a larger interest rate is required to induce households to save more and firms to invest less, to ensure a zero balance in the current account. Further, if the United States were a closed economy, the equilibrium in the rest of the world would be at point C. Of course, like in the United States, the current account in the rest of the world would be zero. Unlike in the United States, however, the equilibrium interest rate in the rest of the world would be below r^*. This is because at r^* the desired current account in the rest of the world is positive, so a fall in the interest rate it faces is required to induce households to increase spending and cut saving in period 1 and to induce firms to expand investment in physical capital.

7.2 An Investment Surge in the United States

Suppose that in period 1, firms in the United States learn that their capital will be more productive in period 2. This could happen, for example, because of a technological improvement, such as fracking, discovered in period 1 and expected to be in place in period 2, or because of a forecast of better weather conditions in the United States in period 2 that will enhance the productivity of farmland. As we analyzed in Section 5.6.3 of Chapter 5, in response to this positive news U.S. firms will desire to increase investment at any given interest rate. Thus, the U.S. investment schedule shifts up and to the right. Also, U.S. households, in anticipation of higher future incomes generated by the investment boom, reduce current saving at any given interest rate, so that the U.S. saving schedule shifts up and to the left (see Figure 5.19 in Chapter 5). This means that the current account schedule of the United States, which is the difference between the saving and investment schedules, shifts up and to the left as shown in Figure 7.2. In the figure, the original U.S. current account schedule is $CA^{US}(r_1)$ and is shown with a solid line, and the new current account schedule is $CA^{US'}(r_1)$ and is shown with a broken line. The current account schedule of the rest of the world, $CA^{RW}(r_1)$, is unaffected by the investment surge in the United States.

The equilibrium prior to the investment surge is at point A, where the U.S. current account equals CA^{US*}, the current account of the rest of the world equals $-CA^{US*}$, and the world interest rate equals r^*. After the investment surge, the

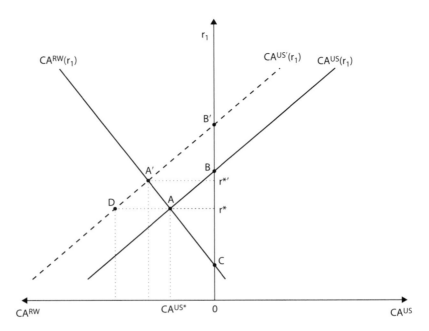

Figure 7.2. Current Account Adjustment to an Investment Surge in the United States
Notes: The figure depicts the effects of an investment surge in the United States on the world interest rate and the current account balances of the United States and the rest of the world. The investment surge shifts the current account schedule of the United States up and to the left, as shown with a broken line. The equilibrium before the investment surge is at point A, and after the investment surge it is at point A′, where the world interest rate is higher, the current account deficit of the United States is larger, and the current account surplus of the rest of the world is higher.

equilibrium is given by point A′, where the schedule $CA^{US'}(r_1)$ and the schedule $CA^{RW}(r_1)$ intersect. In the new equilibrium, the world interest rate is higher and equal to $r^{*'} > r^*$. This is because the higher U.S. demand for funds following the investment surge would result in an excess demand for funds at the original interest rate r^*. In the figure, this excess demand is given by the horizontal distance between points D and A. The increase in the world interest rate from r^* to $r^{*'}$ induces the demand for funds by the United States to shrink and the supply of funds by the rest of the world to increase, thereby eliminating the excess demand for funds in the international financial market. In the new equilibrium, the current account of the United States deteriorates to $CA^{US*'} < CA^{US*}$ and the current account of the rest of the world improves to $-CA^{US*'} > -CA^{US*}$. In sum, because the United States is a large open economy, the investment surge produces a large increase in the demand for loans, which drives world interest rates up. As a result, the deterioration in the U.S. current account is not as pronounced as the one that would have resulted if the interest rate had remained unchanged (point D in the figure).

Note further that the increase in the U.S. interest rate is smaller than the one that would have occurred if the United States were a closed economy. In that case, the increase in the interest rate would be given by the vertical distance between points B and B'.

7.3 Microfoundations of the Two-Country Model

In the previous two sections, the starting point of the analysis was the current account schedule of each country. In this section, we dig deeper and derive the equilibrium levels of the current account and the world interest rate starting from the decisions of individual households. The analysis will provide insight on how different features of the economy, such as disturbances in current and future endowments in the domestic economy and the rest of the world, affect the world interest rate and global imbalances.

To simplify the exposition, we will study an endowment economy (no investment in physical capital). The household's problem in each country is identical to the one we studied in the endowment economy of Chapter 3. So, much of this section runs through familiar territory.

Consider a two-period economy composed of two countries, the United States and the rest of the world. Suppose that each country is populated by a large number of households. In both countries, households derive utility from the consumption of a tradable perishable good. Preferences of households in the United States and the rest of the world are identical and described by the utility functions

$$\ln C_1^{US} + \ln C_2^{US} \tag{7.1}$$

and

$$\ln C_1^{RW} + \ln C_2^{RW},$$

where C_t^{US} and C_t^{RW} denote consumption in period $t = 1, 2$ in the United States and the rest of the world.

Let the endowment of households in the United States and the rest of the world be given by Q_t^{US} and Q_t^{RW} for $t = 1, 2$. Households can borrow or lend at the interest rate r_1. There is free capital mobility in the world, so households in both countries trade financial assets at the same interest rate. Let B_t^{US} and B_t^{RW} for $t = 0, 1, 2$, denote the amount of bonds held in period t by households in the United States and the rest of the world, respectively. Suppose that households start with no debt or assets at the beginning of period 1, that is, $B_0^{US} = B_0^{RW} = 0$. Also, since no one is alive in period 3, asset holdings at the end of period 2 must be zero in both countries; that is, the transversality condition $B_2^{US} = B_2^{RW} = 0$ must hold.

In period 1 the budget constraint of U.S. households is given by

$$C_1^{US} + B_1^{US} = Q_1^{US}. \tag{7.2}$$

According to this expression, households allocate their period 1 endowment to consumption or saving. In period 2, the budget constraint of the U.S. household is

$$C_2^{US} = Q_2^{US} + (1 + r_1)B_1^{US}, \tag{7.3}$$

which says that in period 2 households consume their endowment plus the principal and interest on assets accumulated in period 1.

The U.S. household's problem is to maximize its lifetime utility subject to the budget constraints in each period. The problem of a household in a large open economy is the same as that of a household in a small open economy. Thus, we can proceed in the same way as we did in Chapter 3 to characterize the household's optimal consumption-saving choice. Use the budget constraint in period 1 to eliminate B_1^{US} from the period 2 budget constraint, to obtain the present value budget constraint:

$$C_1^{US} + \frac{C_2^{US}}{1+r_1} = Q_1^{US} + \frac{Q_2^{US}}{1+r_1}. \tag{7.4}$$

Solve this present value budget constraint for C_2^{US} and use it to eliminate C_2^{US} from the utility function (7.1). This yields:

$$\ln C_1^{US} + \ln \left[(1+r_1)(Q_1^{US} - C_1^{US}) + Q_2^{US} \right].$$

Taking the derivative of this expression with respect to C_1^{US}, equating it to 0, and rearranging, we obtain the U.S. household's optimal level of consumption in period 1,

$$C_1^{US} = \frac{1}{2} \left(Q_1^{US} + \frac{Q_2^{US}}{1+r_1} \right). \tag{7.5}$$

This expression is familiar from Chapter 3. Consumption in period 1 is increasing in both endowments as both make the household richer. Also, period 1 consumption is decreasing in the interest rate, as an increase in the interest rate makes saving more attractive; or, equivalently, makes current consumption relatively more expensive than future consumption.

The current account of the United States in period 1 is given by the change in the country's net foreign asset position; that is,

$$CA_1^{US} = B_1^{US} - B_0^{US}.$$

Recalling that $B_0^{US} = 0$, we have that

$$CA_1^{US} = B_1^{US}. \tag{7.6}$$

Using the period 1 budget constraint (7.2) to get rid of B_1^{US}, we have that

$$CA_1^{US} = Q_1^{US} - C_1^{US},$$

which says that the current account in period 1 equals the trade balance in period 1. This is the case because of the maintained assumption of no initial assets, which implies that net investment income in period 1 is nil. Finally, replacing C_1^{US} by its optimal level given in equation (7.5), we obtain the current account schedule of the

United States,

$$CA^{US}(r_1) = \frac{1}{2}Q_1^{US} - \frac{1}{2}\frac{Q_2^{US}}{1+r_1}. \tag{7.7}$$

The current account schedule is increasing in the interest rate r_1. This is because as the interest rate increases, households become more attracted to saving. Also, the current account is increasing in the current endowment, Q_1^{US}, and decreasing in the future endowment, Q_2^{US}. This is because households like to smooth consumption over time, so an increase in the period 1 endowment induces them to save part of it for the future. Similarly, an increase in the period 2 endowment induces them to borrow against part of it to increase period 1 consumption.

Households in the rest of the world are identical to U.S. households except for their endowments. In particular, they have the same preferences, start with zero assets in period 1, must end period 2 with zero assets, and face the same interest rate. This means that the optimal level of consumption in period 1 by households in the rest of the world is given by equation (7.5), with the superscript US replaced by the superscript RW; that is,

$$C_1^{RW} = \frac{1}{2}\left(Q_1^{RW} + \frac{Q_2^{RW}}{1+r_1}\right). \tag{7.8}$$

And the current account schedule of the rest of the world is identical to that of the United States, equation (7.7), with the corresponding change of superscripts,

$$CA^{RW}(r_1) = \frac{1}{2}Q_1^{RW} - \frac{1}{2}\frac{Q_2^{RW}}{1+r_1}. \tag{7.9}$$

Like the current account schedule of the United States, the current account schedule of the rest of the world is increasing in the interest rate and in the period 1 endowment and decreasing in the period 2 endowment. If one were to plot the current account schedules of the United States and the rest of the world, equations (7.7) and (7.9) in the space (CA, r), they would look qualitatively like those shown in Figure 7.1.

The equilibrium world interest rate, r^*, is the interest rate that guarantees that the world current account is zero; that is, it is the interest rate that satisfies

$$CA^{US}(r^*) + CA^{RW}(r^*) = 0. \tag{7.10}$$

Using equations (7.7) and (7.9) to eliminate $CA^{US}(r^*)$ and $CA^{RW}(r^*)$ from this equilibrium condition and solving for r^*, we obtain

$$r^* = \frac{Q_2^{US} + Q_2^{RW}}{Q_1^{US} + Q_1^{RW}} - 1. \tag{7.11}$$

This expression says that the equilibrium world interest rate is increasing in the growth rate of the world endowment. It is intuitive that if the world endowment in period 2, $Q_2^{US} + Q_2^{RW}$, increases relative to the the world endowment in period 1, $Q_1^{US} + Q_1^{RW}$, the world interest rate increases because, on average, households would like to borrow against their period 2 endowment, to smooth consumption across time. The increase in the interest rate is necessary to dissuade the world as a whole from borrowing, as this is impossible. Note that the interest rate is independent of how the endowments are distributed across countries. For example, it does not matter whether one country is richer than the other or whether one country is rich in period 1 and poor in period 2 and vice versa.

To obtain the equilibrium current account of the United States in period 1, use equation (7.11) to eliminate r_1 from equation (7.7). After rearranging terms, this operation yields

$$CA_1^{US} = \frac{1}{2} \frac{Q_1^{RW} Q_2^{RW}}{Q_2^{US} + Q_2^{RW}} \left(\frac{Q_1^{US}}{Q_1^{RW}} - \frac{Q_2^{US}}{Q_2^{RW}} \right).$$

The important part of this expression is the parenthetical object on the right-hand side, as it determines the sign of the U.S. current account. It says that the United States will run a current account surplus when its endowment is relatively more abundant than that of the rest of the world in period 1 relative to period 2; that is, when $\frac{Q_1^{US}}{Q_1^{RW}} > \frac{Q_2^{US}}{Q_2^{RW}}$. This makes sense. If the U.S. endowment in period 1 is large relative to that of the rest of the world in period 1, compared to the relative endowments in period 2, U.S. households end up sharing part of their abundant period 1 endowment with the rest of the world and in return receive in period 2 part of the relatively more abundant endowment of the rest of the world. Notice that this is a relative-relative type condition. What matters for the sign of the current account is the joint relative endowments of the two countries across space and time (the United States relative to the rest of the world, and period 1 relative to period 2).

7.4 International Transmission of Country-Specific Shocks

An important difference between a small and a large economy is that aggregate shocks that originate in the former do not affect the rest of the world, whereas aggregate shocks that originate in the latter impact the rest of the world through changes in international prices, such as the world interest rate.

Consider, for example, how an increase in the period 1 endowment of the United States, Q_1^{US}, transmits to other countries. By equilibrium condition (7.11), the world interest rate falls. This is because households in the United States, to smooth consumption over time, wish to save part of their increased period 1 endowment, elevating the world supply of funds. A fall in the world interest rate eliminates the excess supply of funds in international capital markets by inducing households in the rest of the world and in the United States to increase current spending. In the United States, both the increase in the period 1 endowment and the fall in the interest rate induce households to increase period 1 consumption (equation (7.5)). The rest of the world experiences only a fall in the interest rate (no change in endowments), which stimulates consumption in period 1 (equation (7.8)). Thus, the increase in the current endowment in the United States causes an increase in consumption not only domestically but also abroad.

The cross-country comovement of period 1 consumption is quite different when the shock takes the form of future expected movements in endowments. Consider an expected increase in the U.S. endowment in period 2, Q_2^{US}. By equation (7.11), the world interest rate increases, as U.S. households wish to borrow against their now higher future income. In the rest of the world, the increase in the interest rate depresses period 1 consumption (equation (7.5)). Since the period 1 world endowment $Q_1^{US} + Q_1^{RW}$ did not change, the fall in period 1 consumption in the rest of the world means that period 1 consumption in the United States must increase. Thus, in response to future expected output changes in one country, period 1 consumption moves in opposite directions across countries.

7.5 Country Size and the International Transmission Mechanism

An implicit assumption of the preceding analysis is that the United States and the rest of the world have equal populations. This can be seen from the fact that we assumed that B_1^{US} stands for both the individual and aggregate bond holdings in the United States and that B_1^{RW} stands for both the individual and aggregate bond holdings of the rest of the world. This means that we assumed that both countries had a population of one household. Here, one household could stand for one thousand households, or one million households or, in general, any equal number of households in both countries. But what if the number of households were different in both countries? How would the world interest rate be affected by differences in country size? How would the international transmission of domestic shocks be affected by the size of the country?

To address these questions, let's assume that the United States is populated by N^{US} identical households and the rest of the world by N^{RW} identical households. We continue to assume that households in both countries differ only in their endowments. The U.S. net foreign asset position in period 1 is then given by $N^{US}B_1^{US}$, where, as before, B_1^{US} denotes the bond holdings of the individual U.S. household in period 1. Then, the current account of the United States is given by

$$CA_1^{US} = N^{US}B_1^{US},$$

which is a generalization of equation (7.6) when the country is populated by N^{US} identical households. (Recall that initial assets, B_0^{US}, are assumed to be zero.) Use the period 1 budget constraint of the household, equation (7.2), to eliminate B_1^{US}. This yields

$$CA_1^{US} = N^{US}(Q_1^{US} - C_1^{US}).$$

Now replace C_1^{US} by its optimal level, given in equation (7.5), to obtain

$$CA^{US}(r_1) = \frac{N^{US}}{2}\left(Q_1^{US} - \frac{Q_2^{US}}{1+r_1}\right). \tag{7.12}$$

Since the rest of the world is identical to the United States except for the population size and the endowments, we have that its current account schedule is given by

$$CA^{RW}(r_1) = \frac{N^{RW}}{2}\left(Q_1^{RW} - \frac{Q_2^{RW}}{1+r_1}\right). \tag{7.13}$$

Combine (7.12) and (7.13) with the market clearing condition in the world financial market, given by equation (7.10), to obtain

$$\frac{N^{US}}{2}\left(Q_1^{US} - \frac{Q_2^{US}}{1+r^*}\right) + \frac{N^{RW}}{2}\left(Q_1^{RW} - \frac{Q_2^{RW}}{1+r^*}\right) = 0. \tag{7.14}$$

This is one equation in one unknown, the equilibrium world interest rate r^*. Solving for r^* we obtain

$$1+r^* = \frac{N^{US}Q_2^{US} + N^{RW}Q_2^{RW}}{N^{US}Q_1^{US} + N^{RW}Q_1^{RW}}.$$

Let $\alpha \equiv N^{US}/(N^{US} + N^{RW})$ denote the share of the U.S. population in the world population. Then we can express the world interest rate as

$$r^* = \frac{\alpha Q_2^{US} + (1-\alpha)Q_2^{RW}}{\alpha Q_1^{US} + (1-\alpha)Q_1^{RW}} - 1. \tag{7.15}$$

This expression for the world interest rate is similar to the one we obtained when we assumed that both countries had the same size, equation (7.11), except that now the endowments are weighted by the relative size of the corresponding country. In particular, equation (7.15) says that the larger is the U.S. economy (that is, the larger is α), the more important U.S. endowment shocks will be for the determination of the world interest rate. In the limiting case in which the rest of the world is an infinitesimally small economy so that $1-\alpha$ approaches zero, the world interest rate is determined solely by U.S. conditions and is unaffected by shocks in the rest of the world. Formally, as $1-\alpha$ approaches zero, the world interest rate becomes

$$r^* = \frac{Q_2^{US}}{Q_1^{US}} - 1. \tag{7.16}$$

This result provides a justification for the assumption maintained in previous chapters that a small open economy takes the world interest rate as exogenously given. Furthermore, equation (7.16) shows that shocks in the large economy are transmitted to the small economy through variations in the world interest rate. In particular, a temporary output increase in the United States—that is, an increase in Q_1^{US}— lowers the world interest rate faced by small economies. Also, a future expected increase in U.S. output (that is, an expected increase in Q_2^{US}), causes an increase in the world interest rate, which small economies take as given.

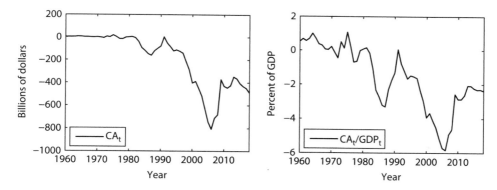

Figure 7.3. The U.S. Current Account Balance, 1960–2018
Data Source: Bureau of Economic Analysis.

7.6   Explaining the U.S. Current Account Deficit: The Global Saving Glut Hypothesis

In the decade preceding the Great Recession of 2007, the U.S. current account deficit experienced a dramatic increase from about $200 billion to $800 billion. (See the left panel of Figure 7.3.) This $600 billion increase brought the deficit from a relatively modest level of 1.5 percent of GDP in 1996 to 6 percent of GDP by 2006. (See the right panel of Figure 7.3.) With the onset of the Great Recession of 2007, the ballooning of the current account deficits came to an abrupt stop. By 2009, the current account deficit had shrunk back to less than 3 percent of GDP. What factors are responsible for these large swings in the U.S. current account? In particular, we wish to know whether the recent rise and fall in the current account deficit was primarily driven by domestic or external factors.

7.6.1   TWO COMPETING HYPOTHESES

Observers have argued that the deterioration in the U.S. current account deficit was caused by external factors.[1] This view is known as the *global saving glut* hypothesis. In particular, it argues that the rest of the world experienced a heightened desire to save but did not have incentives to increase domestic capital formation in a commensurate way. As a result, the current account surpluses of the rest of the world had to be absorbed by current account deficits in the United States.

Much of the increase in the desired current account surpluses in the rest of the world during this period originated in higher desired saving in emerging market economies. In particular, the saving glut hypothesis attributes the increase in the desire of emerging countries to save to two factors. One factor is an increase in foreign reserve accumulation to avoid or be better prepared to face future external crises of the type that had afflicted emerging countries in the 1990s. The second factor is a government-induced foreign currency depreciation aimed at promoting

---

[1] See, among others, Ben S. Bernanke, "The Global Saving Glut and the U.S. Current Account Deficit," Homer Jones Lecture, St. Louis, Missouri, April 14, 2005.

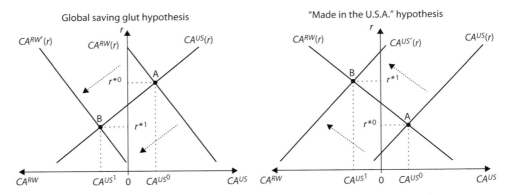

Figure 7.4. U.S. Current Account Deficits: Global Saving Glut or Made in the U.S.A.?

export-led growth. Advocates of the global saving glut view also cite an external factor originating in developed countries; namely, an increase in saving rates in preparation for an aging population.

The global saving glut hypothesis was unconventional at the time. The more standard view was that the large U.S. current account deficits were the results of economic developments inside the United States and unrelated to external factors. In particular, it was argued that financial innovation in the United States had induced low private saving rates and overinvestment in residential housing. This alternative view is known as the *made in the U.S.A. hypothesis.*

How can we tell which view is right, the global saving glut hypothesis or the made in the U.S.A. hypothesis? To address this question, we use the graphical tools developed in Section 7.1. The left panel of Figure 7.4 illustrates the effect of a desired increase in saving in the rest of the world. The initial position of the economy, point A, is at the intersection of the CA^{US} and CA^{RW} schedules. In the initial equilibrium, the U.S. current account equals CA^{US^0} and the world interest rate equals r^{*0}. The increase in the desired saving of the rest of the world shifts the current account schedule of the rest of the world down and to the left as depicted by the schedule $CA^{RW\prime}$. The new equilibrium, point B, features a deterioration in the current account of the United States from CA^{US^0} to CA^{US^1} and a fall in the world interest rate from r^{*0} to r^{*1}. Intuitively, the United States will borrow more from the rest of the world only if it becomes cheaper to do so; that is, only if the interest rate falls. This prediction of the model implies that if the global saving glut hypothesis is valid, then we should have observed a decline in the interest rate.

The made in the U.S.A. hypothesis is illustrated in the right-hand panel of Figure 7.4. Again, in the initial equilibrium, point A, the U.S. current account equals CA^{US^0} and the world interest rate equals r^{*0}. Under this view, the current account schedule of the rest of the world is unchanged. Instead, the current account schedule of the United States shifts up and to the left, as depicted by the schedule $CA^{US\prime}$. The new equilibrium, point B, features a deterioration in the current account of the United States from CA^{US^0} to CA^{US^1} and a rise in the world interest rate from r^{*0} to $r^{*1} > r^{*0}$.

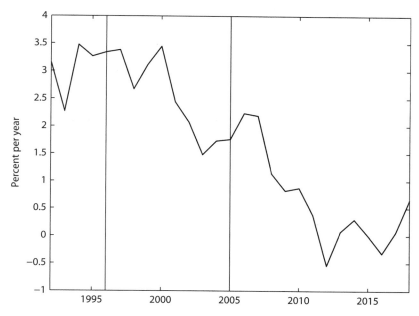

Figure 7.5. The World Interest Rate, 1992–2018

Notes: The world interest rate is measured as the difference between the rate on 10-year U.S. Treasury securities and expected inflation.

Both hypotheses can explain a deterioration in the U.S. current account. However, the global saving glut hypothesis implies that the current account deterioration should have been accompanied by a decline in world interest rates, whereas the made in the U.S.A. hypothesis implies that world interest rates should have gone up. Hence we can use data on the behavior of interest rates to find out which hypothesis is right.

Figure 7.5 plots the world interest rate from 1992 to 2018.[2] It shows that the large current account deterioration in the United States was associated with a significant fall in the interest rate, giving credence to the global saving glut hypothesis.

7.6.2   THE MADE IN THE U.S.A. HYPOTHESIS STRIKES BACK

With the onset of the global financial crisis of 2007, the trajectory of the U.S. current account displayed a sharp reversal. Specifically, as can be seen in Figure 7.3, the current account deficit shrank from a peak of 6 percent of GDP in 2006 to less than 3 percent of GDP in 2009. Can the global saving glut hypothesis also explain this development?

Under the global saving glut hypothesis, the reversal in the current account deficit would be attributed to a decline in desired saving in the rest of the world. Again we can use the graphical tools developed earlier in this chapter to evaluate

---

[2]The world interest rate is computed as the difference between the 10-year constant maturity Treasury rate and expected inflation. Expected inflation in turn is measured as the median CPI inflation forecast over the next 10 years and is taken from the Survey of Professional Forecasters.

the plausibility of this view. Consider the left panel of Figure 7.4. Assume that right before the beginning of the global financial crisis the economy is at point B, where the world interest rate is equal to r^{*1} and the U.S. current account deficit is equal to CA^{US^1}. A decline in desired saving in the rest of the world shifts the current account schedule of the rest of the world up and to the right. For simplicity, assume that the current account schedule of the rest of the world goes back to its original position, given by CA^{RW}. The current account schedule of the United States does not change position. The new equilibrium is given by point A. The shift in the current account schedule of the rest of the world causes the U.S. current account to improve from CA^{US^1} to CA^{US^0} and the interest rate to rise from r^{*1} to r^{*0}. It follows that under the global saving glut hypothesis, the V-shaped U.S. current account balance observed around the global financial crisis should have been accompanied by a V-shaped pattern of the interest rate. However, Figure 7.5 shows that the interest rate does not display such a pattern. In fact, during the crisis the interest rate declined further, rejecting the global saving glut hypothesis as the dominant factor of the U.S. current account reversal.

We conclude that the global saving glut hypothesis presents a plausible explanation for the observed developments in the U.S. current account deficit over the pre-crisis period. At the same time, the behavior of the interest rate suggests that the dynamics of the U.S. current account during the crisis were not primarily driven by external factors.

So what drove the current account improvements during the crisis? Many academic and policy observers have argued that the bursting of a bubble in the U.S. housing market led to a switch in the spending pattern of U.S. households and firms away from current consumption and investment and in favor of saving. In terms of the graphical apparatus developed in this chapter, this expenditure switch shifts the current account schedule of the United States from its position just before the beginning of the global financial crisis down and to the right. In the right panel of Figure 7.4, the position of the economy before the beginning of the crisis is represented by point B. The contraction in domestic spending shifts the U.S. current account schedule down and to the right from $CA^{US'}(r)$ to $CA^{US}(r)$. The current account schedule of the rest of the world does not change position. The new equilibrium is at point A, where the U.S. current account improves and the world interest rate is even lower than it was at the beginning of the crisis. The improvement in the U.S. current account balance in the context of low and declining interest rates is in line with the observed behavior of these two variables in the aftermath of the financial crisis. This analysis suggests that domestic factors might have played a dominant role in explaining the U.S. current account dynamics during the global financial crisis.

7.7 Summing Up

Let's take stock of what we have learned in this chapter.

- We analyze the determination of the current account in a world with large open economies.

- The world interest rate responds to factors affecting saving and investment in large economies.
- A temporary output increase in a large country depresses the world interest rate.
- An expected future increase in output in a large economy drives the world interest rate up.
- The world interest rate is determined by the growth rate of global output. The larger the expected growth in global output is, the higher the world interest rate will be.
- The theoretical framework developed in this chapter suggests that the large increase in U.S. current account deficits between the mid-1990s and the onset of the global financial crisis of 2007 was predominantly driven by an increase in the global supply of saving, known as the "global saving glut."
- The theoretical framework also suggests that the sharp reduction of U.S. current account deficits in the aftermath of the global financial crisis was primarily caused by an increase in U.S. saving and a reduction in U.S. investment triggered by the bursting of the U.S. housing bubble. This explanation is known as the "made in the U.S.A." hypothesis.

7.8 Exercises

Exercise 7.1 (TFU) Indicate whether the following statements are true, false, or uncertain and explain why.

1. In a large open economy, a shock that affects only the saving schedule can give rise to a positive comovement between saving and investment.
2. The larger a country is, the larger the international effects of its domestic disturbances will be.
3. Small economies are unaffected by shocks that are internal to a large economy.
4. News about a future increase in productivity has a larger effect on investment in a small economy than in a large economy.
5. Suppose that in period 1 all small open economies in the world experience an increase in their current endowment, Q_1. This development should have no effect on the large economies of the world.
6. A large closed economy experiences an increase in its period 1 endowment. This should have no effect on the world interest rate, and therefore no effect on other countries in the world.
7. According to the "global saving glut" hypothesis, overborrowing of U.S. households during the housing boom of the late 1990s and early 2000s was a primary driver of the deterioration of the U.S. current account.

Exercise 7.2 (Positive Weather Shock in a Large Economy) Suppose that due to exceptionally good weather in the Midwest, the United States experiences an increase in grain production in period 1. Use a graphical approach to analyze the effect of this shock on the current account, saving, investment, and the world interest rate in the United States and in a small open economy such as El Salvador. Explain.

Exercise 7.3 (External Effects of a Pandemic) The health crisis caused by the coronavirus pandemic of 2020 had supply and demand effects on global economic activity. Consider a two-period economy with two countries, the United States (US) and the Rest of the World (RW). Suppose that the crisis occurs in period 1 and lasts for only one period. Suppose that the shuttering of businesses in period 1 imposed by governments around the world causes output and desired investment to fall globally. In addition, suppose that the uncertainty created by the health crisis in period 1 caused an increase in desired saving worldwide. Use a graphical analysis (one graph for the spaces (I, r), and (S, r), and one for the space (CA, r)), to analyze the effects of the COVID-19 crisis on saving, investment, the current account, and the world interest rate. Distinguish the cases of free capital mobility and of a closed economy. *Hints:* (i) some effects might be ambiguous. In these cases, you should explain what opposing effects are causing the ambiguity; (ii) in analyzing the role of uncertainty, you might want to review Chapter 6, and think about the qualitative effect of an increase in the parameter σ on the saving and current account schedules.

Exercise 7.4 (Protectionist Policy in a Large Economy) Suppose that a protectionist initiative in Congress succeeds in passing a bill closing the U.S. economy to international trade in goods and financial assets. What would be the effect of this policy change on the world interest rate and on saving and investment in the United States and in the rest of the world? Use a graphical analysis and explain.

Exercise 7.5 (A Two-Country Economy) Consider a two-period, two-country, endowment economy. Let one of the countries be the United States (U) and the other Europe (E). Households in the United States have preferences described by the utility function

$$\ln C_1^U + \ln C_2^U,$$

where C_1^U and C_2^U denote consumption of U.S. households in periods 1 and 2, respectively. Europeans have identical preferences, given by

$$\ln C_1^E + \ln C_2^E,$$

where C_1^E and C_2^E denote consumption of European households in periods 1 and 2, respectively. Let Q_1^U and Q_2^U denote the U.S. endowments of goods in periods 1 and 2, respectively. Similarly, let Q_1^E and Q_2^E denote the European endowments of goods in periods 1 and 2, respectively. Assume further that the endowments are nonstorable, that the U.S. and Europe are of equal size, and that there is free capital mobility between the two economies. The United States starts period 1 with a zero net foreign asset position.

1. **Symmetric Equilibrium** Suppose that $Q_1^U = Q_2^U = Q_1^E = Q_2^E = 10$. Calculate the equilibrium world interest rate, and the current accounts in the United States and Europe in period 1.

2. **US-Originated Contraction #1** Suppose that a contraction originates in the United States. Specifically, assume that Q_1^U drops from 10 to 8. All other

endowments (Q_2^U, Q_1^E, and Q_2^E) remain unchanged at 10. This contraction in output has two characteristics: First, it originates in the United States (the European endowments are unchanged). Second, it is temporary (the U.S. endowment is expected to return to its normal value of 10 after one period). Calculate the equilibrium interest rate and the current accounts of the United States and Europe in period 1. Provide intuition.

3. **US-Originated Contraction #2** Consider now a second type of contraction in which the U.S. endowment falls from 10 to 8 in the first period and is expected to continue to fall to 6 in the second period ($Q_1^U = 8$ and $Q_2^U = 6$). The endowments in Europe remain unchanged at 10 each period ($Q_1^E = Q_2^E = 10$). Like the one described in the previous item, this contraction originates in the United States. However, it differs from the one described in the previous item in that it is more protracted. Calculate again the equilibrium interest rate and the two current accounts in period 1. Point out differences in the effects of the two types of contraction and provide intuition.

4. At the beginning of the Great Recession of 2008, interest rates fell sharply around the world. What does the model above say about people's expectations around 2008 regarding the future path of real activity?

Exercise 7.6 (Worldwide Recession) Consider the same economy as described in Exercise 7.5. First solve question 1 of Exercise 7.5. Then answer the following questions:

1. **Worldwide Contraction #1** Consider a global contraction. Specifically, assume that Q_1^U and Q_1^E fall from 10 to 8 and that Q_2^U and Q_2^E are unchanged. Calculate the equilibrium world interest rate.

2. **Worldwide Contraction #2** Consider next a persistent global contraction. Specifically, assume that Q_1^U and Q_1^E fall from 10 to 8 and that Q_2^U and Q_2^E also fall from 10 to 8. Calculate the equilibrium world interest rate.

3. **Worldwide Contraction #3** Finally, consider a global contraction that is expected to get worse over time. Specifically, assume that Q_1^U and Q_1^E fall from 10 to 8 and that Q_2^U and Q_2^E fall from 10 to 6. Calculate the equilibrium world interest rate.

4. Suppose you are a member of a team of economic analysts at an investment bank and observe that both Europe and the United States fall into recession. You would like to know what market participants are expecting about future output. In particular, a third of your team believes that the worldwide output decline is temporary, a third believes that this is the new normal (that is, output will not recover to its original level), and the rest of the team believes that the current recession is just the beginning of a deeper recession to come. How can you use data available in period 1 to tell which view is right?

Exercise 7.7 (Global Uncertainty) Suppose that, for a host of reasons, part of the world suddenly becomes more uncertain (think of wars, political instability, economic crises, or a locally confined pandemic). Refer to this group of more uncertain countries as UC. Assume that the increase in uncertainty is manifested in a higher standard deviation of future output. Refer to the rest of the world as RW. Analyze the effect of this increase in uncertainty on the world interest rate and on consumption, saving, and the current account in the UC and the RW. You might want to accompany your explanation with one or more graphs.

Exercise 7.8 (Effects of World Shocks on Small Economies) Consider a small open economy, say Ecuador. Suppose that the United States experiences an investment surge. Analyze the effects of this development on the Ecuadorian economy. In particular, discuss the effects on the current account, saving, investment, and the domestic interest rate. Consider the following alternative scenarios:

1. All countries in the world are open.
2. Ecuador is a closed economy.
3. The United States is a closed economy.
4. All countries in the world other than the United States and Ecuador are closed economies.

Exercise 7.9 (Determinants of the World Interest Rate) Consider a two-period, two-country, endowment economy. Let one of the countries be the United States (U) and the other the rest of the world (R). Households in the United States have preferences described by the utility function

$$\ln C_1^U + \beta \ln C_2^U,$$

where C_1^U and C_2^U denote consumption of U.S. households in periods 1 and 2, and $\beta \in (0, 1)$ denotes the subjective discount factor. Households in the rest of the world have identical preferences, given by

$$\ln C_1^R + \beta \ln C_2^R,$$

where C_1^R and C_2^R denote consumption of households in the rest of the world in periods 1 and 2. Let Q_1^U and Q_2^U denote the U.S. endowments of goods in periods 1 and 2. Similarly, let Q_1^R and Q_2^R denote the endowments in the rest of the world in periods 1 and 2. Assume further that the endowments are perishable, that the United States and the rest of the world are of equal size, and that there is free capital mobility. The United States starts period 1 with a zero net foreign asset position.

1. Write down and solve the household's optimization problem in the United States, given the interest rate in the United States, denoted r_1^U. Specifically, find expressions for C_1^U, C_2^U, and B_1^U in terms of preference parameters and variables the household takes as given.
2. Write down and solve the household's optimization problem in the rest of the world, given the interest rate in the rest of the world, denoted r_1^R.
3. Derive the equilibrium levels of the trade balance, the current account, and external debt in periods 1 and 2 in country U given the world interest rate, r^*.
4. Derive the equilibrium levels of the trade balance, the current account, and external debt in periods 1 and 2 in country R given r^*.

5. Write down the world resource constraints in periods 1 and 2.

6. Derive the equilibrium level of the world interest rate, r^*. Under what conditions will it satisfy the condition $\beta(1+r)=1$? Provide intuition.

7. Suppose now that output in period 1 increases in both countries from Q_1^i to $(1+x)Q_1^i$ for $i=U,R$ and $x>0$. Derive the effect of this shock on the world interest rate and on the U.S. current account in period 1. Does the global output shock exacerbate global imbalances?

CHAPTER 8

The Twin Deficits: Fiscal Deficits and the Current Account

An important question in macroeconomics is whether fiscal deficits cause current account deficits. The view that fiscal deficits lead to current account deficits is known as the *twin deficit* hypothesis. Consider, for example, a stimulus plan consisting in a tax cut or, equivalently, an increase in government transfers to the public. All else equal, this policy generates an increase in the fiscal deficit. But how does it affect other macroeconomic variables such as private consumption and saving, the trade balance, and the current account?

There are two opposing views. One view maintains that, by putting money in people's pockets, the tax cut increases household income and stimulates consumption spending. In turn, the increase in domestic spending causes a deterioration in the trade balance and the current account. The opposing view maintains that the tax cut has no effect on private consumption or the current account. According to this view, a tax cut is a harbinger of future tax increases: the tax cut generates a fiscal deficit, which must be financed with public debt. In the future the government must repay the public debt including interest, which will require an increase in taxes. Thus under this view, instead of spending the tax cut on consumption goods, households save it to be able to pay the anticipated increase in future taxes. Because consumption spending is unchanged by the tax cut, so are the trade balance and the current account. Thus, this view rejects the twin deficit hypothesis. This fiscal neutrality result is known as *Ricardian equivalence*.

This chapter analyzes conditions under which each of the two views are valid. In addition, it studies whether similar opposing views arise when the fiscal deficit is a consequence of changes in government consumption as opposed to tax cuts or increases in government transfers.

8.1 An Open Economy with a Government Sector

Consider a two-period economy like the one studied in Chapter 5, but now assume the existence of a government that consumes goods (government spending), levies taxes, and issues debt. Let's begin by describing the government sector.

8.1.1 THE GOVERNMENT

Assume that in periods 1 and 2 the government purchases goods and services, denoted G_1 and G_2. These outlays are called government spending. They include goods and services necessary to run the government: goods used in government offices (e.g., paper, computers), defense spending (e.g., weapons, military equipment), public investment (e.g., school buildings, hospitals, roads), and public employment (e.g., public servants, public school teachers, police). We assume that the path of government spending (G_1, G_2) is exogenously given.

Assume that the government levies lump-sum taxes in periods 1 and 2, denoted T_1 and T_2. The term *lump-sum taxes* refers to taxes that do not depend on any economic characteristic of the taxpayer, such as income, spending, or wealth. Lump-sum taxes represent a convenient analytical tool for two reasons. First, because they do not depend on any economic decision taken by private agents, they do not distort economic incentives, which simplifies the characterization of the equilibrium dynamics. Second, lump-sum taxes represent a convenient way to isolate the effects of government spending, because any change in taxes necessary to finance a certain change in government spending does not add real effects, which could in principle be difficult to disentangle. On the down side, lump-sum taxes are rarely seen in real life. Governments do not tell taxpayers "you have to pay x regardless of whether you are a rich or a poor person, a high or low income earner, or a person who spends a lot or little in the supermarket." For this reason, in Section 8.4.3 we study a more realistic environment in which taxes do depend on some economic manifestation. These types of taxes are known as *distortionary taxes*. For the time being, however, we stick to lump-sum taxes.

Assume that the government enters period 1 with financial assets in the amount of B_0^g. If B_0^g is negative, we say that there is *public debt* outstanding at the beginning of period 1 in the amount $-B_0^g$.

The *government budget constraint* in period 1 is given by

$$G_1 + B_1^g - B_0^g = T_1 + r_0 B_0^g, \tag{8.1}$$

where B_1^g denotes the amount of government asset holdings at the end of period 1. If B_1^g is negative, then there is public debt outstanding at the end of period 1. The left-hand side of the government budget constraint represents the government's outlays in period 1, which consist of government purchases of goods, G_1, and purchases of financial assets, $B_1^g - B_0^g$. The right-hand side represents the government's sources of funds in period 1—namely, tax revenues, T_1, and interest income on asset holdings, $r_0 B_0^g$, where r_0 is the interest rate on bonds maturing in period 1.

Similarly, the government budget constraint in period 2 is given by

$$G_2 + B_2^g - B_1^g = T_2 + r_1 B_1^g. \tag{8.2}$$

The government is assumed to be subject to a no-Ponzi-game constraint that prevents it from having debt outstanding at the end of period 2. This means that B_2^g must be greater or equal to zero. At the same time, a benevolent government—that is, a government that cares about the welfare of its citizens—would not find it in its interest to end period 2 with positive asset holdings. This is because the government will not be around in period 3 to spend the accumulated assets in ways that would benefit its constituents. This means that the government will always choose B_2^g to be less than or equal to zero. Taken together, these two arguments imply that

$$B_2^g = 0. \tag{8.3}$$

Combining equations (8.1)–(8.3) to eliminate B_1^g and B_2^g, we obtain the *intertemporal government budget constraint*,

$$G_1 + \frac{G_2}{1+r_1} = (1+r_0)B_0^g + T_1 + \frac{T_2}{1+r_1}. \tag{8.4}$$

This constraint says that the present discounted value of government consumption (the left-hand side) must be equal to initial asset holdings including interest plus the present discounted value of tax revenue (the right-hand side). The intertemporal budget constraint of the government implies that there exist many (in fact a continuum of) tax policies T_1 and T_2 that can finance a given path of government consumption, G_1 and G_2. However, all other things equal, given taxes in one period, the government intertemporal budget constraint uniquely pins down taxes in the other period. In particular, a tax cut in period 1 must be offset by a tax increase in period 2. By the same token, an expected tax cut in period 2 must be accompanied by a tax increase in period 1.

As we mentioned earlier, the path of government spending, (G_1, G_2), is exogenously given. Thus, the only choice of the government is a path of taxes, (T_1, T_2), that satisfies its intertemporal budget constraint, equation (8.4). The government can pick even taxes over time, or lower taxes in period 1 and higher taxes in period 2, or vice versa.

8.1.2 FIRMS

As in Chapter 5, firms borrow in period 1 to invest in capital goods that become productive in period 2. Let I_1 denote investment in period 1. Production takes place in period 2. The production function is of the form

$$Q_2 = A_2 F(I_1),$$

where Q_2 denotes output in period 2, A_2 is an exogenous productivity factor, and $F(\cdot)$ is an increasing and concave production function. In period 2, the firm must repay the loan with interest. Profits are then given by

$$\Pi_2 = A_2 F(I_1) - (1+r_1)I_1.$$

The firm chooses the level of investment, I_1, to maximize profits. The associated first-order optimality condition is

$$A_2 F'(I_1) = 1 + r_1,$$

which equates the marginal product of capital to the marginal cost of capital. Because the production function is concave, the above optimality condition implies a negative relationship between the interest rate r_1 and the optimal level of investment, I_1, which we write as

$$I_1 = I(r_1). \tag{8.5}$$

Note that given r_1, investment is independent of taxes or government spending. Using (8.5), profits can also be expressed as a function of the interest rate, $A_2 F(I(r_1)) - (1 + r_1)I(r_1)$. Further, in Chapter 5 we established that an increase in the interest rate reduces the profitability of firms, so we can write,

$$\Pi_2 = \Pi(r_1). \tag{8.6}$$

Firms are assumed to be owned by households to whom they distribute profits in period 2. We introduce the household sector next.

8.1.3 HOUSEHOLDS

Households are assumed to have preferences over consumption in periods 1 and 2, denoted C_1 and C_2. Their lifetime utility function is of the form

$$\ln C_1 + \ln C_2. \tag{8.7}$$

In period 1, the household receives an exogenous endowment of goods denoted Q_1, and in period 2 it receives profits from firms, denoted $\Pi(r_1)$. In addition, in period $t = 1, 2$, the household can borrow or lend by means of a bond, denoted B_t^h, that pays the interest rate r_t in period $t + 1$. The superscript h distinguishes bond holdings of the household from those held by the government. Each period, the household uses its income to buy consumption goods, buy bonds, and pay taxes. Its budget constraints in periods 1 and 2 are then given by

$$C_1 + B_1^h - B_0^h = r_0 B_0^h + Q_1 - T_1, \tag{8.8}$$

and

$$C_2 + B_2^h - B_1^h = r_1 B_1^h + \Pi(r_1) - T_2. \tag{8.9}$$

Income net of taxes, namely, $Q_1 - T_1$ in period 1 and $\Pi(r_1) - T_2$ in period 2, is called *disposable income*. The household is subject to the no-Ponzi-game condition $B_2^h \geq 0$, which prevents households from leaving debt outstanding at the end of period 2. Optimizing households will not leave any assets at the end of period 2, $B_2^h \leq 0$. Thus, the no-Ponzi-game constraint and household optimization imply the transversality condition

$$B_2^h = 0. \tag{8.10}$$

Combining equations (8.8)–(8.10) to eliminate B_1^h and B_2^h yields the household's intertemporal budget constraint

$$C_1 + \frac{C_2}{1 + r_1} = (1 + r_0)B_0^h + Q_1 - T_1 + \frac{\Pi(r_1) - T_2}{1 + r_1}. \tag{8.11}$$

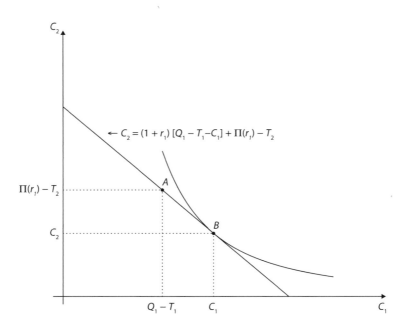

Figure 8.1. Optimal Consumption Choice
Notes: The figure depicts the determination of the optimal path of consumption. The intertemporal budget constraint is a downward-sloping straight line with slope $-(1+r_1)$. It is drawn under the assumption that the household's initial asset position is nil, $B_0^h = 0$. The path of disposable income is point A. The optimal consumption path is given by point B, where the intertemporal budget constraint is tangent to an indifference curve.

This expression says that the present discounted value of lifetime consumption, the left-hand side, must equal the sum of initial wealth and the present discounted value of disposable income, the right-hand side.

Solving (8.11) for C_2 we can rewrite the household's intertemporal budget constraint as

$$C_2 = (1+r_1)\left[(1+r_0)B_0^h + Q_1 - T_1 - C_1\right] + \Pi(r_1) - T_2, \qquad (8.12)$$

which says that if the household increases consumption in period 1 by 1 unit, it must sacrifice $1+r_1$ units of consumption in period 2. Figure 8.1 displays this relationship. For simplicity, the figure is drawn under the assumption that the initial asset position of the household is zero, $B_0^h = 0$. The intertemporal budget constraint is a downward-sloping straight line with slope $-(1+r_1)$. Any point on this line is feasible. Point A represents the path of disposable income, $(Q_1 - T_1, \Pi(r_1) - T_2)$.

The household picks a point on the intertemporal budget constraint to maximize its lifetime utility, given in expression (8.7), taking as given the path of disposable income, $Q_t - T_t$, for $t = 1, 2$, its initial wealth, $(1+r_0)B_0^h$, and the interest rate, r_1. The optimal consumption path is determined by a point on the intertemporal budget constraint that is tangent to an indifference curve. In Figure 8.1 this occurs at point B. As the figure is drawn, the household borrows in period 1, $C_1 > Q_1 - T_1$.

To find the optimal consumption path, use the intertemporal budget constraint (8.12) to eliminate C_2 from the utility function (8.7). This operation gives

$$\ln C_1 + \ln\left[(1+r_1)(\bar{Y}-C_1)\right], \tag{8.13}$$

where

$$\bar{Y} = (1+r_0)B_0^h + Q_1 - T_1 + \frac{\Pi(r_1)-T_2}{1+r_1}$$

denotes the household's lifetime wealth.

The household chooses C_1 to maximize (8.13), taking as given $\bar{Y}$ and r_1. The optimality condition associated with this problem results from taking the derivative of (8.13) with respect to C_1 and equating it to 0. After rearranging, this operation yields $C_1 = \frac{1}{2}\bar{Y}$, or

$$C_1 = \frac{1}{2}\left[(1+r_0)B_0^h + Q_1 - T_1 + \frac{\Pi(r_1)-T_2}{1+r_1}\right]. \tag{8.14}$$

Intuitively, the household consumes half of its lifetime wealth in period 1 and leaves the rest for future consumption. Importantly, consumption is independent of the timing of taxes. It only depends on the size of the present discounted value of tax obligations, $T_1 + T_2/(1+r_1)$. For example, if the government cuts taxes in period 1 and increases taxes in period 2 in such a way as to keep the present discounted value of tax payments constant, the household feels that its lifetime wealth is unchanged. As a result, it will save the tax cut in period 1 to pay for the tax increase in period 2, which allows it to maintain the same optimal path of consumption.

Now using (8.14) to eliminate C_1 from (8.12) gives the optimal value of consumption in period 2,

$$C_2 = \frac{1+r_1}{2}\left[(1+r_0)B_0^h + Q_1 - T_1 + \frac{\Pi(r_1)-T_2}{1+r_1}\right], \tag{8.15}$$

which says that, like consumption in period 1, consumption in period 2 depends on the present discounted value of taxes, $T_1 + T_2/(1+r_1)$.

8.2 Ricardian Equivalence

Assume that the economy is small and that there is free capital mobility. Then the domestic interest rate equals the world interest rate, r^*; that is,

$$r_1 = r^*. \tag{8.16}$$

The country's net foreign asset position at the beginning of period 1, denoted B_0, is given by the sum of private and public asset holdings; that is,

$$B_0 = B_0^h + B_0^g. \tag{8.17}$$

Combining (8.4), (8.14), (8.16), and (8.17) yields the equilibrium level of consumption in period 1,

$$C_1 = \frac{1}{2}\left[(1+r_0)B_0 + Q_1 - G_1 + \frac{\Pi(r^*) - G_2}{1 + r^*}\right]. \tag{8.18}$$

A similar operation using (8.15) delivers the equilibrium level of consumption in period 2,

$$C_2 = \frac{1+r^*}{2}\left[(1+r_0)B_0 + Q_1 - G_1 + \frac{\Pi(r^*) - G_2}{1 + r^*}\right]. \tag{8.19}$$

The trade balance in period 1, denoted TB_1, is given by

$$TB_1 = Q_1 - C_1 - G_1 - I_1.$$

Using (8.5) and (8.18) to eliminate I_1 and C_1, we have that in equilibrium

$$TB_1 = \frac{1}{2}\left[-(1+r_0)B_0 + Q_1 - G_1 - \frac{\Pi(r^*) - G_2}{1 + r^*}\right] - I(r^*). \tag{8.20}$$

The current account equals the trade balance plus net investment income, $CA_1 = TB_1 + r_0 B_0$, so we have that

$$CA_1 = \frac{1}{2}\left[-(1-r_0)B_0 + Q_1 - G_1 - \frac{\Pi(r^*) - G_2}{1 + r^*}\right] - I(r^*). \tag{8.21}$$

Note that neither T_1 nor T_2 appears in equations (8.18)–(8.21). This means that given G_1 and G_2, any combination of taxes T_1 and T_2 satisfying the government's intertemporal budget constraint (8.4) is associated with the same equilibrium levels of private consumption, the trade balance, and the current account. This result is known as Ricardian equivalence. The intuition behind this result is as follows: Suppose the government cuts taxes in period 1, and leaves government spending unchanged in both periods. Since government spending is unchanged, the tax cut must be financed with public debt. With period 2 government spending also unchanged, repaying the higher public debt and the corresponding interest requires increasing taxes in period 2. In period 1, households anticipate that the tax cut will require higher taxes in period 2. Consequently, instead of spending part of the tax cut on consumption goods, households keep consumption unchanged and save all of the tax cut.

This intuition for why Ricardian equivalence holds in this economy is based on the idea that a tax cut (i.e., a reduction in government saving) is exactly offset by an increase in private saving. Let's show this effect more formally.

Government saving, denoted S_1^g, also known as the *secondary fiscal surplus*, is defined as the difference between revenues (taxes plus interest on asset holdings) and government purchases. Formally,

$$S_1^g = r_0 B_0^g + T_1 - G_1.$$

When the secondary fiscal surplus is negative, we say that the government is running a *secondary fiscal deficit* or simply a *fiscal deficit*. The secondary fiscal surplus has two components: interest income on government asset holdings ($r_0 B_0^g$) and the *primary fiscal surplus* ($T_1 - G_1$). The primary fiscal surplus measures the difference between tax revenues and government expenditures. When the primary fiscal surplus is negative—that is, when government expenditures exceed tax revenues—we say that the government is running a *primary deficit.*

Given an exogenous path for government purchases and given the initial condition $r_0 B_0^g$, any change in taxes in period 1 must be reflected one-for-one by a change in government saving; that is,

$$\Delta S_1^g = \Delta T_1. \qquad (8.22)$$

Private saving in period 1, which we denote by S_1^p, is defined as the difference between *disposable income*, given by domestic output plus interest on net bond holdings by the private sector minus taxes, and private consumption:

$$S_1^p = Q_1 + r_0 B_0^h - T_1 - C_1.$$

Because, as we have just shown, for a given time path of government purchases, private consumption is unaffected by changes in the timing of taxes (see equation (8.18)) and because $r_0 B_0^h$ is predetermined in period 1, it follows that changes in lump-sum taxes in period 1 induce changes in private saving of equal size but opposite sign:

$$\Delta S_1^p = -\Delta T_1. \qquad (8.23)$$

National saving in period 1, denoted S_1, is the sum of government and private saving in period 1; that is,

$$S_1 = S_1^g + S_1^p.$$

Changes in national saving are thus equal to the sum of changes in government saving and changes in private saving,

$$\Delta S_1 = \Delta S_1^g + \Delta S_1^p.$$

Combining this expression with equations (8.22) and (8.23), we have that

$$\Delta S_1 = \Delta T_1 - \Delta T_1 = 0.$$

This expression confirms the intuition we gave for why Ricardian equivalence holds in this economy; namely, that given the path of government spending, a change in taxes causes changes in government and private saving that exactly offset each other, leaving national saving unchanged.

An implication of Ricardian equivalence is that the twin deficit hypothesis, whereby an increase in the fiscal deficit causes an increase in the current account deficit, does not hold when fiscal deficits are caused by changes in the timing of taxes. For example, a tax cut in period 1 causes an increase in the fiscal deficit in period 1, but no change in the current account balance in period 1. Does the model predict twin deficits when fiscal deficits are caused by changes in government spending as opposed to changes in taxes? We address this question next.

8.3 Government Spending and Twin Deficits

A change in government spending has the same effect as a change in the endowment but in the opposite direction. Thus, for example, the effect on consumption, the trade balance, and the current account of an increase in government spending in period 1 is the same as the effect of a fall in the endowment in period 1. To see this, take another look at equilibrium conditions (8.18)–(8.21). Notice that G_1 always appears subtracting from Q_1; that is, it always appears in the form $Q_1 - G_1$. It follows that all we have learned about the effects of endowment shocks (Chapter 3) is applicable to understanding the effects of government spending shocks. In particular, a temporary increase in government spending reduces private consumption but by less than the change in government spending itself. Formally, from equation (8.18) we have that

$$\Delta C_1 = -\frac{1}{2}\Delta G_1.$$

Intuitively, the increase in government spending makes households poorer. The reason is that households know that the increase in G_1 must be financed by raising taxes either now or in the future or both, thereby elevating the present discounted value of taxes and reducing the present discounted value of disposable income. Consequently, households cut consumption in both periods. So consumption in period 1 falls. But because the fall in private spending is spread over time, consumption in period 1 falls by less than the increase in government spending.

At the same time, because the world interest rate is unaffected, the change in government spending has no effect on investment,

$$\Delta I_1 = 0.$$

The partial crowding out of private consumption and the absence of an effect on investment imply that the overall effect on domestic absorption following an increase in government spending is positive. Since output in period 1 is fixed at Q_1, the expansion in aggregate demand causes the trade balance and the current account to deteriorate. Formally, from equilibrium conditions (8.20) and (8.21) we have that

$$\Delta TB_1 = \Delta CA_1 = -\frac{1}{2}\Delta G_1.$$

If the increase in government spending is not fully financed by an increase in current taxes, the fiscal deficit in period 1 increases. In this case, the expansion in government spending causes an increase in both the fiscal and the current account deficits. In other words, government spending shocks that are not fully financed with current taxes cause twin deficits. The twins, however, need not have the same size. For example, if current taxes remain unchanged, $\Delta T_1 = 0$, so that the entire government spending shock is financed with future taxes, the deterioration in the current account is only half the size of the increase in the fiscal deficit.

Consider now a future expected change in government spending. This type of shock is akin to a future expected change in income but of the opposite sign. Again, this is evident from the fact that in equilibrium conditions (8.18)–(8.21), G_2 always appears subtracting from profit income; that is, it always appears in the expression $\Pi(r^*) - G_2$. Thus, an expected increase in government spending in period 2 is equivalent to an expected fall in income in that period. It follows that an increase in G_2 causes a fall in consumption in period 1. From equation (8.18), the size of this effect is

$$\Delta C_1 = -\frac{1}{2(1+r^*)}\Delta G_2.$$

The intuition behind this result is that, understanding that the future increase in government spending will cause an increase in the present discounted value of taxes, households feel poorer and consequently cut consumption spending. The fall in consumption is smaller than the increase in government spending because households smooth the adjustment over time. Since the endowment Q_1 and investment $I(r^*)$ are unchanged, it follows that the increase in G_2 leads to an improvement in the trade balance and the current account in period 1. Formally, from equations (8.20) and (8.21) we have that

$$\Delta TB_1 = \Delta CA_1 = \frac{1}{2(1+r^*)}\Delta G_2.$$

Consider now a permanent increase in government spending, say $\Delta G_1 = \Delta G_2 = \Delta G$, where ΔG is a positive number. In response to this innovation, the current account does not change much. The intuition is similar to that behind a permanent fall in the endowment. The permanent increase in government spending lowers the household's income in both periods, so there is no reason to borrow in period 1 to smooth consumption, since the household will become equally more poor in period 2. Consequently, the household adjusts consumption down in both periods by about ΔG. As a result, aggregate demand does not change much, and neither does the current account. Formally, differentiating equation (8.21), we have that the change in the current account in response to a change in G_1 and G_2 equal to ΔG is

$$\Delta CA_1 = -\frac{r^*}{2(1+r^*)}\Delta G,$$

which is a small number if r^* is small. It follows that permanent increases in government spending do not lead to twin deficits.

Summarizing, the present model can capture the twin deficit hypothesis when changes in the fiscal deficit are caused by temporary changes in government spending, but not when they are caused by permanent or future expected changes in government spending. In the next section, we revisit the question of whether fiscal deficits originating in tax cuts can generate twin deficits.

8.4 Failure of Ricardian Equivalence: Tax Cuts and Twin Deficits

The conclusion that twin deficits are impossible in response to tax changes is a consequence of Ricardian equivalence. The conditions under which Ricardian equivalence obtains, however, are special. In particular, the model studied thus far assumes that households face no borrowing constraints, that all households benefiting from a current tax cut expect to be around when taxes are increased in the future, and that all taxes are lump sum. In what follows, we relax each of these assumptions in turn. The main takeaway of this section is that Ricardian equivalence is a fragile result. Relaxing any of the three aforementioned assumptions gives rise to the emergence of twin deficits in response to changes in taxes.

8.4.1 BORROWING CONSTRAINTS

To see why borrowing constraints may lead to a breakdown in Ricardian equivalence, consider as an example a young worker who expects her future income to be significantly higher than her current income, due to on-the-job training or the fact that she is simultaneously attending college. Based on this expectation, she might want to smooth consumption over time by borrowing against her higher future income. However, suppose that because of imperfections in financial markets, such as asymmetric information between borrowers and lenders, she cannot procure a loan. In this case, the young worker is said to be *borrowing constrained*. Suppose now that the government decides to implement a cut in current (lump-sum) taxes, financed by an increase in future taxes. Will the young worker increase saving by the same amount as the tax cut as prescribed by Ricardian equivalence? Most likely not. She will view the tax cut as a welcome relief from her borrowing constraint and allocate the tax cut to consumption. In this case, the decline in government saving causes no change in private saving. As a result, national saving falls. If investment is unaffected by the change in lump-sum taxes, the fall in national saving will be associated with a deterioration in the current account. Twin deficits would thereby emerge. Let's analyze this story more formally.

Suppose households are subject to the following borrowing constraint

$$B_1^h \geq 0, \tag{8.24}$$

which says that they cannot receive any credit in period 1. Borrowing constraints are also called *liquidity constraints*, and we use both terms interchangeably. Figure 8.2 illustrates this case. (For simplicity, it assumes that initial wealth of the household is equal to zero, $B_0^h = 0$.) The downward-sloping solid line is the household's intertemporal budget constraint. Disposable income, $Q_1 - T_1$, is at point A. Suppose that in the absence of borrowing constraints, the consumption allocation is given by point B, where the intertemporal budget constraint is tangent to an indifference curve. At point B, the household in period 1 consumes more than its after-tax income; that is, $C_1 > Q_1 - T_1$. This excess of consumption over disposable income must be financed by borrowing in period 1 ($B_1^h < 0$). In the presence of the borrowing constraint (8.24), point B is no longer feasible. This means that the borrowing constraint is binding, and that the household is forced to choose the consumption allocation given by point A, where

$$C_1 = Q_1 - T_1.$$

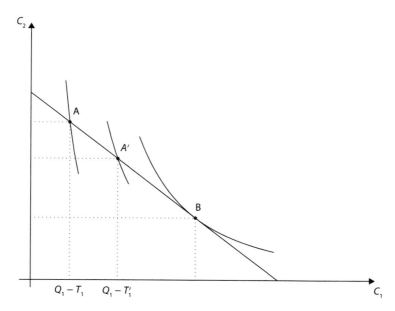

Figure 8.2. Adjustment to a Temporary Tax Cut When Households Are Borrowing Constrained

Notes: The downward-sloping line is the household's intertemporal budget constraint. Initial wealth of the household is assumed to be zero, $B_0^h = 0$. Disposable income is at point A. In the absence of borrowing constraints, the household chooses a consumption allocation given by point B, where an indifference curve is tangent to the intertemporal budget constraint. In the presence of borrowing constraints, only allocations on the intertemporal budget constraint and northwest of point A are feasible. The borrowing constraint forces the household to consume its disposable income, point A. A tax cut equal to $T_1 - T_1'$ increases disposable income to point A'. Since the household is still borrowing constrained, consumption increases by the same amount as the tax cut, and the new allocation is at point A'.

Under these circumstances, a tax cut in period 1 $\Delta T_1 = T_1' - T_1$, with $T_1' < T_1$, produces an increase in consumption in period 1, as it relaxes the household's borrowing constraint. If the household continues to be borrowing constrained after the tax cut, the increase in consumption in period 1 is given by the size of the tax cut itself,

$$\Delta C_1 = -\Delta T_1.$$

In Figure 8.2, the new consumption allocation is given by point A'. The household understands that taxes will be higher in period 2, and that this will negatively affect consumption in that period. But this is precisely what the household would have liked to do in the absence of a borrowing constraint; that is, consume less in period 2 and more in period 1. We have therefore shown that in the presence of borrowing constraints Ricardian equivalence fails.

Assume that neither firms nor the government are liquidity constrained, so that they can borrow at the world interest rate r^*. Then, investment and government purchases are unaffected by the tax cut. Therefore, since output in period 1 is given by an exogenous endowment, the trade balance and the current account deteriorate by the same amount as the increase in consumption,

$$\Delta TB_1 = \Delta CA_1 = \Delta T_1 < 0.$$

Since government spending is assumed to be unchanged, the tax cut causes a reduction in public saving (or an increase in the fiscal deficit) in period 1,

$$\Delta S_1^g = \Delta T_1 < 0.$$

It follows that in the presence of borrowing constraints, tax cuts generate twin deficits.

8.4.2 INTERGENERATIONAL EFFECTS

A second reason why Ricardian equivalence could fail is that those who benefit from a tax cut are not the ones that pay for the tax increase later.

Consider the following example. Suppose the government cuts taxes today and finances the resulting deficit with bonds that mature 30 years later. What should be the reaction of someone who does not expect to be alive 30 years from now when the taxes to repay the debt will be levied? For this group of people, the tax cut is a windfall that elevates their wealth. As a result, they are likely to spend the money received from the tax cut instead of saving it.

To illustrate this idea formally, consider an endowment economy in which households live for only one period. Then, the budget constraint of the generation alive in period 1 is given by $C_1 + T_1 = Q_1$, and similarly, the budget constraint of the generation alive in period 2 is $C_2 + T_2 = Q_2$. Suppose that the government implements a tax cut in period 1 that is financed with a tax increase in period 2. Clearly, $\Delta C_1 = -\Delta T_1$ and $\Delta C_2 = -\Delta T_2$. Thus, the tax cut produces an increase in consumption in period 1 and a decrease in consumption in period 2. As a result, the trade balance and the current account in period 1 decline one-for-one with the decline in taxes. The intuition for this result is that in response to a decline in taxes in period 1, the generation alive in period 1 does not increase saving in anticipation of the tax increase in period 2 because it will not be around when the tax increase is implemented.

8.4.3 DISTORTIONARY TAXATION

Finally, Ricardian equivalence may also break down if taxes are not lump sum. Lump-sum taxes are those that do not depend on agents' decisions. In the economy described in Section 8.1, households are taxed T_1 in period 1 and T_2 in period 2 regardless of their consumption, income, or saving. Thus, in that economy taxes do not distort any of the decisions of the households. In reality, however, taxes are rarely lump sum. Rather, they are typically specified as a fraction of consumption, income, or firms' profits. Thus, changes in tax rates will tend to distort consumption, saving, and investment decisions. These types of taxes are called distortionary taxes.

To see why Ricardian equivalence may fail in the presence of distortionary taxes, suppose, for example, that the government levies a proportional tax on consumption, with a tax rate equal to τ_1 in period 1 and τ_2 in period 2. Then the after-tax cost of consumption is $(1 + \tau_1)C_1$ in period 1 and $(1 + \tau_2)C_2$ in period 2.

If the government lowers τ_1 and finances the tax cut with an increase in future taxes—that is, with an increase in τ_2—current consumption becomes cheaper relative to future consumption. This change will induce households to consume more in period 1 and less in period 2. Thus, unlike changes in lump-sum taxes, changes in distortionary taxes can have real effects.

Let's derive this result more formally by replacing lump-sum taxes with consumption taxes in the model of Section 8.1. With consumption taxes, the budget constraints of the household in periods 1 and 2 become

$$(1 + \tau_1)C_1 + B_1^h - B_0^h = r_0 B_0^h + Q_1, \tag{8.25}$$

and

$$(1 + \tau_2)C_2 + B_2^h - B_1^h = r_1 B_1^h + \Pi(r_1). \tag{8.26}$$

Combining these two budget constraints and the transversality condition (8.10) to eliminate B_1^h and B_2^h yields the following intertemporal budget constraint

$$(1 + \tau_1)C_1 + \frac{(1 + \tau_2)C_2}{1 + r_1} = (1 + r_0)B_0^h + Q_1 + \frac{\Pi(r_1)}{1 + r_1}. \tag{8.27}$$

The household chooses C_1 and C_2 to maximize the lifetime utility function (8.7) subject to the intertemporal budget constraint (8.26), taking as given τ_1, τ_2, Q_1, $(1 + r_0)B_0^h$, and r_1. To obtain the optimal consumption path we proceed as we did in the economy with lump-sum taxes. Solve the intertemporal budget constraint (8.27) for C_2 and use the resulting expression to eliminate C_2 from the lifetime utility function (8.7). The problem of the household then reduces to choosing C_1 to maximize

$$\ln C_1 + \ln \left[\frac{1 + r_1}{1 + \tau_2} \left(\bar{Y} - (1 + \tau_1)C_1 \right) \right],$$

where $\bar{Y} \equiv (1 + r_0)B_0^h + Q_1 + \frac{\Pi(r_1)}{1 + r_1}$. Taking the derivative with respect to C_1 and equating it to zero yields the following Euler equation

$$\frac{C_2}{C_1} = \frac{1 + \tau_1}{1 + \tau_2}(1 + r_1). \tag{8.28}$$

This expression is intuitive. It says that if the government cuts taxes in period 1 and increases taxes in period 2, households will consume relatively more in period 1 and relatively less in period 2. The consumption tax distorts the intertemporal relative price of consumption. The household perceives that one unit of consumption in period 1 costs $\frac{1 + \tau_1}{1 + \tau_2}(1 + r_1)$ units of consumption in period 2, whereas the true relative price is $1 + r_1$. If $\tau_1 > \tau_2$, the intertemporal price of period 1 consumption perceived by the household is greater than the true one, and if $\tau_1 < \tau_2$, it is lower. Only if the government sets $\tau_1 = \tau_2$, does this intertemporal distortion disappear.

The problem of the firm is the same as in the economy with lump-sum taxes because the consumption tax applies only to households. As a result, the investment and profit schedules continue to be given by (8.5) and (8.6) and therefore are independent of the tax rates τ_1 and τ_2. Under free capital mobility, the domestic interest rate equals the world interest rate, $r_1 = r^*$. Now, solve the Euler equation (8.28) for C_2 and use the resulting expression to eliminate C_2 from the household's intertemporal budget constraint (8.27). After replacing r_1 with r^* this operation yields the equilibrium level of consumption in period 1,

$$C_1 = \frac{1}{2(1+\tau_1)}\left[(1+r_0)B_0^h + Q_1 + \frac{\Pi(r^*)}{1+r^*}\right]. \tag{8.29}$$

According to this expression, in equilibrium period 1 consumption is decreasing in τ_1. Intuitively, an increase in τ_1 makes period 1 consumption more expensive, inducing households to cut demand.[1] This result represents a departure from Ricardian equivalence: Given the path of government spending, changes in the timing of distortionary taxes have an effect on the equilibrium level of consumption.

The trade balance in period 1 is $TB_1 = Q_1 - G_1 - I_1 - C_1$. It follows that a tax cut in period 1, holding constant G_1, deteriorates the trade balance through the increase in consumption (recall that investment depends only on the interest rate which in equilibrium is r^*). The current account in period 1, $CA_1 = r_0 B_0 + TB_1$, also deteriorates and by the same magnitude as the trade balance,

$$\Delta CA_1 = \Delta TB_1 = -\Delta C_1 < 0.$$

We have thus established that when taxes are distortionary, a cut in period 1 taxes leads to an increase in the current account deficit.

To establish whether a tax cut causes twin deficits, it remains to show that a tax cut, holding government expenditures constant, leads to a fiscal deficit. Tax revenue in period 1 is given by $\tau_1 C_1$. Government saving in period 1 is then equal to

$$S_1^g = r_0 B_0^g + \tau_1 C_1 - G_1. \tag{8.30}$$

At first glance it is not clear whether a tax cut lowers or increases government saving. On the one hand, a tax cut lowers revenue because the tax rate, τ_1, falls. On the other hand, a fall in τ_1 increases revenue because the tax base, C_1, increases. To determine which of these two effects dominates, use equation (8.29) to eliminate C_1 to get

$$S_1^g = r_0 B_0^g + \frac{\tau_1}{2(1+\tau_1)}\left[(1+r_0)B_0^h + Q_1 + \frac{\Pi(r^*)}{1+r^*}\right] - G_1.$$

---

[1] Note that consumption in period 1 does not depend on taxes in period 2, τ_2. This is a special result due to the assumption of log-linear preferences. Under this type of preference, an increase in τ_2 creates income and substitution effects that exactly offset each other. By the substitution effect, an increase in τ_2 raises the demand for C_1 because it makes it relatively cheaper. By the income effect, an increase in τ_2 makes the household poorer and reduces the demand for C_1. Under different preference specifications, the income and substitution effects associated with a change in τ_2 may not exactly offset each other.

The factor $\tau_1/(1+\tau_1)$ is strictly increasing in τ_1. Therefore, a decline in τ_1 reduces government saving; that is, it increases the fiscal deficit.

We have therefore established that with distortionary consumption taxes, tax cuts can generate twin deficits.

8.5   The Optimality of Twin Deficits

Let's revisit the question of whether an increase in government spending can generate a twin deficit. Section 8.3 shows that this is the case when taxes are lump sum. We now wish to see whether this result is robust to assuming that taxes are distortionary. From equation (8.29), we have that holding τ_1 constant, consumption in period 1, C_1, is independent of G_1. It follows immediately that the current account, $CA_1 = r_0 B_0 + Q_1 - C_1 - I(r^*) - G_1$, falls one for one as G_1 increases. So an increase in G_1, holding τ_1 constant, deteriorates the current account. Now from equation (8.30) we have that, holding τ_1 constant, government saving also deteriorates one for one as G_1 increases. Thus, under distortionary consumption taxes it continues to be the case that an increase in government spending in period 1 holding the tax rate in period 1 constant causes a twin deficit.

But why would the government keep tax rates in period 1 constant when government spending increases? We know that in response to an increase in G_1, the government will have to increase taxes at some point, otherwise it would violate its intertemporal budget constraint. When and by how much should the government increase taxes? The analysis we have conducted thus far is mute in this regard. In fact, given a path for government expenditure, (G_1, G_2), there is an infinite number of tax rate paths, (τ_1, τ_2), that guarantee the satisfaction of the government's intertemporal budget constraint and are consistent with equilibrium. Each of these tax rate paths gives rise to a different consumption path, (C_1, C_2), and as a result generates a different level of welfare for the household. A natural question therefore is which of these tax rate paths a benevolent government should choose. The objective of this section is to address this question.

A *benevolent government* is a government that implements policies that maximize the welfare of households. The equilibrium tax rate path that maximizes the welfare of households is called the *Ramsey optimal* tax policy, after the British economist Frank Plumpton Ramsey, who first solved problems of this type and published the results at the age of 24.[2]

With distortionary taxes on consumption, the intertemporal budget constraint of the government is given by

$$G_1 + \frac{G_2}{1+r^*} = (1+r_0)B_0^g + \tau_1 C_1 + \frac{\tau_2 C_2}{1+r^*}. \qquad (8.31)$$

This expression is identical to the intertemporal government budget constraint with lump-sum taxes given in (8.4) evaluated at $r_1 = r^*$, except that T_1 and T_2, the tax revenues generated by lump-sum taxes, are replaced by $\tau_1 C_1$ and $\tau_2 C_2$, the revenues generated by consumption taxes.

---

[2]Frank P. Ramsey, "A Contribution to the Theory of Taxation," *Economic Journal* 37 (March 1927): 47–61.

Given the path of government spending (G_1, G_2), an equilibrium is a path of tax rates (τ_1, τ_2) and a path of private consumption (C_1, C_2), that satisfy the household's Euler equation (8.28) and intertemporal budget constraint (8.27), both evaluated at $r_1 = r^*$, and the intertemporal government budget constraint (8.31). These are three equations in four unknowns, C_1, C_2, τ_1, and τ_2. It follows that there are in principle an infinite number of equilibria. The government can pick one of the two tax rates arbitrarily. This choice has welfare consequences for the household because, in general, it affects the path of consumption. The question we wish to address is how should the government use this degree of freedom to maximize the household's well-being, or, as Ramsey would have it, "to minimize the decrement of utility."

Formally, the problem of the benevolent government is to pick C_1, C_2, τ_1, and τ_2 to maximize

$$\ln C_1 + \ln C_2 \qquad (8.7\ \text{R})$$

subject to

$$\frac{C_2}{C_1} = \frac{1 + \tau_1}{1 + \tau_2}(1 + r^*), \qquad (8.32)$$

$$(1 + \tau_1)C_1 + \frac{(1 + \tau_2)C_2}{1 + r^*} = (1 + r_0)B_0^h + Q_1 + \frac{\Pi(r^*)}{1 + r^*}, \qquad (8.33)$$

and

$$G_1 + \frac{G_2}{1 + r^*} = (1 + r_0)B_0^g + \tau_1 C_1 + \frac{\tau_2 C_2}{1 + r^*}, \qquad (8.31\ \text{R})$$

given G_1 and G_2. The constraints of this problem make it clear that the benevolent government is restricted to picking the best consumption allocation and the best tax policy among those that can be supported as a competitive equilibrium. This type of maximization problem is known as a *Ramsey problem*.

The Ramsey problem seems daunting, as it involves three constraints and four control variables. However, as it turns out, it is a fairly easy problem to solve. To see this, begin by combining the household's and the government's intertemporal budget constraints, equations (8.33) and (8.31), to obtain the economy's resource constraint

$$C_1 + \frac{C_2}{1 + r^*} = Q_1 - G_1 + \frac{\Pi(r^*) - G_2}{1 + r^*}. \qquad (8.34)$$

Because (8.34) is a combination of (8.33) and (8.31), we have that the restrictions of the Ramsey problem, equations (8.32), (8.33), and (8.31), are satisfied if and only if equations (8.32), (8.33), and (8.34) are satisfied.

So we can restate the Ramsey problem as picking C_1, C_2, τ_1, and τ_2 to maximize the utility function (8.7) subject to restrictions (8.32), (8.33), and (8.34).

Consider now solving the less restricted problem of picking C_1 and C_2 to maximize the utility function (8.7) subject to the economy's resource constraint (8.34). This problem has to deliver at least the same level of utility as the Ramsey problem, because it contains fewer restrictions. If we can show that the solution to the less restricted problem satisfies the omitted restrictions (8.32) and (8.33), we have found the solution to the Ramsey problem. To solve the less restricted problem, first solve the economy's intertemporal resource constraint (8.34) for C_2 to obtain

$$C_2 = (1 + r^*)(\bar{Y} - C_1), \tag{8.35}$$

where $\bar{Y} \equiv (1 + r_0)B_0 + Q_1 - G_1 + [\Pi(r^*) - G_2]/(1 + r^*)$ denotes the economy's lifetime wealth net of government spending. Using (8.35) to eliminate C_2 from the utility function (8.7), the less restricted problem can be stated as choosing C_1 to maximize

$$\ln C_1 + \ln[(1 + r^*)(\bar{Y} - C_1)].$$

Taking the derivative of this objective function with respect to C_1 and setting it to zero yields

$$\frac{1}{C_1} - \frac{1}{\bar{Y} - C_1} = 0. \tag{8.36}$$

Solving for C_1 gives

$$C_1 = \frac{1}{2}\bar{Y}. \tag{8.37}$$

Now using (8.35) to eliminate $\bar{Y} - C_1$ from (8.36) gives

$$\frac{C_2}{C_1} = 1 + r^*. \tag{8.38}$$

This completes the solution of the less restricted utility maximization problem. Let's now show that this solution also solves the Ramsey problem; that is, that it satisfies restrictions (8.32), (8.33), and (8.34). Equation (8.34) is trivially satisfied, as it is the constraint of the less restricted problem. Now pick $\tau_1 = \tau_2 = \tau$. Then, restriction (8.32) collapses to equation (8.38) from the less restricted problem. Finally, replacing τ_1 and τ_2 by τ in equation (8.33) gives the value of τ that makes this equation hold

$$\tau = \frac{(1 + r_0)B_0^h + Q_1 + \frac{\Pi(r^*)}{1+r^*}}{(1 + r_0)B_0 + Q_1 - G_1 + \frac{\Pi(r^*) - G_2}{1+r^*}} - 1. \tag{8.39}$$

This completes the proof that the solution of the less restricted problem is indeed the solution of the Ramsey problem.

Let's interpret what we have obtained. First, equation (8.38) says that the benevolent government picks a tax policy that completely eliminates the distortions introduced by the consumption tax. This is because under the Ramsey optimal tax policy, the intertemporal price of consumption perceived by the household, $\frac{1+\tau_1}{1+\tau_2}(1 + r^*)$, is equal to the intertemporal price of consumption in the world market, $1 + r^*$. Second, the way in which the benevolent government achieves a nondistorted path of consumption is by *tax smoothing*; that is, by setting a constant consumption tax rate over time, $\tau_1 = \tau_2$. Third, the Ramsey optimal allocation is the same as under lump-sum taxes. That is, the household consumes one half of the economy's lifetime resources net of government spending, $\bar{Y}$, in period 1 and leaves the rest for consumption in period 2.

What does all this imply for twin deficits? The current account in period 1 is $CA_1 = r_0 B_0 + Q_1 - C_1 - I(r^*) - G_1$. Replacing C_1 by its Ramsey optimal value $\bar{Y}/2$, we have that the Ramsey optimal current account in period 1 is the same as under lump-sum taxes,

$$CA_1 = \frac{1}{2}\left[-(1-r_0)B_0 + Q_1 - G_1 - \frac{\Pi(r^*) - G_2}{1+r^*}\right] - I(r^*). \qquad (8.21\,\text{R})$$

Government saving in period 1 is given by $S_1^g = r_0 B_0^g + \tau_1 C_1 - G_1$. Replacing τ_1 and C_1 by their Ramsey optimal values, given in equations (8.37) and (8.39), we obtain

$$S_1^g = \frac{1}{2}\left[-(1-r_0)B_0^g - G_1 + \frac{G_2}{1+r^*}\right].$$

According to these two expressions, in response to an increase in G_1, the current account deteriorates and the fiscal deficit increases (or government saving falls), $\Delta CA_1 = \Delta S_1^g = -\frac{1}{2}\Delta G_1$. This means that the benevolent government finds it optimal to run twin deficits.

The intuition behind this result is as follows. As in the economy with lump-sum taxes, the increase in government spending makes households poorer. Because they like to smooth consumption over time, they cut consumption in both periods. So the fall in private consumption in period 1 is less than the increase in government spending. Since investment is constant at $I(r^*)$, the fact that consumption falls by less than government spending increases means that aggregate demand goes up. With the endowment unchanged, the increase in aggregate demand causes a deterioration in the current account. On the fiscal side, in response to the increase in government spending in period 1, the government, to avoid distortions in the allocation of consumption, increases the consumption tax rate in both periods by the same amount. Thus, in period 1 only part of the increase in government spending is financed with higher taxes and the rest by issuing public debt.

8.6   Fiscal Policy in Economies with Imperfect Capital Mobility

A common concern about expansionary fiscal policy is that by driving up interest rates it crowds out investment and private consumption. In the model economy studied thus far, the effect of fiscal policy on interest rates is muted by the assumptions that the economy is small and that it has free capital mobility. We now relax these assumptions. In this section we compare fiscal policy in small economies with different degrees of capital mobility. In the next section, we study fiscal policy in the context of a large economy.

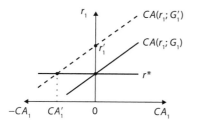
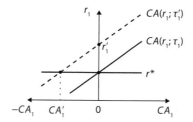

Figure 8.3. Adjustment to Expansionary Fiscal Policy under Free Capital Mobility and Financial Autarky

Notes: The left panel depicts the adjustment of the current account and the interest rate to an increase in government spending from G_1 to $G_1' > G_1$, holding constant the consumption tax rate τ_1. The upward-sloping solid line is the current account schedule before the fiscal expansion. (To avoid clutter, all arguments of the current account schedule other than r_1 and G_1 are omitted.) In the initial equilibrium, the interest rate is $r_1 = r^*$ and the current account is zero. The increase in government spending shifts the current account schedule up and to the left (broken line). Under free capital mobility, the interest rate stays at r^* and the current account deteriorates to $CA_1' < 0$. Under financial autarky, the interest rate increases to $r_1' > r^*$ and the current account stays at zero. The adjustment to a tax cut ($\tau_1' < \tau_1$), holding constant G_1, is shown in the right panel and is qualitatively similar to that of an increase in government spending.

Let's begin by deriving the current account schedule. The current account in period 1 is given by

$$CA_1 = r_0 B_0 + Q_1 - C_1 - I_1 - G_1.$$

Using (8.29) evaluated at r_1 to eliminate C_1 and recognizing that I_1 is a function of r_1 alone, we can write the current account schedule as

$$CA_1 = r_0 B_0 + Q_1 - \frac{1}{2(1+\tau_1)}\left[(1+r_0)B_0^h + Q_1 + \frac{\Pi(r_1)}{1+r_1}\right] - I(r_1) - G_1.$$

According to this expression, the current account is increasing in the interest rate, in the endowment, and in the tax rate, and decreasing in government spending. We write this relationship compactly as

$$CA_1 = CA(r_1; Q_1, \tau_1, G_1). \qquad (8.40)$$
$${+ \quad + \quad + \quad -}$$

Let's compare the effects of fiscal policy in two polar cases, an economy with free capital mobility and an economy in financial autarky, i.e., an economy closed to international capital movements. The left panel of Figure 8.3 displays with a solid upward-sloping line the current account schedule (8.40). The world interest rate is r^*. For expositional simplicity, suppose that at $r_1 = r^*$, the economy runs a zero current account deficit. This means that regardless of whether the economy is open or closed to international capital movements, the equilibrium interest rate happens to be r^* and the equilibrium current account is nil.

Suppose now that government spending increases from G_1 to $G_1' > G_1$ and that the consumption tax rate, τ_1, remains unchanged. At any interest rate, the current account deteriorates. Thus, the current account schedule shifts up and to the left, as shown by the broken line. If the economy is open to international capital markets, the interest rate stays at r^*, and the current account drops from zero to $CA_1' < 0$. Investment remains unchanged at $I(r^*)$, so the increase in government spending does not have a crowding-out effect on capital formation.

If instead the economy is financially closed, then the current account remains at zero after the shock, and the domestic interest rate increases from r^* to $r_1' > r^*$. The increase in the interest rate causes investment to fall from $I(r^*)$ to $I(r_1') < I(r^*)$. It follows that the fiscal expansion crowds out investment. The crowding out is partial, in the sense that investment falls by less than one for one with the increase in government spending. The reason is that consumption is also partially crowded out as the increase in the interest rate discourages private spending and incentivizes private saving. The fall in consumption makes some room for government spending (recall that under financial autarky $Q_1 = C_1 + I_1 + G_1$, and that the endowment, Q_1, is fixed).

The effect of a cut in the consumption tax rate, τ_1, shown in the right panel of Figure 8.3, is qualitatively the same as that of an increase in government spending.

In reality, economies are neither completely open nor completely closed to international capital movements. In such an intermediate situation, expansionary fiscal policy causes an increase in the interest rate, a deterioration in the current account, and some crowding out of investment. To illustrate this case, suppose that the government imposes capital controls to discourage external indebtedness. Specifically, suppose that the interest rate faced by domestic agents is r^* if the country is a net external creditor ($B_1 > 0$), and an increasing function of the country's net debt position, $-B_1$, if the country is a debtor ($B_1 < 0$). Since $B_1 = r_0 B_0 + CA_1$, we have that the country's net external debt increases one for one with the current account deficit, $-CA_1$. For simplicity, in what follows we assume that $B_0 = 0$, so that the country's external debt at the end of period 1 is $-CA_1$.

Figure 8.4 depicts the effect of an increase in government spending in this economy. The domestic interest rate schedule is denoted $\rho(-CA_1)$. It is flat and equal to r^* when CA_1 is positive and increasing in $-CA_1$ when CA_1 is negative. The equilibrium occurs at the intersection of the current account schedule with the interest rate schedule. Initially, government spending equals G_1. The equilibrium is at point A, where the interest rate is r^* and the current account is 0. An increase in government spending from G_1 to G_1' shifts the current account schedule up and to the left, as shown by the broken line. The interest rate schedule is unchanged. The new equilibrium is at point B, where the country runs a current account deficit equal to $CA_1' < 0$, and the interest rate is higher, $r_1' > r^*$. As a consequence of the increase in the interest rate, investment falls from $I(r^*)$ to $I(r_1')$. Equilibrium under free capital mobility and under financial autarky occur at points B' and B'', respectively. Comparing the equilibrium in the economy with imperfect capital mobility (point B) with the equilibria under the two polar cases of free capital mobility (point B') and financial autarky (point B''), we conclude that the more open to international capital mobility the economy is, the smaller the crowding out of investment, the smaller the

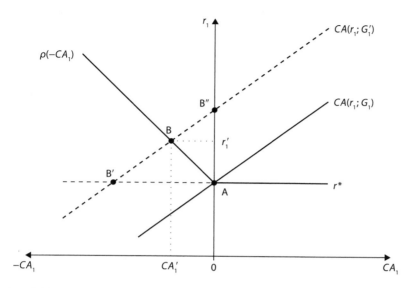

Figure 8.4. Adjustment to an Increase in Government Spending under Imperfect Capital Mobility

Notes: The initial equilibrium occurs at point A, where the current account schedule, $CA(r_1; G_1)$ intersects the interest rate schedule, $\rho(-CA_1)$. (To avoid clutter, all arguments of the current account schedule other than r_1 and G_1 are omitted.) Initially, the interest rate is r^* and the current account is zero. An increase in government spending from G_1 to $G_1' > G_1$ shifts the current account schedule up and to the left (upward-sloping broken line). The interest rate schedule is unchanged. The new equilibrium is at point B, where the interest rate is higher ($r_1' > r^*$), and the current account is negative ($CA_1' < 0$). Equilibria under free capital mobility and financial autarky are at points B' and B'', respectively.

increase in the interest rate, and the larger the deterioration of the current account following an expansion in government spending will be.

8.7 Fiscal Policy in a Large Open Economy

What are the domestic and international effects of fiscal policy in a large economy like the United States? To address this question, suppose that the economy we have been studying thus far is large, in the sense that domestic shocks can affect the world interest rate. Its current account schedule is given by equation (8.40). Let the current account schedule of the rest of the world be given by

$$CA_1^{RW} = CA(r_1; Q_1^{RW}, \tau_1^{RW}, G_1^{RW}). \qquad (8.41)$$
$$\underset{+}{\phantom{CA_1^{RW} = CA(r_1;}} \ \underset{+}{\phantom{Q_1^{RW},}} \ \underset{+}{\phantom{\tau_1^{RW},}} \ \underset{-}{\phantom{G_1^{RW})}}$$

The current account schedule of the rest of the world has the same properties as that of the domestic economy, as it is derived from the same microeconomic foundations.

Figure 8.5 depicts the effects of an increase in government spending in the domestic large economy from G_1 to $G_1' > G_1$. On the horizontal axes, the current

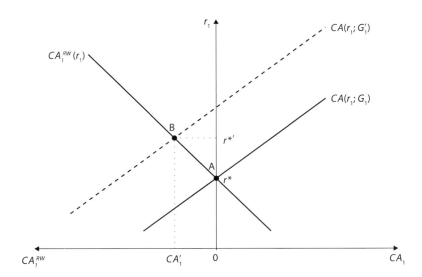

Figure 8.5. Adjustment to an Increase in Government Spending in a Large Open Economy

Notes: The figure depicts the effects of a fiscal expansion in a large open economy. The initial situation is at point A, where the current account schedule of the large economy (the upward-sloping solid line) intersects the current account schedule of the rest of the world (the downward-sloping solid line). At point A, the world interest rate is equal to r^* and the current account deficit is equal to 0. The increase in government spending in the large economy from G_1 to $G_1' > G_1$ shifts the current account schedule of the large economy up and to the left (the upward-sloping broken line). The current account schedule of the rest of the world is unchanged. The new equilibrium is at point B, where the world interest rate is higher, $r^{*'} > r^*$, the large open economy is running a current account deficit, and the rest of the world a current account surplus.

account balance of the domestic large economy is measured from left to right and the current account balance of the rest of the world from right to left. Before the government spending shock, the equilibrium is at point A, where the current account schedule of the domestic large economy (upward-sloping solid line) intersects the current account of the rest of the world (downward-sloping solid line). For simplicity, we assume that at the initial equilibrium the current account is zero (in both countries, of course).

The expansion in government spending in the domestic large economy shifts its current account schedule up and to the left (upward-sloping broken line). The current account schedule of the rest of the world is unchanged. The new equilibrium is at point B, where the interest rate is higher ($r^{*'} > r^*$), the current account of the domestic economy is negative, and the current account of the rest of the world is positive. The increase in the interest rate produces a contraction in investment in both the domestic economy and the rest of the world.

Intuitively, the increase in government spending in the domestic economy reduces national saving. Given the interest rate, this produces a reduction in the global supply of funds, which pushes up the world interest rate. In turn, the increase in the interest rate discourages investment and fosters saving in the domestic economy and in the rest of the world, restoring equilibrium in the international capital market. The effects of a tax cut are qualitatively the same (not shown).

In sum, expansionary fiscal policy in a large economy causes an increase in the world interest rate, a deterioration of the current account of the large economy, and a contraction of investment around the world; that is, in the large economy as well as the rest of the world. Comparing these results with those obtained in the context of a small open economy, we conclude that the larger the economy is, the larger the increase in the world interest rate in response to an expansionary fiscal shock will be. If follows that fiscal stimulus in large economies will be associated with more crowding out of investment than fiscal stimulus in small economies.

8.8 Summing Up

This chapter analyzes how fiscal deficits stemming from tax cuts, increases in government transfers, or increases in government spending affect the current account and other macroeconomic indicators.

- The twin deficit hypothesis states that fiscal deficits cause current account deficits.
- When taxes are lump sum, changes in the timing of taxes, holding the path of government spending unchanged, do not cause changes in the trade balance or the current account. This result is known as Ricardian equivalence.
- Ricardian equivalence is a fragile result. It requires that taxes are lump sum, that households are not borrowing constrained, and that all agents receiving a tax cut expect to pay the future higher taxes required to balance the budget. If any of these conditions is relaxed, Ricardian equivalence fails and tax cuts cause current account deficits (twin deficits).
- A temporary increase in government spending causes a deterioration of the current account (twin deficits).
- If an increase in government spending is perceived to be permanent, the current account is not significantly affected.
- A cut in the consumption tax rate, holding the path of government spending constant, causes a deterioration of the current account (twin deficits).
- A benevolent government finds it desirable to smooth consumption tax rates over time. Consequently, temporary increases in government spending generate both fiscal and current account deficits. In this sense, twin deficits are Ramsey optimal.
- In a small open economy with free capital mobility, temporary increases in government expenditures or tax cuts do not crowd out investment. However, crowding out of investment does occur in small open economies with imperfect international capital mobility.
- In a large open economy with free capital mobility, a temporary increase in government expenditure or a tax cut deteriorates the current account, raises the world interest rates, and crowds out investment domestically and in the rest of the world.

8.9 Exercises

Exercise 8.1 (TFU) Indicate whether the following statements are true, false, or uncertain and explain why.

1. Suppose the current account deficit is 5% of GDP and that half the population is borrowing constrained. Then, the government could eliminate the current account deficit by increasing (lump-sum) taxes by 10% of GDP.

2. A tax cut with current and future government spending unchanged causes an increase in saving as opposed to an increase in consumption because households understand that taxes will have to increase in the future. Since the current account equals saving minus investment, the current account improves.

3. Suppose the government of a small open economy increases current government spending but promises to reduce future government spending in such a way that the present discounted value of government purchases remains unchanged. According to Ricardian equivalence, this policy should have no effect on the current account.

4. The government increases government spending and lump-sum taxes in the same amount, leaving the primary fiscal deficit unchanged. This policy should have no effect on the current account, which is in line with the twin deficit hypothesis.

5. Suppose the world is made up of two countries, the United States and the rest of the world. An increase in government purchases in the rest of the world will lead to an increase in the world interest rate.

6. The fiscal stimulus implemented by the U.S. government in response to the COVID-19 pandemic in 2020 and 2021 was extraordinarily large. This fiscal shock will crowd out investment not only in the United States but also in the rest of the world.

Exercise 8.2 (An Economy with Lump-Sum Taxes) Consider a two-period endowment economy. Assume that households have preferences described by the following utility function

$$\sqrt{C_1} + \frac{1}{1.1}\sqrt{C_2},$$

where C_1 and C_2 denote consumption in periods 1 and 2, respectively. In each period, households are endowed with 10 units of goods. Households pay lump-sum taxes T_1 and T_2, in periods 1 and 2. Finally, households are born with no financial assets ($B_0^h = 0$) and can borrow or lend in the international financial market at the world interest rate $r^* = 0.1$. The government starts period 1 with no outstanding assets or liabilities ($B_0^g = 0$). In period 1, the government collects lump-sum taxes T_1 and consumes $G_1 = 1$ unit of goods. In period 2, it collects lump-sum taxes T_2 and consumes $G_2 = 1$ unit of goods. Like the household, the government has access to the world financial market.

1. Compute the equilibrium levels of consumption, the trade balance, and the current account in periods 1 and 2.

2. Suppose that $T_1 = 0$. What is T_2? What is private, government, and national saving in periods 1 and 2?

3. Suppose now that T_1 increases from 0 to 1 while government purchases are unchanged in both periods. How does this tax hike affect the current account and the fiscal deficit in period 1? Briefly explain your result.

4. Suppose that in period 1 the government increases spending from 1 to 2 and keeps government spending in period 2 unchanged. What is the effect of this policy change on the current account in period 1? Explain.

5. Finally, suppose that there is a permanent increase in government purchases. Specifically, suppose that both G_1 and G_2 increase by 1. Find the response of the current account in period 1. Compare your result with that from the previous question and provide intuition.

Exercise 8.3 (Distortionary Taxation I) Consider an endowment economy populated by identical households with preferences described by the lifetime utility function

$$\ln C_1 + \ln C_2.$$

Households are endowed with 10 units of goods in each period ($Q_1 = Q_2 = 10$) and start period 1 with no assets or debts ($B_0^h = 0$). The world interest rate is 5 percent ($r^* = 0.05$) and the country enjoys free capital mobility. In period 1, taxes are lump sum. In period 2, the government levies a 10 percent tax on consumption ($\tau_2 = 0.1$). Government spending is 1 unit in each period ($G_1 = G_2 = 1$). The government starts period 1 with a zero asset position ($B_0^g = 0$).

1. Compute the equilibrium levels of the primary fiscal deficit and the current account in period 1.

2. Suppose now that the government decides to increase taxes in period 1 by 0.5, leaving government spending unchanged in both periods. The minister of finance argues that this policy change will not affect the current account because the tax being changed is lump sum and therefore nondistortionary. Do you agree or disagree with the minister's opinion, and why? If you disagree, what is your prediction for the current account when the tax reform is applied? Show your work. Relate your answer to the issue of twin deficits.

Exercise 8.4 (Distortionary Taxation II) Consider a two-period, small open endowment economy. Assume that households' preferences are described by the utility function

$$\ln C_1 + \ln C_2,$$

where C_1 and C_2 denote consumption in periods 1 and 2. Households are endowed with 10 units of goods in each period and pay proportional taxes on consumption. Let τ_1 and τ_2 denote the consumption tax rates in periods 1 and 2. Finally, households are born with no financial assets ($B_0^h = 0$) and can borrow or lend in the international financial market at the world interest rate $r^* = 0.1$. The government starts period 1 with no outstanding assets or liabilities ($B_0^g = 0$). It taxes consumption at the same rate in both periods ($\tau_1 = \tau_2$) and consumes 1 unit of goods in each period. That is, $G_1 = G_2 = 1$, where G_1 and G_2 denote government consumption in periods 1 and 2. Like the household, the government has access to the world financial market. In answering the following questions, show your work.

1. Compute the equilibrium tax rate and the equilibrium levels of consumption, the trade balance, private saving, the primary and secondary fiscal deficits, and the current account in periods 1 and 2.
2. Suppose now that the government implements a stimulus package consisting in reducing the tax rate by half in period 1, with government consumption unchanged in both periods. Recalculate the equilibrium of all the variables listed in the previous question. Briefly explain your findings.

Exercise 8.5 (Distortionary Taxation III) Consider a two-period, small open endowment economy populated by a large number of households with preferences described by the utility function

$$\ln C_1 + \beta \ln C_2,$$

where C_1 and C_2 denote consumption in periods 1 and 2, and $\beta = 1/1.1$ is the subjective discount factor. Households receive endowments Q_1 in period 1 and Q_2 in period 2, with $Q_1 = Q_2 = 10$ and can borrow or lend in international financial markets at the interest rate $r^* = 0.1$. The government imposes taxes $T_1 = T^L + \tau_1 C_1$ in period 1 and $T_2 = \tau_2 C_2$ in period 2 and consumes G_1 units of goods in period 1 and G_2 units in period 2. Finally, households and the government start period 1 with no assets or debts carried over from the past.

1. Derive the intertemporal budget constraint of the household, the intertemporal budget constraint of the government, and the intertemporal resource constraint of the economy as a whole.
2. Derive the optimality condition that results from choosing C_1 and C_2 to maximize the household's utility function subject to the household's intertemporal budget constraint.
3. Suppose $G_1 = G_2 = 2$ and $\tau_1 = \tau_2 = 0.2$. Find the equilibrium levels of consumption and the trade balance in periods 1 and 2, and the equilibrium level of lump-sum taxes T^L. Find the level of welfare. Report the primary and secondary fiscal deficits in period 1.
4. Continue to assume that $G_1 = G_2 = 2$. Suppose that the government implements a tax cut in period 1 consisting in lowering the consumption tax rate from 20 to 10 percent. Suppose further that lump-sum taxes, T^L, are kept at the level found in the previous item. Find consumption, the trade balance, and the primary fiscal deficit in period 1, and the consumption tax rate in period 2.
5. Answer the previous question assuming that the cut in consumption taxes in period 1 from 20 to 10 percent is financed with an appropriate change in lump-sum taxes in the same period, while the consumption tax rate in

period 2 is kept constant at its initial level of 20 percent. Compare your answer with the one for the previous item and provide intuition.

6. Suppose that $T^L = 0$. There are many possible equilibrium tax schemes (τ_1, τ_2). Find the pair (τ^1, τ^2) that maximizes the household's lifetime utility. Show your derivation. Refer to your solution as the Ramsey optimal tax policy. Find the level of welfare and compare it to the one obtained in part 3 above. Does the restriction that $T^L = 0$ reduce welfare? Why or why not?

Exercise 8.6 (Imperfect Capital Mobility and Crowding Out) Consider a small open economy with identical households whose preferences are described by the utility function

$$\ln C_1 + \beta \ln C_2,$$

where C_1, C_2, and $\beta = 0.96$ denote consumption in period 1, consumption in period 2, and the subjective discount factor. Households have an endowment of $Q_1 = 20$ units of goods in period 1 and receive profits Π_2 from firms in period 2. They enter period 1 with no assets or debts ($B_0^h = 0$), and can borrow or lend at the interest rate r_1. In period 1, firms borrow at the rate r_1 to invest in I_1 units of capital goods that become productive in period 2. In period 2, they use the production technology

$$6\sqrt{I_1}$$

to produce goods, they pay back their loans, and distribute profits to households. The government enters period 1 with zero debts or assets ($B_0^g = 0$), spends $G_1 = 1$ in period 1, and $G_2 = 7$ in period 2 on goods and levies lump-sum taxes. The interest rate at which the rest of the world is willing to lend to this country is

$$r_1 = \begin{cases} r^* & \text{if } B_1 \geq 0 \\ r^* + p & \text{if } B_1 < 0 \end{cases},$$

where r^* is the world interest rate paid to net external creditors and equals 8 percent ($r^* = 0.08$), p is an interest rate premium charged to net external debtors and equals 2 percent ($p = 0.02$), and B_1 is the country's net foreign asset position at the end of period 1.

1. Calculate the equilibrium values of the interest rate r_1, the current account in period 1, CA_1, and investment in period 1, I_1.
2. Suppose now that because of extraordinary expenses stemming from the COVID-19 pandemic, government spending in period 1 increases by 100 percent (i.e., G_1 goes from 1 to 2). Recalculate r_1, CA_1, and I_1. Does government spending crowd out investment?
3. Suppose now that the increase in government spending in period 1 is not 100 percent but 300 percent (i.e., G_1 goes from 1 to 4). Recalculate r_1, CA_1, and I_1. Does government spending crowd out investment? Provide intuition.
4. Continue to assume that $G_1 = 4$, but suppose that the country premium is 4 percent ($p = 0.04$). Show numerically that an equilibrium does not exist. Explain your finding using a graph.

Exercise 8.7 (A Consumption Tax in a Large Economy) Consider a two-period, two-country model of a large open endowment economy. Households in country 1 are endowed with $Q_1^1 = 0$ goods in period 1 and $Q_2^1 = Q > 0$ goods in period 2. In country 2, the endowments are $Q_1^2 = Q$ and $Q_2^2 = 0$. In both countries, households have preferences defined by the same utility function,

$$\ln C_1^1 + \ln C_2^1,$$

in country 1 and

$$\ln C_1^2 + \ln C_2^2,$$

in country 2, where C_t^i, for $i = 1, 2$ and $t = 1, 2$ denotes consumption in country i in period t. In country 1, households enter period 1 with a zero net asset position $(B_0^1 = 0)$.

1. Calculate the equilibrium levels of consumption in countries 1 and 2 in periods 1 and 2, the current account in countries 1 and 2 in period 1 (CA_1^1 and CA_1^2), and the world interest rate (r^*). Provide intuition.
2. The government of country 1 understands that although individual agents take the interest rate as given, the country as a whole has market power in the international capital market. To take advantage of this situation, it discourages consumption in period 1 by imposing a proportional consumption tax in period 1 at the rate τ_1 equal to 10 percent ($\tau_1 = 0.1$). It does not impose any taxes in period 2. The government of country 1 rebates the tax revenue to its households by means of a lump-sum transfer T_1 in period 1. Suppose that the government of country 2 is passive and does not retaliate. Find the equilibrium value of the world interest rate, r^*. Does the government of country 1 succeed in lowering the world interest rate?
3. Compare the equilibrium paths of consumption in country 1, (C_1^1, C_2^1), with and without the consumption tax. In particular, is the tax welfare increasing for households in country 1? What about for households in country 2? Provide intuition.
4. Generalize your findings to any value of $\tau_1 > 0$. Is there a value of τ_1 that maximizes welfare in country 1? In answering this question, continue to assume that the government of country 2 is passive.

Exercise 8.8 (An Investment Subsidy) Consider a two-period, small open production economy. In period 1, households are endowed with $Q_1 = 2$ units of goods and initial wealth of zero, $B_0^h = 0$. Households are owners of firms. In period 2, households receive profit income of firms in the amount of Π_2 and pay lump-sum taxes, denoted T_2, to the government. Households' preferences over period 1 and period 2 consumption, C_1 and C_2, respectively, are given by $C_1^{\frac{1}{2}} + C_2^{\frac{1}{2}}$. The country enjoys free capital mobility and the world interest rate is zero. Firms invest in period 1 in order to be able to produce in period 2. Investment in physical capital in period 1 is denoted I_1 and the production function for output in period 2 is $F(I_1) = 3I_1^{1/3}$. Assume that the government subsidizes investment by offering firms to borrow at the gross interest rate $1 + \tilde{r}$, such that $1 + \tilde{r} = (1 + r_1)(1 - \tau)$, where r_1 denotes the interest rate in period 1 and $\tau \geq 0$ denotes the investment subsidy. The government finances the investment subsidy by levying a lump-sum tax on households in period 2, T_2. The initial asset position of the government is zero, $B_0^g = 0$.

1. Find the equilibrium value of the firm's profit in period 2, Π_2, for the case that $\tau = 0$ and for the case that $\tau = 0.5$. Interpret your findings.
2. Find the equilibrium value of lump-sum taxes in period 2, T_2, for the case that $\tau = 0$ and for the case that $\tau = 1/2$.
3. Find the value of the household's profit income net of lump-sum taxes in period 2, $\Pi_2 - T_2$, for the case that $\tau = 0$ and for the case that $\tau = 1/2$. Does the subsidy increase after-tax profit income?
4. Find the equilibrium level of period 1 consumption, C_1, for the case that $\tau = 0$ and for the case that $\tau = 1/2$. Does the investment subsidy increase welfare?
5. Find the equilibrium value of the trade balance in period 1, TB_1, for the case that $\tau = 0$ and for the case that $\tau = 1/2$. In equilibrium, does the trade balance move one for one with investment? Why or why not?

Exercise 8.9 (Finite Lives and Fiscal Policy) Consider a two-period, small open endowment economy with free capital mobility. Households live for one period. The endowment is 10 in both periods. The utility function of households living in period 1 is $\ln C_1$ and that of households living in period 2 is $\ln C_2$. The government lives for two periods and has access to the world financial market, where the interest rate is 10 percent, $r^* = 0.1$. Government spending is 2 in both periods ($G_1 = G_2 = 2$). The government levies lump-sum taxes in periods 1 and 2, denoted T_1 and T_2, respectively. Finally, assume that households and the government start their lives with no debts or assets.

1. Suppose that $T_2 = 1$. Calculate T_1. What is the primary fiscal deficit in period 1?
2. Calculate consumption in periods 1 and 2.
3. Calculate the trade balance and the current account in period 1 (TB_1 and CA_1).
4. Suppose now that the government does not have access to lump-sum taxes ($T_1 = T_2 = 0$). Instead, the government levies a proportional tax on consumption at the rates τ_1 and τ_2 in periods 1 and 2. Suppose that $\tau_2 = 0.25$. Calculate τ_1, C_1, C_2, TB_1, and TB_2.

Exercise 8.10 (Optimal Lump-Sum Taxation) Consider the small open economy with finite lives described in Exercise 8.9. In particular, continue to assume that $Q_1 = Q_2 = 10$, $r^* = 0.1$, and $G_1 = G_2 = 2$ and that the government levies lump-sum taxes, T_1 and T_2. Suppose that the government is benevolent and cares equally about the welfare of both generations. Specifically, suppose that the lifetime utility function of the government is given by

$$\ln C_1 + \ln C_2.$$

Calculate the optimal levels of lump-sum taxes in periods 1 and 2 (T_1 and T_2). Provide intuition. In particular, comment on why the government does or does not tax both generations equally.

Exercise 8.11 (Fiscal Expansion in the Rest of the World) Use a graphical approach to analyze the effect of an increase in government spending in the rest of the world on the current account of a large domestic country, the world interest rate, and investment in the domestic country and in the rest of the world. Provide intuition.

PART II

The Real Exchange Rate

CHAPTER 9

The Real Exchange Rate and Purchasing Power Parity

You might have noticed that sometimes Europe seems much cheaper than the United States and sometimes it is the other way around. In the first case, Americans have incentives to visit Europe and to import European goods and services. In the second case, more European tourists should visit America and the United States has an easier time exporting goods and services to Europe. The *real exchange rate* measures how expensive a foreign country is relative to the home country. It tracks the evolution over time of the price of a basket of goods abroad in terms of baskets of goods at home. When prices expressed in the same currency are equalized at home and abroad, the real exchange rate is unity. In this case, the purchasing power of the domestic currency is the same at home and abroad, in the sense that it can buy the same quantity of goods in both countries. When this happens, we say that *purchasing power parity* holds. An important empirical question in international macroeconomics is, how large and persistent are deviations from purchasing power parity? Equally important is the question, what factors determine deviations from purchasing power parity? This chapter is devoted to studying these and other related questions.

9.1 The Law of One Price

When a good costs the same abroad and at home, we say that the *law of one price* (LOOP) holds. Let P denote the domestic currency price of a particular good in the domestic country, P^* the foreign currency price of the same good in the foreign country, and $\mathcal{E}$ the nominal exchange rate, defined as the domestic currency price of one unit of foreign currency. The LOOP holds if

$$P = \mathcal{E}P^*.$$

The good is more expensive in the foreign economy if $\mathcal{E}P^* > P$, and less expensive if $\mathcal{E}P^* < P$.

Why should the law of one price hold? Imagine that a can of Coke costs \$2 in country A and \$1 in country B. In a frictionless world, one could become infinitely rich by buying Coke cans in country B and selling them in country A. This arbitrage opportunity would cause the price of Coke to fall in country A and to increase in country B. This tendency would continue until the price is equalized across countries.

The world, however, is not a frictionless environment. For example, if countries A and B are far apart from each other, transportation costs would have to be taken into account. Or there could be tariffs on imports or exports in either country, which limit arbitrage opportunities. Also, bringing the can from its port of entry in country A to a convenience store involves distribution costs, such as loading and unloading, additional transportation, storage, advertising, and retail services. If buying the can of Coke in country B and making it available to customers in country A costs more than $1, it will not pay for an entrepreneur to exploit the cross-country price difference of $1. Thus, one should expect deviations from the law of one price to persist over time.

For some goods, the law of one price is a better approximation than for others. For example, prices are similar across countries for highly traded commodities, such as gold, oil, soy beans, and wheat. The same is true for luxury consumer goods, such as Rolex watches, Hermès neckties, and Montblanc fountain pens. On the other hand, large differences in prices across countries are observed for goods that are not easily traded internationally—for example, personal services such as health care, education, restaurant meals, domestic services, and personal care (haircuts are a prototypical example). Similarly, prices of local goods such as housing, transportation, and utilities can display large variation across countries or regions.

How large are observed deviations from the law of one price? To answer this question for a particular good, one would need to collect data on its price in different countries and then express all prices in the same currency using the corresponding nominal exchange rate. One easy product to start with is McDonald's Big Mac, because *The Economist* has been collecting data on the price of Big Macs around the world since 1986. The Big Mac is also a good example because it is made pretty much the same way all over the world, so we are sure we are comparing the price of the same good across countries.

Let P^{BigMac} denote the dollar price of a Big Mac in the United States and $P^{\text{BigMac}*}$ the foreign currency price of a Big Mac in a foreign country. Then we can construct a measure of how many U.S. Big Macs it takes to buy one Big Mac abroad. This measure is called the Big Mac real exchange rate, and we denote it by e^{BigMac}. Formally, e^{BigMac} is given by

$$e^{\text{BigMac}} = \frac{\mathcal{E} P^{\text{BigMac}*}}{P^{\text{BigMac}}}.$$

If $e^{\text{BigMac}} > 1$, then the Big Mac is more expensive abroad. In this case, if you exchange the dollar value of one Big Mac in the United States into foreign currency, you would not have enough money to buy one Big Mac abroad. We say that the law of one price holds for Big Macs when the Big Mac real exchange rate is unity,

$$\text{LOOP holds when } e^{\text{BigMac}} = 1.$$

Table 9.1 presents Big Mac real exchange rates for 40 countries measured in January 2019. The table shows that the law of one price does not hold well for the Big Mac. For example, in Russia the least expensive country in the sample, a Big Mac sells for the equivalent of $1.65, whereas in the United States it sells for $5.58. Thus for the price of one Big Mac in Russia one can buy only 0.3 Big Macs in the United States; that is, the Big Mac real exchange rate is 0.3. In Switzerland, the most expensive country in the sample, a Big Mac sells for the equivalent of $6.62. Thus, for the price of one Big Mac in Switzerland one can buy 1.19 Big Macs in the United States, or equivalently, the Big Mac real exchange rate is 1.19.

Why is the Big Mac so expensive in some countries and so cheap in others? Perhaps the most important factor determining the observed price differences is the international tradability of the different items that comprise the cost of producing the Big Mac. Tradable components of a Big Mac include grain (wheat and sesame seeds), meat, and dairy (the cheese on top of the burger). The prices of these items tend to be similar across countries. However, these components combined represent a small fraction of the total cost of producing and serving a Big Mac. Most of the production costs stem from local components such as labor, rent, electricity, and water. These items are not easily tradable across countries, and as a result, their prices can display significant cross-country variation. For example, a worker preparing burgers in Indonesia makes only a fraction of the wage of his or her American counterpart. It follows that we should expect the Big Mac to be more expensive in countries where the aforementioned nontradable components are also more expensive. We will show in Section 9.3.4 that nontradable goods and services tend to be relatively more expensive in richer countries.

Table 9.1 presents a static assessment of deviations from the law of one price for Big Macs across countries. It tells us what these deviations looked like at one point in time—namely, the year 2019. One might wonder whether deviations from the law of one price change over time. In particular, do deviations from the law of one price tend to disappear with time; that is, have countries that were more expensive than the United States in the past become relatively less expensive? Similarly, have countries that were cheaper than the United States in the past become relatively more expensive? Figure 9.1 provides an answer to these questions for the period 2006 to 2019.[1] It plots the change in the Big Mac real exchange rate between 2006 and 2019 against the Big Mac real exchange rate in 2006 for 40 countries. Because the Big Mac real exchange rate is the ratio of the dollar price of a Big Mac in a given country to the dollar price of a Big Mac in the United States, by construction, the coordinate of the United States is $(1, 0)$ (the level of the U.S. Big Mac real exchange rate is always 1 and never changes). Countries located below the horizontal line became cheaper relative to the United States over the period 2006 to 2019 and countries located above the horizontal line became relatively more expensive. The figure also displays a downward-sloping 45-degree line crossing the U.S. position $(1, 0)$. Countries on the 45-degree line converged to the law of one price by 2019.

---

[1] We picked the year 2006 as the starting date because it is the first year in which the database contains Big Mac prices for at least 40 countries.

Table 9.1. The Big Mac Real Exchange Rate, January 2019

Country	$P^{BigMac*}$	$\mathcal{E}$	$\mathcal{E}P^{BigMac*}$	e^{BigMac}	$\mathcal{E}^{BigMac\,PPP}$
Switzerland	6.50	1.02	6.62	1.19	0.86
Norway	50.00	0.12	5.86	1.05	0.11
Sweden	52.00	0.11	5.84	1.05	0.11
United States	5.58	1	5.58	1	1
Canada	6.77	0.75	5.08	0.91	0.82
Euro area	4.05	1.15	4.64	0.83	1.38
Denmark	30.00	0.15	4.60	0.83	0.19
Brazil	16.90	0.27	4.55	0.81	0.33
Australia	6.10	0.71	4.35	0.78	0.91
Uruguay	140.00	0.03	4.31	0.77	0.04
Singapore	5.80	0.74	4.28	0.77	0.96
New Zealand	6.20	0.68	4.19	0.75	0.90
Britain	3.19	1.28	4.07	0.73	1.75
South Korea	4500.00	0.00	4.02	0.72	0.00
Chile	2640.00	0.00	3.89	0.70	0.00
United Arab Emirates	14.00	0.27	3.81	0.68	0.40
Czech Republic	85.00	0.04	3.81	0.68	0.07
Costa Rica	2290.00	0.00	3.77	0.68	0.00
Colombia	11 900.00	0.00	3.73	0.67	0.00
Thailand	119.00	0.03	3.72	0.67	0.05
Japan	390.00	0.01	3.60	0.64	0.01
Pakistan	460.00	0.01	3.31	0.59	0.01
Saudi Arabia	12.00	0.27	3.20	0.57	0.47
Peru	10.50	0.30	3.14	0.56	0.53
China	20.90	0.15	3.05	0.55	0.27
Hungary	850.00	0.00	3.03	0.54	0.01
Poland	10.50	0.27	2.80	0.50	0.53
Philippines	140	0.02	2.67	0.48	0.04
Hong Kong	20	0.13	2.55	0.46	0.28
India	178	0.01	2.55	0.46	0.03
Mexico	49	0.05	2.54	0.45	0.11
Indonesia	33 000.00	0.00	2.34	0.42	0.00
Taiwan	69.00	0.03	2.24	0.40	0.08
South Africa	31.00	0.07	2.24	0.40	0.18
Egypt	40.00	0.06	2.23	0.40	0.14
Malaysia	9.05	0.24	2.20	0.39	0.62
Argentina	75.00	0.03	2.00	0.36	0.07
Turkey	10.75	0.19	2.00	0.36	0.52
Ukraine	54.00	0.04	1.94	0.35	0.10
Russia	110.17	0.01	1.65	0.30	0.05

Notes: $P^{BigMac*}$ denotes the price of a Big Mac in the country's currency; $\mathcal{E}$ denotes the dollar exchange rate, defined as the dollar price of one unit of the country's currency; $e^{BigMac} = \mathcal{E}P^{BigMac*}/P^{BigMac\,US}$ denotes the Big Mac real exchange rate; $P^{BigMac\,US}$ denotes the price of the Big Mac in the United States; and $\mathcal{E}^{BigMac\,PPP}$ denotes the Big Mac PPP exchange rate discussed in Section 9.3. Own calculations based on data from *The Economist*.

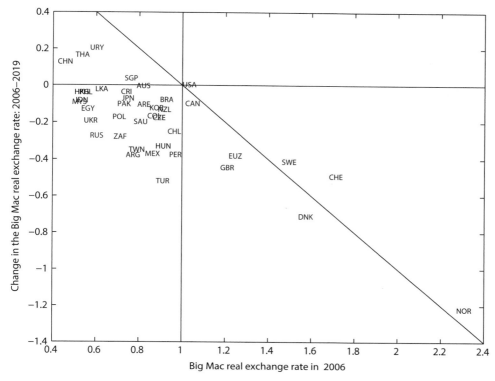

Figure 9.1. Changes in Big Mac Real Exchange Rates from 2006 to 2019
Notes: The figure plots the change in the Big Mac real exchange rate, $e^{BigMac} = \varepsilon p^{BigMac*}/p^{BigMac}$, between 2006 and 2019 against the Big Mac real exchange rate in 2006 for 40 countries. Because by definition the Big Mac real exchange rate is always equal to 1 for the United States, this country is located at coordinate $(1, 0)$. Countries below the horizontal line became relatively cheaper and countries above the horizontal line became relatively more expensive. The figure shows that most countries were cheaper than the United States in 2006 and that many of them became even cheaper by 2019. Country names are shown using ISO abbreviations.
Source: Own calculations based on data from *The Economist*.

The figure shows that deviations from the law of one price are persistent. Most countries were cheaper than the United States in 2006 and continue to be cheaper in 2019 (points to the left of the vertical line and below the 45-degree line). In fact, most countries (28 out of the 40) were cheaper than the United States in 2006 and became even cheaper over the period 2006 to 2019 (points located to the left of the vertical line and below the horizontal line). For these countries, deviations from the law of one price became larger rather than smaller.

The figure suggests that there is convergence to the law of one price for rich developed countries such as Canada, Great Britain, Sweden, Switzerland, Denmark, Norway, and the euro area. In these countries the dollar price of the Big Mac was higher than in the United States in 2006, but over the subsequent 13 years the price difference has narrowed significantly.

9.2 Purchasing Power Parity

Purchasing power parity (PPP) is the generalization of the idea of the law of one price for broad baskets of goods representative of households' actual consumption, as opposed to a single good. Let P denote the domestic currency price of such a basket of goods and P^* the foreign currency price of a basket of goods in the foreign country. The real exchange rate, denoted e, is defined as

$$e = \frac{\mathcal{E}P^*}{P}.$$

The real exchange rate indicates the relative price of a consumption basket in the foreign country in terms of consumption baskets in the home country. When $e > 1$, the foreign country is more expensive than the domestic country and when $e < 1$, the foreign country is less expensive than the domestic country.

We say that *absolute purchasing power parity* holds when the price of the consumption basket expressed in a common currency is the same domestically and abroad, $P = \mathcal{E}P^*$; or equivalently, when the real exchange rate is unity, $e = 1$.

Ascertaining whether absolute PPP holds requires gathering data on the price of the domestic basket, P, the price of the foreign basket, P^*, and the nominal exchange rate, $\mathcal{E}$. Data on price levels of large baskets of goods for many countries is produced by the World Bank's International Comparison Program (ICP).[2] This data has a frequency of about six years. At the writing of the current edition of this book, the most recent ICP release contains data for the year 2011. It reports price level data of more than 1,000 individual goods for 199 countries, including 100 developing and emerging economies and 46 advanced economies. Data on the nominal exchange rate is readily available from many sources including the ICP database. The ICP produces a measure of the level of the real exchange rate and hence allows for testing of absolute PPP.

Table 9.2 shows the dollar real exchange rate of selected developing and advanced economies in 2011. For each country it shows the dollar price of a basket relative to the United States, $e = \mathcal{E}P^*/P^{US}$, where P^{US} denotes the price of a basket of goods in the United States, P^* denotes the price of a basket of goods in a given country, and $\mathcal{E}$ denotes the nominal exchange rate (the dollar price of one unit of currency of the given country). If absolute PPP held, then a basket of goods that costs \$100 in the United States should also cost \$100 in every country. However, as the table shows, this is far from being the case. There are wide deviations from absolute PPP across countries. For example, a basket that in 2011 sold for \$100 in the United States sold for \$163 in Switzerland and for \$27 in Egypt. Thus, in 2011 Switzerland was 63 percent more expensive than the United States, and Egypt was 73 percent cheaper.

How does the ICP real exchange rate shown in Table 9.2 compare with the Big Mac real exchange rate shown in Table 9.1? As we mentioned earlier, one advantage of the real exchange rate measure produced by the World Bank's ICP is that it

---

[2] See the report "Purchasing Power Parities and Real Expenditures of World Economies, Summary of Results and Findings of the 2011 International Comparison Program," especially Table 6.1, The World Bank, 2014.

Table 9.2. Deviations From Absolute PPP in Selected Countries: Evidence from the 2011 International Comparison Program

Country	e	$\mathcal{E}$	$\mathcal{E}^{PPP}$
Switzerland	1.63	1.13	0.69
Norway	1.60	0.18	0.11
Australia	1.56	1.03	0.66
Sweden	1.36	0.15	0.11
Japan	1.35	0.0125	0.00931
Canada	1.26	1.01	0.80
France	1.17	1.39	1.18
New Zealand	1.17	0.79	0.67
Belgium	1.17	1.39	1.19
Netherlands	1.16	1.39	1.20
Austria	1.15	1.39	1.20
Ireland	1.15	1.39	1.21
United Kingdom	1.12	1.60	1.43
Germany	1.08	1.39	1.28
Italy	1.07	1.39	1.30
United States	1	1	1
South Korea	0.7711	0.0009023	0.00117
China	0.54	0.15	0.29
Sierra Leone	0.36	0.000231	0.000644
Sri Lanka	0.35	0.01	0.03
Burundi	0.34	0.000793	0.00235
Gambia, The	0.34	0.03	0.10
Nepal	0.33	0.01	0.04
Madagascar	0.33	0.000494	0.00148
Tanzania	0.33	0.000636	0.00191
Cambodia	0.33	0.000246	0.000742
Uganda	0.33	0.000396	0.0012
Vietnam	0.33	4.88e-05	0.000149
India	0.32	0.02	0.07
Bangladesh	0.31	0.01	0.04
Ethiopia	0.29	0.06	0.20
Pakistan	0.28	0.01	0.04
Egypt	0.27	0.17	0.62

Notes: The table shows the dollar real exchange rate, $e = \mathcal{E}P^*/P^{US}$, the nominal exchange rate, $\mathcal{E}$ (dollar price of one unit of foreign currency), and the PPP exchange rate, $\mathcal{E}^{PPP} = P^{US}/P^*$ in selected countries in 2011. The variable P^* denotes the foreign currency price of a basket in the foreign country, and P^{US} denotes the dollar price of a basket in the United States. The table suggests that there are large deviations from absolute PPP. For example, a basket that in 2011 cost $100 in the United States cost $163 in Switzerland and only $27 in Egypt. The PPP exchange rate will be discussed in Section 9.3.

Data Source: Purchasing Power Parities and Real Expenditures of World Economies, Summary of Results and Findings of the 2011 International Comparison Program, Table 6.1, The World Bank, 2014.

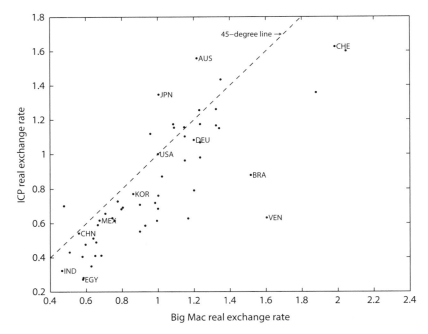

Figure 9.2. Comparing the ICP and Big Mac Real Exchange Rates in 2011
Notes: The figure plots the ICP real exchange rate against the Big Mac real exchange rate for 57 countries in 2011. The figure shows that the Big Mac real exchange rate is highly correlated with the ICP counterpart. This suggests that the Big Mac real exchange rate is a good proxy for how expensive different countries are relative to one another. Selected country names are indicated using ISO abbreviations.
Source: See notes to Tables 9.1 and 9.2.

covers baskets containing hundreds of goods. Its downside is that because the collection of such a large set of prices across many countries is costly, the frequency with which the data is produced is low, about once every six years. As a result, we don't have a good idea of how the cost of living changes in different countries at higher frequency, say yearly. By contrast, the Big Mac real exchange rate is relatively easy to construct because the price of this meal is readily available across countries. This facilitates its publication at a much higher frequency. *The Economist*, for example, publishes this indicator at least once a year. The drawback of the Big Mac real exchange rate is that it is based on a single good, the Big Mac, and therefore may not be representative of the expenditure structure of the overall economy. The ICP and Big Mac real exchange rates therefore present a trade-off between coverage and frequency. For this reason, it is of interest to ask how closely the Big Mac real exchange rate approximates the ICP real exchange rate. If the approximation is good, then the simpler measure could provide a reliable idea of how relative prices move across countries at a higher frequency.

Figure 9.2 compares the Big Mac and ICP real exchange rates in 2011 across 57 countries. Because all real exchange rates are vis-à-vis the United States, the latter is located at the coordinate (1,1) on the 45-degree line. The figure shows that the

Big Mac and ICP real exchange rates are highly correlated. The actual correlation is 0.81, which is pretty close to unity, the value that would obtain if the Big Mac real exchange rate was a perfect proxy for the ICP real exchange rate. This means that the Big Mac real exchange rate provides a reasonable approximation of how expensive countries are relative to one another.

The fact that the majority of countries lie below the 45-degree line means that the Big Mac real exchange rate exaggerates how expensive countries are relative to the United States. Overall, however, this bias is small, about 5 percent. We therefore conclude that, as a quick measure of how expensive countries are, the Big Mac real exchange rate does a pretty good job.

9.3 PPP Exchange Rates

Suppose you work in New York and get a job offer in Mumbai. You want to know whether the offer represents an increase or a decrease in your income. One way to compare the two options is to convert the Mumbai offer from rupees to dollars using the market exchange rate. If the resulting dollar figure is larger than your current salary, the Mumbai offer would represent an income improvement. The problem with this comparison is that prices of goods and services in Mumbai might be quite different from those in New York. A better way to compare income across countries is to convert amounts expressed in local currency to dollars using the *PPP exchange rate,* which takes into account possible price differences. The resulting income amount is said to be PPP adjusted.

The PPP exchange rate is defined as the nominal exchange rate that would make the consumption basket in two countries equally expensive. Put differently, the PPP exchange rate is the nominal exchange rate that would make PPP hold. It is a notional exchange rate. Formally, letting $\mathcal{E}^{PPP}$ denote the PPP exchange rate, we have that

$$\mathcal{E}^{PPP} P^* = P,$$

where, as before, P denotes the price level in the domestic country and P^* denotes the price level in the foreign country. If the PPP exchange rate is higher than the market exchange rate, $\mathcal{E}^{PPP} > \mathcal{E}$, then the domestic country is more expensive than the foreign country, $P > \mathcal{E}P^*$. In this case, it is said that the domestic currency is overvalued (and the foreign currency is undervalued). If $\mathcal{E}^{PPP} < \mathcal{E}$, then the domestic economy is cheaper than the foreign economy, $P < \mathcal{E}P^*$, and we say that the domestic currency is undervalued (and the foreign currency is overvalued).

9.3.1 BIG MAC PPP EXCHANGE RATES

The last column of Table 9.1 shows the PPP exchange rate for Big Macs, which, following the above definition, is given by

$$\mathcal{E}^{BigMac\,PPP} = \frac{P^{BigMac\,US}}{P^{BigMac*}}.$$

For example, the Big Mac PPP exchange rate for Switzerland is $0.86 per Swiss franc, while the market exchange rate is $1.02 per Swiss franc. This means that according to this measure the Swiss franc is overvalued. If one believes that in the long run the law of one price should hold for Big Macs, then one would expect the Swiss franc to depreciate against the dollar by 15.6 percent. By contrast, in the case of India, the Big Mac PPP exchange rate is $0.031 per rupee, whereas the market exchange rate is $0.014 per rupee. This means that according to the Big Mac PPP exchange rate, the rupee is 120 percent undervalued. Again, if one thinks that in the long run the law of one price should hold, then the rupee should appreciate by 120 percent.

A number of policymakers and observers have suggested that China has put in place policies conducive to an undervaluation of its currency with the intention to boost China's competitiveness in international trade. Let's see what the Big Mac PPP exchange rate has to say about the undervaluation of the Chinese yuan. The Big Mac PPP exchange rate is $0.27 per yuan, and the market exchange rate is 0.15. Thus, according to the Big Mac PPP exchange rate, the Chinese yuan is 80 percent undervalued. This result appears to give credence to the critics of China's exchange rate policy. However, in Section 9.3.4, we will show that the observed level of under-valuation of the Chinese yuan is likely to have more to do with China's income per capita than with a deliberate exchange rate manipulation.

9.3.2 PPP EXCHANGE RATES FOR BASKETS OF GOODS

Consider now PPP exchange rates for baskets of goods. The last two columns of Table 9.2 display, respectively, market and PPP exchange rates in 2011 for 33 selected countries. PPP exchange rates are constructed using the price level data from the 2011 ICP program. As we mentioned earlier, the ICP reports prices of baskets containing hundreds of goods. The table suggests a similar pattern of over- and undervaluation of different currencies vis-à-vis the dollar as the one that emerges from Big Mac PPP exchange rates, which should not be surprising given the comparison of ICP and Big Mac real exchange rates presented in Figure 9.2. For example, the market exchange rate of the Swiss franc is $1.13 per franc, whereas the PPP exchange rate is $0.69 per franc. It follows that according to the PPP exchange rate, the Swiss franc is 38.9 percent overvalued. In other words, if the market exchange rate were expected to converge to the PPP exchange rate, then the Swiss franc would be expected to depreciate by 38.9 percent. In India, the market exchange rate is $0.021 per rupee, whereas the PPP exchange rate is $0.066 per rupee, suggesting an undervaluation of the rupee vis-à-vis the dollar of 214 percent. Finally, the yuan also appears to be greatly undervalued when one uses ICP prices, as the market and PPP exchange rates are $0.15 and $0.29 per yuan, respectively.

9.3.3 PPP EXCHANGE RATES AND STANDARD OF LIVING COMPARISONS

Comparing standards of living across countries is complicated by the fact that prices of similar goods vary widely across borders. For example, as shown in Table 9.3, in 2011 GDP per capita was $49,782 in the United States but only $1,533 in India. According to this measure, the average American is 32 times richer than

Table 9.3. GDP Per Capita in U.S. Dollars at Market and PPP Exchange Rates in 2011

Country	GDP	GDP^{PPP}	$\frac{GDP^{US}}{GDP}$	$\frac{GDP^{US}}{GDP^{PPP}}$
Norway	99,035	61,879	0.50	0.80
Switzerland	83,854	51,582	0.59	0.97
Australia	65,464	42,000	0.76	1.19
Sweden	56,704	41,761	0.88	1.19
Canada	51,572	41,069	0.97	1.21
Netherlands	49,888	43,150	1.00	1.15
United States	49,782	49,782	1	1
Austria	49,590	42,978	1.00	1.16
Ireland	49,383	42,942	1.01	1.16
Belgium	46,759	40,093	1.06	1.24
Japan	46,131	34,262	1.08	1.45
Germany	44,365	40,990	1.12	1.21
France	42,728	36,391	1.17	1.37
United Kingdom	39,241	35,091	1.27	1.42
New Zealand	36,591	31,172	1.36	1.60
Italy	36,180	33,870	1.38	1.47
South Korea	22,388	29,035	2.22	1.71
China	5,456	10,057	9.12	4.95
Egypt	2,888	10,599	17.24	4.70
Sri Lanka	2,836	8,111	17.56	6.14
Vietnam	1,543	4,717	32.26	10.55
India	1,533	4,735	32.47	10.51
Pakistan	1,255	4,450	39.68	11.19
Cambodia	902	2,717	55.20	18.32
Bangladesh	874	2,800	56.95	17.78
Nepal	739	2,221	67.35	22.41
Uganda	528	1,597	94.33	31.17
Tanzania	517	1,554	96.37	32.03
Gambia, The	508	1,507	97.94	33.04
Sierra Leone	490	1,369	101.50	36.36
Madagascar	470	1,412	105.98	35.26
Ethiopia	353	1,214	140.85	41.00
Burundi	240	712	207.06	69.91

Notes: GDP stands for *GDP* per capita at market exchange rates and *GDP*^{PPP} stands for GDP per capita at PPP exchange rates.
Date Source: See Table 9.2.

the average Indian. This measure, however, does not take into account the possibility that when expressed in the same currency, goods and services might be cheaper in India than in the United States. In this case, a given dollar amount would buy a larger amount of goods in India than in the United States and Indians would not be as poor as suggested by the ratio of dollar per capita GDPs. Consider, for example, measuring per capita GDPs in units of Big Macs. According to Table 9.1, a Big Mac costs $5.58 in the United States but only $2.55 in India. This implies that one U.S. per capita GDP buys 8,922 Big Macs and one Indian per capita GDP buys 601 Big Macs. According to this measure, the average American is 15 times richer than the average Indian. This is still a big income gap, but not as large as the one suggested by the simple ratio of dollar GDPs.

But the Big Mac is not the only good that is cheaper in India than in the United States. Other items, especially services such as haircuts, domestic services, transportation, and health, are also cheaper in India. We should therefore expect to arrive at a similar conclusion; namely, that the gap in standards of living is not as pronounced as suggested by dollar GDP ratios, when incomes are measured in terms of broader baskets of goods, such as those used in the World Bank's International Comparison Program.

Let GDP^I denote the GDP per capita in India expressed in Indian rupees. Let P^I denote the rupee price of one basket of goods in India. Then, GDP^I/P^I is per capita GDP in India measured in units of baskets of goods. Similarly, letting GDP^{US} and P^{US} denote GDP in the United States and the price of one basket of goods in the United States, both measured in dollars, we have that GDP^{US}/P^{US} represents per capita GDP in the United States measured in units of baskets of goods. The ratio of per capita GDP in the United States to per capita GDP in India measured in units of baskets of goods is then given by

$$\text{Ratio of Incomes in Baskets of Goods} = \frac{GDP^{US}/P^{US}}{GDP^I/P^I}$$

$$= \frac{1}{P^{US}/P^I} \frac{GDP^{US}}{GDP^I}.$$

Now, recall that P^{US}/P^I is the dollar-rupee PPP exchange rate, which we denote by $\mathcal{E}^{PPP,I}$. Then we have that

$$\text{Ratio of Incomes in Baskets of Goods} = \frac{GDP^{US}}{\mathcal{E}^{PPP,I} GDP^I}.$$

The product $\mathcal{E}^{PPP,I} GDP^I$ is called *per capita GDP at PPP exchange rates*, and we denote it by $GDP^{PPP,I}$. It represents per capita GDP in India when baskets of goods are priced in dollar prices of the United States. This measure of GDP per capita is more comparable across countries because in all countries baskets of goods are priced at U.S. prices. Since, of course, all goods in the United States are priced at dollar prices of the United States, we have that $GDP^{PPP,US} = GDP^{US}$. Then we can write

$$\text{Ratio of Incomes in Baskets of Goods} = \frac{GDP^{US}}{GDP^{PPP,I}}.$$

Table 9.3 displays dollar GDP per capita at market exchange rates and at PPP exchange rates for 33 countries in 2011. In India, GDP per capita was $1,533 when measured at market exchange rates but $4,735 when measured at PPP exchange rates. Comparing these figures to per capita GDP in the United States, which in 2011 was \$49,782, we have that the average American is 32 times as rich as the average Indian when GDP is converted into dollars at market exchange rates, but 11 times as rich when GDP is converted at PPP exchange rates. This comparison suggests that failing to adjust for price differences across countries can result in large under- or overestimation of living standards across countries.

9.3.4 RICH COUNTRIES ARE MORE EXPENSIVE THAN POOR COUNTRIES

The comparison of living standards in the United States and India we just performed shows that on average, prices in India are lower than in the United States. It is natural to wonder whether this result belongs to a general pattern whereby poor countries tend to be cheaper than rich countries.

Figure 9.3 shows that this is indeed the case. It plots the dollar real exchange rate, $\mathcal{E}P^*/P^{US}$, against GDP per capita for 177 countries in 2011. The real exchange rate is an appropriate measure of the relative cost of living because it represents the

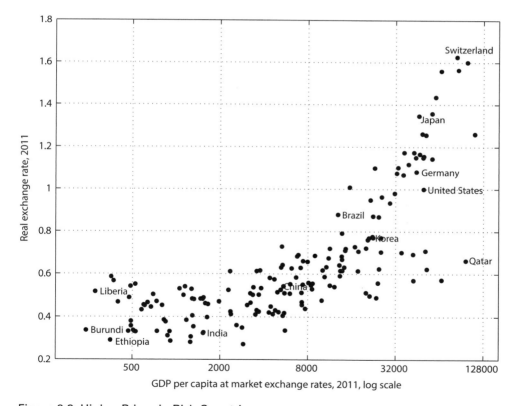

Figure 9.3. Higher Prices in Rich Countries
Notes: The graph plots the dollar real exchange rate, $e = \mathcal{E}P^*/P^{US}$, against per capita GDP at market exchange rates in 2011 for 177 countries. The figure shows that countries with higher per capita incomes tend to be more expensive. The data source is the 2011 ICP. See notes to Table 9.2 for details.

relative price of baskets of goods in two countries. In the figure, each dot represents one country.

The cloud of points is clearly upward sloping, and indeed it appears to be convex. Countries that are much poorer than the United States, such as Burundi, Liberia, and Ethiopia, are also significantly cheaper. By contrast, countries that are as or more developed than the United States, such as Switzerland, are also more expensive.[3]

Note that, consistent with this pattern, China is both poorer and cheaper than the United States. Going back to the claim often made by economic observers that the Chinese yuan is kept artificially undervalued to boost China's competitiveness in export markets, we observe that if this view explained all of the yuan's undervaluation, in the figure China should be an outlier located below the cloud of points, which is clearly not the case.

9.4 Relative Purchasing Power Parity

Most studies of purchasing power parity focus on changes in the real exchange rate, rather than on the level of the real exchange rate. The advantage of focusing on the change in the real exchange rate is that one does not need information on the level of the price of baskets of goods and can instead work with consumer price index data, which is available at higher frequency and for longer periods of time. Price indices, such as the consumer price index, provide information about how prices of large baskets of goods change over time, but not on the absolute price level. This is reflected in the index having a base year at which it takes an arbitrary value, typically 100.

We say that *relative PPP* holds if the real exchange rate does not change over time; that is,

$$\text{relative PPP holds if } \Delta e_t \equiv \Delta \frac{\mathcal{E}_t P^*_t}{P_t} = 0,$$

where e_t denotes the real exchange rate at time t, $\mathcal{E}_t$ denotes the nominal exchange rate at time t, P_t denotes the domestic consumer price index at time t, and P^*_t denotes the foreign consumer price index at time t. The symbol Δ denotes change over time; so, for example, $\Delta e_t = e_t - e_{t-1}$. The notation now introduces time subscripts because relative PPP is all about changes in the real exchange rate over time.

When relative PPP holds, the price of a basket of goods expressed in the same currency need not be the same in the domestic and foreign countries, but changes at the same rate over time in both countries. When Δe_t is negative, we say that the real exchange rate appreciates. In this case the domestic country becomes more expensive over time relative to the foreign country. And when Δe_t is positive, we say that the real exchange rate depreciates. In this case, the domestic country becomes less expensive over time relative to the foreign country.

---

[3]The positive relationship between standards of living and costs of living shown in Figure 9.3 is robust to measuring GDP per capita at PPP exchange rates. Exercise 9.3 asks you to establish this result.

The empirical question of whether relative PPP holds can be divided into two parts: Does relative PPP hold in the long run? And, does relative PPP hold in the short run? Let's begin with the first part.

9.4.1   DOES RELATIVE PPP HOLD IN THE LONG RUN?

Consider the dollar-pound real exchange rate at time t, which is given by

$$e_t = \frac{\mathcal{E}_t P_t^{UK}}{P_t^{US}},$$

where $\mathcal{E}_t$ denotes the dollar-pound nominal exchange rate at time t, defined as the dollar price of one pound, P_t^{UK} denotes the consumer price index in the United Kingdom at time t, and P_t^{US} denotes the consumer price index in the United States at time t. Because consumer price indices are arbitrarily normalized at a base year, the level of e_t, as defined here, is meaningless. However, variations in e_t over time, Δe_t, provide information about changes in the relative costs of living in the two countries, which is precisely why the concept of relative PPP is useful.

Figure 9.4 shows with a solid line the natural logarithm of P_t^{US} and with a broken line the natural logarithm of $\mathcal{E}_t P_t^{UK}$ over the period 1870–2018. To facilitate interpretation, we normalize both P_t^{US} and $\mathcal{E}_t P_t^{UK}$ to 1 in 1870 (i.e., at $t = 1870$), so that their logarithms are zero in that year. The figure shows that over the long run, P_t^{US} and $\mathcal{E}_t P_t^{UK}$ move in tandem. In other words, over the past 148 years the United States did not become systematically cheaper or more expensive than the United Kingdom. This suggests that relative PPP holds in the long run between these two countries.

Let's now see whether relative PPP also holds in the long run for other country pairs. To this end, for a given country, let P_t denote its consumer price index at time t, let $\mathcal{E}_t$ denote its dollar exchange rate at time t, defined as the price of one dollar in terms of the country's currency, and P_t^{US} the U.S. consumer price index at time t. If relative PPP holds between this country and the United States in the long run, then it must be the case that the real exchange rate does not change in the long run. At any time t, the real exchange rate, e_t, is given by

$$e_t = \frac{\mathcal{E}_t P_t^{US}}{P_t}.$$

The rate of change of the real exchange rate, which we denote by ϵ_t^r, is called the *real depreciation rate* of the country's currency against the U.S. dollar and satisfies

$$1 + \epsilon_t^r = \frac{e_t}{e_{t-1}} = \frac{(\mathcal{E}_t/\mathcal{E}_{t-1})(P_t^{US}/P_{t-1}^{US})}{P_t/P_{t-1}}.$$

Let $\epsilon_t = \mathcal{E}_t/\mathcal{E}_{t-1} - 1$ be the rate of change of the nominal exchange rate. This variable is called the *nominal depreciation rate* of the country's currency against the U.S. dollar. Also, let $\pi_t = P_t/P_{t-1} - 1$ and $\pi_t^{US} = P_t^{US}/P_{t-1}^{US} - 1$ be the inflation rates in the country considered and in the United States, respectively. Then, the real

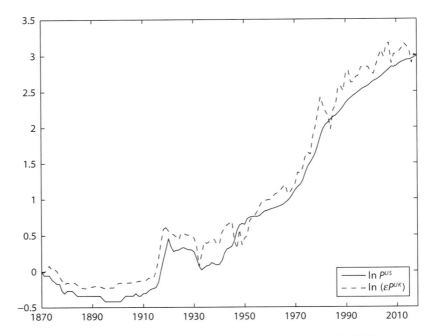

Figure 9.4. U.S. and U.K. Consumer Price Indices in Dollars, 1870–2018

Notes: Both price indices are normalized to 1 in 1870 and are expressed in logarithms. The fact that the two lines keep close to each other over 148 years suggests that relative PPP holds in the long run.

Data Source: Until 2013, Òscar Jordà, Moritz Schularick, and Alan M. Taylor, "Macrofinancial History and the New Business Cycle Facts," in *NBER Macroeconomics Annual 2016*, Volume 31, edited by Martin Eichenbaum and Jonathan A. Parker (Chicago: University of Chicago Press, 2017). After 2013, IFS, FRED, and U.K. Office of National Statistics.

depreciation rate can be written as

$$1 + \epsilon_t^r = \frac{(1 + \epsilon_t)(1 + \pi_t^{US})}{(1 + \pi_t)}. \tag{9.1}$$

Taking the natural logarithm of the left- and right-hand sides of this expression and using the approximation $\ln(1 + x) \approx x$ for any x, we obtain

$$\epsilon_t^r = \epsilon_t + \pi_t^{US} - \pi_t.$$

Relative PPP holds if the real exchange rate does not change over time, which means that the real depreciation rate is nil, $\epsilon_t^r = 0$. So we can write

$$\text{Relative PPP holds if } \epsilon_t = \pi_t - \pi_t^{US}.$$

In words, relative PPP holds if the rate of depreciation of the country's currency against the dollar, ϵ_t, is equal to the inflation differential between the country considered and the United States, $\pi_t - \pi_t^{US}$.

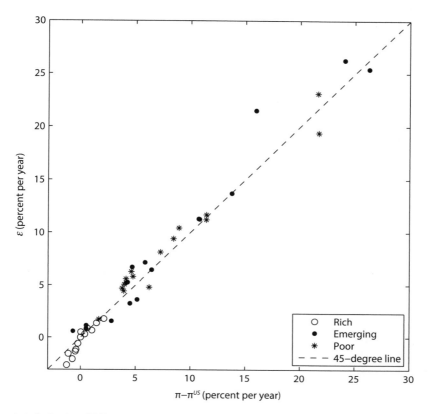

Figure 9.5. Inflation Differentials and Depreciation Rates, 1960 to 2017 Averages
Notes: Each marker represents a country. There are 45 countries in total; 13 rich, 17 emerging, and 15 poor. For a given country, ϵ denotes the average depreciation rate against the U.S. dollar and π denotes the average inflation rate. The variable π^{US} denotes the average U.S. inflation rate. The observations line up close to the 45-degree line, indicating that relative PPP holds well in the long run.
Data Sources: World Development Indicators and FRED. Countries with populations less than 5,000,000, with average inflation rates in excess of 30 percent, with average depreciation rates in excess of 30 percent, or with less than 40 consecutive years of data were excluded.

We say that relative PPP holds in the long run if ϵ_t^r is zero on average over a long period of time. Let ϵ, π, and π^{US} denote the average values of ϵ_t, π_t, and π_t^{US}. Then we can write

$$\text{Relative PPP holds in the long run if } \epsilon = \pi - \pi^{US}.$$

Figure 9.5 plots the average depreciation rate, ϵ, against the average inflation differential, $\pi - \pi^{US}$, for 45 countries. Averages are taken over the period 1960 to 2017. The figure includes 15 poor countries, shown with stars, 17 emerging countries, shown with bullets, and 13 rich countries, shown with circles.[4] The fact that

----

[4]The rich countries are: Australia, Austria, Belgium, Canada, France, Germany, Italy, Japan, Netherlands, Sweden, Switzerland, United Kingdom, and the United States. The emerging countries are: Algeria, Chile,

most observations line up along the 45-degree line suggests that the condition $\epsilon = \pi - \pi^{US}$ holds relatively well. This is particularly the case for rich countries. There are some observations lying relatively far from the 45-degree line. These observations correspond mostly to countries that suffered high inflation during the sample period, such as Chile, Hungary, Poland, and Sudan. In these cases the weakening of the relationship between the inflation differential and the depreciation rate might be due to difficulties measuring prices accurately in high-inflation environments. Overall, however, the clustering of observations close to the 45-degree line is remarkable, which suggests that relative PPP holds fairly well for many countries over the long run.

9.4.2   DOES RELATIVE PPP HOLD IN THE SHORT RUN?

Take another look at Figure 9.4. As discussed before, over the past 150 years prices in the United States and the United Kingdom expressed in the same currency changed by about the same proportion. At the same time, the figure shows that on a period-by-period basis the difference between the two prices displays significant changes. Sometimes the two lines get closer to each other and sometimes they move further apart. This means that sometimes the United States becomes cheaper and sometimes more expensive relative to the United Kingdom. In other words, the real exchange rate changes in the short run.

This fact is shown more clearly in Figure 9.6, which displays the year-over-year real depreciation rate, ϵ_t^r, expressed in percent per year. This variable is the change in the distance between the solid and the broken lines in Figure 9.4. If the real exchange rate were constant over time, Figure 9.6 would display a flat line at zero. But this is far from being the case. The figure shows that the real depreciation rate moves around quite a bit. The standard deviation of ϵ_t^r is 9.3 percent. This means that typically, from one year to the next, the United States becomes almost 10 percent more expensive or cheaper than the United Kingdom. Thus, you should not be surprised if one year you visit the United Kingdom and find it cheap and just a couple of years later you go back and find it quite expensive. The fact that ϵ_t^r is quite volatile means that relative PPP does not hold in the short run.

9.5   How Wide Is the Border?

We just documented that relative PPP does not hold in the short run. Relative costs of living can change significantly across countries from one year to the next. A natural question is whether these time-varying deviations from purchasing power parity are due to the existence of a country border or hold more broadly across different geographic locations. One factor that could explain the failure of relative PPP is transportation costs. It might pay for New York households to shop in Newark

Colombia, Egypt, Greece, Hungary, Iran, South Korea, Malaysia, Mexico, Morocco, Poland, Portugal, South Africa, Spain, Thailand, and Turkey. The poor countries are: Cameroon, Ethiopia, Ghana, India, Indonesia, Kenya, Madagascar, Myanmar, Nepal, Nigeria, Pakistan, Philippines, Sri Lanka, Sudan, and Tanzania. The classification of countries is taken from Uribe and Schmitt-Grohé, *Open Economy Macroeconomics* (Princeton, NJ: Princeton University Press, 2017).

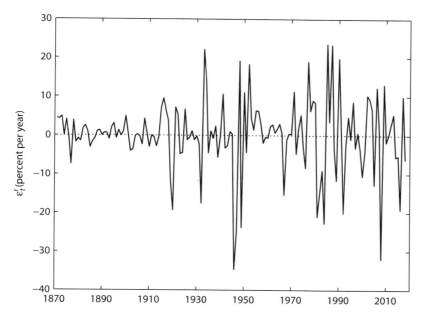

Figure 9.6. Year-Over-Year Percent Change in the Dollar-Pound Real Exchange Rate, 1870–2018
Notes: The figure shows that the dollar-pound real exchange rate changes significantly from one year to the next, suggesting that relative PPP does not hold in the short run.
Data Source: See Figure 9.4.

to exploit relatively small differences in prices between the two cities. However, it would take much larger price differences to induce New York households to shop in Philadelphia. Therefore, differences in prices between New York and Philadelphia are likely to be larger than differences in prices between New York and Newark. Moreover, if transportation costs change over time (say because of changes in the cost of gasoline), price differences are also likely to change over time.

But the mere existence of an international border between two locations could by itself introduce impediments for prices to equalize across locations. Reasons why an international border might matter for the size of deviations from relative PPP include movements in nominal exchange rates in combination with rigidities in local currency prices and trade frictions that contribute to market segmentation across countries such as tariffs, quotas, and government regulation. If these factors are sufficiently pronounced, then we could observe, for example, that even though New York is much farther away from Los Angeles than from Toronto, relative PPPs fail more significantly for the NY-Toronto pair than for the NY-LA pair.

In an influential paper, Charles Engel of the University of Wisconsin and John Rogers of the Board of Governors of the Federal Reserve System set out to quantify how important the international border is for short-run deviations from relative PPP.[5] They consider the consumer price index of 14 baskets of goods in 14 U.S. cities

[5]Charles Engel and John H. Rogers, "How Wide Is the Border?," *American Economic Review* 86 (December 1996): 1112–1124.

and 9 Canadian cities over the period September 1978 to December 1994.[6] Let $P^g_{c,t}$ be the price index of good basket g in city c at time t. Then, the real exchange rate of basket g in the city pair $(c1, c2)$ at time t, which we denote by $e^g_{c1,c2,t}$, is given by

$$e^g_{c1,c2,t} = \frac{\mathcal{E}_{c1,c2,t}P^g_{c2,t}}{P^g_{c1,t}},$$

where $\mathcal{E}_{c1,c2,t}$ is the nominal exchange rate between cities $c1$ and $c2$ in period t defined as the price of one unit of the currency used in city $c2$ in terms of units of the currency used in city $c1$. Of course, if the two cities are located in the same country, then $\mathcal{E}_{c1,c2,t}$ is unity (the U.S. dollar price of one U.S. dollar is 1, and the Canadian dollar price of one Canadian dollar is also 1).

Let $\Delta \ln e^g_{c1,c2,t}$ denote the time difference of the logarithm of the real exchange rate of basket g between cities $c1$ and $c2$. This variable measures the percentage change in the real exchange rate over two months. If relative PPP holds, then $\Delta \ln e^g_{c1,c2,t}$ should be close to zero. Further, let $\sigma^g_{c1,c2}$ be the standard deviation of $\Delta \ln e^g_{c1,c2,t}$ taken across time periods. A large value of $\sigma^g_{c1,c2}$ indicates large violations of relative PPP in the short run.

For each basket of goods g there are as many standard deviations as there are city pairs. Since the dataset contains 14 baskets of goods and 23 cities, the maximum possible number of standard deviations is 3,542.

Engel and Rogers estimate the following regression:[7]

$$\sigma^g_{c1,c2} = \text{constant} + 0.00106 \ln d_{c1,c2} + 0.0119 B_{c1,c2} + \mu^g_{c1,c2},$$

where $d_{c1,c2}$ denotes the distance in miles between cities $c1$ and $c2$, $B_{c1,c2}$ is a variable that takes the value 1 if cities $c1$ and $c2$ are separated by an international border and zero otherwise, and $\mu^g_{c1,c2}$ is a regression residual. The positive coefficient on distance says that the farther apart are cities, the larger the variations in real exchange rate changes will be. The positive coefficient on the border says that, for the same distance between two cities, the standard deviation of changes in real exchange rates is larger for U.S.-Canada city pairs than it is for U.S.-U.S. or Canada-Canada city pairs.

To quantify the impact of the international border on deviations from relative PPP, one could ask what is the required increase in distance between two cities in the same country to obtain the same volatility in real exchange rate changes as two cities separated by the same distance but located on different sides of the U.S.-Canada border. To answer this question, note that the existence of a border between two cities increases the standard deviation of changes in real exchange rates by 0.0119. Increasing the distance between two cities by one mile raises the

---

[6]The baskets of goods are food at home; food away from home; alcoholic beverages; shelter; fuel and other utilities; household furnishings and operations; men's and boys' apparel; women's and girls' apparel; footwear; private transportation; public transportation; medical care; personal care; and entertainment. The U.S. cities included are Baltimore, Boston, Chicago, Dallas, Detroit, Houston, Los Angeles, Miami, New York, Philadelphia, Pittsburgh, San Francisco, St. Louis, and Washington, DC. The Canadian cities included are Calgary, Edmonton, Montreal, Ottawa, Quebec, Regina, Toronto, Vancouver, and Winnipeg.

[7]The term labeled "constant" includes an intercept and city fixed effects.

standard deviation by

$$\frac{\partial \sigma^g_{c1,c2}}{\partial d_{c1,c2}} = 0.00106 \frac{\partial \ln d_{c1,c2}}{\partial d_{c1,c2}} = 0.00106 \frac{1}{d_{c1,c2}}.$$

The average distance between two cities in the Engel-Rogers dataset is about 1,100 miles. Thus, we have that the increase in volatility associated with an increase in distance of one mile is

$$\frac{\partial \sigma^g_{c1,c2}}{\partial d_{c1,c2}} = 0.00106 \frac{1}{1100} = 0.00000096364.$$

Since each mile adds 0.00000096364 to the standard deviation and the border adds 0.0119 to the standard deviation, we have that being separated by the border is equivalent to increasing the distance between two cities by 0.0119/0.00000096364, or about 12,000 miles. This is quite a wide border!

In sum, the evidence presented here suggests that the amplitude of deviations from relative PPP is increasing in the distance separating two locations. In addition, the mere existence of an international border separating two locations adds significantly to this amplitude. This means that factors such as exchange rate volatility, local price rigidities, tariffs, quotas, and cross-border regulations play an important role in determining the size of changes in real exchange rates in the short run.

9.6 Nontradable Goods and Deviations from Purchasing Power Parity

In the preceding sections, we have documented the existence of large and persistent deviations from purchasing power parity. For example, we saw that in 2011 a basket of goods that cost $100 in the United States cost only $32 in India; that is, India was three times as cheap as the United States. One may wonder whether it wouldn't pay for U.S. consumers to import goods from India. This would tend to equalize prices across the two countries.

One reason why price differences tend to persist is that not all goods are internationally tradable. For these goods, transportation costs are too large for international trade to be profitable. For instance, few people would fly from the United States to India just to take advantage of a cheaper haircut. Goods and services with these characteristics are called nontradable goods or nontraded goods. Examples of nontradable goods include services such as haircuts, restaurant meals, housing, some health services, and some educational services. But not all services are nontradables. For instance, the United States exports high-level educational services such as college, master's, and doctoral education. There are also nonservice goods that could be nontradable. For instance, some fresh vegetables, such as lettuce, are typically grown and consumed locally. Tradable goods include agricultural commodities such as wheat, corn, and soybeans, metals, minerals, oil, and many manufacturing goods. In general, nontradables make up a significant share of a country's output, typically above 50 percent.

The existence of nontradables gives rise to systematic deviations from PPP. To see this, note that the consumption price level P is an average of all prices in the economy. Consequently, it includes both the prices of nontradables and the prices of tradables. The prices of nontradables are determined entirely by domestic factors, so one should not expect the law of one price to hold for this type of goods. Let P_T and P_N denote the domestic prices of tradables and nontradables, respectively, and P_T^* and P_N^* the corresponding foreign prices. Suppose that the law of one price holds for tradable goods; that is,

$$P_T = \mathcal{E} P_T^*.$$

By contrast, the law of one price does not hold for nontradable goods

$$P_N \neq \mathcal{E} P_N^*.$$

Suppose the price level, P, is some average of the prices of tradables and nontradables. We can then write

$$P = \phi(P_T, P_N),$$

where the function $\phi(\cdot, \cdot)$ is increasing in P_T and P_N and homogeneous of degree one. The homogeneity property means that if both P_T and P_N increase by the same percentage, then the price level P also increases by the same percentage. For example, if P_T and P_N increase by 5 percent, then P also increases by 5 percent.[8] A number of functional forms satisfy the conditions imposed on $\phi(\cdot, \cdot)$. For instance, if P is a simple average of P_T and P_N, then we have that $\phi(P_T, P_N) = (P_T + P_N)/2$. If instead P is a geometric average of P_T and P_N, then $\phi(P_T, P_N) = (P_T)^\gamma (P_N)^{1-\gamma}$, with $\gamma \in (0, 1)$. Section 9.9 provides microfoundations for this functional form.

Assume that the price level in the foreign country is also constructed as some average of the prices of tradables and nontradables. For simplicity, assume the same functional form as in the domestic country; that is,

$$P^* = \phi(P_T^*, P_N^*).$$

We can then write the real exchange rate, e, as

$$
\begin{aligned}
e &= \frac{\mathcal{E} P^*}{P} \\
&= \frac{\mathcal{E} \phi(P_T^*, P_N^*)}{\phi(P_T, P_N)} \\
&= \frac{\mathcal{E} P_T^* \phi(1, P_N^*/P_T^*)}{P_T \phi(1, P_N/P_T)} \\
&= \frac{\phi(1, P_N^*/P_T^*)}{\phi(1, P_N/P_T)}.
\end{aligned}
\tag{9.2}
$$

The last equality says that the real exchange rate depends on the relative price of nontradables in terms of tradables across countries. The real exchange rate is less

---

[8]Technically, homogeneity of degree one means that $\phi(\lambda P_T, \lambda P_N) = \lambda \phi(P_T, P_N)$ for any $\lambda > 0$.

than one; that is, the consumption basket is less expensive abroad than domestically, if the relative price of nontradables in terms of tradables is lower in the foreign country than domestically. Formally,

$$e < 1 \text{ if } \frac{P_N^*}{P_T^*} < \frac{P_N}{P_T}.$$

Going back to the example of India and the United States, this inequality says that India is cheaper than the United States because in India the relative price of nontradables in terms of tradables is lower than in the United States.

9.7 Trade Barriers and Real Exchange Rates

In the previous section, deviations from PPP occur due to the presence of non-tradable goods. In this section, we investigate deviations from PPP that may arise even when all goods are traded. Specifically, we study deviations from PPP that arise because governments impose trade barriers, such as import tariffs, export subsidies, and quotas, which artificially distort relative prices across countries.

Consider, for simplicity, an economy in which all goods are internationally trad-able. Suppose further that there are two types of tradable goods, importables and exportables. Importable goods are goods that are either imported or produced domestically but coexist in the domestic market with identical or highly substi-tutable imported goods. Exportable goods are goods that are produced domestically and sold in foreign and possibly domestic markets. Let the world price of importa-bles be P_M^*, and the world price of exportables be P_X^*. In the absence of trade barriers, the law of one price must hold for both goods; that is, the domestic prices of exportables and importables, denoted P_X and P_M, must be given by

$$P_X = \mathcal{E} P_X^*$$

and

$$P_M = \mathcal{E} P_M^*,$$

where, as before, $\mathcal{E}$ denotes the nominal exchange rate defined as the domestic cur-rency price of one unit of foreign currency. The domestic price level, P, is an average of P_X and P_M. Specifically, assume that P is given by

$$P = \phi(P_X, P_M),$$

where $\phi(\cdot, \cdot)$ is an increasing and homogeneous-of-degree-one function. A similar relation holds in the foreign country,

$$P^* = \phi(P_X^*, P_M^*).$$

The real exchange rate, $e = \mathcal{E} P^*/P$, can then be written as

$$e = \frac{\mathcal{E} P^*}{P} = \frac{\mathcal{E} \phi(P_X^*, P_M^*)}{\phi(P_X, P_M)} = \frac{\phi(\mathcal{E} P_X^*, \mathcal{E} P_M^*)}{\phi(P_X, P_M)} = \frac{\phi(P_X, P_M)}{\phi(P_X, P_M)} = 1,$$

where the third equality uses the fact that ϕ is homogeneous of degree one and the fourth equality uses the fact that the law of one price holds for both goods. This expression says that if all goods are internationally tradable and no trade barriers are in place, the two countries are equally expensive.

Consider next the consequences of imposing a tariff $\tau > 0$ on imports in the home country. Now an importer of goods pays $\mathcal{E}P_M^*$ to the foreign producer and $\tau\mathcal{E}P_M^*$ in tariffs to the local government. Consequently, the domestic price of the importable good increases by a factor of $1 + \tau$; that is,

$$P_M = (1 + \tau)\mathcal{E}P_M^*.$$

Then the real exchange rate becomes

$$e = \frac{\mathcal{E}\phi(P_X^*, P_M^*)}{\phi(P_X, P_M)} = \frac{\phi(\mathcal{E}P_X^*, \mathcal{E}P_M^*)}{\phi(\mathcal{E}P_X^*, (1 + \tau)\mathcal{E}P_M^*)} < 1,$$

where the inequality follows from the fact that $\phi(\cdot, \cdot)$ is increasing in both arguments and that $1 + \tau > 1$. This expression shows that the imposition of import tariffs leads to an appreciation of the real exchange rate; that is, it makes the domestic consumption basket more expensive relative to the foreign consumption basket. Exercise 9.7 asks you to analyze how the imposition of an export subsidy affects the real exchange rate.

We have established that trade barriers can cause persistent deviations from PPP. According to this analysis, one should expect that protectionist trade policies, like the import tariffs imposed by the Trump administration in 2019, will cause an appreciation of the real exchange rate (a fall in e), making the United States more expensive relative to the rest of the world.

9.8   Home Bias and the Real Exchange Rate

Thus far we have seen that PPP may fail because not all goods are tradable or because of the presence of tariffs. In this section, we introduce a third reason for why PPP fails; namely, that the weights with which a particular good enters in the consumption basket is different across countries. Such differences in weights reflect primarily differences in tastes across countries. And in turn these differences in taste might reflect a preference for goods that the country specializes in. For instance, Argentines might spend a larger fraction of their income on beef than Germans. And Germans might spend a larger fraction of their income on cars than Argentines. Such a preference for domestically produced goods is called *home bias*. To see why home bias can lead to variations in the real exchange rate, suppose that beef becomes more expensive relative to cars. Since beef has a larger share in the Argentine consumption basket, the Argentine basket will become more expensive relative to the German basket. In other words, the Argentine peso will experience a real appreciation against the euro.

To formalize the way in which home bias affects the real exchange rate, suppose that in Argentina and Germany households consume only two goods, beef and cars. Let P_b denote the price of beef and P_c the price of cars in Argentina expressed in Argentine pesos. Similarly, let P_b^* and P_c^* denote the price of beef and cars in Germany expressed in euros. Suppose that the consumer price index in Argentina, denoted P, is the following geometric average of the prices of beef and cars in that country,

$$P = (P_b)^\gamma (P_c)^{1-\gamma},$$

where $\gamma \in (0, 1)$ is a parameter. Similarly, suppose that the consumer price index in Germany, denoted P^*, is given by

$$P^* = (P_b^*)^{\gamma^*} (P_c^*)^{1-\gamma^*},$$

with $\gamma^* \in (0, 1)$. The parameters γ and γ^* capture the weights given to the price of beef in the Argentine and German consumer price indices. Now suppose that Argentines spend a lot on beef and not that much on cars and that Germans spend a lot on cars and relatively little on beef. In this case, the price of beef should have a larger weight in the Argentine price index than in the German one; that is, it should be the case that

$$\gamma > \gamma^*.$$

Suppose further that both beef and cars are freely traded internationally, so that the law of one price holds for both goods; that is,

$$P_b = \mathcal{E} P_b^*$$

and

$$P_c = \mathcal{E} P_c^*,$$

where $\mathcal{E}$ denotes the nominal exchange rate expressed as the peso price of one euro. The real exchange rate can then be written as,

$$e = \frac{\mathcal{E} P^*}{P} = \left(\frac{P_c}{P_b}\right)^{\gamma - \gamma^*}.$$

Because $\gamma > \gamma^*$, an increase in the price of beef in terms of cars causes a real appreciation of the peso (a fall in e). Intuitively, if the relative price of beef increases, then the price of the Argentine consumption basket, P, increases by more than the price of the German consumption basket, P^*, since beef has a larger weight in the Argentine basket than in the German basket. It follows that the Argentine consumption basket becomes relatively more expensive. Note that in the absence of home bias, $\gamma = \gamma^*$, the real exchange rate is one ($e = 1$). It follows that the deviation from purchasing power parity studied here is solely due to home bias.

9.9 Price Indices and Standards of Living

Thus far, we have assumed that the price level, P, is given by some function $\phi(P_T, P_N)$, assumed to be increasing and homogeneous of degree one in the prices of the goods that enter the consumption basket—in this example, the prices of tradables, P_T, and nontradables, P_N. Intuitively, the function $\phi(P_T, P_N)$ is an average of P_T and P_N. But what type of average? What weights should the average place on P_T

and P_N? Is the price index useful to measure standards of living? For example, suppose that your money income increases by 10 percent and the price level increases by 11 percent. Are you better off or worse off? At first glance, we could say that your real income fell by $1 (=10-11)$ percent, suggesting that you are worse off. However, suppose that all of the 11 percent increase in the price level is due to an increase in the price of meat. If you happen to be a vegetarian, the price index that is relevant to you should place a weight of 0 on meat products. Thus, the price index that reflects your preferences would show no movement and you would be better off after the increase in income.

This example suggests that the weights assigned by the price index to different individual prices should reflect consumers' preferences. In this section, we establish this connection.

9.9.1 MICROFOUNDATIONS OF THE PRICE LEVEL

Suppose that the household values consumption according to the utility function

$$U(C),$$

where C denotes current consumption and $U(\cdot)$ is an increasing function. Suppose, in turn, that consumption is a composite of tradable and nontradable consumption given by the aggregator function

$$C = C_T^\gamma C_N^{1-\gamma}, \tag{9.3}$$

where C_T and C_N denote, respectively, consumption of tradable goods and consumption of nontradable goods, and γ is a parameter lying in the interval $(0,1)$. The aggregator function can be interpreted as a subutility function. For instance, we like to consume cars, which are internationally tradable, and haircuts, which are nontradable. Both form a composite good that we call consumption. Another interpretation of the aggregator function is as a technology that combines tradable and nontradable goods to produce the composite consumption good. For example, when we consume a Big Mac, we are consuming a combo made up of tradable goods (beef, wheat, oil, cheese, vegetables) and nontradables (the services provided by the cook, the cashier, etc.). These two interpretations are not mutually exclusive. The form of the above aggregator function is known as *Cobb-Douglas*.[9]

Let's define the consumer price level, P, as the minimum amount of money necessary to purchase one unit of the composite consumption good C. Formally, P is given by

$$P = \min_{\{C_T, C_N\}} \{P_T C_T + P_N C_N\}$$

subject to

$$C_T^\gamma C_N^{1-\gamma} = 1,$$

---

[9]The Cobb-Douglas aggregator is a special case of an aggregator function called *constant elasticity of substitution (CES) aggregator* or *Armington aggregator*, which we introduce in Exercise 9.13.

taking as given P_T and P_N. This is a constrained minimization problem in two variables, C_T and C_N. To transform it into an unconstrained problem in just one variable, solve the constraint for C_N and use the resulting expression to eliminate C_N from the objective function. Then the objective function features just one unknown, C_T. Let's follow these steps one at a time. Solving the constraint for C_N yields

$$C_N = C_T^{\frac{-\gamma}{1-\gamma}}. \tag{9.4}$$

Now using this expression to eliminate C_N from the objective function gives

$$P = \min_{\{C_T\}} \left\{ P_T C_T + P_N C_T^{\frac{-\gamma}{1-\gamma}} \right\}. \tag{9.5}$$

The first term of the objective function is increasing in C_T, reflecting the direct cost of purchasing tradable consumption goods. The second term is decreasing in C_T, because an increase in the consumption of tradables allows for a reduction in the consumption of nontradables while still keeping the amount of composite consumption at unity. The optimality condition associated with the minimization problem given in (9.5) is the derivative with respect to C_T of the objective function set to zero; that is,

$$P_T - \frac{\gamma}{1-\gamma} P_N C_T^{\frac{-1}{1-\gamma}} = 0.$$

Solving for C_T, we obtain

$$C_T = \left[\frac{\gamma}{1-\gamma} \frac{P_N}{P_T} \right]^{1-\gamma}. \tag{9.6}$$

Now using this expression to eliminate C_T in equation (9.4), we get

$$C_N = \left[\frac{\gamma}{1-\gamma} \frac{P_N}{P_T} \right]^{-\gamma}. \tag{9.7}$$

Intuitively, the above two expressions say that as the nontradable good becomes relatively more expensive—that is, as P_N/P_T increases—there is an optimal substitution away from nontradables and toward tradables in the production of the unit of composite consumption. Finally, use (9.6) and (9.7) to eliminate C_T and C_N from the objective function (9.5) to obtain

$$P = P_T^{\gamma} P_N^{1-\gamma} A,$$

where $A \equiv \gamma^{-\gamma} (1-\gamma)^{-(1-\gamma)}$ is a constant independent of prices. The above formula is important because it tells us that the weights assigned to the prices of tradable and nontradable goods in the consumer price level are related to the weights assigned to the corresponding goods in the aggregator function, equation (9.3). The more important the good in the aggregator function is, the larger the weight on its price in the consumer price index will be.

9.9.2 THE PRICE LEVEL, INCOME, AND WELFARE

With the microfoundations of the consumer price index in hand, we can now revisit the question of how changes in income and prices relate to welfare. Let Y denote the amount of money the household allocates to consumption. Because P is the minimum amount of money needed to obtain 1 unit of the composite consumption good, we have that Y dollars can buy

$$C = \frac{Y}{P}$$

units of the composite consumption good. Since utility, $U(C)$, depends on consumption, C, this expression says that if the price level P assigns the correct weight to the price of each of the goods that comprise the consumption basket, in this case P^T and P^N, changes in real income are directly linked to changes in consumers' welfare. That is, the price level constructed here guarantees that if real income, Y/P, goes up, the household can afford a higher level of composite consumption, C, and utility, $U(c)$. Moreover, the percent change in real income tells us the percent increase in consumption the consumer is able to afford. For instance, suppose that $\gamma = 0.25$, and that in the course of one year nominal income increased by 10 percent, the price of tradables by 12 percent, and the price of nontradables by 8 percent; that is, $\%\Delta Y = 0.1$, $\%\Delta P_T = 0.12$, and $\%\Delta P_N = 0.08$. Is the household better off or worse off relative to the previous year? Put differently, can the consumer afford more or less composite consumption in the current year relative to the previous one? Without knowing the price index, this question does not have an answer because, although nominal income increased, and the price of nontradables increased proportionally less than income, the price of tradables increased proportionally more than income. Knowing the weights in the price level, however, the answer is straightforward. The percent increase in the amount of consumption the consumer can enjoy this year is given by

$$\%\Delta C = \%\Delta \frac{Y}{P}$$

$$= \%\Delta Y - \%\Delta P$$

$$= \%\Delta Y - \gamma\%\Delta P_T - (1-\gamma)\%\Delta P_N$$

$$= 0.1 - 0.25 \times 0.12 - 0.75 \times 0.08$$

$$= 1\%.$$

This means that the consumer is better off, as he or she can afford 1 percent more consumption relative to the previous year. The intuition behind this increase in welfare is that the price that increases proportionally more than income corresponds to a good (the tradable good) that is not too important in the generation of composite consumption, as measured by the weight γ.

What could happen if the statistical office used a wrong value of γ in constructing the price level? To answer this question, let us redo the above exercise using a weight

$\tilde{\gamma} = 0.75$. Under this incorrect weight, the change in real income is

$$\%\Delta\frac{Y}{P} = 0.1 - 0.75 \times 0.12 - 0.25 \times 0.08$$

$$= -1\%,$$

which leads to the misleading conclusion that consumers are worse off and can afford 1 percent less consumption than in the previous year. The problem here is that the statistical office is assigning too much weight to the price that increased the most.

It follows from the above example that if price indices are to be informative about changes in standard of living, they must assign the correct weights to individual prices. But how can the statistical agency know what γ is? Even if the government could conduct a survey asking consumers what their individual γ is, people might not know what to answer. The typical individual has never heard anything about utility functions or aggregator functions. Fortunately, there is an indirect and more practical way to infer the value of γ. It consists in observing patterns of consumer expenditure in different types of goods. Specifically, dividing (9.6) by (9.7) and solving for γ yields

$$\gamma = \frac{P_T C_T}{P_T C_T + P_N C_N}.$$

This expression says that γ equals the ratio of expenditure on tradables in total expenditure. Thus, knowing how much individuals spend on each category of goods allows us to obtain the correct weights of each individual price in the aggregate price index P. Statistical agencies periodically conduct surveys asking individuals about their expenditure behavior and use this information as an input in the construction of price indices.

9.10 Summing Up

This chapter is concerned with differences in costs of living across countries. Key concepts introduced in the chapter are the law of one price (LOOP), purchasing power parity (PPP), the real exchange rate, nontradable goods, home bias, and price indices.

- The LOOP states that the same good must have the same price across countries or regions when expressed in a common currency.
- There exist large and systematic deviations from the LOOP.
- Absolute PPP extends the concept of the LOOP to baskets of goods. It says that consumption baskets must have the same price across countries or regions when expressed in a common currency.
- Observed deviations from absolute PPP are large and persistent.
- The real exchange rate is the relative price of a basket of goods in a foreign country in terms of a basket of goods in the domestic country. By definition, when absolute PPP holds, the real exchange rate is one.
- Relative PPP holds when the real exchange rate does not change over time.
- In the data, relative PPP holds over the long run, but fails over the short run.

- Rich countries are systematically more expensive than poor countries.
- The PPP exchange rate is the nominal exchange rate that makes PPP hold. Evaluating GDP per capita at PPP exchange rates allows for meaningful comparisons of standards of living.
- Deviations from PPP across locations are accounted for by a number of factors:

  - Distance between the two locations, which can be a reflection of transportation costs.
  - The existence of an international border separating the two locations. This can reflect the presence of nominal exchange rate volatility, local currency price rigidity, cross-border regulations, import and export tariffs, and trade quotas.
  - The existence of nontradable goods. Nontradable goods are goods that are domestically produced, but are neither importable nor exportable.

- If the weights on prices that enter the consumer price index differ across countries, then variations in relative prices can lead to variations in real exchange rates. If domestically produced goods make up a bigger share of the domestic basket than of the foreign basket and hence receive a larger weight in the home country's price index than in the foreign country's price index, then we say there is home bias in consumption.
- The imposition of import tariffs or export subsidies makes the country more expensive relative to the rest of the world; that is, it causes a real exchange rate appreciation.
- The optimal price index assigns weights to individual prices that correspond to the weight of the associated good in the consumer's utility function. When nominal income is deflated by the optimal price index, variations in real income represent variations in welfare in the same direction.

9.11 Exercises

Exercise 9.1 (International Price Convergence) The figure displays the real exchange rate of 10 hypothetical countries relative to China in 2010 and the change in the real exchange rate between 2010 and 2020.

1. What countries were less expensive than China in 2010 and became even cheaper after 10 years?
2. What countries, if any, were more expensive than China in 2010, but less expensive than China in 2020?
3. What countries, if any, were less expensive than China in 2010, but more expensive than China in 2020?
4. What countries, if any, became as expensive as China in 2020?

Exercise 9.2 (PPP in China) The International Comparison Program (ICP) reported a price level index (PLI) for China of 42 in 2005 and 54 in 2011. Recall that by construction, the PLI for the United States is always equal to 100.

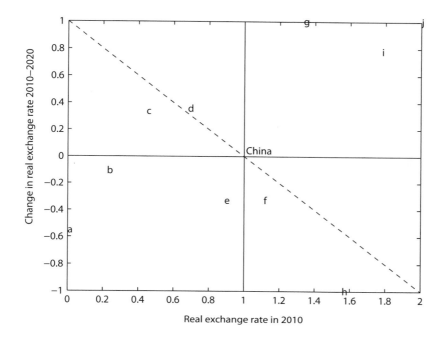

Real exchange rate in 2010

1. Find the percent change in the yuan-dollar real exchange rate between 2005 and 2011.
2. In 2005 the size of the Chinese economy, at PPP exchange rates, was 43 percent that of the U.S. economy. Ignoring growth in physical output, find the size of the Chinese economy, at 2011 PPP exchange rates, relative to that of the U.S. economy.
3. Suppose instead that all of the observed real appreciation of the yuan was due to the imposition of import tariffs by China. Assume that in the United States and China the price level is given by $P = P_X^{\gamma} P_M^{1-\gamma}$, where $\gamma = 0.5$, P_X and P_M denote export and import prices, respectively, and that absent tariffs the law of one price holds. Find the size of the import tariff.

Exercise 9.3 (Higher Prices in Richer Countries) Figure 9.3 plots the real exchange rate against per capita GDP at market exchange rates. Redo this figure using per capita GDP at PPP exchange rates instead. Use red dots. The data are available at the source indicated in the figure. For comparison, the figure should also include, with black dots, the relationship using GDP at market exchange rates. Discuss whether it is still the case that richer countries are more expensive. Explain why the slope changes.

Exercise 9.4 (How Wide Is the Border?) A researcher estimated the following relationship

$$\sigma_{\Delta \ln e} = \text{constant} + 0.001\, d + 12\, B,$$

where $\sigma_{\Delta \ln e}$ stands for the standard deviation of the percent change in the real exchange rate between two cities, d is the distance between the two cities in miles, and B is a variable that takes the value 1 if the two cities are separated by an international border and zero otherwise. Calculate the increase in distance required to keep the standard deviation of $\Delta \ln e$ constant if the international border is removed.

Exercise 9.5 (Nontradable Goods and PPP) In countries A and B, households consume only wheat and haircuts. Wheat is internationally traded, whereas haircuts are not. In country A, a ton of wheat is 10 times as expensive as a haircut, while in country B it is only 5 times as expensive. The consumer price index in country $i = A, B$, denoted P_i, is $P_i = (P_i^W)^{0.25}(P_i^H)^{0.75}$, where P_i^W and P_i^H denote the prices of wheat and haircuts in country i.

1. Calculate the real exchange rate between countries A and B.
2. Which country is more expensive and why?

Exercise 9.6 (Trade Barriers and the Real Exchange Rate I) Suppose that in countries A and B, households consume only cars and spaghetti. Suppose that both goods are internationally traded. Suppose the price index is of the form $P_i = \sqrt{P_i^C P_i^S}$, where P_i, P_i^C, and P_i^S denote, respectively, the consumer price index, the price of cars, and the price of spaghetti in country $i = A, B$.

1. What is the real exchange rate in the absence of trade barriers?
2. What is the real exchange rate if country A imposes a 10 percent import tariff on cars?

Exercise 9.7 (Trade Barriers and the Real Exchange Rate II) In Section 9.7, we deduced that the imposition of an import tariff causes an appreciation of the real exchange rate (i.e., makes the country more expensive relative to other countries). Use a similar analysis to show how the real exchange rate is affected by the following trade barriers:

1. An import subsidy.
2. An export tariff.
3. An export subsidy.

Exercise 9.8 (Import Tariffs) Evaluate the following statement: In April 2018, the United States levied a 25 percent import duty on steel and a 10 percent import duty on aluminum. This policy should make the United States more expensive relative to the rest of the world.

Exercise 9.9 (International Comparison of Standards of Living) The following table displays (fictional) quantities of final goods produced and prices in the United States and Argentina in 2021.

Good	United States		Argentina	
	Quantity	Price	Quantity	Price
Tradable	10	5	4	50
Nontradable	20	15	8	100

U.S. prices are expressed in dollars and Argentine prices in pesos. The typical basket of goods in both countries includes 1 unit of tradable goods and 2 units of nontradable goods. Tradable goods are freely traded internationally. For this type of good PPP holds.

1. Calculate the market exchange rate, expressed as the dollar price of one peso.
2. Calculate the price levels in the United States and Argentina, expressed in dollars and pesos, respectively.
3. What is the dollar/peso real exchange rate? In which country is it cheaper to live?
4. Calculate GDP in the United States and Argentina at market prices. According to this measure, how big is Argentina relative to the United States?
5. Calculate the PPP exchange rate.
6. Calculate GDP at PPP prices.
7. Comment on the numbers you obtained for the two measures of GDP.

Exercise 9.10 (Consumption Baskets and PPP Exchange Rates) Following up with the theme of Exercise 9.9, suppose that the table of quantities and prices is now given by

	United States		Argentina	
Good	Quantity	Price	Quantity	Price
Grain	10	1	10	1
Energy	10	2	10	2

Again, U.S. prices are expressed in dollars and Argentine prices in pesos. The typical consumption basket in the United States contains 1 unit of each good, while the typical consumption basket in Argentina contains 1.5 units of grain and 0.5 units of energy. Both goods are freely traded internationally and the law of one price holds for each type of good. Calculate the dollar value of GDP in Argentina in the following alternative ways:

1. At market exchange rates.
2. At PPP exchange rates using for each country its own basket.
3. At PPP exchange rates using the U.S. basket.
4. At PPP exchange rates using the Argentine basket.

Exercise 9.11 (Prices, Income, and Standards of Living) Suppose the price index, P, is given by $P = P_A^{0.4} P_B^{0.6}$, where P_A and P_B are the prices of goods A and B, the only two goods consumed in the economy. Suppose that over the course of a year, household income increased by 7 percent, the price of good A fell by 1 percent, and the price of good B increased by 12 percent. Are households better off or worse off relative to the previous year? Show your work and provide intuition.

Exercise 9.12 (Cost of Living Comparison) Suppose you work for an investment firm in New York City. You derive utility from consumption, as described by the utility function $U(C)$, where C denotes consumption and $U(\cdot)$ is an increasing function. Consumption is a composite of food and housing given by

$$C = \sqrt{C_F}\sqrt{C_H},$$

where C_F and C_H denote, respectively, consumption of food and housing. Suppose that in your current job, you make \$250,000 per year. Your company offers you a one-year position in its Bolivian branch located in La Paz. In New York City the price of food is \$50 per unit and the price of housing is \$750 per unit. Food is internationally traded, but housing is nontradable. The dollar/Bolivian peso exchange rate is 5 pesos per dollar. The price of housing in La Paz is 2,000 pesos. Suppose that all you care about is to maximize your utility and that you always spend all of your income in consumption (no savings).

1. Your boss would like to know what would be the minimum income (in dollars) you would require to be willing to work in La Paz. What would you answer? Show your work and provide intuition.
2. How many units of food and housing do you consume in New York City and how many would you consume in La Paz with your minimum required income? Provide intuition.

Exercise 9.13 (Microfounded Price Indices) Let C, C_T, and C_N denote consumption, consumption of tradables, and consumption of nontradables. Let P, P_T, and P_N denote the consumer price level, the price of tradables, and the price of nontradables. Find the consumer price level under the following aggregator functions:

1. Leontief aggregator,

$$C = \min\left\{\frac{C_T}{\gamma}, \frac{C_N}{1-\gamma}\right\},$$

where $\gamma \in (0, 1)$ is a parameter.
2. Linear aggregator,

$$C = \gamma C_T + (1-\gamma)C_N,$$

where $\gamma \in (0, 1)$ is a parameter.
3. Constant elasticity of substitution (CES) or Armington aggregator,

$$C = \left[\gamma C_T^{1-\frac{1}{\xi}} + (1-\gamma)C_N^{1-\frac{1}{\xi}}\right]^{\frac{1}{1-\frac{1}{\xi}}},$$

where $\gamma \in (0, 1)$ and $\xi > 0$ are parameters.

CHAPTER 10

Determinants of the Real Exchange Rate

In Chapter 9, we documented that the real exchange rate moves substantially over time. This means that countries sometimes become cheaper than other countries and sometimes more expensive. In this chapter, we investigate what causes the real exchange rate to move over time. We will address this question from two perspectives: the short run and the long run. In the short run, the factors of production, such as labor, cannot move easily from one sector of the economy to another. For example, an accountant cannot become a farmer from one month to the next just because the wage rate went up in the agricultural sector. Similarly, a farmer cannot quickly become an accountant when the wage rate earned by accountants goes up. Technology is also fixed in the short run. It took decades for tractors to replace horses in the farming sector. Thus, in the short run, relative prices are primarily determined by factors driving the demand for goods, such as movements in the interest rate or changes in tastes, or by factors that affect the supply of goods in the short run, such as weather conditions in the agricultural sector. Since the real exchange rate is the relative price of a basket of goods in one country in terms of baskets of goods in another country, we have that these factors will dominate movements in the real exchange rate in the short run.

By contrast, in the long run, factors of production can move more freely across sectors. The accountant can retrain herself and become a farmer, and the farmer can earn a degree in accounting. Even if this transition does not happen in their generation, their children could learn skills useful in sectors other than the one in which their parents specialized. In addition, the adoption of new technologies affects the speed at which production possibilities expand in different sectors of the economy. Thus, in the long run, relative prices—and in particular the real exchange rate—are determined to a large extent by factors affecting the supply of goods.

The short- and long-run approaches to understanding the determination of the real exchange rate have given rise to two important models known as the TNT (Traded-Non-traded) and the Balassa-Samuelson models, respectively. The present chapter is devoted to the analysis of these two models of real exchange rate determination.

10.1 The TNT Model

The TNT model is identical to the open economy model we studied in Chapter 3, except that instead of a single tradable good it features two goods, one tradable and one nontradable. The tradable good can be imported or exported without restrictions. By contrast, the nontradable good is not exchanged in international markets and must be produced and consumed domestically. The presence of two goods introduces a new endogenous variable in the model, the relative price of non-tradable goods in terms of tradable goods. As we saw in Chapter 9 (see especially Section 9.6), this relative price plays a key role in determining the real exchange rate. The reason is that if the law of one price holds for the tradable good, movements in the price of tradables do not introduce changes in relative consumer prices across countries. By contrast, the price of the nontradable good is not equalized across borders, so variations therein do affect relative prices across countries.

10.1.1 HOUSEHOLDS

Consider a two-period economy populated by many identical households whose preferences are described by the utility function

$$\ln C_1 + \beta \ln C_2, \tag{10.1}$$

where C_1 and C_2 denote consumption in periods 1 and 2, and $\beta \in (0,1)$ is a parameter representing the subjective discount factor. As in Section 9.9 of Chapter 9, assume that consumption is a composite of tradable and nontradable goods described by the Cobb-Douglas aggregation technologies

$$C_1 = (C_1^T)^\gamma (C_1^N)^{1-\gamma}, \tag{10.2}$$

and

$$C_2 = (C_2^T)^\gamma (C_2^N)^{1-\gamma}, \tag{10.3}$$

where C_t^T and C_t^N denote consumption of tradables and nontradables in periods $t = 1, 2$, respectively, and $\gamma \in (0,1)$ is a parameter governing the relative importance of tradable consumption in utility.

Suppose that the household is endowed with Q_t^T and Q_t^N units of tradable and nontradable goods in periods $t = 1, 2$. Households start period 1 with no debts or assets. In period 1, households can borrow or lend by means of a bond, denoted B_1, denominated in units of tradables and paying the interest rate r_1 in period 2. For example, if the tradable good is bananas, then the bond costs one banana in period 1 (or P_1^T units of domestic currency) and entitles the holder to $1 + r_1$ bananas in period 2 (or to $(1+r_1)P_2^T$ units of domestic currency). The budget constraint of the household in period 1 is then given by

$$P_1^T C_1^T + P_1^N C_1^N + P_1^T B_1 = P_1^T Q_1^T + P_1^N Q_1^N,$$

where P_t^T and P_t^N denote the prices of tradable and nontradable goods in periods $t = 1, 2$. In period 2, the household's budget constraint is given by

$$P_2^T C_2^T + P_2^N C_2^N = P_2^T Q_2^T + P_2^N Q_2^N + (1 + r_1) P_2^T B_1.$$

Let us now express both budget constraints in terms of tradable goods. To this end, let

$$p_t \equiv \frac{P_t^N}{P_t^T} \qquad (10.4)$$

denote the relative price of the nontradable good in terms of tradable goods in periods $t = 1, 2$. Then, dividing the period 1 budget constraint by P_1^T and the period 2 budget constraint by P_2^T, we obtain

$$C_1^T + p_1 C_1^N + B_1 = Q_1^T + p_1 Q_1^N$$

and

$$C_2^T + p_2 C_2^N = Q_2^T + p_2 Q_2^N + (1 + r_1) B_1.$$

Combining the two budget constraints to eliminate B_1 yields the intertemporal budget constraint

$$C_1^T + p_1 C_1^N + \frac{C_2^T + p_2 C_2^N}{1 + r_1} = Q_1^T + p_1 Q_1^N + \frac{Q_2^T + p_2 Q_2^N}{1 + r_1}. \qquad (10.5)$$

To save notation, let $\bar{Y}$ denote the household's lifetime income expressed in units of tradable goods in period 1; that is, let

$$\bar{Y} \equiv Q_1^T + p_1 Q_1^N + \frac{Q_2^T + p_2 Q_2^N}{1 + r_1}.$$

The intertemporal budget constraint can then be written as

$$C_1^T + p_1 C_1^N + \frac{C_2^T + p_2 C_2^N}{1 + r_1} = \bar{Y}.$$

Using the aggregator functions (10.2) and (10.3) to eliminate C_1 and C_2 from the utility function (10.1) and solving the above intertemporal budget constraint for C_2^T and using the resulting expression to eliminate C_2^T, the household's optimization problem reduces to choosing C_1^T, C_1^N, and C_2^N to maximize

$$\gamma \ln C_1^T + (1 - \gamma) \ln C_1^N + \beta \gamma \ln[(1 + r_1)(\bar{Y} - C_1^T - p_1 C_1^N)$$
$$- p_2 C_2^N] + \beta(1 - \gamma) \ln C_2^N.$$

The first-order conditions associated with this problem are obtained by taking the derivatives of this expression with respect to C_1^T, C_1^N, and C_2^N and equating them to zero. This operation yields

$$\frac{1}{C_1^T} - \frac{\beta(1 + r_1)}{(1 + r_1)(\bar{Y} - C_1^T - p_1 C_1^N) - p_2 C_2^N} = 0,$$

$$\frac{1-\gamma}{C_1^N} - \frac{\gamma\beta(1+r_1)p_1}{(1+r_1)(\bar{Y}-C_1^T-p_1C_1^N)-p_2C_2^N} = 0,$$

and

$$\frac{1-\gamma}{C_2^N} - \frac{\gamma p_2}{(1+r_1)(\bar{Y}-C_1^T-p_1C_1^N)-p_2C_2^N} = 0.$$

Using the fact that $C_2^T = (1+r_1)(\bar{Y}-C_1^T-p_1C_1^N)-p_2C_2^N$ and rearranging, we can write these optimality conditions as

$$C_2^T = \beta(1+r_1)C_1^T, \tag{10.6}$$

$$C_t^N = \frac{1-\gamma}{\gamma}\frac{C_t^T}{p_t}, \tag{10.7}$$

for $t=1,2$. The first optimality condition is the familiar Euler equation stating that as the interest rate increases, households substitute period 2 consumption for period 1 consumption. The second optimality condition says that as nontradables become more expensive, households reduce consumption of nontradables relative to consumption of tradables. Given C_t^T, the second optimality condition represents the demand for nontradables in period t. Figure 10.1 depicts with a solid line the demand schedule (10.7) in the space (C_t^N, p_t). Like any standard demand schedule, this one is downward sloping. An increase in the desired consumption of tradables, C_t^T, shifts the demand schedule out and to the right. In the figure, an increase in tradable consumption from C_t^T to $C_t^{T'}$ gives rise to the demand schedule

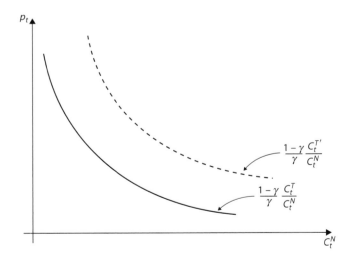

Figure 10.1. The Demand Function for Nontradables

Notes: The figure depicts the demand schedule for nontradables in period t, $p_t = (1-\gamma)/\gamma\, C_t^T/C_t^N$. Holding constant consumption of tradables, C_t^T, the higher is the relative price of nontradables, p_t, the lower the demand for nontradables, C_t^N, will be. An increase in the desired consumption of tradables from C_t^T to $C_t^{T'}$ shifts the demand schedule for nontradables out and to the right.

depicted with a broken line. Intuitively, holding the relative price, p_t, constant, the desired consumptions of tradables and nontradables move in tandem. Of course, consumption of tradables is an endogenous variable that is determined within the model. Shortly, we will see that in the present model the equilibrium level of tradable consumption is identical to its counterpart in the one-good model studied in Chapter 3.

10.1.2 EQUILIBRIUM

In equilibrium, the market for nontradable goods must clear. This means that in each period, consumption of nontradables must equal the endowment of nontradables. Formally,

$$C_t^N = Q_t^N, \qquad (10.8)$$

for $t = 1, 2$.

The country is assumed to have free capital mobility, so in equilibrium the domestic interest rate, r_1, must equal the world interest rate, r^*; that is,

$$r_1 = r^*.$$

We maintain the assumption of free capital mobility throughout this chapter. For this reason, we refer on occasion to r_1 interchangeably as the domestic interest rate or as the world interest rate.

Using the market clearing condition (10.8) to eliminate C_1^N and C_2^N from the intertemporal budget constraint (10.5), we obtain the following intertemporal resource constraint

$$C_1^T + \frac{C_2^T}{1+r_1} = Q_1^T + \frac{Q_2^T}{1+r^*},$$

which is the same as the resource constraint of the one-good economy studied in Chapter 3 (see equation (3.4), and recall that here we are assuming that $B_0 = 0$). Combining this condition with the Euler equation (10.6) yields the equilibrium level of consumption of tradables in period 1,

$$C_1^T = \frac{1}{1+\beta}\left(Q_1^T + \frac{Q_2^T}{1+r^*}\right). \qquad (10.9)$$

Thus, exactly as in the one-good economy of Chapter 3, consumption of tradables depends on the present discounted value of the stream of tradable endowments. In particular, the consumption of tradables is an increasing function of the current and the future expected endowments of tradables and a decreasing function of the interest rate. We summarize this equilibrium relationship by writing

$$C_1^T = C^T(\underset{-}{r^*}, \underset{+}{Q_1^T}, \underset{+}{Q_2^T}). \qquad (10.10)$$

The economy takes all of the variables on the right-hand side as exogenous. In particular, because the country is assumed to be a small player in international financial markets, it takes the world interest rate, r^*, as given.

The trade balance in period 1, denoted TB_1, is the difference between the endowment of tradables and consumption of tradables, $TB_1 = Q_1^T - C^T(r^*, Q_1^T, Q_2^T)$. So we can write

$$TB_1 = TB(\underset{+}{r^*}, \underset{+}{Q_1^T}, \underset{-}{Q_2^T}).$$

This is a familiar result. The trade balance improves in response to an increase in the interest rate or in the current endowment and deteriorates in response to an expected increase in the future endowment. The effects of changes in r^* and Q_2^T are unambiguous. With respect to the effect of changes in Q_1^T, equilibrium condition (10.9) shows that in response to an increase in Q_1^T, C_1^T increases but by less than the increase in Q_1^T (recall that β is positive). Thus, an increase in Q_1^T causes the trade balance to improve. This result was first derived in Chapter 3. Intuitively, C_1^T increases by less than Q_1^T because households save part of the income increase to smooth consumption over time.

Since the economy starts period 1 with a nil asset position, $B_0 = 0$, we have that in period 1 the current account equals the trade balance, $CA_1 = r_0 B_0 + TB_1 = TB_1$. So we can write

$$CA_1 = CA(\underset{+}{r^*}, \underset{+}{Q_1^T}, \underset{-}{Q_2^T}). \tag{10.11}$$

Using the equilibrium level of tradable consumption given in (10.10) to eliminate C_1^T from (10.7), we obtain the following demand schedule for nontradables:

$$C_1^N = \frac{1-\gamma}{\gamma} \frac{C^T(r^*, Q_1^T, Q_2^T)}{p_1}, \tag{10.12}$$

which is plotted in Figure 10.2. The figure also displays the supply of nontradables, Q_1^N. Since the endowment is fixed, the supply schedule is a vertical line. The equilibrium value of the relative price of nontradables, denoted p_1^e, is given by the intersection of the demand and supply schedules, point A in the figure. Combining the market-clearing condition (10.8) and the demand schedule (10.12), we have that the equilibrium relative price of nontradables is given by the solution for p_1 of

$$Q_1^N = \frac{1-\gamma}{\gamma} \frac{C^T(r^*, Q_1^T, Q_2^T)}{p_1}. \tag{10.13}$$

Note that all variables appearing in this expression, except for p_1, are exogenous. We are now ready to analyze how innovations in the interest rate and the different endowments affect the equilibrium value of p_1, a key relative price in open economies.

10.1.3   ADJUSTMENT OF THE RELATIVE PRICE OF NONTRADABLES TO INTEREST RATE AND ENDOWMENT SHOCKS

Suppose the world interest rate increases from r^* to $r^{*\prime} > r^*$. The situation is depicted in the top left panel of Figure 10.3. The initial position is at point A. The increase in the interest rate induces households to postpone consumption and increase savings. Thus, the demand for nontradables shifts down and to the left. At the original equilibrium relative price, p_1^e, there is now an excess supply of

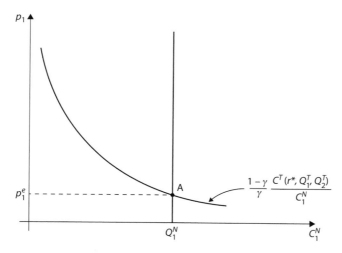

Figure 10.2. The Equilibrium Relative Price of Nontradables
Notes: The figure depicts the demand and supply functions of nontradables. The demand for nontradables is downward sloping and the supply schedule is a vertical line. The equilibrium relative price of nontradables is p_1^e, given by the intersection of the demand and supply schedules, point A.

nontradables, which induces sellers to lower prices. Prices will continue to fall until the demand for nontradables equals the endowment of nontradables. This occurs at point B, where the relative price of nontradables is $p_1^{e'} < p_1^e$. We therefore have that an increase in the world interest rate causes a fall in the equilibrium relative price of nontradables.

Suppose next that the economy experiences an increase in the endowment of tradable goods in period 1 or in period 2 or both. This case is depicted in the top right and bottom left panels of Figure 10.3. The positive endowment shock could be the result, for example, of a larger harvest due to good weather conditions, or of an improvement in the country's terms of trade. The increase in tradable endowment represents a positive income effect for the household, which increases the demand for consumption. As a result, the demand for nontradables shifts up and to the right. At the old equilibrium relative price, p_1^e, there is an excess demand for nontradables, which pushes prices up until the excess demand dissipates. At the new equilibrium, point B in the figure, the relative price of nontradables is $p_1^{e'}$, which is higher than the original price p_1^e. Although the effect of an increase in the endowment of tradables on the relative price of nontradables is qualitatively the same regardless of whether the increase occurs in period 1 or 2, or in both periods, the quantitative effect can be different. Exercise 10.2 asks you to compare the effects of temporary and permanent tradable endowment shocks.

Finally, the bottom right panel of Figure 10.3 illustrates the effect of an increase in the endowment of nontradables in period 1. The increase in the nontradable endowment shifts the supply schedule to the right. At the original price, p_1^e, the economy experiences an excess supply of nontradable goods. Consequently, sellers lower prices until the market clears again. This occurs at point B in the figure. The

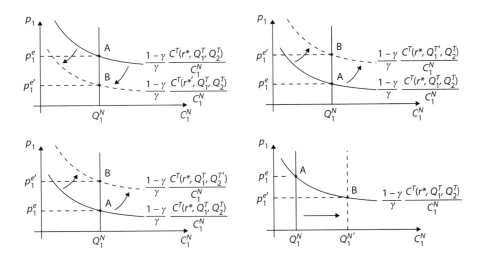

Figure 10.3. Effects of Interest Rate and Endowment Shocks on the Relative Price of Nontradables

Notes: The figure depicts the effect on the relative price of nontradables, p_1, of changes in four exogenous variables. Top left panel: An increase in the interest rate from r^* to $r^{*\prime}$ shifts the demand schedule down and to the left, causing a fall in p_1. Top right and bottom left panels: An increase in the period 1 endowment from Q_1^T to $Q_1^{T\prime}$, or in the period 2 endowment from Q_2^T to $Q_2^{T\prime}$, shifts the demand schedule for nontradables out and to the right, driving p_1 up. Bottom right panel: An increase in the endowment of nontradables from Q_1^N to $Q_1^{N\prime}$, shifts the supply of nontradables to the right, resulting in a fall in the equilibrium value of p_1.

new equilibrium price is $p_1^{e\prime} < p_1^e$. We conclude that increases in the endowment of nontradables cause the relative price of nontradables to decline.

You might have noticed that the equilibrium relative price of nontradables, p_1, does not depend on the future nontradable endowment, Q_2^N. This is somewhat counterintuitive, for one would expect that an increase in Q_2^N would make households feel richer in period 1—just like an increase in Q_2^T does—pushing up the current demand for nontradables and, given the fixed supply of this type of good in period 1, making nontradables relatively more expensive in period 1. But as our derivation of the equilibrium value of p_1 clearly shows, this is not the case. What happens here is that the increase in Q_2^N produces two opposite effects that exactly offset each other. On the one hand, as we just mentioned, an increase in Q_2^N has a positive income effect on the demand for the nontradable good in period 1, which tends to push its price up. On the other hand, the increase in Q_2^N causes the period 2 price of nontradables, p_2, to go down, which produces a substitution effect away from period 1 consumption of nontradables and in favor of future consumption of this type of good. The exact mutual cancellation of these two effects is due to the particular combination of a log-linear utility function and a Cobb-Douglas aggregator.[1]

---

[1] More generally, the two opposing effects exactly offset each other when the intertemporal elasticity of consumption substitution (between C_1 and C_2) equals the intratemporal elasticity of consumption substitution (between C_t^N and C_t^T).

Exercise 10.6 asks you to show how this prediction of the model changes when we move away from the log-linear specification for the lifetime utility function.

Collecting the results obtained in this section and the information conveyed by equation (10.13), we have that the relative price of nontradables in period 1 is increasing in the endowments of tradable goods in both periods, Q_1^T and Q_2^T, and decreasing in the world interest rate, r^*, and the endowment of nontradables in period 1, Q_1^N; that is,

$$p_1 = p(\underset{-}{r^*}, \underset{+}{Q_1^T}, \underset{+}{Q_2^T}, \underset{-}{Q_1^N}). \qquad (10.14)$$

10.2 From the Relative Price of Nontradables to the Real Exchange Rate

There is a tight connection between the relative price of nontradables, p_t, and the real exchange rate, e_t. Recall from Chapter 9 that the real exchange rate is defined as the relative price of a basket of goods abroad in terms of baskets of goods at home. Formally,

$$e_t = \frac{\mathcal{E}_t P_t^*}{P_t},$$

where P_t is the period-t price of a domestic consumption basket in units of domestic currency, P_t^* is the period-t price of the foreign consumption basket in units of foreign currency, and $\mathcal{E}_t$ is the nominal exchange rate defined as the period-t price of one unit of foreign currency in terms of domestic currency.

In the present economy the consumption basket contains tradable and nontradable goods. Its price, P_t, is therefore a function of the prices of tradables and nontradables, P_t^T and P_t^N, respectively. So we can write

$$P_t = \phi(P_t^T, P_t^N),$$

where $\phi(\cdot, \cdot)$ is increasing in both arguments and homogeneous of degree 1. In fact, given the assumed Cobb-Douglas aggregator functions for consumption given in equations (10.2) and (10.3), we know from the analysis of Section 9.9 of Chapter 9 that the price of the consumption basket is also a Cobb-Douglas function and is given by

$$\phi(P_t^T, P_t^N) = (P_t^T)^\gamma (P_t^N)^{1-\gamma} A,$$

where $A \equiv \gamma^{-\gamma}(1-\gamma)^{-(1-\gamma)}$ is a positive constant.

Similarly, the price of the foreign consumption basket is given by $P_t^* = \phi^*(P_t^{T*}, P_t^{N*})$, where P_t^{T*} and P_t^{N*} denote the foreign prices of tradables and nontradables expressed in units of foreign currency, and $\phi^*(\cdot, \cdot)$ is an increasing and homogeneous of degree 1 function. We can then write the real exchange rate as

$$e_t = \frac{\mathcal{E}_t \phi^*(P_t^{T*}, P_t^{N*})}{\phi(P_t^T, P_t^N)}. \qquad (10.15)$$

Exploiting the fact that both $\phi(\cdot,\cdot)$ and $\phi^*(\cdot,\cdot)$ are homogeneous of degree 1, we can rewrite the real exchange rate as

$$e_t = \frac{\mathcal{E}_t P_t^{T*}\phi^*(1, P_t^{N*}/P_t^{T*})}{P_t^T \phi(1, P_t^N/P_t^T)}.$$

Assuming that the law of one price holds for tradable goods, we have that $\mathcal{E}_t P_t^{T*} = P_t^T$. The real exchange rate can then be written as

$$e_t = \frac{\phi^*(1, p_t^*)}{\phi(1, p_t)},$$

where $p_t^* \equiv P_t^{N*}/P_t^{T*}$ and $p_t \equiv P_t^N/P_t^T$ denote the relative price of nontradables in terms of tradables abroad and at home, respectively. Holding constant the foreign relative price of nontradables (p_t^*), the real exchange rate (e_t) is a decreasing function of the domestic relative price of nontradables (p_t). In other words, when nontradables become more expensive relative to tradables, the domestic economy becomes more expensive relative to the rest of the world. For this reason, the relative price of nontradables in terms of tradables, p_t, is often referred to as the real exchange rate, especially in discussions involving small economies for which it is reasonable to take the foreign relative price of nontradables, p_t^*, as given.

The response of the real exchange rate to endowment and world interest rate shocks, holding constant foreign relative prices, can then be read off equation (10.14). We summarize this relationship by writing

$$e_1 = e(\underset{+}{r^*}, \underset{-}{Q_1^T}, \underset{-}{Q_2^T}, \underset{+}{Q_1^N}, \underset{+}{p_1^*}). \tag{10.16}$$

The real exchange rate depreciates in response to an increase in the world interest rate, appreciates in response to increases in the current or future endowment of tradables, and depreciates in response to an increase in the current endowment of nontradables.

10.3 The Terms of Trade and the Real Exchange Rate

Consider an economy that imports food and exports oil. How does an increase in the price of oil affect the relative price of nontradables, such as health care or housing, in terms of food? In Chapter 4, we established that changes in the terms of trade are like changes in the endowment of the exportable good. This result allows us to easily analyze the effects of terms of trade shocks on the relative price of nontradables and the real exchange rate.

Suppose that the tradable consumption good, C_t^T, is imported (food) and that the tradable endowment, Q_t^T, is exported (oil). Then, the value of the tradable endowment in terms of tradable consumption is given by $TOT_t Q_t^T$, where

$$TOT_t = \frac{P_t^X}{P_t^M},$$

P_t^X is the price of the exported traded endowment, and P_t^M is the price of the imported consumption good.

The predictions of the TNT model of Section 10.1 carry over to the present environment except that Q_t^T must be replaced by $TOT_t Q_t^T$. In particular, the equilibrium demand for tradable consumption goods, given by equation (10.10), becomes

$$C_1^T = C^T(\underset{-}{r^*}, \underset{+}{TOT_1 Q_1^T}, \underset{+}{TOT_2 Q_2^T}).$$

The equilibrium demand for nontradables (10.12) becomes

$$C_1^N = \frac{1-\gamma}{\gamma} \frac{C^T(r^*, TOT_1 Q_1^T, TOT_2 Q_2^T)}{p_1}.$$

Using the market-clearing condition $C_1^N = Q_1^N$ to eliminate C_1^N and solving for p_1 yields the equilibrium relative price of the nontradable good in terms of tradable (now imported) consumption goods, $p_1 = \frac{P_1^N}{P_1^M}$,

$$p_1 = \frac{1-\gamma}{\gamma} \frac{C^T(r^*, TOT_1 Q_1^T, TOT_2 Q_2^T)}{Q_1^N}.$$

We can summarize this expression as

$$p_1 = p(\underset{-}{r^*}, \underset{+}{TOT_1 Q_1^T}, \underset{+}{TOT_2 Q_2^T}, \underset{-}{Q_1^N}). \tag{10.17}$$

Thus an increase in the current or the future expected terms of trade (i.e., an increase in TOT_1 or TOT_2) makes nontradable goods relatively more expensive.

The consumer price level is now an average of the prices of imported and nontradable goods

$$P_1 = \phi(P_1^M, P_1^N).$$

Assume that, like domestic households, foreign households consume food and nontradable goods, but do not directly consume oil. Think of oil as an intermediate input in the production of final goods. Then, the consumer price level in the foreign country is given by

$$P_1^* = \phi^*(P_1^{M*}, P_1^{N*}).$$

Following the same steps as in Section 10.2, we can express the real exchange rate, $e_1 = \frac{\mathcal{E}_1 P_1^*}{P_1}$, as

$$e_1 = \frac{\phi^*(1, p_1^*)}{\phi(1, p_1)}.$$

Finally, using (10.17) to eliminate p_1, we can write the real exchange rate as

$$e_1 = e(\underset{+}{r^*}, \underset{-}{TOT_1 Q_1^T}, \underset{-}{TOT_2 Q_2^T}, \underset{+}{Q_1^N}, \underset{+}{p_1^*}),$$

which is just like equation (10.16), but with TOT_t multiplying Q_t^T, for $t = 1, 2$. It follows that an improvement in the current or future expected terms of trade (an increase in either TOT_1 or TOT_2), holding constant r^*, Q_1^T, Q_2^T, Q_1^N, and p_1^*, causes an increase in the equilibrium relative price of nontradables and an appreciation of the real exchange rate. The intuition is that the increase in the price of the export good makes households richer. As a result, they increase the demand for both goods, tradables (imported) and nontradables. Because the supply of nontradables is fixed, the increased demand for this type of good pushes its relative price up. In turn, the increase in the relative price of nontradables makes the country more expensive relative to the rest of the world.

10.4 Sudden Stops

"It is not speed that kills, it is the sudden stop." With this bankers' adage, Rudiger Dornbusch, Ilan Goldfajn, and Rodrigo Valdés baptized a particular type of macroeconomic crisis as a *sudden stop*.[2] A sudden stop occurs when foreign lenders abruptly stop extending credit to a country. This situation manifests itself by a sharp increase in the interest rate that the country faces in international financial markets. A variety of factors can be behind why international credit to a country suddenly dries up. For example, foreign lenders might become worried about the ability of a particular country to honor its external debt obligations, as was the case in the Argentine debt crisis of 2001, which we will examine in more detail in this section. Another reason why international credit to a country may stop is a disruption in credit markets in the developed world, which drives the world interest rate up, as was the case during both the Volcker disinflation of the early 1980s in the United States and the global financial crisis of 2007–2009. Typically, these two factors are concurrent. If the emerging country is highly indebted, foreign lenders might not only pass on the increase in the world interest rate, but also elevate the country's interest-rate premium. Examples of sudden stops include the Latin American debt crisis of the early 1980s, the Mexican Tequila crisis of 1994, the Asian financial crisis of 1997, the Russian crisis of 1998, the Argentine crisis of 2001, and the debt crises in the periphery of Europe and Iceland in the aftermath of the global financial crisis of 2007–2009.

Three hallmark consequences of sudden stops are: (a) a *current account reversal* from a deficit to a surplus or a sizable reduction in the current account deficit; (b) a contraction in aggregate demand; and (c) a real exchange rate depreciation—that is, the country suffering the sudden stop becomes cheaper relative to the rest of the world. This section shows that the TNT model can capture these three stylized facts. It then presents two case studies, the Argentine sudden stop of 2001 and the Icelandic sudden stop of 2008.

10.4.1 A SUDDEN STOP THROUGH THE LENS OF THE TNT MODEL

We model a sudden stop as an increase in the world interest rate, r^*. Figure 10.4 summarizes the effects of an increase in the world interest rate on tradable

[2] See Rudiger Dornbusch, Ilan Goldfajn, and Rodrigo O. Valdés, "Currency Crises and Collapses," *Brookings Papers on Economic Activity* 26, no. 2 (1995): 219–270.

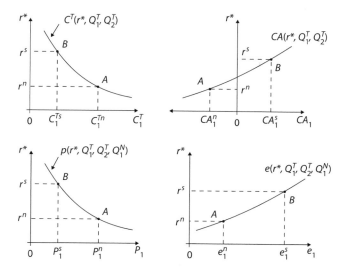

Figure 10.4. Effects of a Sudden Stop as Predicted by the TNT Model
Notes: A sudden stop is modeled as an increase in the world interest rate, r^*, from a normal level, denoted r^n, before the sudden stop to a high level, denoted r^s, after the sudden stop. The sudden stop causes a contraction in the domestic absorption of tradables, a current account reversal, a fall in the relative price of nontradables, and a real exchange rate depreciation.

consumption, the current account, the relative price of nontradables, and the real exchange rate as predicted by the TNT model. The top left panel plots the equilibrium level of tradable consumption in period 1 as a function of the world interest rate. As indicated by equation (10.10), consumption of tradables is a decreasing function of the interest rate. Before the sudden stop, the world interest rate is at its "normal" level, denoted r^n. At this interest rate, tradable consumption is C_1^{Tn}. When the sudden stop occurs, the interest rate jumps to $r^s > r^n$. As a result, the demand for tradable goods experiences a contraction from C_1^{Tn} to $C_1^{Ts} < C_1^{Tn}$. Intuitively, the increase in the interest rate creates an incentive to save in period 1, which requires postponing current spending on goods. The top right panel displays the equilibrium current account in period 1 as a function of the world interest rate, equation (10.11). At the pre-crisis interest rate, the current account is negative and equal to CA_1^n. Thus, foreign lenders are extending credit to the country. The hike in the interest rate following the sudden stop causes an improvement in the current account to $CA_1^s > 0$. As mentioned above, the change of sign in the current account from deficit to surplus is known as a current account reversal. The improvement in the external balance is the result of the contraction in the absorption of tradable goods brought about by the increase in the cost of funds.

The bottom left panel of Figure 10.4 displays the relative price of nontradables in period 1 as a function of the world interest rate. Equation (10.14) shows that in equilibrium the relative price of nontradables is a decreasing function of the world interest rate. In the figure, the sudden stop causes the relative price of nontradables to drop from p_1^n to $p_1^s < p_1^n$. This effect has a clear intuition. The increase in the interest rate induces households to cut the demand for both types of consumption goods, tradable and nontradable. The contraction in tradable consumption is met by an equivalent increase in exports (or reduction in imports). By contrast, nontradables cannot be exported, so the contraction in demand requires a fall in the relative price of nontradables to induce agents to voluntarily consume the entire endowment of this type of goods. The redirection of absorption away from tradables and toward nontradables facilitated by the drop in the relative price of nontradables after the sudden stop is known as an *expenditure switch*. Finally, the bottom right panel plots equation (10.16), which describes a positive relationship between the real exchange rate, e_1, and the world interest rate, r^*. As we just explained, the increase in the interest rate brought about by the sudden stop lowers the price of nontradables, which makes the country cheaper relative to the rest of the world.

10.4.2   THE ARGENTINE SUDDEN STOP OF 2001

To end hyperinflation, in 1991 Argentina implemented an exchange-rate-based inflation stabilization plan. The plan consisted in pegging the peso to the U.S. dollar at a one-to-one parity. This exchange rate policy in fact was written into a law, called the Convertibility Law. Pegging the peso to the dollar quickly brought the inflation rate to low levels. The country was able to maintain the one-to-one parity to the U.S. dollar for an entire decade. But in 2001, Argentina fell into a crisis that culminated in default and devaluation. The default led to a cutoff from international capital markets and hence capital inflows stopped abruptly.

The top left panel of Figure 10.5 displays the interest rate spread of Argentine dollar-denominated bonds over U.S. Treasuries between 1994 and 2001. Prior to 2001, spreads fluctuated around 7 percent (700 basis points). Spreads in other emerging market economies at the time were of similar size (not shown). However, in 2001 Argentine interest rate spreads exploded, reaching over 50 percent (or over 5,000 basis points) by late December. By contrast, during this time interest rate spreads of other emerging market economies did not increase from their prior levels. The fact that the price of foreign credit became prohibitively high meant that in effect the country was shut off from international capital markets. This suggests that in December 2001 Argentina suffered a sudden stop.

The top right panel of the figure shows the Argentine current account to GDP ratio from 1991 to 2002. From 1991 until 2000, Argentina ran current account deficits of around 3 percent of GDP on average. Thus, before the sudden stop the country was the recipient of sustained and sizable capital inflows. In 2002 the current account experienced a sharp and large reversal to 8 percent of GDP. This means that in spite of the fact that the country was technically in default, it transferred large amounts of resources to foreign lenders.

The exchange rate peg was abandoned in December 2001 and the peso suffered a large devaluation, plummeting from 1 peso per dollar to 3.5 pesos per dollar. In 2002 the Argentine consumer price index rose by 41 percent. At the same time, the consumer price index in the United States grew by only 2.5 percent. Recalling that the peso-dollar real exchange rate is given by $e_t = \mathcal{E}_t P_t^{US}/P_t^{AR}$, where $\mathcal{E}_t$ denotes the peso price of one U.S. dollar, P_t^{US} the consumer price index in the United States, and P_t^{AR} the consumer price index in Argentina, we have that the percentage change in

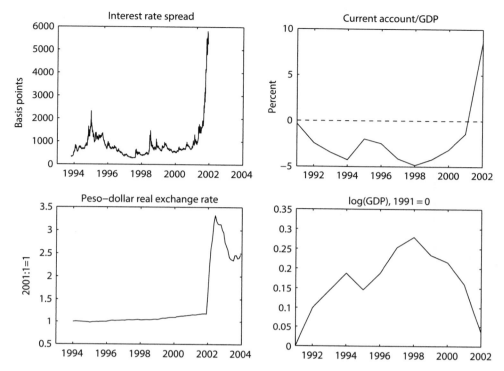

Figure 10.5. The Argentine Sudden Stop of 2001
Notes: The figure displays the behavior of the interest rate spread of Argentine dollar-denominated bonds over U.S. Treasuries, the current account to GDP ratio, the real exchange rate, and real per capita GDP around the Argentine sudden stop of 2001. The sudden stop was characterized by a sharp increase in the country spread, a current account reversal, a real exchange rate depreciation, and a large contraction in GDP.

the real exchange rate is given by

$$\left(\frac{e_t}{e_{t-1}} - 1\right) \times 100 = \left[\frac{(\mathcal{E}_t/\mathcal{E}_{t-1})(P_t^{US}/P_{t-1}^{US})}{P_t^{AR}/P_{t-1}^{AR}} - 1\right] \times 100$$

$$= \left(\frac{3.5 \times 1.025}{1.41} - 1\right) \times 100$$

$$= 154.4 \text{ percent.}$$

This means that the peso depreciated in real terms 154 percent against the dollar. Put differently, in the course of a few months the United States relative to Argentina became 2.5 times as expensive as before the sudden stop. So visitors found Argentina quite expensive in 2001 and a bargain in 2002.

The observed behavior of the current account and the real exchange rate in the aftermath of the Argentine sudden stop are consistent with the predictions of the TNT model. The sudden stop also had significant negative consequences for aggregate activity. In 2002, real GDP per capita fell by 12.5 percent and the number of unemployed people and people working fewer hours than desired reached 35 percent of the labor force. The version of the TNT model developed in Section 10.1 is mute in this respect because tradable and nontradable output are assumed to be fixed. We postpone an analysis of the effects of sudden stops on output and unemployment until Chapter 13, where we will introduce market failures taking the form of nominal rigidities in the labor market.

10.4.3   THE ICELANDIC SUDDEN STOP OF 2008

Sudden stops are not a phenomenon that pertains only to emerging countries. During the global financial crisis of 2007–2009, a number of medium- and high-income European countries with a history of large current account deficits also suffered sudden stops. A case in point is Iceland. Between 2000 and 2008, this country ran large current account deficits, which combined increased its external debt by more than 50 percent of GDP. An immediate consequence of the disruption in financial markets in 2008 was an abrupt cut in the flow of credit to small, highly indebted economies in Europe, including Iceland, Ireland, Greece, Portugal, and Spain.

Here we focus on Iceland as its sudden stop was particularly severe. The root of the Icelandic crisis was its banking sector. The combined balance sheet of the major local banks stood at more than 10 times the country's GDP on the eve of the crisis. With the global financial crisis, the balance sheets of these banks deteriorated significantly as assets lost value relative to liabilities. Fearing default, foreign lenders to the Icelandic banking sector elevated the country's cost of credit. This can be seen in the top left panel of Figure 10.6, which plots Iceland's credit default swap (CDS) spreads over the period 2005 to 2011. A CDS spread is the cost of insuring against default and is measured in basis points. For example, on September 1, 2008, the Icelandic CDS spread was 200 basis points. This means that to insure $100 of Icelandic debt against default, one had to pay $2 per year. CDS spreads represent a measure of borrowing costs on debts with default risk relative to default-free debt. Data on CDS spreads is useful because it is available even when the debtor does not issue new debt or when there are no liquid secondary debt markets. The figure shows that CDS spreads on Icelandic debt grew rapidly from 200 basis points in early September 2008 to over 1,400 basis points by mid-October 2008. At this point Iceland was virtually cut off from the private international capital market. The economy was suffering a full-blown sudden stop.

The large current account deficits of the pre-crisis period turned into current account surpluses virtually overnight, as shown in the top right panel of the figure. Between 2008 and 2009, the current account balance went from a deficit of 17 percent of GDP to a surplus of 8 percent of GDP. Thus the Icelandic crisis conforms to a key characteristic of a sudden stop—namely, a sharp reversal of the current account.

Relative prices, shown in the bottom left panel of the figure, also experienced significant movements around the crisis in the direction predicted by theory. The krona-euro real exchange rate depreciated by 45 percent between January 2008 and

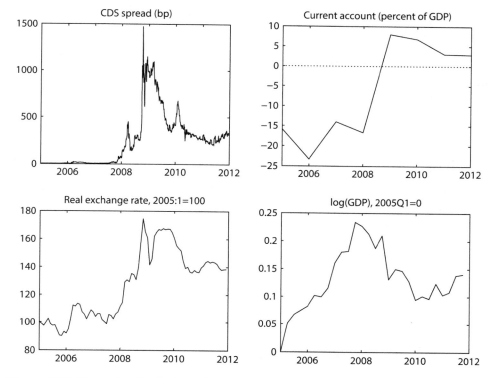

Figure 10.6. The Icelandic Sudden Stop of 2008
Notes: The figure displays the behavior of the Icelandic CDS spread, the current account to GDP ratio, the real exchange rate against the euro, and real GDP around the sudden stop of 2008. The sudden stop was characterized by a sharp increase in the CDS spread, a large current account reversal, a real exchange rate depreciation, and a contraction in the level of real GDP.

January 2009, implying that Iceland became 45 percent cheaper relative to other countries in the euro zone in the aftermath of its sudden stop.

Finally, the bottom right panel of Figure 10.6 shows that real GDP stopped growing as the sudden stop hit the country. While the Icelandic economy had grown on average by 5 percent per year between 2005 and 2007, it contracted by more than 2 percent per year between 2008 and 2011.

10.5 The TNT Model with Sectoral Production

Thus far we have studied a version of the TNT model in which the supplies of tradable and nontradable goods are fixed. This assumption is convenient because it simplifies the analysis of how the real exchange rate responds to different shocks affecting the economy, such as movements in the world interest rate or in the terms of trade. But the assumption is also unrealistic, for it is reasonable to expect that shocks affecting the economy will have consequences for the sectoral levels of output and employment. For example, we saw that an increase in the world interest rate causes a fall in the relative price of nontradables in terms of tradables. It is reasonable to expect that firms in the tradable sector will have an incentive to expand production and that firms in the nontradable sector will have an incentive to scale back production. In turn, these sectoral changes in output would require a reallocation of labor away from the nontraded sector and toward the traded sector. To see whether this intuition materializes in the context of the TNT framework, we now develop a more realistic version of the model in which tradable and nontradable outputs are not exogenous endowments but are produced with labor. In this setup, sectoral employment and output in both sectors adjust endogenously in response to exogenous disturbances such as changes in the world interest rate or the terms of trade.

10.5.1   THE PRODUCTION POSSIBILITY FRONTIER

Assume that tradable and nontradable goods are produced using labor via the production technologies

$$Q_t^T = F_T(L_t^T) \qquad\qquad (10.18)$$

and

$$Q_t^N = F_N(L_t^N), \qquad\qquad (10.19)$$

where L_t^T and L_t^N denote labor in the traded and nontraded sectors in period $t = 1, 2$, and $F_T(\cdot)$ and $F_N(\cdot)$ are production functions. We assume that the production functions are increasing and concave; that is, $F_T' > 0$, $F_N' > 0$, $F_T'' < 0$, and $F_N'' < 0$. The assumption that the production functions are concave means that the marginal productivity of labor is decreasing in the amount of labor used.

The total supply of labor in the economy is assumed to be constant and equal to L in both periods. Therefore, the allocation of labor across sectors must satisfy the following resource constraint:

$$L_t^T + L_t^N = L. \qquad\qquad (10.20)$$

The two production functions along with this resource constraint can be combined into a single equation relating Q_t^T to Q_t^N. This relation is known as the economy's *production possibility frontier* (PPF). To obtain the PPF, solve (10.18) for L_t^T to obtain $L_t^T = F_T^{-1}(Q_t^T)$, where F_T^{-1} denotes the inverse function of F_T and is strictly increasing and convex. Similarly, solve (10.19) for L_t^N to obtain $L_t^N = F_N^{-1}(Q_t^N)$. Then substitute these two expressions into the resource constraint (10.20) to obtain $F_T^{-1}(Q_t^T) + F_N^{-1}(Q_t^N) = L$.

Figure 10.7 plots the PPF in the space (Q_t^N, Q_t^T). The PPF is downward sloping because increasing nontradable output requires moving labor from the tradable sector to the nontradable sector, which causes a fall in tradable output. The PPF is concave because as employment in the nontradable sector increases, the productivity of labor in that sector decreases, which means that more labor is needed to produce each additional unit of nontradable output. This in turn implies that an increasing amount of tradable goods must be sacrificed to produce each additional

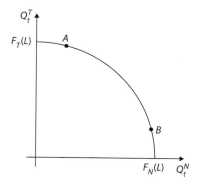

Figure 10.7. The Production Possibility Frontier

Notes: The production possibility frontier (PPF) describes a negative relationship between output of nontradable goods, Q_t^N, and output of tradable goods, Q_t^T. Given the total amount of labor, L, increasing output in one sector requires reducing output in the other sector. If the sectoral production functions exhibit diminishing marginal products of labor, the PPF is concave.

unit of nontradables. In addition, as fewer workers are employed in the traded sector, the productivity of labor in that sector increases, elevating the tradable output loss caused by each unit reduction in employment.

This is intuitive. Suppose that the tradable sector produces wheat and the nontradable sector haircuts. Consider point A in Figure 10.7. At this point, most workers are employed in the traded sector. The most efficient way to increase the output of nontradables is to transfer from the tradable sector the workers with the most experience in hairdressing and with the least training in farming, such as former barbers currently working as wheat farmers. This will result in a relatively large increase in output in the nontradable sector with little sacrifice of output in the traded sector. So in the neighborhood of point A, the PPF is relatively flat. As we continue to increase the output of nontradables, we must remove from the traded sector workers with increasingly less experience in cutting hair. When most workers are employed in the nontraded sector, such as at point B in Figure 10.7, increasing the production of haircuts even further requires moving away from the traded sector farmers who know how to grow wheat but are not good at cutting hair. Each of these workers will add only a small number of haircuts and will cause a large fall in the production of wheat. Thus, in the neighborhood of point B, the PPF has a large negative slope.

Formally, the slope of the PPF can be derived as follows. Differentiate the resource constraint (10.20) to get $dL_t^T + dL_t^N = 0$, or

$$\frac{dL_t^T}{dL_t^N} = -1.$$

This expression says that because the total amount of labor is fixed, any increase in labor input in one sector must be offset one for one by a reduction of labor input in the other sector. Now differentiate the production functions (10.18) and (10.19) to obtain

$$dQ_t^T = F_T'(L_t^T)dL_t^T$$

and

$$dQ_t^N = F_N'(L_t^N)dL_t^N.$$

Combining the above three equations yields the following expression for the slope of the PPF:

$$\frac{dQ_t^T}{dQ_t^N} = -\frac{F_T'(L_t^T)}{F_N'(L_t^N)}.$$

Because the marginal products of labor $F_T'(L_t^T)$ and $F_N'(L_t^N)$ are both positive, we have that the slope of the PPF is negative. Also because both production functions display diminishing marginal products of labor, we have that as L_t^N increases (and hence L_t^T decreases), $F_T'(L_t^T)$ becomes larger and $F_N'(L_t^N)$ becomes smaller, so the slope of the PPF increases in absolute value. This formally establishes that if the production functions exhibit positive but diminishing marginal products of labor, the PPF is downward sloping and concave.

The curvature of the PPF depends on how quickly the marginal product of labor diminishes as employment increases. If the marginal product of labor decreases slowly, the PPF will not have a strong curvature. In the special case in which the production function is linear in labor—that is, $Q_t^T = a_T L_t^T$ and $Q_t^N = a_N L_t^N$, where a_T and a_N are positive constants—the marginal product of labor is constant in both sectors, and the PPF becomes linear, with a slope equal to $-a_T/a_N$, as shown in the left panel of Figure 10.8. When the PPF takes this form, the TNT model has a special name, the Balassa-Samuelson model, which we will study later in this chapter in Section 10.6. On the other hand, if the marginal product of labor falls rapidly with

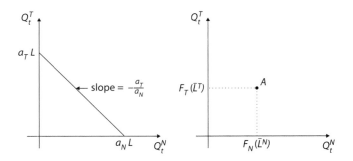

Figure 10.8. The PPF: Two Special Cases
Notes: The slope of the PPF depends on the degree to which the marginal product of labor diminishes with employment. In the special case of a constant marginal product of labor, as when the technologies are $Q_t^T = a_T L_t^T$ and $Q_t^N = a_N L_t^N$, the PPF is linear as shown in the left panel. When labor is fully specialized in the production of one good, as with the technologies $Q_t^T = F_T(\bar{L}^T)$ and $Q_t^N = F_N(\bar{L}^N)$, the PPF collapses to a single point, as shown in the right panel.

employment, the PPF will have a strong curvature. In the special case in which each worker is fully specialized in the production of one good, so that her productivity is positive in one sector and zero in the other sector, the PPF becomes a single point, as illustrated by point A in the right panel of Figure 10.8. In the figure, output in the tradable sector is $F_T(\bar{L}^T)$ and output in the nontraded sector is $F_N(\bar{L}^N)$, where $\bar{L}^T$ and $\bar{L}^N$ denote the number of workers specialized in the production of tradables and nontradables, respectively. This case captures the endowment version of the TNT model studied in Section 10.1.

As an illustration of how the PPF is constructed, consider the following example:

$$Q_t^T = \sqrt{L_t^T}$$

and

$$Q_t^N = \sqrt{L_t^N}.$$

Both of these production technologies display positive but diminishing marginal products of labor, because the square root is an increasing and concave function. Solving both production functions for labor as functions of output yields $L_t^T = (Q_t^T)^2$ and $L_t^N = (Q_t^N)^2$. Then using these two expressions to eliminate L_t^T and L_t^N from the resource constraint (10.20), we obtain the PPF

$$Q_t^T = \sqrt{L - (Q_t^N)^2}.$$

This expression describes a negative and concave relationship between Q_t^T and Q_t^N like the one depicted in Figure 10.7. The slope of this PPF results from taking the derivative of Q_t^T with respect to Q_t^N, which yields $\frac{dQ_t^T}{dQ_t^N} = -\frac{Q_t^N}{Q_t^T}$. Clearly, the slope is negative. Furthermore, as Q_t^N increases (and hence Q_t^T decreases), the slope becomes larger in absolute value.

10.5.2   THE PPF AND THE REAL EXCHANGE RATE

Where on the PPF the economy will operate depends on relative prices. To see this, consider the problem of a firm operating in the traded sector. Its profit, denoted Π_t^T, is given by the difference between revenues from sales of tradables, $P_t^T F_T(L_t^T)$, and the cost of production, $W_t L_t^T$, where W_t denotes the wage rate in period $t = 1, 2$,

$$\Pi_t^T = P_t^T F_T(L_t^T) - W_t L_t^T. \tag{10.21}$$

The firm chooses employment to maximize profits, taking P_t^T and W_t as given. Taking the derivative of profits with respect to L_t^T and setting it to zero, we obtain the first-order optimality condition

$$P_t^T F_T'(L_t^T) - W_t = 0.$$

The intuition behind this condition is that by hiring an extra worker the firm can produce $F_T'(L_t^T)$ additional units of tradable goods. The market value of these goods is $P_t^T F_T'(L_t^T)$, which is known as the *value of the marginal product of labor*. The cost of hiring an extra worker is the wage rate, W_t. Thus, if $P_t^T F_T'(L_t^T)$ is larger than W_t, hiring an extra worker increases the firm's profits. As employment increases, the marginal product of labor falls, and so does the increase in profits stemming from an extra worker. When $P_t^T F_T'(L_t^T)$ equals W_t, hiring an extra worker does not change the firm's profits. Beyond this level of employment, $P_t^T F_T'(L_t^T)$ is less than W_t, so an extra worker reduces profits. It follows that it is optimal for the firm to stop hiring when $P_t^T F_T'(L_t^T) = W_t$; that is, when the value of the marginal product of labor equals the wage rate.

Similarly, the profit of a firm operating in the nontraded sector, denoted Π_t^N, is given by

$$\Pi_t^N = P_t^N F_N(L_t^N) - W_t L_t^N. \tag{10.22}$$

The firm chooses L_t^N to maximize profits, taking as given P_t^N and W_t. The resulting optimality condition is

$$P_t^N F_N'(L_t^N) - W_t = 0.$$

The interpretation of this condition is the same as that of its counterpart in the traded sector. The firm hires workers until the value of the marginal product of labor equals the marginal cost of labor.

Combining the first-order conditions of the firms in the traded and nontraded sectors to eliminate W_t yields

$$\frac{F_T'(L_t^T)}{F_N'(L_t^N)} = \frac{P_t^N}{P_t^T} \equiv p_t. \tag{10.23}$$

The left-hand side of this expression is (minus) the slope of the PPF, and the right-hand side is the relative price of nontradables in terms of tradables, p_t. Thus, the economy produces tradables and nontradables in quantities such that (minus) the slope of the PPF equals the relative price of nontradables in terms of tradables.

Figure 10.9 illustrates how sectoral production responds to a decline in the relative price of nontradables. Suppose that the initial position is at point A, where tradable output is Q_t^{T0}, nontradable output is Q_t^{N0}, and the relative price of nontradables in terms of tradables is p_t^0. Consider a fall in the relative price of nontradables from p_t^0 to $p_t^1 < p_t^0$. Since in equilibrium (minus) the slope of the PPF equals the relative price of nontradables, production moves to a flatter part of the PPF. In the figure, the new position is at point B, where tradable output is higher and nontradable output is lower ($Q_t^{T1} > Q_t^{T0}$ and $Q_t^{N1} < Q_t^{N0}$). Since both goods are produced with labor, as the economy moves from point A to point B, employment falls in the nontraded sector and increases in the traded sector.

We established in Section 10.2 that given the relative price of nontradables in the rest of the world, p_t^*, the relative price of nontradables in terms of tradables, p_t, is negatively related to the real exchange rate, $e_t = \phi^*(1, p_t^*)/\phi(1, p_t)$. It follows that when the real exchange rate depreciates (i.e., when the country becomes cheaper relative to the rest of the world), firms have an incentive to produce more tradables

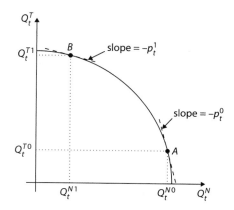

Figure 10.9. The Optimal Production of Tradables and Nontradables
Notes: The optimal production of tradable and nontradable goods occurs at a point where (minus) the slope of the PPF equals the relative price of nontradables in terms of tradables. As the relative price of nontradables falls from p_t^0 to p_t^1, firms find it optimal to produce more tradables and fewer nontradables.

and fewer nontradables. Put differently, as one moves northwest along the PPF (as from point A to point B in Figure 10.9), the real exchange rate depreciates.

10.5.3   THE INCOME EXPANSION PATH

We now study the consumption and saving decisions of the household. Households face the same optimization problem as in the endowment version of the TNT model presented in Section 10.1, except that now their income stems not from the sale of endowments, but from labor income and from profits received from the ownership of firms. To keep the exposition of the model self-contained, we reproduce the household's utility function from Section 10.1

$$\ln C_1 + \beta \ln C_2, \tag{R10.1}$$

with

$$C_1 = (C_1^T)^\gamma (C_1^N)^{1-\gamma}, \tag{R10.2}$$

and

$$C_2 = (C_2^T)^\gamma (C_2^N)^{1-\gamma}, \tag{R10.3}$$

where, as before, C_t, C_t^T, and C_t^N denote consumption of the composite good, consumption of tradables, and consumption of nontradables in period $t = 1, 2$.

Each period $t = 1, 2$, the household works L hours at the wage rate W_t, so its labor income is $W_t L$. In addition, households are assumed to be the owners of firms. Thus, their profit income is $\Pi_t^T + \Pi_t^N$. Households start period 1 with no debts or assets and can borrow or lend via a bond, denoted B_1, which is denominated in units of tradable goods and pays the interest rate r_1. Their budget constraints in periods 1

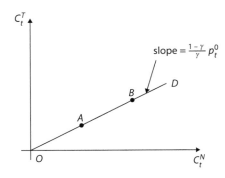

Figure 10.10. The Income Expansion Path

Notes: The figure depicts the income expansion path associated with the relative price p_t^0 as the ray $\overline{OD}$. Given p_t^0, the optimal combination of tradable and nontradable consumption must lie on the income expansion path. What point on the income expansion path the household will pick depends on how much income it allocates to consumption expenditure in period t. At point B, the household allocates more income to consumption in period t than at point A. If both goods are normal, the income expansion path is upward sloping.

and 2 are then given by

$$P_1^T C_1^T + P_1^N C_1^N + P_1^T B_1 = W_1 L + \Pi_1^T + \Pi_1^N, \qquad (10.24)$$

and

$$P_2^T C_2^T + P_2^N C_2^N = W_2 L + \Pi_2^T + \Pi_2^N + (1 + r_1) P_2^T B_1. \qquad (10.25)$$

Let's now follow the same steps we took in subsection 10.1.1 to obtain the household's intertemporal budget constraint. That is, divide the period-t budget constraint by P_t^T, combine the resulting expressions to eliminate B_1, and rearrange terms. This yields

$$C_1^T + p_1 C_1^N + \frac{C_2^T + p_2 C_2^N}{1 + r_1} = \bar{Y},$$

where now the household's lifetime income expressed in units of tradable goods of period 1, $\bar{Y}$, is given by

$$\bar{Y} = \left(\frac{W_1}{P_1^T} L + \frac{\Pi_1^T}{P_1^T} + \frac{\Pi_1^N}{P_1^T} \right) + \frac{\frac{W_2}{P_2^T} L + \frac{\Pi_2^T}{P_2^T} + \frac{\Pi_2^N}{P_2^T}}{1 + r_1}.$$

As in the endowment version of the TNT model, the household takes $\bar{Y}$ as given. This means that the household's utility maximization problem is identical to its counterpart in the endowment version. In particular, we have the following first-order conditions:

$$C_2^T = \beta (1 + r_1) C_1^T, \qquad (10.26)$$

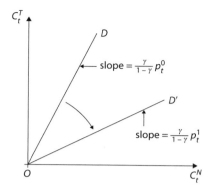

Figure 10.11. The Relative Price of Nontradables and the Income Expansion Path
Notes: The figure displays the income expansion path associated with two values of the relative price of nontradables, p_t^0 and $p_t^1 < p_t^0$ as the rays $\overline{OD}$ and $\overline{OD'}$, respectively. A decline in the relative price of nontradables rotates the income expansion path clockwise around the origin. This rotation is a reflection of households substituting nontradable consumption for tradable consumption as tradables become relatively more expensive.

and

$$C_t^T = \frac{\gamma}{1-\gamma} p_t C_t^N. \tag{10.27}$$

Figure 10.10 plots the optimality condition (10.27) in the space (C_t^N, C_t^T) for a given price p_t^0 as the ray $\overline{OD}$. This relationship is known as the *income expansion path*. Given the relative price p_t^0, the optimal choice of C_t^T and C_t^N must lie on the income expansion path. What point on the income expansion path the household will pick depends on how much income the household allocates to consumption expenditure in period t. Given p_t^0, the higher the amount of income allocated to consumption in period t is, the larger C_t^T and C_t^N will be; that is, the farther away from the origin the optimal consumption choice will lie. For example, consumption expenditure is higher at point B than at point A. The origin is a point on the income expansion path because if the household allocates no income to consumption spending in period t, then $C_t^T = C_t^N = 0$. The fact that the income expansion path is upward sloping means that tradables and nontradables are normal goods.

The slope of the income expansion path is increasing in the relative price of nontradables in terms of tradables, p_t. Figure 10.11 displays the income expansion paths associated with two relative prices, p_t^0 and $p_t^1 < p_t^0$ as the rays $\overline{OD}$ and $\overline{OD'}$, respectively. As the relative price of nontradables falls from p_t^0 to p_t^1, the income expansion path pivots clockwise around the origin. This is intuitive, because a lower price of nontradables induces households to substitute nontradables for tradables in consumption.

10.5.4 PARTIAL EQUILIBRIUM

We now put together the first two building blocks of the model, the production possibility frontier and the income expansion path. Figure 10.12 represents the

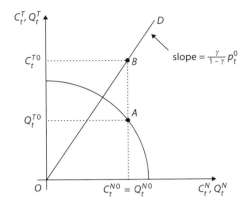

Figure 10.12. Partial Equilibrium
Notes: The figure displays the equilibrium for a given relative price of nontradables p_t^0. Production is at point A, where the slope of the PPF is $-p_t^0$. Consumption is at point B. The trade balance is the vertical distance between points A and B. Because consumption of tradables, C_t^{T0}, is larger than output of tradables, Q_t^{T0}, the country is running a trade deficit in period t.

equilibrium in period t for a given relative price of nontradables, p_t^0. As explained in subsection 10.5.2, to determine production, we must find the output mix (Q_t^N, Q_t^T) at which the slope of the PPF is $-p_t^0$. In the figure, this point is A. At point A, output of nontradables equals Q_t^{N0} and output of tradables equals Q_t^{T0}. The income expansion path corresponding to p_t^0 is the ray $\overline{OD}$. By definition, nontradable goods cannot be imported or exported. Therefore, market clearing in the nontraded sector requires that production equal consumption; that is,

$$Q_t^N = C_t^N. \tag{10.28}$$

Given consumption of nontradables, the income expansion path determines uniquely the level of consumption of tradables, C_t^{T0}, at point B. The trade balance is the difference between production and consumption of tradables,

$$TB_t = Q_t^T - C_t^T. \tag{10.29}$$

In the figure, the trade balance is given by the vertical distance between points A and B. Because in the figure consumption of tradables exceeds production, the country is running a trade balance deficit.

Consider now the effect of a fall in the relative price of nontradables, from p_t^0 to $p_t^1 < p_t^0$. As discussed in Section 10.2, this represents a depreciation of the real exchange rate, as the economy becomes cheaper relative to the rest of the world. Figure 10.13 illustrates this situation. The economy is initially producing at point A and consuming at point B. Because in equilibrium the slope of the PPF must equal the negative of the relative price of nontradables, the depreciation of the real exchange rate induces a change in the production mix to a point like C, where the PPF is flatter than at point A. This shift in the composition of production has a clear intuition: as the price of nontradables falls relative to that of tradables, firms find

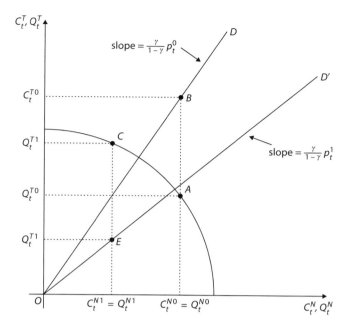

Figure 10.13. Partial Equilibrium: Adjustment to a Real Exchange Rate Depreciation
Notes: The figure displays the adjustment to a fall in the relative price of nontrad-ables from p_t^0 to $p_t^1 < p_t^0$. Initially, production is at point A and consumption is at point B. After the real depreciation, production shifts to point C and consumption to point E. Thus, production of tradables expands, production of nontradables contracts, and consumption of both tradables and nontradables contracts. The new trade balance, given by the vertical distance between C and E, improves.

it profitable to reduce production of nontradable goods and increase production of tradable goods.

On the demand side of the economy, the real exchange rate depreciation causes a clockwise rotation of the income expansion path from $\overline{OD}$ to $\overline{OD'}$ as shown in Figure 10.13. Having determined the new production position and the new income expansion path, we can determine the new equilibrium consumption basket (point E in the figure) and trade balance (the vertical distance between points C and E).

Summing up, in response to a fall in p_t (a real exchange rate depreciation), the economy produces more tradables ($Q_t^{T1} > Q_t^{T0}$) and fewer nontradables ($Q_t^{N1} < Q_t^{N0}$), and consumes fewer tradables as well as nontradables ($C_t^{T1} < C_t^{T0}$ and $C_t^{N1} < C_t^{N0}$). As a result of the expansion in the production of tradables and the contraction in consumption of tradables, the trade balance improves. These effects are illustrated in Figure 10.14.

The analysis we have performed is a partial equilibrium one because we took as given the value of a variable that is endogenously determined in the model—namely, the relative price of nontradables. Equivalently, we could have taken as exogenous any other endogenous variable. Consider, for example, taking as exogenous the trade balance, TB_t. From the bottom right panel of Figure 10.14, we have that the

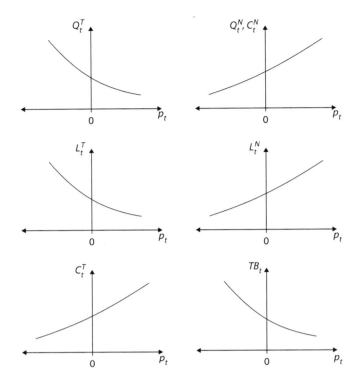

Figure 10.14. Partial Equilibrium: Endogenous Variables as Functions of the Relative Price of Nontradables
Notes: The figure displays the equilibrium values of seven endogenous variables of the TNT model as functions of the relative price of nontradables, which is also an endogenous variable.

relative price of nontradables, p_t, is a decreasing function of the trade balance. Intuitively, if the economy is to have an improvement in the trade balance, the relative price of nontradables must fall to induce firms to move production toward tradables, and consumers to move expenditure away from tradables. We can now easily establish how the other variables of the model relate to the trade balance. For example, the bottom-left panel of Figure 10.14 shows that consumption of tradables, C_t^T, is an increasing function of p_t. Since p_t is a decreasing function of the trade balance, we can write C_t^T as a decreasing function of TB_t. Similarly, all other variables of the model can be written as a function of the trade balance. We can then say that an improvement in the trade balance requires a fall in the relative price of nontradables (a real exchange rate depreciation), an expansion in the production of tradables, a contraction in the production of nontradables, and a contraction in the consumption of both tradables and nontradables. Figure 10.15 illustrates these results. It is important to note that Figures 10.14 and 10.15 convey the same information, just organized in different ways. In one figure the endogenous variable that is taken as exogenous is the relative price of nontradables and in the other it is the trade balance.

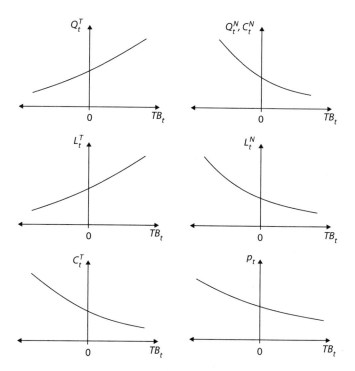

Figure 10.15. Partial Equilibrium: Endogenous Variables as Functions of the Trade Balance

Notes: The figure displays the equilibrium values of seven endogenous variables of the TNT model as functions of the trade balance, which is also an endogenous variable.

10.5.5   GENERAL EQUILIBRIUM

Another way to see that the analysis of Section 10.5.4 pertains to a partial equilibrium is to count equations and unknowns and realize that it does not make use of all the equilibrium conditions of the TNT model with sectoral production. Specifically, it uses seven equations for each period $t = 1, 2$; namely, (10.18)–(10.20), (10.23), and (10.27)–(10.29), which are cast in eight endogenous variables for each period, Q_t^T, Q_t^N, L_t^T, L_t^N, C_t^T, C_t^N, p_t, and TB_t. Thus, we are short two equations.

One of the two equilibrium conditions we have not included in the analysis is the household's Euler equation given in (10.26). We now incorporate this equation into the analysis.

In the partial equilibrium analysis, we deduced that consumption of tradables in period t, C_t^T, can be expressed as a decreasing function of the trade balance in period t, TB_t, as shown in the bottom left panel of Figure 10.15. So, we can write

$$C_t^T = \underset{-}{C^T}(TB_t).$$

We can then rewrite the Euler equation in terms of the trade balances in periods 1 and 2 as

$$C^T(TB_2) = \beta(1 + r^*)C^T(TB_1), \qquad (10.30)$$

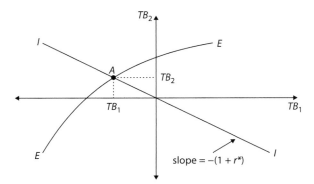

Figure 10.16. General Equilibrium Determination of the Trade Balance
Notes: The locus $\overline{EE}$ depicts the pairs of current and future trade balances TB_1 and TB_2 that are consistent with the household's Euler equation in equilibrium, equation (10.30). The locus $\overline{II}$ depicts the pairs (TB_1, TB_2) that satisfy the economy's intertemporal resource constraint, equation (10.31).

where we used the fact that, by the assumption of free capital mobility, in equilibrium the domestic interest rate is equal to the world interest rate, or

$$r_1 = r^*.$$

The Euler equation (10.30) describes a positive relationship between TB_1 and TB_2. Figure 10.16 depicts this relationship as the locus $\overline{EE}$. We assume that $\beta(1+r^*) < 1$. Under this assumption, the locus $\overline{EE}$ crosses the vertical axis at a positive value of TB_2. To see this, note that if $\beta(1+r^*) < 1$, then by the Euler equation (10.26), we have that $C_2^T < C_1^T$. In turn, since C_t^T is a decreasing function of TB_t, this implies that $TB_2 > TB_1$. Thus, when $TB_1 = 0$, TB_2 must be positive.

The second equilibrium condition that the partial equilibrium analysis leaves out is the economy's intertemporal resource constraint, which we derive next: Use the definitions of profits in the traded and nontraded sectors given in (10.21) and (10.22), the market-clearing condition in the nontraded sector given in (10.28), and the interest rate parity condition, to write the household's budget constraints in periods 1 and 2, equations (10.24) and (10.25), as

$$C_1^T + B_1 = Q_1^T$$

and

$$C_2^T = Q_2^T + (1+r^*)B_1.$$

Combining these two expressions to eliminate B_1 yields the intertemporal resource constraint,

$$C_1^T + \frac{C_2^T}{1+r^*} = Q_1^T + \frac{Q_2^T}{1+r^*},$$

which is identical to the intertemporal resource constraint in the endowment version of the TNT model, except that now Q_1^T and Q_2^T are endogenous variables. It will prove convenient to write the intertemporal resource constraint in terms of the trade balance in periods 1 and 2. To this end, using condition (10.29), we can write

$$TB_2 = -(1+r^*)TB_1. \tag{10.31}$$

Figure 10.16 plots the intertemporal resource constraint in the space (TB_1, TB_2) as the downward sloping line $\overline{II}$. The intertemporal resource constraint crosses the origin and has a slope equal to $-(1+r^*)$. Intuitively, if the country improves its trade balance in period 1 by one unit, it can deposit these savings at the interest rate r^*, allowing for an increase in the trade deficit in period 2 of $1+r^*$ units. The intertemporal resource constraint crosses the origin because of our maintained assumption that households start period 1 with a zero net asset position ($B_0 = 0$). If we had assumed instead that the initial asset position is positive (negative), then the intertemporal budget constraint would cross the vertical axis below (above) the origin.

The equilibrium is at point A, where the loci $\overline{EE}$ and $\overline{II}$ intersect. In equilibrium, the economy runs a trade balance deficit in period 1 ($TB_1 < 0$) and a surplus in period 2 ($TB_2 > 0$).

10.5.6   SUDDEN STOPS AND SECTORAL REALLOCATIONS

We are now ready to analyze the effects of a sudden stop on the sectoral alloca-tion of output and employment. Suppose that the world interest rate increases from r^n to $r^s > r^n$. To capture the effect of a large increase in the interest rate, assume that $\beta(1+r^n) < 1$ and that $\beta(1+r^s) > 1$. The effect of the sudden stop on the trade balance is illustrated in Figure 10.17. The situation under normal times (before the

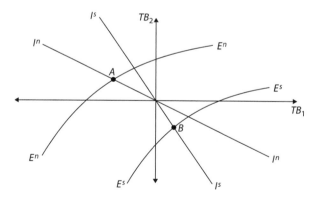

Figure 10.17. A Sudden Stop in the TNT model with Production
Notes: The figure depicts the adjustment of the trade balance to an increase in the interest rate from r^n to $r^s > r^n$. The equilibrium before the sudden stop is at point A, where $\overline{I^nI^n}$ (the locus of pairs (TB_1, TB_2) satisfying (10.31)) intersects $\overline{E^nE^n}$ (the locus of pairs (TB_1, TB_2) satisfying (10.30)). At point A, the country runs a trade deficit in period 1. In response to the increase in the interest rate to r^s, the equilibrium moves to point B, where the loci $\overline{I^sI^s}$ and $\overline{E^sE^s}$ intersect. At point B, the country runs a trade surplus in period 1. Thus, the sudden stop leads to a trade balance reversal.

sudden stop) is like the one illustrated in Figure 10.16. The equilibrium is at point A, where the loci $\overline{E^n E^n}$ and $\overline{I^n I^n}$ intersect. The country runs a trade deficit in period 1. The increase in the interest rate shifts the locus $\overline{EE}$ down and to the right from $\overline{E^n E^n}$ to $\overline{E^s E^s}$. The intercept of $\overline{E^s E^s}$ is negative. To see this, note first that because r^* does not appear in any of the equations used in the partial equilibrium analysis, the function $C^T(TB_t)$ conserves its original form. Next, note that because $\beta(1 + r^s) > 1$, the Euler equation (10.30) implies that $C^T(TB_2) > C^T(TB_1)$. In turn, since $C^T(TB_t)$ is a decreasing function, we have that $TB_2 < TB_1$. Thus, for $TB_1 = 0$, TB_2 (the intercept of the locus $\overline{E^s E^s}$) must be negative. The increase in the interest rate causes the locus $\overline{II}$ to rotate clockwise around the origin from $\overline{I^n I^n}$ to $\overline{I^s I^s}$, as is evident from equation (10.31). The equilibrium after the sudden stop is at point B, where the country runs a trade surplus in period 1. Since in this economy the current account is equal to the trade balance (recall that $B_0 = 0$), the sudden stop causes a current account reversal from a deficit to a surplus.

Having determined the effect of the sudden stop on the trade balance, the effect on all other endogenous variables can be read off directly from Figure 10.15. The model predicts a contraction in aggregate demand, as consumption of both tradables and nontradables falls. The collapse in aggregate demand causes the relative price of nontradables, p_1, to fall, or equivalently, the real exchange rate, e_1, to depreciate. In turn, the fall in p_1 induces firms to reduce output and employment in the nontraded sector and to increase output and employment in the traded sector.

Taking stock, the effects of a sudden stop on the trade balance, the real exchange rate, and the absorption of tradable goods are the same as in the endowment economy. The new prediction stemming from the economy with sectoral production is that the sudden stop also causes a contraction in the absorption of nontradable goods and a reallocation of output and employment away from the nontraded sector and toward the traded sector. In the model the reallocation of workers across sectors happens instantaneously. In real life, however, it is not so easy for workers to move from one sector to another. Such a transition typically involves a period of involuntary unemployment during which the workers that lost their jobs in the nontraded sector search for a new job in the traded sector. The reallocation of labor might also cause some workers to temporarily leave the labor force to acquire new skills to increase their chances of finding a new job in another sector.

The TNT model's prediction of a sectoral reallocation of production away from nontradable sectors and toward tradable sectors is borne out by the data. To document this fact, let's revisit the sudden stops of Argentina in 2001 and Iceland in 2008. Figure 10.18 plots GDP in the construction and the wholesale and retail trade sectors as shares of total GDP in an eight-year window around the Argentine and Icelandic sudden stops. Construction and wholesale and retail trade are two large and labor-intensive nontradable sectors. Their combined share in GDP fell from an average of 20 percent to less than 16 percent during the Argentine sudden stop of 2001 and from an average of 20 percent to less than 15 percent during the Icelandic sudden stop of 2008.

Recalling that in 2002 total GDP in Argentina fell by 12.5 percent, it follows that the crisis in the construction and the wholesale and retail trade sectors was enormous in absolute terms. A similar pattern is observed in the Icelandic sudden stop.

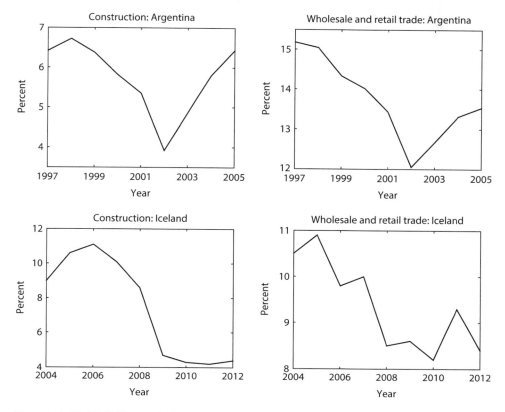

Figure 10.18. GDP Shares in Construction and Wholesale and Retail Trade During Sudden Stops: Argentina 2001 and Iceland 2008

Notes: Construction and wholesale and retail trade are large, labor-intensive, nontradable sectors. Their combined share in GDP fell from an average of 20 percent to less than 16 percent during the Argentine sudden stop of 2001 and from an average of 20 percent to less than 15 percent during the Icelandic sudden stop of 2008. This pattern of sectoral reallocation of production away from nontradable sectors conforms with the predictions of the TNT model.

Because of their labor intensity, these sectors contributed greatly to the surge in involuntary unemployment suffered by Argentina and Iceland in the aftermath of their sudden stops.

10.6 Productivity Differentials and Real Exchange Rates: The Balassa-Samuelson Model

The TNT model assumes no technological progress. For this reason, it is most useful for understanding short-run movements in the real exchange rate and sectoral reallocations of output and employment. In the long run, however, technological improvement generates sustained increases in productivity. In turn, sectoral differences in the speed of productivity growth can generate long-run movements in the real exchange rate and sectoral differences in output growth.

The Balassa-Samuelson model, named after its authors Bela Balassa and Paul Anthony Samuelson, is one of the most widely known theories of long-run determinants of the real exchange rate.[3] It predicts that persistent movements in the real exchange rate are due to cross-country differentials in relative productivities in the traded and nontraded sectors. In this section, we study a simple version of the Balassa-Samuelson model that captures this key result.

Suppose a country produces two kinds of goods, traded goods and nontraded goods. Let Q^T and Q^N denote output in the traded and nontraded sectors, respectively. Suppose that both goods are produced with linear production technologies that take labor as the sole factor input. Labor productivity varies across sectors. Formally, the production technologies in the traded and nontraded sectors are given by

$$Q^T = a_T L^T \tag{10.32}$$

and

$$Q^N = a_N L^N, \tag{10.33}$$

where L^T and L^N denote labor input in the traded and nontraded sectors, and a_T and a_N denote labor productivity in the traded and nontraded sectors, respectively. There are two concepts of labor productivity: average and marginal labor productivity. Average labor productivity is defined as output per worker, Q^T/L^T in the traded sector and Q^N/L^N in the nontraded sector. Marginal labor productivity is defined as the increase in output resulting from a unit increase in labor input. More formally, marginal labor productivity is given by the partial derivative of output with respect to labor, $\partial Q^T/\partial L^T$ in the traded sector and $\partial Q^N/\partial L^N$ in the nontraded sector. For the linear technologies given in (10.32) and (10.33), average and marginal labor productivities are the same, a_T in the traded sector and a_N in the nontraded sector.

Workers are assumed to be able to move freely from one sector to the other, so they will always choose to work in the sector offering the higher wage. This means that if both goods are produced in positive quantities in equilibrium, the wage rate must be the same in the traded and nontraded sectors.

In the traded sector, a firm's profit is given by the difference between revenues from sales of traded goods, $P^T Q^T$, and total cost of production, WL^T, where W denotes the wage rate per worker. That is,

$$\text{profits in the traded sector} = P^T Q^T - WL^T.$$

Similarly, in the nontraded sector we have

$$\text{profits in the nontraded sector} = P^N Q^N - WL^N.$$

---

[3] The first formulations of the model appeared in two separate publications: Bela Balassa, "The Purchasing-Power-Parity Doctrine: A Reappraisal," *Journal of Political Economy* 72 (December 1964): 584–596; and Paul Anthony Samuelson, "Theoretical Notes on Trade Problems," *Review of Economics and Statistics* 46 (March 1964): 145–154. Samuelson went on to win the Nobel Prize in Economics in 1970.

There is perfect competition in both sectors and no restrictions on entry of new firms. This means that as long as profits are positive, existing firms will have an incentive to increase production and new firms will have an incentive to enter, driving prices down and wages up. As a result, profits will go down. This process will continue until profits are zero in both sectors. Thus, in equilibrium it must be the case that

$$P^T Q^T = W L^T$$

and

$$P^N Q^N = W L^N.$$

Using the production functions (10.32) and (10.33) to eliminate Q^T and Q^N from the above zero-profit conditions, one obtains

$$P^T a_T = W$$

and

$$P^N a_N = W.$$

Combining these two expressions to eliminate W yields

$$\frac{P^N}{P^T} = \frac{a_T}{a_N}. \tag{10.34}$$

This expression says that in equilibrium the relative price of nontraded goods, P^N/P^T, is equal to the ratio of labor productivity in the traded sector to that in the nontraded sector, a_T/a_N. The intuition behind this condition is as follows: Suppose that a_T is greater than a_N. This means that one unit of labor produces more units of traded goods than of nontraded goods. Equivalently, producing one unit of tradable goods takes fewer units of labor than producing one unit of nontradable goods ($1/a_T < 1/a_N$). Since the wage rate is the same in both sectors, it follows that producing one unit of traded goods costs less than producing one unit of nontraded goods. Since firms make zero profits, it must be the case that the good that costs less to produce sells at a lower price, $P^T < P^N$.

In the foreign country, the relative price of nontradable goods in terms of tradable goods is determined in a similar fashion; that is,

$$\frac{P^{N*}}{P^{T*}} = \frac{a_T^*}{a_N^*}, \tag{10.35}$$

where P^{N*} and P^{T*} denote the prices of nontradable and tradable goods in the foreign country, and a_N^* and a_T^* denote the labor productivities in the nontraded and traded sectors in the foreign country.

We are now ready to derive the equilibrium real exchange rate, e, which, from equation (10.15), is given by

$$e = \frac{\mathcal{E}\phi^*(P^{T*}, P^{N*})}{\phi(P^T, P^N)}.$$

We assume that the law of one price holds for tradable goods, so that $P^T = \mathcal{E}P^{T*}$. Then, since the price indices $\phi(\cdot, \cdot)$ and $\phi^*(\cdot, \cdot)$ are homogeneous of degree 1, we can express the real exchange rate as

$$e = \frac{\phi^*(1, P^{N*}/P^{T*})}{\phi(1, P^N/P^T)}.$$

Using equation (10.34) to eliminate P^N/P^T and equation (10.35) to eliminate P^{N*}/P^{T*} yields

$$e = \frac{\phi^*(1, a_T^*/a_N^*)}{\phi(1, a_T/a_N)}. \tag{10.36}$$

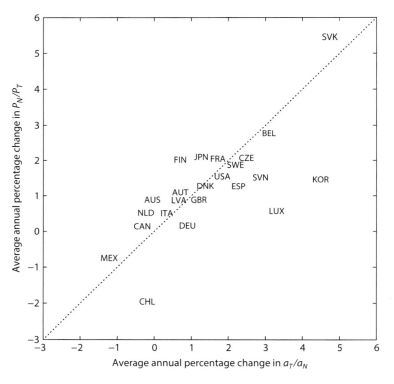

Figure 10.19. Relative Productivity Growth in the Traded and Nontraded Sectors and Changes in the Relative Price on Nontradables
Notes: The figure plots the average annual percentage change in the relative price of nontradables in terms of tradables, P^N/P^T, against the average annual percentage change in productivity in the traded sector relative to the nontraded sector, a_T/a_N, for 23 countries over the period 1996 to 2015. The strong positive relationship provides empirical support to the Balassa-Samuelson model.
Source: Own calculations based on data from KLEMS and OECD STAN. Country names are shown using ISO abbreviations.

This equation captures the main result of the Balassa-Samuelson model; namely, that deviations from PPP (i.e., deviations of e from unity) are due to differences in relative productivities across countries. In particular, if in the domestic country the relative productivity of the traded sector, a_T/a_N, grows faster than in the foreign country, then the real exchange rate will appreciate over time (i.e., e will fall over time), which means that the domestic country will become more expensive relative to the foreign country. This is because in the domestic country nontradables are becoming relatively more expensive to produce than in the foreign country, forcing the relative price of nontradables in the domestic country to grow at a faster rate than in the foreign country.

An important insight of the Balassa-Samuelson model is that in the long run, the relative price of nontradable goods in terms of tradable goods, P^N/P^T, is an increasing function of the relative productivities, a_T/a_N (see equation (10.34)). This prediction implies that countries in which, over a certain period of time, a_T grew faster than a_N should also exhibit a faster growth in P^N than in P^T. Is this prediction borne out by the data? Figure 10.19 plots the average annual percentage change in P^N/P^T against the average annual percentage change in a_T/a_N for 23 countries over the period 1996 to 2015.[4] The figure shows that in the long run there is a strong positive relationship between sectoral differences in productivity growth and sectoral differences in price growth. This evidence provides empirical support for Balassa and Samuelson's theory of the determinants of deviations from PPP.

10.7 Summing Up

This chapter studies the determination of the real exchange rate in the short and long runs.

- The TNT model is an open economy model with tradable and nontradable goods. It is a useful framework for understanding the determinants of the real exchange rate and sectoral reallocations of output and employment in the short run.
- The TNT model predicts that in response to an increase in the world interest rate the real exchange rate depreciates, the relative price of nontradable goods falls, output and employment in the nontradable sector contract, and output and employment in the tradable sector expand.
- The TNT model predicts that in response to positive shocks to the tradable endowment or improvements in the terms of trade, the real exchange rate appreciates and the relative price of nontradables increases. These effects are stronger when the shocks are expected to be persistent.
- A sudden stop is a macroeconomic crisis that occurs when foreign lenders abruptly stop extending credit to a debtor nation. It manifests itself by a steep increase in the country's interest-rate premium.

---

[4]This figure is inspired by figure 3 of José De Gregorio, Alberto Giovannini, and Holger C. Wolf, "International Evidence on Tradable and Nontradable Inflation," *European Economic Review* 38 (June 1994): 1225–1244, which covered 14 OECD countries over the period 1970 to 1985.

- The main observed effects of a sudden stop are a current account reversal from a large deficit to near balance or even surplus, a sharp depreciation of the real exchange rate, and a reallocation of production and employment from the nontradable sector to the tradable sector.
- Two sudden stop episodes are analyzed, Argentina 2001 and Iceland 2008.
- The TNT model explains well the macroeconomic consequences of observed sudden stops.
- The Balassa-Samuelson model is a theory that explains long-run movements in real exchange rates. It explains deviations from PPP as stemming from international differences in relative sectoral productivity growth.
- The Balassa-Samuelson model predicts that for a given country, if productivity grows faster in the traded sector than in the nontraded sector, then the relative price of nontradables in terms of tradables grows over time. This prediction is borne out by the data. Across countries, long-run averages of the growth rate of relative productivities in the tradable and nontradable sectors are positively correlated with long-run averages of the growth rate of the relative price on nontradables in terms of tradables.
- The Balassa-Samuelson model predicts that if in the domestic country productivity in the traded sector relative to productivity in the nontraded sector grows faster than in the foreign country, then the domestic country becomes more expensive; that is, its real exchange rate appreciates.

10.8 Exercises

Exercise 10.1 (A TNT Endowment Economy) Consider an economy populated by identical households with preferences described by the utility function $\ln C_1 + \ln C_2$ where C_t denotes consumption in period $t = 1, 2$. Suppose that consumption is a composite of tradable and nontradable consumption given by $C_t = \sqrt{C_t^T C_t^N}$, where C_t^T and C_t^N denote consumption of tradable and nontradable goods in period $t = 1, 2$. Households receive 1 unit of tradable goods in period 1 and 2 units in period 2 ($Q_1^T = 1$ and $Q_2^T = 2$) and 4 units of nontradables in period 1 and 3 in period 2 ($Q_1^N = 4$ and $Q_2^N = 3$). Suppose further that the country has free capital mobility and that the world interest rate is nil ($r = 0$). Calculate the equilibrium trade balance in periods 1 and 2 (TB_1 and TB_2) and the relative price of nontradables in periods 1 and 2 (p_1 and p_2).

Exercise 10.2 (Endowment Shocks and the Real Exchange Rate) Consider the endowment version of the TNT model studied in Section 10.1. Suppose the endowment of tradables increases in period 1. Analyze the effect of this innovation on the real exchange rate in periods 1 and 2, depending on whether the change in the tradable endowment is temporary or permanent.

Exercise 10.3 (Aging and the Real Exchange Rate) It has been documented that as societies age, the demand for personal and health care services, prime examples of nontradable goods, increases. To capture this phenomenon, suppose that there is an increase in households' preference for nontradable goods, which is reflected in an increase in $1 - \gamma$, the exponent on nontradable consumption in the Armington aggregator (10.2). Using the TNT model of Section 10.1, answer the following questions:

1. What is the effect of this preference shock on the equilibrium consumption of tradable goods in periods 1 and 2? Explain.
2. What is the effect on the trade balance and the current account in periods 1 and 2? Explain.
3. Use a graphical approach to analyze the effect in period 1 of the preference shock on the relative price of nontradables and the real exchange rate.
4. The *old-age dependency ratio* is defined as the ratio of the number of people age 65 or older to the number of people age 15 to 64. Suppose you observe the old-age dependency ratio in a number of countries. Which countries would you expect to be more expensive to live in?

Exercise 10.4 (A Sudden Stop I) Consider a two-period, small open economy populated by a large number of households with preferences captured by the following lifetime utility function,

$$\ln(C_1^T C_1^N) + \ln(C_2^T C_2^N),$$

where C_t^T and C_t^N, for $t = 1, 2$, denote consumption of tradable and nontradable goods in period t, respectively. Households are endowed with $Q_1^T = 1$ and $Q_2^T = 2$ units of tradables and $Q_1^N = Q_2^N = 1$ unit of nontradables in periods 1 and 2. Households start period 1 with no assets or debts. The world interest rate is zero.

1. Calculate the equilibrium levels of the current account and the relative price of nontradables in terms of tradables in period 1, denoted CA_1 and p_1, respectively.
2. Suppose now that suddenly the world interest rate increases from 0 to 10 percent. Calculate the new equilibrium levels of the current account and the relative price of nontradables in terms of tradables in period 1.

Exercise 10.5 (A Sudden Stop II) Consider a two-period, small open economy. In period 1, households receive an endowment of 6 units of tradable goods and 9 units of nontradable goods. In period 2, households receive 13.2 units of tradables and 9 units of nontradables ($Q_1^T = 6$, $Q_2^T = 13.2$, and $Q_1^N = Q_2^N = 9$). Households start period 1 with no assets or liabilities ($B_0 = 0$). The country enjoys free access to world financial markets, where the prevailing interest rate is 10 percent ($r^* = 0.1$). Suppose that the household's preferences are defined over consumption of tradable and nontradable goods in periods 1 and 2, and are described by the following utility function,

$$\ln C_1^T + \ln C_1^N + \ln C_2^T + \ln C_2^N,$$

where C_t^T and C_t^N denote, respectively, consumption of tradables and nontradables in period $t = 1, 2$. Let p_1 and p_2 denote the relative prices of nontradables in terms of tradables in periods 1 and 2, respectively.

1. Write down the budget constraints of the household in periods 1 and 2.

2. Derive the household's intertemporal budget constraint. Assign this expression the number (1).

3. The household chooses consumption of tradables and nontradables in periods 1 and 2 to maximize its lifetime utility function subject to its intertemporal budget constraint. Derive the optimality conditions associated with this problem. To this end, begin by solving (1) for C_1^T and use the resulting expression to eliminate C_1^T from the lifetime utility function. Take the derivatives of the resulting lifetime utility with respect to C_1^N, C_2^T, and C_2^N and set them equal to zero. Assign the resulting three expressions the numbers (2), (3), and (4), respectively.

4. Write down the market-clearing conditions in the nontradable goods market in periods 1 and 2. Assign these expressions the numbers (5) and (6), respectively.

5. Combine expressions (1) to (6) to solve for C_1^T, C_2^T, C_1^N, C_2^N, p_1, and p_2. Explain intuitively why the relative price of nontradables changes over time.

6. Calculate the net foreign asset position of the economy at the end of period 1, B_1.

7. Calculate the equilibrium levels of the current account balance in periods 1 and 2 (CA_1 and CA_2).

8. Assume that the domestic consumer price index in period $t = 1, 2$, denoted P_t, is defined by $P_t = \sqrt{P_t^T P_t^N}$, where P_t^T and P_t^N denote the nominal prices of tradables and nontradables in period $t = 1, 2$, respectively. Similarly, suppose that the foreign consumer price index is given by $P_t^* = \sqrt{P_t^{T*} P_t^{N*}}$, where the superscript $*$ denotes foreign variables. Foreign nominal prices are expressed in terms of foreign currency. Assume that PPP holds for tradable goods. Finally, suppose that the foreign relative price of nontradables in terms of tradables equals unity in both periods. Compute the real exchange rate in periods 1 and 2.

9. Let us sketch a scenario like the one that took place during the Argentine sudden stop of 2001 by assuming that because of fears that the country will not repay its debts in period 2, foreign lenders refuse to extend loans to the domestic economy in period 1. Answer the questions in items 6 through 8 under these new (adverse) circumstances. Compute the equilibrium interest rate. Provide an intuitive explanation of your results.

10. Compute real GDP in period 1 under the sudden stop and no sudden stop scenarios. Consider two alternative measures of real GDP: GDP measured in terms of tradable goods and GDP measured in terms of the basket of goods whose price is the consumer price index P_1. What measure is more economically sensible? Why?

11. Suppose the Inter-American Development Bank (IADB) decided to implement a transfer (gift) to the country to ameliorate the effects of the sudden stop. Specifically, suppose that the IADB gives the country a transfer of F units of tradable goods in period 1. Use the utility function given above to compute the size of F that would make households as happy as in the no

sudden stop scenario. Express F as a percentage of the country's sudden stop and no-aid GDP (in terms of tradables) in period 1.

Exercise 10.6 (Future Nontradable Endowment Shock in the TNT Model) In the endowment economy analyzed in Section 10.1, the period 1 relative price of nontradables in terms of tradables, p_1, is independent of the future endowment of nontradables, Q_2^N. This is a special result due to the assumed log-linear and Cobb-Douglas specifications, respectively, for the utility function and the aggregator function. To see what happens when we move away from this particular combination of functional forms, consider a case in which the aggregator function continues to be Cobb-Douglas, but the utility function is of the form

$$\sqrt{C_1} + \beta\sqrt{C_2}.$$

All other aspects of the economy are as in Section 10.1.

1. Derive the equilibrium relative price of nontradables in terms of tradables in period 1. (Hint: impose the market-clearing conditions $C_t^N = Q_t^N$ for $t = 1, 2$, right after deriving the household's first-order optimality conditions.)
2. What is the effect of an increase in the period 2 nontradable endowment, Q_2^N, on the period 1 relative price of nontradables, p_1? What is the effect on the real exchange rate?
3. Provide intuition.

Exercise 10.7 (The PPF I) Suppose tradable output, Q^T, is produced with labor, L^T, via the production function $Q^T = \sqrt{L^T}$. Similarly, nontradable output, Q^N, is produced with labor, L^N, via the production function $Q^N = \sqrt{L^N}$. Suppose that the economy has 8 workers ($L = 8$) and that output in the nontraded sector is 2 ($Q^N = 2$). Calculate output in the traded sector and the relative price of the nontraded good in terms of traded goods, p.

Exercise 10.8 (The PPF II) Suppose that the production functions in the traded and nontraded sectors are $Q^T = (L^T)^\alpha$ and $Q^N = (L^N)^\alpha$, where Q^i and L^i denote output and employment in sector $i = T, N$, respectively. Let L be the total number of workers in the economy.

1. Find the PPF and its slope.
2. Suppose that $\alpha = 0.25$ and that $L = 1$. Assume further that the relative price of nontradables in terms of tradables, p, equals 2. Find Q^T, Q^N, L^T, and L^N.
3. Suppose that the nominal wage, denoted W, is equal to 5. Find the nominal prices of tradables and nontradables, denoted P^T and P^N, and profits in both sectors.

Exercise 10.9 (Linear Income Expansion Paths) In Section 10.5.3, we showed that when the period utility function is logarithmic, $U(C) = \ln(C)$, and the aggregator function is Cobb-Douglas, $C = (C^T)^\gamma (C^N)^{1-\gamma}$, the income expansion path is linear.

1. Show that the income expansion path is linear in the more general case in which preferences are described by a *constant relative risk aversion (CRRA)*

period utility function and a CES or Armington aggregator function; that is,

$$U(C) = \frac{C^{1-\sigma} - 1}{1 - \sigma}$$

and

$$C = \left[\gamma (C^T)^{1-\frac{1}{\xi}} + (1 - \gamma)(C^N)^{1-\frac{1}{\xi}} \right]^{\frac{1}{1-\frac{1}{\xi}}},$$

with $\sigma, \xi > 0$, and $\gamma \in (0, 1)$.

2. Show that the logarithmic period utility function is a special case of the CRRA period utility function when $\sigma \to 1$.
3. Show that the Cobb-Douglas aggregator is a special case of the CES aggregator when $\xi \to 1$.
4. Even more generally, show that the income expansion path is linear when the period utility function is monotone and the aggregator function is homogeneous. In this case, we say that households have *homothetic preferences* for tradable and nontradable goods.

Exercise 10.10 (Equilibrium in the TNT Model with Production) Consider a two-period, small open economy that produces and consumes tradable and non-tradable goods. In periods $t = 1, 2$, the production possibility frontier (PPF) is of the form

$$Q_t^N = \sqrt{2 - (Q_t^T)^2},$$

where Q_t^T and Q_t^N denote, respectively, tradable and nontradable output in periods $t = 1, 2$. Preferences are described by the utility function

$$\ln\left(C_1^T\right) + \ln\left(C_1^N\right) + \ln\left(C_2^T\right) + \ln\left(C_2^N\right),$$

where C_t^T and C_t^N denote, respectively, tradable and nontradable consumption in periods $t = 1, 2$. Let $p_t \equiv P_t^N / P_t^T$ denote the relative price of nontradable goods in terms of tradable goods in periods $t = 1, 2$.

1. Suppose that p_1 is equal to 1 (i.e., 1 unit of nontradable goods sells for 1 unit of tradable goods). Using the information provided by the PPF, and assuming that firms producing tradables and nontradables are profit maximizers, calculate output of tradables and nontradables in period 1 (Q_1^T and Q_1^N).
2. Using the results obtained thus far, and the market-clearing condition in the nontraded sector, calculate consumption of nontradables in period 1 (C_1^N).
3. Assuming that households are utility maximizers, use the information given above and the results of the previous two questions to calculate consumption of tradables in period 1 (C_1^T).
4. Calculate the country's trade balance in period 1 (TB_1).
5. Suppose that the initial net foreign asset position, B_0, is nil. Calculate the current account in period 1 (CA_1).

6. Suppose that the world interest rate, denoted r^*, equals 0 percent ($r^* = 0$). Assume further that households have access to the world financial market. Calculate consumption of tradables in period 2 (C_2^T).

7. Calculate tradable output in period 2 (Q_2^T). To this end, use the economy's intertemporal resource constraint for tradables.

8. Now calculate output of nontradables in period 2 (Q_2^N).

9. Calculate the relative price of nontradables in terms of tradables in period 2 (p_2).

10. Is the initial guess for p_1, namely, $p_1 = 1$, an equilibrium? Be explicit about what must be verified for this to be the case.

Exercise 10.11 (The Trade Balance in the TNT Model with Sectoral Production)
State whether the following claims about the equilibrium in the TNT model with sectoral production of Section 10.5 are true, false, or uncertain and explain why. In answering this question, assume that the initial international investment position, B_0, is zero.

1. If $\beta(1+r) = 1$, then the trade balance in both periods is nil, $TB_1 = TB_2 = 0$.
2. If $\beta(1+r) > 1$, then the trade balance is positive in period 1, $TB_1 > 0$.
3. If $\beta(1+r) > 1$, then an increase in the world interest rate leads to a trade balance improvement in period 1.

Exercise 10.12 (Equilibrium in the TNT Model with Positive NIIP) Redo Exercise 10.11 under the assumption that the initial net international investment position, B_0, is positive.

Exercise 10.13 (Real Exchange Rate Determination in the Balassa-Samuelson Model) Consider two countries, say the United States and Japan. Both countries produce tradables and nontradables. Suppose that at some point in time the production technology in the United States is described by

$$Q^{T\,US} = a_T^{US} L^{N\,US}; \text{ with } a_T^{US} = 0.4$$

and

$$Q^{N\,US} = a_N^{US} L^{N\,US}; \text{ with } a_N^{US} = 0.1,$$

where $Q^{T\,US}$ and $Q^{N\,US}$ denote, respectively, output of tradables and nontradables in the United States, a_T^{US} and a_N^{US} denote, respectively, labor productivity in the tradable and the nontradable sectors, and $L^{T\,US}$ and $L^{N\,US}$ denote, respectively, the amount of labor employed in the tradable and nontradable sectors in the United States. The total supply of labor in the United States is equal to 1, so that $1 = L^{T\,US} + L^{N\,US}$. At the same point in time, production possibilities in Japan are given by

$$Q_T^J = 0.2 L_T^J$$

and

$$Q_N^J = 0.2 L_N^J,$$

where the superscript J denotes Japan. The total supply of labor in Japan is also equal to 1. Assume that in each country, wages in the traded sector equal wages in the nontraded sector. Suppose that the price index in the United States, which we denote by P^{US}, is given by

$$P^{US} = \sqrt{P_T^{US}}\sqrt{P_N^{US}},$$

where P_T^{US} and P_N^{US} denote, respectively, the dollar prices of tradables and nontradables in the United States. Similarly, the price index in Japan is given by

$$P^J = \sqrt{P_T^J}\sqrt{P_N^J},$$

where Japanese prices are expressed in yen.

1. Calculate the dollar-yen real exchange rate, defined as $e = \mathcal{E}P^J/P^{US}$, where $\mathcal{E}$ denotes the dollar-yen exchange rate (dollar price of 1 yen). The answer to this question is a number, but show your work.
2. Suppose that the U.S. labor productivity in the traded sector, a_T^{US}, grows at a 3 percent rate per year, whereas labor productivity in the nontraded sector, a_N^{US}, grows at 1 percent per year. Assume that labor productivities in Japan are constant over time. Calculate the growth rate of the real exchange rate. Provide an intuitive explanation of your result.

Exercise 10.14 (A Two-Tradable-Good Economy with Linear Technologies) Consider a two-country economy with two goods, A and B. Both goods are traded internationally and produced using labor and linear technologies. The production functions in the domestic economy are

$$Q^A = a_A L^A$$

and

$$Q^B = a_B L^B,$$

where Q^i, L^i, and a_i denote output, labor, and labor productivity in sector $i = A, B$. Assume that labor productivity is exogenous and that the country is endowed with a fixed number of units of labor L. Analogously, in the foreign country the production functions are

$$Q^{A*} = a_{A*} L^{A*}$$

and

$$Q^{B*} = a_{B*} L^{B*},$$

and the labor endowment is L^*.

1. Show that in general, the equilibrium features production specialization in at least one country; that is, one of the two countries produces only one good.

2. Suppose that in equilibrium the domestic country specializes in the production of good A. What relation between labor productivities and relative prices must hold in equilibrium for this to be the case?
3. Suppose that in equilibrium the domestic country specializes in the production of good A and the foreign country in the production of good B. What relation between labor productivities and relative prices must hold in equilibrium for this to be the case?

Exercise 10.15 (A Two-Sector Economy with Linear Technologies) This exercise combines the TNT and Balassa-Samuelson models. Consider a two-period, small open economy populated by a large number of identical households with preferences described by the utility function

$$\ln C_1^T + \ln C_1^N + \ln C_2^T + \ln C_2^N,$$

where C_1^T and C_2^T denote consumption of tradables in periods 1 and 2, respectively, and C_1^N and C_2^N denote consumption of nontradables in periods 1 and 2. Households are born in period 1 with no debts or assets and are endowed with $L_1 = 1$ unit of labor in period 1 and $L_2 = 1$ unit of labor in period 2. Households offer their labor to firms, for which they get paid the wage rate w_1 in period 1 and w_2 in period 2. The wage rate is expressed in terms of tradable goods, that is, $w_t \equiv W_t/P_t^T$. Households can borrow or lend in the international financial market at the world interest rate r^*. Let p_1 and p_2 denote the relative price of nontradable goods in terms of tradable goods in periods 1 and 2, respectively.

Firms in the traded sector produce output with the technology $Q_1^T = a_T L_1^T$ in period 1 and $Q_2^T = a_T L_2^T$ in period 2, where Q_t^T denotes output in period $t = 1, 2$ and L_t^T denotes employment in the traded sector in period $t = 1, 2$. Similarly, production in the nontraded sector in periods 1 and 2 is given by $Q_1^N = a_N L_1^N$ and $Q_2^N = a_N L_2^N$.

1. Write down the budget constraint of the household in periods 1 and 2.
2. Write down the intertemporal budget constraint of the household.
3. State the household's utility maximization problem.
4. Derive the optimality conditions associated with the household's maximization problem.
5. Derive an expression for the optimal levels of consumption of tradables and nontradables in periods 1 and 2 (C_1^T, C_1^N, C_2^T, and C_2^N) as functions of r^*, w_1, w_2, p_1, and p_2.
6. Using the zero-profit conditions on firms, derive expressions for the real wage and the relative price of nontradables (w_t and p_t, $t = 1, 2$), in terms of the parameters a_T and a_N.
7. Write down the market-clearing condition for nontradables.
8. Write down the market-clearing condition for labor.
9. Using the above results, derive the equilibrium levels of consumption, the trade balance, and sectoral employment (C_1^T, C_2^T, C_1^N, C_2^N, TB_1, TB_2, L_1^T, and L_2^T) in terms of the structural parameters a_T, a_N, and r^*.
10. Is there any sectoral labor reallocation over time? If so, explain the intuition behind it.

PART III

International Capital Mobility

CHAPTER 11

International Capital Market Integration

In Chapter 9, we studied whether world goods markets are integrated. We investigated whether there is a tendency for the prices of goods and services to equalize across countries. In this chapter, we study whether international capital markets are integrated and investigate whether under free capital mobility there is a tendency for interest rates to equalize across countries.

Over the past few decades, the world appears to have become more financially globalized. One manifestation of this phenomenon is the explosion in gross international asset and liability positions. For example, as documented in Figure 1.7 of Chapter 1, in the mid-1970s U.S. gross international liabilities were only 15 percent of GDP. By 2018, they had climbed to over 170 percent of GDP. Similarly, the U.S. gross international asset position jumped from 20 percent of GDP in the mid-1970s to over 130 percent in 2018. A similar pattern of growth in gross international asset and liability positions has been observed in many countries around the world.

A number of events have contributed to this phenomenon. Significant advancements in information technologies have reduced the costs of transacting in financial markets and the costs of gathering and storing financial data. These advancements have not only allowed existing market participants to increase the volume of transactions, but have also allowed the entrance of smaller investors, making the financial marketplace more atomistic. Investment funds and other financial intermediaries have facilitated access for this type of investor to international equity and fixed-income markets. The abandonment of the fixed exchange rate system known as Bretton-Woods in the early 1970s allowed many countries and regions of the world to dismantle capital controls aimed at preventing large fluctuations in cross-border capital flows. The creation of the eurozone first generated a large area free of barriers to the movement of financial capital in the mid-1980s, and, since the inception of the euro in 1999, a common currency area. Finally, following deep market-oriented reforms in the early 1980s and accession to the WTO in the early 2000s, China has emerged as a new world economic power that has significantly boosted international trade in goods and financial assets. As we saw in Chapter 1, by running large current account surpluses, China became a major supplier of funds to world capital markets.

11.1 Covered Interest Rate Parity

In a world that enjoys perfect capital mobility, the rate of return on risk-free financial investments should be equalized across countries. Otherwise, arbitrage opportunities would arise, inducing capital to flow out of the low-return countries and into the high-return countries. This movement of capital across national borders will tend to eliminate differences in interest rates. If, on the other hand, one observes that interest rate differentials across countries persist over time, it must be the case that in some countries restrictions on international capital flows are in place.

It follows that a natural empirical test of the degree of capital market integration is to look at cross-country interest rate differentials on assets free of default risk. However, such a test is not as straightforward as it might seem. One difficulty in measuring interest rate differentials is that interest rates across countries are not directly comparable if they relate to investments in different currencies. Suppose, for example, that the interest rate on a 1-year deposit is 7 percent in the United States and 3 percent in Germany. This 4 percent interest rate differential will not necessarily induce capital flows from Germany to the United States even in the absence of any impediments to such flows. The reason is that if the U.S. dollar depreciates sharply within the investment period (by more than 4 percent), an investor who deposited her money in Germany might end up with more dollars at the end of the period than an investor who had invested in the United States. Thus, even in the absence of capital controls, differences in interest rates might exist due to expectations of changes in the exchange rate or as a compensation for exchange rate risk. Therefore, a meaningful measure of interest rate differentials ought to take the exchange rate factor into account.

Suppose at date t a U.S. investor has \$1 and is trying to decide whether to invest it domestically or abroad, say in Germany. Let i_t denote the U.S. interest rate and i_t^* the foreign (German) interest rate at time t. If in period t the investor deposits her money in the United States, then in period $t + 1$ she receives $1 + i_t$ dollars. How many dollars would she get, if instead she invested her \$1 in Germany? In order to invest in Germany, she must first use her dollar to buy euros. Let $\mathcal{E}_t$ denote the spot exchange rate at date t, defined as the dollar price of 1 euro. So, the investor gets $1/\mathcal{E}_t$ euros for her dollar. In period $t + 1$, she will receive $(1 + i_t^*)/\mathcal{E}_t$ euros. At this point she converts the euros back into dollars. Let $\mathcal{E}_{t+1}$ denote the spot exchange rate prevailing in period $t + 1$. Then the $(1 + i_t^*)/\mathcal{E}_t$ euros can be converted into $(1 + i_t^*)\mathcal{E}_{t+1}/\mathcal{E}_t$ dollars in $t + 1$. Therefore, in deciding where to invest, the investor would like to compare the return of investing in the United States, $1 + i_t$, to the dollar return of an equivalent investment in Germany, $(1 + i_t^*)\mathcal{E}_{t+1}/\mathcal{E}_t$. If $1 + i_t$ is greater than $(1 + i_t^*)\mathcal{E}_{t+1}/\mathcal{E}_t$, then it is more profitable to invest in the United States. In fact, in this case, the investor could make unbounded profits by borrowing in Germany and investing in the United States. Similarly, if $1 + i_t$ is less than $(1 + i_t^*)\mathcal{E}_{t+1}/\mathcal{E}_t$, the investor could make infinite profits by borrowing in the United States and investing in Germany.

This investment strategy suffers, however, from a fundamental problem. At time t, the investor does not know $\mathcal{E}_{t+1}$, the exchange rate that will prevail at time $t+1$. This means that the return associated with investing in the United States, $1+i_t$, and the one associated with investing in Germany, $(1+i_t^*)\mathcal{E}_{t+1}/\mathcal{E}_t$, are not directly comparable because the former is known with certainty at the time the investment is made (period t), whereas the latter is uncertain at that time.

Forward exchange markets are designed precisely to allow investors to circumvent the exchange rate risk. The investor can eliminate the exchange rate uncertainty by arranging at the beginning of the investment period, the purchase of the necessary amount of U.S. dollars to be delivered at the end of the investment period for a price determined at the beginning of the period. Such a foreign currency purchase is called a *forward contract*. Let F_t denote the forward rate; that is, the dollar price at time t of €1 delivered and paid for at time $t+1$. Note that when a forward contract is arranged (period t), there is no exchange of money. The exchange of money happens when the forward contract is executed (period $t+1$). The ratio of the forward exchange rate to the spot exchange rate, $F_t/\mathcal{E}_t$, is called the *forward discount*. The dollar return of a \$1 investment in Germany using the forward exchange market is $(1+i_t^*)F_t/\mathcal{E}_t$. This return is known with certainty at time t, making it comparable to the return on the domestic investment, $1+i_t$.

The difference between the domestic return and the foreign return expressed in domestic currency by use of the forward exchange rate is known as the *covered interest rate differential*:

$$\text{covered interest rate differential} = (1+i_t) - (1+i_t^*)\frac{F_t}{\mathcal{E}_t}. \tag{11.1}$$

This interest rate differential is called covered because the use of the forward exchange rate covers the investor against exchange rate risk. It is also known as the *cross-currency basis*.

When the covered interest rate differential is zero, we say that *covered interest rate parity* (CIP) holds. In the absence of barriers to capital mobility and for interest rates and forward rates that are free of default risk, a violation of CIP implies the existence of arbitrage opportunities. When an arbitrage opportunity exists, there is the possibility of making unbounded profits without taking on any risk.

Consider the following example. Suppose that the annual nominal interest rate in the United States is 7 percent ($i_t = 0.07$), that the annual nominal interest rate in Germany is 3 percent ($i_t^* = 0.03$), that the spot exchange rate is \$1.20 per euro ($\mathcal{E}_t = 1.20$), and that the 1-year forward exchange rate is \$1.22 per euro ($F_t = 1.22$). In this case, the forward discount is $F_t/\mathcal{E}_t = 1.22/1.20 = 1.0167$, and the covered interest rate differential is $1+i_t - (1+i_t^*)F_t/\mathcal{E}_t = 1.07 - 1.03 \times 1.0167 = 0.0228$, or 2.28 percent. In the absence of barriers to international capital mobility, this violation of CIP implies that it is possible to make profits by borrowing in Germany, investing in the United States, and buying euros in the forward market to eliminate the exchange rate risk.

To see how one can exploit this arbitrage opportunity, consider the following sequence of trades. (1) Borrow €1 in Germany. (2) Exchange your €1 in the spot market for \$1.20. (3) Invest the \$1.20 in a U.S. deposit. (4) Buy €1.03 in the forward market (you will need this amount of euros to repay your euro loan including interest). Recall that buying euros in the forward market involves no payment at this point. (5) After 1 year, your U.S. investment yields $1.07 \times \$1.20 = \$1.2840$. (6) Execute your forward contract; that is, purchase €1.03 for $1.22 \times 1.03 = \$1.2566$. Use this amount to repay your German loan. The difference between what you receive in (5) and what you pay in (6) is $\$1.2840 - \$1.2566 = \$0.0274 > 0$. Note that this operation involved no exchange rate risk (because you used the forward market), needed no initial capital, and yielded a pure profit of $0.0274.

It is clear from this example that for interest rates and forward rates that are free of default risk, the covered interest rate differential should be zero if there are no barriers to international capital flows. Therefore, the existence of nonzero covered interest rate differentials is an indication of lack of free capital mobility.

11.2 Covered Interest Rate Differentials in China: 1998–2021

In 2001 China became a member of the World Trade Organization. This meant that barriers to international trade in goods and services, including tariffs and quotas, were greatly reduced for transactions involving existing members of the WTO and China. In this way China became more integrated into world markets for goods and services. A natural question is whether this integration process also extended to international capital markets. To address this question, we can examine the behavior of covered interest rate differentials. Specifically, let's analyze the covered interest rate differential between the United States and China. Let i_t denote the dollar interest rate in the United States, i_t^* the renminbi interest rate in China, $\mathcal{E}_t$ the spot exchange rate (dollars per renminbi), and F_t the forward exchange rate (dollars per renminbi).[1] We can then compute the covered interest rate differential between the United States and China using the formula given in equation (11.1).

Figure 11.1 plots weekly data of the dollar-renminbi covered interest rate differential expressed in percent per year. The sample starts on December 11, 1998, and ends on September 24, 2021. The figure shows that deviations from covered interest rate parity are large. The absolute value of the covered interest rate differential was 3.1 percentage points on average. In the last five years of the sample, the absolute value of the differential fell by about 1 percentage point but remained sizable with an average absolute value of 2.1 percentage points. Is there any remarkable change in the covered interest rate differential after China's accession to the WTO? Yes. The sign of the covered interest rate differential flipped. Prior to October 2002 and after August 2015, the covered interest rate differential was positive most of the time, while it was mainly negative in the intervening period. However, the absolute deviation from covered interest rate parity before and after accession to the WTO did not change much, at least until recently. So we cannot conclude that after accession China reduced barriers to international capital flows, for both positive and negative deviations from covered interest rate parity indicate impediments to free capital

---

[1] The measure of F_t is the nondeliverable forward rate from the offshore market.

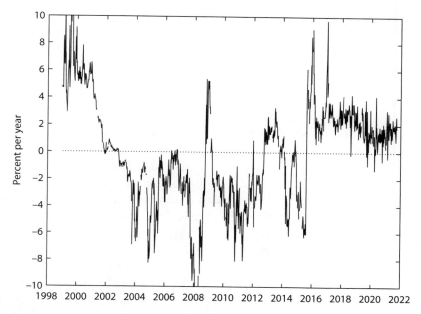

Figure 11.1. U.S. Dollar-Renminbi Covered Interest Rate Differentials, 1998–2021
Notes: The figure plots weekly observations of the dollar-renminbi covered interest rate differential for the period December 11, 1998, to September 24, 2021. Own calculations based on data from Bloomberg.

mobility. A positive covered interest rate differential suggests the presence of impediments to capital outflows from China to the United States and a negative covered interest rate differential suggests the presence of restrictions on capital inflows into China. In other words, the data suggest that prior to accession Chinese investors wanted to take money out of China but could not, whereas in the years following accession they wanted to borrow from abroad to invest domestically, but again could not. Therefore, the observed behavior of the covered interest rate differential suggests that throughout the sample the Chinese economy exhibited impediments to both capital inflows and capital outflows.[2]

11.3   Capital Controls and Interest Rate Differentials: Brazil 2009–2012

Thus far we have argued that covered interest rate differentials can reflect government-imposed impediments to cross-border flows of capital. Impediments to the international flow of capital originating in government regulations are broadly called capital controls. Capital controls can take a variety of forms, including taxes on international inflows or outflows of capital, quotas on international borrowing or lending, or requirements to park capital inflows or outflows in non-remunerated domestic accounts for a given period of time. In this section, we

---

[2] Exercise 12.20 in Chapter 12 asks you to use a publicly available dataset on capital controls to provide a more direct indicator of capital controls on inflows and outflows in China before and after accession to the WTO.

present a case study from Brazil in the aftermath of the global financial crisis of
2007–2009, in which the connection between covered interest rate differentials and
government-imposed impediments to capital flows can be clearly identified.

In the wake of the global financial crisis, interest rates in the United States and
many other developed countries fell to near zero. In response to such low rates,
global investors who were looking for higher yields started sending funds to emerging market economies, where interest rates were higher. One country that was a
recipient of large inflows was Brazil. The Brazilian authorities, concerned that these
capital inflows would destabilize the economy, enacted taxes on capital inflows.
Specifically, between October 2009 and March 2012 Brazil imposed more than
10 major capital control taxes. The measures included taxes on portfolio equity
inflows, taxes on fixed income inflows, and unremunerated reserve requirements.
After March 2012 those restrictions were gradually removed.

When capital inflow taxes are imposed on a specific asset or class of assets there is
always the concern that market participants can find a way to circumvent them. One
way to see if in this instance the capital control taxes were effective is to look at the
covered interest rate differential between the Brazilian real and the U.S. dollar. Let
i_t denote the 360-day interest rate in Brazil on domestic currency deposits (reais),
$\mathcal{E}_t$ the spot exchange rate (that is, the reais price of one U.S. dollar), F_t the 360-
day forward exchange rate of U.S. dollars, and i_t^* the 360-day U.S. dollar Libor rate.
Then the covered interest rate differential between Brazil and the United States is
given by $(1 + i_t)\frac{\mathcal{E}_t}{F_t} - (1 + i_t^*)$. In Brazil, at the time, the first term of this expression
was called the cupom cambial, i_t^{cupom}; that is, $1 + i_t^{cupom} = (1 + i_t)\frac{\mathcal{E}_t}{F_t}$. The cupom
cambial represents the dollar interest rate inside Brazil. We can then express the
covered interest rate differential as

$$\text{covered interest rate differential} = i_t^{cupom} - i_t^*.$$

Figure 11.2 plots daily data for the real-dollar covered interest rate differential for
the period January 1, 2010, to December 31, 2012. If the inflow controls were successful, we should see that dollar interest rates inside Brazil became higher than
outside of Brazil; that is, that the covered interest rate differential increased. The
figure shows that the covered interest rate differential was around half a percentage
point until the fall of 2010. This means that the capital control measures enacted
until then, which targeted mainly portfolio equity investment, were not effective
in restricting arbitrage between the cupom cambial and the Libor rate. However,
starting in the fall of 2010 as the Brazilian government intensified capital controls,
the differential starts rising and reaches a peak of 4 percentage points by April 2011,
after an inflow tax of 6 percent on borrowing from abroad with maturities of less
than 2 years was imposed. The size of the covered interest rate differentials suggests that the latter capital inflow taxes were indeed effective in the sense that they
prevented interest rate equalization. By early 2012, however, arbitragers seem to
have found ways to bypass the capital control tax as differentials return to normal
levels of around 0.5 percentage points. By June 2012, the capital control tax of 6 percent on borrowing from abroad with maturities of less than two years was removed.
The Brazilian experiment with capital controls shows that they can be effective in

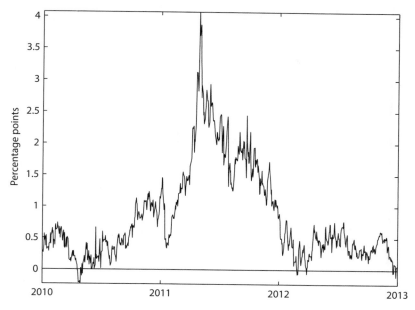

Figure 11.2. Brazilian Real-U.S. Dollar Covered Interest Rate Differentials, 2010–2012
Notes: The figure plots daily real-dollar covered interest rate differentials computed as the spread between the cupom cambial and the U.S. dollar Libor rate for the period January 1, 2010, to December 31, 2012.
Data Source: Marcos Chamon and Márcio Garcia, "Capital Controls in Brazil: Effective?," *Journal of International Money and Finance* 61 (2016): 163–187. We thank the authors for sharing their data.

creating a covered interest rate differential. However, it also shows that if capital controls are imposed on a narrowly defined set of international transactions, their effectiveness can be temporary, as financial investors have an incentive to find ways to avoid them.

The effect of capital controls on covered interest rate differentials can affect the real side of the economy including consumption, saving, investment, and the current account. In turn, these effects can have welfare consequences. Chapter 12 is devoted to analyzing the real consequences of capital controls on small and large economies through the lens of the intertemporal model used throughout the textbook.

11.4 Empirical Evidence on Covered Interest Rate Differentials: A Long-Run Perspective

One can use data on interest rates, spot exchange rates, and forward rates to construct empirical measures of covered interest rate differentials. This indicator can provide useful information about the evolution of international capital mobility across time. In particular, this type of empirical analysis can be used to address the question of whether the world is more globalized now than in the past, and whether globalization progresses over time or is nonmonotone in nature.

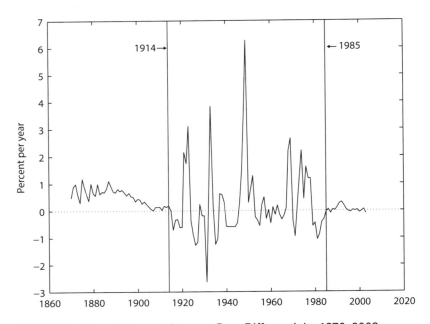

Figure 11.3. Dollar-Pound Covered Interest Rate Differentials, 1870–2003
Notes: The figure plots annual averages of monthly dollar-pound covered interest rate differentials.
Source: Maurice Obstfeld and Alan M. Taylor, "Globalization and Capital Markets," in *Globalization in Historical Perspective*, edited by M. D. Bordo, A. M. Taylor, and J. G. Williamson (Chicago: University of Chicago Press, 2003).

Figure 11.3 displays the dollar-pound sterling covered interest rate differential from 1870 to 2003.[3] Covered interest rate differentials were consistently small before World War I and after 1985, suggesting a high degree of international capital market integration during these two subperiods. The two world wars and the Great Depression threw the international financial system into disarray and led to widespread financial regulations that prevented the free flow of capital across national borders. These impediments to international capital mobility remained more or less in place until the mid-1980s, and led to high and volatile covered interest rate differentials. Low differentials reemerged after the deregulation of financial markets undertaken by the Thatcher and Reagan administrations. A similar pattern emerges when one examines covered interest rate differentials between the United States and Germany, with low differentials before 1914 and after the mid-1980s, and high and volatile differentials in the intervening decades.[4]

The empirical evidence we have examined suggests that capital market integration as measured by covered interest rate differentials is not a modern phenomenon. Like in the 1990s and 2000s, financial capital flowed in a more or less unfettered fashion before World War I. Furthermore, there are no reasons to believe that

---

[3]We thank Alan Taylor for sharing these data. Covered interest rate differentials before 1921 are constructed using a forward exchange instrument called the long bill of exchange. Exercise 11.4 discusses how this instrument works.

[4]See Obstfeld and Taylor, "Globalization and Capital Markets."

the interruptions in capital mobility observed between 1914 and 1985 represent an exceptional event. As we will see shortly, the global financial crisis of 2008 brought about another wave of disruptions and government interventions in financial markets that caused an elevation in covered interest rate differentials around the developed world, albeit less pronounced than the one that occurred in the middle decades of the twentieth century.

11.5 Empirical Evidence on Offshore-Onshore Interest Rate Differentials

An alternative way to construct exchange risk-free interest rate differentials is to use interest rates on instruments denominated in the same currency—for example, the U.S. dollar—issued in financial centers located in different countries.

For example, one can compare the interest rate on dollar time deposits in banks located in New York and London. The interest rate on the domestic instrument is called the onshore rate, and the interest rate on the foreign instrument is called the offshore rate.

Dollar deposits outside of the United States became widespread in the early 1980s. The high inflation rates observed in the 1970s, together with the Federal Reserve's regulation Q that placed a ceiling on the interest rate that U.S. banks could pay on time deposits, led to fast growth of eurocurrency markets. Eurocurrency deposits are foreign currency deposits in a market other than the home market of the currency. For example, a eurodollar deposit is a dollar deposit outside the United States (e.g., a dollar deposit in London). The interest rate on such deposit is called the eurodollar rate. A yen deposit at a bank in Singapore is called a euro yen deposit and the associated interest rate is called the euro yen rate. The biggest market for eurocurrency deposits is London.

Letting i_t be the interest rate in period t on a dollar deposit in the United States and i_t^* the interest rate on a dollar deposit in the foreign country, the offshore-onshore interest rate differential is

$$\text{offshore-onshore differential} = i_t^* - i_t.$$

The fact that both interest rates are on dollar deposits eliminates the exchange rate risk, thereby making them directly comparable. If both deposits are default risk free, then, under free capital mobility, the offshore-onshore differential should be zero. Any difference between i_t and i_t^* would create a pure arbitrage opportunity that investors could exploit to make unbounded profits. This means that in the absence of default risk, nonzero offshore-onshore interest rate differentials are an indication of lack of free capital mobility.

Figure 11.4 plots the three-month U.K.-U.S. offshore-onshore interest rate differential of the U.S. dollar over the period 1981Q1 to 2019Q1. As discussed before, until the mid-1980s, both the United States and the United Kingdom had regulations in place that hindered free international capital mobility. This is reflected in high offshore-onshore differentials during this period. The fact that during this period dollar rates were higher in the United Kingdom than in the United States indicates that investors wanted to borrow in the latter and lend in the former but could not do so to the extent they wished.

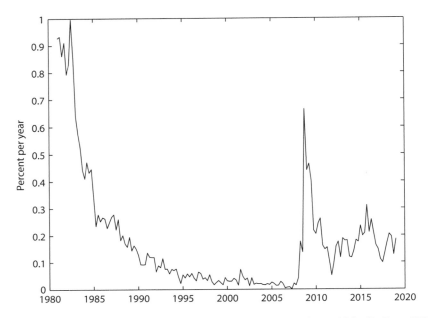

Figure 11.4. Offshore-Onshore Interest Rate Differential of the U.S. Dollar, 1981Q1–2019Q1

Notes: The figure plots the average quarterly offshore-onshore interest rate differential of the U.S. dollar. The offshore rate is the 3-month eurodollar deposit interest rate, Bank of England series: IUQAED3A. The onshore rate is the 3-month certificates of deposit (CD) rate for the United States, OECD MEI series: IR3TIB.

Offshore-onshore differentials fell to practically zero (below 10 basis points) by 1990 and remained at that low level until the onset of the global financial crisis in 2008. In 2008, the interest rate differential spiked briefly at about 60 basis points and then stabilized at a lower level but higher than the one that prevailed prior to the crisis. The lack of convergence to pre-crisis levels can be ascribed to the adoption of prudential regulations in the United States and the United Kingdom that prevent banks from fully arbitraging these differentials away. Such regulations included money market reforms that limited participation of U.S. branches of foreign banks in U.S. CD markets, and the imposition of more stringent bank capital requirements in the United States. Although the global financial crisis had a lasting effect on interest rate differentials, deviations from parity are not nearly as large or volatile as those observed between 1914 and 1985.

The lack of convergence in cross-country interest rate differentials after the global financial crisis is not limited to the U.S.-U.K. country pair, but is a fairly widespread phenomenon. Lack of convergence of interest rate differentials between, for example, the United States and Canada, the euro area, Japan, Norway, New Zealand, and Sweden has also been documented.[5]

---

[5] See Eugenio Cerutti, Maurice Obstfeld, and Haonan Zhou, "Covered Interest Parity Deviations: Macrofinancial Determinants," IMF Working Paper, WP/19/14, January 2019. This study uses covered interest rate differentials as opposed to offshore-onshore interest rate differentials.

11.6 Uncovered Interest Rate Parity

A much discussed concept in international finance is that of *uncovered interest rate parity* (UIP). To understand this concept, suppose first that we could see without uncertainty what the nominal exchange rate will be next period. Then, in deciding whether to invest in the domestic market or abroad, we would compare the return of \$1 invested in the domestic market with the return of \$1 invested in the foreign market. One dollar invested locally pays $1 + i_t$ dollars at the end of the investment period. To invest in the foreign market, we first convert \$1 into $1/\mathcal{E}_t$ units of foreign currency using the exchange rate $\mathcal{E}_t$, and then invest it at the rate i_t^*. This investment yields $(1 + i_t^*)/\mathcal{E}_t$ units of foreign currency in period $t + 1$. Converting this amount into domestic currency yields $(1 + i_t^*)\mathcal{E}_{t+1}/\mathcal{E}_t$ dollars. Lack of arbitrage opportunities would require that $1 + i_t$ equal $(1 + i_t^*)\mathcal{E}_{t+1}/\mathcal{E}_t$. However, as we discussed in Section 11.1, because in period t we do not observe the nominal exchange rate that will occur in $t + 1$, it is impossible to compare the two returns. Consequently, $1 + i_t$ will in general not be equal to $(1 + i_t^*)\mathcal{E}_{t+1}/\mathcal{E}_t$, even if agents could freely arbitrage across countries.

But one might intuitively think that the two returns should be equal to each other on average. Letting E_t denote the expectations operator conditional on information available in period t, we would then have that

$$1 + i_t = (1 + i_t^*)E_t\left(\frac{\mathcal{E}_{t+1}}{\mathcal{E}_t}\right). \tag{11.2}$$

This condition is known as uncovered interest rate parity. The difference between the left-hand side and the right-hand side of this equation is known as the *uncovered interest rate differential*,

$$\text{uncovered interest rate differential} = 1 + i_t - (1 + i_t^*)E_t\left(\frac{\mathcal{E}_{t+1}}{\mathcal{E}_t}\right).$$

In this section we show that the intuition that UIP should hold is not supported by theory or data. This suggests that observing sizable uncovered interest rate differentials is not an indication of the existence of impediments to free capital mobility across countries.

11.6.1 ASSET PRICING IN AN OPEN ECONOMY

Consider a small open endowment economy with free capital mobility. As in Chapter 6, assume that there is no uncertainty in period 1, but that there is uncertainty about period 2. Specifically, in period 2, there are two states of the world—the good state, denoted g, which occurs with probability π, and the bad state, denoted b, which occurs with probability $1 - \pi$.

Let B_1 denote domestic currency bonds purchased in period 1. These bonds pay the nominal interest rate i when held from period 1 to period 2. Suppose that the foreign nominal interest rate is i^*. Let B_1^* denote foreign-currency-denominated bonds purchased by the domestic household in period 1 for which the household buys forward cover. That is, in period 1 the household enters into a contract that allows it to convert in period 2 $(1 + i^*)B_1^*$ units of foreign currency into domestic currency at the forward exchange rate, F_1. Let $\tilde{B}_1^*$ denote the quantity of foreign currency bonds the domestic household acquires in period 1 for which it does not buy forward cover and hence is exposed to exchange rate risk.

Let $\mathcal{E}_t$ denote the nominal exchange rate in period $t = 1, 2$, defined as the domestic currency price of one unit of foreign currency in period t. We can then express the period 1 budget constraint of the domestic household as

$$P_1 C_1 + B_1 + \mathcal{E}_1 B_1^* + \mathcal{E}_1 \tilde{B}_1^* = P_1 Q_1, \tag{11.3}$$

where P_1 denotes the domestic price level in period 1 and Q_1 denotes the endowment of goods in period 1. Here we have assumed that the household entered period 1 without any asset holdings, $B_0 = B_0^* = \tilde{B}_0^* = 0$.

The budget constraint in the good state in period 2 is

$$P_2^g C_2^g = P_2^g Q_2^g + (1 + i)B_1 + F_1(1 + i^*)B_1^* + \mathcal{E}_2^g(1 + i^*)\tilde{B}_1^*, \tag{11.4}$$

where P_2^g denotes the price level in the good state in period 2, C_2^g denotes the level of consumption in the good state in period 2, Q_2^g denotes the endowment in the good state in period 2, and $\mathcal{E}_2^g$ denotes the exchange rate in the good state in period 2. Similarly, the budget constraint in the bad state in period 2 is given by

$$P_2^b C_2^b = P_2^b Q_2^b + (1 + i)B_1 + F_1(1 + i^*)B_1^* + \mathcal{E}_2^b(1 + i^*)\tilde{B}_1^*, \tag{11.5}$$

with a notation analogous to the one for the good state.

Assume that the household's expected utility function is

$$U(C_1) + \pi \, U(C_2^g) + (1 - \pi)U(C_2^b), \tag{11.6}$$

where $U(\cdot)$ is an increasing and concave period utility function.

The household's utility maximization problem consists in choosing C_1, C_2^g, C_2^b, B_1, B_1^*, and $\tilde{B}_1^*$ to maximize (11.6) subject to the budget constraints (11.3), (11.4), and (11.5), taking as given $P_1, P_2^g, P_2^b, \mathcal{E}_1, \mathcal{E}_2^g, \mathcal{E}_2^b, F_1, i, i^*, Q_1, Q_2^g$, and Q_2^b. To obtain the optimality conditions associated with this problem, first solve the period 1 budget constraint for C_1, the period 2 good-state budget constraint for C_2^g, and the period 2 bad-state budget constraint for C_2^b. This yields

$$C_1(B_1, B_1^*, \tilde{B}_1^*) = \frac{P_1 Q_1 - B_1 - \mathcal{E}_1 B_1^* - \mathcal{E}_1 \tilde{B}_1^*}{P_1},$$

$$C_2^g(B_1, B_1^*, \tilde{B}_1^*) = \frac{P_2^g Q_2^g + (1 + i)B_1 + (1 + i^*)\left(F_1 B_1^* + \mathcal{E}_2^g \tilde{B}_1^*\right)}{P_2^g},$$

and

$$C_2^b(B_1, B_1^*, \tilde{B}_1^*) = \frac{P_2^b Q_2^b + (1 + i)B_1 + (1 + i^*)\left(F_1 B_1^* + \mathcal{E}_2^b \tilde{B}_1^*\right)}{P_2^b}.$$

Then use these three expressions to eliminate consumption from the utility function to obtain

$$U(C_1(B_1, B_1^*, \tilde{B}_1^*)) + \pi\ U(C_2^g(B_1, B_1^*, \tilde{B}_1^*)) + (1-\pi)U(C_2^b(B_1, B_1^*, \tilde{B}_1^*)).$$

The first-order condition with respect to B_1 is

$$U'(C_1)\frac{1}{P_1} = \pi U'(C_2^g)\frac{1+i}{P_2^g} + (1-\pi)U'(C_2^b)\frac{1+i}{P_2^b}.$$

The left-hand side of this expression indicates the marginal utility of one unit of domestic currency in period 1: One unit of domestic currency buys $1/P_1$ units of goods, each of which provides $U'(C_1)$ units of utility. The right-hand side also indicates the marginal utility of one unit of currency in period 1; but in this case, the one unit of currency is used to buy a domestic bond. This investment returns $(1+i)$ units of currency in period 2 regardless of the state of the economy. In the good state, this buys $1/P_2^g$ units of goods, which each provides $U'(C_2^g)$ units of utility and in the bad state this buys $1/P_2^b$ units of goods, which each provides $U'(C_2^b)$ units of utility. The right-hand side thus gives the expected marginal utility of investing one unit of domestic currency in period 1 in the domestic bond and consuming the proceeds in period 2. At the optimum, the expected utility of investing one unit of domestic currency in the domestic bond (the right-hand side) or converting it into consumption goods already in period 1 (the left-hand side) must generate the same level of utility. This optimality condition is known as the Euler equation for domestic bonds. Rewrite this Euler equation as

$$1 = (1+i)\left[\pi\frac{U'(C_2^g)}{U'(C_1)}\frac{P_1}{P_2^g} + (1-\pi)\frac{U'(C_2^b)}{U'(C_1)}\frac{P_1}{P_2^b}\right].$$

Notice that the expression within square brackets is an expected value. Thus, using the expectations operator E_1, we can write

$$1 = (1+i)E_1\left\{\frac{U'(C_2)}{U'(C_1)}\frac{P_1}{P_2}\right\}.$$

The object

$$M_2 \equiv \left\{\frac{U'(C_2)}{U'(C_1)}\frac{P_1}{P_2}\right\}$$

is known as the household's pricing kernel. It is the ratio of the marginal utility of one unit of domestic currency in period 2, $U'(C_2)/P_2$, to the marginal utility of one unit of domestic currency in period 1, $U'(C_1)/P_1$. It is a pricing kernel because multiplying any nominal payment in a given state of the world in period 2 by M_2 returns the period 1 value of such payment. Using the pricing kernel, the Euler equation for domestic bonds becomes

$$1 = (1+i)E_1\{M_2\}. \tag{11.7}$$

The first-order condition with respect to foreign bonds for which the household buys forward cover, B_1^*, is

$$U'(C_1)\frac{\mathcal{E}_1}{P_1} = \pi(1+i^*)U'(C_2^g)\frac{F_1}{P_2^g} + (1-\pi)(1+i^*)U'(C_2^b)\frac{F_1}{P_2^b}.$$

The left-hand side of this expression is the utility of using one unit of foreign currency to purchase consumption goods in period 1. The right-hand side is the expected utility of using one unit of foreign currency to purchase foreign bonds with forward cover, and spending the proceeds on consumption in period 2. This optimality condition is known as the Euler equation for foreign bonds. As we did with the Euler equation for domestic bonds, we use the pricing kernel to write the Euler equation for foreign bonds as

$$1 = (1+i^*)\frac{F_1}{\mathcal{E}_1}E_1\{M_2\}. \tag{11.8}$$

Finally, the household's optimality condition with respect to bonds purchased without forward cover, $\tilde{B}_1^*$, is

$$U'(C_1)\frac{\mathcal{E}_1}{P_1} = \pi(1+i^*)U'(C_2^g)\frac{\mathcal{E}_2^g}{P_2^g} + (1-\pi)(1+i^*)U'(C_2^b)\frac{\mathcal{E}_2^b}{P_2^b}.$$

The left-hand side of this optimality condition is the utility of one unit of foreign currency used for consumption in period 1. The right-hand side is the expected utility of investing one unit of foreign currency in the foreign bond without forward cover. Note that the domestic currency return of this investment depends on the realization of the nominal exchange rate in period 2. In other words, this investment has exposure to exchange rate risk. Using the pricing kernel M_2, we can rewrite this condition as

$$1 = (1+i^*)E_1\left\{\left(\frac{\mathcal{E}_2}{\mathcal{E}_1}\right)M_2\right\}. \tag{11.9}$$

11.6.2   CIP AS AN EQUILIBRIUM CONDITION

Combining the Euler equations for domestic and foreign bonds, equations (11.7) and (11.8), we obtain

$$(1+i) = (1+i^*)\frac{F_1}{\mathcal{E}_1}, \tag{11.10}$$

which is the CIP condition discussed in Section 11.1. This result shows that CIP is not only a no-arbitrage condition, as we argued in Section 11.1, but also an equilibrium condition.

11.6.3   IS UIP AN EQUILIBRIUM CONDITION?

Can we derive the UIP condition given in equation (11.2) as an equilibrium condition of the present model? As it turns out, the answer to this question is no.

Optimization on the part of households implies that in general the rate of return on domestic bonds will not be equal to the expected exchange-rate adjusted rate of return on foreign bonds.

To see this, let's begin by comparing the UIP condition, equation (11.2), to the CIP condition, equation (11.10). It is clear from this comparison that UIP holds if and only if

$$F_1 = E_1 \mathcal{E}_2; \tag{11.11}$$

that is, if and only if the forward rate, F_1, is equal to the expected future exchange rate, $E_1 \mathcal{E}_2$.

The question of whether UIP holds in equilibrium then boils down to the question of whether the forward rate equals the expected future exchange rate. To answer this question, combine optimality conditions (11.8) and (11.9) to obtain

$$F_1 E_1 \{M_2\} = E_1 \{\mathcal{E}_2 M_2\}.$$

This expression implies that in general the forward rate, F_1, will not equal the expected future exchange rate, $E_1 \mathcal{E}_2$,

$$F_1 \neq E_1 \mathcal{E}_2.$$

This establishes that under free capital mobility, UIP in general fails to hold. Formally, we have that in general,

$$1 + i \neq (1 + i^*) E_1 \left(\frac{\mathcal{E}_2}{\mathcal{E}_1} \right).$$

Put differently, observing deviations from UIP in the data is not necessarily an indication of lack of free capital mobility.

Although UIP does not hold in general, it does hold in the special case in which the pricing kernel is uncorrelated with the exchange rate. To see this, recall that for any pair of random variables a and b, their covariance conditional on information available in period 1, denoted $\text{cov}_1(a, b)$, is given by $\text{cov}_1(a, b) = E_1(ab) - E_1(a)E_1(b)$. We then can express (11.9) as

$$1 = (1 + i^*) \left[\text{cov}_1 \left(\frac{\mathcal{E}_2}{\mathcal{E}_1}, M_2 \right) + E_1 \left(\frac{\mathcal{E}_2}{\mathcal{E}_1} \right) E_1(M_2) \right].$$

If the depreciation rate, $\mathcal{E}_2 / \mathcal{E}_1$, is uncorrelated with the pricing kernel, M_2; that is, if $\text{cov}_1 \left(\frac{\mathcal{E}_2}{\mathcal{E}_1}, M_2 \right) = 0$, then equation (11.9) becomes

$$1 = (1 + i^*) E_1 \left(\frac{\mathcal{E}_2}{\mathcal{E}_1} \right) E_1(M_2).$$

Combining this expression with optimality condition (11.7), we have

$$(1 + i) = (1 + i^*) E_1 \left\{ \frac{\mathcal{E}_2}{\mathcal{E}_1} \right\},$$

which is the UIP condition. We have therefore shown that while UIP need not hold in general, it does obtain under the special case in which the pricing kernel is uncorrelated with the depreciation rate of the domestic currency.

11.6.4   CARRY TRADE AS A TEST OF UIP

Suppose that UIP holds—that is, that $1 + i_t = (1 + i_t^*)E_t[\mathcal{E}_{t+1}/\mathcal{E}_t]$. It is clear from this expression that if $i_t > i_t^*$, then $E_t[\mathcal{E}_{t+1}/\mathcal{E}_t] > 1$. In words, if UIP holds, then the high interest rate currency is expected to depreciate. This means that one should not be able to make systematic profits from borrowing at the low interest rate and lending at the high interest rate, since exchange rate movements would exactly offset the interest rate differential on average. Yet, this trading strategy, known as *carry trade*, is widely used by practitioners, suggesting that it does indeed yield positive payoffs on average.

Empirical studies confirm that carry trade does yield positive profits on average. The payoff from carry trade is given by

$$\text{payoff from carry trade} = (1 + i_t) - (1 + i_t^*)\frac{\mathcal{E}_{t+1}}{\mathcal{E}_t},$$

where i_t is the high interest rate currency; that is, $i_t > i_t^*$. Burnside, Eichenbaum, Kleshchelski, and Rebelo (2006) document returns to carry trade for the pound sterling against 10 currencies using monthly data covering the period 1976:1 to 2005:12.[6] They find that the average payoffs from carry trade are positive but low, 0.0029 for £1 invested for one month. This means that to generate substantial profits, carry traders must wager large sums of money. For example, suppose a trader invests £1 billion in carry trade, then after one month the carry trade has a payoff of £2.9 million on average. The fact that the average payoff from carry trade is nonzero means that on average, the uncovered interest rate differential is not zero and that UIP fails.

Carry trade does not seem to be a more risky investment than other investments, such as the stock market. A commonly used measure of the risk-adjusted return is the *Sharpe ratio*, which is defined as the ratio of the average payoff divided by the standard deviation of the payoff; that is,

$$\text{Sharpe ratio} = \frac{\text{mean(payoff)}}{\text{std(payoff)}}.$$

The lower the Sharpe ratio, the lower the risk-adjusted return of the investment. Burnside et al. report a Sharpe ratio for carry trades that is relatively high, 0.145. This figure is similar to the Sharpe ratio of 0.14 corresponding to investing in the S&P 500 Index over the same period.

---

[6]See Craig Burnside, Martin Eichenbaum, Isaac Kleshchelski, and Sergio Rebelo, "The Returns to Currency Speculation," NBER Working Paper 12489, August 2006. The study considers the payoff from carry trade between the British pound and the currencies of Belgium, Canada, France, Germany, Italy, Japan, the Netherlands, Switzerland, the United States, and the euro area.

Like the stock market, carry trade is subject to crash risk. Crashes in carry trade are the result of sudden large movements in exchange rates. For example, on October 6–8, 1998, there was a large surprise appreciation of the Japanese yen against the U.S. dollar. The yen appreciated by 14 percent (or equivalently the U.S. dollar depreciated by 14 percent). Suppose that you were a carry trader with $1 billion short in yen and long in U.S. dollars. The payoff of that carry trade in the span of 2 days was −$140 million. Because of this crash risk and because of its low payoff relative to the large gross positions it requires, *The Economist* magazine has likened carry trade to "picking up nickels in front of steamrollers."[7]

11.6.5   THE FORWARD PREMIUM PUZZLE

When a foreign currency is "more expensive" in the forward market than in the spot market—that is, when

$$F_t > \mathcal{E}_t,$$

we say that the foreign currency is at a *premium in the forward market*, or equivalently, that the domestic currency is at a *discount in the forward market*.

We have already established that conditional on CIP holding, UIP holds if and only if the forward rate equals the expected future spot exchange rate; that is, if and only if $F_t = E_t \mathcal{E}_{t+1}$ (see equation (11.11)). Dividing both sides by $\mathcal{E}_t$ and rearranging, we have that

$$E_t \frac{\mathcal{E}_{t+1}}{\mathcal{E}_t} = \frac{F_t}{\mathcal{E}_t},$$

which says that conditional on CIP holding, UIP holds if and only if the domestic currency is expected to depreciate when the foreign currency trades at a premium in the forward market.

We saw in Section 11.4 that CIP holds reasonably well in the data. Therefore, the above expression represents a testable implication of UIP. Consider estimating the following equation by ordinary least squares (OLS):

$$\frac{\mathcal{E}_{t+1}}{\mathcal{E}_t} = a + b \frac{F_t}{\mathcal{E}_t} + \mu_{t+1},$$

where a and b are the regression coefficients and μ_{t+1} is a regression residual. Under UIP, the estimation should yield $a = 0$ and $b = 1$. This result, however, is strongly rejected in the data. For example, Burnside (2018) estimates this regression for the U.S. dollar against the currencies of 10 industrialized economies using monthly observations over the period 1976:1 to 2018:3.[8] He reports cross-country average estimates of a and b of 0.00055 and −0.75, respectively. For most countries (7 out

[7] See "Carry on Speculating," Economic Focus, *The Economist*, February 24, 2007, page 90.

[8] See Craig Burnside, "Exchange Rates, Interest Parity, and the Carry Trade," draft for publication in the *Oxford Research Encyclopedia of Economics and Finance*, June 2018. The countries included in the analysis are Australia, Canada, Denmark, Germany/euro area, Japan, New Zealand, Norway, Sweden, Switzerland, United Kingdom.

of 10), the null hypothesis that $a = 0$ and $b = 1$ is rejected at high significance levels of 1 percent or less. This result is known as the *forward premium puzzle*.

Like the evidence on returns to carry trade analyzed in Section 11.6.4, the forward premium puzzle indicates that UIP is strongly rejected by the data.

11.7 Real Interest Rate Parity

A natural question is whether free capital mobility creates a tendency for real interest rates to equalize across countries. The purpose of this section is to show that the answer to this question is no, except under special circumstances. To illustrate one such special case, consider an economy that produces and trades a single good, say apples. Let the domestic real interest rate be denoted r and the foreign real interest rate r^*. Then, if $r > r^*$, a household could borrow X apples in period t at the rate r^* in the foreign country and ship them to the home country. In the home country the household could lend out these X apples at the interest rate r. Next period the household collects $(1 + r)X$ apples on its loan. The household then ships $(1 + r^*)X$ apples abroad to repay the loan. The remainder $[(1 + r) - (1 + r^*)]X = (r - r^*)X > 0$ apples is pure profit. This investment strategy required no initial capital, did not involve any risk, and yielded a profit of $(r - r^*)X$ apples. Thus it represents a pure arbitrage opportunity that market participants would exploit until the real interest rate differential, $r - r^*$, is nil. In this economy, therefore, free capital mobility leads to real interest rate parity. Deviations from real interest rate parity would indicate the existence of impediments to the movement of capital across borders.

In a more realistic economy, however, in which there is more than one good and in which purchasing power parity does not hold, nonzero real interest rate differentials need not imply the absence of free capital mobility. To derive this result, consider a two-period open economy with two assets. Assume that in period 1, households have access to a domestic real bond, denoted b_1, that pays $(1 + r)b_1$ units of the domestic consumption basket in period 2. The second asset is a foreign real bond, denoted b_1^*, that pays $(1 + r^*)b_1^*$ units of the foreign consumption basket in period 2.

Let

$$e_t = \frac{\mathcal{E}_t P_t^*}{P_t}$$

denote the real exchange rate in period $t = 1, 2$, where P_t is the nominal price of a domestic basket of goods, P_t^* is the nominal price of a foreign basket of goods expressed in foreign currency, and $\mathcal{E}_t$ is the nominal exchange rate, defined as the domestic currency price of one unit of foreign currency. Think of this economy as one in which there are many goods. These goods form baskets. The household derives utility from the consumption of baskets of goods and is endowed with a number of such baskets each period. In the rest of the world, the basket of goods might have a different composition or might even contain different items. In addition, there might be tariffs or other barriers to international trade, creating differences in goods prices across countries. For all these reasons, the price of a basket of goods might be different in the domestic economy and in the rest of the world.

As we saw in Chapter 9, the real exchange rate, e_t, is the relative price of one foreign basket of goods in terms of domestic baskets of goods.

The budget constraint of the household in period 1 is

$$C_1 + b_1 + e_1 b_1^* = Q_1,$$

where C_1 denotes domestic consumption in period 1, and Q_1 denotes the endowment in period 1, both expressed in units of the domestic consumption basket. The remaining terms in the budget constraint are also expressed in units of domestic baskets. In particular, since the foreign real bond, b_1^*, is denominated in units of foreign baskets of goods, we have that $e_1 b_1^*$ expresses the cost of purchasing b_1^* units of the foreign bond in terms of domestic baskets of goods.

The household's budget constraint in period 2 is given by

$$C_2 = Q_2 + (1+r)b_1 + (1+r^*)e_2 b_1^*,$$

where C_2 denotes consumption in period 2, Q_2 denotes the endowment in period 2, and e_2 denotes the real exchange rate in period 2.

The household's utility function is assumed to be given by

$$U(C_1) + U(C_2),$$

where $U(\cdot)$ is an increasing and concave period utility function. The household chooses C_1, C_2, b_1, and b_1^* to maximize this utility function subject to the budget constraints in periods 1 and 2. To derive the optimality conditions associated with this problem, solve the period 1 budget constraint for C_1 and the period 2 budget constraint for C_2 and use the resulting expressions to eliminate consumption from the utility function. This yields

$$U(Q_1 - b_1 - e_1 b_1^*) + U(Q_2 + (1+r)b_1 + (1+r^*)b_1^*).$$

Taking derivatives with respect to b_1 and b_1^* and equating them to zero, we obtain the following Euler equations associated with the optimal choice of domestic and foreign real bonds:

$$U'(C_1) = (1+r)U'(C_2)$$

and

$$U'(C_1) = (1+r^*)U'(C_2)\frac{e_2}{e_1}.$$

The left-hand side of the first Euler equation is the increase in utility of consuming one additional basket of goods in period 1. The right-hand side gives the increase in utility if the household saves one basket of goods in domestic bonds. This investment yields $1+r$ baskets of goods in period 2, each of which produces $U'(C_2)$ units of utility. At the optimum the household must be indifferent between consuming and saving the marginal basket of goods. Likewise, the second Euler equation equates the utility derived from consuming an extra basket of goods in period 1 with the utility of saving the basket in foreign bonds. One basket of goods in period 1 buys $1/e_1$ baskets of foreign goods. Invested in the foreign bond, these baskets become $(1+r^*)/e_1$ baskets of foreign goods in period 2. In turn, with these baskets of foreign goods, the household can purchase $(1+r^*)e_2/e_1$ baskets of domestic goods in period 2.

Combining the two Euler equations we obtain

$$1+r = (1+r^*)\frac{e_2}{e_1}. \tag{11.12}$$

This expression says that r will in general not equal r^*. Even though the economy has free capital mobility, the real interest rate differential is in general different from zero. Instead, the (gross) domestic real interest rate, $1+r$, equals the (gross) foreign real interest rate adjusted by the real depreciation of the domestic currency, e_2/e_1. Intuitively, if e_2/e_1 is bigger than 1, the foreign basket is becoming more expensive over time. So one domestic basket invested in the foreign bond yields more than $1+r^*$ units of domestic baskets in period 2. We conclude that observing nonzero real interest rate differentials need not be indicative of restrictions to capital mobility.

This conclusion is empirically quite relevant. In Section 9.4 of Chapter 9, we documented that there are large deviations from relative PPP in the short run. This means that e_t/e_{t-1} changes significantly from one quarter to the next. These movements in the real exchange rate create a wedge between the domestic and the foreign real interest rates. Thus, tests of free capital mobility based on real interest rate differentials should be interpreted with caution, especially during periods of large and frequent movements in real exchange rates.

For simplicity, in this section we abstract from uncertainty. With uncertainty about the state of the world in period 2, equation (11.12) changes, as it incorporates the effect of expected comovements between the real exchange rate and consumption. However, the result that deviations from real interest rate parity are not indicative of lack of capital mobility continues to hold.[9]

11.8 Saving-Investment Correlations

In 1980, Martin Feldstein (1939–2019) and Charles Horioka published a provocative empirical paper documenting that national saving rates are highly correlated with investment rates.[10] They examined data on average investment-to-GDP and saving-to-GDP ratios from 16 industrial countries over the period 1960–1974. The data used in their study are shown in Figure 11.5.

Feldstein and Horioka estimate by OLS the following linear relation between investment and saving rates:

$$\left(\frac{I}{GDP}\right)_i = 0.035 + 0.887\left(\frac{S}{GDP}\right)_i + v_i; \qquad R^2 = 0.91,$$

where $(I/GDP)_i$ and $(S/GDP)_i$ denote, respectively, the average investment-to-GDP and saving-to-GDP ratios in country i over the period 1960–1974. Figure 11.5 shows the fitted relationship as a solid line. Feldstein and Horioka use data on 16

---

[9]Exercise 11.6 asks you to characterize an economy like the one discussed in this section, augmented with uncertainty.

[10]M. Feldstein and C. Horioka, "Domestic Saving and International Capital Flows," *Economic Journal* 90 (June 1980): 314–329.

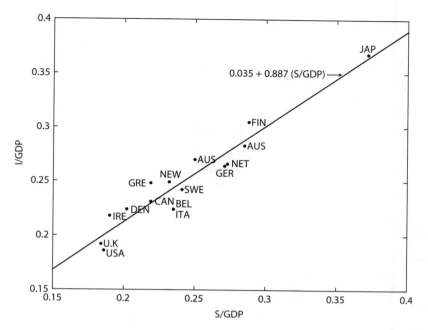

Figure 11.5. Saving and Investment Rates for 16 Industrialized Countries, 1960–1974 Averages

Data Source: M. Feldstein and C. Horioka, "Domestic Saving and International Capital Flows," *Economic Journal* 90 (June 1980): 314–329. Country names are shown using ISO abbreviations.

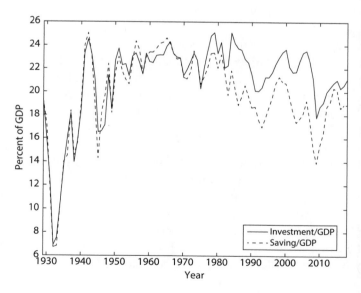

Figure 11.6. U.S. National Saving and Investment Rates, 1929–2018
Data Source: Bureau of Economic Analysis, NIPA Table 1.1.5 and Table 5.1.

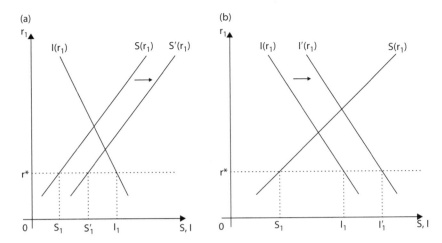

Figure 11.7. Response of *S* and *I* to Independent Shifts in (a) the Saving Schedule and (b) the Investment Schedule

OECD countries, so that their regression was based on 16 observations. The high value of the coefficient on S/GDP of 0.887 means that there is almost a one-to-one positive association between average saving rates and average investment rates. The reported R^2 statistic of 0.91 means that the estimated equation fits the data quite well, as 91 percent of the cross-country variation in I/GDP is explained by variations in S/GDP.

A positive relationship between saving and investment rates is observed not only across countries but also across time. For example, Figure 11.6 shows the U.S. saving and investment rates from 1929 to 2018. The two series move closely together over time, although the comovement has weakened somewhat since the emergence of large current account deficits in the 1980s.

Feldstein and Horioka argued that if capital was highly mobile across countries, then the correlation between saving and investment should be close to zero, and therefore interpreted their findings as evidence of low capital mobility. The reason why Feldstein and Horioka arrived at this conclusion can be seen by considering the identity,

$$CA = S - I,$$

where CA denotes the current account balance, S denotes national saving, and I denotes investment. In a closed economy—that is, in an economy without capital mobility—the current account is always zero, so that $S = I$ and changes in national saving are perfectly correlated with changes in investment. On the other hand, in a small open economy with perfect capital mobility, the interest rate is exogenously given by the world interest rate, so that if the saving and investment schedules are affected by independent factors, then the correlation between saving and investment will be zero. Figure 11.7 illustrates this point. Events that change only the saving schedule will result in changes in the equilibrium level of saving but will not affect the equilibrium level of investment (panel (a)). Similarly, events that affect only the investment schedule will result in changes in the equilibrium level of investment but will not affect the equilibrium level of national saving (panel (b)).

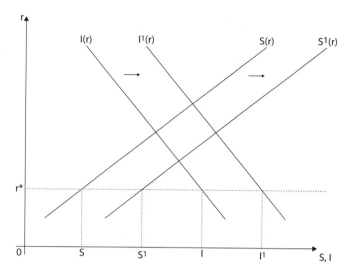

Figure 11.8. Response of *S* and *I* to a Persistent Productivity Shock

But do the Feldstein-Horioka findings of high saving-investment correlations really imply imperfect capital mobility? Feldstein and Horioka's interpretation has been criticized on at least two grounds. First, even under perfect capital mobility, a positive association between saving and investment may arise because the same events might shift the saving and investment schedules. For example, suppose that in a small open economy, the production functions in periods 1 and 2 are given by $Q_1 = A_1 F(I_0)$ and $Q_2 = A_2 F(I_1)$, respectively. Here Q_1 and Q_2 denote output in periods 1 and 2. The variable I_t, for $t = 0, 1$, denotes physical capital (like machines and structures) invested in period t that becomes productive in $t + 1$. The function $F(\cdot)$ represents the production technology and is assumed to be increasing and concave. And A_1 and A_2 are exogenous efficiency parameters capturing the state of technology, the effects of weather on the productivity of capital, and so forth. Consider a persistent productivity shock. Specifically, assume that A_1 and A_2 increase and that A_1 increases by more than A_2. This situation is illustrated in Figure 11.8, where the initial situation is one in which the saving schedule is given by $S(r)$ and the investment schedule by $I(r)$. At the world interest rate r^*, the equilibrium levels of saving and investment are given by S and I. In response to the expected increase in A_2, firms are induced to increase next period's capital stock, I_1, to take advantage of the expected rise in productivity. Thus, I_1 goes up for every level of the interest rate. This implies that in response to the increase in A_2, the investment schedule shifts to the right to $I^1(r)$. At the same time, the increase in A_2 produces a positive wealth effect that induces households to increase consumption and reduce saving in period 1. As a result, the increase in A_2 shifts the saving schedule to the left. Now consider the effect of the increase in A_1. This should have no effect on desired investment because the capital stock in period 1, I_0, is predetermined. However, the increase in A_1 produces an increase in output in period 1. Consumption-smoothing households will want to save part of the increase in Q_1. Therefore, the effect of an increase in A_1 is a rightward shift in the saving schedule. Because we assumed that

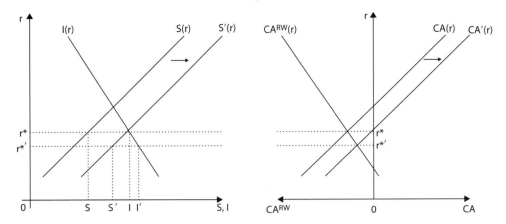

Figure 11.9. Large Open Economy: Response of *S* and *I* to a Shift in the Saving Schedule

A_1 increases by more than A_2, on net the saving schedule is likely to shift to the right. In the figure, the new saving schedule is given by $S^1(r)$. Because the economy is small, the interest rate is unaffected by the changes in A_1 and A_2. As a result, both saving and investment increase (to S^1 and I^1). Thus, in this economy we would see that saving and investment are positively correlated even though the economy has free capital mobility.

A second reason why saving and investment may be positively correlated in spite of free capital mobility is the presence of large country effects. Consider, for example, an event that affects only the saving schedule in a large open economy like the one represented in Figure 11.9. In response to a shock that shifts the saving schedule to the right from $S(r)$ to $S'(r)$, the current account schedule also shifts to the right from $CA(r)$ to $CA'(r)$. As a result, the world interest rate falls from r^* to $r^{*'}$. The fall in the interest rate leads to an increase in investment from I to I'. Thus, in a large open economy, a shock that affects only the saving schedule results in positive comovement between saving and investment.

We conclude that observing a positive correlation between saving and investment is not necessarily an indication of lack of capital mobility.

11.9 Summing Up

- The forward exchange rate, F_t, is the domestic currency price of one unit of foreign currency to be delivered and paid for in a future period.
- The forward discount is the ratio of the forward exchange rate to the spot exchange rate, $F_t/\mathcal{E}_t$. When the forward discount is greater than one, we say that the foreign currency trades at a premium and the domestic currency at a discount in the forward market.
- Covered interest rate parity (CIP) says that the domestic interest rate, i_t, must equal the foreign interest rate, i_t^*, adjusted for the forward discount, $1 + i_t = (1 + i_t^*)F_t/\mathcal{E}_t$.
- The covered interest rate differential, or cross-currency basis, is defined as $1 + i_t - (1 + i_t^*)F_t/\mathcal{E}_t$.

- Under free capital mobility, absent default risk, covered interest rate differentials should be near zero.
- The offshore-onshore interest rate differential is the difference between the interest rate on domestic currency denominated assets in a foreign market and the interest rate on domestic currency denominated assets in the domestic market.
- Under free capital mobility, absent default risk, offshore-onshore interest rate differentials should be near zero.
- The US dollar-renminbi covered interest rate differentials have been large in absolute value since 1998, suggesting impediments to international capital flows in China.
- Government-imposed impediments to international capital flows are called capital controls. Capital controls can take a variety of forms, including taxes, quotas, and unremunerated reserve requirements.
- The imposition of capital controls can create deviations from covered interest rate parity. However, if imposed on a narrow set of transactions, their effectiveness can be temporary, as investors can find ways to circumvent them. A case in point is the imposition of capital controls in Brazil in the aftermath of the global financial crisis of 2007–2009.
- Based on observed cross-country covered interest rate differentials, the developed world displayed a high degree of capital mobility between 1870 and 1914 and again after 1985. The period 1914–1985 was characterized by large disruptions in international capital market integration. This suggests that capital market integration is not a monotonic process.
- As a consequence of new financial regulations, covered interest rate differentials have displayed a slight elevation since the global financial crisis of 2008.
- Uncovered interest rate parity (UIP) says that the domestic interest rate must equal the foreign interest rate adjusted for expected depreciation, $1 + i_t = (1 + i_t^*)E_t \mathcal{E}_{t+1}/\mathcal{E}_t$.
- UIP is in general not implied by an equilibrium asset pricing model.
- UIP is strongly rejected by the data.
- Deviations from real interest rate parity can arise even under free capital mobility.
- Observing a positive correlation between saving and investment is not necessarily an indication of lack of capital mobility.

11.10 Exercises

Exercise 11.1 (TFU) Indicate whether the statement is true, false, or uncertain and explain why.

1. If there is free capital mobility between the United States and Germany, then dollar deposits in New York and Frankfurt should have the same interest rate.
2. If uncovered interest rate parity holds, then returns to carry trade must be zero not only on average but period by period.

3. The interest rate in Japan is 0 percent and the interest rate in the United States is 1.75 percent. There is clearly an arbitrage opportunity, as one can become infinitely rich without taking any risk by borrowing in yen and investing in dollars.
4. When the U.S. dollar (the domestic currency) is selling at a premium in the forward market, $F_t/\mathcal{E}_t < 1$, one should expect the dollar to depreciate, $E_t\mathcal{E}_{t+1}/\mathcal{E}_t > 1$.

Exercise 11.2 (Returns to Carry Trade) Suppose in month t the annual nominal interest rate is $i_t = 0.02$ in the United States and $i_t^* = 0.05$ in Germany. Suppose further that in month t a speculator invests \$400 million in carry trade for one month. Let $\mathcal{E}_t$ be the nominal exchange rate in month t, defined as the dollar price of one euro. Suppose that between month t and month $t+1$ the dollar appreciates by 2.8 percent. Find the payoff from the carry trade. Express your answer in dollars.

Exercise 11.3 (Interest Rate Differentials) Suppose that the spot exchange rate, $\mathcal{E}_t$, is \$1.5 per euro, that the forward exchange rate, F_t, is \$2 per euro, that the nominal interest rate in the United States is 3 percent per year, and that the nominal interest rate on euro deposits in Frankfurt is 1 percent per year. The time unit is one year. Assume further that with probability one half $\mathcal{E}_{t+1}$ is 2 and with equal probability it equals 1.

1. Calculate the covered interest rate differential.
2. Calculate the uncovered interest rate differential.
3. Calculate the forward discount.
4. Suppose a carry trade investor decides to invest \$1 million. How much money would she make or lose under each of the two possible realizations of $\mathcal{E}_{t+1}$?

Exercise 11.4 (The Long Bill of Exchange) As mentioned in the body of the chapter, prior to 1920 the covered interest rate differentials shown in Figure 11.3 are constructed using data on an instrument called the long bill of exchange. The long bill consists in purchasing with domestic currency in the current period one unit of foreign currency to be delivered 90 days later. Contrary to a forward contract, in the long bill the buyer of foreign currency must make a domestic currency payment at the beginning of the investment period. Let b_t denote the long bill rate, which is defined as the date-t dollar price in New York of one British pound deliverable in London after 90 days. (Note that b_t is paid 90 days prior to the date of delivery of the £1.) Let i_t^* denote the 90-day deposit rate in London, i_t the 90-day deposit rate in New York, and $\mathcal{E}_t$ the spot exchange rate; that is, the dollar price of one British pound. Suppose you had time series data for b_t, $\mathcal{E}_t$, i_t, and i_t^*. How can you construct a test of free capital mobility between the United States and Great Britain?

Exercise 11.5 (UIP Regression) Let $y_{t+1} = \mathcal{E}_{t+1}/\mathcal{E}_t$ and $x_t = F_t/\mathcal{E}_t$, where $\mathcal{E}_t$ denotes the nominal exchange rate in period t and F_t denotes the forward rate in period t. Consider estimating via OLS

$$y_{t+1} = a + bx_t + \mu_{t+1}.$$

Show that if UIP holds, then it must be the case that $a = 0$ and $b = 1$.

Exercise 11.6 (Real Interest Rate Parity and Uncertainty) Consider the two-period, small open endowment economy studied in Section 11.6.1 and introduce two additional assets. Specifically, assume that households have access to a domestic risk-free real bond, denoted b_1, that pays in period 2 $(1+r)b_1$ units of the domestic consumption basket. The second real asset is a foreign risk-free real bond, denoted b_1^*. The foreign real bond is denominated in units of the foreign consumption basket. It pays $(1+r^*)b_1^*$ units of the foreign consumption basket in period 2 when held from period 1 to period 2. Let $e_2^j = \mathcal{E}_2^j P_2^{*j}/P_2^j$ denote the real exchange rate in period 2 in state j for $j = g, b$. Assume that free capital mobility holds.

1. State the household's budget constraints in period 1, in the good state in period 2, and in the bad state in period 2, assuming (for simplicity) that the only assets the household has access to are real domestic and real foreign bonds.

2. Find the household's Euler equations associated with the optimal choice of b_1 and b_1^*, respectively.

3. Suppose that $cov(C_2, e_2/e_1) \neq 0$. Does real interest rate parity hold under free capital mobility?

4. Assume now that the real depreciation rate is uncorrelated with period 2 consumption; that is, assume that $cov(C_2, e_2/e_1) = 0$. Does real interest rate parity hold under free capital mobility?

CHAPTER 12

Capital Controls

Over the past 120 years, international capital markets have experienced periods in which capital flowed fairly freely across countries as well as periods with significant deviations from free capital mobility. For example, in Section 11.4 of Chapter 11, we documented that the United States was highly integrated with international capital markets between 1870 and 1914 and between 1985 and 2008, as reflected by low covered interest rate differentials. The period starting with World War I and ending in the mid-1980s displayed low degrees of international capital market integration as a result of disruptions created by the two world wars and a number of capital control policies that impeded the free flow of financial capital across borders. The global financial crisis of 2008 triggered new government regulations of financial markets that resulted in the reemergence of cross-country covered interest rate differentials, albeit small in size.

Capital control policies are also widespread in emerging countries. For example, in Section 11.3 of Chapter 11 we document how Brazil's imposition of capital control taxes aimed at reducing the large inflows of capital stemming from low interest rate regions (especially the United States and Europe) during the global financial crisis caused a significant elevation in covered interest rate differentials.

A natural question is whether capital controls can have consequences for real economic activity. This chapter takes up this question. It characterizes the effects of capital controls on the current account, consumption, and welfare in the context of an extension of the open-economy framework developed in Chapters 3–8. We consider controls that take the form of a tax on international financial transactions or a limit on the level of international borrowing or lending. We show that capital controls can be an effective tool to reduce current account deficits but that absent any distortions they are welfare decreasing. Thus, in these environments free capital mobility is optimal. We then study cases in which imperfections in financial markets, including externalities and market power of large economies, can provide a rationale for welfare-improving capital control taxes. In these environments, free capital mobility ceases to be optimal.[1]

---

[1] The analysis in the present chapter focuses on real economies; that is, economies without nominal frictions. The role of capital controls in monetary economies is analyzed in Chapter 14. There, capital controls can serve in addition as a stabilization tool when the exchange rate lacks flexibility.

The chapter closes with a discussion of empirical evidence suggesting that capital controls are ubiquitous and employed more intensively in low- and middle-income countries than in rich countries.

12.1 Capital Controls and Interest Rate Differentials

Capital controls are restrictions imposed by governments on the flow of financial capital into or out of a country. Capital controls can take the form of quantitative limits to the amount of funds that can flow through the border or of a tax on international capital flows. The imposition of capital controls gives rise to interest rate differentials that cannot be arbitraged away.

Suppose, for example, that the country is borrowing from the rest of the world and that initially there are no capital controls. Let i be the domestic interest rate on dollar loans (the onshore rate) and i^* the foreign interest rate on dollar loans (the offshore rate). Clearly, i cannot be lower than i^*, because if this were the case, no one would borrow internationally since it is cheaper to borrow domestically, contradicting the assumption that the country is borrowing from the rest of the world. Also, the domestic interest rate cannot be higher than the offshore interest rate, because in this case anybody could become infinitely rich by borrowing internationally at the rate i^* and lending domestically at the rate i. Thus, the onshore interest rate must equal the offshore interest rate,

$$i = i^*.$$

Suppose now that the government imposes a tax τ per dollar borrowed internationally. Suppose further that the tax is not large enough to completely discourage international borrowing, so that the country continues to borrow from abroad in spite of the capital control tax. Now the cost of borrowing one dollar internationally is $i^* + \tau$. If the domestic banks were to offer dollar loans at a rate lower than $i^* + \tau$, then no one would borrow internationally, contradicting the assumption that the country continues to borrow from the rest of the world after the imposition of the capital control tax. The domestic interest rate cannot be higher than $i^* + \tau$ either, because in this case an arbitrage opportunity would arise, consisting in borrowing internationally at the cost $i^* + \tau$ and lending domestically at the rate i. So the domestic interest rate must equal the sum of the foreign interest rate and the capital control tax rate,

$$i = i^* + \tau.$$

This establishes that when capital controls are imposed on capital inflows—that is, on international borrowing—the domestic interest rate will be higher than the foreign interest rate,

$$\text{Controls on capital inflows} \Rightarrow i > i^*.$$

The resulting interest rate differential, $i - i^*$, equals the capital control tax rate, τ. The larger the capital control tax rate is, the larger the interest rate differential will be.

When the capital control tax is imposed on capital outflows—that is, on international lending—it also creates an interest rate differential, but in the opposite direction. To see this, suppose that the country is lending to the rest of the world and that the government imposes a tax τ per unit lent internationally. In this case, the after-tax rate of return on lending one dollar abroad is $i^* - \tau$. By the same logic given in the analysis of controls on capital inflows, the domestic interest rate must equal the after-tax rate of return of lending abroad, otherwise arbitrage opportunities would arise, allowing agents to become infinitely rich. So we have that

$$i = i^* - \tau.$$

As in the case of controls on capital inflows, the imposition of controls on capital outflows creates an interest rate differential. However, unlike the case of controls on capital inflows, controls on capital outflows cause the domestic interest rate to be lower than the world interest rate,

$$\text{Controls on capital outflows} \Rightarrow i < i^*.$$

The analysis in this section shows that the introduction of capital controls creates a wedge between the domestic and the foreign interest rate. This distortion in financial markets will in general affect the real side of the economy, because key macroeconomic indicators, such as consumption, saving, investment, and the current account, depend on interest rates.

12.2 Macroeconomic Effects of Capital Controls

Current account deficits are often viewed as bad for a country. The idea behind this view is that by running a current account deficit, the economy is living beyond its means. By accumulating external debt, the argument goes, the country imposes future economic hardship on itself in the form of reduced consumption and investment spending when the external debt becomes due. A policy recommendation sometimes offered to countries undergoing external imbalances is the imposition of capital controls, which can take the form of taxes on international capital flows or quotas on external borrowing.

12.2.1 EFFECTS OF CAPITAL CONTROLS ON CONSUMPTION, SAVINGS, AND THE CURRENT ACCOUNT

Consider a two-period economy populated by a large number of households with preferences over consumption described by the utility function

$$U(C_1) + U(C_2),$$

where C_1 and C_2 denote consumption in periods 1 and 2, respectively, and $U(\cdot)$ is an increasing and concave period utility function. Suppose that households start period 1 without any debts or assets. In period 1, they receive an endowment of Q_1 units of goods. In addition, they can borrow or lend at the interest rate i. Then the budget constraint in period 1 is given by

$$P_1 C_1 + B_1 = P_1 Q_1,$$

where P_1 denotes the price of the good in period 1 and B_1 denotes the number of bonds purchased in period 1.

In period 2, the household receives an endowment of Q_2 units of goods and a transfer from the government equal to T units of goods. In addition, in period 2 the household receives the principal and interest on its period 1 savings. Because the world ends in period 2, there is no borrowing or lending in this period. Consequently, the budget constraint in period 2 is given by

$$P_2 C_2 = P_2 Q_2 + P_2 T + (1+i)B_1,$$

where P_2 denotes the price of the good in period 2. Assume that there is no inflation and normalize the price of goods in both periods to 1; that is, $P_1 = P_2 = 1$. Combining the period 1 and period 2 budget constraints to eliminate B_1 yields the household's intertemporal budget constraint

$$C_2 = Q_2 + T + (Q_1 - C_1)(1+i). \tag{12.1}$$

This expression says that in period 2 the household can consume its period 2 non-financial, disposable income, $Q_2 + T$, plus its period 1 savings including interest, $(Q_1 - C_1)(1+i)$.

Using the period 2 budget constraint to eliminate C_2 from the utility function, we obtain

$$U(C_1) + U(Q_2 + T + (Q_1 - C_1)(1+i)).$$

The household chooses C_1 to maximize this expression, taking Q_1, Q_2, T, and i as given. Taking the derivative of this expression with respect to C_1 and equating it to zero, we obtain the first-order optimality condition

$$U'(C_1) = (1+i)U'(Q_2 + T + (Q_1 - C_1)(1+i)).$$

Noticing that $Q_2 + T + (Q_1 - C_1)(1+i)$ is C_2, we can write the first-order condition as

$$\frac{U'(C_1)}{U'(C_2)} = 1 + i. \tag{12.2}$$

This is the familiar consumption Euler equation. It says that if the interest rate increases, the household has an incentive to reduce current consumption relative to future consumption. This follows from the fact that $U'(\cdot)$ is a decreasing function.

Suppose that the government imposes a capital control tax on international borrowing. Let $\tau > 0$ be the capital control tax rate. Then, by the analysis of Section 12.1, we have that if the economy is borrowing in period 1, then

$$i = i^* + \tau,$$

where i^* is the world interest rate. Using the Euler equation (12.2) to eliminate i from the household's optimality condition, we obtain

$$\frac{U'(C_1)}{U'(C_2)} = 1 + i^* + \tau. \tag{12.3}$$

This expression says that a capital control tax on international borrowing creates an incentive to reduce current consumption in favor of future consumption.

Let's assume that the government returns the proceeds of the capital control tax to households. Tax revenue equals $-\tau B_1$. To understand why this expression is preceded by a minus sign, recall that if the country is borrowing, then asset holdings, B_1, are negative, and tax revenue is positive. The amount of transfers received by each household is

$$T = -\tau B_1. \tag{12.4}$$

The household takes the transfer T as exogenously given. That is, the household does not internalize that the more capital control taxes it pays the larger its transfer will be. This type of transfer is called a lump-sum transfer. The idea is that in this economy there are many households, all of which pay capital control taxes. The government then divides total tax receipts equally among all households. So an individual household receives the same transfer regardless of how much capital control taxes it paid. Because all households are identical, it happens that in equilibrium transfers are exactly equal to the amount of taxes the household paid.

Using equation (12.4) to eliminate T from the intertemporal budget constraint (12.1), we obtain the economy's intertemporal resource constraint

$$C_2 = Q_2 + (Q_1 - C_1)(1 + i^*). \tag{12.5}$$

Note that the economy's intertemporal resource constraint is independent of the capital control tax rate, τ. This is because the government's tax revenue is returned to households, so no resources are lost as a consequence of the imposition of capital controls. This does not mean, however, that capital controls have no macroeconomic consequences. As can be seen from the optimality condition (12.3), capital controls distort the intertemporal allocation of consumption.

Figure 12.1 depicts the equilibrium effects of imposing the capital control tax τ. The downward sloping straight line is the economy's intertemporal resource constraint, given by equation (12.5). The slope of this line is $-(1 + i^*)$. It reflects the fact that if the country sacrifices 1 unit of consumption in period 1, in period 2 it can consume $1 + i^*$ additional units of consumption. Point A represents the endowment path, (Q_1, Q_2). Point B represents the optimal consumption path in the absence of capital controls, $\tau = 0$. At point B, the indifference curve is tangent to the intertemporal resource constraint. In particular, the slope of the indifference curve is $-(1 + i^*)$, which equals the slope of the intertemporal resource constraint. In this example, when capital controls are zero, the economy runs a trade deficit equal to $C_1^* - Q_1 > 0$. Because the initial asset position is assumed to be nil, $B_0 = 0$, both the current account and external debt equal the trade balance. This means that in period 1 the economy runs a current account deficit and becomes a net debtor

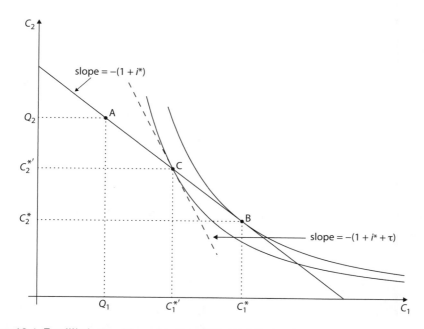

Figure 12.1. Equilibrium with and without Capital Controls
Notes: Point A represents the endowment path, point B the equilibrium consumption path in the absence of capital controls, and point C the equilibrium consumption path with capital controls. The capital control tax on international borrowing causes a fall in period 1 consumption, an improvement in the trade balance and the current account, and a reduction in net external debt. The equilibrium under capital controls yields a lower level of welfare than the equilibrium without capital controls.

to the rest of the world. In period 2, the household chooses a level of consumption, C_2^*, lower than its period 2 endowment, Q_2, to allow for the repayment of the debt contracted in period 1 plus the corresponding interest.

Point C in Figure 12.1 represents the equilibrium when the government imposes a capital control tax τ per unit borrowed internationally. The economy's resource constraint is unchanged. However, individually, households perceive an increase in the cost of borrowing from i^* to $i^* + \tau$. As a result, they reduce borrowing and move to a consumption bundle containing less consumption in period 1 and more in period 2 (see optimality condition (12.3)). In the figure, in response to the imposition of the capital control tax τ, consumption in period 1 falls from C_1^* to $C_1^{*'}$ and the trade and current account deficits shrink from $C_1^* - Q_1$ to $C_1^{*'} - Q_1$. Note that the slope of the indifference curve that crosses point C is steeper than the slope of the indifference curve that crosses point B. The difference in slopes is given by the capital control tax, τ.

In sum, the imposition of a capital control tax on international borrowing discourages current consumption and causes a reduction in the trade deficit, a reduction in the current account deficit, and a reduction in the country's net external debt. Next, we analyze how capital controls affect investment in physical capital.

12.2.2 EFFECTS OF CAPITAL CONTROLS ON INVESTMENT

Suppose that in the economy we have been studying thus far there are firms that borrow in period 1 to buy physical capital, which they use in period 2 to produce goods. The setup is identical to the one introduced in Chapter 5. To keep the present analysis self-contained, we go over its main elements.

Specifically, suppose that output in period 2 is given by

$$Q_2 = \sqrt{I_1},$$

where I_1 is the stock of capital available in period 2. To build this stock of capital, firms invest in period 1. The investment process requires funding, which firms procure by tapping the financial market. Accordingly, in period 1 firms borrow the amount I_1 at the interest rate i. In period 2, firms must pay back these loans, including interest. Thus, profits in period 2 are given by

$$\sqrt{I_1} - (1+i)I_1.$$

The firm chooses I_1 to maximize profits. The optimality condition associated with this maximization problem is the derivative of profits with respect to I_1 equated to zero, which slightly rearranged yields,

$$\frac{1}{2\sqrt{I_1}} = 1 + i.$$

Solving for I_1, we obtain the optimal level of investment

$$I_1 = \left(\frac{1}{2(1+i)}\right)^2,$$

which says that investment in physical capital is a decreasing function of the interest rate.

Recalling that we are considering an economy that borrows internationally and in which the government imposes capital controls on inflows, we have that in equilibrium the domestic interest rate must equal the world interest rate plus the capital control tax,

$$i = i^* + \tau.$$

Combining the above two expressions, we obtain

$$I_1 = \left(\frac{1}{2(1+i^*+\tau)}\right)^2.$$

This expression says that the imposition of capital controls on inflows has a negative effect on investment, as it increases the cost of financing the purchase of physical capital. We conclude that capital control taxes distort not only the consumption-saving choice of households but also the investment choice of firms.

12.2.3   WELFARE CONSEQUENCES OF CAPITAL CONTROLS

We have established that capital controls can be an effective tool to reduce external debt and current account deficits. We now ask whether these effects are desirable. To answer this question, note that the equilibrium under capital controls, given by point C in Figure 12.1, is on an indifference curve located closer to the origin than the indifference curve associated with the equilibrium without capital controls, point B. This means that the capital control tax is welfare decreasing. It follows that if the government wants to maximize the household's happiness, the best it can do is to set the capital control tax rate to zero. In other words, the optimal capital control tax is zero, or equivalently, free capital mobility is optimal.

The reason why capital controls are welfare decreasing in this economy is that they create a distortion in the domestic financial market by introducing a wedge between the true cost of borrowing for the economy, given by i^*, and the perceived cost of borrowing at the individual level, $i^* + \tau > i^*$. Households borrow less than is socially optimal because the capital control tax makes them feel that the cost of borrowing is higher than it really is. In Section 12.5, we will consider a large economy that has market power in world financial markets. In this environment, capital controls might be welfare increasing, as they can be used to manipulate the world interest rate in the country's favor. Before addressing this issue, however, we will consider the macroeconomic effects of capital controls that take the form of limits on the total amount of borrowing a country can undertake.

12.3   Quantitative Restrictions on Capital Flows

Capital controls can also take the form of quantitative restrictions on international borrowing and lending. In this section, we show that this form of capital controls is equivalent to those based on taxes on international flows. Suppose that the government imposes a cap on the total amount of external debt the country is allowed to have. The situation is depicted in Figure 12.2. The endowment point is represented by point A and the optimal consumption path in the absence of quantitative restrictions is given by point B. The figure is drawn under the assumption that the economy starts period 1 with a zero asset position ($B_0 = 0$). In the unconstrained equilibrium, point B, households optimally choose to borrow from the rest of the world in period 1 in order to finance a level of consumption, C_1^*, that exceeds their period 1 endowment, Q_1. As a result, in period 1 the trade balance, $Q_1 - C_1^*$, the current account, $Q_1 - C_1^*$, and the net foreign asset position, $B_1 = Q_1 - C_1^*$, are all negative.

Assume now that the government prohibits international borrowing beyond the amount D. That is, the policymaker imposes financial restriction

$$B_1 \geq -D.$$

As a result of this borrowing limit, consumption in period 1 can be at most as large as $Q_1 + D$. It is clear from Figure 12.2 that any point on the intertemporal budget constraint containing less period 1 consumption than at point C (i.e., any point on the intertemporal budget constraint located northwest of C) is less preferred than point

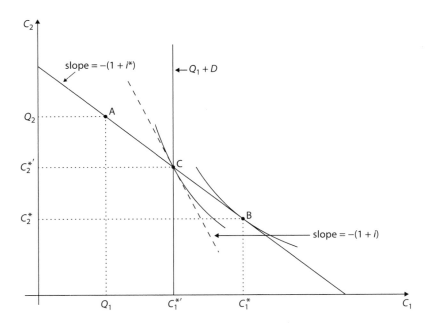

Figure 12.2. Equilibrium under Quantitative Capital Controls
Notes: The equilibrium under free capital mobility is at point B. At this point, period 1 consumption exceeds the endowment, and the economy borrows from the rest of the world. Quantitative capital controls forbid borrowing more than D, pushing households to consume $Q_1 + D$ in period 1, point C. The domestic interest rate under capital controls is given by the slope of the indifference curve at point C and is higher than the world interest rate i^*.

C itself. This means that when quantitative capital controls are imposed, households choose point C, and the borrowing constraint is binding, $B_1 = -D$. In the constrained equilibrium, in period 1 the household consumes the endowment plus the maximum amount of borrowing allowed, D, so $C_1^{*'} = Q_1 + D$. In period 2, the household consumes its endowment, Q_2, net of debt obligations including interest, $(1 + i^*)D$; that is, $C_2 = Q_2 - (1 + i^*)D$. So we have that in response to the quantitative restrictions on capital inflows, current consumption falls from C_1^* to $C_1^{*'}$, the trade balance and the current account shrink from $Q_1 - C_1^*$ to $Q_1 - C_1^{*'} = -D$, and external debt falls from $C_1^* - Q_1$ to $C_1^{*'} - Q_1 = D$.

In the absence of quantitative restrictions, the domestic interest rate, i, equals the world interest rate i^*. Upon the imposition of the binding borrowing limit D, the domestic interest rate increases above the world interest rate. To see this, note that at the world interest rate, domestic households would like to borrow more than D. But capital controls make international funds unavailable beyond this limit. Thus, the domestic interest rate must rise above the world interest rate to bring about equilibrium in the domestic financial market. Graphically, $1 + i$ is given by the negative of the slope of the indifference curve at point C in Figure 12.2, indicated by the negative of the slope of the broken line. Only at that interest rate are households willing to consume exactly $Q_1 + D$ in period 1.

Formally, the domestic interest rate under quantitative capital controls is given by optimality condition (12.2) evaluated at the equilibrium levels of consumption, $C_1^{*'} = Q_1 + D$ and $C_2^{*'} = Q_2 - (1 + i^*)D$. That is, the domestic interest rate satisfies

$$\frac{U'(Q_1 + D)}{U'(Q_2 - (1 + i^*)D)} = 1 + i.$$

Because Q_1, Q_2, D, and i^* are exogenously given, this expression represents one equation in one unknown, i. Further, because $U'(\cdot)$ is a decreasing function, if D decreases—that is, if the government tightens quantitative capital controls—the numerator of the left-hand side goes up and the denominator goes down. Consequently, the more stringent capital controls are, the higher the domestic interest rate will be. We therefore have that the interest rate differential $i - i^*$ is an increasing function of the severity of quantitative restrictions on capital inflows.

Comparing Figures 12.1 and 12.2, it is clear that quantity-based and tax-based capital controls give rise to the same equilibrium, in the sense that given a capital control tax τ one can find a quantitative restriction D, such that in equilibrium, consumption, the trade balance, the current account, the stock of external debt, and the interest rate differential are the same under both capital control policies.

This equivalence result depends on how the quantitative restrictions are implemented. Suppose, for example, that the government allocates the entire quota of external debt to one bank. All households must channel their own borrowing through this bank. The owner of the bank earns a rent equal to $(i - i^*)$ on each domestic loan. In this case the quantitative restriction has distributional effects against households and in favor of the owner of the bank, which causes the equivalence result to break down. This type of arrangement is common in countries run by kleptocrats, where policy is contaminated by corruption and rent seeking. Alternatively, the quantitative restrictions on capital inflows could be implemented by allocating a quota of D to each household. In this case, the rent $(i - i^*)D$ is distributed equally across all households. This rent is identical to the tax rebate $T = \tau D = (i - i^*)D$ in the tax-based capital control policy studied in Section 12.2. Under this modality the equivalence result obtains.

A market-based way to implement quantitative capital controls while preserving the equivalence with the tax-based form is to auction the quota D. The market price of this quota is $(i - i^*)D$, the pure rent it generates. In this case, even if all the quotas are sold to a single bank, the buyer makes zero profits. If the government distributes the proceeds of the auction to households in an egalitarian and lump-sum fashion, the resulting equilibrium is identical to the one in which each individual household is allotted a borrowing quota of D.

12.4   Borrowing Externalities and Optimal Capital Controls

The main message of Sections 12.2 and 12.3 is that capital controls can be an effective instrument to curb external imbalances but if the economy is small and has well-functioning markets, they are welfare decreasing. In this section, we study an economy identical to the one considered in those two sections, except for an imperfection in its financial market. Specifically, in the present economy, foreign lenders charge an interest rate that is increasing in the country's external debt.

The assumption that the interest rate that the country faces in international markets is debt elastic is empirically plausible, especially for emerging economies. Perhaps the most compelling explanation of why international creditors charge a higher interest rate to more indebted countries is that as the level of debt grows, the probability of default increases. So a higher rate of interest is required to make the expected return of investing in the emerging country similar to that of safer alternatives.

The debt-elastic interest rate creates an externality in the country's market for international funds. The reason is that individual households, being atomistic participants in financial markets, take the country's external debt as exogenously determined. In particular, they don't internalize the fact that their individual borrowing decisions collectively determine the level of the interest rate. As a result, in equilibrium the economy borrows more than is socially optimal. Under these circumstances, the government has an incentive to impose capital controls as a way to make households internalize the fact that their borrowing drives the interest rate up. We show that there is an optimal level of capital controls that reduces external borrowing and is welfare increasing. We now proceed to formally establish these results.

12.4.1   AN ECONOMY WITH A DEBT-ELASTIC INTEREST RATE

Consider a two-period open economy populated by households with preferences for consumption described by the utility function

$$U(C_1) + U(C_2).$$

The household starts period 1 with no debts or assets and receives endowments of goods in the amounts Q_1 and Q_2 in periods 1 and 2, respectively. In period 1, the household can borrow or lend at the domestic interest rate i via a bond, denoted B_1. The household's budget constraints in periods 1 and 2 are then given by

$$B_1 = Q_1 - C_1,$$

and

$$C_2 = Q_2 + (1+i)B_1.$$

Combining these two period budget constraints to eliminate B_1 yields the familiar intertemporal budget constraint

$$C_2 = Q_2 + (1+i)(Q_1 - C_1). \tag{12.6}$$

Using this expression to eliminate C_2 from the utility function, we obtain

$$U(C_1) + U(Q_2 + (1+i)(Q_1 - C_1)).$$

The household chooses C_1 to maximize this function. Taking derivative with respect to C_1 and equating it to zero, we obtain the optimality condition

$$U'(C_1) - U'(Q_2 + (1+i)(Q_1 - C_1))(1+i) = 0.$$

Using the fact that $Q_2 + (1+i)(Q_1 - C_1) = C_2$ and rearranging, we obtain the Euler equation

$$\frac{U'(C_1)}{U'(C_2)} = 1 + i. \tag{12.7}$$

Suppose that the country has free capital mobility. Let i^* be the interest rate charged by foreign lenders to the country in international capital markets. Then, free capital mobility implies that the onshore and offshore interest rates, i and i^*, must be equal to each other, or

$$i = i^*. \tag{12.8}$$

Suppose further that the interest rate at which the country can borrow in international markets, i^*, is an increasing function of the external debt per capita. From the period 1 budget constraint, we have that the debt of the individual household is given by $-B_1 = C_1 - Q_1$. Let $\bar{Q}_1$ and $\bar{C}_1$ denote cross-sectional averages of output and consumption in period 1. Then the per capita level of debt in period 1 is given by $\bar{C}_1 - \bar{Q}_1$. Thus, we are assuming that i^* is an increasing function of $\bar{C}_1 - \bar{Q}_1$. Given the endowment, the higher is consumption per capita, the higher the level of debt per capita will be. In turn, the higher is the per capita debt level, the higher the interest rate will be. So we can write the debt-elastic interest rate charged by foreign lenders to the country as

$$i^* = I(\bar{C}_1),$$

where $I(\cdot)$ is a weakly increasing function. To economize notation, we omit $\bar{Q}_1$ in the argument of this function. This is not a problem for the present analysis, because $\bar{Q}_1$ is an exogenous variable, which we will keep constant throughout. Using the fact that by free capital mobility the domestic interest rate, i, equals the interest rate the country faces in world capital markets, i^*, we can write this expression as

$$i = I(\bar{C}_1). \tag{12.9}$$

As an example of a debt-elastic interest rate, consider the function

$$I(\bar{C}_1) = \begin{cases} \underline{i} & \text{for } \bar{C}_1 \leq \bar{Q}_1 \\ \underline{i} + \delta(\bar{C}_1 - \bar{Q}_1) & \text{for } \bar{C}_1 > \bar{Q}_1 \end{cases}, \tag{12.10}$$

where $\underline{i}$ and δ are positive parameters. In this example, depicted in Figure 12.3, the country lends at the constant interest rate $\underline{i}$ but borrows at an interest rate that increases linearly with the level of debt, $\bar{C}_1 - \bar{Q}_1$.

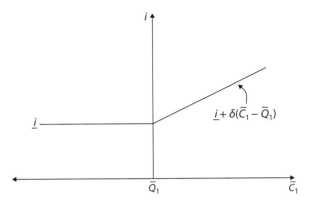

Figure 12.3. A Debt-Elastic Interest Rate

Notes: The figure displays an interest rate schedule that is weakly increasing in the level of external debt. For $\bar{C}_1 < \bar{Q}_1$, the country is a net external lender, and the interest rate is constant and equal to $\underline{i}$. For $\bar{C}_1 > \bar{Q}_1$, the country is a net external borrower, and the interest rate is an increasing function of the level of debt, $\bar{C}_1 - \bar{Q}_1$.

12.4.2   COMPETITIVE EQUILIBRIUM WITHOUT GOVERNMENT INTERVENTION

Because all households are identical in preferences and endowments, in equilibrium they all consume the same amount of goods. This means that consumption per capita equals the individual level of consumption, $\bar{C}_1 = C_1$. So we can write the interest rate as

$$i = I(C_1).$$

It is important to understand why in deriving the household's optimality condition (12.7) we do not take into account that the interest rate depends on consumption. The reason is that the interest rate depends on aggregate per capita consumption, not on the household's individual level of consumption, and the household takes aggregate per capital consumption as given. Only in equilibrium is aggregate consumption per capita equal to individual consumption.

Use equation (12.9) to eliminate the interest rate i from the intertemporal budget constraint (12.6) and the optimality condition (12.7) to obtain

$$C_2 = Q_2 + (1 + I(C_1))(Q_1 - C_1) \tag{12.11}$$

and

$$\frac{U'(C_1)}{U'(C_2)} = 1 + I(C_1). \tag{12.12}$$

These are two equations determining the equilibrium levels of consumption in periods 1 and 2.

Figure 12.4 depicts the equilibrium in the space (C_1, C_2). Equation (12.11), shown as the locus AA, is the economy's intertemporal resource constraint. Like

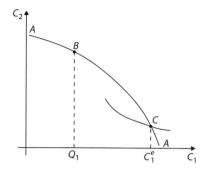

Figure 12.4. Equilibrium in an Economy with Borrowing Externalities
Notes: The locus AA represents the economy's resource constraint. The endowment is at point B. The competitive equilibrium without government intervention is at point C. This equilibrium is inefficient because there are other allocations on the resource constraint that yield higher utility than point C.

in the case of a constant interest rate, the resource constraint is downward sloping. Increasing consumption in period 1 requires sacrificing some consumption in period 2. The key difference with the case of a constant interest rate is the slope. When the interest rate is constant, the slope of the resource constraint is constant and equal to minus $1 + i$. By contrast, in this economy the slope of the resource constraint is always larger than $1 + i$ in absolute value. More precisely, taking the derivative of C_2 with respect to C_1 in equation (12.11), we see that the slope of the intertemporal resource constraint is given by minus $1 + i + I'(C_1)(C_1 - Q_1)$, which is always greater than $1 + i$ if the country is a borrower; that is, if $C_1 > Q_1$, because $I'(C_1)$ is positive. Intuitively, the reason why the slope of the intertemporal resource constraint is greater than $1 + i$ in absolute value is that if the country borrows an additional unit for consumption in period 1, in period 2 it must pay not only $1 + i$ but also the increase in the interest rate, $I'(C_1)$, caused by the increase in debt. This increase in the interest rate applies not only to the extra unit borrowed, but also to the entire debt, $C_1 - Q_1$.

The endowment is at point B, and the equilibrium is at point C where consumption in period 1 is C_1^e. Because $C_1^e > Q_1$, the country is a borrower. At point C, the indifference curve has a slope equal to minus $1 + i$, as dictated by the Euler equation (12.12). This means that at point C the indifference curve is flatter than the resource constraint, $1 + i < 1 + i + I'(C_1)(C_1 - Q_1)$. The discrepancy between the slope of the intertemporal resource constraint and that of the indifference curve renders the competitive equilibrium inefficient. It is clear from Figure 12.4 that there are points on the intertemporal resource constraint that deliver higher levels of utility than point C. The inefficiency originates in the fact that private households fail to internalize the full marginal cost of current consumption. Because the interest rate does not depend on individual consumption, but on aggregate per capita consumption, households perceive an opportunity cost of current consumption equal to $1 + i$, which is lower than the social cost of $1 + i + I'(C_1)(C_1 - Q_1)$. This induces households to consume more than is socially optimal.

12.4.3 THE EFFICIENT ALLOCATION

Imagine a benevolent *social planner* that can allocate consumption in periods 1 and 2 to maximize households' utility subject to the economy's resource constraint (12.11). The planner gives all households the same path of consumption. The planner's optimization problem then is to maximize

$$U(C_1) + U(C_2),$$

subject to

$$C_2 = Q_2 + (1 + I(C_1))(Q_1 - C_1).$$

As before, use the resource constraint to get rid of C_2 in the utility function to restate the planner's problem as one of choosing C_1 to maximize

$$U(C_1) + U(Q_2 + (1 + I(C_1))(Q_1 - C_1)).$$

There are two key differences between this optimization problem and that of an individual household in a market economy. First, the planner understands that C_1 is both individual and aggregate per capita consumption. Second, the household takes the interest rate as given, whereas the social planner internalizes the fact that changes in C_1 move the interest rate $I(C_1)$. The first-order condition associated with the social planner's optimization problem is

$$U'(C_1) - U'(Q_2 + (1 + I(C_1))(Q_1 - C_1))[1 + I(C_1) + I'(C_1)(C_1 - Q_1)] = 0.$$

Using the fact that $C_2 = Q_2 + (1 + I(C_1))(Q_1 - C_1)$ and rearranging we can write the planner's optimality condition as

$$\frac{U'(C_1)}{U'(C_2)} = 1 + I(C_1) + I'(C_1)(C_1 - Q_1). \qquad (12.13)$$

This expression says that at the efficient allocation the slope of the indifference curve equals the slope of the economy's intertemporal resource constraint. It is of interest to compare this optimality condition to its counterpart in the competitive equilibrium, given by equation (12.12). In the competitive equilibrium, the marginal rate of substitution of current for future consumption, $U'(C_1)/U'(C_2)$, is equated to the private cost of funds, $1 + I(C_1)$, whereas in the efficient allocation it is equated to the social cost of funds, $1 + I(C_1) + I'(C_1)(C_1 - Q_1)$, which is higher than the private cost.

The efficient allocation is given by the values of C_1 and C_2 that solve the economy's resource constraint (12.11) and the social planner's optimality condition (12.13). Figure 12.5 provides a graphical representation of the solution to the social planner's optimality conditions. The efficient allocation is at point D. At this point, consumption satisfies the resource constraint and in addition, the resource constraint is tangent to an indifference curve. Clearly, at point D households attain the highest possible level of welfare given the economy's resources. For comparison, the figure also displays the endowment, given by point B, and the competitive equilibrium, given by point C. The efficient level of consumption in period 1

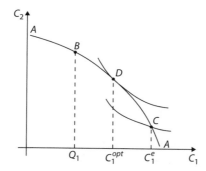

Figure 12.5. The Efficient Allocation in an Economy with Borrowing Externalities
Notes: The locus AA represents the economy's resource constraint. The endowment is at point B. The competitive equilibrium without government intervention is at point C. The efficient allocation is at point D, where an indifference curve is tangent to the resource constraint. This allocation can be supported by an appropriately chosen capital control tax.

is C_1^{opt}, which is higher than the endowment, Q_1, but lower than the level of consumption attained in the competitive equilibrium, C_1^e. Accordingly, in the efficient allocation (point D), the external debt is lower than in the competitive equilibrium (point C), $C_1^{opt} - Q_1 < C_1^e - Q_1$. The excess external borrowing in the competitive equilibrium is known as *overborrowing*.

12.4.4   OPTIMAL CAPITAL CONTROL POLICY

Can the efficient allocation be achieved in a market economy as opposed to a centrally planned economy like the one we just studied? The answer is yes. The government can eliminate overborrowing and achieve the efficient allocation by imposing a capital control tax like the one analyzed in Section 12.2. Specifically, suppose that the government imposes a tax on external borrowing at the rate τ. By the arguments given in Section 12.2, the capital control tax introduces a wedge between the domestic interest rate, i, and the interest rate at which the country can borrow in international financial markets, i^*. Specifically, the interest parity condition (12.8) changes to

$$i = i^* + \tau.$$

Suppose that the government sets $\tau = I'(\bar{C}_1)(\bar{C}_1 - \bar{Q}_1)$. Because the tax rate depends on aggregate per capita variables, the household takes the tax as exogenously given, exactly as in the case studied in Section 12.2. We then have that

$$i = i^* + I'(\bar{C}_1)(\bar{C}_1 - \bar{Q}_1).$$

Since $i^* = I(\bar{C}_1)$ and since in equilibrium $\bar{C}_1 = C_1$ and $\bar{Q}_1 = Q_1$, this expression becomes

$$i = I(C_1) + I'(C_1)(C_1 - Q_1).$$

Using this expression, the household's optimality condition (12.7) can be written as

$$\frac{U'(C_1)}{U'(C_2)} = 1 + I(C_1) + I'(C_1)(C_1 - Q_1),$$

which is identical to the optimality condition of the social planner, given by (12.13). Further, if, as assumed in Section 12.2, the government rebates the revenue generated by the capital control tax to the households in a lump-sum fashion, the economy's resource constraint (12.11) is unchanged. So the equilibrium values of C_1 and C_2 are determined by the solution to equations (12.11) and (12.13), which are the two equations determining the efficient allocation.

This establishes that the capital control policy $\tau = I'(\bar{C}_1)(\bar{C}_1 - \bar{Q}_1)$ supports the efficient allocation as a competitive equilibrium outcome. In other words, the proposed capital control tax places the economy at point D in Figure 12.5. Intuitively, the capital control tax increases the effective cost of borrowing perceived by households, which induces them to cut consumption in period 1. Thus, the role of the capital control tax is to make households internalize that the social cost of an extra unit of consumption is not just $1 + I(C_1)$, but $1 + I(C_1) + I'(C_1)(C_1 - Q_1)$.

Summarizing, in the presence of a borrowing externality free capital mobility ceases to be optimal. Households consume more and borrow more in period 1 than is socially optimal. Capital controls become desirable as a way to eliminate overborrowing and bring about the socially optimal allocation.

12.5 Capital Mobility in a Large Economy

When a large economy like the United States, the eurozone, or China increases its demand for international funds, the world interest rate will in general experience upward pressure. Each individual household in the large economy takes the interest rate as given, but for the country as a whole, the interest rate is an endogenous variable. This means that the government of a large economy might be able to apply policies to manipulate world interest rates in the country's favor. For example, if the country is running a current account deficit, the government could impose capital controls to curb the country's aggregate external borrowing and induce a fall in the world interest rate.

Before analyzing the ability of capital controls to manipulate the current account and the world interest rate, we will characterize the equilibrium in a large economy under free capital mobility. This analysis will serve as a useful benchmark to evaluate national policies aimed at managing international capital flows, which we will take up in Section 12.7.

The model of a large economy we present here builds on the two-country model introduced in Section 7.3 of Chapter 7. Consider a two-period economy composed of two countries—the home country, denoted h, and the foreign country, denoted f. The home country receives a constant endowment in both periods. By contrast, the foreign country receives a lower endowment in period 1 than in period 2. The two economies are identical in all other respects. In particular, both have the same preferences for consumption and start period 1 with no assets or debts. If both countries had identical endowment streams, they would be content consuming their respective endowments each period and would not benefit from engaging in intertemporal trade with each other. However, because in the foreign country the endowment in period 1 is lower than in period 2, all households in the foreign country would like to borrow in period 1 against their period 2 endowment. The collective demand for funds from the foreign country will drive the world interest rate up and result in an equilibrium in which the foreign country borrows from the home country in period 1.

Assume that preferences in both countries take the form

$$\ln C_1^j + \ln C_2^j, \tag{12.14}$$

where C_1^j and C_2^j denote consumption in periods 1 and 2, respectively, in country $j = h, f$.

The budget constraint of households in country j in period 1 is given by

$$C_1^j + B_1^j = Q_1^j, \tag{12.15}$$

where B_1^j denotes bonds purchased in period 1. Because the world ends in period 2, households cannot borrow or lend in that period, so the budget constraint in period 2 takes the form

$$C_2^j = Q_2^j + (1 + i^j)B_1^j, \tag{12.16}$$

where i^j denotes the interest rate in country j, for $j = h, f$.

Solving the budget constraint in period 1 for B_1^j to eliminate B_1^j from the period 2 budget constraint, one obtains the following intertemporal budget constraint

$$C_2^j = Q_2^j + (1 + i^j)(Q_1^j - C_1^j). \tag{12.17}$$

Using this expression to eliminate C_2^j from the utility function (12.14) yields

$$\ln C_1^j + \ln[Q_2^j + (1 + i^j)(Q_1^j - C_1^j)].$$

The objective of the household in country j is to choose C_1^j to maximize this expression, taking as given the interest rate and the endowments. Taking the derivative with respect to C_1^j and equating the resulting expression to zero, we obtain the household's optimality condition

$$\frac{1}{C_1^j} = \frac{1 + i^j}{Q_2^j + (1 + i^j)(Q_1^j - C_1^j)}.$$

Realizing that the denominator of the right-hand side is C_2^j, we can rewrite the optimality condition as the consumption Euler equation,

$$\frac{C_2^j}{C_1^j} = 1 + i^j. \tag{12.18}$$

Now solve this optimality condition for C_2^j to eliminate C_2^j from the intertemporal budget constraint (12.17). This yields the optimal level of consumption in period 1,

$$C_1^j = \frac{1}{2}\left(Q_1^j + \frac{Q_2^j}{1+i^j}\right). \tag{12.19}$$

Let us now consider the home country; that is, set $j=h$. Assume that the endowment in the home country is equal to Q in both periods. Then, by equation (12.19), consumption in period 1 in the home country satisfies

$$C_1^h = \frac{1}{2}\left(Q + \frac{Q}{1+i^h}\right). \tag{12.20}$$

This expression says that consumption is a decreasing function of the interest rate.

The trade balance, denoted TB_1^h, is the difference between the endowment and current consumption,

$$TB_1^h = \frac{Q}{2}\frac{i^h}{1+i^h}.$$

And, because the initial net asset position is assumed to be nil ($B_0^h = 0$), in period 1 the current account in the home country, denoted CA_1^h, equals the trade balance,

$$CA_1^h = \frac{Q}{2}\frac{i^h}{1+i^h}.$$

Intuitively, as the interest rate increases, households save an increasing part of their endowments, generating surpluses in the trade balance and the current account. Recalling that the current account equals the change in the country's net foreign asset position, $CA_1^h = B_1^h - B_0^h$, and that by assumption the initial asset position is nil, $B_0^h = 0$, we have that the country's net foreign asset position at the end of period 1 equals the current account. So we can write

$$B_1^h = \frac{Q}{2}\frac{i^h}{1+i^h}. \tag{12.21}$$

This expression says that the demand for bonds is an increasing function of their rate of return.

In the foreign country the endowment is $Q/2$ in period 1 and Q in period 2. Thus, from equation (12.19) we have that foreign consumption in period 1 is given by

$$C_1^f = Q\frac{3+i^f}{4(1+i^f)}. \tag{12.22}$$

It is straightforward to see from this expression that in period 1 consumption exceeds the endowment, $C_1^f > Q/2$, for any interest rate below 100 percent (i.e., for any $i^f < 1$). It makes sense that foreign households choose to borrow for a wide range of interest rates because their endowment in period 2 is twice as large as in period 1 (Q versus $Q/2$). So households borrow against their future endowment in order to smooth consumption over time.

Because the foreign country starts period 1 with no assets or debts, the period 1 trade balance and current account are both given by the difference between the endowment and consumption in period 1. Using the above expression for period 1 consumption we can write,

$$TB_1^f = \frac{Q}{4} \frac{i^f - 1}{(1 + i^f)},$$

and

$$CA_1^f = \frac{Q}{4} \frac{i^f - 1}{(1 + i^f)}.$$

This expression says that as long as the interest rate in the foreign country is below 100 percent ($i^f < 1$), the current account in period 1 will be negative. This is in line with the fact that households, facing an increasing path of endowments, borrow in period 1 to smooth consumption. Because the foreign country starts period 1 with no assets or debts, its net foreign asset position at the end of period 1, B_1^f, is equal to the current account. So we can write

$$B_1^f = \frac{Q}{4} \frac{i^f - 1}{(1 + i^f)}. \tag{12.23}$$

In equilibrium the world asset demand, given by the sum of the bond demands of the home and foreign countries, must be zero; that is,

$$B_1^h + B_1^f = 0. \tag{12.24}$$

Under free capital mobility, the interest rate must be the same in both countries. Let this common interest rate be denoted i^*. We refer to i^* as the world interest rate. So we have

$$i^h = i^f = i^*. \tag{12.25}$$

Use this expression to replace i^h and i^f by i^* in equations (12.21) and (12.23), respectively. Then, use the resulting expressions to eliminate B_1^h and B_1^f from (12.24) to obtain

$$\frac{Q}{2} \frac{i^*}{1 + i^*} + \frac{Q}{2} \frac{i^* - 1}{2(1 + i^*)} = 0.$$

Solving for i^*, we obtain the equilibrium level of the world interest rate

$$i^* = \frac{1}{3},$$

so under free capital mobility the world interest rate is 33 percent. Because the world interest rate is less than 100 percent, we know from the bond demand of the foreign household (equation (12.23)) that the foreign country borrows internationally in period 1. In turn, if the foreign country borrows the domestic country must save in period 1.

Setting $i^h = 1/3$ in equations (12.20) and (12.21), we obtain the equilibrium levels of period 1 consumption and bond holdings in the home economy,

$$C_1^h = \frac{7}{8}Q < Q$$

and

$$B_1^h = \frac{1}{8}Q > 0.$$

In spite of having a flat path of endowments, which, if consumed, would produce a perfectly smooth path of consumption, households in the home country choose to consume less than their endowment in period 1 and to save. This is because foreign demand for funds (discussed next) drives the world interest rate up, inducing the home country to postpone consumption. As a result, in period 2 the home country can enjoy a level of consumption higher than its endowment. This can be verified by setting $j = h$ and $i^j = 1/3$ in optimality condition (12.17), which yields

$$C_2^h = \frac{7}{6}Q > Q > C_1^h.$$

Proceeding in an analogous fashion, we obtain the following equilibrium values for the foreign country's levels of consumption and bond holdings:

$$C_1^f = \frac{5}{8}Q > \frac{1}{2}Q,$$

$$C_2^f = \frac{5}{6}Q < Q,$$

and

$$B_1^f = -\frac{1}{8}Q < 0.$$

Intuitively, facing an upward sloping path of endowments, the foreign country borrows in period 1 to smooth consumption. So it consumes above its endowment in period 1, below its endowment in period 2, and maintains a short bond position in period 1.

Welfare under free capital mobility can be found by evaluating the utility function (12.14) at the respective equilibrium consumption levels. This yields

$$\ln C_1^h + \ln C_2^h = \ln \left(\frac{49}{48}Q^2 \right) \tag{12.26}$$

for the home country, and

$$\ln C_1^f + \ln C_2^f = \ln \left(\frac{25}{48}Q^2 \right)$$

for the foreign country.

Exercise 12.10 asks you to show that both countries are better off under free capital mobility than under financial autarky, which is an environment in which both economies are closed to international trade in financial assets. An implication of this result is that it does not pay for either country to impose capital controls so high that all intertemporal trade is killed. The main question we will address shortly is whether there is a capital control policy on the part of one country that induces an equilibrium in which the level of welfare of the households it represents is higher than under free capital mobility.

12.6 Graphical Analysis of Equilibrium under Free Capital Mobility in a Large Economy

To visualize how the equilibrium under free capital mobility is determined in a two-country world as well as its implications for consumption, international borrowing, and welfare, we begin by presenting two powerful graphical objects in general equilibrium analysis, the *offer curve* and the *Edgeworth box*, both created by the Irish economist Francis Ysidro Edgeworth (1845–1926).

Consider the optimal choice of consumption in periods 1 and 2 by country $j=h,f$, C_1^j and C_2^j, for different levels of the interest rate. Figure 12.6 displays these optimal choices for three different interest rates, i^0, i^1, and i^2, satisfying $i^0 > i^1 > i^2$. The household's endowment, (Q_1^j, Q_2^j), is given by point A^0. Each of the three interest rates considered defines a different intertemporal budget constraint, $C_2^j = Q_2^j + (1+i)(Q_1^j - C_1^j)$. Each budget constraint is a downward-sloping line that crosses the endowment point A^0 and has slope $-(1+i)$. The higher the interest rate is, the steeper the budget constraint will be. In the figure, the budget constraint $\overline{I^0 I^0}$ corresponds to the interest rate i^0 at which it is optimal for the household to consume its endowment. This can be seen from the fact that the indifference curve that crosses point A^0 is tangent to the budget constraint $\overline{I^0 I^0}$ at point A^0. As the interest rate falls, the intertemporal budget constraint pivots counterclockwise around point A^0. The budget constraint $\overline{I^1 I^1}$ corresponds to the interest rate i^1. The optimal consumption choice at the interest rate i^1 is given by point A^1. At this point, the household consumes more than its endowment in period 1 and less than its endowment in period 2. The household achieves this consumption allocation by borrowing in period 1. Finally, the budget constraint $\overline{I^2 I^2}$ corresponds to the interest rate i^2. The optimal consumption choice induced by this interest rate is given by point A^2 that contains more consumption in period 1, less consumption in period 2, and more borrowing in period 1 than point A^1.[2]

---

[2] At a sufficiently low level of the interest rate, it could happen that a fall in the interest rate causes an increase in consumption in both periods. This is because when the household is indebted, a fall in the interest rate has a positive income effect, which calls for increasing consumption in both periods. If the household is highly indebted, this effect might more than offset the substitution effect, which calls for increasing consumption in period 1 and cutting consumption in period 2. Under the log-linear utility function given in (12.14), however, the substitution effect always dominates the income effect. See also the discussion of income and substitution effects associated with changes in interest rates in Section 4.4 of Chapter 4, Exercise 4.4 in Chapter 4, and Exercise 12.13 at the end of the present chapter.

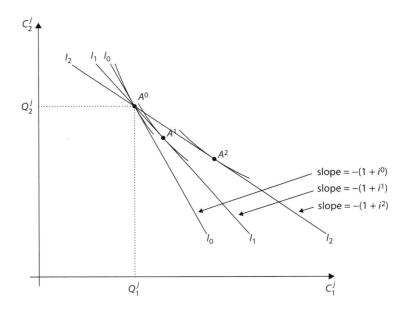

Figure 12.6. Optimal Intertemporal Consumption Choice at Different Interest Rates
Notes: The figure displays the optimal consumption choice for three different values of the interest rate, i^0, i^1, and i^2, satisfying $i^0 > i^1 > i^2$. Each interest rate is associated with a different intertemporal budget constraint. The higher the interest rate is, the steeper the intertemporal budget constraint will be. The intertemporal budget constraint $\overline{I^0 I^0}$ is induced by the highest of the three interest rates, and the intertemporal budget constraint $\overline{I^2 I^2}$ by the lowest. The associated optimal consumption path induced by the interest rate associated with budget constraint $\overline{I^0 I^0}$ is the endowment point, A^0. The intertemporal budget constraints $\overline{I^1 I^1}$ and $\overline{I^2 I^2}$ produce optimal consumption choices given by points A^1 and A^2, respectively. The offer curve (not shown) connects points A^0, A^1, A^2.

Now imagine doing the same not just for three interest rates, but for all possible levels of the interest rate. The offer curve is the locus that connects all the associated optimal consumption choices. Figure 12.7 displays the offer curve of country j as the locus JJ. By construction, points A^0, A^1, and A^2 are on the offer curve. Each point on the offer curve is associated with a different value of the interest rate, i. The interest rate associated with any given point on the offer curve can be found as follows: draw the line that connects the point on the offer curve with the endowment point, A^0. This line is the intertemporal budget constraint of the household at the interest rate i and therefore its slope equals $-(1 + i)$. At the point it intersects the offer curve, this intertemporal budget constraint is tangent to an indifference curve.

In addition to the offer curve, Figure 12.7 displays the indifference curve that crosses the endowment point, A^0. All points on the offer curve other than the endowment point are strictly preferred to the endowment point itself. This is because at any interest rate, consuming the endowment is feasible.

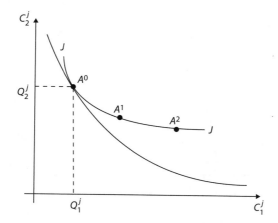

Figure 12.7. The Offer Curve
Notes: The offer curve is the locus *JJ*, which connects all optimal consumption allocations at different interest rates. The offer curve crosses the endowment point A^0. The figure also shows the indifference curve that crosses the endowment point. All points on the offer curve other than the endowment point are preferred to the endowment point itself.

We are now ready to analyze the equilibrium under free capital mobility. Figure 12.8 displays a box known as the Edgeworth box. The length of the horizontal side of the box is the global endowment of goods in period 1, $Q_1^h + Q_1^f$. The height of the box is the global endowment in period 2, $Q_2^h + Q_2^f$. The southwest corner of the box is the origin of the foreign country and is indicated by the symbol O^f. For the foreign country, consumption and the endowment in period 1 are measured on the horizontal axis from the origin O^f to the right, and consumption and the endowment in period 2 are measured on the vertical axis from O^f upward. The northeast corner of the box is the origin of the home country and is indicated by the symbol O^h. For this country, consumption and the endowment in period 1 are measured on the horizontal axis from O^h to the left, and consumption and the endowment in period 2 are measured on the vertical axis from O^h downward. So households in the foreign country become happier as one moves northeast in the box and households in the home country become happier as one moves southwest in the box. In the figure, the endowments of the two countries are given by point A^0. In this example, the home country is abundant in period 1 goods, and the foreign country is abundant in period 2 goods. Any point in the box represents an allocation of consumption across time and countries that can be achieved with the existing global endowments.

The offer curve of the foreign country is the locus *FF* and the offer curve of the home country is the locus *HH*. Clearly, both offer curves must cross the endowment point A^0. The equilibrium under free capital mobility is given by point B, where the two offer curves intersect for a second time. In equilibrium, the foreign country, which has a relatively low endowment in period 1, borrows from the home

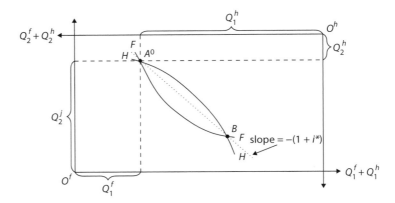

Figure 12.8. Equilibrium under Free Capital Mobility in a Two-Country Model
Notes: This type of graph is known as an Edgeworth box. The origin of the foreign country is O^f and the origin of the home country is O^h. The endowment point is A^0. The offer curve of the foreign country is the locus FF, and the offer curve of the home country is the locus HH. The equilibrium under free capital mobility is point B. The slope of the line that connects points A^0 and point B is $-(1 + i^*)$, where i^* is the equilibrium world interest rate under free capital mobility.

country. The equilibrium world interest rate, i^*, is determined by the slope of the line that connects points A^0 and B. This line is the intertemporal budget constraint faced by the domestic and foreign households at the equilibrium world interest rate i^*. This interest rate is lower than the domestic interest rate in the foreign country under financial autarky, which is determined by the slope of the foreign household's indifference curve at the endowment point A^0. By the same logic, we have that the equilibrium interest rate under free capital mobility, i^*, is higher than the domestic interest rate in the home country under financial autarky. We have therefore established that allowing for free capital mobility eliminates interest rate differentials by causing a fall in the interest rate in the borrowing country and an increase in the interest rate in the lending country.

Because in equilibrium both countries are on their respective offer curves, they are both better off than under autarky. This means that in this economy, free capital mobility is welfare improving for both countries. Further, at point B the indifference curves of the home and foreign households both have a slope equal to $-(1 + i^*)$. Thus, at point B the indifference curves of the home and foreign households are tangent to each other. This implies that at no point inside the Edgeworth box can both countries be better off than at point B. In other words, any other attainable consumption allocation makes at least one country worse off relative to the allocation associated with the equilibrium under free capital mobility. When an equilibrium has this property, we say that it is *Pareto optimal*.[3]

---

[3] This name is given after the Italian economist Vilfredo Federico Pareto (1848–1923), who first discussed this notion of efficiency.

12.7 Optimal Capital Controls in a Large Economy

Suppose that the government of the foreign country behaves strategically and manipulates capital flows by imposing capital controls to obtain a value of the world interest rate, i^*, that maximizes the welfare of its citizens. It can do so because the country is large and therefore has monopsony power in international funds markets. Unlike the country as a whole, individual households do not have market power in financial markets as they are atomistically small. Thus, exploiting the country's market power can only be achieved via government intervention.

Capital controls have two opposing macroeconomic effects. First, as we studied in Section 12.1, they create a wedge between the domestic and the foreign interest rate, which is welfare decreasing because it distorts the intertemporal allocation of consumption and investment. Second, because the country is borrowing, the fall in the world interest rate caused by the imposition of capital controls is welfare increasing, for it reduces the cost of servicing the external debt. In a small open economy, the second effect is nil, because the country cannot affect the world interest rate; so, as we saw in Section 12.2, the resolution of the policy trade-off calls for no capital controls. In a large economy, however, the government will in general find it optimal to impose capital controls to push the world interest rate down. The main purpose of this section is to establish this result and to study how optimal capital controls affect the current account and welfare in both countries.

Assume that in response to capital controls imposed by the foreign country, the home country does not retaliate by imposing its own capital controls. In Section 12.9 we will analyze the case of retaliation. This means that the demand for international funds by the home country continues to be given by (12.21) evaluated at the world interest rate i^*,

$$B_1^h = \frac{Q}{2} \frac{i^*}{1+i^*}. \tag{12.27}$$

The foreign country imposes a tax τ on international borrowing. The budget constraint of the foreign household in period 1 is unchanged by this tax,

$$C_1^f + B_1^f = \frac{Q}{2}. \tag{12.28}$$

The budget constraint in period 2 is now given by

$$C_2^f = Q + T + (1 + i^f)B_1^f,$$

where T denotes a lump-sum transfer received from the government.

By the analysis of Section 12.1, the capital control tax creates a wedge between the world interest rate and the interest rate in the foreign country,

$$i^f = i^* + \tau. \tag{12.29}$$

Tax revenue is given by $-\tau B_1^f$. The government rebates these resources to households via lump-sum transfers,

$$T = -\tau B_1^f.$$

Thus, combining the above three expressions, the budget constraint in period 2 becomes

$$C_2^f = Q + (1 + i^*)B_1^f. \tag{12.30}$$

The government internalizes that in equilibrium the international bond market must clear; that is, that $B_1^f = -B_1^h$, as indicated by the market-clearing condition (12.24). The government also internalizes that the supply of funds by the home country, B_1^h, is an increasing function of the world interest rate, i^*, as shown in equation (12.27). So using (12.24) and (12.27) to express C_1^f and C_2^f in equations (12.28) and (12.30) as functions of the world interest rate, we have that

$$C_1^f = \frac{Q}{2}\frac{1 + 2i^*}{1 + i^*} \tag{12.31}$$

and

$$C_2^f = \frac{Q}{2}(2 - i^*). \tag{12.32}$$

Now use these two expressions to eliminate C_1^f and C_2^f from the utility function of the foreign household to obtain

$$\ln\left(\frac{Q}{2}\frac{1 + 2i^*}{1 + i^*}\right) + \ln\left(\frac{Q}{2}(2 - i^*)\right).$$

This object is known as (the foreign household's) *indirect utility function*. It is the lifetime utility function of the foreign household expressed in terms of the world interest rate, i^*, instead of consumption, C_1^f and C_2^f. The objective of the foreign government is to pick the world interest rate i^* to maximize the indirect utility function of the foreign household. The optimality condition associated with this maximization problem results from taking the derivative of the indirect utility function with respect to i^* and setting it to zero. Performing this operation and rearranging yields

$$i^{*2} + 2i^* - \frac{1}{2} = 0.$$

Solving this quadratic expression for i^*, we obtain two candidate values,

$$-1 \pm \sqrt{\frac{3}{2}}.$$

We can discard the root that implies a value for the interest rate below -1, because an interest rate cannot be below -100 percent. So the only economically sensible solution is

$$i^* = -1 + \sqrt{\frac{3}{2}} = 0.22,$$

or 22 percent. This confirms the conjecture that under optimal capital controls by the foreign government the world interest rate is lower than under free capital mobility (22 versus 33 percent). Intuitively, the foreign government picks a lower interest rate to induce a positive income effect on its residents who are net borrowers in the international market. Plugging the interest rate of 0.22 into the indirect utility function of the foreign household yields a welfare of $\ln(\frac{25.2122}{48}Q^2)$ under optimal capital controls, which, compared with a welfare of $\ln(\frac{25}{48}Q^2)$ under free capital mobility, confirms that the policy is welfare increasing for foreign residents.

The foreign government induces the required fall in the world interest rate by imposing controls on capital inflows. To obtain the optimal capital control tax, τ, plug the optimal world interest rate of 0.22 into equations (12.31) and (12.32) and use the result to eliminate C_1^f and C_2^f from the household's optimality condition (12.18) to obtain

$$i^f = 0.5.$$

Then equation (12.29) gives the optimal capital control tax as the difference between the domestic interest rate in the foreign country and the world interest rate, which yields,

$$\tau = 0.28,$$

or a tax rate on capital inflows of 28 percent. By taxing international borrowing, the government causes an increase in the domestic interest rate in the foreign country, i^f. A domestic interest rate in excess of the world interest rate causes an inefficient allocation of consumption over time, as households feel the cost of borrowing went up, when in reality it went down. In addition, the increase in the domestic interest rate in the foreign country, i^f, causes a negative income effect on households, as they are net debtors. How do these negative effects square with the result that capital controls are welfare increasing in the foreign country? The reason why households are better off is that the government rebates all of the capital control tax revenue to the households. As it turns out, the positive income effect resulting from this transfer more than offsets the aforementioned negative effects. The reason why, overall, households in the foreign country are better off under capital controls is that the country as a whole experiences a positive income effect: The fall in the world interest rate, i^*, implies that the foreign country as a whole transfers less resources to the home country in the form of interest payments on the external debt.

The imposition of optimal capital controls by the foreign country causes an improvement of the current account in the foreign country and a deterioration of the current account in the home country. To see this, recall that the change in the current account is equal to the change in bond holdings (i.e., the change in B_1^h). In turn, bond holdings of the home country are increasing in the world interest rate (see equation (12.27)). Thus, when the capital controls in the foreign country push the world interest rate down from 33 to 22 percent, bond holdings and the current account in the home country decline. By the same token, the current account in the foreign country must improve, since market clearing requires that the sum of the current accounts of the two countries be zero, $CA_1^h + CA_1^f = 0$. It follows that by imposing controls on capital inflows, the foreign government manages to improve its own current account to the detriment of the home country's.

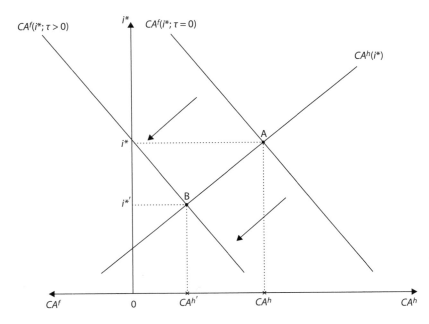

Figure 12.9. Effect of Capital Controls on the Current Account
Notes: The equilibrium without capital controls is at point A. The imposition of capital controls in the foreign country shifts the current account schedule of the foreign country, $CA^f(i^*, \tau)$ down and to the left and leaves the current account schedule of the home country, $CA^h(i^*)$, unchanged. The equilibrium with capital controls is at point B, where the world interest rate, i^*, is lower, the current account of the foreign country improves, and the current account of the home country deteriorates.

The situation is illustrated in Figure 12.9 in the space (CA, i^*). On the horizontal axis, the current account of the home country is measured from left to right, and the current account of the foreign country from right to left. Thus, the current account schedule of the home country is upward sloping and that of the foreign country is downward sloping. The equilibrium in the absence of capital controls ($\tau = 0$), is at point A. In this equilibrium the home country runs a current account surplus and the foreign country a current account deficit.

When the foreign country imposes capital controls ($\tau > 0$), the current account schedule of the home country remains unchanged. The current account schedule of the foreign country shifts down and to the left, reflecting the fact that at each level of the world interest rate, i^*, the domestic interest rate in the foreign country increases by τ, causing a contraction in the aggregate demand for goods and an increase in the trade balance and the current account. At the original level of the world interest rate, the imposition of the capital control tax generates an excess supply of funds in the world. Restoring equilibrium in the international financial market requires a fall in the world interest rate as indicated by point B in the figure. A lower level of the world interest rate induces an expansion in the demand for goods in the home country, which causes its trade balance and current account to deteriorate. In the foreign country, the capital control tax leads to an increase in the domestic interest rate, i^f, despite the fact that the world interest rate falls. The higher domestic interest rate, in turn, causes a contraction in the aggregate absorption of goods and an improvement in the trade balance and the current account.[4]

Going back to the algebraic example, the imposition of optimal capital controls in the foreign country is welfare decreasing for the home country. To see this, first use the world's resource constraint to write consumption in the home country as $C_1^h = Q_1^h + Q_1^f - C_1^f$ and $C_2^h = Q_2^h + Q_2^f - C_2^f$. Then eliminate C_1^f and C_2^f by using equilibrium conditions (12.31) and (12.32) evaluated at $i^* = 0.22$ to get $C_1^h = 0.9082Q$ and $C_2^h = 1.1124Q$. Finally, plug these consumption values into the utility function of the home country to obtain $\ln C_1^h + \ln C_2^h = \ln(1.0103Q^2)$. Recalling that under free capital mobility the utility level of the home household is $\ln(1.0208Q^2)$, we conclude that the home country is hurt by the optimal capital controls in the foreign country.

Finally, the equilibrium under optimal capital controls in the foreign country is *Pareto inefficient*; that is, the equilibrium allocation of consumption across time and countries could be rearranged in such a way that the foreign country maintains the welfare level associated with the optimal capital control, but the home country is made better off relative to its situation under optimal capital controls. To establish this result, we resort to the graphical apparatus developed earlier in Section 12.6.

12.8 Graphical Analysis of Optimal Capital Controls in a Large Economy

Figure 12.10 reproduces from Figure 12.8 the offer curves of the home country and the foreign country, given by the loci *HH* and *FF*, respectively. The endowment point is marked A^0, and the equilibrium under free capital mobility is at point B. The world interest rate under free capital mobility, denoted i^*, is defined by the slope of the line connecting points A^0 and B. In setting capital controls, the objective of the foreign country is to attain a point on the home country's offer curve, *HH*, that maximizes the foreign country's utility. The foreign country is constrained to pick a point on the home country's offer curve because, by construction, only the allocations on the offer curve can be obtained as a market outcome; that is, by an appropriate choice of the world interest rate. Consequently, the allocation associated with the optimal capital control policy is one at which an indifference curve of the foreign country is tangent to the offer curve of the home country. This allocation is point C in the figure.

The world interest rate under optimal capital controls, denoted $i^{*'}$, is defined by the slope of the line that connects points A^0 and C. Clearly, this line is flatter than the one connecting points A^0 and B. This means that the imposition of optimal capital controls causes the world interest rate to fall. Also, the optimal capital control policy in the foreign country makes the foreign country better off at the expense of

---

[4]One might be tempted to think that the capital control tax rate, τ, is given by the vertical distance from point B to the original current account schedule of the foreign country. However, this is not the case, because as Exercise 12.18 asks you to show, the current account of the foreign country does not depend on $i^* + \tau$, but on i^* and τ separately.

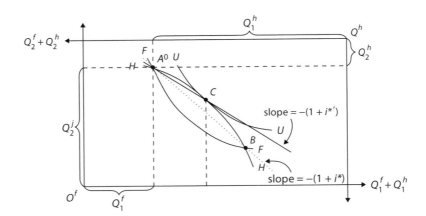

Figure 12.10. Optimal Capital Controls in a Large Economy
Notes: The offer curve of the home country is *HH* and that of the foreign country is *FF*. The endowment is at point A^0. The equilibrium under free capital mobility is at point B, and the equilibrium under optimal capital controls in the foreign country is at point C. The interest rate under free capital mobility is $i*$ and under optimal capital controls $i*'$. The indifference curve attained by the foreign country under optimal capital controls is *UU*. The fact that this indifference curve is not tangent to the intertemporal budget constraint that crosses point C implies that the equilibrium with capital controls is Pareto inefficient.

the home country, whose welfare goes down. To see this, recall that the equilibrium under free capital mobility is Pareto optimal, so the improvement in the foreign country's welfare must be welfare decreasing for the home country. These results echo those obtained algebraically in Section 12.7.

We wish to show that the equilibrium under optimal capital controls in the foreign country fails to be Pareto optimal. To see this, note that at point C, the indifference curve of the home country is tangent to the intertemporal budget constraint associated with the interest rate $i*'$, whereas the indifference curve of the foreign country is tangent to the offer curve of country H (the locus *HH*). Since the budget constraint and *HH* cross each other at point C, it must be the case that the slopes of the home and foreign indifference curves at point C are not the same. This implies that the equilibrium allocation under capital controls is inefficient in the sense that the home country could be made better off without making the foreign country worse off.

12.9 Retaliation

Thus far, we have assumed that as the foreign country imposes controls on capital inflows, the home country responds passively, without retaliating by imposing its own restrictions on capital flows. This assumption is reasonable if the home country is a small country or a region composed of small countries, each without market power in international capital markets. As we saw in Section 12.2.3, the best policy for a small country in the environment studied in this chapter is to allow for free capital mobility. However, if the home country is a large economy, it will in general have an incentive to retaliate. Recall that the home country is a net lender in international markets. So it might be in its own interest to restrict the supply of funds to induce an increase in the world interest rate. In turn, the foreign country would have an incentive to readjust its capital control policy in response to the reaction of the home country. The equilibrium that will emerge under this strategic interaction depends on what type of game the two countries play in setting capital controls. We will focus on one type of game known as *Nash equilibrium*. Essentially, in a Nash equilibrium each country sets its own capital control tax optimally, taking as given the capital tax rate of the other country. An equilibrium is reached when the capital control tax that each country takes as given is indeed the tax rate that is optimal for the other country.

We saw that when the government rebates tax revenues to the public, capital control taxes entail no loss of resources, so for country $j = f, h$, the intertemporal resource constraint is the same as in the case without capital controls; that is,

$$C_1^j + \frac{C_2^j}{1+i^*} = Q_1^j + \frac{Q_2^j}{1+i^*}.$$

Also, by the familiar Euler equation we have that

$$\frac{C_2^j}{C_1^j} = 1 + i^j.$$

The foreign country imposes controls on capital inflows, so its domestic interest rate is given by

$$i^f = i^* + \tau^f,$$

where τ^f denotes the capital control tax rate imposed by the foreign country. It now carries the superscript f to distinguish it from the capital control tax rate of the home country, τ^h. Setting $j = f$ and solving for C_1^f and C_2^f yields

$$C_1^f = \frac{Q_1^f + \frac{Q_2^f}{1+i^*}}{1 + \frac{1+i^*+\tau^f}{1+i^*}}$$

and

$$C_2^f = (1 + i^* + \tau^f) \frac{Q_1^f + \frac{Q_2^f}{1+i^*}}{1 + \frac{1+i^*+\tau^f}{1+i^*}}.$$

Note that consumption depends on two endogenous variables, i^* and τ^f. So, to abbreviate notation we can write

$$C_1^f = K^f(i^*, \tau^f),$$

and

$$C_2^f = L^f(i^*, \tau^f).$$

For the home country, the derivation of the optimal levels of consumption in periods 1 and 2 is analogous, except that because the country is a lender in the international financial market, a tax on capital outflows creates a negative differential between the domestic and the world interest rate,

$$i^h = i^* - \tau^h.$$

Combining this expression with the above intertemporal budget constraint and Euler equation and solving for consumption in periods 1 and 2, we obtain

$$C_1^h = \frac{Q_1^h + \frac{Q_2^h}{1+i^*}}{1 + \frac{1+i^*-\tau^h}{1+i^*}}$$

and

$$C_2^h = (1+i^* - \tau^h)\frac{Q_1^h + \frac{Q_2^h}{1+i^*}}{1 + \frac{1+i^*-\tau^h}{1+i^*}}.$$

As in the case of the foreign country, consumption in both periods is a function of the world interest rate and the country's capital control tax rate. Accordingly, we write these relations as

$$C_1^h = K^h(i^*, \tau^h)$$

and

$$C_2^h = L^h(i^*, \tau^h).$$

Market clearing in the goods market in period 1 requires that global consumption equal the global endowment,

$$K^f(i^*, \tau^f) + K^h(i^*, \tau^h) - Q_1^f - Q_1^h = 0.$$

This equation expresses the world interest rate as an implicit function of the tax rates in the home and foreign countries. We then write

$$i^* = I(\tau^f, \tau^h).$$

Using this relation to eliminate i^* from consumption in both periods in the home and foreign countries, we can write

$$C_1^f = \tilde{K}^f(\tau^f, \tau^h) \equiv K^f(I(\tau^f, \tau^h), \tau^f),$$

$$C_2^f = \tilde{L}^f(\tau^f, \tau^h) \equiv L^f(I(\tau^f, \tau^h), \tau^f),$$

$$C_1^h = \tilde{K}^h(\tau^f, \tau^h) \equiv K^h(I(\tau^f, \tau^h), \tau^h),$$

$$C_2^h = \tilde{L}^h(\tau^f, \tau^h) \equiv L^h(I(\tau^f, \tau^h), \tau^h).$$

The government of the foreign country picks τ^f to maximize the utility of the foreign household, taking as given the tax rate in the home country, τ^h. Thus, the objective function of the foreign country is

$$\ln \tilde{K}^f(\tau^f, \tau^h) + \ln \tilde{L}^f(\tau^f, \tau^h).$$

The first-order condition associated with the foreign government's maximization problem is the derivative of the objective function with respect to τ^f, equalized to zero. Formally,

$$\frac{\tilde{K}_1^f(\tau^f, \tau^h)}{\tilde{K}^f(\tau^f, \tau^h)} + \frac{\tilde{L}_1^f(\tau^f, \tau^h)}{\tilde{L}^f(\tau^f, \tau^h)} = 0,$$

where $\tilde{K}_1^f(\tau^f, \tau^h)$ and $\tilde{L}_1^f(\tau^f, \tau^h)$ denote, respectively, the partial derivatives of $\tilde{K}^f(\tau^f, \tau^h)$ and $\tilde{L}^f(\tau^f, \tau^h)$ with respect to the first argument, τ^f. This optimality condition implicitly defines the tax rate in the foreign country, τ^f, as a function of the tax rate in the home country, τ^h. We write the solution for τ^f as

$$\tau^f = R^f(\tau^h).$$

This relationship is called the *reaction function* of the foreign country. It represents the optimal tax response of the foreign country as a function of the tax rate in the home country.

Likewise, the objective of the home country is to choose τ^h to maximize

$$\ln \tilde{K}^h(\tau^f, \tau^h) + \ln \tilde{L}^h(\tau^f, \tau^h),$$

taking as given τ^f. The associated first-order condition is

$$\frac{\tilde{K}_1^h(\tau^f, \tau^h)}{\tilde{K}^h(\tau^f, \tau^h)} + \frac{\tilde{L}_1^h(\tau^f, \tau^h)}{\tilde{L}^h(\tau^f, \tau^h)} = 0.$$

Solving this expression for τ^h, we can write

$$\tau^h = R^h(\tau^f),$$

which is the reaction function of the home country.

Figure 12.11 displays the reaction functions of the home and foreign countries in the space (τ^h, τ^f). The Nash equilibrium is at point A, where the two reaction functions intersect. At this point, the tax rate of the foreign country maximizes the foreign government's objective function given the equilibrium tax rate in the home country, and the tax rate in the home country maximizes the objective function of the home government given the equilibrium tax rate in the foreign country. The equilibrium tax rate in the foreign country is 18 percent and in the home country it is 30 percent. This means that the retaliation of the home country is quite substantial. Also, the cross-country domestic interest rate differential, $i^f - i^h = \tau^f + \tau^h$, widens from 28(=28+0) percent when the home country is passive to 48(=18+30) percent when the home country retaliates.

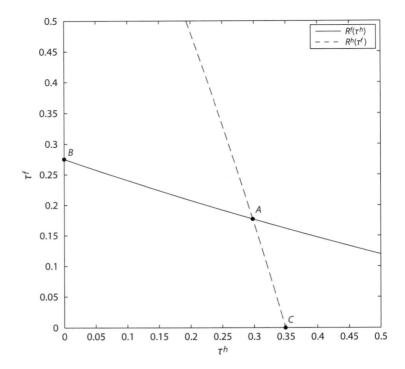

Figure 12.11. Capital Control Reaction Functions of the Home and Foreign Governments

Notes: The function $R^f(\tau^h)$ is the reaction function of the foreign country. It expresses the optimal capital control tax rate of the foreign country as a function of the tax rate of the home country. Similarly, $R^h(\tau^f)$ is the reaction function of the home country, representing the optimal tax rate in the home country as a function of the foreign country's tax rate. The intersection of the two reaction functions gives the Nash equilibrium capital control tax rates in the two countries.

Point B in the figure corresponds to the case in which the foreign country behaves strategically and the home country is passive, which is the case we studied in Section 12.7. Comparing points A and B, we see that retaliation by the home country makes the foreign country lower its capital control tax rate (28 versus 18 percent). Point C in the figure corresponds to the case in which the home country behaves strategically and the foreign country is passive.[5] Comparing points A and C shows that retaliation by the foreign country also makes the home country lower its capital control tax rate. We conclude that regardless of whether a country is borrowing or lending, retaliation by the other country lowers its own capital control taxes relative to the situation in which the other country is passive.

Table 12.1 compares equilibrium macroeconomic outcomes under alternative capital control arrangements. Not surprisingly, intertemporal trade, as measured

[5]Exercise 12.17 asks you to characterize the equilibrium in this case.

Table 12.1. Comparison of Equilibria under Alternative Capital Control Policies

Policy	i^*	τ^f	τ^h	CA^f	Welfare f	h
Autarky	–	–	–	0	$\ln(0.5000Q^2)$	$\ln(1.0000Q^2)$
Free Capital Mobility	0.33	0	0	−0.125Q	$\ln(0.5208Q^2)$	$\ln(1.0208Q^2)$
Home Country Passive	0.22	0.28	0	−0.092Q	$\ln(0.5253Q^2)$	$\ln(1.0103Q^2)$
Foreign Country Passive	0.55	0	0.35	−0.073Q	$\ln(0.5082Q^2)$	$\ln(1.0318Q^2)$
Retaliation—Nash Eqm	0.45	0.18	0.30	−0.060Q	$\ln(0.5111Q^2)$	$\ln(1.0219Q^2)$

by the absolute size of the current account, is the largest under free capital mobility and the smallest under optimal capital controls with Nash retaliation. Also not surprisingly, a country's welfare is the highest when it imposes optimal capital controls and the other country is passive. It is somewhat surprising, however, that the home country is better off under optimal capital controls with retaliation than under free capital mobility. Thus, it is optimal for the home country to impose capital controls regardless of whether this triggers a capital control war or not. This is not the case for the foreign country, which prefers free capital mobility to a capital control war. An interesting question is whether it pays for the foreign country to compensate the home country for abiding in free capital mobility. Exercise 12.19 asks you to address this issue. Finally, if one country imposes optimal capital controls unilaterally, it is in the interest of the other country to retaliate. To see this, note that in both countries welfare is higher under retaliation than in the absence thereof.

12.10 Empirical Evidence on Capital Controls around the World

Thus far, this chapter has argued on theoretical grounds that capital controls can affect aggregate activity, the current account, and welfare. A natural question is whether this type of instrument is used in practice by countries around the world. Chapter 11 provides some indirect evidence indicating that this is indeed the case. It begins by establishing that under free capital mobility, covered interest rate parity should hold and that deviations from covered interest rate parity can be an indication of impediments to the free flow of capital across borders. It then presents empirical evidence on observed deviations from covered interest rate parity between the U.S. dollar and the pound sterling, the Brazilian real, and the Chinese renminbi at different points in history. All three of these case studies point to the empirical relevance of capital controls. But how widespread are these type of restrictions to the international flow of capital?

This section answers this question by focusing on a more direct measure of capital controls available for a large set of countries. The information comes from the dataset on capital control indicators developed by Fernández, Klein, Rebucci, Schindler, and Uribe (2016) (hereafter FKRSU),[6] who translate into a binary index, 0 or 1, the narrative descriptions of capital-control regulations in place in IMF member countries. These narratives are published in the IMF's Annual Report on Exchange Arrangements and Exchange Restrictions (AREAER). A value of 0 indicates no restriction and a value of 1 the existence of a restriction. The frequency of the index is annual. The FKRSU dataset contains separate capital control indices for inflows and outflows disaggregated into 10 categories of assets: money market instruments; bonds; equity; collective investment securities; financial credits; derivatives; commercial credits; guarantees and sureties; real estate; and direct investment. The dataset covers 100 countries, including low-, middle-, and high-income countries, and ranges from 1995 to 2019. The FKRSU capital control indices reflect *de jure measures of capital controls*, as opposed to de facto measures, because they reflect regulations in place in a given country at a given point in time, but do not provide information on how strictly these regulations are enforced. Also, the FKRSU indices reflect the extensive margin of capital controls, as they provide information on how many categories of assets are subject to restrictions but do not reflect the intensive margin, as they do not provide information on the degree to which international asset transactions are limited or taxed.

Table 12.2 displays for each country and in descending order an average over the period 1995 to 2019 of an aggregate capital control indicator. This indicator, denoted *ka* in the FKRSU dataset, is the arithmetic mean of the granular binary index (0 or 1) across all 10 asset categories and across the direction of flow (inflow and outflow). The table also shows the maximum and minimum of the *ka* index over the sample period.

The first fact that emerges from the table is that the capital control index varies significantly across countries. For example, Tunisia (0.99), Sri Lanka (0.99), India (0.97), and China (0.96) all have indices above 0.95, indicating that they had restrictions in place on virtually all asset categories, on both directions of flow, and throughout the entire 25 years covered in the sample. Put differently, de jure, these countries impose significant impediments to international capital mobility. The fact that China appears in the group of countries with a high capital control index is consistent with the large observed deviations from covered interest rate parity documented in Section 11.2 of Chapter 11.

At the other extreme, Nicaragua (0.04), Costa Rica (0.04), Spain (0.03), Italy (0.03), Guatemala (0.02), Hong Kong (0.02), United Kingdom (0.02), Peru (0.01), Uruguay (0), Japan (0), Netherlands (0), Panama (0), and Zambia (0), all have indices below 5 percent, indicating that, at least on paper, they impose virtually no restrictions on capital flows.

A second fact that emerges from Table 12.2 is that countries that on average are neither very closed nor very open to capital flows tend to vary their degree of openness over time quite significantly. That is, this intermediate set of countries is sometimes relatively closed and sometimes relatively open to capital flows. This fact

[6]Andrés Fernández, Michael Klein, Alessandro Rebucci, Martin Schindler, and Martín Uribe, "Capital Control Measures: A New Dataset," *IMF Economic Review* (64), 2016: 548–574.

Table 12.2. The FKRSU Capital Control Index by Country, 1995–2019

Country	Mean	Min	Max	Country	Mean	Min	Max
Tunisia	0.99	0.90	1.00	Australia	0.27	0.13	0.35
Sri Lanka	0.99	0.95	1.00	Kyrgyz Republic	0.27	0.06	0.44
India	0.97	0.95	1.00	Dominican Republic	0.26	0.17	0.38
China	0.96	0.80	1.00	Bahrain	0.25	0.00	0.43
Tanzania	0.92	0.65	1.00	Hungary	0.24	0.00	0.75
Uzbekistan	0.90	0.75	0.97	Nigeria	0.22	0.13	1.00
Vietnam	0.89	0.39	0.95	United Arab Emirates	0.22	0.20	0.22
Angola	0.86	0.78	0.93	Germany	0.19	0.00	0.30
Philippines	0.85	0.75	0.97	Switzerland	0.19	0.05	0.35
Algeria	0.85	0.70	1.00	Bulgaria	0.18	0.05	0.70
Kingdom of Eswatini	0.84	0.80	1.00	Greece	0.17	0.00	0.68
Bangladesh	0.83	0.53	0.95	Egypt	0.17	0.03	0.25
Malaysia	0.81	0.72	0.88	Bolivia	0.17	0.10	0.33
Ukraine	0.80	0.75	0.94	Portugal	0.17	0.00	0.40
Ethiopia	0.79	0.31	1.00	Oman	0.16	0.06	0.22
Myanmar	0.78	0.52	1.00	Finland	0.15	0.05	0.33
Côte d'Ivoire	0.77	0.69	0.80	Austria	0.15	0.05	0.25
Morocco	0.76	0.67	0.77	Singapore	0.14	0.11	0.22
Togo	0.75	0.70	0.94	United States	0.13	0.11	0.15
Thailand	0.73	0.58	0.82	Israel	0.13	0.00	0.55
Pakistan	0.73	0.63	0.88	Qatar	0.12	0.05	0.20
Poland	0.72	0.55	1.00	Mauritius	0.12	0.06	0.13
Saudi Arabia	0.67	0.31	0.88	Yemen	0.11	0.05	0.19
Iran, Islamic Republic of	0.66	0.45	1.00	Paraguay	0.10	0.00	0.23
Moldova	0.65	0.53	0.88	New Zealand	0.10	0.10	0.13
South Africa	0.65	0.57	0.75	Uganda	0.10	0.05	0.61
Burkina Faso	0.65	0.53	0.70	El Salvador	0.10	0.00	0.22
Indonesia	0.64	0.50	0.70	Sweden	0.09	0.00	0.23
Colombia	0.63	0.47	0.82	France	0.07	0.00	0.20
Brazil	0.63	0.28	0.88	Belgium	0.07	0.00	0.17
Russia	0.61	0.20	1.00	Latvia	0.06	0.05	0.20
Lebanon	0.61	0.17	0.82	Georgia	0.06	0.00	0.14
Mexico	0.60	0.53	0.94	Denmark	0.06	0.05	0.08
Ghana	0.52	0.33	0.88	Canada	0.06	0.05	0.10
Argentina	0.51	0.06	0.90	Brunei Darussalam	0.05	0.05	0.11
Kazakhstan	0.48	0.08	0.81	Norway	0.05	0.00	0.08
Jamaica	0.48	0.14	0.75	Ireland	0.05	0.00	0.06
Iceland	0.47	0.15	0.90	Nicaragua	0.04	0.00	0.10
Turkey	0.46	0.23	0.70	Costa Rica	0.04	0.00	0.13
Cyprus	0.45	0.05	0.95	Spain	0.03	0.00	0.15
Venezuela	0.41	0.14	0.69	Italy	0.03	0.03	0.03
Chile	0.39	0.22	0.93	Guatemala	0.02	0.00	0.07
Ecuador	0.39	0.10	0.53	Hong Kong	0.02	0.00	0.08
Slovenia	0.37	0.10	0.80	United Kingdom	0.02	0.00	0.13
Kuwait	0.35	0.11	0.45	Peru	0.01	0.00	0.05
Korea	0.35	0.13	0.94	Uruguay	0.00	0.00	0.03
Malta	0.32	0.08	0.88	Japan	0.00	0.00	0.05
Kenya	0.32	0.30	0.35	Netherlands	0.00	0.00	0.00
Romania	0.32	0.05	0.85	Panama	0.00	0.00	0.00
Czech Republic	0.29	0.05	0.47	Zambia	0.00	0.00	0.00

Notes: The table displays the mean, the minimum, and the maximum value of the FKRSU aggregate capital control index *ka* over the period 1995 to 2019 by country. The capital control index can take values in the interval [0, 1]. The table is sorted by the level of the average capital control index, with Tunisia displaying the highest level of capital controls (0.99) and Zambia displaying the lowest level (0). Own calculations based on the capital control database of Fernández, Klein, Rebucci, Schindler, and Uribe (2016). The latest update of this dataset is available online at http://www.columbia.edu/~mu2166/fkrsu/.

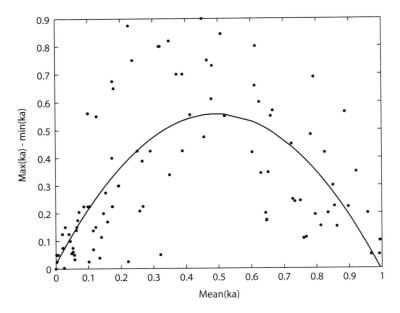

Figure 12.12. Relationship between Variability and Mean of the Capital Control Index
Notes: The figure plots with dots the range of the capital control index, given by the difference between the maximum and the minimum value of the *ka* index across time, against its mean value. Each dot represents one country. The solid line is the quadratic polynomial that best fits the cloud of points in the ordinary least squares sense. The data come from Table 12.2. The figure suggests that countries that are neither very closed nor very open to capital flows change the number of restrictions on capital flows significantly over time.

is illustrated in Figure 12.12. It plots with dots the difference between the maximum and the minimum values of the capital control index *ka* (i.e., the difference between the third and second columns of Table 12.2, also known as the range) against the mean value of *ka* (the first column of Table 12.2). Each dot represents a country. The solid line is the quadratic polynomial that best fits the cloud of points. Both the cloud of points and the fitted line have an inverted-U shape. It is not surprising that in a short sample (in our case 25 annual observations), at the extremes of the cloud the range of variation of the index is close to zero—if the index is near 1 on average, it has to be near 1 most of the time; and similarly, if it is near 0 on average, it must be near 0 almost all the time. What is remarkable in the figure is that countries with intermediate average levels of capital controls, say those with a mean *ka* index between 0.2 and 0.8, display significant variation in the index across time. This doesn't necessarily have to be the case. The cloud of points could have been flat. Instead, it displays significant curvature. For example, the fitted line suggests that a country with a mean value of the capital control index of 0.5 exhibits values of the index ranging from 0.25 to 0.75 over time. The figure therefore suggests that there are a few countries that are always either quite closed or quite open to capital flows and that the rest of the countries tend to vary their degree of openness significantly over

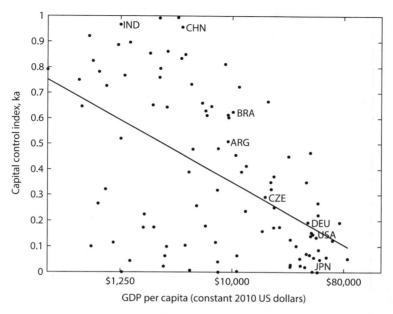

Figure 12.13. Capital Controls and Real GDP per Capita, 1995–2019
Notes: The figure plots the average FKRSU capital control index (*ka*) against the average of real GDP per capita over the period 1995 to 2019 for 100 countries. Country names are shown using ISO abbreviations. Own calculations based on GDP data from WDI and the capital control database of Fernández, Klein, Rebucci, Schindler, and Uribe (2021 update, http://www.columbia.edu/~mu2166/fkrsu/).

time. This result is robust to using the standard deviation instead of the range as the variable plotted on the vertical axis in Figure 12.12.[7]

A third fact that emerges from Table 12.2 is that there appears to be a negative relationship between income per capita and capital controls. Put differently, richer countries tend to be more open to capital flows than poorer countries. This fact is illustrated in Figure 12.13, which plots the average level of the capital control index *ka* over the sample period 1995–2019 against the average level of real GDP per capita over the same period. In the figure, each point represents a country. The horizontal axis, which measures real GDP per capita, is in logarithmic scale. The solid line is the straight line that best fits the cloud of points. The points display a downward sloping pattern, which is picked up by the fitted line. Specifically, the fitted line is given by

$$mean(ka) = 1.4304 - 0.1174 \times \ln\left(mean(GDP)\right).$$

This means that a country that has twice the GDP per capita of another country has on average a capital control index that is 0.1174 lower than the capital control index of the other country. For example, consider Germany and the Czech Republic. Over the sample period, the average real GDP per capita of Germany was $40,958 and that

---

[7] Exercise 12.21 asks you to establish this claim.

of the Czech Republic was $18,516, so that Germany was about twice as rich as the Czech Republic. In Germany the average capital control index was 0.1937 and in the Czech Republic it was 0.2914, which is 0.0978 higher than in Germany, a value close to the slope of the fitted line.

If the fitted line correctly represents the relationship between capital controls and GDP, then the high capital control index of China, 0.96, cannot be accounted for solely by the fact that China is an emerging country with a relatively low average real GDP per capita over the sample period, $3,932. This interpretation follows from the fact that the dot corresponding to China in the figure lies significantly above the fitted line. If the capital control index of China were accounted for solely by income, it should be 0.46, roughly half the actual one. This means that there must be factors other than the level of economic development that explain why the Chinese government imposes so many restrictions on the international flow of capital.

12.11 Summing Up

- Capital controls drive a wedge between the domestic interest rate and the world interest rate.
- If under free capital mobility, a small country borrows from the rest of the world, then the imposition of capital controls drives domestic interest rates up, depresses current consumption, and improves the current account.
- If under free capital mobility, a small country lends to the rest of the world, then the imposition of capital outflow controls lowers domestic interest rates, increases current consumption, and worsens the current account.
- In a small open economy without distortions, capital controls are always welfare decreasing.
- In the presence of borrowing externalities, capital controls can be welfare increasing, as they can be effective in eliminating overborrowing.
- In a two-country world, free capital mobility is in general preferred to financial autarky.
- In a two-country world, free capital mobility results in a Pareto optimal allocation; that is, any other feasible allocation makes at least one country worse off.
- For an economy that has market power in global financial markets it might be welfare improving to impose capital controls to move the world interest rate in its favor.
- A large economy that runs a current account deficit benefits from imposing controls on capital inflows that drive the world interest rate down, provided the rest of the world does not retaliate.
- A large economy that runs a current account surplus benefits from imposing controls on capital outflows that drive the world interest rate up, provided the rest of the world does not retaliate.
- In a two-country world, the allocation under optimal capital controls fails to be Pareto efficient; that is, there is a feasible reallocation of resources that would make at least one country better off without making the other country worse off.

- In a two-country world, if one country imposes optimal capital controls unilaterally, it is in the interest of the other country to retaliate.
- In a two-country world, it may be welfare improving for one country to initiate a capital control war.
- Empirical studies show that many countries in the world have significant de jure capital controls.
- There appears to be a strong negative empirical relationship between the level of economic development and the use of capital controls.

12.12 Exercises

Exercise 12.1 (TFU) Indicate whether the statements are true, false, or uncertain and explain why.

1. In a two-country world, if the interest rate in both countries is the same under financial autarky, then there are no welfare gains from changing to a regime of free international capital mobility.
2. In a two-country world, if under financial autarky the interest rate in one country is higher than in the other country, then welfare in the country with the low interest rate under autarky will increase and welfare in the country with the high interest rate under autarky will decrease if both countries switch to free capital mobility.

Exercise 12.2 (Capital Controls and the Current Account) Consider a two-period, small open economy populated by identical households with preferences given by

$$\ln C_1 + \ln C_2,$$

where C_1 and C_2 denote consumption in periods 1 and 2, respectively. Households are endowed with $Q_1 = 5$ units of goods in period 1 and $Q_2 = 10$ units in period 2. In period 1, households can borrow or lend at the interest rate i. Let D_1 denote the amount of debt of the household in period 1. Assume that the initial level of debt is zero, $D_0 = 0$. The world interest rate, denoted i^*, is 10 percent.

1. Calculate the equilibrium current account in period 1 under free capital mobility.
2. Now assume that the government introduces capital controls in period 1. Specifically, the government charges foreign lenders a proportional tax τ on the amount of debt extended to domestic residents. So foreign lenders pay τD_1 to the government in period 1. Suppose that the tax rate is 10 percent. In period 1, the government transfers all of these revenues to households via a lump-sum transfer denoted T. The government does not intervene in the economy in period 2.
   (a) Calculate the interest rate differential.
   (b) Calculate the equilibrium current account balance in period 1. Compare this situation to what happens under free capital mobility and provide intuition.

(c) Suppose now that instead of setting it at 10 percent, the government sets τ to a level consistent with a 50 percent reduction in the current account relative to the level prevailing under free capital mobility (i.e., when $\tau = 0$). Calculate the equilibrium capital control tax rate. Calculate the new interest rate differential. Discuss your results.

Exercise 12.3 (Effectiveness of Taxes on Capital Inflows) In Section 12.2, we saw that an increase in the tax rate on capital inflows, τ, affects real variables, such as consumption in periods 1 and 2, the trade balance, the current account, and the level of external debt. Assume that $B_0 = 0$. Show that there is a level $\bar{\tau}$ beyond which the tax on capital inflows has no effect on real variables. Derive a formula expressing $\bar{\tau}$ as a function of Q_1, Q_2, and i^*. Provide intuition on how $\bar{\tau}$ depends on each of these exogenous variables.

Exercise 12.4 (Quantitative Capital Flow Restrictions) Consider a two-period model of a small open economy with a single good each period and no investment. Let preferences of the household be described by the lifetime utility function

$$\sqrt{C_1} + \beta\sqrt{C_2}.$$

Assume that $\beta = 1/1.1$. The household has initial net foreign wealth of $(1 + i_0^*)B_0 = 1$, with $i_0^* = 0.1$, and is endowed with $Q_1 = 5$ units of goods in period 1 and $Q_2 = 10$ units in period 2. The world interest rate paid on assets held from period 1 to period 2, i^*, equals 10 percent (i.e., $i^* = 0.1$) and there is free international capital mobility.

1. Calculate the equilibrium levels of consumption in period 1, C_1, consumption in period 2, C_2, the trade balance in period 1, TB_1, and the current account balance in period 1, CA_1.
2. Suppose now that the government imposes quantitative restrictions on capital flows limiting the country's net foreign asset position at the end of period 1 to be nonnegative ($B_1 \geq 0$). Compute the equilibrium value of the domestic interest rate, i, consumption in periods 1 and 2, and the trade and current account balances in period 1.
3. Evaluate the effect of quantitative capital controls on welfare. Specifically, find the level of lifetime utility under capital controls and compare it to the level of utility obtained under free capital mobility.
4. For this question and the next, suppose that the country experiences a temporary increase in the endowment of period 1 to $Q_1 = 9$, with the period 2 endowment unchanged. Calculate the effect of this output shock on C_1, C_2, TB_1, CA_1, and i in the case that capital is freely mobile across countries.
5. Finally, suppose that the capital controls described in question 2 are in place. Will they still be binding (i.e., affect household behavior)?

Exercise 12.5 (Quantitative Controls on Capital Outflows) Consider the equilibrium with quantitative capital controls analyzed in Section 12.3 and depicted in Figure 12.2. Suppose the equilibrium allocation under free capital mobility is at a point on the intertemporal budget constraint located northwest of the endowment point A. Suppose that capital controls prohibit borrowing or lending internationally. Would it still be true that capital controls are welfare decreasing? Why or why not?

Exercise 12.6 (Forced Savings) Consider a two-period model of a small open endowment economy populated by households with preferences given by

$$\sqrt{C_1} + \sqrt{C_2},$$

where C_1 and C_2 denote consumption in periods 1 and 2, respectively. Households' endowments are 5 units of goods in period 1 and 10 units of goods in period 2. Households start period 1 with a zero net asset position, $B_0 = 0$, and the world interest rate is zero, $i^* = 0$.

1. Find consumption in periods 1 and 2, the country's net foreign asset position at the end of period 1, and the trade balance in periods 1 and 2.
2. Find the level of welfare in the economy.
3. Now assume that the government announces in period 1 that a strong nation is one with a positive net foreign asset position and that therefore the country must save more. In particular, assume that the government requires that the net foreign asset position at the end of period 1 be greater or equal to 2. That is, the government imposes capital controls of the form $B_1 \geq 2$. Find the domestic interest rate that supports this allocation.
4. Find the level of welfare under capital controls and compare it to the level of welfare under free capital mobility. Provide intuition.

Exercise 12.7 (Borrowing Externalities) Consider a two-period, small open economy populated by a large number of identical households with preferences given by

$$\ln C_1 + \ln C_2.$$

Households are endowed with $Q_1 = 1$ unit of consumption in period 1 and with $Q_2 = 2$ units in period 2. They start period 1 with no debts or assets and can borrow or lend at the interest rate i. The interest rate at which the country can borrow or lend in international markets is given by

$$i^* = \begin{cases} 0 & \text{for } \bar{C}_1 \leq \bar{Q}_1 \\ \delta(\bar{C}_1 - \bar{Q}_1) & \text{for } \bar{C}_1 > \bar{Q}_1 \end{cases},$$

where $\delta = 0.5$ and $\bar{C}_1$ and $\bar{Q}_1$ denote the aggregate per capital levels of consumption and output in period 1. The country operates under free capital mobility.

1. Show that the country is not a lender in period 1.
2. Calculate the equilibrium levels of consumption in period 1, external debt in period 1, and the interest rate.
3. Compute the efficient allocation. Compare it with that of the competitive equilibrium.
4. Calculate the capital control tax, denoted τ, that supports the efficient allocation as a competitive equilibrium. Assume that the government rebates

the tax revenue to households in a lump-sum fashion. Calculate also the domestic and foreign interest rate that obtain in this equilibrium.

Exercise 12.8 (Financial Exclusion) Consider a two-period, small open economy identical to that of Exercise 12.7, except that the interest rate at which the country can borrow or lend in international markets is given by

$$i^* = \begin{cases} 10\% & \text{for } \bar{C}_1 \leq \bar{Q}_1 \\ 120\% & \text{for } \bar{C}_1 > \bar{Q}_1 \end{cases}.$$

1. Show that the country is not a lender in period 1.
2. Show that the country does not borrow in period 1.
3. Calculate the equilibrium levels of consumption and the interest rate.
4. Show that the allocation that obtains in the competitive equilibrium is efficient.

Exercise 12.9 (Market Clearing in the Two-Country Model) Show that the market-clearing condition in the world financial market, given by equation (12.24), implies a market-clearing condition in the world goods market requiring that in equilibrium the world endowment of goods equals the world consumption of goods in both periods,

$$C_1^h + C_1^f = Q_1^h + Q_1^f,$$

and

$$C_2^h + C_2^f = Q_2^h + Q_2^f.$$

Exercise 12.10 (Autarky in the Two-Country Economy) Show that in the two-country economy of Section 12.5, both countries are better off under capital mobility than under autarky.

Exercise 12.11 (The Offer Curve with Log-Linear Preferences) Show that in the two-country economy of Section 12.5 the offer curve of country $j = h, f$ is given by

$$C_2^j = \frac{C_1^j Q_2^j}{2C_1^j - Q_1^j}.$$

Exercise 12.12 (Tangency of Offer and Indifference Curves at the Endowment Point) Show that at the endowment point, the slope of the offer curve is equal to the slope of the indifference curve.

Exercise 12.13 (An Upward-Sloping Offer Curve) The beginning of this exercise is the same as Exercise 4.4 of Chapter 4. Consider an individual who lives for two periods, $t = 1, 2$. Her preferences for consumption in each period are described by the lifetime utility function $U(C_1) + U(C_2)$, where C_1 and C_2 denote consumption in periods 1 and 2 and

$$U(C) = \frac{C^{1-\sigma} - 1}{1 - \sigma}.$$

The parameter $\sigma > 0$ denotes the inverse of the intertemporal elasticity of substitution. Suppose that the individual starts period 1 with no financial wealth, $B_0 = 0$. Suppose further that the individual receives endowments of goods in the amounts Q_1 and Q_2 in periods 1 and 2. In period 1, the individual can borrow or lend at the interest rate i_1 via a bond denoted B_1.

1. Find the optimal levels of consumption in periods 1 and 2 as functions of the individual's endowments, Q_1 and Q_2, the intertemporal elasticity of substitution $1/\sigma$, and the interest rate i_1.
2. Find the optimal level of saving in period 1 as a function of the individual's endowments, Q_1 and Q_2, the intertemporal elasticity of substitution $1/\sigma$, and the interest rate i_1. Characterize conditions under which the individual will save in period 1; that is, conditions such that $S_1 > 0$. Provide intuition.
3. Find the partial derivative of the optimal level of consumption in period 1 with respect to the interest rate i_1.
4. Find the partial derivative of the optimal level of consumption in period 2 with respect to the interest rate i_1.
5. Characterize conditions on $1/\sigma$, i_1, Q_1, and Q_2 such that an increase in the interest rate i_1 reduces desired consumption in both periods. Provide an intuitive explanation of your finding.
6. Assume that $\sigma = 2$, $Q_1 = 1$, and $Q_2 = 2$. Consider values of $i_1 > -1$. Using a software, such as Matlab, construct the offer curve. At what interest rate would the individual choose the endowment point as the optimal consumption path? Do there exist feasible values of i_1 such that the offer curve changes from downward to upward sloping as the interest rate declines, as suggested in footnote 2? If so, find the value of i_1 at which the sign of the slope of the offer curve changes.

Exercise 12.14 (Capital Controls and Welfare in the Two-Country Economy) This question is concerned with the analysis in Section 12.7. Show that the home country is better off in the equilibrium with optimal capital controls set by the foreign country and no capital controls in the home country than in the autarkic equilibrium.

Exercise 12.15 (Capital Controls in a Large Economy) Consider a two-period, two-country model of a large open endowment economy. Households in country 1 are endowed with $Q_1^1 = 0$ goods in period 1 and $Q_2^1 = Q > 0$ goods in period 2. In country 2, the endowments are $Q_1^2 = Q$ and $Q_2^2 = 0$. In both countries, households have preferences defined by the same utility function,

$$\ln C_1^1 + \ln C_2^1,$$

in country 1 and

$$\ln C_1^2 + \ln C_2^2,$$

in country 2, where C_t^i, for $i = 1, 2$ and $t = 1, 2$, denotes consumption in country i in period t. In country 1, households enter period 1 with a zero net asset position ($B_0^1 = 0$).

1. Calculate the equilibrium levels of consumption in countries 1 and 2 in periods 1 and 2, the current account in countries 1 and 2 in period 1, (CA_1^1 and CA_1^2), and the world interest rate (r^*). Provide intuition.

2. The government of country 1 understands that although individual agents take the interest rate as given, the country as a whole has market power in the international capital market. To take advantage of this situation, it restricts capital inflows by imposing capital controls as follows. Let τ denote a tax on capital inflows such that the domestic interest rate in country 1, denoted r, becomes $1+r = (1+r^*)/(1-\tau)$. Suppose that the tax is 10 percent ($\tau = 0.1$). The government of country 1 rebates the tax to its households by means of a lump-sum transfer T_2 in period 2 given by $T_2 = -(1+r)\tau B_1^1$, where B_1^1 denotes the net foreign asset position of country 1 at the end of period 1. (Note that if $B_1^1 < 0$, then $T_2 > 0$, so T_2 is a proper transfer.) Suppose that the government of country 2 is passive and does not retaliate. Find the equilibrium values of the world interest rate, r^*, and of the domestic interest rate in country 1, r. Does the government of country 1 succeed in lowering the world interest rate?

3. Compare the equilibrium paths of consumption in country 1, (C_1^1, C_2^1), with and without capital controls. In particular, is the tax welfare increasing for households in country 1? What about for households in country 2? Provide intuition.

4. Generalize your findings to any value of $\tau \in (0, 1)$. Is there a value of τ that maximizes welfare in country 1? In answering this question, continue to assume that the government of country 2 is passive.

Exercise 12.16 (Equivalence Between Capital Controls and Consumption Taxes) Compare Exercise 12.15 with Exercise 8.7 in Chapter 8.

1. Derive an equivalence between capital control taxes and consumption taxes.

2. Generalize the equivalence to the case in which a consumption tax is applied in both periods at rates τ_1 and τ_2.

Exercise 12.17 (Optimal Capital Controls in a Large Lending Country) Section 12.7 characterizes optimal capital controls in a large borrowing country (the foreign country) assuming that the lending country (the home country) adopts a passive stance. This question asks you to characterize optimal capital controls in the home country when the foreign country is passive. Specifically,

1. Find the world interest rate i^* when there is free capital mobility.

2. Find the level of welfare in each country.

Suppose now that country h taxes capital outflows optimally. Assume that country f does not retaliate when country h imposes capital controls. The fiscal authority of country h rebates any revenue from the capital control tax in a lump-sum fashion to its citizens.

1. Find the world interest rate i^* and compare it to the world interest rate under free capital mobility. Provide intuition.

2. Find i^h and compare it to the world interest rate.
3. Find τ, the capital control tax on outflows.
4. Find the level of welfare in country f. Compare it to the level of welfare under free capital mobility.

Exercise 12.18 (Capital Controls and the Current Account Schedule) Consider the two-country economy of Section 12.7.

1. Show that the current account schedules of the home and foreign countries are given, respectively, by

$$CA_1^h = \frac{1}{2}\left(Q_1^h - \frac{Q_2^h}{1+i^*}\right)$$

and

$$CA_1^f = \frac{(1+i^*+\tau)Q_1^f - Q_2^f}{2(1+i^*)+\tau}.$$

2. Show that as long as the current account of the foreign country is negative, its current account schedule is an increasing function of the world interest rate i^*, holding τ constant. *Hint: Take the partial derivative of CA_1^f with respect to i^* and show that it is positive if $2Q_2^f - \tau Q_1^f > 0$. Then show that if $CA_1^f < 0$, then $Q_2^f - \tau Q_1^f > 0$.*
3. Show that the current account schedule of the foreign country is an increasing function of the capital control tax rate τ, holding constant i^*.

Exercise 12.19 (Country Compensation) In the two-country model with Nash retaliation studied in Section 12.9, calculate whether it pays for the foreign country to give a lump-sum compensation to the home country in period 2 in exchange for the home country to maintain free capital mobility. Denote this compensation by G and assume that it is proportional to the foreign country's endowment in period 2; that is, $G = \gamma Q$, where $\gamma > 0$ is a parameter, whose value you are asked to find. To answer this question, you can proceed as follows:

1. Compute welfare in the two countries under free capital mobility. These should be two functions of γ (and Q).
2. Find the value of γ that makes the home country indifferent between free capital mobility and receiving the gift and a capital control war and not receiving the gift (the latter welfare level can be read off Table 12.1). The answer should be a number for γ.
3. With γ in hand, evaluate the level of welfare of the foreign country under capital mobility and paying the gift. Then compare this number with the foreign country's level of welfare under a capital control war and not paying the gift. (The latter number can also be read off Table 12.1.)

Exercise 12.20 (Capital Control Indicators for China) In Section 11.2 of Chapter 11, we argued, based on the observed behavior of the covered interest rate differential, that China must have had in place restrictions on both capital inflows and capital outflows before and after accession to the WTO. Section 12.10 of this chapter (see in particular Table 12.2) shows evidence indicating that China had high capital controls on average over the period 1995 to 2019. The data in Table 12.2, however, represents an average across both time and the direction of flows (inflow and outflow). This exercise asks you to provide more direct evidence in favor or against the inference that both restrictions on outflows and inflows were in place in China prior to and after accession to the WTO. Specifically, use the database of Fernández, Klein, Rebucci, Schindler, and Uribe (2016, updated to 2019) available at http://www.columbia.edu/~mu2166/fkrsu/ and download the time series *kai* and *kao* for China, measuring, respectively, capital controls on inflows and outflows in that country over the period 1995 to 2019. Make a plot of the two time series and discuss whether they do or do not support the inference made in Section 11.2 of Chapter 11.

Exercise 12.21 (Mean and Volatility of Capital Controls) Section 12.10 suggests that countries that are neither very closed nor very open to capital flows tend to vary capital controls over time. Specifically, Figure 12.12 plots the mean value of the *ka* index of capital controls against its range, and shows that the pattern has an inverted-U shape. Investigate whether this result is robust to using the standard deviation of the index *ka* across time instead of its range as a measure of variability. Specifically, redo Figure 12.12 using the standard deviation as opposed to the range as the variable plotted on the vertical axis.

PART IV

Monetary Policy and Exchange Rates

CHAPTER 13

Nominal Rigidity, Exchange Rate Policy, and Unemployment

The nominal exchange rate is a central variable in open economies. Thus far, we have studied how the real exchange rate is determined, but not how the nominal exchange rate is determined. In Chapter 10, we introduced the TNT (Traded-Nontraded) model of real exchange rate determination and analyzed responses of the real exchange rate to various shocks. For example, a deterioration of the terms of trade reduces aggregate demand, which causes a fall in the relative price of goods that cannot be sold abroad (nontradable goods). As a result, the country becomes cheaper relative to the rest of the world; that is, the real exchange rate depreciates. In the TNT model, monetary policy plays no role for the determination of real variables such as employment, consumption, the real wage, and the real exchange rate. This is because of a key assumption—namely, that all prices adjust flexibly to bring about market clearing in labor and goods markets. Thus, the TNT model displays a dichotomy in the determination of real and nominal variables. Real variables are determined by real factors, such as preferences, technology, and real shocks, but not by *monetary policy*, which can only affect nominal variables, such as the consumer price level and nominal wages.

In this chapter, we are concerned with environments in which some prices suffer from *nominal rigidity*. When this is the case, monetary policy can have real effects, in the sense that it can affect the level of real variables, such as consumption, employment, the real wage, and the real exchange rate. Consider again the example of a deterioration in a country's terms of trade. The contraction in aggregate demand caused by this shock triggers a decline in the demand for labor by firms. Equilibrium in the labor market thus requires a fall in the real wage; that is, in the wage rate measured in terms of goods. A fall in the real wage can happen either through a fall in the nominal wage or through an increase in the consumer price level. Suppose that, for some reason, the nominal wage is downwardly rigid. Then, the price level must rise for the labor market to clear. Otherwise, the real wage would be too high and involuntary unemployment would emerge. In turn, an increase in the price level could be brought about by expansionary monetary policy. Thus, in the presence of nominal rigidity, the economy ceases to be dichotomic, and relative prices, the real allocation, and welfare can depend on monetary policy.

The analysis in this chapter builds on the two-period TNT model of Chapter 10. The economy we study here departs from the TNT model in that it features downward nominal wage rigidity (DNWR).[1] We refer to this variant of the TNT model as the *TNT-DNWR model*. For convenience, we keep the presentation self-contained, so that you don't necessarily have to refresh the material of Chapter 10 before proceeding.

13.1 The TNT-DNWR Model

In low inflation countries, whether developed or emerging, we observe that each year only a small fraction of workers experience a wage cut. Almost half of all workers experience an exact zero change in their wages, and almost half experience a wage increase. Moreover, the fraction of workers whose wages don't change from one year to the next is countercyclical; that is, it goes up during recessions and down during booms. This pattern of wage changes has been interpreted as evidence of downward nominal wage rigidity. Section 13.7 expands on these empirical regularities.

The question of why nominal wages have a hard time falling is still a matter of investigation. Truman Bewley of Yale University set out to find an answer directly from firm managers.[2] During the U.S. recession of the early 1990s, he interviewed more than 300 managers in the northeastern United States about their firms' wage policies. The most common answer Bewley received was that they don't cut wages because wage cuts undermine the morale of workers, which disrupts productivity in the workplace. Managers seem to prefer layoffs over wage cuts because, although layoffs also reduce workers' morale, the effect on the workers that remain in the firm is not as strong.

We model *downward nominal wage rigidity* as the inability of firms to cut wages,

$$W_t \geq W_{t-1}, \tag{13.1}$$

where W_t denotes the nominal hourly wage rate in period t.

The economy produces and consumes two goods. One good is internationally traded and the other is nontradable. Let P_t^T and P_t^N denote the prices of tradable and nontradable goods. The price of the nontradable good is determined by domestic demand and supply conditions, which we will analyze below. The price of the tradable good is determined by the law of one price,

$$P_t^T = \mathcal{E}_t P_t^{T*}.$$

Here, $\mathcal{E}_t$ denotes the nominal exchange rate defined as the domestic currency price of one unit of foreign currency so that an increase in $\mathcal{E}_t$ corresponds to a

---

[1] The theoretical framework is a two-period adaptation of the infinite horizon model developed in Stephanie Schmitt-Grohé and Martín Uribe, "Downward Nominal Wage Rigidity, Currency Pegs, and Involuntary Unemployment," *Journal of Political Economy* 124 (2016): 1466–1514.

[2] Truman F. Bewley, *Why Wages Don't Fall during a Recession* (Cambridge, MA: Harvard University Press, 1999).

depreciation of the domestic currency, and P_t^{T*} is the foreign currency price of tradable goods. As discussed in Chapter 9, the law of one price says that when prices are expressed in the same currency, the traded good sells for the same price domestically and internationally. The domestic economy is assumed to be small, so it takes the foreign price of the tradable good as given. For simplicity, we assume that P_t^{T*} is constant over time and equal to 1; that is, $P_t^{T*} = 1$. This implies that $P_t^T = \mathcal{E}_t$ and we therefore use P_t^T and $\mathcal{E}_t$ interchangeably in what follows.

13.1.1 THE SUPPLY SCHEDULE

Output of tradable goods, denoted Q_t^T, is an exogenous endowment. Think of trees that each period produce an exogenous amount of fruit Q_t^T. Nontraded goods are produced by perfectly competitive firms using labor, h_t. The quantity of nontraded goods produced in period t is given by

$$Q_t^N = F(h_t),$$

where $F(\cdot)$ is a production function assumed to be increasing and concave. Concavity implies that the marginal product of labor, $F'(h_t)$, is decreasing in labor; that is, that an extra hour of work increases output but at a decreasing rate.

Nominal profits of firms operating in the nontraded sector, Π_t, are given by

$$\Pi_t = P_t^N F(h_t) - W_t h_t. \tag{13.2}$$

Firms choose employment, h_t, to maximize profits, taking as given P_t^N and W_t. The profit-maximizing choice of employment results from taking the derivative of profits with respect to employment and equating it to zero. This yields

$$P_t^N F'(h_t) = W_t. \tag{13.3}$$

This optimality condition says that firms hire labor until the value of the marginal product of labor, $P_t^N F'(h_t)$, equals its marginal cost, W_t.

It is convenient to express prices in terms of tradable goods. Let

$$p_t \equiv \frac{P_t^N}{P_t^T}$$

denote the relative price of nontradable goods in terms of tradable goods. For example, if the nontradable good is haircuts and the tradable good is bushels of wheat, then p_t indicates that one haircut sells for p_t bushels of wheat. Dividing the left- and right-hand sides of the firm's optimality condition (13.3) by P_t^T, recalling that $P_t^T = \mathcal{E}_t$, and rearranging gives

$$p_t = \frac{W_t/\mathcal{E}_t}{F'(h_t)}. \tag{13.4}$$

This condition says that at the optimal level of employment, firms equate the relative price of the nontraded good, p_t, to its marginal cost of production, $\frac{W_t/\mathcal{E}_t}{F'(h_t)}$.

Figure 13.1 displays equation (13.4) in the space (h_t, p_t). We refer to this locus as the supply schedule. The supply schedule is upward sloping. To see why, note

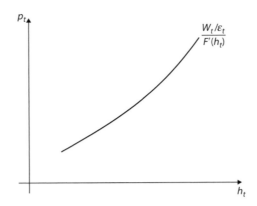

Figure 13.1. The Supply Schedule
Notes: The supply schedule is an increasing relationship between the relative price of nontradables in terms of tradables, p_t, and employment, h_t. All other things equal, an increase in p_t opens up a positive gap between marginal revenue and marginal cost, $p_t - (W_t/\mathcal{E}_t)/F'(h_t)$, which induces firms to expand production and employment until the gap disappears.

that an increase in p_t raises the left-hand side of (13.4). Given $W_t/\mathcal{E}_t$, the marginal product of labor, $F'(h_t)$, must fall to restore equality. Since the production function is concave, a decrease in $F'(h_t)$ requires an expansion in employment, h_t. Intuitively, holding the real wage constant, a higher price makes marginal revenue exceed marginal cost, $(p_t > (W_t/\mathcal{E}_t)/F'(h_t))$. This induces firms to expand the production of nontraded goods, which in turn requires hiring more workers.

Holding the nominal exchange rate constant, an increase in the nominal wage, W_t, pushes the supply schedule up and to the left, as shown in the left panel of Figure 13.2. This is because, given $\mathcal{E}_t$, an increase in W_t raises the firm's marginal cost, which discourages production and employment. By contrast, a depreciation of the domestic currency—that is, an increase in $\mathcal{E}_t$—holding the nominal wage constant, shifts the supply schedule down and to the right as shown in the right panel of the figure. Intuitively, a depreciation reduces the real wage, $W_t/\mathcal{E}_t$, which lowers the marginal cost of production. As a result, for any given level of the relative price, p_t, firms find it profitable to expand production and employment.

13.1.2 THE DEMAND SCHEDULE

The economy is assumed to be populated by a large number of identical two-period lived households, which derive utility from consumption, denoted C_t, for $t = 1, 2$. Preferences are described by the utility function

$$\ln C_1 + \beta \ln C_2, \qquad (13.5)$$

where $\beta \in (0, 1)$ is the subjective discount factor. The consumption good, C_t, is assumed to be a composite of tradable consumption, denoted C_t^T, and nontradable consumption, denoted C_t^N. Households aggregate these two types of goods into the

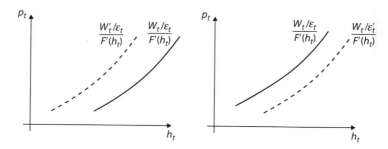

Figure 13.2. Shifters of the Supply Schedule
Notes: The left panel shows that an increase in the nominal wage from W_t to $W'_t >$ W_t, holding constant the nominal exchange rate, $\mathcal{E}_t$, shifts the supply schedule up and to the left. Given $\mathcal{E}_t$, an increase in W_t raises marginal cost, which discourages production and employment for any given relative price, p_t. The right panel shows that holding constant the nominal wage, W_t, an increase in $\mathcal{E}_t$ to $\mathcal{E}'_t > \mathcal{E}_t$ (a depreciation of the domestic currency) shifts the supply schedule down and to the right. Given W_t, a depreciation lowers the real wage, which induces firms to expand output and employment at any given level of p_t.

composite good by means of the following Cobb-Douglas aggregator function

$$C_t = (C_t^T)^\gamma (C_t^N)^{1-\gamma}, \tag{13.6}$$

for $t = 1, 2$. This expression is known as a *subutility function*. The parameter $\gamma \in (0, 1)$ governs the consumer's taste for each type of good. We will see that at the optimal consumption choice, the expenditure share of tradables in total consumption equals γ (see also the analysis in Chapter 9, Section 9.9).

Households can borrow or lend by buying or selling a bond denominated in foreign currency denoted B_t. The household's budget constraint in period 1 expressed in domestic currency is then given by

$$P_1^T C_1^T + P_1^N C_1^N + \mathcal{E}_1 B_1 = \mathcal{E}_1(1 + r_0)B_0 + P_1^T Q_1^T + W_1 h_1 + \Pi_1.$$

The left-hand side of the budget constraint represents the uses of income: expenditure on tradable goods, $P_1^T C_1^T$, expenditure on nontradable goods, $P_1^N C_1^N$, and bond purchases, $\mathcal{E}_1 B_1$. Because the bond is denominated in foreign currency, B_1 is multiplied by the nominal exchange rate, $\mathcal{E}_1$, to express its value in units of domestic currency. The right-hand side represents the sources of income: initial bond holdings including interest, $\mathcal{E}_1(1 + r_0)B_0$, the endowment of tradables, $P_1^T Q_1^T$, labor income, $W_1 h_1$, and profit income from the ownership of firms, Π_1.

The budget constraint in period 2 is given by

$$P_2^T C_2^T + P_2^N C_2^N = P_2^T Q_2^T + W_2 h_2 + \Pi_2 + (1 + r^*)\mathcal{E}_2 B_1,$$

where r^* is the world interest rate on bonds held from period 1 to period 2. Here we are assuming that there is free capital mobility, so domestic households borrow or lend at the world interest rate. Also assume that there is no inflation in the rest of the world, $P_1^* = P_2^*$. This means that r^* is both the real and the nominal interest rate prevailing in the rest of the world. (In the notation of Chapter 11, $i^* = r^*$.)

In each period, the household supplies inelastically a constant number of hours of work $\bar{h}$ to the labor market. However, sometimes there is unemployment and workers get to work less than $\bar{h}$ hours, so that we have

$$h_t \leq \bar{h}. \tag{13.7}$$

As a result, the workers of the household take h_t as given, as it depends on labor market conditions, which they don't control. We will analyze shortly how h_t is determined.

To obtain the intertemporal budget constraint, first divide the budget constraint in period $t = 1, 2$ by P_t^T (recalling that $P_t^T = \mathcal{E}_t$). Then, combine the budget constraints in periods 1 and 2 to eliminate B_1. This is a familiar procedure by now, so we will skip the intermediate steps. The intertemporal budget constraint can then be written as

$$C_1^T + p_1 C_1^N + \frac{C_2^T + p_2 C_2^N}{1 + r^*} = \bar{Y}, \tag{13.8}$$

where

$$\bar{Y} \equiv (1 + r_0) B_0 + Q_1^T + \frac{W_1}{\mathcal{E}_1} h_1 + \frac{\Pi_1}{\mathcal{E}_1} + \frac{Q_2^T + W_2 / \mathcal{E}_2 h_2 + \Pi_2 / \mathcal{E}_2}{1 + r^*}$$

represents lifetime wealth, which the household takes as given. The intertemporal budget constraint says that the household's present discounted value of consumption expenditure must equal its lifetime wealth.

The optimization problem of the household consists in choosing C_t, C_t^T, and C_t^N, for $t = 1, 2$, to maximize the utility function (13.5) subject to the subutility function (13.6), for $t = 1, 2$, and to the intertemporal budget constraint (13.8). As usual, we reduce this constrained maximization problem to an unconstrained problem by using (13.6), for $t = 1, 2$, and (13.8) to eliminate C_t, for $t = 1, 2$, and C_2^T from the lifetime utility function. This yields the following objective function

$$\gamma \ln C_1^T + (1 - \gamma) \ln C_1^N + \beta \gamma \ln \left[(1 + r^*) \bar{Y} - p_2 C_2^N - (1 + r^*)(C_1^T + p_1 C_1^N) \right]$$
$$+ \beta (1 - \gamma) \ln C_2^N.$$

The household chooses C_1^T, C_1^N, and C_2^N to maximize this expression, taking as given its lifetime wealth $\bar{Y}$, the relative price of nontradables in periods 1 and 2, p_1 and p_2, and the world interest rate, r^*. The optimality conditions with respect to C_1^T, C_1^N, and C_2^N, after some rearranging, are, respectively,

$$\frac{C_2^T}{C_1^T} = \beta (1 + r^*), \tag{13.9}$$

$$\frac{1 - \gamma}{C_1^N} = \beta \gamma (1 + r^*) \frac{p_1}{C_2^T}, \tag{13.10}$$

and

$$\frac{C_2^N}{C_2^T} = \frac{1-\gamma}{\gamma}\frac{1}{p_2}. \tag{13.11}$$

Optimality condition (13.9) is the familiar Euler equation. It says that the growth rate of tradable consumption is increasing in the interest rate. This makes sense: The higher is the interest rate, the stronger will be the incentive to save, by consuming relatively less in period 1 and relatively more in period 2.[3] Combining optimality conditions (13.9) and (13.10) yields

$$\frac{C_1^N}{C_1^T} = \frac{1-\gamma}{\gamma}\frac{1}{p_1}. \tag{13.12}$$

This expression says that as the relative price of nontradables increases, the household consumes relatively less nontradables and more tradables. Optimality condition (13.11) has a similar interpretation for period 2.

In equilibrium, the market for nontraded goods must clear; that is, domestic consumption must equal domestic production, or

$$C_t^N = F(h_t), \tag{13.13}$$

for $t = 1, 2$. Using this market-clearing condition and the definition of the profits of firms (13.2) to eliminate C_t^N and Π_t from the intertemporal budget constraint (13.8) yields the familiar economy-wide resource constraint for tradable goods

$$C_1^T + \frac{C_2^T}{1+r^*} = (1+r_0)B_0 + Q_1^T + \frac{Q_2^T}{1+r^*}, \tag{13.14}$$

which says that in equilibrium the present discounted value of tradable consumption must equal the sum of the initial asset position and the present discounted value of the endowment of tradable goods. Using the Euler equation (13.9) to eliminate C_2^T from this expression yields the equilibrium value of consumption of tradables in period 1,

$$C_1^T = \frac{1}{1+\beta}\left[(1+r_0)B_0 + Q_1^T + \frac{Q_2^T}{1+r^*}\right]. \tag{13.15}$$

This is also a familiar expression. Consumption of tradables depends only on the household's lifetime tradable wealth, given by the initial bond position and the present discounted value of the endowment of tradables. It is therefore increasing in the current endowment, Q_1^T, in the future endowment, Q_2^T, and in the initial financial wealth, $(1+r_0)B_0$, and decreasing in the interest rate r^*. Notice that the equilibrium value of C_1^T is independent of the exchange rate regime. This result

---

[3] Note that the Euler equation (13.9) does not depend on nontradable consumption. This feature obtains when the intertemporal and intratemporal elasticities of consumption substitution are equal to each other. Our assumption of a logarithmic utility function and a Cobb-Douglas aggregator function is a special case in which these two elasticities are equal to one.

is a consequence of the assumption that preferences are such that the intertemporal and the intratemporal elasticities of consumption substitution are equal to each other (see also footnote 3). We summarize equation (13.15) by writing

$$C_1^T = C^T(\underset{-}{r^*}, \underset{+}{Q_1^T}, \underset{+}{Q_2^T}, \underset{+}{(1+r_0)B_0}). \tag{13.16}$$

Now use this expression and the market-clearing condition (13.13) to eliminate C_1^T and C_1^N from (13.12), to obtain

$$p_1 = \frac{1-\gamma}{\gamma} \frac{C^T(r^*, Q_1^T, Q_2^T, (1+r_0)B_0)}{F(h_1)}. \tag{13.17}$$

The intuition behind this expression is as follows: All else equal, an increase in the relative price of nontradables, p_1, reduces the nontradable consumption, C_1^N. In equilibrium, consumption of nontradable goods must equal nontradable output, $C_1^N = Q_1^N$. In turn, nontradable output is produced with labor, by means of the increasing production function $F(\cdot)$, $Q_1^N = F(h_1)$. Thus, an increase in p_1 is associated with a fall in h_1. In words, an increase in p_1 causes a fall in the demand for nontradable goods, which requires a reduction in employment to clear the market for nontradable goods. We refer to this relationship between p_1 and h_1 as the demand schedule. The demand schedule is a downward-sloping curve in the space (h_1, p_1), as shown in Figure 13.3.

An increase in the world interest rate r^* shifts the demand schedule down and to the left, as shown in the left panel of Figure 13.4. (To avoid clutter, for the remainder of the chapter, we omit the argument $(1+r_0)B_0$, except when we analyze changes in the initial wealth position.) In the figure, the interest rate increases from r^* to $r^{*\prime} > r^*$. The reason why the demand schedule moves to the left is that, by the intertemporal substitution effect, the increase in r^* induces households to save more and consume less in period 1. As a result, at any level of the relative price, p_1, the

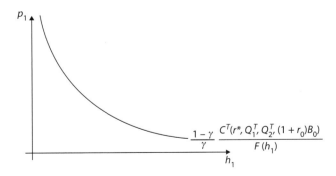

Figure 13.3. The Demand Schedule
Notes: The figure depicts the demand schedule in period 1. Holding constant r^*, Q_1^T, Q_2^T, and $(1+r_0)B_0$, the higher is the relative price of nontradables, p_1, the lower will be the demand for nontradables, C_1^N. If the nontradable market is in equilibrium, a lower demand for nontradables implies lower nontradable output, $F(h_1)$, and hence lower employment, h_1.

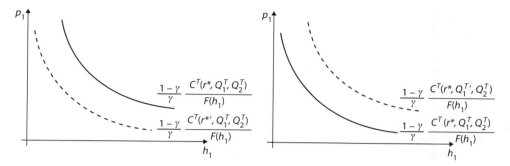

Figure 13.4. Shifters of the Demand Schedule

Notes: The left panel shows that an increase in the world interest rate from r^* to $r^{*\prime} > r^*$ shifts the demand schedule down and to the left. By the intertemporal substitution effect, a higher interest rate reduces the demand for tradable goods, C_1^T, which, for every level of the relative price p_1 lowers the demand for nontradable goods, C_1^N, and thereby the implied demand for labor, h_1. The right panel shows that an increase in the period 1 endowment of tradable goods from Q_1^T to $Q_1^{T\prime} > Q_1^T$ shifts the demand schedule up and to the right. By the income effect, an increase in the endowment increases the demand for tradable and nontradable goods for every level of the relative price p_1 and thereby the demand for labor, h_1.

demand for nontradables is lower; which, for the market for nontradables to clear, requires a reduction in both output, $F(h_1)$, and employment, h_1.

The right panel of Figure 13.4 shows the effect on the demand schedule of an increase in the endowment of tradables in period 1 from Q_1^T to $Q_1^{T\prime} > Q_1^T$. In response to this shock, the demand schedule shifts up and to the right. Intuitively, the increase in the endowment has a positive income effect, which boosts demand for both tradable and nontradable goods for any given price p_1. In turn, for the nontradable market to clear, the expansion in the demand for nontradable goods requires an increase in the production of nontradable goods and employment. The effect of an increase in the endowment of tradables in period 2 (not graphed) is qualitatively identical to an increase in the period 1 endowment. This is because in equilibrium, consumption of tradables is an increasing function of both Q_1^T and Q_2^T.

13.1.3   THE LABOR MARKET SLACKNESS CONDITION

We assume that in periods in which there is involuntary unemployment, $h_t < \bar{h}$, the wage constraint (13.1) is binding; that is, $W_t = W_{t-1}$. The intuition behind this assumption is that involuntary unemployment in period t puts downward pressure on the nominal wage, W_t. As a consequence W_t would be driven down to its lowest possible value, W_{t-1}. We also assume that if the wage constraint is slack— that is, if $W_t > W_{t-1}$—then the economy is operating at full employment, $h_t = \bar{h}$. This makes sense because if, on the contrary, $W_t > W_{t-1}$ and there was involuntary unemployment, $h_t < \bar{h}$, then W_t would fall until either $h_t = \bar{h}$ or $W_t = W_{t-1}$.

We summarize these assumptions by writing

$$(W_t - W_{t-1})(\bar{h} - h_t) = 0. \tag{13.18}$$

This expression is called the *labor market slackness condition*. In this model economy the labor market does not necessarily clear every period. That is, the structure of the labor market leaves open the possibility that under certain circumstances the equilibrium displays excess labor supply, or in other words involuntary unemployment, $h_t < \bar{h}$. This happens when the wage rate cannot adjust to equate the demand and supply of labor, so that employment is rationed. Models in which some markets can fail to clear and rationing occurs in equilibrium are known as *non-Walrasian models*. The TNT-DNWR model belongs to this class. By contrast, models in which prices (in this case the nominal wage) adjust so that all markets clear at all times are known as *neoclassical models*. The TNT-DNWR model collapses to a neoclassical model when conditions (13.1), (13.7), and (13.18) are replaced by the labor market clearing condition $h_t = \bar{h}$ for $t = 1, 2$. Imposing this condition results in the TNT model of Chapter 10. That is, in the present chapter we study a non-Walrasian variant of the TNT model. As discussed earlier and as we will show shortly, the key difference between the TNT-DNWR and the TNT models is that while in the TNT model monetary policy plays no role, in the TNT-DNWR model monetary policy can affect the equilibrium levels of real variables, including output, employment, the real wage, consumption, and the real exchange rate.

13.1.4   EQUILIBRIUM IN THE TNT-DNWR MODEL

Gathering the results obtained thus far, we can define the equilibrium in the TNT-DNWR model as paths for the endogenous variables C_t^T, h_t, W_t, and p_t, for $t = 1, 2$, satisfying

$$C_1^T = \frac{1}{1+\beta}\left[(1+r_0)B_0 + Q_1^T + \frac{Q_2^T}{1+r^*}\right], \tag{13.19}$$

$$C_2^T = \beta(1+r^*)C_1^T, \tag{13.20}$$

$$p_t = \frac{1-\gamma}{\gamma}\frac{C_t^T}{F(h_t)}, \tag{13.21}$$

$$p_t = \frac{W_t/\mathcal{E}_t}{F'(h_t)}, \tag{13.22}$$

$$h_t \leq \bar{h}, \tag{13.23}$$

$$W_t \geq W_{t-1}, \tag{13.24}$$

and

$$(W_t - W_{t-1})(\bar{h} - h_t) = 0, \tag{13.25}$$

given initial conditions W_0 and B_0, an exogenous path for the endowment of tradable goods Q_t^T for $t = 1, 2$, a value for the world interest rate, r^*, and an exchange rate policy $\mathcal{E}_t$ for $t = 1, 2$. You will notice that all of these conditions are repeated from the preceding analysis with the exception of equation (13.21), which results from using the market-clearing condition (13.13) to replace C_t^N with $F(h_t)$ in equations (13.11) and (13.12). The definition of equilibrium given above is useful for solving the TNT-DNWR model analytically or numerically. The appendix to this chapter provides step-by-step directions for how to go about doing this.

With the equilibrium paths of C_t^T, h_t, W_t, and p_t for $t = 1, 2$ in hand, obtaining the equilibrium values for the remaining endogenous variables is straightforward. By the market-clearing condition (13.13), consumption of nontradables equals production of nontradables,

$$C_t^N = F(h_t). \tag{13.26}$$

The trade balance is the difference between tradable output and tradable consumption,

$$TB_t = Q_t^T - C_t^T. \tag{13.27}$$

The country's net foreign asset position at the end of period 1, B_1, is given by

$$B_1 = (1 + r_0)B_0 + TB_1. \tag{13.28}$$

The net foreign asset position at the end of period 2, B_2, is zero because period 2 is the last period of the economy so no one holds assets or debts payable after period 2. The current account in period t, for $t = 1, 2$, equals the change in the country's net foreign asset position,

$$CA_t = B_t - B_{t-1}. \tag{13.29}$$

13.2 Adjustment to Shocks with a Fixed Exchange Rate

Having derived the supply and demand schedules, we now use them to analyze the determination of prices, wages, and employment. Because of the presence of nominal rigidities, the nominal exchange rate will play a central role in the adjustment process.

In this section, we consider a *fixed exchange rate regime*, also known as a *currency peg*. Under a fixed exchange rate regime, the central bank keeps the nominal exchange rate constant over time by standing ready to buy or sell any quantity of foreign currency desired by the public at the predetermined exchange rate. This monetary arrangement may sound rather special but, with nuances, it is quite common. The classic case of a fixed exchange rate policy is one in which the domestic currency is convertible to a foreign currency. For example, between April 1991 and December 2001 Argentina operated under a convertibility law obliging the central bank to exchange 1 Argentine peso for 1 U.S. dollar and vice versa. A variant of convertibility is a *crawling peg*, whereby the central bank specifies a time path of the exchange rate at which the domestic currency is convertible. A second form of a fixed exchange rate occurs when a group of countries forms a currency union. Under this arrangement, the members of the union share a common currency. A case in point is the euro area created in 1999, which introduced the euro as sole legal tender in 11 western European countries. By 2022, the euro area had expanded to 19 countries. Each member of the union has a fixed exchange rate arrangement with the other members. For example, trivially, the exchange rate between the Portuguese currency and the German currency is one. A third version of a fixed exchange rate is dollarization, which occurs when a country unilaterally adopts the currency of another country as legal tender. Examples of dollarization include Ecuador, El Salvador, and Panama, where the U.S. dollar is the official currency. A fourth and more wide spread version of a fixed exchange rate occurs in countries that claim to have a floating exchange rate regime *(de jure floaters)* but in fact keep their exchange rate nearly fixed over time *(de facto peggers)*. Carmen Reinhart and Guillermo Calvo, who first identified this phenomenon, gave it the name *fear of floating*.[4]

To understand how the economy adjusts to shocks under a fixed exchange rate arrangement, suppose that the central bank fixes the exchange rate at the value $\bar{\mathcal{E}}$; that is,

$$\mathcal{E}_t = \bar{\mathcal{E}},$$

for $t = 1, 2$.

13.2.1   AN INCREASE IN THE WORLD INTEREST RATE

Consider the effect of an increase in the world interest rate, r^*. Suppose that prior to the shock the economy has been stable with full employment and a constant nominal wage rate. Thus, prior to the shock $h_1 = \bar{h}$ and $W_1 = W_0$. The equilibrium is as displayed in Figure 13.5. The demand and supply schedules intersect at point A. At this point, there is full employment, $h_1 = \bar{h}$, the relative price of nontradables is p_1^A, and the real wage is $W_0/\bar{\mathcal{E}}$. To avoid clutter, we omit the arguments Q_1^T and Q_2^T in the function $C^T(r^*, Q_1^T, Q_2^T)$ of the demand schedule, as they are held constant throughout this analysis.

Suppose now that the world interest rate increases from r^* to $r^{*\prime} > r^*$. This shock induces households to increase savings and cut consumption of tradable and nontradable goods in period 1. The excess supply of tradable goods created by the decline in domestic demand can be exported. In the nontradable sector, the adjustment is quite different because by definition, nontradable goods cannot be exported; in equilibrium domestic production must equal domestic demand. The contraction in the demand for nontradables therefore puts downward pressure on the relative price of nontradables. Absent nominal rigidities, the price of nontradables would experience a large enough fall to induce households to switch expenditures away from tradables and toward nontradables by an amount large enough to guarantee that all firms continue to operate at full employment. However, the combination of nominal wage rigidity and a fixed exchange rate prevents this adjustment from taking place fully. Because labor costs don't fall, firms cannot cut prices to the necessary degree, as doing so would generate losses and put them out of business. Instead, firms cut production and lay off workers.

---

[4]Guillermo A. Calvo and Carmen M. Reinhart, "Fear of Floating," Quarterly Journal of Economics 117, May 2002, 379–408.

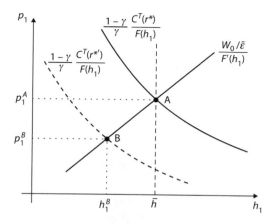

Figure 13.5. Adjustment to an Increase in the World Interest Rate under a Fixed Exchange Rate

Notes: Prior to the increase in the world interest rate from r^* to $r^{*\prime} > r^*$, the equilibrium is at point A, where there is full employment, $h_1 = \bar{h}$. The nominal wage is W_0 and the nominal exchange rate is fixed at $\bar{\mathcal{E}}$. The increase in r^* shifts the demand schedule down and to the left. The supply schedule is unchanged, however, because the combination of downward nominal wage rigidity and a fixed exchange rate prevents a decline in the real wage, $W_0/\bar{\mathcal{E}}$. As a result, unemployment in the amount $\bar{h} - h_1^B$ emerges at the new equilibrium, point B.

The adjustment is illustrated in Figure 13.5. In response to the increase in r^*, the demand schedule shifts down and to the left, as shown by the broken line. The new equilibrium is at point B, where both employment and the relative price of non-tradables are lower, $h_1^B < \bar{h}$ and $p_1^B < p_1^A$. Thus, the increase in the world interest rate causes unemployment in the amount $\bar{h} - h_1^B > 0$. Firms are forced to lay off workers because the real price of the good they sell falls from p_1^A to p_1^B, while labor costs, given by $W_0/\bar{\mathcal{E}}$, remain constant. Unemployment is involuntary, because at the market wage workers would like to work $\bar{h}$ hours. The real wage, $W_0/\bar{\mathcal{E}}$, does not fall to clear the labor market for two reasons: First, the nominal wage cannot fall because it is downwardly rigid; see constraint (13.1). Second, the nominal exchange rate does not increase (the domestic currency does not depreciate) because the central bank follows a fixed exchange rate policy. The presence of two nominal rigidities (in the nominal wage and the nominal exchange rate) gives rise to a real rigidity (in the real wage).

The increase in unemployment following the interest rate hike is welfare decreasing. This is because at point B the economy suffers a fall in the production of nontradable goods, $F(h_1^B) < F(\bar{h})$. In equilibrium the fall in nontradable output implies an equivalent fall in consumption of nontradable goods, which lowers the household's level of utility.

As the equilibrium moves from point A to point B, the country becomes cheaper relative to the rest of the world; that is, the real exchange rate depreciates. To see why, recall from Section 10.2 of Chapter 10 that there is a tight relationship between the relative price of nontradables, p_t, and the real exchange rate,

$$e_t \equiv \frac{\mathcal{E}_t P_t^*}{P_t},$$

where P_t and P_t^* are the consumer price levels in the domestic country and the rest of the world, respectively. As explained there, the essence of this relationship is the following: The country's price level is an average of the price of the tradable good and the price of the nontradable good. The price of the tradable good, when expressed in the same currency, is the same domestically and abroad, by the law of one price. By contrast, the price of the nontradable good is determined by market conditions in each country. This means that an increase in the relative price of the nontraded good in terms of the traded good makes the country more expensive relative to the rest of the world; that is, it is associated with a real exchange rate appreciation. Similarly, a decrease in the relative price of nontradables makes the country cheaper relative to the rest of the world; that is, it is associated with a depreciation of the real exchange rate. Since the relative price of nontradables is decreasing in the world interest rate, the real exchange rate, e_t, is increasing in this variable. We can then write

$$e_t = e(\underset{+}{r^*}). \tag{13.30}$$

In response to the r^* shock, p_1 falls from p_1^A to p_1^B (see Figure 13.5). This means that e_1 depreciates (the country becomes cheaper relative to the rest of the world). However, as we will see next, because of downward nominal wage rigidity, the real depreciation is insufficient in the sense that the economy does not become as cheap as would be necessary to avoid involuntary unemployment.

If the nominal wage were downwardly flexible, it would fall to clear the excess supply of labor created by the contraction in the demand for labor after the interest rate shock. The situation is illustrated in Figure 13.6. The equilibrium before the shock is at point A. The increase in the world interest rate shifts the demand schedule down and to the left. Under wage flexibility, however, the nominal wage falls from W_0 to $W_1 < W_0$. The real wage falls in the same proportion because the nominal exchange rate is fixed at $\bar{\mathcal{E}}$. The new equilibrium is at point C, where full employment is restored. At the new equilibrium, the relative price of nontradables is lower than at point B, the equilibrium with downward nominal wage rigidity. This is because the fall in real labor costs (from $W_0/\bar{\mathcal{E}}$ to $W_1/\bar{\mathcal{E}}$) allows firms to lower the price of the nontradable good. The larger decline in p_1 induces households to engage in a larger expenditure switch away from tradable goods and toward nontradable goods. In fact, the expenditure switch under flexible wages is large enough to support full employment in the nontradable sector.

13.2.2   ASYMMETRIC ADJUSTMENT: A DECREASE IN THE WORLD INTEREST RATE

The TNT-DNWR model has an asymmetry in the response of the nominal wage. Constraint (13.1) says that the wage rate cannot fall, but it imposes no impediments

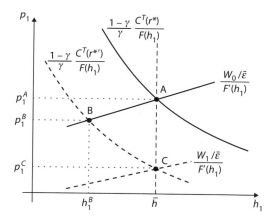

Figure 13.6. Adjustment to an Increase in the World Interest Rate under Wage Flexibility

Notes: Prior to the increase in the world interest rate the equilibrium is at point A, where the labor market operates at full employment. The increase in the world interest rate from r^* to $r^{*\prime}$ shifts the demand schedule down and to the left. Under downward nominal wage rigidity the equilibrium is at point B, where the economy suffers involuntary unemployment. Under wage flexibility, the nominal wage falls from W_0 to W_1, shifting the supply schedule down and to the right. The new equilibrium is at point C, where the economy continues to operate at full employment, and the relative price of nontradables is lower than at the pre-shock equilibrium or at the equilibrium with downward nominal wage rigidity, $p_1^C < p_1^B < p_1^A$.

to wage increases. As a result, the response of other variables to positive and negative shocks need not be symmetric. To see this, consider a decrease in the world interest rate. Figure 13.7 illustrates the adjustment. The initial equilibrium is at point A, where the interest rate is r^* and the economy is at full employment, $h_1 = \bar{h}$. Suppose that the interest rate falls to $r^{*\prime} < r^*$. The fall in the interest rate shifts the demand schedule up and to the right. This is because in response to the fall in r^*, households in period 1 cut saving and increase demand for both tradable and nontradable goods at any given relative price, p_1. At the original wage W_0, the demand and supply schedules would intersect at point B. However, at point B the economy experiences an excess demand for labor equal to $h_1^B - \bar{h} > 0$. This would put upward pressure on the nominal wage. Since the wage is upwardly flexible, it will increase, shifting the supply schedule up and to the left. The new equilibrium is at point C, where the wage rate, W_1, is higher than W_0, and the excess demand for labor is nil. At the new equilibrium, the real wage, $W_1/\bar{\mathcal{E}}$, is higher (recall that the nominal exchange rate is fixed at $\bar{\mathcal{E}}$). The relative price of nontradables is also higher, $p_1^C > p_1^A$. This is because of the expansion in the demand for nontradables and because of the increase in labor costs. In turn, the increase in p_1 implies that the real exchange rate appreciates; that is, that the economy becomes more expensive relative to the rest of the world.

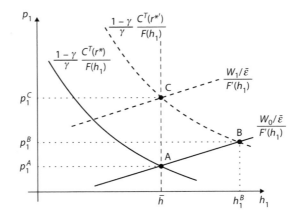

Figure 13.7. Adjustment to a Decrease in the World Interest Rate under a Fixed Exchange Rate

Notes: The nominal exchange rate is fixed at $\bar{\mathcal{E}}$. Prior to the decrease in the world interest rate from r^* to $r^{*\prime} < r^*$, the equilibrium is at point A, where there is full employment, $h_1 = \bar{h}$, and the nominal wage is W_0. The fall in r^* shifts the demand schedule up and to the right. Absent an increase in nominal wages, the equilibrium would be at point B, where labor demand exceeds labor supply, $h_1^B > \bar{h}$. As a result, wages will rise until the excess demand is eliminated. The increase in wages shifts the supply schedule up and to the left. The new equilibrium is at point C, where there is full employment, $h_1 = \bar{h}$, the nominal wage rate is equal to $W_1 > W_0$, and the relative price of nontradables is higher, $p_1^C > p_1^A$.

13.2.3   OUTPUT AND TERMS OF TRADE SHOCKS

When the nominal wage is downwardly rigid and the monetary authority fixes the nominal exchange rate, a fall in the endowment of tradables either in period 1, Q_1^T, or in period 2, Q_2^T, or in both periods, causes involuntary unemployment. To see this, take a look at Figure 13.8. The economy is initially at point A, where there is full employment, $h_1 = \bar{h}$, and the relative price of nontradables equals p_1^A. Suppose that the endowment of tradables in period 1 falls from Q_1^T to $Q_1^{T\prime} < Q_1^T$. This shock shifts the demand schedule down and to the left, as shown with a broken line. (For visual clarity, the figure omits the arguments r^* and Q_2^T from $C^T(r^*, Q_1^T, Q_2^T)$.) The supply schedule does not change position because neither the wage rate nor the nominal exchange rate changes. The former cannot fall, in spite of the contractionary effect of the shock, because of downward nominal wage rigidity, and the latter does not change because, under a currency peg, the central bank is committed to keeping it constant over time. The new equilibrium is therefore at point B, where the new demand schedule intersects the supply schedule. At point B, the economy suffers involuntary unemployment in the amount $\bar{h} - h_1^B > 0$ and the real exchange rate depreciates, $p_1^B < p_1^A$. Intuitively, the fall in the endowment of tradables makes households poorer, so they cut their desired demand for both types of goods, tradable and nontradable. The fall in the demand for nontradables induces a contraction in the demand for labor by firms. Market clearing in the labor market

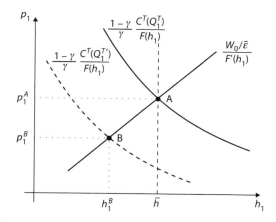

Figure 13.8. Adjustment to a Fall in Tradable Output under a Fixed Exchange Rate

Notes: Prior to the fall in tradable output from Q_1^T to $Q_1^{T'} < Q_1^T$, the equilibrium is at point A, where there is full employment, $h_1 = \bar{h}$. The nominal wage is W_0 and the nominal exchange rate is fixed at $\bar{\mathcal{E}}$. The decrease in Q_1^T shifts the demand schedule down and to the left. The supply schedule is unchanged, however, because the combination of downward nominal wage rigidity and a fixed exchange rate prevents a decline in the real wage, $W_0/\bar{\mathcal{E}}$. As a result, unemployment in the amount $\bar{h} - h_1^B$ emerges at the new equilibrium, point B.

requires a fall in the real wage. However, the combination of downward nominal wage rigidity and a fixed exchange rate prevents this from happening. The result is an excess supply of labor in equilibrium.

The effect of an anticipated fall in the endowment of tradables in period 2, Q_2^T, is qualitatively identical. This is because changes in Q_1^T and Q_2^T shift the demand for tradable goods, $C^T(r^*, Q_1^T, Q_2^T)$, in the same direction. Further, a deterioration in the terms of trade—a fall in the relative price of exports in terms of imports—has the same effect as a contraction in the endowment of tradables. You might recall from Chapter 4 that changes in the terms of trade have the same effects on the demand for tradable goods as changes in the endowment of tradables. Thus, if we assume that Q_1^T and Q_2^T represent the endowments of oil in periods 1 and 2 and TT_1 and TT_2 represent the relative price of oil in terms of wheat (the consumption good, now imported), then a fall in TT_1 causes unemployment and a real exchange rate depreciation just like a fall in Q_1^T does. Intuitively, in deciding how much to save and consume, households do not care whether their period 1 income, $TT_1 Q_1^T$, falls because the world price of oil falls (because of a large oil discovery in a third country, say) or because the domestic country's endowment of oil falls (because of the breaking of an oil pipeline, say). The same is true for the effect of anticipated changes in the terms of trade in period 2, TT_2. In sum, when the endowment (oil) is a different good from the traded consumption good (wheat), the demand function for tradable consumption goods takes the form $C^T(r^*, TT_1 Q_1^T, TT_2 Q_2^T)$. All other elements of the model are unchanged. So what matters is the value of the tradable endowment each period, $TT_1 Q_1^T$ and $TT_2 Q_2^T$, rather than the breakdown into price and quantity.

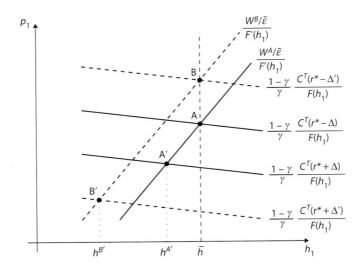

Figure 13.9. Volatility and Average Unemployment under a Fixed Exchange Rate
Notes: The figure illustrates the effect of an increase in volatility of the world interest rate on average unemployment. In the low volatility environment, the interest rate
fluctuates between $r^* + \Delta$ and $r^* - \Delta$, and the equilibrium level of employment fluctuates between $h^{A'}$ and $\bar{h}$. In the high volatility environment, the interest rate fluctuates
between $r^* + \Delta'$ and $r^* - \Delta'$, where $\Delta' > \Delta$, and the equilibrium level of employment
between $h^{B'}$ and $\bar{h}$. The average rate of unemployment is larger in the high volatility
environment.

13.2.4   VOLATILITY AND AVERAGE UNEMPLOYMENT

We have seen that under a fixed exchange rate regime, the adjustment of the economy to positive and negative shocks is asymmetric. For example, a fall in the world
interest rate causes an increase in wages, whereas an increase in the world interest
rate is not accompanied by a decline in the nominal wage but instead by an increase
in involuntary unemployment. As a result, over the business cycle, the economy
fluctuates between periods of unemployment, $h_t < \bar{h}$, and periods with full employment, $h_t = \bar{h}$. On average, therefore, the economy experiences unemployment; that
is, on average, h_t is less than $\bar{h}$.

Furthermore, the larger the size of the shocks buffeting the economy is, the larger
the rate of unemployment during contractions will be. This means that an economy
with more volatile shocks will experience a higher average level of unemployment.
The positive relationship between volatility and average unemployment is illustrated in Figure 13.9. Consider two world interest rate environments, a tranquil one
and a turbulent one. In both environments the interest rate fluctuates over time, but
it fluctuates more widely in the turbulent one.

Consider first the tranquil interest rate environment. In this environment, the
interest rate is r^* on average, but it fluctuates between $r^* + \Delta$ and $r^* - \Delta$, where
$\Delta > 0$ is a parameter reflecting the volatility of the world interest rate. Suppose that
the nominal exchange rate is pegged at $\bar{\mathcal{E}}$ and that the nominal wage rate is W^A.

In the figure, when the interest rate is $r^* - \Delta$ the equilibrium is at point A, where the economy enjoys full employment. When the interest rate increases to $r^* + \Delta$, the demand schedule shifts down and to the left and the supply schedule remains unchanged (because the wage rate is downwardly rigid, and the nominal exchange rate is pegged). The new equilibrium is at point A', and the economy suffers involuntary unemployment in the amount $\bar{h} - h^{A'}$. If the world interest rate is half of the time $r^* - \Delta$ and half of the time $r^* + \Delta$, the average rate of unemployment is positive and equal to $(\bar{h} - h^{A'})/2$.

Consider now the turbulent interest rate environment. Suppose that for some reason (say, a war in some parts of the world that exacerbates global economic uncertainty) the world interest rate is highly volatile. Specifically, suppose that the world interest rate continues to be r^* on average, but that it now fluctuates between $r^* + \Delta'$ and $r^* - \Delta'$, with $\Delta' > \Delta$. When the interest rate is at its new low, $r^* - \Delta'$, the equilibrium is at point B in Figure 13.9. At point B the economy operates at full employment, and the wage rate is $W^B > W^A$. When the interest rate is at its new high value, $r^* + \Delta'$, the equilibrium is at point B', and the economy experiences unemployment in the amount $\bar{h} - h^{B'}$. If the interest rate is with equal probability at $r^* + \Delta'$ and $r^* - \Delta'$, the average rate of unemployment is $(\bar{h} - h^{B'})/2$. Since $h^{B'}$ is lower than $h^{A'}$, we have that the average rate of unemployment is larger in the turbulent environment, in spite of the fact that the average interest rate is the same in both environments.

We conclude that under downward nominal wage rigidity and a fixed exchange rate regime, the average rate of unemployment is increasing in the amount of uncertainty in the economy.

13.3 Adjustment to Shocks with a Floating Exchange Rate

We now consider a policy regime in which the nominal exchange rate is flexible. This type of exchange rate arrangement is also known as a *floating exchange rate regime*. Under a floating exchange rate regime, the nominal exchange rate can change over time. There is an infinite number of floating exchange rate regimes, depending on how much the central bank allows the exchange rate to move. In this section, we focus on a particular member of this large family.

Specifically, we assume that the central bank conducts monetary policy to ensure full employment and price stability. A *dual mandate* of this type is common for central banks around the world. Generally, central banks aim to stabilize what is known as *core inflation*, a measure of inflation of a basket of goods that excludes food and energy. The motivation for using core inflation as the policy target is that food and energy prices tend to be volatile, blurring the trend path of the overall price level. Changes in the prices of food and energy often reverse themselves quickly, without requiring a monetary policy action.

The bulk of food and energy products are internationally traded commodities. In terms of the model analyzed in this chapter, food and energy products would be represented by C_t^T and Q_t^T. For example, if we assume, as we just did in subsection 13.2.3, that the tradable consumption good, C_t^T, is wheat and that the tradable

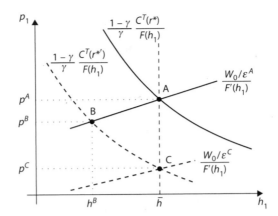

Figure 13.10. Adjustment to an Increase in the World Interest Rate with a Floating Exchange Rate

Notes: Prior to the increase in the world interest rate the equilibrium is at point A, where the labor market operates at full employment, the nominal wage is W_0, the nominal exchange rate is $\mathcal{E}^A$, and the nominal price of nontradables is $W_0/F'(\bar{h})$. The increase in the world interest rate from r^* to $r^{*\prime}$ shifts the demand schedule down and to the left. Absent a change in the exchange rate, the equilibrium would be at point B, where employment is $h^B < \bar{h}$. The central bank can achieve its objectives of full employment and price stability by depreciating the exchange rate to $\mathcal{E}^C > \mathcal{E}^A$. At point C, $h_1 = \bar{h}$ and $P_1^N = W_0/F'(\bar{h})$, which are the same values as at point A.

endowment good, Q_t^T, is oil, then food would be C_t^T and energy would be Q_t^T. In any case, in the context of the model, a central bank that targets a price index that excludes food and energy would focus on stabilizing the price of nontradable goods, P_t^N. Achieving the two objectives of the central bank will in general require the nominal exchange rate to move in response to shocks impinging on the economy. The resulting exchange rate regime will therefore belong to the family of floating exchange rates.

13.3.1   ADJUSTMENT TO EXTERNAL SHOCKS

Consider the adjustment of the economy to external shocks such as the world interest rate or the terms of trade, when the monetary authority, trying to achieve its full employment and price stability goals, allows the nominal exchange rate to float.

Suppose that in period 1 the world interest rate increases from r^* to $r^{*\prime} > r^*$. The effect of this shock is depicted in Figure 13.10. Initially, the economy is at point A, where there is full employment, $h_1 = \bar{h}$, the nominal exchange rate is $\mathcal{E}_1 = \mathcal{E}^A$, and the relative price of the nontraded good is $p_1 = p^A$. From the firm's optimality condition (13.3), it follows that at point A the nominal price of nontradables, P_1^N, is equal to $W_0/F'(\bar{h})$. The increase in the world interest rate shifts the demand schedule down and to the left. If the central bank were to keep the nominal exchange rate pegged at $\mathcal{E}^A$, the new equilibrium would be at point B, with involuntary unemployment, $h^B < \bar{h}$. The presence of involuntary unemployment would put downward pressure on the nominal wage, but downward nominal wage rigidity would prevent the wage from falling. At point B, both the relative and the nominal price of nontradables is lower, $p^B < p^A$, and $P_1^N = W_0/F'(h^B) < W_0/F'(\bar{h})$ (recall that $F(\cdot)$ is concave). Thus, at point B both objectives of the central bank, full employment and price stability, are compromised.

To achieve its objectives, the central bank must let the currency depreciate. An increase in $\mathcal{E}_1$ shifts the supply schedule down and to the right. The position of the demand schedule is unaffected. Thus, a devaluation moves the intersection of the demand and supply schedules to the right. The exchange rate that restores full employment and price stability is $\mathcal{E}^C$, which makes the new supply schedule intersect with the new demand schedule exactly at $\bar{h}$, point C in Figure 13.10. At point C, the nominal price of nontradables, P_1^N, is the same as at point A, namely, $W_0/F'(\bar{h})$. This means that by letting the currency depreciate, the monetary authority achieves both of its objectives.

The intuition behind why a devaluation is necessary to achieve full employment when the economy is hit by an increase in the world interest rate is as follows. The higher interest rate causes a reduction in desired private consumption in period 1, as households have an incentive to postpone spending and increase saving. Given the relative price of nontradables, households would cut their demand for both types of goods, tradable and nontradable. Faced with a fall in the demand for their product, firms reduce their demand for labor. Since workers continue to supply $\bar{h}$ hours of labor, equilibrium in the labor market would require that the real wage, $W_0/\mathcal{E}_1$, fall. In turn, a fall in the real wage requires either a fall in the nominal wage, W_0, or a currency depreciation, an increase in $\mathcal{E}_1$. Because the nominal wage is downwardly rigid, the only way in which the real wage can fall and full employment can be restored is via a depreciation.

The size of the currency depreciation that achieves both policy objectives is uniquely pinned down. To see this, suppose that the central bank depreciates the currency by less than $\mathcal{E}^C - \mathcal{E}^A$ (see again Figure 13.10). In this case, the supply schedule would experience a smaller shift to the right than the one shown in the figure, and the equilibrium would occur at a point between points B and C on the new demand schedule. The equilibrium would feature involuntary unemployment and a fall in P_1^N. So the central bank would fall short of achieving its goals.

Suppose instead that the government depreciates the currency by more than $\mathcal{E}^C - \mathcal{E}^A$. In this case, the supply schedule would shift to the right by more than shown in the figure and would intersect the new demand schedule at a point located to the right and below point C. At such a point, the economy would experience an excess demand for labor that would push the nominal wage up. The increase in the wage rate would push the supply schedule back to the left. The excess demand will disappear and the nominal wage will stop rising when the supply schedule crosses the new demand schedule at point C. Let the new nominal wage be $W_1 > W_0$. Thus, an excessive depreciation does achieve the full employment objective of the central bank. But what about the price stability objective? The nominal price of the nontradable good, P_1^N, would be $W_1/F'(\bar{h})$. Since W_1 is greater than W_0, we have that an excessive depreciation causes price inflation in the nontraded sector, so that the central bank would fail to achieve its price stability goal.

The adjustment to current or future expected changes in the endowment of tradable goods (Q_1^T or Q_2^T) or in the country's terms of trade (TT_1 or TT_2) under the present floating exchange rate regime is qualitatively the same as the adjustment to changes in the world interest rate. This is because r^*, Q_t^T, and TT_t all affect the economy only through their effect on the desired consumption of tradable goods, $C^T(r^*, TT_1 Q_1^T, TT_2 Q_2^T)$. We therefore conclude that in response to a fall in the endowment of tradable goods or a deterioration of the terms of trade in period 1 or 2, a central bank whose objectives are to maintain full employment and stability in the price of nontradables would let the domestic currency depreciate.

It is important to note that the currency depreciation cannot completely undo the contractionary effects of negative external shocks. Specifically, the depreciation cannot avoid a contraction in the demand for tradable goods, $C^T(r^*, TT_1 Q_1^T, TT_2 Q_2^T)$, that results from an increase in r^* or from a fall in $TT_t Q_t^T$ for $t = 1$ or 2. The role of the depreciation is to prevent the contraction in the tradable sector created by an external shock from spilling over to the nontradable sector. Put differently, the depreciation prevents the negative effect of an adverse shock from becoming even larger. In this regard, the depreciation plays a significant but limited role in stabilizing the economy. This result is important because it helps us to correctly interpret the empirical evidence, and not arrive at spurious conclusions about the role of changes in the exchange rate over the business cycle. To see this, suppose that you are given the task of analyzing macroeconomic data from some country. Suppose that you observe that periods in which aggregate demand is depressed coincide with periods in which the currency experiences devaluations. Concluding from this evidence that devaluations are contractionary may be misleading. As the analysis in this section suggests, if the contractions in aggregate demand are the results of negative external shocks (hikes in the interest rate that the country faces in world financial markets, deteriorations in the terms of trade, or drops in the country's output of exportable goods due to adverse weather conditions), devaluations could be exactly the opposite of contractionary. In this case, the correct interpretation of the data would not be that devaluations are contractionary, but rather that contractions are devaluatory.

13.3.2 SUPPLY SHOCKS, THE INFLATION-UNEMPLOYMENT TRADE-OFF, AND STAGFLATION

Thus far, we have analyzed shocks that shift the demand schedule. We established that in response to such shocks, appropriate movements in the nominal exchange rate can achieve both objectives of the central bank—price stability and full employment. In this section, we study shocks that can create a policy conflict, in the sense that attainment of both objectives is impossible. In response to such shocks, the monetary authority has to choose between fulfilling one objective or the other or fulfilling both only partially.

Consider, for example, a shock to the supply of nontradables. Specifically, suppose that now the production function of nontradables takes the form

$$Q_t^N = A_t F(h_t),$$

where A_t is an exogenous productivity factor, reflecting a variety of determinants of productivity in the nontraded sector, such as changes in the pace of technological progress or government regulation. We can interpret the model studied thus far as a special case in which $A_t = 1$ for $t = 1, 2$. For simplicity, suppose that $F(h_t)$ takes the form h_t^α, where $\alpha \in (0, 1)$ is a parameter. Then we have that nontradable output is given by

$$Q_t^N = A_t h_t^\alpha.$$

This production technology is increasing in h_t and concave.

Consider the effect of a negative productivity shock in period 1; that is, a reduction in A_1. This movement in A_1 represents a negative supply shock in the nontraded sector because, given the level of employment, it reduces output and increases the marginal cost of production. Higher marginal costs of production put upward pressure on prices and discourage employment. As we will see, these two forces create a trade-off between inflation and unemployment, which the monetary authority must negotiate.

Suppose that prior to the negative productivity shock, the nominal wage is $W_1 = W_0$. From the optimality condition (13.3), we then have that

$$P_1^N \alpha A_1 h_1^{\alpha-1} = W_0. \tag{13.31}$$

In this expression, $\alpha A_1 h_1^{\alpha-1}$ is the marginal product of labor in period 1. So, like equation (13.3), this expression says that firms hire workers up to the point where the value of the marginal product of labor (the left-hand side) equals the marginal cost of labor (the right-hand side).

Suppose that before the shock the economy is at full employment, so that $h_1 = \bar{h}$. It follows from (13.31) that if the central bank fulfills its price stability goal (i.e., keeps P_1^N constant), the fall in A_1 has to result in either a contraction in employment (a fall in h_1) or a fall in the nominal wage. Due to downward nominal wage rigidity, the nominal wage cannot fall. As a result, maintaining price stability necessitates a decline in employment.

If instead the central bank decides to prioritize full employment, then we see from equation (13.31) that either the price level, P_1^N, must increase or the nominal wage must decrease. Again, a fall in the nominal wage is negated because nominal wages are downwardly rigid. Thus, if the central bank prioritizes full employment, the fall in productivity is inflationary.

In the two policy options we analyzed, in response to the negative productivity shock in the nontraded sector, the central bank must resign either the price stability goal or the full employment goal. In other words, the objective of price stability is in conflict with the objective of full employment and vice versa. The central bank can also achieve a range of intermediate outcomes in which the economy experiences some unemployment and some inflation. When an economy experiences simultaneously unemployment and inflation it is said to suffer from *stagflation*.

Let's analyze now how exchange rate policy can achieve the desired compromise. To achieve price stability, the central bank must appreciate the domestic currency;

that is, it must bring about a fall in the nominal exchange rate $\mathcal{E}_1$. To see this, write equilibrium condition (13.17) as

$$\frac{P_1^N}{\mathcal{E}_1} = \frac{1-\gamma}{\gamma} \frac{C^T(r^*, Q_1^T, Q_2^T)}{A_1 h_1^\alpha}. \tag{13.32}$$

Using (13.31) to eliminate P_1^N from this expression gives

$$\frac{W_0}{\mathcal{E}_1} = \frac{1-\gamma}{\gamma} \frac{\alpha C^T(r^*, Q_1^T, Q_2^T)}{h_1}.$$

In this expression, all variables are constant, except for $\mathcal{E}_1$ and h_1. As we just showed, maintaining price stability implies a fall in h_1. It follows from the above equation that $\mathcal{E}_1$ falls—that is, the currency appreciates.

Intuitively, a decline in productivity in the nontradable sector (a fall in A_1) reduces the supply of the nontradable good causing an increase in its relative price (an increase in $p_1 = P_1^N/\mathcal{E}_1$). In turn, an increase in the relative price of nontradables can occur either by an increase in the nominal price of nontradables (an increase in P_1^N) or by a fall in the nominal price of tradables (a fall in $\mathcal{E}_1$). Since the monetary authority chooses to stabilize the nominal price of nontradables, the increase in the relative price of nontradables must necessarily occur via a fall in the nominal price of tradables, or a nominal exchange rate appreciation.

Suppose now that in response to the fall in productivity in the nontraded sector, the central bank opts to defend its full employment mandate; that is, it decides to keep h_1 at $\bar{h}$. We have already shown that this requires letting the price of nontradables, P_1^N, increase. To see what exchange rate is compatible with full employment, note that by equilibrium condition (13.31), under full employment and given W_0, the product $P_1^N A_1$ does not change in response to the fall in productivity. Now evaluate the demand schedule (13.32) at $h_1 = \bar{h}$ to get

$$\frac{P_1^N}{\mathcal{E}_1} = \frac{1-\gamma}{\gamma} \frac{C^T(r^*, Q_1^T, Q_2^T)}{A_1 \bar{h}^\alpha}.$$

Taken together, this expression and the fact that $P_1^N A_1$ is unchanged imply that the nominal exchange rate is unaffected by the decline in A_1. Thus, keeping the nominal exchange rate constant in response to a fall in productivity in the nontraded sector ensures full employment. This result is somewhat special. It is a consequence of assuming that the utility function is log-linear in consumption and that the aggregator function is Cobb-Douglas. Relaxing these assumptions can result in either a depreciation or an appreciation. Exercise 13.5 addresses this issue.

In sum, we have shown that when the economy is hit by a negative productivity shock in the nontraded sector, it can maintain price stability at the cost of some unemployment or it can maintain full employment at the cost of some price inflation. The central bank can also allow for some inflation and some unemployment. In this case, the economy experiences stagflation. In the present environment, stagflation occurs when in response to the fall in productivity in the nontraded sector, the central bank appreciates the currency but by less than is required to maintain price stability.

In this section we have shown that the central bank must induce appropriate changes in the exchange rate to achieve its goals of (or compromises between) full employment and price stability in response to various shocks. But how can the central bank engineer these exchange rate movements? In practice, the central bank can do this either directly or indirectly. In the former case, the central bank announces a level for the nominal exchange rate, which might depend on the realization of the different shocks, and stands ready to buy or sell any quantity of foreign currency desired by the private sector at the announced exchange rate. In the latter case, the central bank affects the foreign exchange market by altering the domestic nominal interest rate. Sections 13.5 and 13.6 shed light on how changes in the nominal interest rate affect the nominal exchange rate.

13.4   A Numerical Example: A World Interest Rate Hike

Let's analyze numerically the effects of an increase in the world interest rate, r^*, under a fixed and a floating exchange rate regime.

Suppose that the endowment of tradable goods is 1 in both periods, $Q_1^T = Q_2^T = 1$, that the time endowment is 1, $\bar{h} = 1$, that the initial net foreign asset position is 0, $B_0 = 0$, that the world interest rate is 25 percent, $r^* = 0.25$, that the initial nominal wage is 0.75, $W_0 = 0.75$, that the subjective discount factor is 0.8, $\beta = 0.8$, and that the parameter of the Cobb-Douglas consumption aggregator is 0.5, $\gamma = 0.5$. Assume that the production technology for nontradables takes the form

$$F(h_t) = h_t^\alpha$$

and that α is 0.75. Table 13.1 summarizes the calibration of the TNT-DNWR model.

Table 13.1. Numerical Example: Calibration

Parameter	Value	Description
Q_1^T	1	Endowment of tradable goods in period 1
Q_2^T	1	Endowment of tradable goods in period 2
$\bar{h}$	1	Time endowment
B_0	0	Net foreign asset position at beginning of period 1
r^*	0.25	World interest rate
W_0	0.75	Nominal wage in period 0
β	0.8	Subjective discount factor
γ	0.5	Expenditure share of tradable consumption
α	0.75	Labor share in the nontraded sector

Suppose that initially the economy is in an equilibrium in which the nominal exchange rate is equal to 1 in both periods

$$\mathcal{E}_1 = \mathcal{E}_2 = 1.$$

13.4.1 THE PRE-SHOCK EQUILIBRIUM

From equilibrium conditions (13.19)–(13.20), we have that the equilibrium path of tradable consumption is given by

$$C_1^T = \frac{1}{1+\beta}\left[Q_1^T + \frac{Q_2^T}{1+r^*}\right]$$

$$= \frac{1}{1+0.8}\left[1 + \frac{1}{1+0.25}\right]$$

$$= 1$$

and

$$C_2^T = \beta(1+r^*)C_1^T$$

$$= 0.8 \times (1+0.25) \times 1$$

$$= 1.$$

Intuitively, in this economy the subjective discount factor β and the financial-market discount factor $1/(1+r^*)$ are equal to each other, so households choose a smooth path of tradable consumption. Since the endowment of tradables is the same in both periods and the household starts with no assets or debts, the only way to have a flat path for tradable consumption is to consume the endowment in each period. Accordingly, the trade balance is nil in both periods, $TB_t = Q_t^T - C_t^T = 0$, for $t = 1, 2$. It follows that the household chooses not to borrow or lend in the international financial market even though it has free access to it. The country's net foreign asset position at the end of period 1 is therefore equal to zero, $B_1 = 0$. The current accounts in both periods are also zero, $CA_1 = r_0 B_0 + TB_1 = 0$ and $CA_2 = r^* B_1 + TB_2 = 0$.

Let's guess that the equilibrium features full employment in both periods, $h_1 = h_2 = \bar{h} = 1$. We must check that equilibrium conditions (13.21)–(13.25) hold for $t = 1, 2$. Clearly, this guess implies that the time constraint (13.23) and the slackness condition (13.25) are satisfied in both periods. From the demand schedule (13.21) we have that under the guess, the relative price of nontradables is 1, $p_t = 1$. Next solve the supply schedule (13.22) for the nominal wage

$$W_t = p_t \mathcal{E}_t F'(h_t)$$

$$= p_t \mathcal{E}_t \alpha h_t^{\alpha-1}$$

$$= 0.75,$$

which is the same as W_0. Therefore, the downward wage rigidity constraint (13.24) is satisfied. This completes the proof that the pre-shock equilibrium features full employment in both periods.

13.4.2   ADJUSTMENT WITH A FIXED EXCHANGE RATE

Suppose now that the world interest rate increases to 50 percent, $r^{*'} = 0.5$. Suppose further that the central bank follows a fixed exchange rate regime whereby $\mathcal{E}_t = 1$ for $t = 1, 2$. By equilibrium conditions (13.19) and (13.20), $C_1^T = 0.9259$ and $C_2^T = 1.1111$. With higher interest rates, households choose to consume more in period 2 and less in period 1; C_1^T falls 7.4 percent and C_2^T increases by 11 percent. As a result, the trade balance improves to $TB_1 = 0.0741$ in period 1 and deteriorates to $TB_2 = -0.1111$ in period 2. The trade surplus in period 1 generates an improvement in the country's net foreign asset position from 0 to $B_1 = (1 + r_0)B_0 + TB_1 = TB_1 = 0.0741$. The current account in period 1 is $CA_1 = B_1 - B_0 = B_1 = 0.0741$. The current account in period 2 is $CA_2 = B_2 - B_1 = -B_1 = -0.0741$.

The increase in the world interest rate lowers not only the demand for tradable goods in period 1 but also the demand for nontradable goods. In turn, facing a weaker demand, firms wish to hire fewer workers. This puts downward pressure on the real wage, $W_1 / \mathcal{E}_1$. Since $\mathcal{E}_1$ is fixed, there will be downward pressure on the nominal wage rate, W_1. We therefore guess that the downward nominal wage constraint is binding; that is, we guess $W_1 = W_0 = 0.75$. Again, we need to check that equilibrium conditions (13.21)–(13.25) are satisfied. Obviously, equilibrium condition (13.24) holds and so does the slackness condition (13.25). Combining (13.21) and (13.22) to eliminate p_1 and solving for h_1 yields $h_1 = 0.9259$. Thus, the interest rate hike generates 7.4 percent of involuntary unemployment. Since $h_1 < 1$, the time constraint (13.23) is satisfied. Now evaluate either equation (13.21) or equation (13.22) to obtain $p_1 = 0.9809$. Intuitively, the relative price of nontradables falls because the interest rate hike weakens the demand for nontradables. As a result, the economy becomes cheaper relative to the rest of the world, or the real exchange rate depreciates. From the definition of the relative price of nontradables, $p_1 \equiv P_1^N / \mathcal{E}_1$, and the fact that $\mathcal{E}_1 = 1$, it follows that $P_1^N = p_1 = 0.9809$. So in response to the interest rate hike, the TNT-DNWR economy experiences deflation in core prices of 1.91 percent.

Consider now equilibrium in period 2. The increase in the world interest rate induces households to substitute demand for goods away from period 1 and toward period 2. Thus, it makes sense to conjecture that in period 2 the economy returns to full employment, $h_2 = \bar{h} = 1$. One more time we need to check that equilibrium conditions (13.21)–(13.25) hold; this time, for period 2. Trivially, the time constraint (13.23) and the slackness condition (13.25) hold. Evaluate the demand schedule (13.21) at $t = 2$ to obtain $p_2 = 1.1111$. Thus, as the economy recovers from the recession in period 1, the real exchange rate appreciates and the economy becomes more expensive. Solve the supply schedule (13.22) in period 2 for the nominal wage to get $W_2 = 0.8333$, so the recovery brings about an increase in the nominal wage and because the exchange rate is pegged, also an increase in the real wage measured in units of tradables. Since $W_2 > W_1$, we have that the downward nominal wage constraint (13.24) is satisfied in period 2. The nominal price of nontradables, P_2^N, increases by the same proproportion as p_2 because the nominal exchange rate, $\mathcal{E}_2$, is fixed at 1.

Table 13.2. Effects of an Interest Rate Hike in the
TNT-DNWR Model: A Numerical Example

		Post-Shock Equilibrium	
	Pre-Shock Equilibrium	Fixed Exchange Rate	Floating Exchange Rate
r^*	0.25	0.5	0.5
$\mathcal{E}_1$	1	1	1.0800
$\mathcal{E}_2$	1	1	0.9000
h_1	1	0.9259	1
h_2	1	1	1
$W_1/\mathcal{E}_1$	0.75	0.75	0.6944
$W_2/\mathcal{E}_2$	0.75	0.8333	0.8333
W_1	0.75	0.75	0.75
W_2	0.75	0.8333	0.75
p_1	1	0.9809	0.9259
p_2	1	1.1111	1.1111
P_1^N	1	0.9809	1
P_2^N	1	1.1111	1
C_1^T	1	0.9259	0.9259
C_2^T	1	1.1111	1.1111
TB_1	0	0.0741	0.0741
TB_2	0	−0.1111	−0.1111
CA_1	0	0.0741	0.0741
CA_2	0	−0.0741	−0.0741
B_1	0	0.0741	0.0741

Notes: The table displays the quantitative effects of an increase in the world interest rate, r^*, from 25 percent to 50 percent in the TNT-DNWR model. The calibration of the model is shown in Table 13.1.

The adjustment of the TNT-DNWR economy to the world interest rate hike under a fixed exchange rate regime is summarized in Table 13.2. The increase in the interest rate causes a contraction in aggregate demand in period 1, so consumption of tradables and nontradables falls. This causes involuntary unemployment, a depreciation of the real exchange rate, improvements in the trade balance, the current account, and the country's net foreign asset position in period 1, and deflation in core prices. In period 2, the economy recovers. Consumption of tradables and nontradables is higher than in period 1 and full employment is restored. The recovery is accompanied by a real exchange rate appreciation and a rise in nominal and real wages and core inflation.

13.4.3   ADJUSTMENT WITH A FLOATING EXCHANGE RATE

In response to the interest rate hike, the central bank can bring about a much bet-ter outcome than the one associated with a currency peg. As we analyzed graphically in Section 13.3.1, the central bank can fulfill its dual mandate of full employment and stable core prices in both periods by depreciating the currency during the downturn in period 1 and appreciating it during the recovery in period 2.

Let's confirm that the equilibrium features a constant nominal price of nontrad-ables, $P_t^N = 1$, and full employment, $h_t = \bar{h} = 1$, for $t = 1, 2$. In our economy the path of consumption of tradables is independent of monetary policy, so we continue to have that $C_1^T = 0.9259$ and $C_2^T = 1.1111$. It remains to check that equilibrium conditions (13.21)–(13.25) are satisfied. Clearly, the time constraint (13.23) and the slackness condition (13.25) hold for $t = 1, 2$ because the economy operates at full employment in both periods. Set p_t to satisfy equilibrium condition (13.21). This yields $p_1 = 0.9259$ and $p_2 = 1.1111$. Note that in the period of the inter-est rate hike, the relative price of nontradables falls by more under the floating exchange rate regime than under the peg. As explained earlier this allows for a larger expenditure switch away from tradables and toward nontradables, which contributes to maintaining full employment. Also because the nominal price of nontradables is constant, all of the real depreciation (fall in p_1) must be brought about by a nominal depreciation. Specifically, $\mathcal{E}_1 = 1.0800$, which means that the domestic currency depreciates by 8 percent. When the economy recovers in period 2, the real exchange rate appreciates ($p_2 > p_1$). Again, all of this real appreciation must come from a nominal appreciation. The nominal exchange rate in period 2 is $\mathcal{E}_2 = 0.9000$, which implies a nominal appreciation of 16.67 percent between peri-ods 1 and 2. The supply schedule (13.22) implies that $P_t^N = W_t/(\alpha \bar{h}^{\alpha-1})$, which in turn implies that $W_t = \alpha = W_0$ for $t = 1, 2$. Hence, the downward nominal wage rigidity constraint (13.24) is satisfied in both periods. This completes the proof that the equilibrium features full employment and core price stability. The fact that the nominal wage is constant over time implies that the real wage expressed in terms of tradables, $W_t/\mathcal{E}_t$, is inversely proportional to the nominal exchange rate. In par-ticular, the 8 percent depreciation of the domestic currency in period 1 causes the real wage to fall from 0.75 to 0.6944. This fall in the real cost of labor allows firms to maintain full employment in period 1 in spite of the contraction in aggregate demand following the interest rate hike. The last column of Table 13.2 summarizes these results.

13.4.4   THE WELFARE COST OF A CURRENCY PEG

The household is better off in the economy with the flexible exchange rate than in the economy with the currency peg. To see why this is so, note first that the path of tradable consumption is the same under both exchange rate regimes. However, consumption of nontradables is lower in period 1 under the peg than under the float. This is because in period 1, the currency peg economy experiences involun-tary unemployment, which implies a lower level of production and consumption of nontradable goods.

We have already calculated the equilibrium levels of consumption of tradables and nontradables in both periods and under both exchange rate regimes. We can therefore calculate the level of utility for each exchange rate regime. To this end, first evaluate the consumption aggregator function (13.6) to obtain the path of total consumption, C_t, for $t = 1, 2$. Letting C_t^p for $t = 1, 2$ denote the level of consumption under the peg and C_t^f for $t = 1, 2$ the level of consumption under flexible exchange rates, we obtain $C_1^p = 0.9349$, $C_1^f = 0.9623$, and $C_2^p = C_2^f = 1.0541$. Consumption is the same in period 2 under the peg and the float, because in period 2 the economy operates at full employment in both regimes and because, as we already mentioned, consumption of tradables is also the same across regimes. We are now ready to compute lifetime utility under each regime. Evaluating the lifetime utility function (13.5) using the path of consumption for each regime yields -0.0252 utils for the peg and 0.0037 utils for the float. This confirms that households are better off under the floating exchange rate regime than under the peg.

One problem with measuring welfare in terms of utils is that it does not give us much of an idea of how costly the peg is. To solve this problem, Robert E. Lucas, Jr., of the University of Chicago proposes to translate utils into units of consumption.[5] Following Lucas's approach, we define the welfare cost of currency pegs as the percent increase in consumption in each period that a household living under a currency peg would require to be as happy as a household living under the flexible exchange rate regime. Let λ denote the welfare cost of a currency peg. Then λ is implicitly given by

$$\ln\left[(1 + \lambda)C_1^p\right] + \beta \ln\left[(1 + \lambda)C_2^p\right] = \ln C_1^f + \beta \ln C_2^f.$$

Now let U^p and U^f denote the lifetime utility under a currency peg and under a float and solve the above expression for λ to obtain

$$\ln(1 + \lambda) = \frac{U^f - U^p}{1 + \beta}$$
$$= \frac{0.0037 + 0.0252}{1 + 0.8}$$
$$= 0.016.$$

Using the approximation $\ln(1 + \lambda) \approx \lambda$, we have that $\lambda = 0.016$. This means that households living under a currency peg require a 1.6 percent increase in consumption each period to be indifferent between staying in the currency peg economy or moving to a floating exchange rate regime.

13.5 The Monetary Policy Trilemma

There is a limit to the number of monetary instruments that the central bank can simultaneously control. In an open economy, this limit is determined in part

---

[5] Robert E. Lucas, Jr., *Models of Business Cycles* (Oxford: Basil Blackwell, 1987).

by the ability of the private sector to borrow or lend internationally. These policy constraints are known as the *monetary policy trilemma* or as the *impossible trinity*. The monetary policy trilemma says that the monetary authority can achieve simultaneously only two of the following three things:[6]

(1) A fixed exchange rate.
(2) Monetary autonomy; that is, the ability to set the nominal interest rate as it wishes.
(3) Free capital mobility.

To show the validity of the monetary policy trilemma, suppose first that the central bank has (1) and (3); that is, it pegs the exchange rate and has free capital mobility. Let i denote the interest rate in period 1 on a bond denominated in domestic currency. Free capital mobility implies that after correcting for changes in the nominal exchange rate, i must equal r^*, the interest rate on assets denominated in foreign currency prevailing in the world market. Formally, we have that

$$1 + i = \frac{\mathcal{E}_2}{\mathcal{E}_1}(1 + r^*). \tag{13.33}$$

This interest parity condition is a special case of the covered interest parity condition studied in Chapter 11 (equation (11.10)), for an environment without uncertainty like the one we are considering here.

To demonstrate the validity of the monetary policy trilemma, consider in turn all three situations in which two of its conditions are satisfied and check that the third one is impossible. Let's start by analyzing the case in which (1) and (3) hold. By (1) the monetary authority pegs the currency at, say, $\bar{\mathcal{E}}$. Then, replacing $\mathcal{E}_1$ and $\mathcal{E}_2$ by $\bar{\mathcal{E}}$ in the interest rate parity condition (13.33) yields

$$i = r^*.$$

Because the economy we are studying is assumed to be small, the world interest rate r^* is exogenously given. As a result, the monetary authority cannot pick i independently: in equilibrium, i must equal r^*. In other words, if the central bank pegs the currency and allows for free capital mobility—that is, if (1) and (3) hold—then it loses monetary autonomy and (2) cannot hold.

Suppose now that the central bank conducts monetary policy autonomously and guarantees free capital mobility; that is, (2) and (3) hold. In this case, we have that, given the value of r^* determined in the world market and the value of i picked by the central bank, the interest parity condition (13.33) uniquely determines the depreciation rate of the domestic currency, $\mathcal{E}_2/\mathcal{E}_1$, as

$$\frac{\mathcal{E}_2}{\mathcal{E}_1} = \frac{1 + i}{1 + r^*}.$$

[6] Early formalizations of the trilemma can be found in J. Marcus Fleming, "Domestic Financial Policies Under Fixed and Under Floating Exchange Rates," *Staff Papers, International Monetary Fund* 9 (November 1962): 369–379, and in Robert A. Mundell, "Capital Mobility and Stabilization Policy under Fixed and Flexible Exchange Rates," *Canadian Journal of Economics and Political Science* 29 (November 1963): 475–485.

In this case, the central bank loses the ability to control the path of the exchange rate. In particular, if $i \neq r^*$, it will not be able to peg the exchange rate, $\mathcal{E}_1 \neq \mathcal{E}_2$, which means that (1) cannot hold.

Finally, suppose that the central bank pegs the exchange rate and has monetary autonomy—that is, (1) and (2) hold. Under these assumptions, $\mathcal{E}_2/\mathcal{E}_1 = 1$, and i takes a value that is independent of the world interest rate or the exchange rate policy. Since r^* is determined independently of i or $\mathcal{E}_2/\mathcal{E}_1$, it follows that in general the interest rate parity condition (13.33) will fail to hold. That is, in general there cannot be free capital mobility. Thus, if (1) and (2) hold, then (3) cannot hold. This completes the proof of the monetary policy trilemma.

13.6 Exchange Rate Overshooting

Under certain monetary arrangements, the nominal exchange rate can be more volatile than other prices in the economy. In particular, exchange rates tend to over-react to movements in monetary policy. This property is known as *exchange rate overshooting*. An early model of this phenomenon was offered by Dornbusch in 1976.[7] Two important elements in Dornbusch's model are a demand for money and the assumption that prices are rigid in the short run but flexible in the long run. In this section, we adapt the TNT-DNWR model to accommodate these two elements. We will add a third ingredient to the model that is going to prove important to obtain the overshooting result in our model; namely, an intratemporal elasticity of substitution between tradable and nontradable consumption of less than unity.

Consider a monetary arrangement in which the central bank controls the quantity of money. Since the monetary authority does not directly control the exchange rate, this monetary arrangement pertains to the family of floating exchange rates. Let's begin by introducing a demand for money. Assume that consumers face a *cash-in-advance constraint*, whereby they need money (cash) to purchase consumption goods.[8] For simplicity, assume that money is needed only to purchase nontradable goods. Specifically, letting M_t denote money holdings in period t, the cash-in-advance constraint takes the form

$$M_t = P_t^N C_t^N. \tag{13.34}$$

Using the firm's optimality condition (13.3) to eliminate P_t^N, the market-clearing condition (13.13) to eliminate C_t^N, and assuming that the production function is of the form $F(h_t) = h_t^\alpha$, with $\alpha \in (0, 1)$, we can write the cash-in-advance constraint (13.34) as

$$M_t = \frac{1}{\alpha} W_t h_t. \tag{13.35}$$

---

[7] Rüdiger Dornbusch, "Expectations and Exchange Rate Dynamics," *Journal of Political Economy* 84 (December 1976): 1161–1171.

[8] A cash-in-advance constraint as a way to motivate a demand for money was proposed by Robert Clower in "A Reconsideration of the Microfoundations of Monetary Theory," *Western Economic Journal* 6 (1967): 1–9. Robert E. Lucas, Jr., in "Equilibrium in a Pure Currency Economy," *Economic Inquiry* 18 (April 1980): 203–220, introduces a cash-in-advance constraint in a general equilibrium model of the determination of the price level.

Suppose that in period 1 the central bank unexpectedly implements a once-and-for-all cut in the money supply by a factor λ. Let variables with the superscript $'$ refer to the equilibrium with the monetary shock and variables without this superscript refer to the equilibrium without the shock. We then have that

$$M'_t = (1 - \lambda)M_t.$$

Suppose that prior to the monetary contraction the economy is at full employment, $h_1 = \bar{h}$, with a constant nominal wage W_0 inherited from the past, $W_1 = W_0$. We then have that in period 1, in the equilibrium without the monetary shock

$$M_1 = \frac{1}{\alpha} W_0 \bar{h}. \tag{13.36}$$

Since the nominal wage is downwardly rigid, equation (13.35) implies that after the shock, employment in period 1 must fall by the same factor as the money supply

$$\frac{h'_1}{h_1} = 1 - \lambda. \tag{13.37}$$

From optimality condition (13.3), we then have that

$$\frac{P_1^{N'}}{P_1^N} = \left(\frac{h'_1}{h_1}\right)^{1-\alpha} = (1-\lambda)^{1-\alpha} < 1, \tag{13.38}$$

which means that the monetary tightening causes a fall in the nominal price of nontradable goods.

Now consider the following generalization of the demand schedule (13.17):

$$p_t = \frac{1-\gamma}{\gamma} \left(\frac{C^T(r^*, Q_1^T, Q_2^T)}{h_t^\alpha}\right)^{1/\xi}, \tag{13.39}$$

where $\xi > 0$ is the intratemporal elasticity of substitution between tradable and nontradable goods. This demand schedule becomes the one given in (13.17) when $\xi = 1$.[9] Since r^*, Q_1^T, and Q_2^T are unaffected by the monetary shock, the demand schedule implies that

$$\frac{p'_t}{p_t} = \left(\frac{h'_t}{h_t}\right)^{-\alpha/\xi}.$$

Combining this expression evaluated at $t = 1$ with (13.37) yields that the proportional change in the relative price of nontradables is given by

$$\frac{p'_1}{p_1} = (1-\lambda)^{-\alpha/\xi} > 1. \tag{13.40}$$

---

[9] Exercise 13.4 asks you to show that this demand schedule arises when the intratemporal and intertemporal elasticities of consumption substitution are equal to each other (which is also assumed in deriving (13.17)), but not equal to 1. Also, for simplicity we are assuming that the cash-in-advance constraint does not distort the intratemporal marginal rate of substitution between nontradables (the cash good) and tradables (the credit good).

It follows that the decline in the money supply causes an increase in the relative price of nontradables and hence an appreciation of the real exchange rate—the economy becomes more expensive relative to the rest of the world. Intuitively, a fall in the consumption of nontradables can be supported in equilibrium only if its relative price increases. The increase in the relative price of nontradables occurs despite the fact that the nominal price of nontradables falls. It follows that the nominal price of tradables must fall by even more than the nominal price of nontradables. Formally, since $p_t = P_t^N / \mathcal{E}_t$, we have that

$$\frac{\mathcal{E}_t'}{\mathcal{E}_t} = \frac{P_t^{N'}/P_t^N}{p_t'/p_t}.$$

Combining this expression evaluated at $t = 1$ with (13.38) and (13.40) yields that the proportional change in the nominal exchange rate is given by

$$\frac{\mathcal{E}_1'}{\mathcal{E}_1} = (1 - \lambda)^{1 - \alpha + \frac{\alpha}{\xi}}. \tag{13.41}$$

Since $0 < \alpha < 1$ and $\xi > 0$, the nominal exchange rate falls. We have therefore shown that the reduction in the money supply leads to an appreciation of both the nominal and the real exchange rate in period 1.

To establish whether there is exchange rate overshooting, we need to see what happens to the nominal exchange rate in the long run. In Dornbusch's model, prices (in our case wages) are flexible in the long run. Our model has only two periods, so we will assume that the short run is period 1 and that the long run is period 2. As we saw in Section 13.3, when the nominal wage is flexible, full employment obtains regardless of monetary policy. Evaluating equation (13.35) at $t = 2$, we then have that

$$\frac{W_2'}{W_2} = \frac{M_2'}{M_2} = (1 - \lambda).$$

In words, in the long run, the nominal wage falls by the same proportion as the money supply. Similarly, the cash-in-advance constraint (13.34) in period 2 implies that

$$\frac{P_2^{N'}}{P_2^N} = \frac{M_2'}{M_2} = (1 - \lambda).$$

Thus, in the long run, a cut in the money supply in the proportion λ produces deflation in core prices of λ. Finally, the demand schedule (13.39), together with the fact that $p_t = P_t^N / \mathcal{E}_t$, implies that in the long run the nominal exchange rate appreciates in the same proportion as the fall in the money supply

$$\frac{\mathcal{E}_2'}{\mathcal{E}_2} = \frac{P_2^{N'}}{P_2^N} = (1 - \lambda). \tag{13.42}$$

Comparing the short- and long-run effects of the monetary contraction on the nominal exchange rate, equations (13.41) and (13.42), respectively, we have that if

$\xi < 1$, the nominal exchange rate appreciation is larger in the short run than in the long run. Thus, when the intratemporal elasticity of substitution is less than one, the TNT-DNWR model predicts an overshooting of the nominal exchange rate.

The intuition behind the exchange rate overshooting result in the TNT-DNWR model is as follows. Let's first consider the long run. Because all nominal prices (including the nominal wage) are flexible in the long run, the fall in the money supply has no effects on real variables. For *real money balances*, M_2/P_2^N, to be unchanged, the nominal price of nontradables must decline by the same proportion as the money supply. Similarly, for the relative price of nontradables, $p_2 = P_2^N/\mathcal{E}_2$, to be unchanged, $\mathcal{E}_2$ must fall by the same proportion as the nominal price of nontradables. This implies that in the long run, the nominal exchange rate falls (appreciates) by the same proportion as the money supply. Consider now the short-run effects of the monetary tightening. In the short run, nominal wages are downwardly rigid. As a result the contraction in the money supply causes a contraction in real money balances, M_1/P_1^N. In turn, by the cash-in-advance constraint the fall in real balances reduces the consumption of nontradables; that is, C_1^N declines. Since the price elasticity of the demand for nontradables is less than one ($\xi < 1$), the fall in C_1^N is associated with an increase in real expenditures on nontradables ($p_1 C_1^N$ increases).[10] Now real expenditures on nontradable goods equal the ratio of nominal expenditures on nontradables to the nominal exchange rate, $P_1^N C_1^N/\mathcal{E}_1$. In turn, by the cash-in-advance constraint we have that $P_1^N C_1^N/\mathcal{E}_1 = M_1/\mathcal{E}_1$. That is, in the short run real balances measured in units of tradables must go up. But this can only happen if the nominal exchange rate falls (appreciates) by more than the money supply. We therefore have that in the short run the nominal exchange rate appreciates by more than in the long run; that is, the exchange rate overshoots.

Finally, the overshooting of the exchange rate implies that the nominal interest rate jumps up when the central bank cuts the money supply. To see this, use the interest parity condition (13.33) to express the nominal interest rate in the equilibria with and without the monetary shock as $1 + i' = (\mathcal{E}_2'/\mathcal{E}_1')(1 + r^*)$ and $1 + i = (\mathcal{E}_2/\mathcal{E}_1)(1 + r^*)$. This implies that

$$\frac{1+i'}{1+i} = \frac{\mathcal{E}_2'/\mathcal{E}_2}{\mathcal{E}_1'/\mathcal{E}_1} = (1-\lambda)^{\alpha(1-1/\xi)} > 1,$$

where the second equality uses equations (13.41) and (13.42) and the inequality uses the assumption that $\xi < 1$. The increase in the nominal interest rate makes sense: By the overshooting effect, the cut in the money supply triggers an expected depreciation of the domestic currency between periods 1 and 2 relative to the equilibrium without the shock. If the domestic interest rate does not go up to compensate domestic depositors for the expected depreciation of the domestic currency, an arbitrage opportunity would open up whereby infinite profits could be made by borrowing domestically and investing abroad.

---

[10]To see this, recall that a price elasticity less than 1 means that if the price increases by 1 percent, the quantity demanded falls by less than 1 percent, so expenditure (the product of price times quantity) increases.

13.7 Empirical Evidence on Downward Nominal Wage Rigidity

Downward nominal wage rigidity is the central friction in the TNT-DNWR model. It is therefore natural to ask whether it is empirically relevant. The available evidence appears to suggest that it is. The presence of downward nominal wage rigidity has been documented from a number of perspectives, including micro data, macro data, economies with predominantly formal labor markets, economies with large informal sectors, developed countries, emerging countries, early data, and more recent data.

13.7.1 EVIDENCE FROM U.S. MICRO DATA

Consider first micro evidence stemming from a developed country. Figure 13.11 displays the distribution of wage changes for individual workers from 1997 to 2016 in the United States. Wage changes are measured as year-over-year log changes in nominal hourly wages of hourly paid job stayers. Each distribution is based on a sample of about 5,000 workers who did not lose their job (job stayers). In each panel, the horizontal axis measures the year-over-year percent change in the nominal hourly wage of an hourly paid job stayer. The vertical axis measures the share of workers in each bin. The bin size is 2 percent, with the exception of a wage freeze, which is defined as an exact zero change.

There are a number of characteristics of the wage change distributions that are consistent with the hypothesis of downward nominal wage rigidity. All of the distributions have a large spike at zero wage changes. Also, the distributions are not symmetric. There are many more wage increases than wage cuts. Finally, the fraction of wage freezes is cyclical. It increases during recessions and decreases during booms. For example, the fraction of wage freezes rose from 15 percent in 2007, the year prior to the onset of the Great Recession, to 20 percent in 2009, the year in which the unemployment rate peaked at 10 percent. At the same time, the fraction of workers receiving a wage cut did not change significantly between 2007 and 2009. Taken together, this evidence paints a picture that is consistent with an environment in which nominal wages increase during booms, but fail to fall during recessions.

13.7.2 EVIDENCE FROM THE GREAT DEPRESSION

Downward nominal wage rigidity is sometimes ascribed to regulation (minimum wage laws) or market power in labor markets (labor unions). A natural question is therefore whether downward nominal wage rigidity is also observed during periods in which these factors did not play a major role. To address this question, here we examine the behavior of prices and wages during the Great Depression of 1929–1933. The Great Depression is relevant in this regard because at the time enforceable union contracts did not exist in the United States and because regulations requiring nominal wage increases were only enacted after mid-1933.[11]

---

[11] See Christopher Hanes, "Nominal Wage Rigidity and Industry Characteristics in the Downturns of 1893, 1929, and 1981," *American Economic Review* 90 (2000): 1432–1446.

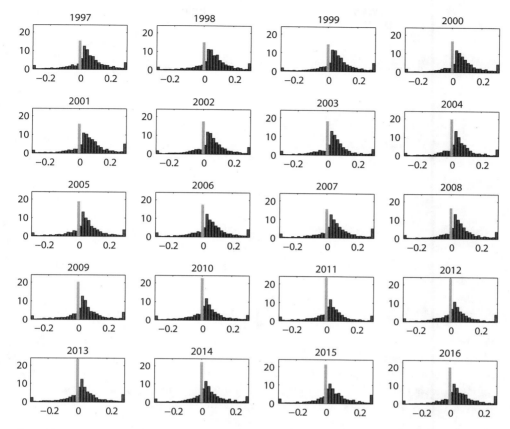

Figure 13.11. Nominal Wage Change Distributions: United States, 1997–2016
Notes: The wage change distributions display three key characteristics that are consistent with an environment in which nominal wages increase during expansions but fail to fall during recessions: (1) they all display a spike at 0; (2) there are more wage increases than wage cuts; and (3) the spike at 0 increased during the Great Recession (the global financial crisis of 2007–2009).
Source: Yoon Jo, Stephanie Schmitt-Grohé, and Martín Uribe, "Does Nominal Wage Rigidity of Job Stayers Matter? Evidence from the Great Recession," manuscript, Columbia University, 2021, based on data from the Current Population Survey.

During the Great Depression, the U.S. economy experienced unprecedented levels of unemployment, with almost one third of workers losing their jobs. If nominal wages were downwardly flexible, one would expect them to fall by much more than the price level. This would lower the real wage, reduce marginal costs of firms, and allow the labor market to clear. However, this is not what happened.

Figure 13.12 displays the nominal wage rate in the manufacturing sector and the consumer price index in the United States from January 1923 to July 1935. Vertical lines mark the beginning and end of the Great Depression, August 1929 and March 1933, according to the Business Cycle Dating Committee of the NBER. Between 1929 and 1931, employment fell by 31 percent. In spite of this large contraction

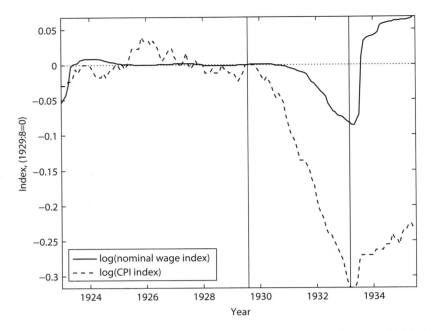

Figure 13.12. Nominal Wage Rate and Consumer Prices, United States, 1923:1–1935:7
Notes: The thick solid line depicts the natural logarithm of an index of manufacturing money wage rates. The broken line depicts the logarithm of the consumer price index. The two vertical lines mark the beginning and end of the Great Depression, August 1929 and March 1933, according to the National Bureau of Economic Research (NBER). The figure shows that during the Great Depression nominal wages fell by only 6 percent, whereas nominal prices fell by 32 percent, leading to an increase in the real wage of 26 percent, in spite of a contraction in employment of more than one third of the labor force.
Data source: NBER for the wage rate and BLS for the price index.

in aggregate activity, nominal hourly wages fell by only 0.6 percent per year, while consumer prices fell by 6.6 percent per year. Thus, the real wage rose by 6 percent per year in the context of a massive excess supply of workers. A similar pattern is observed during the second half of the Depression. By 1933, real wages were 26 percent higher than in 1929, in spite of the fact that the labor market continued to be highly distressed. This evidence is consistent with downward nominal wage rigidity, taking the form of an inability of the nominal wage to fall enough to reduce real wages when the economy experiences widespread involuntary unemployment.

13.7.3   EVIDENCE FROM EMERGING COUNTRIES

We now return to the time of the Great Recession of 2008 but look at what happened with unemployment and nominal wages outside the United States. We focus on a group of countries on the periphery of Europe. These countries are of particular interest because at the time of the crisis they were either on the euro or pegging their currencies to it. Table 13.3 displays the unemployment rate in 2008:Q1 and in

Table 13.3. Unemployment and Nominal Wages:
Peripheral Europe, 2008–2011

| Country | Unemployment Rate | | Wage Growth |
	2008Q1 (in percent)	2011Q2 (in percent)	$\frac{W_{2011Q2}}{W_{2008Q1}}$ (in percent)
Bulgaria	6.1	11.3	43.3
Cyprus	3.8	6.9	10.7
Estonia	4.1	12.8	2.5
Greece	7.8	16.7	−2.3
Ireland	4.9	14.3	0.5
Italy	6.4	8.2	10.0
Lithuania	4.1	15.6	−5.1
Latvia	6.1	16.2	−0.6
Portugal	8.3	12.5	1.9
Spain	9.2	20.8	8.0
Slovenia	4.7	7.9	12.5
Slovakia	10.2	13.3	13.4

Notes: The table shows that during the global financial crisis, unemployment increased in all countries on the periphery of Europe. However, no country experienced sizable declines in nominal wages. The joint behavior of unemployment and wages, together with the fact that both productivity growth and inflation were small during this period, is consistent with the presence of downward nominal wage rigidity. In the third column, W is an index of nominal average hourly labor cost in manufacturing, construction, and services, including the public sector (except for Spain).

Source: Stephanie Schmitt-Grohé and Martín Uribe, "Downward Nominal Wage Rigidity, Currency Pegs, and Involuntary Unemployment," *Journal of Political Economy* 124 (October 2016): 1466–1514.

2011:Q2 and the cumulative growth rate of the nominal hourly wage rate over this period. The picture that emerges is quite uniform across countries. All countries experienced an increase in the unemployment rate. In some countries the increase was large. For example, in Ireland, the unemployment rate went from 4.9 percent in 2008:Q1 to 14.3 percent in 2011:Q2. In spite of the significant increase in unemployment, the nominal wage increased in most countries, and in the few countries in which it fell, the decline was modest. The joint occurrence of an increase in unemployment and nondeclining wages in countries whose currencies are tied to those of other countries either by a currency union or by a currency peg is consistent with downward nominal wage rigidity.

We close this section by revisiting the Argentine currency peg of 1991 to 2001, known as the Convertibility Plan. During this period, the Argentine peso was convertible into dollars at a one-to-one rate. In Section 10.4.2 of Chapter 10, we saw that the peg ended in a sudden stop—that is, in a sharp reversal of the current account

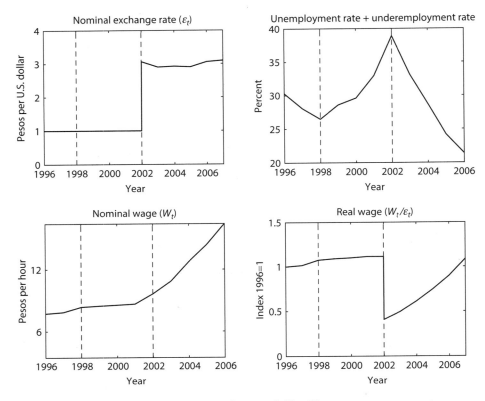

Figure 13.13. The End of the Argentine Convertibility Plan

Notes: The figure shows that the large increase in unemployment that characterized the last three years of the Argentine peg occurred in the context of remarkably stable nominal wages.

Source: Stephanie Schmitt-Grohé and Martín Uribe, "Downward Nominal Wage Rigidity, Currency Pegs, and Involuntary Unemployment," *Journal of Political Economy* 124 (October 2016): 1466–1514.

(from negative to positive) and a large real exchange rate depreciation—and default. We now focus on the dynamics of the nominal wage and unemployment during the last three years of the currency peg, to show that they too provide evidence consistent with the hypothesis of downward nominal wage rigidity.

Figure 13.13 displays the paths of the nominal exchange rate (pesos per dollar), the subemployment rate (the sum of unemployed workers and workers working fewer hours than desired at the going wage), the nominal hourly wage rate in pesos, and the nominal hourly wage deflated by the nominal exchange rate. Starting in 1998, the economy was buffeted by a number of large negative shocks, including weak commodity prices, a large devaluation in Brazil (Argentina's largest trading partner), and a large increase in the country premium, reflecting foreign investors' perception that the government would default on its debt. Not surprisingly, between 1998 and 2001, unemployment rose sharply, as shown in the top right panel of the figure. Nonetheless, like in the periphery of Europe during the global financial crisis, nominal wages remained remarkably flat. Since the nominal exchange rate was fixed at one peso per dollar throughout this period, the real wage measured in units of tradables, which we denoted $W_t/\mathcal{E}_t$ in previous sections, also displayed a flat path during the contraction. Viewed through the lens of the TNT-DNWR model, the lack of downward adjustment of the nominal wage in the context of a currency peg and rising unemployment is consistent with the presence of downward nominal wage rigidity.

13.8 Appendix

This appendix shows how to solve the TNT-DNWR model of Section 13.1. The equilibrium conditions are (13.19) to (13.25). They constitute a system of 12 conditions, because the last 5 expressions hold for $t = 1, 2$. This system, however, is in only 8 unknowns, C_t^T, h_t, W_t, and p_t, for $t = 1, 2$. The reason why there are more equilibrium conditions than unknowns is that the system contains four inequalities—namely, (13.23) and (13.24) for $t = 1, 2$. These inequalities serve to constrain the possible equilibrium paths but do not dictate the mathematical determinacy or consistency of the system.

To find the equilibrium, proceed as follows.

1. The equilibrium value of C_1^T is given by (13.19).
2. The equilibrium value of C_2^T can then be read off equation (13.20).
3. From this point on one can proceed sequentially, first solving for period 1 and then for period 2. We explain in detail how to solve for the equilibrium in period 1. The solution of the equilibrium in period 2 is along similar lines.

    (a) Begin by guessing that there is full employment in period 1 by setting $h_1 = \bar{h}$. Then conditions (13.23) and (13.25) are satisfied. The relative price, p_1, can be obtained by evaluating condition (13.21) for $t = 1$. Evaluating (13.22) yields W_1. Now check whether $W_1 \geq W_0$. If so, the wage rigidity constraint (13.24) is satisfied and the equilibrium in period 1 has been found.

    (b) If, on the other hand, condition (13.24) is not satisfied, then set $W_1 = W_0$. This guarantees satisfaction of (13.24) and (13.25). Next, combine (13.21) and (13.22) to obtain $(1 - \gamma)/\gamma\, C_1^T/F(h_1) = W_0/\mathcal{E}_1/F'(h_1)$ and solve for h_1. This value of h_1 will satisfy the time constraint (13.23) with a strict inequality because the real wage, $W_0/\mathcal{E}_1$, is, by construction, above the one associated with full employment. Finally, the relative price p_1 can be read off either condition (13.21) or (13.22).

13.9 Summing Up

This chapter shows that in the presence of nominal rigidity, monetary and exchange rate policy can affect the equilibrium levels of inflation, unemployment, aggregate activity, and the real exchange rate. It considers separately two exchange rate regimes: a fixed exchange rate regime and a floating exchange rate regime in which the central bank pursues the dual mandate of full employment and price stability.

- The chapter embeds downward nominal wage rigidity into the TNT model of Chapter 10. The resulting model is called the TNT-DNWR model.
- In the TNT-DNWR model, nominal wages are downwardly rigid. They can go up, but they cannot go down.
- Under a fixed exchange rate regime, negative external shocks, such as an increase in the world interest rate or a deterioration of the terms of trade, cause involuntary unemployment and a real exchange rate depreciation (the country becomes cheaper).
- Under a floating exchange rate regime, in response to negative external shocks the central bank can preserve full employment and price stability by depreciating the domestic currency.
- When the economy is buffeted by external shocks, welfare is higher under a floating exchange rate that preserves full employment and price stability than under a currency peg.
- The central bank cannot achieve both price stability and full employment in response to negative supply shocks, such as a fall in productivity in the non-traded sector. In this case the monetary authority faces a trade-off between inflation and unemployment. When the central bank negotiates this trade-off by allowing for some inflation and some unemployment, the economy is said to experience stagflation.
- The monetary policy trilemma says that the monetary authority can achieve only two of the following: (1) a fixed exchange rate; (2) monetary autonomy (setting the nominal interest rate or the money supply independently); and (3) free capital mobility.
- Under a flexible exchange rate regime, a monetary tightening (a contraction in the money supply or an increase in the nominal interest rate) causes an appreciation of the currency. Importantly, the appreciation is larger in the short run than in the long run. This result is known as exchange rate overshooting.
- There is empirical evidence consistent with the presence of downward nominal wage rigidity. This evidence can be found in data from developed countries, emerging countries, and from periods in which labor market regulations and labor unions did not play a major role in the determination of nominal wages.

13.10 Exercises

Exercise 13.1 (External Shocks and the Real Wage I) Suppose that due to a fall in the world interest rate, the equilibrium consumption of tradables, $C^T(r^*, Q_1^T, Q_2^T)$, increases by 10 percent. Assume that prior to the fall in the world interest rate the economy was operating at full employment. Show that the equilibrium real wage also increases by 10 percent. Show that this result is independent of the exchange rate arrangement. To answer this question, you can use a graphical or a mathematical approach.

Exercise 13.2 (External Shocks and the Real Wage II) Suppose that due to an increase in the world interest rate, the equilibrium consumption of tradables, $C^T(r^*, Q_1^T, Q_2^T)$, falls by 10 percent. Show that in the TNT-DNWR model, the equilibrium real wage also falls by 10 percent if the central bank follows a floating exchange rate regime and has as objectives full employment and price stability in the nontraded market. To answer this question, you can use a graphical or mathematical approach.

Exercise 13.3 (A Natural Rate Shock) Suppose the economy is initially at full employment. Suppose further that in period 1 households experience an increase in their subjective discount factor from β to $\beta' > \beta$. This type of shock is known as a *natural rate shock*. Characterize graphically the effect in period 1 on consumption of nontradables, unemployment, the relative price of nontradables, and the real wage measured in units of tradable goods under two alternative monetary policy regimes:

1. A fixed exchange rate regime.
2. A floating exchange rate regime in which the central bank pursues full employment and price stability.

Exercise 13.4 (The Demand Schedule with CRRA Utility and CES Aggregator) Assume that the utility function is of the constant relative risk aversion (CRRA) form

$$\frac{C_1^{1-\sigma}}{1-\sigma} + \beta \frac{C_2^{1-\sigma}}{1-\sigma},$$

where $1/\sigma > 0$ is a parameter known as the intertemporal elasticity of consumption substitution. Suppose also that the Armington aggregator function is of the constant elasticity of substitution (CES) form

$$C_t = \left[C_t^{T\,1-1/\xi} + C_t^{N\,1-1/\xi} \right]^{1/(1-1/\xi)},$$

where $\xi > 0$ is a parameter known as the (intratemporal) elasticity of substitution between tradable and nontradable goods.

1. Show that the optimality conditions of the household imply that

$$\frac{C_t^N}{C_t^T} = p_t^{-\xi}.$$

Interpret this result. In particular, discuss why it makes sense that ξ is called the elasticity of substitution between tradable and nontradable consumption. [Hint: If p_t increases by 1 percent, what is the percentage change in C_t^N/C_t^T?]

2. Consider the case in which the intra- and intertemporal elasticities of substitution are equal to each other,

$$\xi = \frac{1}{\sigma}.$$

Show that in this case the demand schedule derived in Section 13.1.2 takes the form

$$p_1 = \left(\frac{C^T(r^*, Q_1^T, Q_2^T)}{h_1^\alpha} \right)^{1/\xi}.$$

Exercise 13.5 (Supply Shocks with CRRA Utility and CES Aggregator) Subsection 13.3.2 shows that in response to a negative productivity shock in the nontradable sector (a fall in A_1), the central bank can ensure full employment without having to change the nominal exchange rate. This result depends on the assumption of a log-linear utility function and a Cobb-Douglas aggregator function. Assume instead that the utility function is CRRA and that the Armington aggregator is CES, as in Exercise 13.4, and that $\xi = 1/\sigma$. Redo the analysis in subsection 13.3.2. In particular, establish under what conditions on the parameter ξ the full employment equilibrium is accompanied by no change in the exchange rate, an appreciation of the exchange rate, or a depreciation of the exchange rate.

Exercise 13.6 (Expected Income Shock in a TNT Economy) Consider a two-period, small open economy with free capital mobility. The economy produces tradable and nontradable goods. Tradable output is an exogenous endowment in both periods. Nontradable output is produced using labor via an increasing and concave production function. Households have preferences for tradable and non-tradable goods in both periods described by a lifetime utility function that is separable across time and goods, like the log preferences analyzed in the body of this chapter. Suppose that in period 1 households learn that the endowment of tradables in period 2 will be significantly lower than expected. Analyze, using graphs to complement your explanation, the effect of this shock on consumption, employment, the real exchange rate, and the current account in period 1, under two alternative environments: (a) flexible nominal wages; and (b) downwardly rigid nominal wages coupled with a currency peg. Discuss optimal exchange rate policy in scenario (b).

Exercise 13.7 (Adjustment to an Intratemporal Preference Shock) Suppose that there is an increase in households' preference for nontradable goods, which is reflected in an increase in $1 - \gamma$, the exponent on nontradable consumption in the Armington aggregator (13.6).

1. What is the effect of this preference shock on equilibrium consumption of tradable goods in periods 1 and 2? Explain.
2. Use a graphical approach to analyze the effect in period 1 of the preference shock on employment, the nominal wage, the real wage, the relative price of nontradables, the nominal exchange rate, and the real exchange rate under two alternative monetary arrangements:

(a) A currency peg.

(b) A floating exchange rate regime in which the central bank aims to achieve price stability in the nontraded sector and full employment.

3. Consider now a fall in $1 - \gamma$. Answer question 2 under this scenario. Comment on possible asymmetries with respect to the case of an increase in $1 - \gamma$.

Exercise 13.8 (Capital Controls and the Monetary Policy Trilemma) Suppose the domestic nominal interest rate is 3 percent ($i = 0.03$), that the foreign interest rate is 5 percent ($r^* = 0.05$), and that the central bank pegs the nominal exchange rate ($\mathcal{E}_1 = \mathcal{E}_2$). Suppose further that the government imposes capital controls in the form of a proportional tax τ on interest income from holdings of foreign bonds. The tax does not apply to interest payments on foreign debts.

1. Explain investors' incentives in the absence of capital controls ($\tau = 0$).
2. Write a modified interest parity condition that incorporates the capital control tax. This condition should be in terms of i, r^*, τ, $\mathcal{E}_1$, and $\mathcal{E}_2$.
3. Using the given values of i, r^*, and $\mathcal{E}_2/\mathcal{E}_1$, find the value of τ consistent with the modified interest parity condition.
4. Explain investors' incentives if τ is higher or lower than the value you found.
5. Suppose the central bank depreciates the currency by 1 percent in period 1 and leaves the exchange rate in period 2 unchanged. Find the new value of τ consistent with the modified interest parity condition. Provide intuition.

Exercise 13.9 (Adjustment under Financial Autarky) Suppose that possibly due to prohibitive capital controls, households cannot borrow or lend internationally ($B_0 = B_1 = 0$). When an economy is in this situation, we say that it is in *financial autarky*. Analyze the effects of a fall in the endowment of tradables in period 1 on unemployment, the real exchange rate, and the real wage rate expressed in units of tradable goods. Distinguish the cases of fixed and floating exchange rates. Compare your answer to the case of free capital mobility: in which economy are the effects larger?

Exercise 13.10 (A Monetary Tightening) Suppose the economy is initially operating at full employment. Suppose also that the exchange rate in period 2, $\mathcal{E}_2$, is fixed. Analyze graphically the consequences of an increase in the nominal interest rate in period 1 from i to $i' > i$ for unemployment, the real exchange rate, the real wage expressed in units of tradable goods, and inflation.

Exercise 13.11 (A Monetary Easing) This exercise builds on Exercise 13.10. It is meant to explore possible asymmetries in the effects of monetary policy. Suppose the economy is initially operating at full employment. Suppose also that the exchange rate in period 2, $\mathcal{E}_2$, is fixed.

1. Analyze graphically the consequences of a decrease in the nominal interest rate in period 1 from i to $i' < i$ for unemployment, the real exchange rate, the real wage expressed in units of tradable goods, and inflation.

2. Compare your answer to that for Exercise 13.10, commenting on possible asymmetries in the effect of monetary policy. How would your answer change if in the present exercise prior to the monetary shock the economy suffered involuntary unemployment?

Exercise 13.12 (Estimating the Degree of Downward Nominal Wage Rigidity)
Consider the following more general version of the wage constraint (13.1):

$$W_t \geq \gamma W_{t-1},$$

where $\gamma \geq 0$ is a parameter.

1. Provide an interpretation of the parameter γ. What does $\gamma = 0$ mean? What does $\gamma > 1$ mean?
2. Use the information displayed in Table 13.3 to estimate a value of γ for each country at the quarterly frequency. Hint: Use the fact that, according to the TNT-DNWR model, when unemployment increases, the nominal wage constraint must be binding.

Exercise 13.13 (Optimality of Constant Nominal Interest Rates under a Float)
Suppose that the monetary authority follows a flexible exchange rate regime and cares about full employment and core price stability. Suppose further that the only shocks hitting the economy are movements in the world interest rate, r^*, or in the tradable endowments, Q_t^T, for $t = 1, 2$. Show that the nominal interest rate, i, that supports the equilibrium is independent of these shocks and equal to $\beta^{-1} - 1$.

CHAPTER 14

Managing Currency Pegs

In countries with fixed exchange rates, a positive shock can be the prelude to a crisis. Consider, for example, the effect of a temporary fall in the world interest rate. The lower cost of funds attracts capital inflows, boosts consumption spending, and deteriorates the current account. The increase in aggregate demand fosters employment and drives up nominal wages. This is the happy part of the story. When the interest rate goes back up to its normal level, aggregate demand contracts, and so does the demand for labor. Equilibrium in the labor market requires a fall in the real wage. However, if the nominal wage is downwardly rigid and the central bank pegs the currency, the real wage is unable to fall. As a result, the economy experiences an excess supply of labor, or involuntary unemployment. This type of dynamics is known as a *boom-bust cycle.*

Most peripheral European countries, including Cyprus, Greece, Ireland, Spain, and Portugal, experienced a boom-bust cycle between 2000 and 2011. The boom part of the cycle started in 1999 with the introduction of the euro as the common currency. The bust part of the cycle was triggered by the *global financial crisis* of 2007–2009. The severity of the contraction gave the bust all of the characteristics of a sudden stop, a phenomenon we studied in Chapter 10. In subsection 14.4 below, we will study the boom-bust cycle in the periphery of Europe in more detail.

We begin by analyzing the mechanics of a boom-bust cycle. The analysis is conducted in the context of the TNT-DNWR model developed in Chapter 13. We then show that when the exchange rate is pegged, the TNT-DNWR model has an externality stemming from the fact that households fail to internalize that booms place the economy in a weak position to weather the next downturn. This externality motivates policy interventions to reduce the welfare costs of boom-bust cycles. We study a number of such interventions including *fiscal devaluations* and *macroprudential policies* taking the form of capital controls.

14.1 A Boom-Bust Cycle in the TNT-DNWR Model

Consider the TNT-DNWR economy developed in Chapter 13. Figure 14.1 illustrates the mechanics of a typical boom-bust cycle. Initially, the world interest rate is r^* and the nominal wage is W^A. The monetary authority pegs the nominal

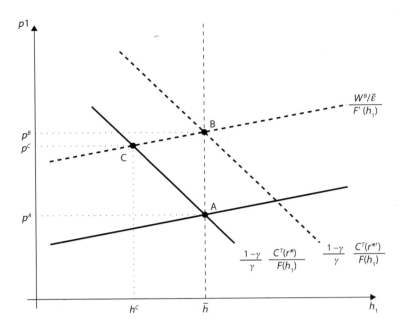

Figure 14.1. A Boom-Bust Cycle in the TNT-DNWR Model under a Fixed Exchange Rate
Notes: The economy starts at point A, where there is full employment and the wage rate is W^A. The nominal exchange rate is fixed at $\bar{\mathcal{E}}$. A decline in the world interest rate from r^* to $r^{*\prime} < r^*$ sets off a boom. The demand schedule shifts up and to the right. Wages rise to W^B and the supply schedule shifts up and to the left. In the boom equilibrium (point B) there is full employment and the relative price of nontradables rises to $p^B > p^A$. The bust occurs when the interest rate goes back to r^*. The demand schedule shifts down and to the left back to its original position. The new equilibrium is at point C, where there is involuntary unemployment in the amount $\bar{h} - h^C$ and the relative price of nontradables falls to p^C.

exchange rate at $\bar{\mathcal{E}}$. The equilibrium is at point A. Suppose that the interest rate falls to $r^{*\prime} < r^*$. As a result, consumption of tradables increases from $C^T(r^*)$ to $C^T(r^{*\prime})$. Because the endowment of tradables has not changed, the trade balance, $TB_1 = Q_1^T - C^T(r^{*\prime})$, deteriorates. The current account, $CA_1 = r_0 B_0 + TB_1$, also deteriorates, since $r_0 B_0$ is given. The increase in the desired consumption of tradables shifts the demand schedule up and to the right, as indicated by the broken downward-sloping line. At the original nominal wage rate W^A, there would be an excess demand for labor. Because the nominal wage is upwardly flexible, it increases to a level that clears the labor market. Let the new wage be $W^B > W^A$. The increase in the nominal wage shifts the supply schedule up and to the left, as shown by the broken upward-sloping line. The new equilibrium is at point B, where the economy is at full employment, $h_1 = \bar{h}$, and the relative price of nontradable goods is higher, $p_1 = p^B > p^A$. The increase in the relative price of nontradables means that the real exchange rate appreciates; that is, the country becomes more expensive relative to the rest of the world. This completes the expansionary phase of the boom-bust cycle.

Suppose now that the world interest rate goes back up to its original level r^*. Consumers react by cutting spending, which shifts the demand schedule down and to the left. For simplicity, Figure 14.1 assumes that the demand schedule goes back to its original position.[1] By contrast, the supply schedule does not shift back to its original position. This would require a fall in the nominal wage from W^B to W^A, which cannot happen because wages are downwardly rigid. As a consequence, the new equilibrium is at point C. At this point, the economy experiences involuntary unemployment in the amount $\bar{h} - h^C$, because the real wage, $W^B/\bar{\mathcal{E}}$, is too high to clear the labor market. The relative price of nontradables falls from p^B to p^C. Thus, the real exchange rate depreciates (nontradable goods, and the economy in general, become cheaper). However, the real exchange rate depreciation is not large enough—that is, the relative price of nontradables doesn't fall all the way down to p^A—to induce an expenditure switch from tradable to nontradable goods and a corresponding increase in the production of nontradables and in the demand for labor to eliminate involuntary unemployment.

In sum, under a currency peg, booms sow the seeds of busts, in the sense that what could be a soft landing at the end of a positive shock turns into a period of protracted unemployment. The source of the problem is an insufficient downward adjustment in real wages caused by the combination of downward nominal wage rigidity and a fixed exchange rate.

14.2 The Currency Peg Externality

It follows from the above analysis of a boom-bust cycle that the combination of downward nominal wage rigidity and a fixed exchange rate causes the economy to expand by more than is desirable or efficient in response to positive shocks. When the interest rate falls, individual agents know that the expansion in aggregate consumption and the capital inflows that finance it will result in an increase in nominal wages that, once the boom is over, will cause unemployment. Yet, individual agents do not take this aggregate effect into account; that is, they do not restrain their own rise in consumption when the interest rate falls with the intention to curb the rise in nominal wages. The reason is that each household is too small to affect the equilibrium dynamics of wages. Thus, the economy suffers from an externality.

If households were to moderate the increase in consumption during the boom phase of the cycle, the increase in the nominal wage would be smaller, and therefore the level of unemployment in the bust phase of the cycle would also be lower. The *currency peg externality* implies that there is room for welfare-improving government intervention aimed at making households internalize the cost that their own consumption choices during booms have in terms of unemployment when the boom is over. In Section 14.3, we study policy tools, including taxes and capital controls, that can achieve this goal.

---

[1] Strictly speaking, because households consume a larger part of their permanent income during the low-interest-rate period, tradable consumption does not go back exactly to the level prior to the interest rate fall, but to a lower level, so that the new demand schedule should be located left of the original one.

14.3   Managing a Currency Peg

What policies could a government of an economy with a fixed exchange rate implement to avoid involuntary unemployment following a negative shock? The most obvious solution perhaps would be to devalue; that is, to increase $\mathcal{E}_t$, and in this way lower the real wage in terms of tradables to a level consistent with full employment (see Section 13.3 of Chapter 13). However, for some countries this is not an option. For example, for members of the euro area this would mean breaking away from the European Union, which could entail large political and economic costs.

If devaluations are not possible, what other policy options are there? The main obstacle in achieving full employment is that the wage rate in terms of tradables, $W_1/\mathcal{E}_1$, is too high during recessions. One strategy might be to introduce structural reforms in the labor market, such as reducing hiring and firing costs. Such measures tend to facilitate the reallocation of workers from sectors hardest hit by negative shocks to less affected sectors. This type of policy pertains to government agencies responsible for the design of the labor market architecture. Typically, structural reforms take years to negotiate and implement. We will not study structural reforms in detail because the focus of the present analysis is on tools that can be applied by the fiscal and monetary authorities at a business cycle frequency.

Within the class of policies that can be deployed over the business cycle to improve the functioning of a currency peg, we will distinguish two types. One type of policy achieves both full employment and an efficient intertemporal allocation of consumption expenditure. We refer to this class of policies as *first-best policies*. The second type of policy we will consider reduces unemployment during recessions, but at the cost of distorting the intertemporal allocation of consumption. We will refer to this type of policy as *second-best policies*. A second distinction between the first- and second-best policies we consider here is that the former are ex post policies, in the sense that they are applied once the economy is in recession, whereas the latter are ex ante policies (or *macroprudential policies*), in the sense that they are applied preemptively before the economy enters into recession.

First-best policies are policies that directly address the core of the problem in this economy—namely, the downward rigidity in the real wage caused by the combination of a downwardly rigid nominal wage and a fixed exchange rate. As we will see, these policies perfectly substitute for a flexible exchange rate regime that guarantees full employment without affecting the efficient allocation of consumption across time.

Promising as they sound, recent crises have shown that first-best policies might not be the panacea. The reason is that they can be impractical, as they require that subsidies or taxes be introduced and removed at different phases of the business cycle. Changing the tax code at business cycle frequency is difficult both from an administrative point of view, as it requires parliamentary approval, and also from a political point of view, because taxes are difficult to pass and subsidies are difficult to remove.

By contrast, second-best polices, although not fully effective in reducing the costs of currency pegs, are easier to implement. This is because they involve taxing international capital flows, which in most countries does not require parliamentary approval and has less of a political charge. This may explain why second-best policies, especially movements in capital controls, are more commonly observed in real life. For this reason, we begin by analyzing this class of policy tool in Section 14.3.1 and then turn in Sections 14.3.2 and 14.3.3 to first-best policies.[2]

14.3.1 MACROPRUDENTIAL CAPITAL CONTROL POLICY

In Section 14.2, we demonstrated that the combination of downward nominal wage rigidity and a currency peg creates an externality. During booms, nominal wages rise, which puts the economy in a vulnerable position when the expansion ends. The return to a normal level of activity requires the real wage, $W_t/\mathcal{E}_t$, to fall back to its normal value. But because the nominal wage is downwardly rigid and the exchange rate is pegged, the real wage has a hard time falling. As a result, firms cannot employ all the workers that are willing to work at the going wage, and involuntary unemployment emerges. Households understand that the increase in consumption during the boom has this negative side effect. Nonetheless, during expansions (periods of low world interest rates, say), they increase their own consumption because they know that they are too small to make a difference by cutting their individual spending.

The currency peg externality implies that a benevolent *social planner* facing as constraints a currency peg and downward nominal wage rigidity and with powers to determine individual consumption in each period would pick a path of consumption that expands by less during booms than under a *laissez-faire* (competitive) equilibrium. Under the planner's allocation, the economy would experience less capital inflows and a smaller increase in the nominal wage during booms. In exchange, the bust phase of the cycle would be milder, with less unemployment and with a smaller contraction in the consumption of tradable and nontradable goods. The *benevolent government* could achieve this outcome in a variety of ways. For example, it could impose quantitative limits on international borrowing and lending, or it could impose a tax on capital inflows or on external debt. These instruments fall under the rubric *capital controls*. In fact, in Chapter 12, Section 12.4, we established the result that capital controls can be welfare improving for a small open economy in the presence of borrowing externalities.

The idea of how capital controls can alleviate the currency peg externality is illustrated in Figure 14.2.

The situation is a boom-bust cycle like the one studied in Section 14.1 and illustrated in Figure 14.1. Initially the world interest rate is r^* and the nominal wage is W^A. The exchange rate is fixed at $\bar{\mathcal{E}}$. The initial equilibrium is point A, where the economy has full employment and the relative price of nontradables is p^A. The boom phase of the cycle is triggered by a fall in the world interest rate from r^* to $r^{*\prime} < r^*$, which shifts the demand schedule out and to the right as shown with

[2]The analysis in this section is based on Stephanie Schmitt-Grohé and Martín Uribe, "Managing Currency Pegs," *American Economic Review: Papers and Proceedings* 102 (May 2012): 28-45. An infinite-horizon approach can be found in Stephanie Schmitt-Grohé and Martín Uribe, "Downward Nominal Wage Rigidity, Currency Pegs, and Involuntary Unemployment," *Journal of Political Economy* 124 (2016): 1466-1514.

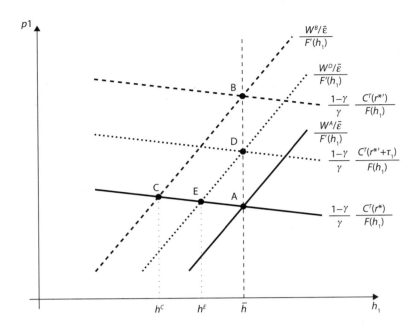

Figure 14.2. Capital Control Intervention during a Boom-Bust Cycle in a Currency Peg
Notes: The boom-bust dynamics under free capital mobility are identical to those shown in Figure 14.1: the initial equilibrium is at point A. A fall in the interest rate from r^* to $r^{*\prime} < r^*$ moves the equilibrium to point B, where wages and consumption of tradables are higher ($W^B > W^A$ and $C^T(r^{*\prime}) > C^T(r^*)$). When the interest rate goes back to r^*, the equilibrium shifts to point C, where there is unemployment in the amount $\bar{h} - h^C$. During the boom, the government imposes a capital control tax τ_1, which raises the effective interest rate to $r^{*\prime} + \tau_1 \in (r^{*\prime}, r^*)$. The fall in the interest rate shifts the demand schedule to the right but by less than under free capital mobility. The equilibrium is at point D, where the wage and consumption of tradables are higher but lower than under free capital mobility ($W^D \in (W^A, W^B)$ and $C^T(r^{*\prime} + \tau_1) \in (C^T(r^*), C^T(r^{*\prime}))$). When the interest rate goes back to r^*, the government removes the capital control tax ($\tau_1 = 0$), and the equilibrium is at point E, where there is unemployment but less than under free capital mobility ($\bar{h} - h^E < \bar{h} - h^C$).

a broken downward-sloping line. The expansion in aggregate demand pushes the nominal wage up to $W^B > W^A$, which shifts the supply schedule up and to the left, as shown with a broken upward-sloping line. The new equilibrium is at point B, where the economy operates at full employment, the nontradable good is more expensive ($p^B > p^A$), and the real wage is higher, $W^B/\bar{\mathcal{E}} > W^A/\bar{\mathcal{E}}$. The boom is led by an increase in the consumption of tradables, $C^T(r^{*\prime}, Q_1^T, Q_2^T) > C^T(r^*, Q_1^T, Q_2^T)$, and a deterioration of the trade balance, $Q_1^T - C^T(r^{*\prime}, Q_1^T, Q_2^T) < Q_1^T - C^T(r^*, Q_1^T, Q_2^T)$, and the current account. The current account deficit is financed by an increase in external debt (or a reduction in net foreign assets), a fall in $B_1 - B_0$.

The bust phase of the cycle occurs when the interest rate goes back to its initial level r^*. The increase in the interest rate causes consumption of tradables to fall, which shifts the demand schedule down and to the left. We assume, for simplicity, that the demand schedule shifts back to its original position. The fall in aggregate demand puts downward pressure on the real wage. However, due to downward nominal wage rigidity and a fixed exchange rate, the real wage stays at its boom level $W^B/\bar{\mathcal{E}}$. As a result, the equilibrium is at point C, where the economy experiences involuntary unemployment in the amount $\bar{h} - h^C$.

Let's now analyze how the boom-bust cycle looks with government intervention. Suppose that during the boom, the government imposes capital controls in the form of a tax on external debt. Let the tax rate be τ_1. A household that borrows 1 unit of the tradable good receives, after paying the debt tax, only $1 - \tau_1$ units of the tradable good. Next period, the household must pay $1 + r^{*\prime}$. So the effective interest rate is $r^{*\prime} + \tau_1$.[3] The introduction of capital controls hinders international capital mobility. In particular, with capital controls, the fall in the world interest rate causes a smaller expansion in consumption of tradable goods in period 1, $C^T(r^{*\prime} + \tau_1, Q_1^T, Q_2^T) < C^T(r^{*\prime}, Q_1^T, Q_2^T)$, a smaller deterioration of both the trade balance and the current account, and a smaller elevation in external debt. Consequently, following the fall in the world interest rate, the demand schedule shifts up and to the right (dash-dotted downward-sloping line in Figure 14.2), but by less than under free capital mobility. This demand schedule is located in between the pre-shock demand schedule and the post-shock demand schedule under free capital mobility. The expansion in aggregate demand following the fall in the world interest rate pushes the nominal wage up to W^D. However, the wage increase is smaller than in the absence of capital controls, $W^D < W^B$. As a result, the supply schedule shifts up and to the left, as shown by the dash-dotted upward-sloping line, but by less than under free capital mobility. The equilibrium in the boom phase of the cycle with capital controls is at point D.

Consider now the bust phase of the cycle with government intervention. Assume that when the world interest rate goes back up to its original level $r^* > r^{*\prime}$, the government removes the capital controls. Suppose that the demand schedule shifts down and to the left to its original position, indicated by the downward-sloping solid line. The nominal wage stays at W^D, because downward rigidity prevents it from falling. As a result, the supply schedule continues to be the upward-sloping dash-dotted line. The equilibrium is at point E, where there is involuntary unemployment in the amount $\bar{h} - h^E$. The key result is that the level of unemployment is lower than under free capital mobility, $\bar{h} - h^E < \bar{h} - h^C$.

By imposing capital controls during the boom phase of the cycle, the government allows for a softer landing. The government does not prevent a contraction; it simply makes it less pronounced. It is important to note that the government must intervene during the expansionary phase of the cycle to make the boom smaller. This kind of capital control policy in which the government "takes the punch bowl away just when the party is getting good" as opposed to "picking up the broken pieces once the party is over" is known as *macroprudential policy*.

Capital controls can be welfare improving, but do not represent a first-best solution to the inefficiencies caused by the combination of downward nominal wage

---

[3]Strictly speaking, the effective interest rate is $(1 + r^{*\prime})/(1 - \tau_1) - 1$, which is approximately equal to $r^{*\prime} + \tau_1$.

rigidity and a fixed exchange rate. This is because by distorting the domestic interest rate (recall that under capital controls the interest rate perceived by households is $r^{*\prime} + \tau_1$ instead of $r^{*\prime}$), capital controls lead to an inefficient allocation of consumption over time. Put differently, households don't take full advantage of the fall in the world interest rate. For this reason, in this context capital controls represent a second-best solution.

Next, we analyze a number of policy interventions that have the advantage of achieving the first-best allocation—which in the context of the TNT-DNWR model means full employment without distorting the intertemporal allocation of tradable consumption—but that, as mentioned in the introduction to this section, can be more difficult to implement in practice.

14.3.2 FISCAL DEVALUATIONS

One way to make up for the inefficiencies caused by the lack of movement in the nominal exchange rate in a currency peg is to apply subsidies or taxes that affect the incentives to employ workers. Consider, for example, a wage subsidy. Let s_t denote a wage subsidy paid to firms in the nontraded sector in period $t = 1, 2$. Specifically, assume that the government pays a fraction s_t of the wage bill of firms in period t. In this case profits in the nontraded sector are given by

$$\Pi_t = P_t^N F(h_t) - (1 - s_t) W_t h_t. \tag{14.1}$$

The first-order optimality condition of the firm is $P_t^N F'(h_t) = (1 - s_t) W_t$. Dividing both sides by $\mathcal{E}_t$ and recalling that $p_t \equiv P_t^N / \mathcal{E}_t$, we can write this optimality condition as:

$$p_t = \frac{(1 - s_t)(W_t/\mathcal{E}_t)}{F'(h_t)}. \tag{14.2}$$

This is the supply schedule of the TNT-DNWR economy with a wage subsidy. It says that at the optimum level of employment, the firm equates the price to the after-subsidy marginal cost of production. All else equal, the higher the subsidy is, the lower the after-subsidy marginal cost will be. Thus, the imposition of a labor subsidy shifts the supply schedule down and to the right. From the point of view of a nontraded goods producer, given p_t, a wage subsidy is identical to a decline in the nominal wage or to a devaluation. The firm does not care whether a fall in the marginal cost comes about because the government subsidizes wages, or because the nominal wage falls, or because the central bank devalues the currency. For this reason, when a labor subsidy is used as a way to foster employment in a currency peg economy, it is called a *fiscal devaluation*.

Next, we show that the demand schedule is unchanged by the introduction of the wage subsidy. Assume that the wage subsidy is financed by a proportional income tax, τ_t^y, imposed on households. The government budget constraint is then given by

$$s_t W_t h_t = \tau_t^y (\bar{\mathcal{E}} Q_t^T + W_t h_t + \Pi_t), \tag{14.3}$$

in period $t = 1, 2$. The left-hand side is the expenditure on subsidies. The right-hand side is the revenue from the income tax. The household's budget constraints in periods 1 and 2 are

$$\bar{\mathcal{E}}C_1^T + P_1^N C_1^N + \bar{\mathcal{E}}B_1 = (1 - \tau_1^y)(\bar{\mathcal{E}}Q_1^T + W_1 h_1 + \Pi_1)$$

and

$$\bar{\mathcal{E}}C_2^T + P_2^N C_2^N = (1 - \tau_2^y)(\bar{\mathcal{E}}Q_2^T + W_2 h_2 + \Pi_2) + (1 + r^*)\bar{\mathcal{E}}B_1.$$

The novel element in each of these budget constraints is that the right-hand sides feature *disposable income*, defined as income net of tax payments. Now proceed exactly as we did in Section 13.1.2 of Chapter 13 to derive the demand schedule. To obtain the household's intertemporal budget constraint, first divide the right- and left-hand sides of the above two budget constraints by the nominal exchange rate in the corresponding period (which now is pegged at $\bar{\mathcal{E}}$) to express all quantities in terms of tradable goods. Then combine the resulting expressions to eliminate B_1. This yields the following intertemporal budget constraint

$$C_1^T + p_1 C_1^N + \frac{C_2^T + p_2 C_2^N}{1 + r^*} = \bar{Y}, \tag{14.4}$$

which is identical to its counterpart without taxes or subsidies, equation (13.8) in Chapter 13, except that now $\bar{Y}$ is given by the present discounted value of disposable income,

$$\bar{Y} \equiv (1 - \tau_1^y)(Q_1^T + W_1/\bar{\mathcal{E}}h_1 + \Pi_1/\bar{\mathcal{E}}) + \frac{(1 - \tau_2^y)(Q_2^T + W_2/\bar{\mathcal{E}}h_2 + \Pi_2/\bar{\mathcal{E}})}{1 + r^*}. \tag{14.5}$$

As in the economy without taxes, the household takes $\bar{Y}$ as exogenously given. The household chooses C_t^T and C_t^N for $t = 1, 2$, to maximize the lifetime utility function

$$\ln C_1 + \beta \ln C_2 \tag{14.6}$$

subject to the Armington aggregator

$$C_t = (C_t^T)^\gamma (C_t^N)^{1-\gamma} \tag{14.7}$$

and to the intertemporal budget constraint (14.4), with $\bar{Y}$ given by (14.5). Given $\bar{Y}$, the household's problem is identical to that of the economy without taxes. As a result, the optimality conditions are also the same. In particular, we have that

$$\frac{C_2^T}{C_1^T} = \beta(1 + r^*) \tag{14.8}$$

and

$$\frac{C_1^N}{C_1^T} = \frac{1-\gamma}{\gamma}\frac{1}{p_1}. \tag{14.9}$$

Combining the market-clearing condition in the nontraded sector,

$$C_t^N = F(h_t),$$ (14.10)

with the firm's profits (14.1), the government budget constraint (14.3), and the household's intertemporal budget constraint (14.4), with $\bar{Y}$ given by (14.5), yields the economy's intertemporal resource constraint for tradable goods,

$$C_1^T + \frac{C_2^T}{1+r^*} = Q_1^T + \frac{Q_2^T}{1+r^*},$$ (14.11)

which is identical to the one obtained in the economy without taxes, equation (13.14) in Chapter 13. (Make sure you can derive equation (14.11).) Note that neither the subsidy rate s_t nor the income tax rate τ_t^y appears in this constraint. The reason is that in equilibrium the reduction in disposable income due to the income tax is exactly offset by the increase in profit income due to the wage subsidy.

Now, combining the Euler equation (14.8) and the intertemporal resource constraint (14.11) yields the equilibrium consumption of tradable goods in period 1,

$$C_1^T = \frac{1}{1+\beta}\left[Q_1^T + \frac{Q_2^T}{1+r^*}\right],$$ (14.12)

which is identical to equation (13.15) in Chapter 13 under the assumption that $B_0 = 0$. Again, we summarize this equilibrium condition as

$$C_1^T = C^T(r^*, Q_1^T, Q_2^T),$$ (14.13)

where the function $C^T(\cdot)$ is increasing in Q_1^T and Q_2^T and decreasing in r^*.

To obtain the demand schedule, use (14.13) and (14.10) to eliminate C_1^T and C_1^N, respectively, from (14.9). This yields the demand schedule

$$p_1 = \frac{1-\gamma}{\gamma}\frac{C^T(r^*, Q_1^T, Q_2^T)}{F(h_1)},$$ (14.14)

which is the same as the demand schedule without wage subsidies or income taxes. This demonstrates that in the TNT-DNWR economy, the introduction of a wage subsidy for firms financed with an income tax on households does not affect the demand schedule.

Figure 14.3 illustrates the adjustment of the economy to an increase in the world interest rate. The initial position is at point A, where there is full employment and the relative price of the nontraded good is p^A. The currency is pegged at $\bar{\mathcal{E}}$, and the nominal wage rate is W^A. Suppose that the world interest rate increases from r^* to $r^{*\prime} > r^*$. The negative external shock shifts the demand schedule down and to the left, as shown by the downward-sloping broken line. In the absence of government intervention, the new equilibrium is at point B, where there is involuntary unemployment in the amount $\bar{h} - h^B$. In spite of the excess supply of labor, the wage rate remains at its initial value W^A. It fails to fall because it is downwardly rigid. The introduction of a wage subsidy $s_1 > 0$ shifts the supply schedule down and to the right, as indicated by the upward-sloping broken line. As shown above, the subsidy

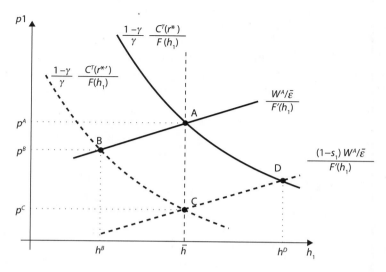

Figure 14.3. A Fiscal Devaluation in the TNT-DNWR Economy
Notes: The figure shows the effect of a wage subsidy in the adjustment to an interest rate hike in the TNT-DNWR economy with a fixed exchange rate. Initially, the world interest rate is r^*, and the equilibrium is at point A. When the interest rate increases to $r^{*\prime} > r^*$, the demand schedule shifts down and to the left. The new equilibrium without a subsidy is point B and features involuntary unemployment. The wage subsidy, $s_1 > 0$, shifts the supply schedule down and to the right and leaves the demand schedule unchanged. The equilibrium with the subsidy is point C, where full employment is restored and the price of nontradables is lower, $p^C < p^B$.

leaves the demand schedule unchanged. If the size of the subsidy is just right, the new supply and demand schedules will cross at point C, where full employment is restored.

The intuition why a fiscal devaluation is effective in maintaining full employment is as follows: the negative external shock produces a contraction in the demand for nontradables. At the same time, the wage subsidy increases the supply of nontradables. These two effects offset each other, so the quantity of goods produced is unchanged by the shock. Since the economy was at full employment prior to the shock, it remains at full employment afterward. Both the contraction in demand and the increase in supply push the relative price down (in the figure, p_1 falls from p^A to p^C). The fall in the relative price is larger than in the absence of government intervention ($p^C < p^B$), which allows for a larger expenditure switch in favor of nontradable consumption. Put differently, the introduction of the labor subsidy allows for a larger depreciation of the real exchange rate. All of these effects are exactly the same as those associated with a nominal depreciation that restores full employment in a floating exchange rate regime (see Section 13.3 of Chapter 13), giving credence to the term fiscal devaluation. The only difference between a fiscal devaluation and a currency devaluation has to do with the behavior of core inflation. In the fiscal devaluation, the nominal price of the nontraded good in period 1 is given by $P_1^N = (1 - s_1) W_1 / F'(\bar{h})$. Thus, the imposition of the subsidy has a deflationary effect, as it produces a fall in P_1^N (recall that due to downward nominal wage rigidity, the wage rate stays at W^A). By contrast, a currency devaluation, as shown in Section 13.3 of Chapter 13, can preserve price stability in the nontraded sector.

How large is the minimum wage subsidy that ensures full employment? Equating the supply and demand schedules, equations (14.2) and (14.14), evaluated at $h_1 = \bar{h}$ and solving for s_1, we obtain[4]

$$s_1 = 1 - F'(\bar{h}) \frac{1-\gamma}{\gamma} \frac{C^T(r^{*\prime})}{F(\bar{h})} \frac{\bar{\mathcal{E}}}{W^A} = 1 - \frac{C^T(r^{*\prime})}{C^T(r^*)}.$$

Thus, if the external shock causes a fall in the consumption of tradables of, say, 10 percent, then the subsidy should equal 10 percent. More generally, this expression shows that the wage subsidy is an increasing function of the change in the world interest rate. That is, the larger the negative external shock is, the larger the wage subsidy that ensures full employment has to be.

It is important that when the interest rate hike dissipates, the fiscal authority remove the subsidy. Keeping the subsidy in place for too long has the unintended consequence of having to increase subsidies even further when the next negative shock comes around. To see this, suppose that the interest rate goes back to r^*. For simplicity, let's assume that the demand schedule goes back up to its original position, the downward-sloping solid line in Figure 14.3. If the nominal wage stayed the same, the economy would experience an excess demand for labor equal to $h^D - \bar{h} > 0$. Thus, the nominal wage increases, shifting the supply schedule up and to the left to its original position, the upward-sloping solid line. The equilibrium is back at point A. The difference with the pre-shock equilibrium is that now the subsidy is positive (as opposed to zero), and the nominal wage is higher. Suppose now that the economy suffers another increase in the world interest rate. As before, the demand schedule shifts down and to the left as indicated by the downward-sloping broken line. If the fiscal authority keeps the subsidy unchanged, the equilibrium is at point B, where there is involuntary unemployment. To eliminate the unemployment, the government would have to increase the subsidy again. Continuing with this logic, we have that as time goes by and more ups and downs in the world interest rate happen, the subsidy will become bigger and bigger. In the limit, the government would end up subsidizing the entire wage bill (that is, s_t would converge to 1). To avoid this, the government must remove the subsidy as soon as the interest rate hike is over. Eliminating the subsidy, however, has a political downside because once a subsidy is given, it is typically regarded as an acquired right by the beneficiaries (firms in the nontraded sector in this case). This suggests that it is important that right from the outset, the subsidy comes with an expiration date.

Many countries have payroll taxes that are paid in part by firms. In this case, fiscal devaluations can be implemented by cutting the employer's part of the payroll tax. This is because a wage subsidy has the same effect as a cut in wage taxes. For example, if prior to the shock firms faced a proportional tax τ_t on wages, then profits

---

[4]The second equality follows from the fact that prior to the interest rate shock, equations (14.2) and (14.14) imply that $1/C^T(r^*) = [(1-\gamma)/\gamma][F'(\bar{h})/F(\bar{h})]\bar{\mathcal{E}}/W^A$.

are given by $P_t^N F(h_t) - (1 + \tau_t) W_t h_t$. The firm's optimality condition is then

$$p_t = (1 + \tau_t) \frac{W_t / \bar{\mathcal{E}}}{F'(h_t)}.$$

It is apparent from this expression that a cut in τ_t reduces the marginal cost just like a wage subsidy does. Put differently, a cut in τ_t shifts the supply schedule down and to the right in the same way as an increase in the wage subsidy does. It follows that in response to an adverse external shock, like the increase in the world interest rate considered in this section, a cut in wage taxes can preserve full employment. Like a wage subsidy, the cut in wage taxes would have to be financed somehow (e.g., by an increase in the income tax τ_t^y).

Fiscal devaluations can also be implemented through other taxes or subsidies. Exercise 14.9 asks you to show that a cut in sales taxes (or an increase in sales subsidies) in the nontraded sector has the same effect on employment as the cut in wage taxes (increase in wage subsidies) studied in this section. Exercise 14.10 asks you to prove a similar result for taxes on the consumption of nontradable goods.

Fiscal devaluations were part of the menu of policy options discussed for the periphery of Europe in the aftermath of the global financial crisis of 2008. A cut in wage taxes financed by an increase in the value-added tax was proposed by Cavallo and Cottani (2010) for Greece—the economy hit hardest by the crisis—as a substitute for exiting the monetary union and devaluing.[5] The Portuguese government also took this idea seriously. In 2011 it proposed to shift part of the employers' social security contributions to the employees' social security contributions. In terms of our model, this is equivalent to a reduction in the wage tax τ_t and an increase in the income tax τ_t^y applied to the household's labor income. In the face of widespread protests, this proposal was quickly discarded.

14.3.3   HIGHER INFLATION IN A MONETARY UNION

Another first-best policy that can bring about full employment in an economy suffering unemployment due to a fixed exchange rate and downward nominal wage rigidity is an increase in the international price of the tradable good, P^{T*}. This policy option is relevant for countries belonging to a monetary union such as the eurozone. Suppose, for example, that a country or a set of countries in a monetary union suffers a negative shock. Think of the periphery of Europe in the aftermath of the global financial crisis of 2008. The affected countries could lobby the monetary authority of the currency union to increase inflation in the union as a whole; that is, to increase P^{T*}. This would lower the real wage measured in units of the tradable good and raise the demand for labor by firms.

Thus far, we have assumed that the foreign price of the tradable good, P^{T*}, is equal to 1. Suppose now that it can take different values, depending on how expansionary the union-wide monetary policy is. In a monetary union, all member countries use the same currency. For example, in all countries in the euro area the

---

[5] See Domingo Cavallo and Joaquín Cottani, "For Greece, A 'Fiscal Devaluation' Is a Better Solution Than a Temporary Holiday from the Eurozone," VoxEU, February 22, 2010.

euro is legal tender. Thus, the exchange rate between the currencies of two member countries is 1. Therefore, we can interpret a currency union as a currency peg in which the exchange rate is fixed at unity. Accordingly, throughout this subsection think of $\bar{\mathcal{E}}$ as being equal to 1.

By the law of one price, the domestic price of the tradable good in period 1, P_1^T, must equal $\mathcal{E}_1 P^{T*}$. Further, because the exchange rate is fixed at $\bar{\mathcal{E}}$, we have that $P_1^T = \bar{\mathcal{E}} P^{T*}$. The supply schedule in period 1 then becomes

$$p_1 = \frac{W_1/(\bar{\mathcal{E}} P^{T*})}{F'(h_1)}.$$

Assume first that the initial asset position is zero, $B_0 = 0$. In this case, the demand schedule is unchanged,

$$p_1 = \frac{1-\gamma}{\gamma} \frac{C^T(r^*, Q_1^T, Q_2^T)}{F(h_1)}.$$

It is clear from these two expressions that an increase in the union-wide price level has the same effect as a devaluation. That is, it shifts the supply schedule down and to the right without affecting the position of the demand schedule.

It follows that if a country that belongs to a currency union is hit by a negative external shock, such as an increase in the world interest rate, some inflation in the monetary union can lift it out of unemployment. The adjustment is illustrated in Figure 14.4. The economy starts at point A, where the foreign price of the tradable good is P^{T*}, the world interest rate is r^*, and the nominal wage is W^A. At point A, the economy enjoys full employment and the relative price of nontradables is p^A. Suppose now that the world interest rate increases to $r^{*\prime} > r^*$. As a consequence of this shock, the demand schedule shifts down and to the left (broken downward-sloping line). If the monetary union's central bank, the European Central Bank, say, remains unresponsive, the new equilibrium is at point B, where the economy is in a recession with unemployment equal to $\bar{h} - h^B$ and the real exchange rate is somewhat depreciated ($p^B < p^A$). If instead the union's central bank eases monetary policy and increases the union-wide price of tradable goods to $P^{T*\prime} > P^{T*}$, the supply schedule shifts down and to the right (broken upward-sloping line). The right amount of external inflation will make the new supply and demand schedules intersect at point C, where the economy retains full employment. The equilibrium with intervention of the union's central bank features a more depreciated real exchange rate than the equilibrium without intervention ($p^C < p^B$). This extra depreciation allows for a larger expenditure switch in favor of nontradable goods, which contributes to preserving full employment.

For countries that are net external debtors—like most peripheral European countries during the global financial crisis of 2008—union-wide inflation can have an additional expansionary effect via a reduction of the real value of net external liabilities. Thus far, we have assumed that the country starts with no assets or liabilities, $B_0 = 0$. Suppose instead that the country begins period 1 as a net debtor, so that $B_0 < 0$. The asset position B_0 is a nominal quantity; that is, it is measured in units of foreign currency. Its real value in units of tradable goods is B_0/P^{T*}. The country's

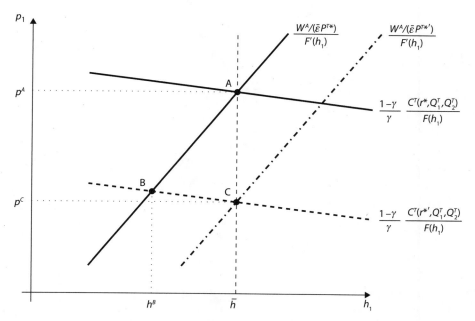

Figure 14.4. Adjustment to an Interest Rate Shock with Union-Wide Inflation

Notes: The figure shows the adjustment to an increase in the world interest rate from r^* to $r^{*\prime}$ in a country that is a member of a currency union, when the union's central bank intervenes by generating inflation. The initial equilibrium is at point A, where the union-wide price of tradable goods is P^{T*}, the nominal wage is W^A, the exchange rate is fixed at $\bar{\mathcal{E}}(= 1$ in a monetary union), and there is full employment. The increase in r^* shifts the demand schedule down and to the left. In response to the rise in r^*, the monetary authority increases the price level to $P^{T*\prime} > P^{T*}$. The increase in P^{T*} shifts the supply schedule down and to the right. The new equilibrium is at point C, where full employment is preserved and the real exchange rate depreciates.

intertemporal resource constraint then becomes

$$C_1^T + \frac{C_2^T}{1+r^*} = (1+r_0)B_0/P^{T*} + Q_1^T + \frac{Q_2^T}{1+r^*}.$$

If the country is a net external debtor, $B_0 < 0$, an increase in the external price level lowers the real value of its debt, making domestic households richer. We can then write the equilibrium level of consumption of tradable goods in period 1 as

$$C_1^T = C^T(\underset{-}{r^*}, \underset{+}{Q_1^T}, \underset{+}{Q_2^T}, \underset{+}{(1+r_0)B_0/P^{T*}}).$$

If the country is a net external debtor, an increase in the external price level, P^{T*}, shifts the demand schedule up and to the right. This is because at a given relative price, p_1, the increase in P^{T*} generates a positive wealth effect, which boosts the demand for goods.

Consider again the adjustment to an increase in the world interest rate. The situation is illustrated in Figure 14.5. Initially, the world interest rate is r^*, the external

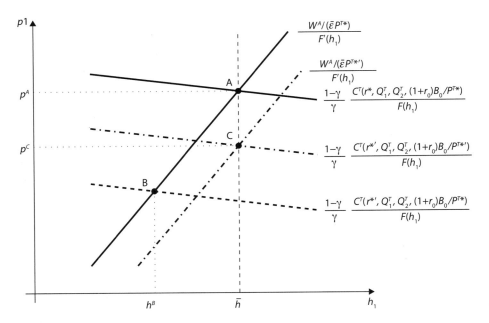

Figure 14.5. Adjustment to an Interest Rate Shock with External Inflation and Initial Debts

Notes: The figure shows the adjustment to an increase in the world interest rate from r^* to $r^{*\prime}$ for a member of a monetary union that starts with external debt, $B_0 < 0$. The initial equilibrium is at point A, where the nominal wage is W^A, the exchange rate is fixed at $\bar{\mathcal{E}}$, and the external price level is P^{T*}. Absent any policy intervention, after the increase in the world interest rate, the new equilibrium would be at point B. Suppose that in response to the rise in r^*, the monetary authority of the currency union increases the price level to $P^{T*\prime} > P^{T*}$. The increase in P^{T*} shifts the demand schedule up and to the right (the downward-sloping dash-dotted line) and the supply schedule down and to the right (the upward-sloping dash-dotted line). The new equilibrium is at point C.

price of the tradable good is P^{T*}, and the nominal wage is W^A. The initial equilibrium is at point A, where there is full employment and the relative price of the nontradable good is p^A. Suppose that the world interest rate increases to $r^{*\prime} > r^*$. As a result of this negative external shock, the demand schedule shifts down and to the left, as shown with a broken downward-sloping line. If the monetary union's central bank does not intervene, the new equilibrium is at point B, where the economy suffers involuntary unemployment. Suppose now that the central bank intervenes by creating union-wide inflation. Specifically, suppose that the external price level increases from P^{T*} to $P^{T*\prime} > P^{T*}$. As a result of this policy intervention, the supply schedule shifts down and to the right, as indicated by the dash-dotted upward-sloping line, and the demand schedule shifts up and to the right, as indicated by the dash-dotted downward-sloping schedule. If the increase in the external price of tradables is just right, the new supply and demand schedules will intersect at point C, where full employment is restored. As the economy moves from point A to point C, the nontraded good becomes cheaper (the real exchange rate depreciates). This change in relative prices is necessary to induce an expenditure switch away from tradables and toward nontradables. However, the required expenditure switch—and therefore the real exchange rate depreciation—is smaller compared to a situation in which the country starts with a zero net asset position ($B_0 = 0$). The reason is that the fall in the real value of debt created by the increase in P^{T*} partially offsets the contraction in aggregate demand caused by the increase in the world interest rate.

In sum, external inflation boosts equilibrium employment through two channels. First, it lowers real labor costs measured in terms of tradables, $W^A/(\bar{\mathcal{E}}P^{T*'}) < W^A/(\bar{\mathcal{E}}P^{T*})$. Second, it inflates away part of the real value of the country's initial net external liabilities, $(1 + r_0)B_0/P^{T*'} > (1 + r_0)B_0/P^{T*}$. During the global financial crisis of 2008, a number of economists advocated for an increase in inflation in the euro area as a way to provide relief to the highly indebted peripheral members of the eurozone. However, in spite of the stated intention of the European Central Bank to boost the price level, the eurozone consistently undershot its inflation target of close to but below 2 percent throughout the global financial crisis and for many years thereafter.

14.4 The Boom-Bust Cycle in Peripheral Europe, 2000–2011

Throughout this chapter we have focused on economies with a fixed exchange rate experiencing a boom-bust cycle. In this section, we present a case study of an actual boom-bust cycle—namely, the one that took place between 2000 and 2011 in the periphery of Europe. The case study suggests that the boom-bust cycle predicted by the TNT-DNWR model with fixed exchange rates analyzed in Section 14.1 shares a number of characteristics with the one observed in peripheral Europe.

In 1999, a number of countries in western Europe formed a monetary union known as the eurozone. A key element of the eurozone is the common currency, the euro. Member countries relinquished their local currencies (Spain the peseta, Greece the drachma, Portugal the escudo, and so on) and adopted the common one. At the time of its creation, the level of income within the eurozone was somewhat heterogeneous. There was a core of highly developed countries, including Germany, France, and the Low Countries, and a periphery of relatively less developed countries including, among others, Cyprus, Greece, Ireland, Portugal, and Spain. In effect, by joining the eurozone, the peripheral countries adopted a currency peg vis-à-vis the core countries at a unit exchange rate. In addition, a number of nonmember peripheral European countries pegged their currencies to the newly created euro in preparation for possible future accession to the eurozone (Estonia, Lithuania, Latvia, Slovenia, and Slovakia, among others).

The international community interpreted the creation of the eurozone as a signal that the periphery of Europe would embark on a convergence path toward the living standards of the core countries. Foreign lenders viewed the region as a safe investment opportunity. As a result, between 2000 and 2008, the periphery experienced a sustained boom in aggregate activity fueled by large international capital inflows at low interest rates. As shown in the top left panel of Figure 14.6, countries in the

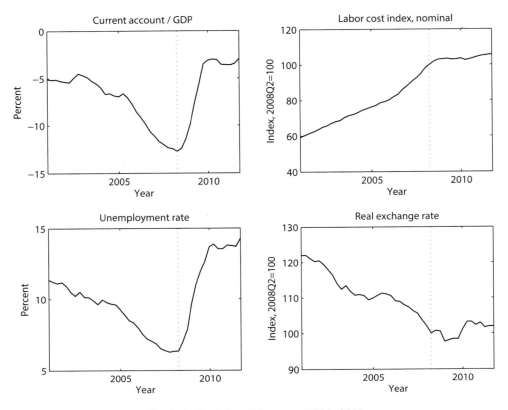

Figure 14.6. Boom-Bust Cycle in Peripheral Europe, 2000–2011

Notes: Arithmetic mean of Bulgaria, Cyprus, Estonia, Greece, Ireland, Lithuania, Latvia, Portugal, Spain, Slovenia, and Slovakia. The vertical line indicates 2008Q2, the beginning of the recession according to the Euro Area Business Cycle Dating Committee.

Data Source: Eurostat.

periphery experienced large increases in current account deficits of about 8 percent of GDP. These external imbalances financed a rapid growth in the aggregate demand for goods and services. In turn, the expansion in aggregate demand was accompanied by a sharp increase in nominal wages of about 60 percent between 2000 and 2008 (top right panel) and a significant fall in unemployment of about 5 percentage points (bottom left panel). During the boom, the prices of nontradable goods (personal services, housing, etc.) grew rapidly, resulting in a large real exchange rate appreciation of about 25 percent (bottom right panel). This means that countries in the periphery of Europe became significantly more expensive relative to the core countries.

In terms of the graphical characterization of a boom-bust cycle in Figure 14.1, these developments correspond to the boom phase of the cycle, captured by the move from point A to point B. Along the transition from point A to point B, like in the data, the TNT-DNWR economy experiences capital inflows, a deterioration in the current account, a rise in nominal wages, and a real exchange rate appreciation.

Unlike in the data, however, the move from point A to point B does not feature a fall in unemployment. This is because to avoid clutter, the economy is assumed to enter the boom at full employment. But the model can capture this fact if one assumes that there is some unemployment prior to the shock, as Exercise 14.5 asks you to demonstrate.

The boom in peripheral Europe came to an abrupt end with the onset of the global financial crisis, which arguably originated in the United States in the last quarter of 2007 and quickly spread to Europe. For the periphery of the eurozone, the global financial crisis meant that foreign investors suddenly stopped extending credit. As a result, as shown in the top left panel of Figure 14.6, the current account experienced a sharp reversal and aggregate demand froze. The large contraction in aggregate demand, however, was not accompanied by a fall in nominal wages, which remained as high as at the peak of the boom. The lack of downward adjustment in nominal wages in the context of a severe recession and near-zero inflation is an indication of downward nominal wage rigidity. In this context, the unemployment rate rose sharply. In addition, during the contraction, countries in the periphery became somewhat cheaper. The real exchange rate depreciated by about 5 percent between 2008 and 2011. However, the real exchange rate did not return to its pre-boom level, but remained about 20 percent more appreciated in 2011 than in 2000. Viewed through the lens of the TNT-DNWR model, the contraction in the aftermath of the global financial crisis corresponds to the move from point B to point C in Figure 14.1. As in the data, the model predicts that when financial market conditions deteriorate, the current account improves, the wage rate fails to fall, the real exchange rate depreciates but does not reach its pre-boom level, and involuntary unemployment rises.

The boom-bust cycle in the periphery of Europe conforms closely to the predictions of the model. This suggests that the combination of downward nominal wage rigidity and a fixed exchange rate can be a relevant factor in the adjustment of open economies to external shocks.

Two key building blocks of the eurozone are a common currency and free capital mobility. These two elements have served as vehicles for achieving convergence across its heterogeneous members. However, the global financial crisis of 2008 revealed that these two key elements can also be the Achilles heel of the union. By the monetary policy trilemma (studied in Section 13.5 of Chapter 13), a country with a fixed exchange rate and free capital mobility cannot have an autonomous monetary policy: if its currency is pegged to that of a core country and capital can flow freely across borders, its domestic interest rate is determined by the interest rate in the core country. As a result, the peripheral country has no monetary policy tools to respond to aggregate shocks. It is precisely in this sense that alternative policies, such as macroprudential capital controls, fiscal devaluations, and union-wide inflation, might fill the void left by the loss of monetary autonomy.

14.5 Summing Up

In the presence of nominal rigidity and free capital mobility, the exchange rate can be a powerful tool to stabilize aggregate activity and prices over the business cycle. When the central bank pegs the currency, it gives up this tool. This chapter analyzes alternative stabilization policies that can substitute for the loss of monetary autonomy.

- In a currency peg, a positive external shock can be a Trojan horse. When the economy expands, the real wage goes up. Once the boom is over, the real wage must fall to equilibrate the labor market. The combination of downward nominal wage rigidity and a fixed exchange rate makes the real wage downwardly rigid, giving rise to involuntary unemployment. This is called a boom-bust cycle.
- Downward nominal wage rigidity and a currency peg combined produce an externality, originating in the fact that individual agents fail to internalize that capital inflows in the expansionary phase of the business cycle push wages up, placing the economy in a vulnerable position to adjust in the contractionary phase of the cycle.
- Capital controls can help reduce the amplitude of the business cycle in economies with a currency peg.
- Capital controls must be raised during booms and lowered during contractions, to reduce the volatility of capital inflows. This type of preemptive policy is called macroprudential, as it acts before the economy enters a downturn.
- Capital controls do not achieve the first-best allocation, as they represent a trade-off between reducing unemployment and hindering the free flow of capital. For this reason, they are known as second-best instruments.
- One advantage of capital controls is that they are relatively easy to change over the business cycle.
- Labor subsidies or cuts in labor taxes can also be used to stabilize an economy subject to a currency peg and free capital mobility. An increase in a labor subsidy acts as a devaluation, as it lowers the labor cost of firms.
- Because changes in labor subsidies (labor taxes) mimic changes in the exchange rate, they are called fiscal devaluations.
- Unlike capital controls, labor subsidies (taxes) do not hinder the free flow of capital.
- Appropriate movements in labor subsidies (taxes) can achieve the first-best allocation—namely, full employment and an efficient intertemporal allocation of resources.
- Labor subsidies (labor tax cuts) are politically easy to pass but difficult to remove. In addition, they require parliamentary approval, which is often slow. These issues render fiscal devaluations impractical for stabilization purposes, as the optimal policy requires introducing subsidies (tax cuts) during recessions and removing them during booms. This might explain why fiscal devaluations are not commonly observed in practice.
- In a currency union, all members use the same currency as legal tender. For this reason, from the perspective of a member country, a currency union can be thought of as a currency peg in which the exchange rate is fixed at 1.
- An increase in union-wide inflation acts as a devaluation, because it increases the price of the internationally traded good.

- For this reason, union-wide inflation can reduce unemployment in member countries hit by negative external shocks.
- The 2000–2011 boom-bust cycle in the periphery of the eurozone (Ireland, Spain, Portugal, Greece, the Baltics, etc.) shares a number of features with the boom-bust cycle predicted by the TNT-DNWR model: Current account deficits, rising real wages, expansions in consumption and employment, and real exchange rate appreciation during the boom phase and a current account reversal, failure of real wages to decline, a collapse in consumption, and unemployment during the contractionary phase.

14.6 Exercises

Exercise 14.1 (Sudden Stops with Downward Wage Rigidity) Consider a TNT-DNWR economy. Households are endowed with 10 units of tradables in period 1 and 13.2 units in period 2 ($Q_1^T = 10$ and $Q_2^T = 13.2$). The country interest rate is 10 percent ($r^* = 0.1$), and the nominal exchange rate is fixed at 1 ($\mathcal{E}_0 = \mathcal{E}_1 = \mathcal{E}_2 = 1$). Suppose that the nominal wage is downwardly rigid ($W_t \geq W_{t-1}$, for $t = 1, 2$), and that $W_0 = 8.25$. Suppose the economy starts period 1 with no assets or debts carried over from the past ($B_0 = 0$). Suppose that the household's preferences are defined over consumption of tradable and nontradable goods in periods 1 and 2, and are described by the following utility function,

$$\ln C_1^T + \ln C_1^N + \ln C_2^T + \ln C_2^N,$$

where C_t^T and C_t^N denote consumption of tradable and nontradable goods in period $t = 1, 2$. Let p_1 and p_2 denote the relative prices of nontradables in terms of tradables in periods 1 and 2. Households supply inelastically $\bar{h} = 1$ units of labor each period. Firms produce nontradable goods using labor as the sole input. The production technology is given by $Q_t^N = h_t^\alpha$, where Q_t^N and h_t denote nontradable output and hours employed in period $t = 1, 2$. The parameter α is equal to 0.75.

1. Compute the equilibrium levels of consumption of tradables and the trade balance in periods 1 and 2.
2. Compute the equilibrium levels of employment, nontradable output, and the relative price of nontradables in periods 1 and 2.
3. Suppose now that the country interest rate increases to 32 percent. Calculate the equilibrium levels of consumption of tradables, the trade balance, consumption of nontradables, unemployment, the nominal and real wage, and the relative price of nontradables in periods 1 and 2, and the nominal interest rate on domestic currency bonds. Provide intuition for why unemployment and wages behave differently in periods 1 and 2.
4. Given the situation in question 3, find the devaluation rates in periods 1 and 2, $\frac{\mathcal{E}_t - \mathcal{E}_{t-1}}{\mathcal{E}_{t-1}} \times 100$, that are consistent with full employment and price stability in the nontraded market. Explain.

Exercise 14.2 (A Boom-Bust Cycle I) This exercise analyzes a boom-bust cycle through a numerical example. Consider the TNT-DNWR economy. Suppose that the endowment of tradable goods is 1 in both periods, $Q_1^T = Q_2^T = 1$, the time endowment is 1, $\bar{h} = 1$, the initial net asset position is 0, $B_0 = 0$, and the initial nominal wage is 0.75, $W_0 = 0.75$. The utility function is $\ln C_1 + \beta \ln C_2$. Assume further that the subjective discount factor β is 0.8. Consumption is a composite good made of tradable and nontradable goods, via the Cobb-Douglas aggregator $C_t = (C_t^T)^\gamma (C_t^N)^{1-\gamma}$, with $\gamma = 0.5$. Assume that the production technology for nontraded goods is $F(h_t) = h_t^\alpha$, with $\alpha = 0.75$. The central bank pegs the nominal exchange rate at $\mathcal{E}_t = 1$, for $t = 1, 2$. In Section 13.4 of Chapter 13, we showed that under this calibration, when the world interest rate is 25 percent, the equilibrium paths of the current account, the relative price of nontradables, the nominal wage, and unemployment are $CA_t = 0$, $p_t = 1$, $W_t = 0.75$, and $\bar{h} - h_t = 0$, for $t = 1, 2$.

1. Suppose the world interest rate is 10 percent, $r^* = 0.1$. Find the equilibrium values of the current account, the relative price of nontradables, the nominal wage, and the unemployment rate in periods 1 and 2.
2. State whether when r^* is 10 percent the economy experiences a boom-bust cycle and provide intuition.

Exercise 14.3 (A Boom-Bust Cycle II) Redo Exercise 14.2 under the assumption that the utility function is $-\frac{1}{C_1} - \beta \frac{1}{C_2}$ and the aggregator function is $C_t = \left[C_t^{T-1} + C_t^{N-1} \right]^{-1}$ for $t = 1, 2$. As a first step, compute the equilibrium when $r^* = 0.25$. Explain why it is or is not the same as the one given in Exercise 14.2.

Exercise 14.4 (Impossible Equilibria) Using the calibration of the TNT-DNWR model given in Exercise 14.2, show that when the world interest rate is 10 percent ($r^* = 0.1$):

1. An equilibrium with unemployment in period 1 is impossible.
2. An equilibrium with full employment in periods 1 and 2 is impossible.

Exercise 14.5 (Boom-Bust Cycle with Initial Unemployment) Use a graphical approach to analyze a boom-bust cycle under a currency peg from an initial position in which the economy suffers involuntary unemployment. Show that if the fall in the world interest rate is sufficiently large, the boom will feature a drop in unemployment, an increase in the nominal wage, and a real exchange rate appreciation. Assume for simplicity that when the world interest rate goes back up to its pre-boom level, the demand schedule returns to its initial position. Will the economy necessarily experience a larger level of unemployment during the bust than in the pre-boom situation?

Exercise 14.6 (Capital Controls, Downward Wage Rigidity, and Currency Pegs) Consider a two-period, small open economy with free capital mobility. Households are endowed with 10 units of tradables in period 1 and 10 units in period 2 ($Q_1^T = 10$ and $Q_2^T = 10$). The world interest rate is 0, $r^* = 0$; the nominal exchange rate, defined as the price of foreign currency in terms of domestic currency, is fixed and equal to 1 in both periods ($\mathcal{E}_1 = \mathcal{E}_2 = 1$). Suppose that the foreign currency price of tradable goods is constant and equal to 1 in both periods, and that the law of one price holds for tradable goods. Nominal wages are downwardly rigid. Specifically, assume that the nominal wage in periods 1 and 2, measured in terms of domestic currency, cannot fall below the past wage rate, $W_t \geq W_{t-1}$ for $t = 1, 2$, with $W_0 = 5$. Suppose the economy starts period 1 with no assets or debts carried over from the past ($B_0 = 0$). Suppose that the household's preferences are defined over consumption of tradable and nontradable goods in periods 1 and 2, and are described by the following utility function,

$$\ln C_1^T + \ln C_1^N + \ln C_2^T + \ln C_2^N,$$

where C_t^T and C_t^N denote consumption of tradables and nontradables in period $t = 1, 2$. Let p_1 and p_2 denote the relative prices of nontradables in terms of tradables in periods 1 and 2. Households supply inelastically $\bar{h} = 1$ units of labor each period. Finally, firms produce nontradable goods using labor as the sole factor input. The production technology is given by

$$Q_1^N = h_1^\alpha$$

and

$$Q_2^N = h_2^\alpha$$

in periods 1 and 2, where Q_t^N and h_t denote nontradable output and hours employed in period $t = 1, 2$. The parameter α is equal to 0.5.

1. Compute the equilibrium level of consumption of tradables and the trade balance in periods 1 and 2. Interpret your findings.
2. Compute the equilibrium levels of employment and nontradable output in periods 1 and 2.

For the remainder of the problem consider the case that the world interest rate falls to $r^* = -0.5$.

3. Compute the equilibrium level of consumption of tradables and the trade balance in periods 1 and 2.
4. Compute the equilibrium level of nontraded consumption in periods 1 and 2 and the wage rate in period 1. Provide a discussion of your findings.
5. Compute the level of welfare.
6. Suppose wages were fully flexible. Find the level of nontradable consumption in periods 1 and 2. Compute the level of welfare.

Suppose now that the government imposes capital controls that prevent households from borrowing in international capital markets in period 1; that is, the government imposes $B_1 \geq 0$. Continue to assume that the world interest rate is $r^* = -0.5$.

7. Find consumption of tradables and nontradables in periods 1 and 2.
8. Find the level of welfare under capital controls. Are capital controls welfare decreasing? Explain why or why not.
9. Compare the level of welfare under capital controls and under wage flexibility.

10. Suppose the only instrument the government has to influence capital inflows is a proportional capital control tax, denoted τ. In particular, individual households face an interest rate $1 + \tilde{r} = (1 + r^*)/(1 - \tau)$. Any capital control tax revenue is rebated to households in a lump-sum fashion.
    (a) What is the minimum value of τ consistent with an equilibrium in which $B_1 = 0$?
    (b) Does there exist a value of τ that implements the flexible wage allocation? If so, what is the value of τ?

Exercise 14.7 (Excessive Fiscal Devaluations) Using a graphical approach, consider the effect of an increase in the world interest rate from r^* to $r^{*\prime} > r^*$. Suppose that the currency is pegged at $\bar{\mathcal{E}}$ and that the initial nominal wage is W^A. Assume further that prior to the shock the economy operates at full employment. Suppose that in response to the shock, the government subsidizes wages at the rate s_1. Suppose further that s_1 is larger than the minimum subsidy that ensures full employment. Compare the equilibrium under the excessive wage subsidy to the one associated with the minimum wage subsidy that ensures full employment, discussed in Section 14.3.2. In particular, discuss possible differences in the equilibrium levels of employment, h_1, the nominal price of nontradables, P_1^N, the nominal wage, W_1, and the relative price of nontradables, p_1.

Exercise 14.8 (Insufficient Fiscal Devaluations) Using a graphical approach, consider the effect of an increase in the world interest rate from r^* to $r^{*\prime} > r^*$. Suppose that the currency is pegged at $\bar{\mathcal{E}}$ and that the initial nominal wage is W^A. Assume further that prior to the shock, the economy operates at full employment. Suppose that in response to the shock, the government subsidizes wages at the rate s_1. Suppose further that s_1 is smaller than the minimum subsidy that ensures full employment. Compare the equilibrium under the insufficient wage subsidy to the one associated with the minimum wage subsidy that ensures full employment, discussed in Section 14.3.2. In particular, discuss possible differences in the equilibrium levels of employment, h_1, the nominal price of nontradables, P_1^N, the nominal wage, W_1, and the relative price of nontradables, p_1.

Exercise 14.9 (Fiscal Devaluation through Sales Tax Cuts) Suppose an economy with a fixed exchange rate and downward nominal wage rigidity is hit by an increase in the world interest rate from r^* to $r^{*\prime} > r^*$, as in the example of Section 14.3.2. Show that the government can restore full employment by cutting taxes on sales in the nontraded sector. To this end, proceed as follows:

1. Let τ_t^s and τ_t^y denote the tax rates on sales and income, respectively. Derive the supply and demand schedules. Discuss how the schedules shift in response to a reduction in the sales tax.
2. Use a graphical approach to show that the sales tax cut is effective in maintaining full employment in response to the negative external shock.
3. Derive a formula for the minimum change in the sales tax that guarantees full employment as a function of exogenous variables only.

Exercise 14.10 (Fiscal Devaluation through Nontradable Consumption Tax Cuts) Suppose an economy with a fixed exchange rate and downward nominal wage rigidity is hit by an increase in the world interest rate from r^* to $r^{*\prime} > r^*$ as in the example of Section 14.3.2. Show that the government can restore full employment by cutting taxes on the consumption of nontraded goods. To this end, proceed as follows:

1. Let τ_t^c and τ_t^y denote the tax rates on consumption of nontraded goods and income, respectively. Derive the supply and demand schedules. Discuss how the schedules shift in response to a reduction in the nontradable consumption tax.
2. Use a graphical approach to show that the consumption tax cut is effective in maintaining full employment in response to the negative external shock.
3. Derive a formula for the minimum change in the consumption tax that guarantees full employment as a function of exogenous variables only.

Exercise 14.11 (External Price Inflation) Consider a country that is a member of a currency union. Suppose that households start period 1 with a positive net asset position, $B_0 > 0$. Show, following the analysis of Section 14.3.3, that in response to an increase in the world interest rate r^*, the country would be worse off if the monetary union's central bank were to increase the union's price level, P^{T*}.

CHAPTER 15

Inflationary Finance and Balance of Payments Crises

This chapter explores the connection between fiscal deficits, money creation, and the exchange rate. It begins by studying a theory of exchange rate determination that is rooted in a monetary theory known as the *quantity theory of money*. In the quantity theory of money, presented in Section 15.1, money creation by the central bank plays a key role in determining the price level and the exchange rate. The idea in this framework is that if the central bank prints too much money, prices would rise. All else equal, the country would become more expensive relative to the rest of the world. In turn, this creates incentives for people to buy goods abroad for which they need foreign currency. Given the quantity of money abroad, the elevated demand for foreign currency drives up its price relative to the domestic currency. That is, the foreign currency appreciates and the domestic currency depreciates. At the end of the day, money creation causes domestic inflation and a currency depreciation.

The next natural question is why would a central bank print too much money? One reason, studied in Section 15.2, is that some countries finance part of their fiscal deficits by money creation. In this case, the higher the fiscal deficit is, the more pressing the need to print money will be. In turn, by the arguments given in the previous paragraph, the higher the rate of money creation is, the higher inflation and currency depreciation will be. In other words, inflationary financing of the fiscal deficit causes exchange rate depreciation.

The connection between fiscal deficits and money creation, inflation, and devaluation need not be instantaneous or contemporaneous. Sometimes central banks engage in monetary and exchange rate arrangements that delay this connection, often with unintended consequences. In Section 15.7, we study a situation of this type, in which the treasury runs fiscal deficits and the central bank pegs the exchange rate. While the peg lasts, money creation, the price level, and obviously the exchange rate are under control. The fiscal deficits, however, cause a continuous deterioration in the government's asset position. When the asset position of the government gets sufficiently close to being unsustainable, there is a *speculative attack* against the domestic currency. The government loses massive amounts of assets in a short period of time and access to credit. At this point, it can no longer defend the currency peg. This situation is known as a *balance of payments crisis*.

We will organize ideas around using a theoretical framework (model) that is similar to the one presented in previous chapters, with one important modification: there is a demand for money.

15.1 The Quantity Theory of Money

The quantity theory of money (or just quantity theory) asserts that a key determinant of the nominal price level is the quantity of money printed by the central bank. A central building block of this theory is the *demand for money*. According to the quantity theory, people hold a more or less stable fraction of their income in the form of money. Formally, let M_t^d denote desired money holdings, P_t the price level, Y_t real income, and $1/V > 0$ the fraction of income that households desire to hold in the form of money balances, then the demand for money is assumed to take the form

$$M_t^d = \frac{1}{V} P_t Y_t. \tag{15.1}$$

The parameter V is known as *money velocity*. The intuition behind the name "velocity," is that V, being the ratio of nominal income, $P_t Y_t$, to desired money holdings, M_t^d, represents the number of times that each dollar must be used to purchase the entire income. For example, if V equals 5, each dollar is used to make five transactions; that is, it "circulates" five times from buyers to sellers.

But why would people want to hold money? This is an important question in macroeconomics. In the modern world, this question arises because money takes the form of unbacked paper notes printed by the government, unlike in former times, when paper money was convertible into specie (gold or silver coins). Paper money that the government is not obliged to exchange for goods is called *fiat money* and is intrinsically valueless.

One reason why people value fiat money is that it facilitates transactions. When money plays this role, we say that it is a *medium of exchange*. In the absence of money, all purchases of goods must take the form of barter. However, barter exchanges can be difficult to arrange because they require a double coincidence of wants. For example, a carpenter who wants to eat an ice cream must find an ice cream maker who is in need of a carpenter. Money eliminates the need for a double coincidence of wants.

Money also serves as the *unit of account*, which means that prices are quoted in units of currency. This is also the case in reality. For example, in the United States, prices of goods, services, and assets are expressed in dollars. Similarly, in countries belonging to the eurozone, prices are expressed in euros and so on.

A third possible use of money is as a *store of value*, which means that people may hold part of their savings in the form of money. A reason why money might be chosen as a store of value in spite of having a zero nominal rate of return is that it is a highly liquid asset; that is, it is easy to find someone who would be willing to accept it in exchange for other assets or goods.

In sum, money has three main uses: medium of exchange, unit of account, and store of value.

Let M_t denote the nominal *money supply*; that is, M_t represents the quantity of bills and coins in circulation plus checking deposits. Equilibrium in the money market requires that money demand be equal to money supply,

$$M_t = M_t^d.$$

Combining this market-clearing condition with the money demand function (15.1) to eliminate M_t^d gives

$$M_t = \frac{1}{V} P_t Y_t. \tag{15.2}$$

The quantity theory maintains that there is a dichotomy between the quantity of money, M_t, and real income, Y_t. In its strongest formulation, the quantity theory asserts that real income, which in equilibrium is real output, is determined by real factors such as population growth, technological progress, taxes, and openness to trade. This means that the equilibrium condition (15.2) has two endogenous variables, P_t and M_t, one exogenous variable, Y_t, and one parameter, V. Thus, if the central bank decides to double the quantity of money in period t, then the price level will also double, since neither V nor Y_t is affected by changes in the supply of money. The intuition behind this result is that when the central bank injects money into the economy, households find themselves with more money than they wish to hold. As a result, they try to get rid of the excess money balances by purchasing goods. However, the supply of goods is not affected, as it is determined by non-monetary factors. As a result, there is a generalized excess demand for goods that pushes all prices up. It is in this precise sense that the quantity theory predicts that inflation is a monetary phenomenon.

To understand how the nominal exchange rate is determined in the quantity theory, let's recall that the real exchange rate is defined as the relative price of a basket of consumption goods abroad in terms of baskets of consumption goods at home. Formally, letting e_t denote the real exchange rate, $\mathcal{E}_t$ the nominal exchange rate, and P_t^* the foreign price level, the real exchange rate is defined as

$$e_t = \frac{\mathcal{E}_t P_t^*}{P_t}. \tag{15.3}$$

The quantity theory maintains that the real exchange rate, like real output, is determined by real factors—such as technological progress, as, for example, in the Balassa-Samuelson model of Section 10.6 of Chapter 10, and real external shocks, as in the TNT model of Section 10.1 of the same chapter. Thus, in the quantity theory e_t is an exogenous variable.

Combining equations (15.2) and (15.3) to eliminate P_t and solving for the nominal exchange rate yields

$$\mathcal{E}_t = M_t \frac{V e_t}{P_t^* Y_t}. \tag{15.4}$$

In equation (15.4) the only two endogenous variables are the nominal exchange rate, $\mathcal{E}_t$, and the money supply, M_t. The real exchange rate, real output, and the foreign price level are exogenously determined. As we did in Chapter 13, we distinguish two exchange rate regimes, a flexible or floating exchange rate regime and a fixed exchange rate regime, depending on whether the central bank controls the path of the money supply or the path of the nominal exchange rate.

15.1.1   A FLEXIBLE EXCHANGE RATE REGIME

Under a flexible exchange rate regime, the central bank controls the quantity of money, M_t, and the market determines the nominal exchange rate, $\mathcal{E}_t$.

Let's analyze how monetary policy affects the exchange rate. Suppose that the central bank decides to increase the money supply. It is clear from equation (15.4) that, all other things constant, the monetary expansion causes the domestic currency to depreciate by the same proportion as the increase in the money supply; that is, $\mathcal{E}_t$ increases by the same proportion as M_t. The intuition behind this effect is simple. We already saw that an increase in the supply of money causes the price level, P_t, to increase by the same proportion as M_t. Since P_t^* is unaffected by the increase in M_t, given $\mathcal{E}_t$, the country becomes more expensive. As a result, households increase their demand for foreign currency to purchase goods abroad, where they are cheaper. As households dump the domestic currency, its value falls, or it depreciates relative to the foreign currency.

Suppose now that the country experiences a recession, so that real output, Y_t, falls. Suppose first that the monetary authority does not respond to this shock and keeps the money supply unchanged. By equations (15.2) and (15.4), the price level, P_t, and the nominal exchange rate, $\mathcal{E}$, increase in the same proportion. Intuitively, the fall in real income reduces the desired demand for money. As a result, households try to get rid of their excess money holdings by buying goods, which pushes the price level up. In turn, the increase in the price level makes the country more expensive, inducing households to increase their demand for foreign goods. In their attempt to buy more foreign goods, households exchange domestic currency for foreign currency, which drives up the price of foreign currency. Thus, a recession without central bank intervention results in inflation and exchange rate depreciation. What should the central bank do to avoid these effects? To stabilize the price level, the central bank should contract the money supply in the same proportion as the fall in real output. The intuition is that by cutting the money supply, the central bank accommodates the fall in the demand for money stemming from the lower level in aggregate activity.

Thus far, we have considered two shocks (an increase in M_t and a fall in Y_t) in response to which the price level and the nominal exchange rate move in tandem. But there are other shocks in which this is not the case. Suppose, for example, that the real exchange rate depreciates; that is, e_t goes up. This means that a foreign basket of goods becomes more expensive relative to a domestic basket of goods. A depreciation of the real exchange rate can be due to a variety of reasons, such as a terms-of-trade shock or the removal of import barriers. If the central bank keeps the money supply unchanged, then by equation (15.4) the real exchange rate depreciation causes a depreciation of the domestic currency (an increase in $\mathcal{E}_t$). In fact, e_t and $\mathcal{E}_t$ increase by the same proportion. By contrast, the price level P_t is unaffected because neither M_t nor Y_t has changed (see equation (15.2)). A similar disconnect in the reaction of $\mathcal{E}_t$ and P_t occurs in response to changes in the foreign price level P_t^*.

15.1.2 A FIXED EXCHANGE RATE REGIME

Under a fixed exchange rate regime, the central bank determines the path of $\mathcal{E}_t$. So given $\mathcal{E}_t$, e_t, P_t^*, and Y_t, condition (15.4) determines what M_t ought to be in equilibrium. Thus, under a fixed exchange rate regime, the money supply is an endogenous variable. Put differently, by controlling the path of the nominal exchange rate, the central bank gives up control of the money supply.

To see how under a fixed exchange rate regime the money supply changes endogenously in response to exogenous shocks, consider a fall in real output. Suppose that the central bank keeps the nominal exchange rate constant. By equation (15.4), the fall in Y_t requires M_t to decline in the same proportion as Y_t. Intuitively, the fall in real output reduces the demand for money. If the central bank kept the money supply constant, households' attempts to get rid of some of their money holdings would cause the exchange rate to depreciate. To avoid this, the central bank has to accommodate by reducing the amount of money in circulation.

Under a fixed exchange rate regime, the fall in Y_t does not affect the price level. To see this, look at equilibrium condition (15.2), and recall that M_t falls in the same proportion as Y_t. Note how different the effect of a fall in real output on the price level and the exchange rate is under the two exchange rate regimes considered. Under a flexible exchange rate in which the central bank keeps the money supply constant, the decline in Y_t causes inflation and an exchange rate depreciation, whereas under a fixed exchange rate regime the decline in Y_t has no effect on either variable. Similar asymmetries take place in response to other shocks: A real exchange depreciation (an increase in e_t) or a decrease in the foreign price level P_t^* cause an exchange rate depreciation and no change in the domestic price level under a flexible exchange rate regime in which the central bank keeps the money supply constant, but no change in the exchange rate and price deflation under a fixed exchange rate regime.

15.2 A Monetary Economy with a Government Sector

The quantity theory of money provides a simple and insightful analysis of the relationship between money, prices, the nominal exchange rate, and real variables. However, it leaves a number of questions unanswered. For example, what is the effect of fiscal policy on inflation? What role do expectations about future changes in monetary and fiscal policy play for the determination of prices, exchange rates, and real balances? To address these questions, it is necessary to use a richer model. One that incorporates a more realistic money demand specification and that explicitly considers the relationship between monetary and fiscal policy.

In this section, we embed a money demand function into a model with a government sector, similar to the one used in Chapter 8, to analyze the effects of fiscal deficits on inflation and the exchange rate. The model features four building blocks: (1) an interest-elastic demand for money; (2) purchasing power parity; (3) interest rate parity; and (4) the government budget constraint. We present each building block in turn.

15.2.1   AN INTEREST-ELASTIC DEMAND FOR MONEY

In the quantity theory, the demand for money is assumed to depend only on the level of real activity. In reality, however, the demand for money also depends, negatively, on the nominal interest rate. The reason why the demand for money is decreasing in the nominal interest rate is that money is a non-interest-bearing asset. As a result, the opportunity cost of holding money is the nominal interest rate on alternative interest-bearing liquid assets such as time deposits, government bonds, and money market mutual funds. Thus, the higher the nominal interest rate is, the lower the demand for real money balances will be. An important consequence of assuming that the demand for money is interest elastic is that the demand for real balances becomes a function not only of current but also of future expected monetary policy. This is because, as will become clear shortly, the interest rate factors in people's expectations about the future path of monetary variables. Formally, we assume a money demand function of the form:

$$\frac{M_t^d}{P_t} = L(\underset{+}{C_t}, \underset{-}{i_t}), \tag{15.5}$$

where C_t denotes consumption in period t, and i_t denotes the domestic nominal interest rate in period t. The function $L(\cdot, \cdot)$ is increasing in consumption and decreasing in the nominal interest rate. The motivation for having consumption as an argument of the money demand function is that households use money to purchase consumption goods.[1] We assume that consumption is constant over time and therefore drop its time subscript in what follows. The money demand function $L(\cdot, \cdot)$ is also known as the *liquidity preference function*.

In equilibrium the demand for money must equal the supply of money. Letting M_t denote the money supply in period t, equilibrium in the money market requires that $M_t = M_t^d$. Using this expression to replace M_t^d from (15.5), we have that

$$\frac{M_t}{P_t} = L(C, i_t). \tag{15.6}$$

This expression says that in equilibrium the real supply of money must equal the demand for real money balances.

15.2.2   PURCHASING POWER PARITY

We assume that there is a single traded good and no barriers to international trade. Therefore, purchasing power parity must hold; that is, the domestic and

---

[1] Readers interested in learning how a money demand like equation (15.5) can be derived from the utility maximization problem of the household can skip to Appendix 15.8 and then resume reading from here.

foreign price levels must be equal to each other when expressed in the same currency.[2] Formally,

$$P_t = \mathcal{E}_t P_t^*.$$

For simplicity, assume that the foreign currency price of the good is constant and equal to 1 ($P_t^* = 1$ for all t). In this case, it follows from purchasing power parity that the domestic price level is equal to the nominal exchange rate,

$$P_t = \mathcal{E}_t. \tag{15.7}$$

Using this relationship, we can write the money market-clearing condition (15.6) as

$$\frac{M_t}{\mathcal{E}_t} = L(C, i_t). \tag{15.8}$$

15.2.3 THE INTEREST PARITY CONDITION

We assume that there is free capital mobility and no uncertainty. These assumptions imply that the domestic and foreign interest rates must be equal to each other after compensating for changes in the nominal exchange rate. Formally,[3]

$$1 + i_t = (1 + i_t^*)\frac{\mathcal{E}_{t+1}}{\mathcal{E}_t}, \tag{15.9}$$

where i_t^* denotes the foreign interest rate. This interest parity condition says that there are no arbitrage opportunities between domestic and foreign bond markets. It has an intuitive interpretation. The left-hand side is the gross rate of return of investing 1 unit of domestic currency in a domestic currency denominated bond. Because there is free capital mobility, this investment must yield the same return as investing 1 unit of domestic currency in foreign bonds. One unit of domestic currency buys $1/\mathcal{E}_t$ units of foreign currency. In turn, $1/\mathcal{E}_t$ units of foreign currency invested in foreign bonds pay $(1 + i_t^*)/\mathcal{E}_t$ units of foreign currency in period $t + 1$, which can then be exchanged for $(1 + i_t^*)\mathcal{E}_{t+1}/\mathcal{E}_t$ units of domestic currency. Throughout the analysis that follows, we assume that the world interest rate i_t^* is constant. For this reason we drop its time subscript and write i^*.

15.2.4 THE GOVERNMENT BUDGET CONSTRAINT

The government is assumed to have three sources of income: tax revenue, T_t, money creation, $M_t - M_{t-1}$, and interest earnings from holdings of international bonds, $\mathcal{E}_t i^* B_{t-1}^g$, where B_{t-1}^g denotes the government's holdings of foreign currency denominated bonds carried over from period $t - 1$ into period t. The government allocates its income to finance government purchases, $P_t G_t$, where G_t denotes real government consumption of goods in period t, and to changes in its holdings of foreign bonds, $\mathcal{E}_t(B_t^g - B_{t-1}^g)$. Thus, in period t, the government budget

---

[2]For a more extended exposition of purchasing power parity, see Section 9.2 of Chapter 9.

[3]Appendix 15.8 derives this interest parity condition in an infinite horizon model with utility-maximizing households.

constraint is

$$\mathcal{E}_t(B_t^g - B_{t-1}^g) + P_t G_t = P_t T_t + (M_t - M_{t-1}) + \mathcal{E}_t i^* B_{t-1}^g.$$

The left-hand side of this expression represents the government's uses of revenue and the right-hand side the sources. Note that B_t^g is not restricted to be positive. If B_t^g is positive, then the government is a creditor, whereas if it is negative, then the government is a debtor. Taxes and government spending are measured in units of goods. This is why G_t and T_t are multiplied by P_t in the government budget constraint.

We can express the government budget constraint in real terms by dividing the left- and right-hand sides of the above equation by the price level P_t. Using the result that $\mathcal{E}_t = P_t$ (equation (15.7)) and after rearranging terms, we have

$$B_t^g - B_{t-1}^g = \frac{M_t - M_{t-1}}{P_t} - \left(G_t - T_t - i^* B_{t-1}^g\right). \qquad (15.10)$$

The first term on the right-hand side measures the government's real revenue from money creation and is called *seignorage revenue*,

$$\text{seignorage revenue} = \frac{M_t - M_{t-1}}{P_t}.$$

The second term on the right-hand side of (15.10) is the *secondary fiscal deficit* and we denote it by DEF_t. Recall from Chapter 8 that the secondary fiscal deficit is given by the difference between government expenditures and income from the collection of taxes and interest income from bond holdings. Formally, DEF_t is defined as

$$DEF_t = (G_t - T_t) - i^* B_{t-1}^g.$$

In Chapter 8, we also defined the primary fiscal deficit as the difference between government expenditures and tax revenues (primary fiscal deficit $= G_t - T_t$), so that the secondary fiscal deficit equals the difference between the primary fiscal deficit and interest income from government holdings of interest-bearing assets.

Using the definition of secondary fiscal deficit and the fact that by purchasing power parity $P_t = \mathcal{E}_t$, the government budget constraint can be written as

$$B_t^g - B_{t-1}^g = \frac{M_t - M_{t-1}}{\mathcal{E}_t} - DEF_t. \qquad (15.11)$$

This equation makes it transparent that a fiscal deficit ($DEF_t > 0$) must be associated with money creation ($M_t - M_{t-1} > 0$) or with a decline in the government's asset position ($B_t^g - B_{t-1}^g < 0$), or both.

To complete the description of the economy, we must specify the exchange rate regime, to which we turn next.

15.3 Fiscal Deficits and the Sustainability of Currency Pegs

Under a fixed exchange rate regime, the government intervenes in the foreign exchange market in order to keep the exchange rate at a fixed level. Let that fixed level be denoted by $\mathcal{E}$. Then $\mathcal{E}_t = \mathcal{E}$ for all t. When the government pegs the exchange rate, the money supply becomes an endogenous variable because the central bank must stand ready to exchange domestic for foreign currency at the fixed rate $\mathcal{E}$.

With the nominal exchange rate pegged at $\mathcal{E}$, the purchasing power parity condition, given in equation (15.7), implies that the price level, P_t, is also constant and equal to $\mathcal{E}$ for all t. This result explains why almost all stabilization programs aimed at ending high inflation or hyperinflation involve some form of currency peg. By fixing the exchange rate between the domestic currency and the currency of a low inflation country, the central bank induces a rapid convergence of domestic inflation to foreign inflation. The analysis that follows shows, however, that if a peg is not accompanied by fiscal reform, an *exchange rate–based stabilization program* represents a short-lived remedy to the inflation problem.

Because the nominal exchange rate is constant, the expected rate of devaluation is zero. This implies, by the interest parity condition (15.9), that the domestic nominal interest rate, i_t, is constant and equal to the world interest rate i^*. It then follows from the liquidity preference equation (15.8) that the demand for nominal balances is constant and equal to $\mathcal{E}L(C, i^*)$. Since in equilibrium money demand must equal money supply, we have that the money supply is also constant over time: $M_t = M_{t-1} = \mathcal{E}L(C, i^*)$. Using the fact that the money supply is constant, the government budget constraint (15.11) becomes

$$B_t^g - B_{t-1}^g = -DEF_t. \tag{15.12}$$

In words, when the government pegs the exchange rate, it loses one source of revenue—namely, seignorage. Therefore, fiscal deficits must be entirely financed through the sale of interest-bearing assets.

For a fixed exchange rate regime to be sustainable over time, it is necessary that the government displays fiscal discipline. To see this, suppose that the government runs a constant secondary fiscal deficit, say $DEF_t = DEF > 0$ for all t. Equation (15.12) then implies that government assets are falling over time ($B_t^g - B_{t-1}^g = -DEF < 0$). At some point, B_t^g will become negative, which implies that the government is a debtor. Suppose that there is an upper limit on the size of the public debt. When the public debt hits this limit, the government is forced to either eliminate the fiscal deficit (i.e., set $DEF = 0$), default on its debt, or abandon the exchange rate peg. A situation in which the government reaches this point is called a *balance of payments crisis*. We analyze balance of payments crises in Section 15.7.

15.4 Fiscal Consequences of a Devaluation

An unexpected devaluation acts as a tax that generates revenue for the government. To see this, assume that in period 1 the government unexpectedly announces a devaluation of the currency by raising the exchange rate from $\mathcal{E}$ to $\mathcal{E}' > \mathcal{E}$, so that $\mathcal{E}_t = \mathcal{E}'$ for all $t \geq 1$. "Unexpected" here means that prior to period 1, the path of the nominal exchange rate was expected to be $\mathcal{E}_t = \mathcal{E}$ for all t.

By the purchasing power parity condition, equation (15.7), the domestic price level, P_t, jumps up in period 1 from $\mathcal{E}$ to $\mathcal{E}'$ and remains at that level thereafter. Thus, the devaluation is inflationary.

The one-time unexpected devaluation has no effect on the nominal interest rate. To see this, consider first the nominal interest rate in period 0, just before the policy change. At that time, everyone is expecting the exchange rate to be constant and equal to $\mathcal{E}$ for all t. Thus, the interest rate parity condition (15.9) implies that

$$1 + i_0 = (1 + i^*)\frac{\mathcal{E}_1}{\mathcal{E}_0} = (1 + i^*)\frac{\mathcal{E}}{\mathcal{E}} = 1 + i^*.$$

Now consider any period $t \geq 1$. The exchange rate has changed to $\mathcal{E}'$ and is expected to remain at that level. The interest parity condition (15.9) therefore implies that

$$1 + i_t = (1 + i^*)\frac{\mathcal{E}_{t+1}}{\mathcal{E}_t} = (1 + i^*)\frac{\mathcal{E}'}{\mathcal{E}'} = 1 + i^*.$$

Intuitively, the nominal interest rate does not change because it only factors in expected changes in the exchange rate. Since during, before, and after period 1 everybody expects the exchange rate to be constant over time, the depreciation rate is always expected to be 0.

Using the fact that the nominal interest rate is unchanged, the liquidity preference equation (15.8) then implies that in period 1 the demand for nominal money balances increases from $\mathcal{E}L(C, i^*)$ to $\mathcal{E}'L(C, i^*)$. This means that the demand for nominal balances increases by the same proportion as the nominal exchange rate. Consider now the government budget constraint (15.11) evaluated in period 1,

$$
\begin{aligned}
B_1^g - B_0^g &= \frac{M_1 - M_0}{\mathcal{E}'} - DEF \\
&= \frac{\mathcal{E}'L(C, i^*) - \mathcal{E}L(C, i^*)}{\mathcal{E}'} - DEF.
\end{aligned}
$$

The numerator of the first term on the right-hand side of the last equality is positive, since $\mathcal{E}' > \mathcal{E}$. Therefore, in period 1 seignorage revenue is positive. As a result, the government asset position improves; that is, $B_1^g - B_0^g$ increases. In the absence of a devaluation, seignorage revenue would have been nil because in that case $M_1 - M_0 = \mathcal{E}L(C, i^*) - \mathcal{E}L(C, i^*) = 0$. Therefore, a surprise devaluation increases government revenue in the period in which the devaluation takes place. In the periods after the devaluation, $t = 2, 3, 4, \ldots$, the nominal money demand is constant and equal to $\mathcal{E}'L(C, i^*)$, so that $M_t - M_{t-1} = 0$ for all $t \geq 2$ and seignorage revenue is nil.

Summarizing, an unexpected once-and-for-all devaluation produces an increase in the domestic price level of the same proportion as the increase in the nominal exchange rate. Given the households' holdings of nominal money balances, the increase in the price level erodes their real value. Thus, a devaluation acts like a tax on real balances. In order to rebuild their desired real balances, which don't change because the nominal interest rate is unaffected by the devaluation, households sell part of their foreign bonds to the central bank in return for domestic currency. The net effect of a devaluation is, therefore, that the private sector ends up with a lower foreign asset position, whereas the government gains real resources as it exchanges money—a non-interest-bearing asset created by itself—for interest-bearing foreign assets.

15.5 A Constant Money Growth Rate Regime

We now consider a floating exchange rate regime in which the central bank targets a path for the money supply. Suppose that the central bank expands the quantity of money at a constant, positive rate μ each period, so that

$$M_t = (1 + \mu)M_{t-1}. \tag{15.13}$$

The goal is to find out how the endogenous variables of the model, such as the nominal exchange rate, the price level, real balances, and the domestic nominal interest rate, behave under the money growth rate rule specified in equation (15.13). To do this, we conjecture (or guess) that in equilibrium the nominal exchange rate depreciates at the rate μ. We will then verify that this guess is correct. Formally, the guess is that

$$\frac{\mathcal{E}_{t+1}}{\mathcal{E}_t} = 1 + \mu,$$

for $t = 1, 2, \ldots$. By the purchasing power parity condition (15.7), the domestic price level must also grow at the rate of monetary expansion μ,

$$\frac{P_{t+1}}{P_t} = 1 + \mu,$$

for $t = 1, 2, \ldots$. This expression says that under the guess, the rate of inflation must equal the rate of growth of the money supply.

To determine the domestic nominal interest rate i_t, use the interest parity condition (15.9)

$$1 + i_t = (1 + i^*)\frac{\mathcal{E}_{t+1}}{\mathcal{E}_t} = (1 + i^*)(1 + \mu),$$

which implies that the nominal interest rate is constant and increasing in μ. When μ is positive, the domestic nominal interest rate exceeds the world interest rate i^* because the domestic currency is depreciating over time. We summarize the positive relationship between i_t and μ by writing

$$i_t = i(\mu).$$
$$+$$

Substituting this expression into the money market-clearing condition (15.8) yields

$$\frac{M_t}{\mathcal{E}_t} = L(C, i(\mu)). \tag{15.14}$$

Because the money growth rate μ is constant, the nominal interest rate $i(\mu)$ is also constant. Therefore, the right-hand side of (15.14) is constant. For the money market to be in equilibrium, the left-hand side of (15.14) must also be constant. This will be the case only if the exchange rate depreciates—grows—at the same rate as the money supply. This confirms the initial conjecture that $\mathcal{E}_{t+1}/\mathcal{E}_t = 1 + \mu$. Equation (15.14) says that in equilibrium, real money balances must be constant and that the higher the money growth rate μ is, the lower the equilibrium level of real balances will be. Intuitively, as the money growth rate goes up, the interest rate, which is the opportunity cost of holding money, also goes up, inducing households to economize on the use of money in performing transactions. In real life, households do this by holding less money in their pockets, lowering balances in their sight deposit accounts, and making more frequent transfers from their interest-bearing accounts to their deposit accounts.

15.6 Fiscal Consequences of Money Creation

We just established that money creation generates inflation and currency depreciation, and that it decreases real money balances. These are all potentially negative effects. For example, a reduction in real money holdings hinders transactions of goods. So why do some governments nevertheless choose to increase the money supply at high rates? One reason is that printing money is a way to collect resources to finance fiscal deficits. This section explores this issue.

15.6.1 THE INFLATION TAX

Take another look at the government budget constraint (15.11), which we reproduce for convenience

$$B_t^g - B_{t-1}^g = \frac{M_t - M_{t-1}}{\mathcal{E}_t} - DEF_t. \qquad (15.11 \text{ R})$$

Let's analyze the first term on the right-hand side of this expression, seignorage revenue. Using the result that under a constant money growth rate rule $M_t = \mathcal{E}_t L(C, i(\mu))$ (see equation (15.14)), we can write

$$\frac{M_t - M_{t-1}}{\mathcal{E}_t} = \frac{\mathcal{E}_t L(C, i(\mu)) - \mathcal{E}_{t-1} L(C, i(\mu))}{\mathcal{E}_t}$$

$$= L(C, i(\mu)) \left(\frac{\mathcal{E}_t - \mathcal{E}_{t-1}}{\mathcal{E}_t} \right).$$

Now using the result that when the money supply grows at the rate μ, in equilibrium $(\mathcal{E}_t - \mathcal{E}_{t-1})/\mathcal{E}_t = \mu/(1 + \mu)$, we can write seignorage revenue as

$$\frac{M_t - M_{t-1}}{\mathcal{E}_t} = L(C, i(\mu)) \left(\frac{\mu}{1 + \mu} \right). \qquad (15.15)$$

Recalling that in equilibrium μ is the inflation rate, the right-hand side of equation (15.15) can be interpreted as the government's *inflation tax revenue*. The idea is that inflation acts as a tax on the public's holdings of real money balances, with the tax base being real money holdings, $L(C, i(\mu))$, and the tax rate being the factor $\mu/(1 + \mu)$.

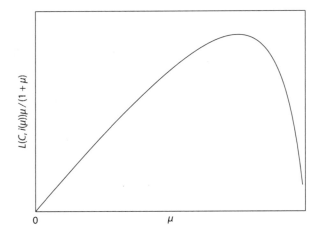

Figure 15.1. The Inflation Tax Laffer Curve
Notes: The inflation tax Laffer curve depicts the relationship between the money growth rate, μ, and seignorage income, $(M_t - M_{t-1})/P_t$, in an economy in which the government expands the money supply at a constant rate. In equilibrium, seignorage income equals $L(C, i(\mu)) \frac{\mu}{1+\mu}$. The first factor is decreasing in μ and the second increasing. This feature can give rise to a nonmonotonic relationship between the money growth rate and seignorage income, like the one depicted in the figure. In equilibrium, inflation equals the money growth rate, so the horizontal axis can be interpreted as measuring either variable.

15.6.2   THE INFLATION TAX LAFFER CURVE

Because the tax base, $L(C, i(\mu))$, is decreasing in μ and the tax rate, $\mu/(1 + \mu)$, is increasing in μ, it is not clear whether seignorage increases or decreases with the rate of expansion of the money supply. Whether seignorage revenue is increasing or decreasing in μ depends on the form of the liquidity preference function $L(\cdot, \cdot)$, as well as on the level of μ itself. Typically, for low values of μ seignorage revenue is increasing in μ. However, as μ gets large the contraction in the tax base (the money demand) dominates the increase in the tax rate and therefore seignorage revenue falls as μ increases. Thus, there exists a maximum level of revenue a government can collect from printing money. The resulting relationship between the growth rate of the money supply and seignorage revenue has the shape of an inverted U and is called the *inflation tax Laffer curve* (see Figure 15.1).

15.6.3   INFLATIONARY FINANCE

Consider a situation in which the government is running constant fiscal deficits, $DEF_t = DEF > 0$ for all t. Furthermore, assume that the government has reached its borrowing limit and thus cannot finance the fiscal deficit by issuing additional debt, so that $B_t^g - B_{t-1}^g$ must be equal to zero. Under these circumstances, the government

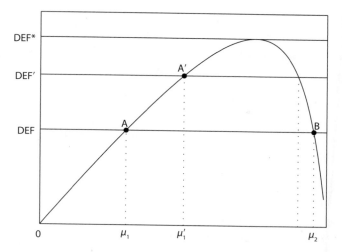

Figure 15.2. Inflationary Finance and the Laffer Curve of Inflation
Notes: The figure shows that there are two values of the money growth rate, μ_1 and μ_2, that generate enough seignorage revenue to finance the fiscal deficit *DEF*. In one equilibrium inflation is high (point B), and in the other it is relatively low (point A). Typically, economies are on the upward-sloping side of the Laffer curve, so point A is more relevant. An increase in the deficit from *DEF* to *DEF'* requires a higher rate of monetary expansion, $\mu_1' > \mu_1$, and results in higher inflation. Deficits above *DEF*** cannot be financed by printing money and lead the economy into hyperinflation if the economy has exhausted its ability to issue debt.

budget constraint (15.11) becomes

$$DEF = \frac{M_t - M_{t-1}}{\mathcal{E}_t}.$$

This expression says that a country that has exhausted its ability to issue public debt must resort to printing money in order to finance the fiscal deficit. This way of financing the public sector is called *monetization of the fiscal deficit*. Combining the above expression with (15.15), we obtain

$$DEF = L(C, i(\mu)) \left(\frac{\mu}{1 + \mu} \right). \tag{15.16}$$

Figure 15.2 illustrates the relationship between the fiscal deficit and the rate of monetary expansion necessary to finance it. Keeping in mind that in equilibrium inflation and the depreciation rate are equal to the money growth rate, we can think of the horizontal axis as measuring either the money growth rate, inflation, or the depreciation rate. The Laffer curve of inflation corresponds to the right-hand side of (15.16). The horizontal line plots the left-hand side of (15.16), or *DEF*.

There are two rates of monetary expansion, μ_1 and μ_2, that generate enough seignorage revenue to finance the fiscal deficit *DEF*. In the μ_2 equilibrium, point B in the figure, the money growth rate is relatively high, whereas in the μ_1 equilibrium, point A in the figure, the money growth rate is lower. Empirical studies show that in reality, economies tend to be located on the upward-sloping branch of the Laffer curve. Thus, the more realistic scenario is described by point A.

Consider now the effect of an increase in the fiscal deficit from DEF to $DEF' > DEF$. To finance the larger fiscal deficit, the government is forced to increase the money supply at a faster rate. At the new equilibrium, point A', the rate of monetary expansion, μ_1', is greater than at the old equilibrium, point A. As a result, the inflation rate, the rate of depreciation of the domestic currency, and the nominal interest rate all go up as the deficit increases from DEF to DEF'.

In some instances, inflationary finance can degenerate into hyperinflation. A hyperinflationary situation arises when the fiscal deficit reaches a level that can no longer be financed by seignorage revenue alone. In terms of Figure 15.2, this is the case when the fiscal deficit is larger than DEF^*, the level of deficit associated with the peak of the Laffer curve. What happens in practice is that the government is initially unaware of the fact that no rate of monetary expansion will suffice to finance the deficit. In its attempt to close the fiscal gap, the government accelerates the rate of money creation. But this measure is counterproductive because the government has entered the downward-sloping side of the Laffer curve, so the increase in the money growth rate lowers seignorage revenue instead of raising it, further widening the fiscal gap. The decline in seignorage revenue leads the government to increase the money supply at an even faster rate. These dynamics turn into a vicious cycle that ends in an accelerating inflationary spiral.

The most fundamental step in ending hyperinflation is to eliminate the underlying budgetary imbalances that are at the root of the problem. When this type of structural fiscal reform is undertaken and is understood by the public, hyperinflation typically stops abruptly.

15.7   Balance of Payments Crises

A balance of payments (or BOP) crisis is a situation in which the government is unable or unwilling to meet its financial obligations. These difficulties may manifest themselves in a variety of ways, such as the failure to honor the domestic or foreign public debt or the suspension of currency convertibility.

What causes BOP crises? Sometimes a BOP crisis arises as the inevitable consequence of an unsustainable combination of monetary and fiscal policy. A classic example of such a policy mix is a situation in which a government pegs the nominal exchange rate and at the same time runs a fiscal deficit. As we discussed in Section 15.3, under a fixed exchange rate regime, the government must finance any fiscal deficit by running down its stock of interest-bearing assets (see equation (15.12)). To the extent that there is a limit to the amount of debt a government is able to issue, this situation cannot continue indefinitely. When the public debt hits its upper limit, the government is forced to change policy. One possibility is that the government stops servicing the debt (i.e., stops paying interest on its outstanding financial obligations), thereby reducing the size of the secondary deficit. A second possibility is that the government adopts a fiscal adjustment program by cutting government spending and raising regular taxes and in that way reduces the primary deficit. Finally, the government can abandon the exchange rate peg and resort to monetizing the fiscal deficit. This third alternative has been the fate of the vast majority of currency pegs adopted in developing countries.

An empirical regularity associated with the collapse of fixed exchange rate regimes is that in the days immediately before the peg is abandoned, the central bank loses vast amounts of reserves in a short period of time. The loss of reserves is the consequence of a run by the public against the domestic currency in anticipation of the impending devaluation. The stampede of people trying to massively get rid of domestic currency in exchange for foreign currency is driven by the desire to avoid the loss of real value of domestic currency denominated assets that is expected to take place when the currency is devalued.

The first formal models of the dynamics of a balance of payments crisis are due to Stephen Salant and Dale Henderson in 1978 and Paul Krugman in 1979.[4] In this section, we analyze the dynamics of a balance of payments crisis using the tools developed in Sections 15.2 to 15.6.

Consider a country that is running a constant fiscal deficit $DEF > 0$ each period. Suppose that in period 1, the country embarks on a currency peg. Specifically, assume that the government fixes the nominal exchange rate at $\mathcal{E}$ units of domestic currency per unit of foreign currency. Suppose that in period 1, when the currency peg is announced, the government has a positive stock of foreign assets carried over from period 0, $B_0^g > 0$. Further, assume that the government does not have access to credit. That is, the government asset holdings are constrained to being nonnegative, or $B_t^g \geq 0$ for all t. It follows from the discussion of the sustainability of currency pegs in Section 15.3 that as long as the currency peg is in effect, the fiscal deficit produces a continuous drain of assets, which at some point will be completely depleted. Put differently, if the fiscal deficit is not eliminated, at some point the government will be forced to abandon the currency peg and start printing money in order to finance the deficit. Let T denote the period in which, as a result of having run out of reserves, the government abandons the peg and begins to monetize the fiscal deficit.

The dynamics of the balance of payments crisis are characterized by three distinct phases. (1) The pre-collapse phase: during this phase, which lasts from $t = 1$ to $t = T - 2$, the currency peg is in effect and is expected to continue to be in effect the next period. (2) The BOP crisis: it takes place in period $t = T - 1$, and is the period in which the central bank, while still defending the peg, faces a run against the domestic currency, resulting in massive losses of foreign reserves. And (3) The post-collapse phase: it encompasses the period from $t = T$ onward. In this phase, the nominal exchange rate floats freely and the central bank expands the money supply at a rate consistent with the monetization of the fiscal deficit.

(1) THE PRE-CRISIS PHASE: FROM $T = 1$ TO $T = T - 2$

In period $t = 1, 2, \ldots, T - 2$, the exchange rate is pegged and is expected to also be pegged in period $t + 1$. Consequently, the variables of interest behave as

[4]Stephen W. Salant and Dale W. Henderson, "Market Anticipations of Government Policies and the Price of Gold," *Journal of Political Economy* 86 (August 1978): 627–648; and Paul R. Krugman, "A Model of Balance-of-Payments Crisis," *Journal of Money, Credit and Banking* 11 (August 1979): 311–325.

described in Section 15.3. In particular, the nominal exchange rate is constant and equal to $\mathcal{E}$; that is, $\mathcal{E}_t = \mathcal{E}$ for $t = 1, 2, \ldots, T-2$. By purchasing power parity, and given our assumption that $P_t^* = 1$, the domestic price level is also constant over time and equal to $\mathcal{E}$ ($P_t = \mathcal{E}$ for $t = 1, 2, \ldots, T-2$). Because the exchange rate is fixed, the devaluation rate $(\mathcal{E}_t - \mathcal{E}_{t-1})/\mathcal{E}_{t-1}$ is equal to 0. The nominal interest, i_t, which by the interest parity condition (15.9) satisfies $1 + i_t = (1 + i^*)\mathcal{E}_{t+1}/\mathcal{E}_t$, is equal to the world interest rate i^*. Note that the nominal interest rate in period $T-2$ is also equal to i^* because the exchange rate peg is still in place in period $T-1$. Thus, $i_t = i^*$ for $t = 1, 2, \ldots, T-2$.

As discussed in Section 15.3, by pegging the exchange rate the government relinquishes its ability to monetize the deficit. This is because the nominal money supply, M_t, which in equilibrium equals $\mathcal{E}L(C, i^*)$, is constant, and as a result seignorage revenue, given by $(M_t - M_{t-1})/\mathcal{E}$, is nil. Consider now the dynamics of government assets, B_t^g. Following the tradition in the balance of payments literature, think of B_t^g as consisting of foreign reserves. By equation (15.12),

$$B_t^g - B_{t-1}^g = -DEF; \quad \text{for } t = 1, 2, \ldots, T-2.$$

This expression shows that the fiscal deficit causes the central bank to lose DEF units of foreign reserves per period. The continuous loss of reserves in combination with the lower bound on the central bank's assets, $B_t^g \geq 0$, makes it clear that the currency peg is unsustainable in the presence of persistent fiscal imbalances.

(3) THE POST-CRISIS PHASE: FROM $T = T$ ONWARD

The government starts period T without any foreign reserves ($B_{T-1}^g = 0$). Given our assumptions that the government cannot borrow (that is, B_t^g cannot be negative) and that it is unable to eliminate the fiscal deficit, it follows that in period T the monetary authority is forced to abandon the currency peg and to print money in order to finance the fiscal deficit. Thus, in the post-crisis phase the government lets the exchange rate float. In particular, assume that the government expands the money supply at a constant rate μ that generates enough seignorage revenue to finance the fiscal deficit. In Section 15.6, we deduced that μ is determined by equation (15.16), which we reproduce here for convenience

$$DEF = L(C, i(\mu)) \left(\frac{\mu}{1 + \mu} \right). \tag{15.16 R}$$

Note that because the fiscal deficit is positive, the money growth rate must also be positive. In the post-crisis phase, real balances, $M_t/\mathcal{E}_t$, are constant and equal to $L(C, i(\mu))$. Therefore, the nominal exchange rate, $\mathcal{E}_t$, must depreciate at the rate μ. Because by purchasing power parity $P_t = \mathcal{E}_t$, the price level also grows at the rate μ; that is, the inflation rate is positive and equal to μ. Finally, the nominal interest rate satisfies $1 + i_t = (1 + i^*)(1 + \mu)$.

Let's compare the economy's pre- and post-crisis behavior. The first thing to note is that with the demise of the fixed exchange rate regime, price level stability disappears as inflation sets in. In the pre-crisis phase, the rate of monetary expansion, the rate of devaluation, and the rate of inflation are all equal to zero. By contrast, in the post-crisis phase these variables are all positive and equal to μ. Second, the sources of deficit finance are different in each of the two phases. In the pre-crisis phase, the deficit is financed entirely with foreign reserves. As a result, foreign reserves display a steady decline during this phase. On the other hand, in the post-crisis phase the fiscal deficit is financed through seignorage income and foreign reserves are constant (and in the present example equal to zero). Finally, in the post-crisis phase real balances are lower than in the pre-crisis phase because the nominal interest rate is higher.

(2) THE BOP CRISIS: PERIOD $T-1$

In period $T-1$, the exchange rate peg has not yet collapsed. Thus, the nominal exchange rate and the price level are both equal to $\mathcal{E}$; that is $\mathcal{E}_{T-1} = P_{T-1} = \mathcal{E}$. However, the nominal interest rate is not i^*, as in the pre-crisis phase because in period $T-1$ the public expects a depreciation of the domestic currency in period T. The rate of depreciation of the domestic currency between periods $T-1$ and T is μ; that is,

$$\frac{\mathcal{E}_T - \mathcal{E}_{T-1}}{\mathcal{E}_{T-1}} = \mu.$$

To see this, use the facts that in $T-1$ the nominal interest rate satisfies

$$1 + i_{T-1} = (1 + i^*)\frac{\mathcal{E}_T}{\mathcal{E}_{T-1}}, \tag{15.17}$$

that real balances in $T-1$ are given by

$$\frac{M_{T-1}}{\mathcal{E}_{T-1}} = L(C, i_{T-1}), \tag{15.18}$$

and that in period T the government budget constraint is

$$DEF = \frac{M_T - M_{T-1}}{\mathcal{E}_T} = L(C, i(\mu)) - \frac{M_{T-1}}{\mathcal{E}_{T-1}}\frac{\mathcal{E}_{T-1}}{\mathcal{E}_T}. \tag{15.19}$$

These are three equations in three unknowns: i_{T-1}, $M_{T-1}/\mathcal{E}_{T-1}$, and $\mathcal{E}_T/\mathcal{E}_{T-1}$. Guess that the solution is $\mathcal{E}_T/\mathcal{E}_{T-1} = 1 + \mu$. Then by (15.17) $i_{T-1} = i(\mu)$. In turn, by equation (15.18) $M_{T-1}/\mathcal{E}_{T-1} = L(C, i(\mu))$. Finally, equation (15.19) becomes $DEF = L(C, i(\mu))\frac{\mu}{1+\mu}$, which is identical to equation (15.16), confirming that the guess is correct.

We have established that in period $T-1$, the nominal interest rate increases to its post-crisis level, $i(\mu) > i^*$, and that real balances fall to their post-crisis level, $L(C, i(\mu)) < L(C, i^*)$. Because the nominal exchange rate does not change in period $T-1$, as the central bank is still defending the peg, the decline in real balances is entirely brought about through a fall in nominal balances. The public runs to the central bank to exchange domestic currency for foreign reserves. Thus, in period $T-1$ foreign reserves at the central bank fall by more than DEF, which is the amount by which they had been falling each period prior to $T-1$. To see this more formally, evaluate the government budget constraint (15.11) at $t = T-1$ to get

$$B_{T-1}^g - B_{T-2}^g = \frac{M_{T-1} - M_{T-2}}{\mathcal{E}} - DEF$$

$$= L(C, i(\mu)) - L(C, i^*) - DEF$$

$$< -DEF.$$

The second equality follows from the fact that $M_{T-1}/\mathcal{E} = L(C, i(\mu))$ and $M_{T-2}/\mathcal{E} = L(C, i^*)$. The inequality follows from the fact that $i(\mu) = (1 + i^*)(1 + \mu) - 1 > i^*$ and the fact that the liquidity preference function $L(\cdot, \cdot)$ is decreasing in the nominal interest rate.

Figure 15.3 illustrates the predicted dynamics of a balance of payments crisis. Inflation and the depreciation rate are zero until period $T-1$ inclusive. In period T they jump to a permanently higher level. The nominal interest rate jumps one period earlier, in period $T-1$, because it factors in the expected depreciation in period T. Real money balances, $M_t/\mathcal{E}_t$, are flat until period $T-2$. In period $T-1$, the increase in the nominal interest rate induces agents to reduce their real money holdings to a permanently lower level. The nominal money supply mimics the flat path of the real money supply until period $T-2$ inclusive, since the price level is constant over this period. In period $T-1$, the speculative attack against the currency causes a drop in the money supply. Starting in period T, the nominal money supply grows at the rate μ, reflecting the fact that the central bank is collecting seignorage revenue. Finally, foreign reserves, B_t^g, fall at the constant rate DEF between periods 1 and $T-2$. In period $T-1$, foreign reserves experience a larger drop. This collapse in the stock of foreign reserves represents the model's central insight on why in real life the demise of currency pegs is typically preceded by a speculative run against the domestic currency and large losses of foreign reserves by the central bank: Even though the exchange rate is pegged in $T-1$, the nominal interest rate rises in anticipation of a devaluation in period T, causing a contraction in the demand for real money balances. Because in period $T-1$ the domestic currency is still fully convertible, the central bank must absorb the entire decline in the demand for money by selling foreign reserves. In period T the peg is abandoned and the central bank is forced to print money to finance the fiscal deficit, which causes an increase in the rate of inflation.

15.8 Appendix: A Dynamic Optimizing Model of the Demand for Money

This appendix develops a dynamic optimizing model underlying the liquidity preference function $L(C, i_t)$ given in equation (15.5) and the interest rate parity condition given in equation (15.9). This material is a bit more advanced than the rest of the chapter and can be skipped without losing any of the key concepts treated therein.

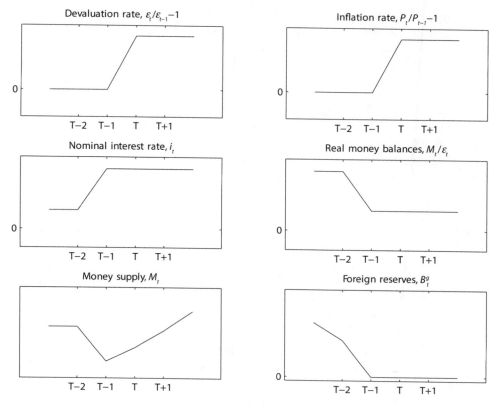

Figure 15.3. The Dynamics of a Balance of Payments Crisis
Notes: The figure depicts the dynamics of a balance of payments crisis. The central bank initially pegs the currency, which results in zero inflation. However, fiscal deficits cause the stock of foreign reserves to fall steadily. In period $T-1$ there is a speculative attack in which the central bank loses an unusually large volume of foreign reserves. In period T the peg is abandoned and the central bank is forced to print money to finance the fiscal deficit, which causes an increase in the inflation rate.

We motivate a demand for money by assuming that money facilitates transactions. We capture the fact that money facilitates transactions by assuming that agents derive utility not only from consumption of goods but also from holdings of real balances. Specifically, in each period $t = 1, 2, 3, \ldots$ preferences are described by the following single-period utility function,

$$u(C_t) + z\left(\frac{M_t^d}{P_t}\right),$$

where C_t denotes the household's consumption in period t and M_t^d/P_t denotes the household's real money holdings in period t. The functions $u(\cdot)$ and $z(\cdot)$ are strictly increasing and strictly concave functions ($u' > 0$, $z' > 0$, $u'' < 0$, $z'' < 0$).

Households are assumed to be infinitely lived and to care about their entire stream of single-period utilities. However, households discount the future by assigning a greater weight to consumption and real money holdings the closer they are to the present. Specifically, their lifetime utility function is given by

$$u(C_t) + z\left(\frac{M_t^d}{P_t}\right) + \beta\left[u(C_{t+1}) + z\left(\frac{M_{t+1}^d}{P_{t+1}}\right)\right] + \beta^2\left[u(C_{t+2}) + z\left(\frac{M_{t+2}^d}{P_{t+2}}\right)\right] + \dots$$

The parameter $\beta \in (0, 1)$ is the subjective discount factor. The fact that households care more about the present than about the future is reflected in β being less than 1.

Let's now analyze the budget constraint of the household. In period t, the household allocates its wealth to purchase consumption goods, P_tC_t, to hold money balances, M_t^d, to pay taxes, P_tT_t, and to buy domestic currency bonds, B_t^d, and foreign currency bonds, $\mathcal{E}_tB_t^f$. Taxes, T_t, are lump sum and measured in units of goods. The domestic bond is denominated in domestic currency and pays the interest rate i_t when held from period t to period $t + 1$. The superscript d in B_t^d indicates that these are domestic currency bonds to distinguish them from foreign currency bonds. The foreign bond is denominated in foreign currency. Each unit of foreign bonds costs 1 unit of the foreign currency, so each unit of the foreign bond costs $\mathcal{E}_t$ units of domestic currency. Foreign bonds pay the constant world interest rate i^* in foreign currency. The superscript f in B_t^f indicates that these are foreign currency bond holdings of private households.

The household's nominal wealth at the beginning of period t is given by the sum of its money holdings carried over from the previous period, M_{t-1}^d, domestic and foreign currency bonds purchased in the previous period plus interest, $(1 + i_{t-1})B_{t-1}^d + \mathcal{E}_t(1 + i^*)B_{t-1}^f$, and income from the sale of its endowment of goods, P_tQ_t, where Q_t denotes the household's endowment of goods in period t. This endowment is assumed to be exogenous; that is, determined outside of the model. The budget constraint of the household in period t is then given by

$$P_tC_t + M_t^d + P_tT_t + B_t^d + \mathcal{E}_tB_t^f = M_{t-1}^d + (1 + i_{t-1})B_{t-1}^d + (1 + i^*)\mathcal{E}_tB_{t-1}^f + P_tQ_t.$$

$$(15.20)$$

The left-hand side of the budget constraint represents the uses of wealth and the right-hand side the sources of wealth. The budget constraint is expressed in nominal terms; that is, in terms of units of domestic currency. To express the budget constraint in real terms—that is, in units of goods—divide the left- and right-hand sides of (15.20) by P_t, which yields

$$C_t + \frac{M_t^d}{P_t} + T_t + \frac{B_t^d}{P_t} + \frac{\mathcal{E}_t}{P_t}B_t^f = \frac{M_{t-1}^d}{P_{t-1}}\frac{P_{t-1}}{P_t} + (1 + i_{t-1})\frac{B_{t-1}^d}{P_t}$$

$$+ (1 + i^*)\frac{\mathcal{E}_t}{P_t}B_{t-1}^f + Q_t.$$

Note that real money balances carried over from period $t - 1$, M_{t-1}^d/P_{t-1}, appear multiplied by P_{t-1}/P_t. In an inflationary environment, P_t is greater than P_{t-1}, so inflation erodes a fraction $1 - P_{t-1}/P_t$ of the household's real balances. As discussed in Section 15.6.1, this loss of resources due to inflation is called the inflation tax.

The higher the rate of inflation is, the larger the fraction of wealth that households must allocate to maintaining a certain level of real balances will be.

Use the purchasing power parity condition (15.7) to eliminate P_t from the utility function and the budget constraint to obtain

$$u(C_t) + z\left(\frac{M_t^d}{\mathcal{E}_t}\right) + \beta\left[u(C_{t+1}) + z\left(\frac{M_{t+1}^d}{\mathcal{E}_{t+1}}\right)\right] + \beta^2\left[u(C_{t+2}) + z\left(\frac{M_{t+2}^d}{\mathcal{E}_{t+2}}\right)\right] + \cdots$$

$$(15.21)$$

and

$$C_t + \frac{M_t^d}{\mathcal{E}_t} + T_t + \frac{B_t^d}{\mathcal{E}_t} + B_t^f = \frac{M_{t-1}^d}{\mathcal{E}_t} + (1 + i_{t-1})\frac{B_{t-1}^d}{\mathcal{E}_t} + (1 + i^*)B_{t-1}^f + Q_t.$$

$$(15.22)$$

Households choose C_t, M_t^d, B_t^d, and B_t^f to maximize the utility function (15.21) subject to a sequence of budget constraints like (15.22), one for each period, taking as given the time paths of $\mathcal{E}_t$, i_t, T_t, and Q_t. In choosing streams of consumption, money balances, and bonds, the household faces three trade-offs. The first trade-off is between consuming today and saving in the form of foreign currency bonds. The second trade-off is between consuming today and saving by means of domestic currency bonds. And the third trade-off is between consuming today and holding money.

Consider first the trade-off between consuming one extra unit of the good today and investing it in foreign currency bonds to consume the proceeds tomorrow. If the household chooses to consume an extra unit of goods today, then its utility increases by $u'(C_t)$. Alternatively, the household could sell the unit of good for 1 unit of foreign currency and with the proceeds buy 1 unit of the foreign bond. In period $t + 1$, the bond pays $1 + i^*$ units of foreign currency, with which the household can buy $(1 + i^*)$ units of goods. This amount of goods increases utility in period $t + 1$ by $(1 + i^*)u'(C_{t+1})$. Because households discount future utility at the rate β, from the point of view of period t, lifetime utility increases by $\beta(1 + i^*)u'(C_{t+1})$. If the first alternative yields more utility than the second, the household will increase consumption in period t, and lower consumption in period $t + 1$. This will tend to eliminate the difference between the two alternatives because it will lower $u'(C_t)$ and increase $u'(C_{t+1})$ (recall that $u(\cdot)$ is concave, so that $u'(\cdot)$ is decreasing). On the other hand, if the second alternative yields more utility than the first, the household will increase consumption in period $t + 1$ and decrease consumption in period t. An optimum occurs at a point where the household cannot increase utility further by shifting consumption across time; that is, at an optimum the household is, on the margin, indifferent between consuming an extra unit of good today or saving it and consuming the proceeds in the next period. Formally, the optimal allocation of consumption across time satisfies

$$u'(C_t) = \beta(1 + i^*)u'(C_{t+1}), \qquad (15.23)$$

which is the Euler equation associated with foreign currency bonds.

If $\beta(1+i^*) > 1$, then since $u'(\cdot)$ is a decreasing function, we have that consumption grows over time, $C_{t+1} > C_t$. Conversely, if $\beta(1+i^*) < 1$, then consumption falls over time, $C_{t+1} < C_t$. Put differently, consumption grows over time if the subjective discount factor, β, is larger than the market discount factor, $1/(1+i^*)$, and falls over time if the subjective discount factor is smaller than the market discount factor. Intuitively, when households are relatively patient, they tend to postpone consumption and when they are relatively impatient, they tend to frontload consumption.

To simplify the equilibrium dynamics, assume that the subjective discount factor equals the market discount factor,

$$\beta = \frac{1}{1+i^*}.$$

Combining this equation with the Euler equation (15.23) yields

$$u'(C_t) = u'(C_{t+1}). \tag{15.24}$$

This expression implies that consumption is constant over time, $C_t = C_{t+1}$ for all $t = 1, 2, \ldots$. Let C be that optimal level of consumption. Then we have

$$C_t = C_{t+1} = C_{t+2} = \cdots = C.$$

Consider next the trade-off between allocating 1 unit of good to consumption today and using the unit of good to buy domestic currency bonds. One additional unit of consumption increases utility by $u'(C_t)$. Alternatively, with that 1 unit of good one can buy $\mathcal{E}_t$ domestic currency bonds, which pay $(1+i_t)\mathcal{E}_t$ units of domestic currency in the next period. In turn, $(1+i_t)\mathcal{E}_t$ units of domestic currency buy $(1+i_t)\mathcal{E}_t/\mathcal{E}_{t+1}$ units of goods in the next period, which increases lifetime utility by $\beta u'(C_{t+1})(1+i_t)\mathcal{E}_t/\mathcal{E}_{t+1}$. At the optimum, the household must be indifferent between allocating the unit of good to consumption in the current period or saving in the form of domestic currency bonds and consuming the proceeds of this investment in the next period. That is, at the optimum it must be the case that

$$u'(C_t) = \beta(1+i_t)u'(C_{t+1})\frac{\mathcal{E}_t}{\mathcal{E}_{t+1}}.$$

This optimality condition is the Euler equation for domestic currency bonds. Combining it with the Euler equation for foreign currency bonds, equation (15.23), we have that

$$(1+i_t) = (1+i^*)\frac{\mathcal{E}_{t+1}}{\mathcal{E}_t}. \tag{15.25}$$

This expression is the interest rate parity condition (15.9).

Now consider the trade-off between spending 1 unit of good on consumption and allocating it to holding money. If the household chooses to spend the unit of good on consumption, its utility goes up by $u'(C_t)$. If instead the household chooses to allocate the unit of good to holding money, it must exchange it for cash, which yields $\mathcal{E}_t$ units of money. This amount of money increases its utility by $z'(M_t^d/\mathcal{E}_t)$.

In period $t+1$, the household can use the $\mathcal{E}_t$ units of money to buy consumption at the price $\mathcal{E}_{t+1}$. Thus, the household can buy $\mathcal{E}_t/\mathcal{E}_{t+1}$ units of consumption in period $t+1$, which yields $\beta u'(C_{t+1})\mathcal{E}_t/\mathcal{E}_{t+1}$ utils. Thus, the total increase in utility from allocating the unit of good to holding money is $z'(M_t^d/\mathcal{E}_t) + \beta u'(C_{t+1})\mathcal{E}_t/\mathcal{E}_{t+1}$ utils. At the optimal allocation, the household must be indifferent between allocating the unit of good to current consumption and holding it in the form of money for one period. That is, at the optimum, it must be the case that

$$u'(C_t) = z'\left(\frac{M_t^d}{\mathcal{E}_t}\right) + \beta \frac{\mathcal{E}_t}{\mathcal{E}_{t+1}} u'(C_{t+1}).$$

Using the fact that $u'(C_t) = u'(C_{t+1}) = u'(C)$ and the assumption that $\beta = 1/(1+i^*)$, we have, after some rearranging, that

$$z'\left(\frac{M_t^d}{\mathcal{E}_t}\right) = u'(C)\left[1 - \frac{\mathcal{E}_t}{(1+i^*)\mathcal{E}_{t+1}}\right].$$

Now by optimality condition (15.25), we can write

$$z'\left(\frac{M_t^d}{\mathcal{E}_t}\right) = u'(C)\left(\frac{i_t}{1+i_t}\right). \tag{15.26}$$

This equation relates the demand for real money balances, $M_t^d/\mathcal{E}_t$, to the level of consumption and the domestic nominal interest rate. Inspecting equation (15.26) and recalling that both u and z are strictly concave, reveals that the demand for real balances, $M_t^d/\mathcal{E}_t$, is decreasing in the level of the nominal interest rate, i_t, and increasing in consumption, C. This relationship is the liquidity preference function. We write it in a compact form as

$$\frac{M_t^d}{\mathcal{E}_t} = L(\underset{+}{C}, \underset{-}{i_t}),$$

which is precisely equation (15.5).

The following example derives the liquidity preference function for a particular functional form of the period utility function. Assume that

$$u(C_t) + z(M_t^d/\mathcal{E}_t) = \ln C_t + \gamma \ln(M_t^d/\mathcal{E}_t).$$

Then we have $u'(C) = 1/C$ and $z'(M_t^d/\mathcal{E}_t) = \gamma/(M_t^d/\mathcal{E}_t)$. Therefore, equation (15.26) becomes

$$\frac{\gamma}{M_t^d/\mathcal{E}_t} = \frac{1}{C}\left(\frac{i_t}{1+i_t}\right).$$

The liquidity preference function can be found by solving this expression for $M_t^d/\mathcal{E}_t$, which yields

$$\frac{M_t^d}{\mathcal{E}_t} = L(C, i_t) = \gamma C\left(\frac{1+i_t}{i_t}\right). \tag{15.27}$$

This is the liquidity preference function used in Exercises 15.4 and 15.5. In this money demand function, $M_t^d/\mathcal{E}_t$ is linear and increasing in consumption and convex and decreasing in i_t.

15.9 Summing Up

- The quantity theory of money states that a key determinant of the price level and the nominal exchange rate is the money supply.
- The quantity theory assumes that real output and the real exchange rate are independent of monetary policy.
- In the quantity theory, an increase in the money supply causes an increase in the price level and a depreciation of the domestic currency.
- If the central bank follows a fixed exchange rate regime, it loses control over the money supply.
- Governments finance fiscal deficits either by issuing debt or by printing money.
- By pegging the currency to that of a low inflation country, the government can control the inflation rate. This policy is known as an exchange rate–based inflation stabilization program.
- Chronic fiscal deficits render currency pegs unsustainable.
- A once-and-for-all unexpected devaluation causes an increase in the price level, has no effect on the nominal interest rate, and acts like a tax on private money holdings, redistributing real resources from households to the government.
- If the central bank expands the money supply at the constant rate μ, in equilibrium inflation and the depreciation rate are both equal to μ, the difference between the domestic and the foreign interest rate is μ, and real money balances are constant over time and decreasing in μ.
- Inflation acts like a tax on real money holdings, where the tax base is real balances and the tax rate is an increasing function of inflation.
- When a government exhausts its ability to issue debt, it must finance the fiscal deficit by printing money.
- The inflation tax Laffer curve describes the relationship between the rate of money growth and seignorage income. It has an inverted U shape.
- Financing a higher fiscal deficit requires increasing the money growth rate and therefore increasing the equilibrium level of inflation.
- There is a maximum level of deficit that can be financed with money creation. Fiscal deficits beyond this level lead the economy into hyperinflation.
- A currency peg combined with fiscal deficits produces dynamics ending in a balance of payments crisis. Before the crisis, inflation is low and the government loses foreign reserves at a steady rate. In the period of the crisis, there is a speculative attack against the currency in which the government loses an unusually large amount of reserves. Then, the government is forced to abandon the peg and print money to finance the deficit, which increases the rate of inflation.

15.10 Exercises

Exercise 15.1 (TFU) Indicate whether the following statements are true, false, or uncertain, and explain why.

1. If the money supply grows at the same rate as GDP, the nominal exchange rate is constant.
2. In the quantity theory, the maximum fiscal deficit that the government can finance by printing money is a fraction $1/V$ of GDP.
3. In the quantity theory, the Laffer curve is upward sloping. This means that the country can never fall into hyperinflation, regardless of the level of the fiscal deficit, DEF.

Exercise 15.2 (The Quantity Theory and Economic Growth) Suppose that the growth rate of GDP is 4 percent ($Y_t/Y_{t-1} = 1.04$), that the money supply grows at 6 percent ($M_t/M_{t-1} = 1.06$), that foreign inflation is 1 percent ($P_t^*/P_{t-1}^* = 1.01$), and that the real exchange rate is constant.

1. Calculate the equilibrium rate of inflation, $P_t/P_{t-1} - 1$.
2. Calculate the equilibrium depreciation rate, $\mathcal{E}_t/\mathcal{E}_{t-1} - 1$.
3. Generalize this result. Specifically, let μ be the money growth rate, g the growth rate of output, π the inflation rate, π^* the foreign inflation rate, and ϵ the depreciation rate. Continue to assume that the real exchange rate is constant. Derive two formulas, one expressing the equilibrium inflation rate, π, as a function of μ and g, and the other expressing the equilibrium depreciation rate, ϵ, as a function of μ, g, and π^*.
4. Rewrite the two formulas in the previous question using the approximation $\ln(1+x) \approx x$, for $x = \mu, \pi, \pi^*, \epsilon$. Provide intuition for the role of economic growth in determining the rates of inflation and currency depreciation.

Exercise 15.3 (The Quantity Theory of Money in a Large Economy) Consider a two-country world. Assume that money demand in country i for $i = 1, 2$ is given by

$$M_t^{di} = \frac{1}{V^i} P_t^i Y_t^i,$$

where M_t^{di} denotes the money demand, P_t^i the price level, and Y_t^i real output. Let M_t^i denote the money supply in country i, and $\mathcal{E}_t$ the nominal exchange rate, defined as the price of one unit of currency of country 2 in units of currency of country 1.

1. Assume that both countries control their respective money supplies. Show that the monetary authority in country 2 cannot influence the price level in country 1, P_t^1.
2. Continue to assume that each country controls its own money supply. Analyze the effect on the nominal exchange rate of an increase in the money supply in both countries. Consider separately the following three cases:
   (a) Both countries increase their money supply in the same proportion.
   (b) Country 1 increases its money supply by a larger proportion than country 2.

(c) Country 1 increases its money supply by a smaller proportion than country 2.

3. Assume that country 1 pegs the exchange rate at $\mathcal{E}_t = \mathcal{E}$ and that monetary policy in country 2 consists in controlling the money supply, M_t^2. Show that the monetary authority in country 1 cannot influence P_t^2, whereas the monetary authority in country 2 can influence the value of P_t^1.

Hint: Use the definition of the real exchange rate, $e_t = \mathcal{E}_t P_t^2 / P_t^1$, and assume that e_t is exogenously determined.

Exercise 15.4 (Inflationary Finance) Suppose that the liquidity preference function is given by

$$L(C, i_t) = \gamma C \left(\frac{1 + i_t}{i_t} \right).$$

(Appendix 15.8 provides the microfoundations of this liquidity preference function; see equation (15.27).) Suppose also that the government runs a fiscal deficit of 10 percent of GDP $(DEF/GDP = 0.1)$, that the share of consumption in GDP is 65 percent $(C/GDP = 0.65)$, that the world interest rate is 5 percent per year $(i^* = 0.05)$, and that γ is equal to 0.2.

1. Calculate the rate of monetary expansion, μ, necessary to monetize the fiscal deficit.
2. Calculate the inflation rate, the depreciation rate, and the nominal interest rate.

Exercise 15.5 (Inflationary Finance and Economic Growth) Assume that the demand for money is $L(C_t, i_t) = \gamma C_t \frac{1 + i_t}{i_t}$. Suppose that consumption grows at the rate g $(C_t/C_{t-1} - 1 = g)$. Suppose the central bank expands the money supply at the constant rate μ $(M_t/M_{t-1} - 1 = \mu)$ and that the world interest rate is constant and equal to i^*.

1. Derive formulas for the equilibrium values of the inflation rate, the devaluation rate, and the nominal interest rate as functions of i^*, μ, and g. Provide intuition. Hint: follow the guess-and-verify method.
2. Suppose that the secondary fiscal deficit is a constant fraction δ of GDP, and that GDP grows at the same rate of consumption. Suppose further that consumption is a constant fraction c of GDP. Derive a formula for the money growth rate necessary to finance the fiscal deficit. Hint: μ should be a function of g, δ, c, γ, and i^*.
3. Suppose that as in Exercise 15.4, the secondary fiscal deficit is 10 percent of GDP, consumption is 5 percent of GDP, the world interest rate is 5 percent, and γ is 0.2. Assume further that GDP grows at 2 percent. Calculate the equilibrium money growth rate, μ. Compare this number to the one obtained in Exercise 15.4 and provide intuition.

Exercise 15.6 Suppose that in Costa Rica the liquidity preference function (or money demand function) is given by $0.5C - 100i_t$, where C denotes consumption and i_t denotes the nominal interest rate. Suppose that consumption equals 100. Also, assume that the government is expanding the money supply at a rate of 10 percent per year and that the real secondary deficit equals 4. In Costa Rica PPP holds and the world interest rate, i^*, is 5 percent per year.

1. What is the nominal interest rate in Costa Rica?
2. How much seignorage revenue is the government collecting per year?
3. Is seignorage revenue enough to finance the deficit? If not, then by how much are government asset holdings changing each period?

Exercise 15.7 (The Gold Standard) Consider two countries, Germany and the United States. Money demand in Germany is given by $\frac{M_t}{P_t} = Y_t$, where M_t denotes nominal money balances, P_t denotes the price level, and Y_t denotes output. In the United States, money demand is given by $\frac{M_t^*}{P_t^*} = Y_t^*$, where starred variables refer to U.S. variables. Assume that both countries are on the gold standard, so think back to the 1920s. This means that the central bank in each country has to back the money supply with gold reserves and must stand ready to exchange money for gold at a fixed price. Formally, $M_t = P_t^g G_t$ and $M_t^* = P_t^{g*} G_t^*$, where P_t^g is the gold price in marks, G_t are the German gold reserves, P_t^{g*} is the gold price in dollars, and G_t^* are the U.S. gold reserves. In Germany, the Reichsbank fixes the price of 1 ounce of gold at DM40 ($P_t^g = 40$) and in the United States the Federal Reserve fixes the price of 1 ounce of gold at \$20 ($P_t^{g*} = 20$). The world supply of gold, $\bar{G}$, is 200 ounces and is equal to the sum of the gold reserves of the Reichsbank and the Federal Reserve, $\bar{G} = G_t + G_t^*$. Assume further that PPP holds—that is, $P_t = \mathcal{E}_t P_t^*$—and that the law of one price holds for gold, $P_t^g = \mathcal{E}_t P_t^{g*}$, where $\mathcal{E}_t$ denotes the nominal exchange rate defined as marks per dollar. Output in Germany is 100 units of goods and output in the United States is 400 units of goods.

1. Show that in equilibrium it must be the case that $G_t/\bar{G} = Y_t/(Y_t + Y_t^*)$.
2. Find the gold reserves of the German and U.S. central banks, G_t and G_t^*, that make the gold standard a viable arrangement and find M_t, M_t^*, $\mathcal{E}_t$, P_t, and P_t^*.
3. Suppose now that output in Germany increases by 10 percent while output in the United States remains unchanged. What is the effect on the distribution of gold across countries? That is, find G_t and G_t^*, such that the gold standard remains viable. Also solve for M_t, M_t^*, P_t, and P_t^*. Provide intuition. [Hint: Use the fact that P_t^g and P_t^{g*} are fixed under the gold standard.]
4. Suppose that in response to the increase in output described in the previous question, Germany changes the price of gold in such a way as to preserve domestic goods price stability. What is the increase in the price of gold that achieves this goal? What is the effect of this policy on the nominal exchange rate and on the U.S. price level? Would this policy affect the world distribution of gold? Provide intuition.
5. Answer the previous question assuming that now both countries change the price of gold in terms of their domestic currencies so as to maintain domestic price stability.

6. Does there exist a gold price that would prevent the loss of U.S. gold reserves to Germany?

Exercise 15.8 (The Fiscal Consequences of a Devaluation) Consider a small open endowment economy with a single traded good and free capital mobility. Assume that purchasing power parity and interest rate parity hold. The world interest rate i_t^* is equal to 20 percent. Agents hold money to facilitate transactions. The liquidity preference function of households is given by

$$L(C, i_t) = C\frac{1 + i_t}{i_t},$$

where $C = 2$ denotes the constant level of consumption and i_t denotes the domestic nominal interest rate. Suppose that the government follows a balanced budget fiscal policy whereby it sets the secondary deficit equal to zero each period ($DEF_t = 0$ for all t). Assume that in period 1, the government's initial holdings of foreign reserves are equal to 100 ($B_0^g = 100$). The government pegs the nominal exchange rate at 1 unit of domestic currency per unit of foreign currency ($\mathcal{E} = 1$). The government contemplates the following two alternative once-and-for-all devaluation schemes to raise its stock of foreign reserves: (1) In period 1, it surprises the public with a permanent 100 percent devaluation (that is, $\mathcal{E}_t = 2$ for all periods $t \geq 1$). (2) In period 1, the government announces that beginning in period 2, the exchange rate will be 2 forever (that is, $\mathcal{E}_1 = 1$ and $\mathcal{E}_t = 2$ for all periods $t \geq 2$).

1. Suppose the government implements devaluation scheme (1). Find the level of foreign reserves at the end of period 2, B_2^g.
2. Suppose the government implements instead devaluation scheme (2). Again, find the level of foreign reserves at the end of period 2, B_2^g.
3. Under which devaluation scheme, (1) or (2), is the level of foreign reserves of the government higher in the long run and by how much? Explain your answer and provide intuition.

Exercise 15.9 (Balance of Payments Crisis) Consider a small open economy with a single traded good and free capital mobility. Suppose that the government is running a permanent real secondary deficit of 10 units of goods per period ($DEF = 10$). Because the government has defaulted on its debt in the past, it cannot borrow; that is, the stock of assets of the government, B_t^g, cannot be negative. In period 1, the government's initial asset holdings are positive and equal to 150 units of goods; that is, $B_0^g = 150$. Suppose in period 1, the government decides to peg the nominal exchange rate, defined as the price of 1 unit of foreign currency in terms of domestic currency. Households demand money for transactions purposes. Their liquidity preference function is given by

$$L(C, i_t) = 0.2\, C \left(\frac{1 + i_t}{i_t}\right),$$

where $C = 100$ denotes consumption and i_t denotes the domestic nominal interest rate. Assume that PPP and interest rate parity hold, that the world interest rate i^*

is 10% per period, and that the foreign currency price of the single traded good is constant and equal to 1 (i.e., $P_t^* = 1$ for all t).

1. Explain in words why in this economy the exchange rate peg is unsustainable.
2. Assume that once the government is forced to abandon the peg, it will finance the entire fiscal deficit through seignorage revenue. At what rate μ will the government have to expand the domestic money supply? Find the level of real balances, the rate of depreciation of the domestic currency, the rate of inflation, and the domestic nominal interest rate after the collapse of the currency peg.
3. Let period $T - 1$ be the last period in which the currency peg is in place. Find the demand for real balances, seignorage revenue, and the change in government assets in any period $t \le T - 2$.
4. Find the demand for real balances, seignorage revenue, and the change in government assets in period $T - 1$.
5. Finally, determine T. To do this, assume that the government keeps pegging the domestic currency until it lost all its reserves; that is, at the end of the last period in which the peg is still in place, $T - 1$, government assets are zero; that is, $B_{T-1}^g = 0$. [Hint: Take into account that in period $T - 1$ the government loses an unusually large amount of foreign reserves.]

Exercise 15.10 (Permanent Money-Based Inflation Stabilization) Consider a small open economy with a single traded good and free capital mobility. Assume that monetary policy takes the form of a money growth rate peg: $M_t = (1 + \mu)M_{t-1}$ for all t. The liquidity preference function is given by $L(C, i_t) = C/(1 + i_t)^2$, where i_t denotes the domestic nominal interest rates on assets held between periods t and $t + 1$ and $C = 1$ is a constant. Assume that the money growth rate is 10 percent per year, that PPP and interest rate parity hold, that the world interest rate i^* is 5 percent per period, and that the foreign currency price of the single traded good is constant and equal to 1 (i.e., $P_t^* = 1$ for all t). The fiscal authority adjusts the secondary fiscal deficit so as to keep reserves constant.

1. Find the rate of inflation, the rate of depreciation of the domestic currency, and the level of seignorage income in any period t.

Now suppose that in period 0, the central bank surprises the public by announcing that it will implement an inflation stabilization plan. Specifically, the money supply will be held constant from now on; that is, $M_t = M_0$ for all $t \ge 0$.

2. Find the rate of inflation between periods $t = -1$ and $t = 0$ and between periods $t = 0$ and $t = 1$. Will inflation be zero immediately? Explain why or why not.
3. Find seignorage income in period 0. Compare the level of seignorage in period $t = 0$ to that in periods $t = -1$ as well as $t = 1$. Provide an intuitive explanation for your results.

4. Find the rate of exchange rate depreciation in periods $t = -1, 0, 1$.
5. What could the central bank have done to achieve zero inflation immediately; that is, to ensure that $P_t = P_{-1}$ for any $t \geq 0$?

Exercise 15.11 (Temporary Money-Based Inflation Stabilization) Consider a small open economy with a single traded good and free capital mobility. Suppose that the government is running a permanent real secondary deficit of 10 units of goods per period ($DEF = 10$). Because the government has defaulted on its debt in the past, it cannot borrow—that is, the stock of assets of the government, B_t^g, cannot be negative. In period 1, the government's initial asset holdings are positive and equal to 150 units of goods; that is, $B_0^g = 150$. Suppose in period 1, the government decides to follow a monetary policy of keeping the money supply constant over time—that is, $M_t = M_0$, for any period t in which the constant money supply policy is in place. Households demand money for transactions purposes. Their liquidity preference function is given by

$$L(C, i_t) = 0.2\, C \left(\frac{1 + i_t}{i_t} \right),$$

where $C = 100$ denotes consumption and i_t denotes the domestic nominal interest rate. Assume that PPP and interest rate parity hold, that the world interest rate i^* is 10 percent per period, and that the foreign currency price of the single traded good is constant and equal to 1 (i.e., $P_t^* = 1$ for all t).

1. Explain in words why in this economy the policy of keeping the money supply constant is unsustainable in the long run.
2. Assume that once the government is forced to abandon the policy of holding the money supply constant, it will switch to a policy of constant money growth at the rate $\mu > 0$ and finance the entire fiscal deficit through seignorage revenue. Let period $T - 1$ be the last period in which the money supply is constant; that is, $M_{T-1} = M_0$, and $M_t/M_{t-1} = 1 + \mu$ for all $t \geq T$. Find seignorage income for any period $t \geq T$ as a function of μ. Then determine at what rate μ the government will have to expand the domestic money supply to be able to finance the deficit.
3. Find the rate of inflation, the rate of depreciation of the domestic currency, the domestic nominal interest rate, and the level of real balances after the collapse of the constant money policy; that is, for any period $t \geq T$.
4. Find seignorage revenue and the change in government assets in any period $t \leq T - 1$. Will the country experience a balance of payments crisis—that is, will the country lose an unusally large amount of reserves in $T - 1$, the last period the money supply is held constant?
5. Determine T. To do this, assume that the government keeps the money supply constant until it loses all its reserves—that is, assume that at the end of the last period in which the money supply is constant (period $T - 1$) $B_{T-1}^g = 0$.

6. Find the time path of inflation. Give an intuitive explanation for the behavior of prices during the time that the money supply is held constant. [Hint: Recall that above we determined inflation for any period $t \geq T$. So all you need to find now is P_t/P_{t-1} for any $2 \leq t < T$. First, find inflation in period $T - 1$. Thereafter, inflation in period $T - 2$, and so on until period 2.]

7. Compare the dynamics of the temporary money-based inflation stabilization program with the dynamics triggered by a temporary exchange rate–based inflation stabilization program.

Index

income taxes, 405–7, 410

India: capital controls in, 338; as emerging large open economy, 44; real exchange rate with, 202–5, 213, 215

indifference map/curves: defined, 48; in intertemporal theory of current account, 48, 48–52, 51, 54, 54, 60; offer curve and, 324, 325; tariff shock effects on, 77–79, 78

indirect utility function, 328–29

Indonesia, as small open economy, 45

infinite horizon economies: perpetual current account deficit in, 36, 40–41; perpetual trade balance deficit in, 35, 38–40

inflation: core, 371; hyperinflation, 240, 431, 436, 437; increasing in monetary union, 410–14, 412, 413; monetary policy effects on, 371, 410–14, 412, 413; real exchange rate and, 208–10, 209, 240; supply shocks and, 376; as tax, 434–35, 435, 443; unemployment and, 375, 376, 410–14, 412

inflationary finance, 423–47; balance of payments crises and, 424, 431, 437–41, 442; in constant money growth rate regime, 433–34; fiscal consequences of devaluations and, 431–33, 438; fiscal consequences of money creation and, 434–37, 435; fiscal deficits and, 423, 430–31, 434–41; fixed exchange rate and, 427, 430–31, 437–39; interest rate parity condition and, 429; in monetary economy with government sector, 427–30; money demand and, 424, 425, 427–30, 432, 435, 441–47; overview of, 423–24, 447; purchasing power parity and, 428–29; quantity theory of money and, 423, 424–27

inflation/inflation tax Laffer curves, 435, 435–37, 436

inflation tax revenue, 434

interest rate: capital controls and (see capital controls); ceiling on, 126; consumption and, 68, 72–75, 74, 101, 101–2, 230, 305, 314, 323–24, 324–26, 398–400, 399; covered interest rate differentials, 277–84, 279, 281, 282, 284, 302, 303–4; covered interest rate parity, 276–78, 288; current account schedule and, 105–6; debt-elastic, 312–13, 314; fiscal policy and, 178–83, 179, 181, 182; free capital mobility and, 52–53, 61, 77, 145, 179–80, 231, 275, 276, 289, 292–94, 313, 318–26; interest-elastic money demand, 428; interest rate parity condition, 52–53, 61, 77, 429 (see also covered, real, and uncovered interest rate parity subentries); interest rate shock effects, 68, 72–75, 74, 107–8, 108, 114, 232–35, 234, 243–44, 364–68, 365, 367, 368, 370–71, 370, 372–74, 372, 377–82, 377, 380 (see also world interest rate); investments and, 68, 92, 92, 93–94, 93–94, 142–45, 144; large open economy, 141–55, 142, 144, 152–53, 182–83, 318–23, 327; monetary policy and, 382–84, 386–87; net investment income and (see net investment income); real exchange rate and, 227, 231, 232–35, 234, 236, 243–44; real interest rate parity, 292–94; savings and, 68, 73–74, 103, 103, 142–43; small open economies and, 141, 150; sudden stops and, 238–43, 239, 241, 257, 257–59;

on trade balance deficit, 33–35; uncovered interest rate differentials, 285; uncovered interest rate parity, 285–92; world (see world interest rate)

international capital: capital account of transfers of, 4; capital controls on (see capital controls); free capital mobility (see free capital mobility); imperfect capital mobility, 180–81, 181; market integration for (see international capital market integration)

international capital market integration, 275–99; with Brazil, 279–81; capital controls and, 275, 279–81, 281, 282–84 (see also capital controls); with China, 275–76, 278–79; covered interest rate differentials and, 277–84, 279, 281, 282, 284, 302; covered interest rate parity and, 276–78, 288; free capital mobility and, 275, 276, 289, 292–98; overview of, 275–76, 299; real interest rate parity and, 292–94; saving-investment correlation and, 294–98, 295–98; uncovered interest rate parity and, 285–92

International Comparison Program (ICP), 198–201, 199–200, 204

International Monetary Fund, Annual Report on Exchange Arrangements and Exchange Restrictions, 338

international transactions account. See balance of payments account

intertemporal marginal rate of substitution, 50, 52

intertemporal theory of current account, 44–63; anticipated income shocks in, 59–61, 60; for economy with logarithmic preferences, 61–62; equilibrium in small open economy in, 53–54, 54; interest rate parity condition in, 52–53, 61; intertemporal budget constraint in, 45–47, 46, 50–51, 51, 53, 54, 57, 57, 59–61; intertemporal resource constraint in, 53–54, 54; lifetime utility function in, 47–50, 48, 61; optimal intertemporal allocation of consumption in, 50–52, 51, 98, 163–65, 164; optimal intertemporal allocation of expenditure in, 44; output shocks adjustment in, 56–61, 57–60, 62; overview of, 44–45, 62–63; shock effects and (see shock adjustments); simplified assumptions with, 68–69; trade balance and current account in, 55–56

investment: capital control effects on, 308; carry trade, 290–91; current account and, 36–38, 87–96, 104, 105–6, 106, 143–45, 144; firm decisions on, 87–93, 88, 90–93, 162–63; fiscal deficits and, 162–63, 168, 171–72, 174, 182–83; giant oil discovery effects on, 118, 118–19; interest rates and, 68, 92, 92, 93–94, 93–94, 142–45, 144; international capital market integration for (see international capital market integration); in large open economies, 143–45, 144; net income from (see net investment income); net international position on (see net international investment position); optimal level of, 90–92, 91–92, 162–63; productivity shock adjustments to, 89–90, 90, 92–93, 93, 95, 108–10, 297, 297; profit and, 90–96, 91–95, 133–34, 162–63; saving correlations with, 294–98, 295–98; schedule of, 93–96, 94, 112; terms of trade and, 116–17

Iran, as closed economy, 44